A HISTORY OF
INDIAN CRICKET

Other books by the author

Cricket
Keith Miller: A Cricketing Biography
All in a Day: Great Moments in Cup Cricket
A Maidan View: The Magic of Indian Cricket
Cricket Voices

History and Biography
The Lost Hero: A Biography of Subhas Bose
The Aga Khans
Michael Grade: Screening the Image
Sporting Colours: Sport and Politics in South Africa (runner-up in
the 1994 William Hill Sports Book of the Year)
Sports Babylon (The story of drugs and corruption in sport)
Memons: A History

Football
Behind Closed Doors: Dreams and Nightmares at Spurs (Irving
Scholar's years at Tottenham)
False Messiah: The Life and Times of Terry Venables
Manchester Unlimited: The Rise and Rise of Manchester United

Business
The Crash: The 1987–88 World Market Slump
A New Money Crisis (children's guide to money)
Are You Covered? An insurance guide
Fraud – The Growth Industry of the 1980s
How to Invest in a Bear Market

Autobiography
The Sporting Alien

A HISTORY OF
INDIAN CRICKET

MIHIR BOSE

Foreword by Sunil Gavaskar   **REVISED EDITION**

ANDRE DEUTSCH

First published 1990 by
André Deutsch Limited
20 Mortimer Street, London W1T 3JW

Revised edition 2002

A CIP catalogue record for this book is available
from the British Library

ISBN 0 233 05040 X

Printed in Great Britain

Foreword to the First Edition
SUNIL GAVASKAR

Compared with England and Australia, India is a cricketing babe. And what a babe she has been, the joy and despair of her millions of followers! She has come through a turbulent growing-up, interrupted by a war and then a divorce of sorts when part of her body was separated from her. The adolescent years were tentative, a period of learning with the occasional win, but as she entered her forties, the triumphs she had worked for and craved were hers. But all too soon the failures returned, and thereafter it has been a period of ups and downs – like a roller coaster to use Mihir Bose's words – as she has tried to adjust to the changing face of cricket. Now, in the last decade of the century, India finds herself at a crossroads, keen as always but a trifle uncertain how to proceed.

The task of trying to piece together the events that have brought India to its current cricketing status is not only an exciting but an enormous job. The intrigue and manoeuvering of today is no more devious that it was in the earlier years. Yet it has to be seen in the context of the times. Then, it was the maharajahs who patronised the game and thus wanted to concentrate power in their hands; today's 'maharajahs' are more suave and more subtle as they seek to control the 'fiefdom' that is Indian cricket.

The players have always been pawns in the hands of these manoeuverers, some willing, as you will find out in this book, some unwittingly so. Yes, and there have been some players who have given the Board of Control as good as it gave, but they were a rare breed because, in India, bowing to authority is the easy way out. And it is because those who bow far outnumber those who do not, that the Board gets away with imposing its will on the players.

This one aspect of Indian cricket (perhaps its most crucial aspect), the Board/players relationship, is seldom given the importance in books that it deserves. The reason it is so crucial is that the players have always had to play with a Damoclean sword hanging over their heads. It could fall on them not because of their cricketing form but for reasons unconnected with the happenings on the field. To perform in spite of this additional pressure is no easy task. In fact, it is often easier to guess what international bowlers are going to bowl that what the Board is going to throw at you! This lack of understanding, due to unwillingness to have a regular dialogue with the players, has been Indian cricket's greatest trajedy. No Test player has ever been at the helm of the Board, indeed the Indian Board must be the only Board of Control in the world which has non-cricketers not just occupying the highest positions on the Board but also representing various affiliated associations. A cricketer's viewpoint is thus seldom, if ever, heard. He has no control over playing conditions or other matters important to his performance. I mention this only to emphasise how the deeds of Indian cricketers have to be seen in this light whe Indian cricket history is being written.

Having said that, it must be admitted that the Board gives plenty of opportunities for the young player to display his skills. Nowhere in the world do youngsters get as many chances to play in the tourneys the Board organises. At this level, there is no problem as the young player is so keen to gain his national colours that he will ignore any inconvenience he may have to face. It is when a player attains Test status, and then goes on to make a name for himself internationally, that the problems with the Board start. This is the time the player's opinion is sought about how to improve the facilities and playing conditions; but when he makes his point, the Board immediately moves to silence him. This, too, is a game that has been played ever since Indian cricket entered the international arena. The participants may change as age catches up with the players and they retire; but unfortunately, changes on the Board's side occur mainly on a signal from the Great Umpire.

Amid all this the game of cricket goes on because the majority of Indians love it with a rare passion, especially now that radio and television have taken the game to the remotest parts of the country. With the following thus increased, with people able to watch the game on their TV sets at home, expectations have multiplied and this too is an important factor in the performance of the players. Some revel in this pressure, many more crumble under it and, as you read Mihir Bose's book, you will realise that there are many players who have felt most uncomfortable playing before the crowds in certain centres.

While it is unrealistic to expect all eleven players to do well in a game, there are some of whom the expectations are greater. These are the players who have gained a permanent place in the hearts of the cricket lovers of India. From Colonel C.K. Nayudu to the young Sachin Tendulkar, they are the ones the crowd has come to watch more than the others and, when they do not do well, the disappointment is not always expressed but it is most certainly felt. On the other hand, to do well in front of Indian crowds is to be in a heaven. The sense of joy and fulfilment that one feels after such an achievement has to be experienced to be believed. There can be no higher 'high' than this anywhere else in the cricketing world. It has been a great privilege for me to have felt this on more than one occasion and to have contributed in some way to the history of Indian cricket. Now, with the one-day game taking root all over the world and Test-match crowds dwindling even in India, that wondrous sense of achievement is considerably reduced.

Many attempts have been made to write a book on the history of Indian cricket. They have mostly been statistical works which, for that very reason, do not fully satisfy the curiosity of the avid cricket lover who wants to know more about the circumstances and conditions of the times, and the nature and personalities of the players.

In this pioneering book, Mihir Bose has drawn all these strands together to produce a narrative and a chronology so far unrivalled and which, with its statistical appendixes, has made this book a must for all those interested in the development and the history of cricket in India.

I sincerely hope this book will inspire many an Indian to take up the bat and the ball, and with them carve a name for himself to be printed in its future editions.

Contents

List of Illustrations

Plate section 1

18 a) A.L. Wadekar; b) E. Solkar; c) F.M. Engineer
19 The great quartet of Indian spinners
20 Sunil Gavaskar
21 a) Mohinder Amarnath; b) D.B. Vengsarkar; c) Kapil Dev
22 a) G.R. Viswanath; b) Indian spectators crossing the border to Lahore
23 a) Chetan Chauhan; b) Gavaskar during his innings of 221
24 a) Groudsman sweeping the wicket at Eden Gardens; b) Viswanath recalls Taylor in Jubilee Test

Plate section 4

25 a) R.J. Shastri; b) S.H. Kirmani; c) D.R. Doshi
26 a) Kapil Dev; b) K. Srikkanth; c) scooter park at Bangalore
27 1983 World Cup
28 Views of the Azad Maidan, Bombay, 1984
29 a) Sivaramakrishnan; b) Robinson caught at the wicket; c) Celebrations after Indians win World Championship of Cricket, Melbourne 1985
30 Vengsarkar, Kapil Dev, and the Cornhill Trophy, 1986
31 Reliance Cup, 1987: a) Wankhede Stadium, Bombay, during England v. India semi-final; b) Eden Gardens, Calcutta, during the final
32 a) Mohammed Azharuddin; b) Narendra Hirwani; c) Sanjay Manjrekar

Plate section 5

33 a) Mohammad Azharuddin; b) Poster of Tendulkar
34 Mohammad Azharuddin
35 a) Sachin Tendulkar; b) Vinod Kambli
36 a) Javagal Srinath; b) Ventkatesh Prasad
37 a) Sachin Tendulkar; b) Vavjot Singh Sidhu
38 a) Saurav Ganguly and Rahul Dravid; b) Anil Kumble; c) Manoj Prabhakar
39 a) Nayan Mognia; b) V.V.S. Laxman
40 a) Harbhajan Singh; b) Jagmohan Dalmiya

Author's Acknowledgements

One afternoon, quite out of the blue, I received a phone call from Tom Rosenthal of André Deutsch. He suggested that I might like to write this history. The thought had never entered my mind but, once he had made it, his proposal seemed both logical and sensible. So my first thanks go to him.

I am also grateful to him for choosing John Bright-Holmes as the book's editor, for he combines knowledge with a patience almost as great as that of certain legendary Indian batsmen.

Writing this book has given me an unrivalled opportunity to meet some of the cricketing heroes of my youth: men I had been brought up on, even idolised, but whom I had never met. Quite the most enchanting of these meetings was in San Fernando, Trinidad, where I spent a morning with Subash Gupte. Old spinners never die, they merely recall the different ways they set the leg-trap, and that morning with Subash and his family was an education. I am also grateful to George Bickerstaff of *The Director* magazine for providing a perfect excuse to go to Trinidad just when the Indians were playing a Test match there.

Sunil Gavaskar kindly agreed to write a Foreword, and many other cricketers have shared their memories with me. My thanks go to them all: Mohinder Amarnath, the late Leslie Ames, B.S. Chandrasekhar, Charlie Davis, Dilip Doshi, Gerry Gomez, Prior Jones, Kapil Dev, Budhi Kunderan, W.H.V. Levett, Tony Lewis, Alan Moss, Kailash Pattani, Gulabrai Ramchand, Willie Rodriguez, Pankaj Roy, Dilip Sardesai, Ravi Shastri, Dilip Vengsarkar. Only one famous cricketer felt he still could not unburden himself after all these years: Lala Amarnath. That was a real disappointment.

Cricket officials in Britain, India and, indeed, around the world have given me their time very readily: Raman Subba Row, Ted Dexter, Ralph Gosein. Nor can I thank Anant Gaundalkar enough for the help he provided. His statistics form a vital part of this book but, more, he responded to my frequent, often inconvenient long-distance calls with alacrity. I was introduced to Anant, as the rising star of Indian statisticians, by Sharad Kotnis who remains a dear friend and one of the most valued sources on contemporary Indian cricket. I am also grateful to Vinod Mehta, quite the best editor in India for his sympathetic understanding of cricket, and to the many Indian cricket journalists whose writings, not always well-known outside India, have over the years shaped my understanding of the Indian game, in particular K.N. Prabhu, N.S. Ramaswami, Raju Bharatan, R. Mohan, and Kishore

Bhimani. Dickie Rutnagur, whose voice is part of my Bombay cricket memory, provided invaluable comments and suggestions.

Kate Shakir provided much-needed typing skills at very short notice and, as ever, Sue Cairncross was a source of great help not only with the typing but a whole host of other matters. My thanks, too, to Professor Derek West for compiling the index. My nephew Abhijit gave me fresh insights into Indian cricket thinking; and my wife Kalpana bore the progress of the book with remarkable fortitude given that she was simultaneously bearing our child who turned out to be neither a Sunil nor a Dilip, but Indira Ellora. But who knows? By the time she grows up, India may require a female cricket captain.

Author's Preface

The hardback edition of this book was published in 1990 when India were about to tour England. I could not have asked for a better reception with the book receiving much critical acclaim and winning the Cricket Society Literary Award. Since then, wherever I have gone in India or England, I have been told the book is a source of reference. In recent years the book has also been a source material for a film called *Laagan*, the only film made in India which is built round cricket. Aamir Khan, the producer of the film, has very kindly said that my book was an inspiration for him and he kept it in the dressing room, which is immensely gratifying.

All this would justify a paperback edition. But the real justification for it is that the last ten years have seen tremendous changes in Indian cricket both on and off the field, not least in the emergence of Sachin Tendulkar, thre greatest phenomenon Indian cricket has known, and I felt there was a real need to update it.

Nowhere is this more evident than in the way Indians now bet on cricket. To judge that better, I visited India during the Bangalore Test between India and England in December 2001 and was staggered to find that illegal betting on cricket was alive and well and keeping the Indian bookmakers busy.

Massive amounts of money were bet on the India-England series with odds changing by the minute as the play fluctuated. By the time the series was over a total of £420m had been bet. According to bookmakers I spoke to in Bombay, which is the centre of this illegal cricket activity, £140m of bets were taken in each of the three Tests. In contrast, Graham Sharp of William Hill reckoned the entire bookmaking industry in England took no more than £100,000 for the entire series.

However, what makes this Indian betting very different is that with it being illegal in India the Indian police are always on the look out for bookies. According to Shirish Immamdar, the Inspector in charge of the Bombay Police's Social Security Cell which tackles illegal betting, in 2001 alone 33 illegal bookmakers were arrested.

And what makes it dangerous is that many of India's most notorious underworld characters, who are wanted on a variety of charges, bet heavily on cricket matches. One bookmaker I spoke to said that there had been 19 murders involved with cricket betting and as I finished my conversation he even warned me to be careful, saying that I was probing into very dangerous areas.

While I was in Bombay investigating the betting industry, an associate of one of the underworld dons, who had been involved in illegal cricket betting, was shot dead in what the police termed an 'encounter', and while there is nothing to suggest he was involved in cricket betting, it showed the link between illegal betting and the underworld. This link is now being investigated by the Indian Central Bureau of Investigation and has caused concern to Lord Condon who heads the International Cricket Council's Anti Corruption Unit.

The only legal form of betting allowed in India is on-course race betting, but even here the Indian government's imposition of a tax on winnings has made bookmakers and punters conceal their real bets. One bookmaker told me, 'The government taxes winnings by 34.5 per cent on winnings over Rupees 2,500 (£35) and if you have a big win then the Income Tax authorities will come around asking where you got the money. So we have a code for betting. You are Mihir, your account will be called Charlie. Your basic bet is Rupees 200 (£3). That will be 1 and when you bet you say Charlie 1 plus 4 which means that you are really betting Rupees 500 (£7). Or you can bet one plus 9 which is Rupees 1,000 (£14), 1 plus 49 is rupees 5,000 (£70) or 1 plus 99 which is Rupees 10,000 (£140). The bet that will be written down will only be 1.'

This way punters not only avoid income tax but also the betting tax of 26 per cent, although bookmakers charge an illegal betting tax of 9 per cent to meet their expenses.

All cricket betting is illegal and is done on mobile phones. To place a bet you have to hire a betting line. These lines are supplied illegally by telephone workers. On these lines you can hear continuous commentary on the cricket betting. The more expensive the line the more information you get, and for the right amount you can not only hear the constantly changing odds but also what the big punters are betting on.

The punters are constantly hedging their bets. Having decided to back India, they could in a couple of overs switch to a draw or an England victory as the odds change reflecting the fluctuations of the play. I had dramatic evidence of this on the second day of the Bangalore Test as India began their reply to England. The odds were draw: evens, 12/10 India, 10/1 England.

But as I rang the bookmaker, V.V.S. Laxman got out and the bookmaker said, 'Are you not watching the cricket. A wicket has fallen, the odds will change. Ring me in ten minutes.' When I rang in ten minutes he said India 1/4, draw 1/4 England 5/1.

It is this ability to place bets on constantly changing fixed price odds that provides the scope to nobble players. The aim is not so much to fix the result of the match but to do something that could alter the odds.

The bookmaker explained, 'Let us say in a match Pakistan starts on half money (1/2 or 2/1 on) and India is 2/1. If in the first fifteen overs Pakistan loses two wickets then the odds change and the punter 'eats' (meaning hedges) his position as Pakistan will become 2/1 and India will become half money.'

This means, said the bookmaker, all you need to do is get a couple of batsmen to agree to lose their wickets, or a fielder to drop a catch or a bowler to bowl badly for a few overs, particularly in a one-day match, and it can make all the difference. The bookies I spoke to said they were not involved in trying to nobble players, but that this was done by the underworld dons (the bettors), many of them operating from outside India.

However in the last six months of 2001 attempts to nobble players have led to enormous problems for Bombay bookmakers and huge losses. In July 2001, a one-day match between Sri Lanka and New Zealand played in Colombo saw tremendous fluctuations with first New Zealand then Sri Lanka becoming favourite. One don, who lives outside India and had bet heavily, suspected a rival don had fixed the match and put out an order for sauda fok (stop payments) on the entire match. No bets he said were to be honoured. Bookmakers were threatened with retributions if they did not obey and they held a crisis meeting to discuss what to do. One bookmaker told me the stop payment led to bets totalling £300m being lost. He himself lost £51,000.

In November 2001 when Pakistan played Sri Lanka in a tournament in Sharjah there was much talk of match fixing and the Joint Commissioner of Bombay Police, Bhujangrao Mohite, let it be known that his policemen would stop bets being laid. When I asked him how he did it he got quite angry and said, 'That is an operational matter. Why do you want to know?'

However his assistant Shirish Immamdar told me, 'The first time this sauda fok happened was in 1996, just before the World Cup. There was a tournament in Sharjah and a number of upsets. The underworld dons said sauda fok, do not pay and even threatened some bookies. And with their lives in danger they came to us asking for protection. While the underworld dons are wanted in India for various murders, the bookies are small traders in Bombay.'

The biggest such bookie, according to Immamdar, is believed to travel around Bombay in a car equipped with several mobile phones and with his own security guards. All the bookmakers have nicknames and they tend to take the name of the place they operate from. The police have never managed to catch the infamous bookmakers.

Whether Lord Condon's outfit can catch them seems doubtful. None of the bookies I met had heard of Lord Condon, although the day after I met one of them, quite intriguingly, he received a call from London asking whether he would meet one of Condon's officers who is shortly to visit Bombay.

The England players were warned of the activities of Indian bookies before they went to India, although Condon and his men had not spoken to the Indians by the time the series was over. Lord Condon has confessed that match fixing still goes on and my investigation suggests that given the huge amounts bet in India, unless the Indian government can be persuaded to make it legal, it may be impossible to control.

I mention all this in my introduction because no history of Indian cricket can be written without some attention to betting which is both an integral part of it, yet being illegal is impossible to control and regulate. This makes Indian cricket all the more unique.

I owe thanks to many people for making this paperback possible. They include Martin Corteel for taking it on and proving so patient, Wendy Wimbush for her wonderful statistics, Gulu Advani for his generosity with both time and contacts, Noel Rands, as ever, for more things than I can list, Amrit Mathur, Raj Singh, G. Viswanath, Sabanayakan, Vijay Lokaphally, Rajaraman, Ehsan Mani and many others too numerous to name who have so generously given me their time and answered my many inquiries.

Above all I owe far more than I can express to my wife Caroline, who did not know who Sachin Tendulkar was before I began on this venture but has shown exemplary patience, kindness, thoughtfulness and devotion to a sport with which she does not readily identify with. More in the style of the British pioneers taking the game to the Indians, she has doled out both carrots and sticks in judicious measures to make sure I finished the project.

Bombay,
December 2001

Preface to the First Edition

When I was young I used to imagine I would play for India one day and score a hundred at Lord's. Indian defeats then would reduce me to tears and I would return to my bedroom mirror determined to perfect the cover drive that would scatter Trueman and his ring of slips.

I never got further than damaging the bedroom furniture but in retrospect I feel that a tussle against Trueman might almost have been easier than writing a history of Indian cricket. Carlyle, when writing his study of Oliver Cromwell, said he had to drag the life of the Lord Protector out from under a mountain of dead dogs, a huge load of calumny and oblivion. My task has been similar except that Indian cricket is not so much maligned as simply not properly known. Even when you look under the mountain of press cuttings, published material, books and records it is difficult to construct a logical, coherent narrative for what must be the most extraordinary story in cricket.

Much of this is due to the fact that Indians have never much cared for recording history. One of the earliest and greatest of the country's historians, Kalhana, shared Aristotle's view that poetry was a higher form of learning than history. 'Who else but the poet, who like the creator knows how to bring forth magically the most pleasant figures, could make the past ages appear like the present?' Not being a poet myself, I have had to work hard on what material is available.

Cricket literature may be vast, but Indian cricket literature has contributed little to it. The historian of English cricket has a wealth of material to work with, including county histories, biographies of leading cricketers, accounts of tours and home Test series. There is nothing remotely comparable in India. Cricket literature is growing but just as an historian of ancient India cannot construct a complete list of kings and their reigns, so even today it is not possible to compile a definitive list of all first-class cricket matches that have been played in India since the game was introduced by the British. The best guide to first-class cricket matches in India has been prepared by a man who lives in Orpington.

So the historian of Indian cricket needs also to be a bit of a detective.

If that has imposed an unexpected obligation, perhaps the greater problem has been that I had to construct a framework in which to present the history. Altham and Swanton, writing *A History of Cricket*, a classic of its kind, did not need to explain England to their readers, but for this book I felt that, without some explanation of the larger Indian context, this history would be, as Masefield said, 'one damn thing after another'. Worse, one confusing damn thing after another. Thus, while this is a book about Indian cricket, it cannot help being also a book about India itself. It is impossible to understand the intrigues of the princes or even the essential roller-coaster nature of the story, full of paradoxes and surprises, without some idea that this is a basic feature too of Indian life and society.

Nothing illustrates this better than the events which have taken place since the book was completed. The narrative takes Indian cricket to the end of 1989 when, under the leadership of Srikkanth, India earned a draw in Pakistan – a creditable performance in a country which has seen shattering Indian defeats in the past. The tour seemed to promise a new beginning but within weeks Srikkanth was sacked as captain and Azharuddin was appointed in his place to lead India to New Zealand in the early part of 1990. His side lost the three-Test series 1–0 and this has once again led to recriminations. Just as it seemed Indian cricket might have entered the 1990s with some stability, everything is again in turmoil. To the student of Indian history this is all too familiar, moments of glory alternating with moments of despair; but if there is one lesson which Indian history teaches us, then it is not to be surprised by anything that happens. Indian cricket may be strong or weak, pedestrian or joyous. It is never predictable.

March 1990

In memory of Baba, my father for all those early mornings when he took me to Bombay's Oval Maidan where I learnt my cricket; for that magical day when he took me to Ella Aunty's flat, whose balcony overlooked the Brabourne Stadium, and from where I saw Ridgeway injure Hazare; and for the many, many hot afternoons when he sat with me in overcrowded stands and once, on New Year's Day watching Australia in a Test, was nearly crushed by the crowds. I miss him terribly and regret not ever telling him how much I loved him and how much he meant to me.

India in 1930

India in 2000

1

The day the elephant came to The Oval

Just after 12.30 pm on Monday 23 August 1971 Brian Luckhurst and John Jameson walked out at The Oval to begin England's second innings against India in the third and final Test of the series. The previous two matches had been drawn but now England, leading by 71 runs on the first innings, appeared to have worked themselves into a position where the only tricky question for the English captain, Ray Illingworth, was when to make his declaration.

Illingworth was worried about the slowness of the Oval wicket. Over the weekend he had grumbled that right through the summer England had done their cause little good by preparing pitches which blunted England's own superior pace attack and now helped the Indian spinners. But in the first innings Illingworth, himself, had bowled his off-breaks quite beautifully; and that very morning he had taken two more wickets to finish with 5 for 70, encouraging for England, ominous for India, as the Indians would have to bat last. As Luckhurst and Jameson followed the Indians on to the field Denis Compton, then the expert on BBC television, speculated that a declaration would come soon after tea and warned Illingworth to leave sufficient time to have a chance of bowling the Indians out. Compton's record as forecaster was a poor one that season. In the first Test of the summer, after Pakistan had declared at 608 for 7, Compton had confidently predicted a big England score and a draw. England made 353, followed-on, and were saved by rain.

But such details were forgotten in the general optimism about the outcome of the match and the series. Defeat was almost a forgotten factor, for England had not lost a Test since being beaten by Australia in June 1968 – no defeat in 26 matches. In that time they had beaten the West Indies in England and won back the Ashes, the previous winter, in Australia. Illingworth had captained England in 19 Tests and not lost once. He had been beaten by a Rest of the World side in 1970 but not by the Test team of another country.

Also Illingworth had the ideal batsman to score runs quickly. Boycott had played in the first Test but was then injured and his replacement, John Jameson, had brought a touch of Colin Milburn to England's

1

opening partnership. Luckhurst defended, Jameson attacked: ferociously. In his short Test career he had taken the attack to the Indian spinners and they had avoided an even greater punishment only because in three Test innings so far he had been run out twice. There was something ironical in all this, although the Indians probably did not appreciate it. Jameson was born in Bombay of Anglo-Indian stock and his father was still a leading figure in that city's hockey and athletics circles.

Jameson, with Luckhurst very much the silent partner, quickly put on runs against the opening 'pace attack' of Abid Ali and Solkar. Convention demands they be described as a pace attack but those words hardly represent their bowling. Abid was the happy soldier of the Indian team: he had opened the batting, opened the bowling and done just about everything. His bearing conveyed something of a quartermaster in the army and, appropriately, his pace was military medium. Solkar was a lithe young man, a wonderful close-in fielder – probably the best in the world then – and a stylish attacking batsman who looked for all the world as if he had been tossed the ball by his captain, Wadekar, because he could not think of anyone else who could bowl. He had started life as a left-arm spinner only to discover that he was competing against Bishan Singh Bedi. He quickly abandoned spin to become India's opening bowler. Both Solkar and Abid had had their successes on the tour, Abid getting Boycott in the first innings of the Lord's Test for 3 and then in the second at Old Trafford reducing England to 41 for 4. But this had surprised him as much as the English batsmen. Both he and Solkar were there, primarily, to take the shine off the ball. The quicker they did that the better, so that the spinners could get on with the main burden of bowling.

As Jameson set about the bowling there was some speculation as to whether Wadekar might follow his tactics at Old Trafford in the previous Test. There, with England leading by 174 runs, Abid had bowled 26 overs and, when Solkar bruised his hand trying to catch a cut by Jameson, Wadekar turned to Gavaskar as his main bowler. In one of his longest spells in Test cricket Gavaskar bowled twelve overs of seam while Bedi bowled five overs of spin, and Chandrasekhar two. True it was a green top and conditions were so wet that the spinners could not grip the ball, but it was clear that Wadekar was buying time.

Nobody could have blamed Wadekar had he been just as defensive at The Oval. Over the weekend he had hoped the series would be left drawn: 'If we can return to Bombay on the ninth of next month having beaten the West Indies in the Caribbean and held England it will be a wonderful boost for cricket throughout India,' Basil Easterbrook quoted him as saying in *Playfair Cricket Monthly*. It would mean that India, in the course of six months, had suddenly, almost unaccountably, acquired the look of world beaters. At home they had always been determined opponents, but away from home they were the rabbits of international cricket. At the beginning of 1971, after nearly forty years of Test cricket, they had only won one series abroad, against New Zealand in 1968; and the three Tests they had won on that tour had been their only overseas Test victories. Now they had suddenly beaten the West Indies in the West Indies, and looked like drawing a series in England. India had never before won a Test against the West Indies, let alone a series, and at that stage they had lost all the six series they had played in England.

But at The Oval Gavaskar did not bowl. Abid Ali and Solkar had six overs between them before Chandrasekhar came on from the Vauxhall End. There were ten minutes to go for lunch. England, at 23 for 0, were 94 runs ahead and Wadekar thought it would do no harm. If things went horribly wrong he could always fall back on defence.

Chandrasekhar was the great unpredictable of the Indian side, a potent match-winner one day, extremely profligate the next. His very presence on a cricket field was something of a miracle. His right arm was so withered by an attack of polio at the age of five that it did not have the strength to throw a cricket ball. He just had sufficient strength to bowl with it. Perhaps this explained why he was such an unusual leg-spinner. There was nothing of the classical mould of spinners who lured batsmen to destruction with their flighted leg-breaks. He rarely bowled the leg-break, and if he did, he did not turn it much. His stock ball was the googly, his main wicket-taker the top-spinner which skidded through. And all this at near medium-pace – he had even once bowled a bouncer at Charlie Griffith. The theory was that the thinness of his withered arm made it like a whipcord and gave his top-spinner extra bite.

If Chandrasekhar's bowling was a miracle, then his presence on this tour was a gamble and his selection for this Test very much a last-minute choice. He had played no Test cricket for three-and-a-half years, indeed only two Tests since his 1967 tour of England. It was on that tour that he had acquired his name of 'Chandra' as English tongues, struggling to cope with his full name Bhagwat Chandrasekhar, simply shortened it, as they did with Venkataraghavan who became Venkat. Chandra had been the mainstay of the bowling: 461 overs for 57 wickets, including 16 in Tests. On the short tour in the wet, early part of the summer, Chandra would have done much better had the Indians been even a reasonable fielding side; but this was a young, experimental Indian side and heavily outclassed by an England team just reaching its peak under Brian Close.

The next few months were to prove very busy for Indian cricket and disastrous for Chandrasekhar. On the way home from England India toured East Africa, then played a domestic season at home. Immediately after that they went to Australia. The burden was too much. Chandrasekhar sustained a leg injury and was sent home. To make matters worse he was soon involved in a nasty accident in his home town of Bangalore. He was riding pillion on a scooter – a common mode of transport in Bangalore – when it was hit by a truck, the wheel coming agonisingly close to running over him.

Chandrasekhar quickly became the forgotten man of Indian cricket. In 1969, when New Zealand and Australia visited India, there was no Chandrasekhar; in early 1971 the Indians went to the West Indies and left Chandrasekhar at home. He was now taking wickets voraciously in domestic cricket and the West Indies did not always play leg-spin well, but it seemed he would be another Indian player whose promise would never be fulfilled. Before the West Indies tour the chairman of the selectors, Vijay Merchant, had backed his hunch that it was time to sack Pataudi, the long-standing captain, and replace him with Wadekar. That having worked successfully, he now thought that Chandra was a 'calculated risk' who could just make the difference to the tour in England.

Chandrasekhar's selection meant that India had four world-class spinners. While he had been in the wilderness Bedi, Prasanna, and Venkataraghavan had established themselves as the three main spinners. Although both Bedi and Venkat had come into the Indian side long after Chandra had made his reputation, Bedi was now the star left-armer, the master of flight and spin, Prasanna was rated by the Australians as the best off-spinner in the world, and Venkat was the ideal foil for these two attacking spinners, bowling more in what the Indians called the English mould: mean, tight, keeping one end in control while Bedi and Prasanna lured batsmen to destruction at the other.

But if three spinners were good company, four was a crowd and the Indians could never bring themselves to play all four, except in emergencies like the Edgbaston Test of 1967. In 1971 Venkataraghavan was the vice-captain, which meant that his place was secure, Bedi as the left-armer was an automatic selection, so that left a choice between Prasanna and Chandrasekhar. Chandra had played in the first two Tests but, before the third, Wadekar was undecided as to whether he should be replaced by Prasanna. Wadekar only made up his mind when, in the final county game before the Test, Chandra caused a sensational Nottinghamshire collapse. The Notts openers put on 56 runs against Abid Ali and Govindraj, the reserve Indian seamer. Then Chandra took over and, in 20 overs, he took 6 for 34, with Notts hanging on for dear life at 115 for 6. Wadekar realised that, while Chandra could be wayward and unpredictable – the ball he bowled was said to be as much of a surprise to him as to the batsman – he could also be a match winner.

Chandrasekhar's first over, a maiden, produced no surprises. The drama began in his second. Luckhurst hit the second ball hard back at the bowler. Chandra half-stopped it and in the process deflected it on to the stumps. Jameson, backing up, was well out of his crease and run out for the third time in four Test innings.

It was just the stroke of luck India needed. Chandrasekhar was now mesmerising Edrich, who survived only five balls before he was bowled. Fletcher came into bat at the most awkward moment, just over two minutes before lunch. With his crab-like stance and his cap pulled low over his eyes he looked like a startled rabbit who had just emerged into the sunlight. He prodded forward to the very first ball from Chandra and was superbly caught by Solkar at forward short-leg. 24 for 3. Chandra was on a hat-trick.

Suddenly the optimism that Compton had expressed seemed to be ebbing away. Fletcher's wicket also meant lunch. During the break Chandra, listening to his tapes of Indian music, did not worry too much about his hat-trick, but England had a very anxious meal. Over lunch Wadekar, a naturally phlegmatic person, reflected that the two Chandra wickets were very like the wickets Salim Durani had taken six months earlier in Port of Spain: the wickets of Sobers and Lloyd which had led to India's first victory over the West Indies. The previous night Durani had promised Wadekar the wickets. Chandra had made no such promises, but had he turned the match India's way?

Chandrasekhar, nodding his head in that Indian way, resumed his unfinished over to D'Oliveira after lunch and beat him; but he was saved by his pads. The hat-trick had been avoided. But the very next ball D'Oliveira sliced a shortish delivery to Sardesai – a hard, fast, difficult chance. Sardesai could not hold on to it, and in the process injured his hand. In the past such missed chances had often deflated the Indians. But Chandra now seemed to be in a world of his own. With Venkat keeping it tight from the pavilion end, Chandra used his extra pace to make the most of the sluggish pitch. A bowler of his type who bowls googlies and top-spinners at such speed can often be inaccurate but now the batsmen found it almost impossible to get him away. The missed chance had convinced D'Oliveira that he should attack, but he never looked convincing and, after he had made 17, he tried to loft Venkat and was caught by Jayantilal, substitute for Sardesai, at mid-on – 49 for 4.

Knott had not so far failed that summer against the Indians: 222 runs in four innings, 67, 24, 41 and 90. The Indians had almost despaired as he used his broad pads to frustrate the spinners and then employed hefty swipes to leg to score most of his runs as they tired. But this time, after just three balls, he pushed forward to Venkat. It was a reasonable defensive shot but Solkar from short-leg dived full-length almost on to the popping crease to make the catch. It was quite breathtaking. Solkar later saw this as the greatest catch he ever took, and this was the moment too when the reputation of Indian spinners and their preying fieldsmen at short-leg was born.

Now every ball that Chandra bowled seemed to spell English doom. Illingworth survived, precariously, for seventeen balls. Then Chandra bowled a rare but well-controlled leg-spinner and Illingworth was caught and bowled: 65 for 6. The next over Luckhurst, who had batted 110 minutes for 33, was so mesmerised by Chandra that he refused a single – trying to protect Richard Hutton who had made 81 in the first innings – and then edged the very next ball to Venkat at slip. The over after that Snow was also caught and bowled by Chandra – he had lasted just four balls. England were 72 for 8, just 143 runs ahead.

Even now, however, the Indians could not be sure. Right through the series the top order of England had collapsed only for Knott, Illingworth and the tail to repair the innings. In the process seventh-wicket and eighth-wicket records had been set for England-India Tests, and John Snow and Peter Lever, in the side to open the bowling, had made their highest first-class scores. It was a recurring Indian nightmare. The spinners would slice through the main batting but then they would tire and could not finish the job off. Indeed, on the very first morning of the first Test at Lord's England were 71 for 5 before Knott and then Snow helped to take England to 304. In the first innings of the Old Trafford Test, after first Abid Ali and then the spinners reduced England to 187 for 7, Illingworth and Lever put on 148 runs for the eighth wicket. Just as Snow made his highest first-class score at Lord's with 73, so Lever, with 88 not out, made his highest first-class score at Old Trafford. Even in the first innings of the Oval Test, after six wickets had gone for 175, Hutton and Knott had put on 103 for the seventh wicket, a record that stood for more than ten years.

This time Hutton and Underwood threatened to hijack the game, except that, unlike in previous Tests, there was something unconvincing about this performance. They had put on 24, the best stand since Luckhurst and D'Oliveira for the fourth wicket, when Wadekar changed Chandra and brought on Bedi for his first bowl of the innings. Underwood tried to swing him away but only succeeded in finding Mankad. It was a simple enough catch but, at the beginning of the tour not many would have bet on Ashok Mankad taking it. He had been one of those Indian fielders whose catching had revived memories of previous Indian tours. But Colonel Hemu Adhikari, the Indian team manager and one of India's great fielders, had organised regular fielding practice and Mankad was now more confident. He certainly took the catch with some ease.

The change of bowling having worked, Chandra returned the very next over and immediately had Price lbw. Just before four o'clock, after two-and-a-half hours batting, England were all out for 101, their lowest-ever score against India, their third lowest since the war. Only five batsmen had made double figures, only three survived longer than half an hour, and Chandrasekhar had finished with 6 for 38, and match figures of 8 for 114, still the best by any Indian bowler in England.

India required 173 runs to win and they had plenty of time available, more than two hours on Monday, and the whole of Tuesday: eight hours at roughly 21 runs an hour. At last the Indians could begin to believe that they would win a Test in England. When Brian Johnston asked Colonel Adhikari, who had also been the somewhat delphic Indian expert on *Test Match Special* that summer, he said sternly, 'If India do not win now they will never deserve to win'. The force with which he uttered those words surprised Johnston. Indian supporters were not so sure. They knew the Indian record in England and how fickle their cricketing gods could be.

In six previous visits to England, starting in 1932, India had failed to win a single Test. In 1952 they lost three of the four Tests – saved by rain in the fourth – and on the two previous visits in 1959 and 1967 they lost each and every Test they played. In the first Test at Leeds in 1952 they started their second innings in a reasonable position, 41 runs behind, but lost their first four wickets without putting a run on the board. This created the myth of Indian batsmen so terrified of Fred Trueman that they almost trampled the square-leg umpire in their rush to get out of the line of the ball.

The 1971 tour had already been different. Instead of the Indians being continually surprised, the Indians had surprised others. On the Sunday during the Lord's Test, the TV presenter Frank Bough, seemingly perplexed that England's top batsmen should fall to spinners whose names nobody could pronounce, had used the tea interval of a Sunday league match to quiz Peter Walker, the Glamorgan all-rounder. Just before the Test the Indians had beaten Glamorgan and Walker reassured Bough that these were world-class spinners and it was no disgrace to get out to them.

In the Lord's Test, India had even gained a first-innings lead of 9 runs. This was so intoxicating that one Indian journalist distributed sweets in the Lord's press box, provoking derision from Robin Marlar in the next day's *Sunday Times*. Marlar wrote that not all the sweets in India could make up for the slow batting the Indians had inflicted on the 20,000 or more people who had packed Lord's that Saturday. His criticism missed the point that, in the conditions – frequent stoppages for bad light and rain – previous Indian teams would have collapsed. This Indian side, unlike its predecessors, would no longer collapse abjectly when the conditions went against them.

Right through the early summer of 1971 the Indian first innings took place on Saturdays and every one of those Saturdays that summer turned out dank, miserable and wet. The teams of the 1950s would have taken one look at the skies and surrendered mentally in the dressing-room. But perhaps because they had won in the West Indies in 1970-71, perhaps because this was the first generation of cricketers to be brought up in independent India, there was a new resolve, a new willingness and ability to fight. At Old Trafford some crucial late resistance from Solkar, who made a stylish 50, prevented the follow-on. This was to prove vital. Then, on the Saturday of this Oval Test, as dank and wretched a day as any that summer, Engineer, the wicket-keeper batsman, and Solkar came together with India at 125 for 5 and in some danger of having to follow-on. The outfield was so wet that Engineer did not hit a single four in his 59, although his innings contained three sixes. Solkar, maturing fast as a batsman, missed his third successive 50 by only six runs and their 97-run stand not only saved the follow-on but kept India within sight of England, scoring finally 284 to England's 355. The Indians had not, perhaps, provided the greatest Saturday entertainment possible but they had kept their side in the game.

There was also a psychological importance in the 9-run first-innings lead at Lord's. In India the Ranji Trophy matches are often decided on first-innings lead and this was only the second time in Tests in England that India had gained a lead on the first innings. The worth of that stubborn batting became evident on the Tuesday morning of that Test. India bowled out England for 191, the last five wickets falling for 46 runs in an hour and a half, and left themselves 183 to win. Wadekar and Adhikari checked with the weather bureau and were told rain was expected at tea-time. So it was not 183 in 4 hours 20 minutes but, more likely, 2 hours 20 minutes. Two wickets fell early and then Engineer was promoted up the order to take the attack to England.

He and Gavaskar did this superbly, adding 66 runs in 50 minutes, so that there was an almost joyous disbelief that India could win. At last India were giving England a match and this was borne out, in a curious way, when John Snow shoulder-charged Gavaskar as the

Indian went for a quick single. Snow is over six feet tall, Gavaskar 5ft 4in; this was almost the classical, even comical confrontation of one large Englishman versus one small Indian. Snow compounded it by throwing the bat at Gavaskar. The pavilion disapproved, Snow was made to apologise, and dropped for the second Test, but amongst some of the Indians the feeling was that India had got under England's skin. No longer was there that English condescension, where a pat on the back or a murmur of 'hard luck' was meant to soothe the pang of defeat. Now England knew they were in a match and Snow's reaction showed they cared.

That day I was sitting in the Grandstand next to a West Indian. On the previous Saturday, during the slow Indian batting, a couple of West Indians had left Lord's muttering about the cricket and recalling the glory of Gary Sobers. Now this West Indian, quickly downing neat whiskies, was convinced India would win: 'Man, you going to win, man, you is whipping England.' I was not so sure, this was my first Lord's Test and I had seen any number of spectacular Indian collapses. The Indians around me shared my doubts. This was a young Indian crowd, the second generation of immigrants too young to remember the 1950s and early 1960s, but still unable to believe that India could win. As India tried to get those 183 runs before the weather closed in I could hear the old Indian cries that I had heard so often in Bombay – at once expressing hope and fear. 'Dhiré, Dhiré, aré bhai Farouk jara rookay kelo,' shouted the Gujerati crowd around me in Hindi as they saw Engineer charging down the wicket to Gifford. 'Take it easy, Farouk, take it easy.' But that was alien to Engineer's dashing style, and he charged out to Gifford once too often and was stumped. This started a steady Indian decline and by the time the drizzle set in at tea-time England had the initiative.

As the rain grew in intensity so did the arguments. The English argued that rain had saved India, the Indians countered that it was the threat of rain that had made the Indians, at times, throw their wickets away recklessly in the chase for the elusive 183. Even then some Indians were confident that the last two wickets could make the runs. This was probably being fanciful, but the Test had already provided a tantalising glimpse of what might just be possible. This was the closest India had come to winning a Test in England, only the first of seven Tests at Lord's which they had managed to draw. Previously they had played six and lost all of them.

This new mood, this new spirit of belief – a feeling that 1971 was not going to be like 1952 or 1959 or 1967 – was sensed by a *Guardian* writer as he went around Lord's talking to the Indians in the crowd. But then on this tour India was doing things it had never before achieved in England. India had started the tour with a

9

victory, the first time an Indian team had won the first match of an English tour. They had gone on to beat four other counties before the first Test. It was modest compared to Australian performances but no Indian team had ever gone into a Test series in England with such an impressive record. And there was Gavaskar, who had arrived from the West Indies with a Bradman-like average. Just twenty-one, and in his first Test series, he had scored 774 runs, at an average of 154.80. If he could score even half that number of runs now, that would provide a platform for the spinners.

But Gavaskar, while playing some very promising innings, never quite recaptured his West Indian form and by the time India returned to London, England were the favourites. At Old Trafford England clearly had the advantage, apart from the first morning when Abid Ali shook England's top-order batsmen. However, England then recovered so splendidly, probably helped by a couple of dubious umpiring decisions, that on Saturday India were struggling to save the follow-on and in the end rain almost definitely saved India. Set to make 420 to win in eight hours they were 65 for 3 by Monday evening. On Monday night Wadekar heard the sound of raindrops on the window awnings and could have been forgiven for thinking he was back in Bombay. This was not so much tepid Manchester rain as a full-blown Indian monsoon: it rained for fourteen hours and the match was called off at half-past one on the Tuesday.

The first day of the Oval Test seemed to confirm that the series had swung towards England. In the most exciting day's play of the summer under, probably, the bluest of its skies, Illingworth won the toss for the third successive time and saw his side make 355 all out in a day. The sun, having done its bit, then disappeared for the rest of the match. Friday was entirely lost due to rain and on the Saturday India's batting was very like what it had been at Old Trafford: bad start, recovery, collapse, then another recovery. On the Monday morning the last three wickets lasted for another 65 minutes to add 50 runs and, while this was more than England had bargained for, it still gave them a lead of 71 runs.

Chandrasekhar's bowling had almost miraculously transformed the picture. As in the great Indian fables India was on the threshold of a famous victory, the anticipatory joy all the sweeter because it would be so unexpected, but despite this the nagging feeling persisted that England would escape. Illingworth's team had quite a record for doing just that. Six weeks earlier, in the third Test against Pakistan at Headingley, Pakistan, chasing 231, had reached 160 for 4. England looked doomed but in the end won by 25 runs. Illingworth had proved the master tactician and bowler. Could he do it again? It looked very likely when, with the score on 2, Snow, who had returned after his one-Test ban, had Gavaskar lbw. In the first innings Gavaskar had been bowled by Snow for 6, just after the good luck charm he wore round his neck, and which was presented to him by a guru, had broken; now his luck seemed to desert him completely as he padded up and was given out for a duck. It was his first duck in Test cricket.

However, Mankad, whose previous innings in the series had been 1, 5, 8, 7, and 10 (in the first innings Indian wags in the Oval crowd had shouted at Wadekar: 'What does he pay you to keep him in the side?') now played his longest innings of the series. India required someone to stay with Wadekar, and Mankad did just that. He made only 11, but he stayed for an hour and by the time he was out the score was 37. Another 136 to go. Sardesai continued the old Bombay partnership – the first four in the Indian order were all from Bombay – and India ended the day at 76 for 2, requiring 97 runs more.

At Lord's, on the Tuesday, only a few West Indian spectators had believed India could win and the depth of their feelings depended on how long they had been drinking. But on the Tuesday of the Oval Test most of the 7,000 crowd were Indians, making Illingworth almost feel he was playing away from home. He must have felt even more alienated when, just before the match restarted, an elephant, brought specially from Chessington Zoo, was paraded round the ground. As Wadekar and Sardesai walked out to bat there was a growing belief that this was the day the elephant would dance at The Oval.

But in the very second over of the day there was a shock. Sardesai cut Underwood to third man, the batsmen hesitated and Wadekar could not beat D'Oliveira's direct throw to Knott. The two had played together for Bombay for more than a decade, they knew each other's batting intimately, both spoke the same Indian language, but their running between the wickets was still dreadful. They regularly ran each other out in Bombay, now they had done it at The Oval, even though, later, evidence was to emerge to show Wadekar had just got in. India had not added a run to the overnight score.

Wadekar showed no emotion. He returned to the dressing-room, took off his pads, then, after a few shakes of his head, jumped on to the massage table and went to sleep. Wadekar later explained that, while the run-out was a harrowing experience for the Indians present, he was not unduly alarmed: 'For I knew when it came to the crunch Sardesai, Viswanath, Solkar and Engineer would face up to the challenge and carry us to victory'. Like most Indians he believes in fate, and he was now convinced that fate was on his side. After all, had he not done everything to appease the gods?

August 24 was the festival of Ganesh, the elephant-headed god who is considered a source of great good luck in India and worshipped

11

with tremendous fervour in Wadekar's native Bombay. Before the tour Wadekar had consulted the astrologers and made sure they were happy. A Bombay doctor, who was also an astrologer, had predicted an Indian victory in the West Indies. Such predictions on all and sundry matters are cheap in India, but when the Indians won in the West Indies the Bombay doctor immediately became a great seer. Now his word was law and he had predicted victory in England if the team left India on 17 June. The team, due to leave on 15 June, delayed its departure by two days to make sure the stars were right. So Wadekar slept confident he could do no more.

Also, in Sardesai and Viswanath India now had their best batsmen in the middle – both used to spin, both capable of monumental patience. Illingworth had opened with Underwood, he tried D'Oliveira, then himself and even Snow who could get nothing out of the slow wicket. The Indians waited for the bad ball, nudging and deflecting most of their runs. In 105 minutes they put on 48. The tension was unbearable, every ball required careful watching. Sardesai was slightly more enterprising than Viswanath but both batsmen gave the impression they were climbing Everest by the near-impregnable north col: runs were not so much stroked as chiselled out of the hard, granite English attack led by Illingworth and Underwood. Ian Wooldridge in the *Daily Mail* pictured the Indians as a hardy Sepoy unit, with England 'conceding singles as unwillingly as some Douglas Fairbanks retreating inch by inch to the cliff edge, the last act was as gripping as some Hollywood sword-play scene'.

Just 49 runs were needed, seven wickets were still in hand, and the pressure seemed to ease a little. Then Illingworth brought back Underwood. Almost immediately Sardesai, playing forward to a good-length ball that straightened, was brilliantly caught by Knott. The pressure was back on. Solkar stayed twenty minutes for a single before trying to break free: he was caught and bowled by Underwood.

134 for 5. What would Engineer do? He could be devastating. He could also be so irresponsible. He played a horrible whoosh at his first ball. Indians held their breath. He missed the ball, the ball missed the stumps. As if infected by this Viswanath, who had been rectitude itself, did the same a few balls later. Would nerves prove England's best bowler? But Indian nerves steadied. Engineer, curbing his attacking instincts and waiting for the short ball he could punch off his back foot, provided the only batting sparkle of the day.

His confidence transmitted itself to the crowd. Shocked by the dismissal of Sardesai and Solkar they found their voices again. Now, every time a stroke was played, there was an excited hubbub. In the twenty minutes before lunch Engineer and Viswanath put on 12 runs.

This was almost a run feast given what had gone before. At lunch India were 146 for 5, just 22 runs away.

Over lunch the crowd relaxed. Take-away Indian food had not yet made its mark in England, but some tandooris and samosas were being eaten. Surely now victory could not be denied? At lunch the elephant paraded again in some style. The confidence seemed fully justified when, at twenty minutes to three, Engineer and Viswanath were still there with the score 170. Three runs needed. The turbans and the saris gathered along the boundary for the victory charge and it seemed an act of concession when Illingworth brought on Luckhurst. Viswanath, who had batted so patiently – 2 hours and 35 minutes for 33 – decided to have a mighty heave to score the four that would bring India victory. Instead he edged a catch to Knott.

Abid Ali came in and nearly provided a catch to mid-wicket. Illingworth seemed to curse himself for not bringing Luckhurst on earlier, he was doing more than any other bowler. The crowd on the boundary line hesitated. Could it still end in tears? Engineer walked down the wicket and had a word with Abid. The buccaneer had turned man of caution. Luckhurst's next ball was short, outside the off stump. Abid Ali square-cut, and it flashed past Snow and disappeared. Probably it never reached the boundary, but that did not matter. India had won and the crowds were now swarming on to the ground to acclaim the heroes.

At some stage during all this Wadekar woke up and, as he lay on the couch – it is not clear when he had shifted from the massage table to the couch – Ken Barrington, England's assistant team manager, entered the dressing-room and said, 'It's all over. The match is yours. They'll want you up there on the balcony.' Wadekar thought of his mother. Three months ago in the early hours of a monsoon morning, as the team waited to board the flight to England, she had blessed him as he, in that very traditional Indian way, touched her feet and promised to repeat his West Indian triumph in England.

Now he put on his India blazer and came on to the Oval pavilion balcony, at almost the same spot where, in 1953, Len Hutton had stood to accept English cheers on regaining the Ashes. For the first time in the match Wadekar smiled. That smile made a deep impression on Clive Taylor of the *Sun*: 'Old Stone Face stood in front of the balcony and smiled. He might never stop smiling for the rest of his life.'

It was 2.42pm in London, a dull grey afternoon. It was nearly 7.15 in India, a night of heavy monsoon rain. It was the time when Indians would be sitting down for the evening meal, listening to Hindi film songs on the radio. India then had little or no television.

It had been a fraught time. All day Indians had waited for the match to restart. It had done so at 3.30 in the afternoon, Indian

13

time, and through the late afternoon and evening listeners had hung on to every word from the Radio 3 ball-by-ball commentary. As Brian Johnston declared that India had won, the celebrations began. Radios were garlanded. Crowds poured out on to the streets of Bombay, shouting, gesticulating, blowing horns, not in anger as they often did, but in joy. Buses were stopped and commandeered for the celebrations. Mrs Gandhi, one Indian at The Oval speculated to the *Guardian*, would fly over to kiss the team, then hastily corrected himself and suggested she would perhaps send a telegram. Two weeks later, when the team flew home, she had the plane diverted from Bombay to Delhi. India was in the middle of the Bangladesh crisis which in a few months was to lead to war with Pakistan; but this was a rare triumph.

Indians hailed the team as world champions. There was some logic in this, even if the reasoning was tenuous. India had defeated the West Indies and England who in turn had just defeated Australia and Pakistan. England, while not going that far, acknowledged this was a new India, an India that did not collapse at the first sight of a green wicket or the arrival of a cloud. But the Indian claim to be world champions had a wider resonance. The victory not only changed her cricket and marked her emergence in the big league of England, Australia and the West Indies, it was also a significant moment for international cricket. It marked the end of world cricket's unofficial divide into a first and a second division.

This was the first series victory in England by a team that had hitherto been seen as part of the second division – comprising India, Pakistan and New Zealand. New Zealand had been playing Test cricket longer than India but had never won a Test or a series in England. Pakistan had won a Test but never a series. In subsequent years Pakistan and New Zealand were also to win series in England, though it took them another decade. India's victory marked the end of the almost effortless superiority England had exercised over such countries. Before 24 August 1971, the English supporter could routinely expect a win over India, Pakistan, and New Zealand at home. The crunch matches were with Australia and, from 1950, the West Indies. From now on all the Test-playing countries would provide tough opposition. There were no more easy international matches for England. The myth of English invincibility had been exploded.

For India it marked her emergence from the shadow of English cricket. Even as the cricketers had set out from India, the retired Indian cricketers who had suffered such humiliating defeats predicted doom and gloom. The English were too perfect. Their batsmen always played straight, never left a gap between bat and pad, their fielders never dropped catches. Earlier that summer Imran Khan, then a seventeen-year-old touring with Pakistan, was told that if he ever snicked a ball he should not bother to look back to see if the fielder took the catch. An English slip-fielder never missed a catch. One young Pakistani player was so convinced of English superiority that he asked an older player: 'Will I be able to see the ball as it leaves Alan Ward's hand?' At official dinners the Pakistan team manager thanked their English hosts for 'civilising' them, teaching them to play cricket and to eat with knives and forks. Imran cringed. India's victory meant that such craven sentiments had no place.

As ever John Arlott, writing in the *Guardian*, provided the historical perspective. 'This team, admirably captained and sustained by Wadekar, have succeeded where since their Tests began in 1932, the great names of Indian cricket – Wazir Ali, C. K. Nayudu, Nazir Ali, Mohammed Nissar, the Pataudis, Merchant, the elder Mankad, Hazare, Mushtaq Ali, Manjrekar, Amarnath and many more – had failed. Or perhaps it is fairer to say the side of today reaped the harvest these elders and, in their quite different way, Ranjitsinhji and Duleepsinhji sowed in earlier times.'

2

Middle-men as promoters
1792-1920

Cricket, that very English game, is now one of the most prized of Indian institutions. It is the strangest, certainly the most unexpected, legacy created by Imperial rule. Nothing could be more English than cricket, yet nothing could be more Indian in the way the sub-continent has taken to the game and fashioned out of it something unique and very different to the English game.

Indian cricket started, as did all overseas cricket, with expatriate Britons – in this case British sailors playing on a beach in western India. The beginning could not have been more casual. It was 1721. A boat had been lying for a fortnight in some channel off the 'gulf of Cambay' and as Downing, one of the players, recorded, 'Every day we diverted ourselves with playing Cricket and other Exercises'. A few Indians might have gathered round and wondered why these strange men from far lands should want to exert themselves in this fashion in the hot sun – Indians aware of how the sun can burn never do. But if Downing or any of the other players were to return to the bay now they would be astonished to discover how many Indians are prepared to play cricket. Of course it is more than a mere exercise for diversion. It is now a multi-billion-pound business, live television coverage carries the game into millions of homes, the radio listenership for important matches can run into tens of millions and, at least in urban India, cricket matches are played on almost every available bit of space and in all kinds of weather. It is rare to find an urban Indian who does not care deeply about the game. Often his knowledge and zeal for the game match that of Brazilians for soccer. Indeed, cricket in Bombay, Calcutta and the other major centres generates much the same level of passion and skill that soccer does in Rio de Janeiro.

There is an Indian mystery here which requires some explanation. While the Indians were fighting the British for their independence, one of the most popular games in the country was football. Logically, after Independence, football should have become India's number one sport. It is cheaper, it certainly permeated more layers of Indian society – even down to the semi-rural areas – than cricket and, as in other parts of the world, could have been a metaphor for nationalism. It is possible that, had India won its independence from Britain in different circumstances, cricket might not have occupied the position it does in India today. Had the British been thrown out of India in the violent, revolutionary way proposed by the Indian nationalist Subhas Bose (1897-1945), rather than agreed to withdraw peacefully, football rather than cricket would have become the major game.

But while there was no revolutionary overthrow the British withdrew because of a combination of factors: exhaustion from the war, the potential revolutionary situation, and an astute Nationalist movement, led by Gandhi and his western Indian allies who were based round Bombay where cricket was strong. Cricket's path was also smoothed by the fact that Gandhi's campaign was motivated by love, or at least so it appeared. He wanted Indians to hate the actions and results of British policy in India, not the British themselves. Unique amongst nationalist movements, Gandhi taught the Indians to accept the good that was in the British, while rejecting the harm that they were doing to India and its people. This meant that, after Independence, there was no contradiction in accepting cricket – it could very simply be seen as one of the British 'good things' which ought to be retained. Cricket, without any fuss or much debate, was seen as a part of the British system of which Indians approved.

Cricket never became a metaphor for an India v. England contest as did football. In Nationalist history the match between a barefoot team of Indians from the famous Calcutta club Mohun Bagan, and an East Yorkshire regiment in the Indian Football Association Shield final, is legendary. It was played on 29 June 1911 on Calcutta's 'maidan', the vast expanse of green just in front of Fort William which, since the days of Robert Clive, had symbolised the British military presence in Calcutta with the Union Jack proudly flying over it. The day the flag was unfurled had marked the start of British rule and both Indians and British knew that, if it ever came down, that would mean the Raj was over.

The match was a classic David v. Goliath affair. The Mohun Bagan players looked puny compared to the beefy, strong, virile English. This contrast was heightened by the fact that, like all Indian teams then, Mohun Bagan played in bare feet. How could these small barefooted players match the East Yorkshire players who looked and acted so superior? At half-time Mohun Bagan were 1-0 down, but in an incredible second half they came back to win 2-1. (It is, of course, well known that one barefooted Indian equals ten Englishmen in shoes. Indians lose their virility when they put on shoes!) The club's historian would later describe the match as 'a red-letter day in the history of Indian football – a day that has gone down in the history of the nation's struggle for freedom and independence . . . it gave hope and pride to all Indians and sustained and strengthened the peoples' feelings of patriotism and helped to rouse national consciousness'. The story goes that one spectator ran up to the Mohun Bagan captain and suggested the next step was to bring down the flag over Fort William. That romantic legends should attach to this match is understandable, but what is significant is that no cricket match ever attained such a status. Yet today while football is popular – at the common level, probably, more popular – it is cricket that is the pre-eminent Indian sport. It gets all the glory and the attention.

But cricket did not develop in India along conventional lines. The British came as traders, then seized political power. Bengal, in the east, was the first province to fall to the British, the native Bengalis the first to take to British ways. The Calcutta Cricket Club was in existence by 1792 and is, probably, the second oldest cricket club in the world after the MCC. All the early mention of cricket in India centres around Calcutta: the first match of which there is any detailed record was played there on 18 and 19 January 1804, the first recorded century on Indian soil was in Calcutta. It was not Calcutta, however, but Bombay, 1,200 miles away on the other, western, side of the sub-continent which took to the game, making it the centre for Indian cricket. While Calcutta continues to show immense enthusiasm for the game and Eden Gardens is one of the great Test match centres of the world, only a handful of Bengalis has played Test cricket. Calcutta provides the best, the most committed, spectators, but very few players.

The explanation lies at the heart of the contradictory development of Indian cricket. In Calcutta the game never developed beyond the English. That first match in 1804 was between Old Etonians and the Rest of Calcutta, all the players were English and the first century came from Robert Vansittart, the son of a former Governor of Bengal. For good measure he also took seven wickets as the Old Etonians won by an innings. There might have been a few Bengali spectators at the match but they would have made little of it. The Bengalis had taken to English ways early and with great eagerness, but that was essentially in the arts. It inspired Bengali literature, producing some of the great literary figures of the country like the Nobel-prize winner Rabindranath Tagore and Bankim Chatterjee. The tradition of Bengali literary eminence has continued down the ages with Satyajit Ray, the film maker, and Nirad Chaudhuri – probably the finest Anglo-Indian writer in the English language today. But this interest in English literature did not extend to the sporting field. There was a certain amount of Bengali distrust of team games, reflecting not only a highly individualistic approach but also a definite social barrier between the rulers and the ruled.

The early British scorned the Bengalis for the ease with which they had allowed Clive and his East India Company men to conquer them, and the later, imperial, Raj ridiculed their efforts to imbibe English culture and education. In the eighteenth century Luke Scrafton could write of the Bengalis as a 'slightly made people' with 'dejected minds' that 'fall an easy prey to every invader'. By the time Kipling arrived the Bengali Babu proudly flaunting his 'BA failed' and claiming acquaintance with Shakespeare was a finely honed figure of Raj fun.

Cricket is essentially a social game. A. G. Macdonell's *England, Their England* may exaggerate the charms and humours of village cricket but the village pub and the village cricket green go together. In India, however, the British saw cricket as a way of keeping their own community together with little or no place there for the Indians. Till the end of their rule, as Nirad Chaudhuri points out in *Thy Hand, Great Anarch*, the British in India practised a form of racial apartheid; even as late as 1928, just six years before India played a Test match there, he was told off for walking on the wrong side of the Eden Gardens – the side reserved for Europeans:

The Whites in India lived in quarters in the big cities to which it was very difficult to gain admittance. For all practical purposes there was complete racial segregation. The clubs and other social institutions were reserved for the Whites. The railway carriages were marked 'Europeans' in the lower classes and if Indians entered first-class carriages they were either not allowed to go in by the white passengers or thrown out. Even the most eminent Indians were. The public conveniences were marked 'European' and 'Natives' (afterwards 'Indians'). I have also heard that Indian Christians were not allowed to sit in the coolest places under the fans in the Anglican churches.

Chaudhuri writes with evident bitterness about the behaviour of the British in India but this did not diminish his love for the British Empire to which he dedicated his autobiography 'because all that was good and living within us was shaped and quickened by the same British Rule'. Chaudhuri's praise of the British has given him an undeserved reputation in India for being anti-Indian and it shows the contradictory response the Raj produced in India. Chaudhuri could hate the local English community in Calcutta – indeed he went out of his way to avoid them – but he could admire the England of Shakespeare and Milton and Macaulay. If the local English upset him he found consolation in England's great poets and novelists. They represented the real England he cherished. Till the age of fifty-five, when he first came to England, his main contact with England was through books. This can work in literature but how can a social game like cricket take root in such a strange situation?

It did so, because an intermediary stepped in to convert cricket from a diversion of the British in India to the Indians' national game. This intermediary group was the Parsees. The Parsees had fled Iran in the sixth century AD from the incoming forces of Islam, and been given sanctuary in western India. The local King allowed them to live in India provided they did not try to proselytise. They were allowed to maintain their own customs and traditions and this was so successful that, while they lived in India for centuries, they never became wholly part of it. When the European traders and mercenaries started arriving in India they found the Parsees willing collaborators. By the time the British had assumed control the Parsees were the ideal middle-men, as much in trade as in the social field. Despite having lived in India for 1,200 years by then, they portrayed themselves as fellow interlopers. They took to British ideas so passionately that even today many Indians see them as the Raj's last representatives in the country. The popular joke in Bombay is about the Parsee matron talking about 'our Queen' but referring to 'your Indian President'.

The British, keen to get local support for their rule, cultivated the Parsees, a process that continued right through the Raj with the British showering honours on the Parsees: by the end of 1943, sixty-three Parsee knights had been created and of the four Indians made hereditary baronets by 1908, three were Parsees. However, this encouragement stopped short of the cricket field. Here there was no master plan to make the Parsees, let alone other Indians, take to the game. It was the Parsees, anxious to cultivate and copy what the new masters did, who took to the game on their own initiative. Shapoorjee Sorabjee has left a picture in *A Chronicle of Cricket amongst Parsees*, published in 1897, of how this process began:

Parsee boys began with a mock and farcical imitation of European soldiers and officers playing at Fort George, Bombay, their chimney-pot hats serving as wickets, and their umbrellas as bats in hitting elliptical balls stuffed with old rags and sewn by veritably unskilful cobblers. Some enthusiastic boys at first only gleefully watched from a distance the game played at Fort George, and then hunted after and returned the balls from the field to the players. For such gratis services rendered heartily and joyfully the officers sometimes called them to handle the bat, which was done with extreme pleasure and delight. Thus were learnt the initiatory practical lessons in cricket by the Parsees . . . The more they watched the game the intenser grew their desire to play it. And they did begin with a make-shift of cricket – quaint bats unskilfully hewn out of old logs or cut out of planks that once served as lids or bottoms of dealwood boxes, and balls as artistically turned out of materials foreign to ball-making. The height and shape of stumps were matters of absolutely no moment.

As cricket grew in popularity amongst Parsees there were attempts to show that the ancient Persians had played cricket except that it was called chowgan. About the only common element was that, in both cases, a ball was used. Later, as other Indians took to the game, there were similar attempts to prove that the game of gilli-danda, popular in western India, could have been a forerunner of cricket. Gilli-danda was played with a short wooden baton and a wooden cylinder of the same thickness as the baton but it was a hit and catch affair which had no real connection with cricket.

Nor, to be honest, was there much similarity between the early cricket that the Parsees were playing and the game as played in England. For a start there was the problem of pitches. Early Parsee cricket was played on uneven patches of ground, overgrown with weeds or tufty kinds of grass. This made batting impossible, every batsman was of necessity a slogger but the fielding was sharp. And even if Bombay never had the heightened sense of racial separation that the English in Calcutta developed, the English in Bombay did not always take kindly to attempts by the Parsees to play cricket.

As it happens, in both Bombay and Calcutta cricket was played on a ground which had great strategic importance. The English may have come to India as traders but even as merchants they developed armies and constructed forts. In Calcutta and Bombay the constructions were very similar. In both cities the British kept the water at their back – the river in Calcutta, the sea in Bombay – and trained their guns on the Indian hordes likely to emerge from the interior. In Calcutta the area in front of Fort William was an open space, kept free of any encumbrance to provide a clear field of fire. This is now the great 'maidan' where, on a Sunday, a million matches will take place, but even now no permanent construction is allowed – the strategic consideration of one age providing environmental comfort in another. In Bombay, similarly, there was the Esplanade which was outside the walls of the Fort that marked the entrance to the fortified English city. In the mid-eighteenth century, a hundred years before the Parsees took to cricket, the British had cleared the Esplanade to provide an open field of fire.

Emma Roberts, writing about the Esplanade in 1840, saw it as a 'wide plain stretching from the ramparts to the sea'. Today the sea has receded as Bombay, reversing the processes of Venice, has reclaimed land and built on it, but there are still some open spaces, the maidans, which are the heart of Indian cricket. It was here that the Parsees first saw the Europeans play and tried to copy them.

But to gain the necessary space they had to dispute with the local English. Out of the total open area of 180,000 square yards, a third was taken by the Bombay Gymkhana to which, of course, the Parsees and other Indians did not have access. This already meant that, while at best twenty-two people occupied a third of the ground, some 500 or more were squeezed into the remaining two-thirds forcing them, complained the Parsees, 'to pitch their wickets so close to one another that anything like a free play of the game is impossible'. But in addition to that the Gymkhana's polo players used the remaining part of the ground to play two nights a week and this, as the Parsee petitioners to the Governor said in 1881, meant 'the polo ponies completely ruin the turf and render the ground unsuited for cricket'.

Thus started a familiar Raj battle of petition and counter-petition interspersed with letters to the press between the Parsees, the Gymkhana and the government and, while the intricacies of the argument are no longer relevant, it revealed both Parsee tenacity and their ability to use the Raj system. The local English, as ever, quickly saw this as a challenge to the very existence of the Raj. N. F. Symons, secretary of the Polo club, wrote in a letter to the *Times of India* on 15 September 1884, 'Do not allow the preposterous notion to take root that a few young Parsee cricketers are going to be allowed to oppose the whole European community and jostle the Europeans off the Esplanade, whether at polo, sports or anything else . . . the sooner these young Parsees come to their senses and become a little modest, the better'.

Then there was the problem of dress. The Parsees as a community may have had fewer restrictions compared to the Hindus and the Muslims, but even so they did not dress in the British way. Parsee men wore the orthodox sudra, a white shirt reaching almost to the knees and worn under the coat. One player, J. M. Patel, tried to conceal the sudra under the flannel dress but this met with opposition from fellow Parsees. To the English this gave the Parsee cricketers a rather ridiculous air, and Lord Harris, who took over as Governor of Bombay in 1890, thought it looked as if they were playing with their 'shirt-tails' flying in the breeze. It was also inconvenient for players. The handle of the bat could get caught up when players made the drive. Mehellasha Pavri, probably the greatest Parsee cricketer of the early days, once hit the ball into his sudra and was caught out. On another occasion, so legend has it, as the ball lodged there fielders gathered around the batsman waiting for it to drop so that they could catch it. When it would not drop they got hold of the poor batsman's legs and shook him like a mango tree and as the ball dropped took the catch.

If this suggests that early Parsee cricket developed its own rules, then it also, sometimes, took liberties with the rules. Pavri recalled an early occasion when 'a Parsee batsman went in but did not score. He was a good batsman. Some of the best men on his side were out for about 30 runs; so this batsman put on a different dress, and tied a handkerchief round his head to escape being identified by his opponents, and went in to bat again. He made a big score and won the match for his club. But he was put to great shame when it was found out that he had played this trick.'

By the mid-1840s Parsee cricket began to establish itself on a proper footing. In 1848 the Orient Club was formed with the high ambition of pioneering ventures such as overseas tours and professional coaching. It was dissolved two years later but, in 1850, the Young Zoroastrian Club was formed. All they possessed were two broken bats, four stumps and some old cricket balls. Despite Bombay Gymkhana's arrogance and the polo players' opposition they had found a space on the maidan and they rolled and watered this patch of once barren land to make a usable pitch. They were also beginning to attract the support of men of money. This was an era when the great Parsee businessmen, who dominated the early Indian economic scene, were emerging and the earliest – and best – of them, the Tatas and Wadias, provided money. In technique Parsee cricket followed the English but at a respectful distance. In 1828 round-arm bowling was legalised in England, it only reached Parsee cricket around 1867, some three years after over-arm bowling was permitted in the English game. It was still some years before the Parsee caught up with that fundamental bowling change.

But what mattered was the spirit of these early Parsees. With a determination that was remarkable they continued to play the game. In 1877 the Parsees were granted a first match against the English at Bombay Gymkhana. They lost and were the butt of English sarcasm. The Governor, Sir Philip Woodhouse, much amused his dinner guests when he said, 'I have no doubt the Parsees expect to be able in a year or two to encounter an All-England Eleven'.

But much as the English in India scoffed at their ambitions the Parsees were not downcast. Within a decade they were touring England, first in 1886 and then again in 1888. The tours produced that mixture of levity and hope that such pioneering efforts often do. On the eve of one Parsee tour the *London Graphic* had wondered if, after the drubbing from 'our Australian cousins', perhaps 'we are next destined to be knocked (cricketically) into a cocked hat by the descendants of the Fire Worshippers of Persia'. But the first tour did not make much of an impression. The Parsees lost 19 of the 28 matches they played, won only one and failed to impress either *Wisden* – which did not think it worthwhile to print the scores – or W. G. Grace. He played against them at Lord's, scored 65, and took 7 for 18 and

4 for 26 as they were bowled out for 23 and 66, losing by an innings and 224 runs.

However, unlike the English in India, the English at home were generous with the Parsees, keen to cultivate them. On Saturday 7 August 1886 they played in Windsor Great Park, in the vicinity of the Royal residence, against a team captained by Prince Victor, Queen Victoria's grandson, with Princess Victoria and Princess Louise as interested spectators. The entertainment at Cumberland Lodge was on the invitation of Queen Victoria who in 1876, encouraged by Disraeli, had assumed the title of Empress of India. She had an Indian servant and was keen to see the first cricketers to come out of this land, which was the subject of so much fantasy but about which she knew little. The Parsees bowled out the Prince's XI, which included the great hitter C. I. Thornton, for 90, Prince Victor making 24 and his brother Prince Albert 11. But the Parsees could only make 33 and the royals had much the better of the encounter with 95 for 1 in their second innings, Thornton 61 not out.

The Parsees must have been surprised by the civility and warmth with which they were received – after the years of aloof, almost haughty disdain the English had shown in India. It showed, as Nirad Chaudhuri was to find out, how very differently the English could behave with the Indians in England. Here the Indians were no threat and as the band of the Life Guards played, there was a luncheon where Prince Victor drank a toast to the Parsees and, according to the *Windsor and Eton Express*, the match was attended by 'numerous and brilliant company'.

Some were quick to see political capital in all this. The magazine *Cricket Chat* commented that year that this was a visit of 'no small significance, not only from the standpoint of cricket, but also from the political point of view. Anything which can tend to promote an assimilation of tastes and habits between the English and the native subjects of our Empress-Queen cannot fail to conduce to the solidity of the British Empire . . . the zeal with which the natives of India are working to secure proficiency in the chief as well as the best of our sports, cannot be overestimated. The Parsee fraternity is the most intelligent as well as the most loyal of the races scattered over our Indian possession.'

Two years later the loyal Parsees were back, eager to learn more but also to show what they had learnt. Wearing blazers which had black and yellow stripes they were soon dubbed the 'Bengal Tigers' but there was a certain tenacity in the play on this tour which was missing on the previous visit. Eight of the 31 matches were won, 11 lost, 12 drawn. Grace was still not very impressed: not equal to our second- and third-rate clubs, he said, but they had shown the quality the Victorians most admired, 'pluck in adversity', and Grace and many

24

of the Victorians acknowledged this. Some of the displays of Parsee 'pluck' were remarkable. At Scarborough their opponents wanted 4 runs to win with four wickets to fall and half an hour left. But in that half an hour the Parsees captured three wickets and restricted their opponents to three runs, earning a draw. Even more remarkable was what happened at Eastbourne. The Parsees followed-on against the Gentlemen of Eastbourne but then batted so well that Eastbourne had to make 123 to win and collapsed for 56, the Parsees winning by 66.

It was this match which announced the arrival of Mehellasha Pavri, who took six wickets and bowled one batsman with such ferocity that the bail travelled a full fifty yards. In another match in Norwich he uprooted a stump and sent it flying – it somersaulted, then pitched the right way up. On the tour his pacy round-arm bowling was so successful that he took 170 wickets at an average of 11.66. During the three-month tour he bowled over 5,000 deliveries at a cost of just under 2,000 runs.

Pavri, like Grace a doctor, later returned to England to practise his profession – probably the first such Indian doctor – and played cricket for Forest Hill, Surrey Club and Ground, and even Middlesex. He was without doubt the first great Indian cricketer and his devotion to the game was all the more remarkable because there was so little encouragement. When he was thirteen cricket had been introduced into his school in Navsari, the little Gujerat town which has produced such famous Parsee families as the business group Tatas and the musical Mehtas, whose son Zubin was to become the famous conductor. But, as he later told an English journalist:

> My grandfather, who was of orthodox views, did not at all like the idea of my playing cricket, which was a great innovation in India at that time. Accordingly he put my bat into the fire. I said nothing, but stole quietly away to the timber yard of my uncle, a contractor. There I found a big log of wood which seemed suitable for my purpose, and gave it to a carpenter, with instructions to make a bat out of it. The value of the whole log was ten times greater than the piece which eventually appeared in the shape of a bat, so that my uncle, who did not quite understand my enthusiasm, took good care to express his feelings by giving me a severe beating.

Later his batting feats at school – he was then a cricketer of the barndoor type – won him a bat and by the time he came on the English tour he was a round-arm bowler with a slingy action; on the tour he learnt to vary his pace, carefully watching Lockwood and Sharpe, both of Surrey. Lockwood took him to one side and showed him how to bowl the breakback.

All this came in very useful when, in 1889-90, G. F. Vernon led the first English team to tour India. Vernon had played for Middlesex and the team included Lord Hawke but only three players who had regularly played first-class cricket in 1889. Modern cricket research suggests that the matches were not first-class. In any case all the matches were against Englishmen in India, but the Parsees managed to wangle a fixture against them. It was played in Bombay in January 1890.

This was, perhaps, the first great cricket match played in India, the start of what has been called the golden age of Parsee cricket. Some 12,000 people – a 'variegated Oriental crowd', wrote Framji Patel, who captained the Parsees that day – gathered to watch the match. Along the maidan, shamianas – Indian-style marquees – were erected to house the glittering members of society. There were Parsee priests present in their ceremonial dress invoking the assistance of their prophet Zoroaster and, as one observer noted, 'dark-eyed daughters of the land for the first time mustered strongly'. The first innings showed fairly level pegging, Vernon's XI making 97, Parsees 80, but in the second Pavri took 7 for 34 and the Parsees were left 78 to win. They won by four wickets. It was Vernon's only defeat of the tour and the victory produced amongst the Parsees the sort of sporting hyperbole that rare triumphs can inspire. One of the leaders of the community felt it was the greatest Parsee show since they had been beaten by the Arabs in the battle of Nahavand, a defeat which led to their exile in India. Parsee women garlanded the victors and the Parsee rich of Bombay held lavish parties. It was as if a people, which had lost its country in a battle long ago, had suddenly rediscovered itself on a cricket field.

Two years later in the winter of 1892–93 Lord Hawke returned leading a team which was much stronger. It included Stanley Jackson, who was later to become Governor of Bengal, and eleven players in all who were playing or had played first-class cricket. Again nearly all the matches were against the local English but there were two matches against the Parsees: the first on 22 December was dominated by Pavri. He took ten wickets and the Parsees won by 109 runs, the first defeat on the tour for the Englishmen. Lord Hawke had disapproved of some of the Parsee batsmen having frequent drinks intervals. It was a blazing hot day and, every time the ball was hit for four, 'a bucket was brought out for the hero to have a drink and, of course, the time thus wasted gave him a rest'. Hawke soon put a stop to such 'violation' of the rules. Whether this affected the return match is not clear but in a nail-biting finish the Parsees lost by 7 runs. Hawke observed with some sardonic pleasure that 'the Parsee ladies cried like babies and the crowd did not take the result in a good spirit'. There was much comment in the English press in India about such unsportsmanlike behaviour, the inability to take defeat graciously but, as Pavri explained, the Parsees were just 'paralysed by the result . . . the crowd had not at that time been educated up to taking defeat in a philosophical manner'.

One of the spectators at this match was Lord Harris whose invitation it was that had brought Lord Hawke and his team to India. Harris had not played against the Parsees on either of their English tours of 1886 and 1888 and only really got to know them when he arrived in Bombay. The Parsees of that era and Harris's rather uncritical biographers have hailed him as a great promoter of cricket in Bombay. There is some truth in that. He got on well with Framji Patel, the legendary Parsee captain. In the row about the polo players using cricket grounds he did favour the Europeans, but he persuaded the government to set aside sites along the sea front in Bombay for the Parsees, the Hindus and the Muslims where they could build their own gymkhanas – these still stand and have seen some of the best club cricket in Bombay.

In his first year as governor Harris went to see the Parsees play the Bombay Gymkhana. This fixture had started three years before Harris arrived, with the Parsees playing one match against Bombay Gymkhana and one against Poona Gymkhana, Poona being 120 miles from Bombay in the hills overlooking Bombay. As Parsee cricket grew in strength the English found it difficult to maintain face – so important to colonial rulers – when defeated. Harris quickly saw that it would make sense to have an annual fixture that would pit the combined strength of the English against the Parsees. Despite some opposition from Bombay Gymkhana he convinced the Europeans that it would be a good idea to have a joint European side to represent the Presidency of Bombay and to challenge the Parsees: it would attract good crowds and provide a decent match. The first match was held in 1892 and was called the Presidency match. Two matches were played, one in Bombay, the other in Poona.

The first Presidency match in July 1892 illustrated some of the problems that the Parsees faced – problems that have continued to dog Indian cricket to this day. The English insisted, understandably, that the Parsees should select their best team. This meant, wrote one Parsee notable to another, that the old Indian habit of 'dictating' would not be tolerated. The team must be selected on merit and the Indian habit of 'if you take so and so then alone I will play' would not be tolerated. The first match was dubbed the 'fire engine match' as the fire brigade had to be called to the ground to draw the rain water off and permit the match to take place; but there was more rain and it ended in a draw. The Parsees and the Europeans were, in general, evenly matched. Between 1892 and 1906 they played 26 matches, the Parsees won 11, the Europeans 10, and 5 were drawn.

Twice the matches were abandoned, once due to rain, once due to the plague.

If these matches presented problems for the Parsees, then they were also a headache for the local English. The early matches generated 'a good deal of feeling'. The 1890 match between the Parsees and Bombay Gymkhana was cancelled at very short notice by the Bombay Gymkhana because, said its secretary, A. P. Gould, the match had led to a 'display of feeling' which was 'rather too high and it caused a great deal of dissatisfaction as anything of the kind naturally takes away most of the pleasures of a cricket match'. Gould did not specify how this feeling manifested itself but, as Framji Patel wrote in reply, that a match between two different nationalities would evoke partisan spirit was hardly a reason to abandon it. The real cause appears to have been the fact that the Europeans had made it clear they would not play the match unless the Parsees agreed to 'appoint European umpires'. This seems an extraordinary demand, which the Parsees saw as a reflection on themselves.

Umpiring continued to be a problem even when the Presidency matches started, with the local English unwilling to accept that the Parsees were competent to umpire. It was one thing playing cricket with the Parsees, but umpiring meant an Indian, a subject race, giving decisions on an Englishman, the master race. This was anathema to many local English. Just before the 1898 Presidency match the Parsees were told they could nominate one of the two umpires but whoever was nominated had to be an Englishman. The reply of the Parsee Gymkhana secretary, J. M. Divecha, with its mixture of hope and humility, 'Please, sir, do give us a chance', provides an insight into how the two cricketing communities related to each other:

We must say it is very difficult for us to find one fitted with the task, especially as our acquaintance with such persons is very limited. In deference to the strong public opinion on this point we now wish to approach you with the following proposal and trust that your committee will see its way to accepting it. While it may be admitted that at one time it was necessary, for one reason or another, to have both European umpires, it is perfectly evident that this has now changed and that good cricketers such as Framji Patel, D. J. Tata, B. B. Spenser, R. E. Mody, M. D. Kanga and a few others can efficiently and honourably perform the arduous duties of umpiring in the Presidency Match and we shall certainly consider it a compliment to Parsee cricket if men like the above are asked to umpire the match.

The English relented to allow the Parsees to nominate a panel of three Parsee names but if all three proved unsuitable then an English umpire would have to officiate. It was 1900, eight years after the Presidency matches had started, before the first Parsee was accepted as an umpire. Harris did try to break down social barriers. Before the first match at Poona he asked the English team whether they would mind if he invited the Parsee cricketers as his guests during the luncheon. They agreed and this strengthened the bond between Harris and the Parsee cricketers. Harris acknowledged the 'humble but always loyal and active' support of the community, particularly Framji Patel, and he in turn described Harris as the 'guru' of Indian cricket.

Certainly it is doubtful whether, without Harris, the annual Presidency match between the Parsees and the Europeans – which later became a great Bombay tournament involving other communities – could have got started. Also the senior inter-schools tournament in Bombay (there is a different junior school competition) owes much to Harris and the schools still play for the 'Harris Shield'. This has led his biographer to present his role in the promotion of cricket in India in almost heroic terms. The radicals in England criticised him, the Indian press attacked him, but he, Harris, was the lone champion who 'encouraged the diverse Indian youth to play cricket together'. This is so far from the truth as to be almost farcical. Harris, a true-blue Conservative who loved to tangle with the radicals in England, had succeeded Lord Reay as governor. Reay was a friend of Gladstone and ranks with Ripon as one of the most popular British officials ever to rule India. British rulers fell into two broad patterns. For all the high-sounding phrases they uttered when they set sail on the P&O liners to India, once there they had to struggle constantly not to become prisoners of the local British who, as Nirad Chaudhuri has written, were driven by the pathological fear that one day the Indians would rise up en masse and drive them out of the country. So while the British could be marvellously even-handed when it came to administering justice between Indians, in any case which involved an Englishman and an Indian, however gross the English behaviour, the Indian was always wrong. The community closed ranks. Ripon, as Viceroy from 1880-84, had tried to stand up to the local British community over the Ilbert Bill which proposed that Europeans could be tried by Indian judges. But the English in India raised such a howl of protest that Ripon had to back down. Yet the very fact that Ripon had dared to defy the collective British doctrine in India won him amongst Indians a glowing reputation as a friend.

Reay did much the same in the Crawford case in 1888-89 when he prosecuted Crawford, a senior member of the Civil Service who had evolved a ruthless technique of extorting bribes from his juniors by threatening to demote them or transfer them to inconvenient places.

29

The English judges in Bombay found him not guilty but Reay refused to accept the verdict and eventually Crawford's guilt was proved to the hilt. His conviction was secured by promising a free pardon to the junior Indian officers who had been victims of Crawford's extortions, but the English press in India and *The Times* in London whipped up a campaign to dismiss these men. In the process Reay was presented as that most dangerous of Englishmen, going soft on the natives. The Indians held public meetings supporting Reay and the whole affair was very fresh in everyone's minds when Harris took over from Reay.

There was never any danger of Harris going soft on the natives. Harris, as his own writings show, could not think of the Indians as a nation (but then neither could the majority of British officials) and had nothing but contempt for the great majority of the people of the sub-continent. As he wrote to Lord Cross on 4 June 1891, just over a year after he had arrived:

You asked me what I think . . . the feelings of the people to us are . . . I should say that ninety per cent of the population i.e. the agricultural class – don't care two pence to what nationality the Surcar [i.e. Government] belongs as long as the [revenue] assessment is a fair one . . . and that a large proportion of that percentage is quite in the dark as to who the English are, or where they came from . . . I should say that they don't hate us more than they hate each other . . . Hindus hate Muhammedans and Parsees hate both. Each is ready to get up a free fight about nothing at all . . . We can do infinitely more work in their climate than they can, and they get fat and lazy as they rise in rank, whilst our civilians are as active as young men.

Harris had a splendid chance to build on the trust Reay had created between the Raj and the educated Indians but in every educated Indian he tended to see a conspirator.

The Ripon-Reay period was a time when Indians, particularly educated ones, could feel that their voices would be heard in the governor's house and the Viceregal palace. The men who succeeded them soon found it easier to give in to the prejudices of the local British community. Any demand by Indians nearly always became a contest of India versus England, and in that there could be only one winner.

Harris and later successors of Ripon and Reay, like the English in India generally, reserved special scorn for educated Indians. These were the Indians emerging from the British-inspired schools and colleges set up following Macaulay's idea of raising Indians who would be English in everything – thoughts, ideas, feeling – but the colour of their skins. When these very same Indians started demanding a greater say in their own affairs they provoked hostility and anger from British officials. It is astonishing how moderate these early Indians were, how touching their belief in the goodness of British rule, and their faith that, if the Indians proved themselves worthy of the British, they would – as Dadabhai Naoroji, a Parsee and one of the founders of the Indian National Congress, said – become 'British citizens'. He was, himself, a Member of Parliament for Central Finsbury, and the desire to be accepted by the British was the height of nationalist Indian aspirations. It is fascinating to speculate how differently the Indian Nationalist struggle might have turned out if there had been more British rulers like Ripon and Reay to respond to the early nationalists.

Irish Home Rule, and Parnell, was a live political argument in England then and it became fashionable to label every Indian politician, even moderates like Ranade who saw divine inspiration in the connection between Britain and India, as an Indian Parnell. Ten years before Harris arrived a predecessor as governor had toured the Western Ghats, the mountain region that forms the hinterland to Bombay. Armed with a history book that detailed how the people of the region had fought the great Mughal, he had searched the lairs, the retreats and strongholds of this mountainous region trying to picture how another generation of rebels might torment the British Raj. What he missed was that the rebellion would come through the modern word, not through the medieval sword, and that it would be led by Indians who had been taught ideas of freedom, liberalism and justice by their British tutors.

Harris used the Parsees as a counterweight to the increasing criticism which his insensitive rule provoked from educated Indians. The Indian press, which had so often praised Reay, now just as often criticised Harris, and Gokhale, the great leader of the Indian Moderates – and the guru of Gandhi – described Harris's rule as 'an unsympathetic and reactionary administration'. Cricket, which fulfilled the Victorian ideal of the manly game, was, for Harris, just the 'healthy, active pastime as a counter-attraction to pice [Indian for penny] and politics'. One of the ironies of Indian cricket was that the viceroys and governors who were the least sympathetic to Indian political aspirations had the greatest impact on Indian cricket. Reay and Ripon were held in high esteem by educated Indians but they made no contribution to the development of Indian cricket. Harris and other 'reactionary' politicians did. This meant that in the early stages of its development in India, cricket was effectively shut out to the best minds of the country. In Calcutta the game made no impact on the Bengali literary world which was then flowering as never before. In Bombay it was shunned by the growing, influential, educated classes. So, unlike in England, where cricket became part of literature and an element of educated life, in India it did not. It was many years before it did. Even now, in the 1990s, cricket has made very little literary impact in India.

To be fair to Harris, he was reflecting the prejudices of his time. Soon after he returned to England, after completing his term as Governor of Bombay, an Oxford University Authentics team visited India. Again the crucial match was against the Parsees, who beat them by eight wickets. The Authentics, who included the last of the great lob bowlers, G. H. Simpson-Hayward, were missing a couple of their best players, but the Parsees too were without Mistry, their top player – so probably the odds evened out. What was especially interesting was the attitude of the English team. One of the players, Cecil Headlam, later wrote a book about the tour which was more of a travel book as the title, *Ten Thousand Miles through India and Burma* (1903), suggests. He took an active dislike to the babu, as the British-educated Indian was derisively referred to. Headlam met one in the shape of a clerk and, at one Indian railway station, he had had to wait a long time to buy some cheap railway tickets. What would have taken him 'a minute and a half' at Euston had taken him an hour. He was finally directed to a 'narrow, narrow, dark, dirty office' where a 'babu' told him to go back to the stationmaster. When Headlam said he had just come from the stationmaster, the babu 'read the letter out in loud, unintelligent voice', repeated his command, and put the letter in front of him and went on counting the rupees. Headlam wrote:

> This was too much. I put the toe of my riding boot round the near leg of his three-legged stool and gave it a sharp jerk. In a second it capsized and my Aryan brother capsized with it. Never shall I forget the look of mingled astonishment and awe upon the faces of his gaping underlings, never the look of fear and injured pride upon the countenance of that sprawling and obese black gentleman. Without saying a word he got up and bowed and deferentially led the way to the ticket office. In two minutes I had got my tickets and paid for them.

Compared to this Harris was a shining liberal and, by encouraging the Parsees, he had unlocked a door to the development of Indian cricket: communal ambition. First the Hindus, then the Muslims, watched the growth of Parsee cricket and were determined to copy it. What the Parsee could do the Hindu and the Muslim could certainly do better.

The annual Presidency matches effectively generated the first Indian cricket tournament. Over the years it acquired different names, the Triangular Tournament, the Quadrangular and, ultimately, the Pentangular. These changes in names indicated that yet another team had joined. In 1905 and 1906 the Hindus had played in place of the Parsees, but it was in 1907 that they formally joined and thus the annual Presidency match became a Triangular tournament. The Hindus were followed by the Muslims in 1912 to make it a Quadrangular and then in 1937 a team called 'The Rest', comprising Indian Christians, Anglo-Indians (i.e. those of mixed Indian and British stock) and Jews joined. As the Pentangular it continued in this form up to 1945.

By the time the tournament was abandoned the idea of different communities playing against each other on a cricket field was considered politically dangerous. Communal – whose dictionary meaning is no more than 'relating to a community or a commune' – had come to imply a man or a woman who was such a fanatical supporter of his or her own religious community that they would be prepared to kill for it. The word communal had become a term of abuse in India, just as in the 1990s in Europe one might use the word racist or fascist. But in those early days the development of Bombay cricket, and thereby Indian cricket, was due to the different communities sharpening their competitive instincts on the cricket field. This process did not take place to quite that extent anywhere else, which explains why Bombay cricket expanded so quickly, so vigorously, and why Bombay became a centre of Indian cricket. Not merely Bombay cricket but Indian cricket benefited from the tournament. Until well into the 1930s it was almost the only Indian tournament of any significance. Even after the Ranji Trophy, the national championships, were started in 1934-35 it remained the one tournament in which every player wanted to participate. It produced some excellent cricket and a platform for cricketers who dominated Indian cricket well into the 1950s. Communal cricket in the end, denounced by Gandhi, fell victim to the times but in its early years the development of Indian cricket would have been a lot slower but for the competitive spark that it provided.

The Hindus were eager enough to play cricket. They were keen to drink the 'milk of the tigress', as English education was called, but this education stressed book-learning, and cricket or any other sport was shunned. Professor D. B. Deodhar, one of the last of the great Indian cricketers before the Test match era began, has described some of the problems: lack of grass wickets, the sheer effort involved in even producing matting wickets – the Poona Young Cricketers Club used to carry their own net and matting over their shoulders to the pitch and then off again every day to make sure it was safe – and no encouragement from school or college authorities except the odd teacher who had been exposed to the Victorian ideals of developing manly virtues through games.

Some of the problems of Hindu cricket were also caused by the caste system. Caste restrictions, which were even more rigidly enforced then,

33

meant, as Harris discovered, that one team had only twelve players because the team, based on a particular caste, only had twelve members of the caste who could play cricket. The first of the great left-arm spinners, Palwankar Baloo, also had to fight caste. He was an untouchable who worked for three rupees per month (just under five shillings then in English money) as a groundsman in a Bombay club. His low caste meant he could not play for the prestigious Bombay Hindu club, the Hindu Gymkhana, but the Parsees gave him an opportunity and, when the Hindus discovered the magic in his fingers, he was quickly made a member and he went on to captain the Hindus. Professor Deodhar believes that he was as fine a bowler as Rhodes or Verity. Even if that may be an exaggeration, on the 1911 All-India tour of England he took over a hundred wickets in all matches.

Despite Baloo's presence in that team one Faguram, from Calcutta, was excluded because he was not of the right caste and another high-caste member decided not to tour because he feared ex-communication from his caste. Indians at the time were gripped by the fear of 'kala pani', literally 'black water'. In the Middle Ages a pernicious doctrine had grown up which said that Hindus would lose caste if they crossed the seas. It led to the ruinous isolation of the country, and those who defied it, like Gandhi, had formally to purify themselves.

If, as Lord Harris and Lord Hawke had noted, the early Parsee cricketers were rather too keen on drinks and drinks intervals, then the early Hindu and Muslim cricketers liked the idea of hitting a cricket ball but did not fancy running between the wickets. One observer recorded, 'During the matches with the native soldiers, the robust, stalwart sepoys took pride in hitting the balls as high as they could, and then instead of running, would gaze in admiration, with exclamations of Wah-wah [Indian for bravo] at the result of their prowess and get run out'.

Some of the early Hindu players also disdained the use of boots, leg-guards and gloves, but their attitude changed when they faced Pavri and went home with 'crushed toes and fingers'. Nor was the early development of Indian cricket helped by the fact that cricket, in Bombay at least, was played just after the monsoon. The theory, as Harris explained it, was that 'after the heavy monsoon rains the monsoon leaves behind thick, damp, atmosphere which moderates the directness of the sun's rays and by wearing a topee and a spinal pad and keeping one's sleeves turned down, one could play cricket comfortably'. The rain-sodden, soft wickets meant, however, that any bowler maintaining a good length and supported by smart fielding could run through a side. It also encouraged slogging. Curiously, in Calcutta cricket was always a winter game but it was 1917 before Bombay became converted to the idea. This explains why, between 1892 and 1918 when the Bombay tournament was played just after the monsoon, there were so few memorable batting feats: only eight centuries and only one a double-century. A monsoon cricket tournament is still played in the city, appropriately called the Kanga League after the Parsee cricketer, but it produces some of the most extraordinary play. Suddenly a ground, which has been a lake the previous day, is somehow passed fit for play and bowlers hold sway with batting very much a lottery.

The communal series also saw the development of the first neutral umpires, although this came about in rather regrettable circumstances. In 1916 the Hindus were playing the Europeans. John Greig, known affectionately as 'Jungly', was batting against C. K. Nayudu. This was Nayudu's first big match at the age of twenty-one, while Greig was already the great hero of English cricket in the sub-continent. Born in 1871, a year before Ranji, he came to India in his early twenties and lived there till 1921. He arrived in India as a captain and returned to England as a colonel, then for good measure became a Roman Catholic and was ordained a priest in Rome in 1935. On his regular visits home he played for Hampshire and his *Wisden* obituary entry reads 'Greig, Canon John Glennie', because in 1947 he was made an honorary canon of the Diocese of Portsmouth. In India he saw the rise of Parsee cricket, its decline and the assumption of the Parsee mantle by the Hindus and the Muslims. During this period he was always the Englishman the Indians had to get out if they wanted to beat the Europeans. In 36 innings in the Presidency Tournament he scored 1,478 runs, including two centuries, at an average of 41.05 and took 55 wickets for 670 runs at an average of 12.18.

On this particular occasion Greig was stumped off Nayudu. The decision was given by an umpire called M. F. Pai, a Hindu, but Greig and his partner Goldie did not like the decision, claiming that the bails had not been properly removed. The implication was that a Hindu would support a Hindu and eventually the committee that ran the tournament met and decided that, in future matches, umpires should come from a community not involved in the match. Today such a decision, given the controversy about neutral umpires, might be regarded as a good decision, even a progressive one. But the Hindus saw it as a reflection on their ability to be objective and even thirty years later Professor Deodhar could not forget the implied insult:

The inborn and dormant prejudice as well as the superiority complex of Britishers in India, was clearly brought out by this incident which showed that they thought us incompetent to get over our communal bias and prejudice. But I am not and was not surprised at this incident. Even though British officials high up in the military and civilian hierarchy carefully refrained from exhibiting this complex in the least manner, it was there all the time and one sensed it all over – on the field of play, in the dressing-room and at the lunch and tea tables. Most of them always assumed an attitude of reserve and aloofness which was the natural outcome of a presumed superiority, not only in games, but even in race and culture.

Perhaps Deodhar was being unusually sensitive. He came from Poona, the capital of the great Maratta power which had offered such fierce resistance to the British. Born in 1892, and growing up in the late nineteenth and early twentieth centuries, Deodhar was influenced by the Maratta lore of having fought the Mughals and the British and some of this is reflected in his comments. His attitude is conditioned by the English in Poona behaving even more aloofly than in Bombay. Every year the Hindus used to play a number of matches against the Poona European Club. But the matches were always played at the ground of the European club, never at any of the grounds owned by the Hindus. It was only in 1925 that Sir Leslie Wilson, then Governor of Bombay, for the first time brought a team to the Poona Young Cricketers Hindu Gymkhana ground and then it was a special occasion. The Poona Young Cricketers Hindu Gymkhana was celebrating twenty-five years of existence.

So cricket prospered, not because the different communities mixed but because they did not. Competition, not co-operation, was the spur. When the Hindus first played the Parsees they were astonished to discover how advanced they were not only in playing skills but in the art of captaincy and field setting. Parsee crowds, brought up on the great victories of their team, had also developed a fine line in barracking. Every Hindu batsman was a 'Tatya', which can mean 'wally', but also has more complimentary and affectionate connotations. But all this only increased the Hindu urge to do better next time and if such development meant that it intensified the divisions of India, cricket was the gainer. Had this not happened it is doubtful if cricket would have developed in quite the way it did. Over the years, as the fierceness of the Quadrangular and Pentangular tournaments intensified, the Hindus and the Muslims gathered players from all over the country and this provided a further boost to cricket.

One of the main problems with developing a proper English-style game in India was the nature of the Indian crowd. Descriptions of the early matches, like the one between the Parsees and the Europeans, speak of large crowds. Certainly vast numbers gathered to watch the match and many of them were becoming increasingly knowledgeable about the game, but even then there was an element about the game of 'tamasha'. 'Tamasha' is a rich Indian word which conveys fun, glamour, suspense, excitement all rolled into one. In India anything can become a tamasha. It could be a policeman chasing a hawker down the sidestreets, it is generally a film star attending a public function, it is increasingly cricketers whether on or off the field. India is a country which lives on the streets – the streets provide a sort of living theatre that dwarfs, in variety and colour, anything seen in the English National Theatre. From morning to night the streets provide a rising volume of noise: the hawkers selling their goods shouting to get attention, the incessant car honks, the cries of newspaper vendors, the general hubbub of a people who talk, argue and gesticulate as they go about their normal business.

In such a situation cricket could never be a polite Victorian game played before a respectful audience. Here the cricketer who did well was appreciated, the one who failed was shunned. The successful cricketer instantly became a hero, the man who failed was hounded as a villain. But since street theatre in India is free, open to anybody who wants to watch, so in the beginning Indian cricket was free. Large crowds came but it was almost impossible to take a 'gate' in the English sense. It meant that Indian cricket could never capitalise on its early popularity, it was always short of money and Harris, writing as late as 1921, felt that this would always prevent it from arranging tours of England. Without such tours, he felt, 'notwithstanding their multitudes I doubt if they are going to turn out a team of all India as good as the best of our County Clubs'.

Indeed this formed one of the underlying points of dispute between the English and the Indian. When the Bombay Gymkhana cancelled the 1890 match against the Parsees they may have been upset by boisterous Indian crowds, but one of their unstated grievances was that they could not make the large crowd that came to watch the match pay for the privilege. Bombay Gymkhana was closed on one side where the clubhouse was – open only to the English members – but the other three sides and particularly the far side which opened on to the rest of the maidan would have to be enclosed if the crowd was to be made to pay. The Victorians with their shrewd sense of money had been chafing at this inability to take a 'gate'. The polo executive of the Gymkhana had requested the government 'for leave to reserve an enclosure on the west side and charge a small fee for admission thereto' and the editor of the Gymkhana newsletter had urged in May 1897 'the necessity of charging gate money at all important polo and football tournaments and important cricket matches'.

Twelve years after Harris had expressed doubts if Indians could ever become a cricket nation because of lack of finance, the first ever Test match played in India was held at the Bombay Gymkhana and temporary stands and shamainas were erected. A gate was possible even if the ground was never big enough to accommodate all those who wanted to see, while the spectators who climbed up the surrounding trees could not be made to pay. So while the setting was charming, and Indians who saw the Test still recall it in terms of wonder, the Test grounds on the sub-continent which began to be developed, concentrated on the need to convert open fields into stadiums: concrete bowls with permanent covered stands enveloping the ground. What had been like English county grounds became something more resembling a huge football stadium. The game that was played within the stadiums was inspired by England, but local needs meant that the setting was very far from being English.

3

The strange princely light

Indian history always seems to be a muddle. As a child reading Rawlinson's *History of India* I could hardly restrain my tears, upset not so much by the Indian defeats – unexpected and staggering as they often were – but by the sheer inconsistency of it all. Every now and again it would be proceeding along a broad avenue of triumphs and settled policy only to turn a corner and end in a cul-de-sac, which seemed to undo everything that had gone before. Indian cricket history is not dissimilar, wonderful victories ruined by amazing defeats. But occasionally, in the middle of the most desperate gloom, a figure emerges who, however briefly, lights up the whole scene.

Kumar Sri Ranjitsinhji ('kumar' literally means 'young prince') was one such light: suddenly a dark alley is lit up to reveal the most handsome of boulevards. His leg-side play, particularly the leg-glance, revolutionised the game and he, along with W. G. Grace and Victor Trumper, are part of the great golden age of cricket: men who both changed the game and defined an era. Gilbert Jessop wrote, 'He was indisputably the greatest genius who ever stepped on to a cricket field, the most brilliant figure in what, I believe, was cricket's most brilliant period'.

There is something magical about the Ranji story. Before he emerged there was nothing to suggest that India was ready to produce such a cricketer. There had been a number of fine Parsee cricketers but they were little known beyond a very select circle. Ranji himself came to England unheralded and unknown. He was seen as a prince though he was neither brought up at court nor did he look like succeeding to the throne of the western Indian state of Nawanagar, which in any case was a fairly small princely state. A rival was ensconced on the 'gadi' and, indeed, it was because Ranji's chances of succeeding to the throne were slim, if not non-existent, that at the age of sixteen he made the hazardous journey to England and to Cambridge. Initially he was ignored at Cambridge. F. S. Jackson thought little of his habit of nearly going down on his knee to sweep to leg, but a trip to India with Lord Hawke's team made Jackson more sympathetic to Indians

39

generally and, when in 1893 Jackson became the Cambridge captain, Ranji was awarded a blue.

Ranji used his bat like a wand to charm even those who had at first spurned him, and by the end of the summer of 1896 he was being hailed as the 'most popular man in England'. That summer, in his first Test against Australia at Old Trafford, he scored 62 and followed it with 154 not out which not only saved England from an innings defeat but almost brought them victory as Australia struggled to make the 125 required in the final innings. If this represented a touch of Victorian romanticism – and in dinners and functions held in his honour at the end of that summer there was a great deal of such rhetoric – there is no doubt that, as John Lord wrote in *The Maharajahs*, Ranji was 'the first Indian of any kind to become universally known and popular'.

Ranji had, in effect, become India's cricket ambassador. Not since the days of the great Mughal had another Indian made such an impact. Even then the Mughal was part of the fantasy of pearls and spices that India always evoked. Ranji was flesh and blood, captivating English cricket crowds, charming English socialites by playing an English game better, certainly more inventively, than any Englishman. The full story of how he conquered first the English cricket world and then its social world has no place in Indian cricket history, however, for Ranji played no first-class cricket in India whatsoever. During his playing career in England he occasionally went back to India, but the cricket he played there was purely social and when he finally returned to take up the throne of Nawanagar his cricketing days were over.

He did play cricket after becoming the Jam Saheb of Nawanagar but even then, in 1920 aged forty-eight, it was for his beloved Sussex. It was as if he had divided his life into two compartments. He reserved his cricket for England, and his princely duties for India, a rather novel version of 'East is East and West is West and never the twain shall meet'. In England he was a cricketer, in India he was a ruler of men. But such a duality at once makes him an awkward subject in the history of Indian cricket. For India's greatest ever cricketer played no cricket in India, unless you include his schoolboy cricket at Rajkumar College in Rajkot.

Indeed Indian cricket administrators who played a major part in establishing the game in India received no assistance from Ranji. Anthony De Mello, who helped set up the Indian Cricket Board, wrote with evident bitterness many years later that 'Ranji did absolutely nothing for Indian sport and sportsmen. To all our requests for aid, encouragement and advice, Ranji gave but one answer: Duleep [his nephew] and I are English cricketers. Ranji could not have been more blunt. In short, Ranji was a different man in England and in India . . . in most other walks of life he was a model Indian Prince. But the Ranji who settled in Jamnagar after the first world war was an altogether different man from the great cricketer who delighted English crowds in earlier years.'

Ranji's biographers accept that he felt more at home in England than in India. His official biographer Roland Wild, in a biography published in 1934, a year after Ranji's death, wrote, 'More than once it is remarked that the Jam Saheb seemed to attain the peak of his enjoyment only when in the company of his English guests'. Wild, perhaps, did not appreciate how ironic this was. Some years after Ranji left Rajkumar College for Cambridge, Lord Curzon, then Viceroy of India, came to the college to make a speech-day address and reiterated the philosophy that guided the institution. The aim, he said, was not like Macaulay's, to turn Indians into Englishmen: 'The Anglicised Indian is not a more attractive spectacle in my eyes than the Indianised Englishman. Both are hybrids of an unnatural type. No . . . After all, those Kumars who became Chiefs are called upon to rule, not an English but an Indian people; and as a Prince who is to have any influence and to justify his own existence, must be one with his subjects, it is clear that it is not by English models alone, but by an adaption of Eastern prescriptions to the Western standard, that he can hope to succeed'. Ranji, educated to be an Indian who could use English methods to improve his rule, turned out to be an Indian who could teach the English something about their own national game.

Ranji's love for England was deepened by his love for an English-woman, the daughter of the Reverend Louis Borissow, the chaplain of Trinity College, Cambridge. For obvious reasons this was a love he could not declare when he was alive. The love had to be so clandestine that he had a secret passage built in his palace connecting their two rooms. The idea of intermarriage scandalised both the English and the Indians, and the idea of an Indian ruler marrying a European seriously alarmed the India Office. It raised all sorts of diplomatic and social problems. This love affair was long rumoured in India but has only recently been confirmed in the latest biography by Simon Wilde, who also paints a much more critical picture of Ranji than his previous biographers – at times he makes Ranji out to be quite Machiavellian.

This is less than fair, but certainly Ranji's cricketing story is more than just a case, as Sir Edwin Arnold said indulging in the height of Victorian sentimentality, of a 'star from the east' bursting upon the cricketing world. If such a star did burst it was a cool, calculating star which knew exactly where it was going to land and how. Ranji had wonderful natural gifts, perhaps no other cricketer before or since has had such gifts. His dedication and his discipline were exemplary, enabling him to harness those gifts and create a batting revolution. But at the same time he saw cricket as a weapon – a weapon for his own personal advancement. There need be no dishonour in that. For in a sense Ranji's is a very modern story of an immigrant who seeks fame, glory and money in a foreign land, and then returns to his own land to use his foreign money and prestige to establish himself. Ranji did not earn money in England, but the prestige he earned from cricket was invaluable.

The modern immigrant does it by setting up business or, occasionally, winning success in the field of sciences or medicine. Ranji was the first to do it on a cricket field. Like many an immigrant Ranji did, perhaps, create an impression of wealth and standing back home that may not have passed critical, modern scrutiny. Strictly speaking, Ranji was not a prince, nor a direct descendant of the rulers, but the grandson of an officer who had served the state and hailed from a village that, in comparison, makes Bradman's Bowral look rich. He was adopted by the ruler as his successor and was then ignored. When he came to England he had no official status. Nawanagar was an insignificant kingdom where plague alternated with famine – in the ten years after Ranji became ruler in 1907 there were four famines – nature had given it little, nor had its rulers done much better. But in England all this was obscured by a life-style that lived up to every occidental's idea of Indian princely behaviour. While this meant that Ranji was often in debt, that was a small price to pay to establish the princely cricketer. Cricket, Ranji quickly sensed, was the key that could unlock the door to social acceptability in the highest class in England.

The making of Ranji as the prince among cricketers also helped with establishing Ranji the ruler. When he returned to India in November 1904, his fame as one of the great cricketers of the world established, there seemed no chance that he would become the ruler. But Ranji kept up his socialising both of fellow princes and, more particularly, of British officials who would have to decide should a successor become necessary. This seemed unlikely as the then ruler was younger than Ranji, but suddenly he died of typhoid and British officials ruled in Ranji's favour as the natural choice. On 10 March 1907 Ranji became the ruler of Nawanagar.

After that he discouraged all talk of cricket, but whenever the need arose he used cricket to further his plans. Thus, just after the first world war, he returned to England to play cricket. He was forty-eight, had lost an eye in a shooting accident, and had no other cricket fields left to conquer. But he played thrice for Sussex – scoring 16, 9 and 13 – a pale, rotund shadow of the pre-war Ranji. He explained that he wanted to write a book on the art of batting with one eye, and that the King wished him to play.

That, perhaps, was the real reason. For years Ranji had harboured the ambition of making his state a major princely power. Before Ranji it was too small to merit more than passing reference. Only about 40 out of the 562 princely Indian states had a direct relationship with the Raj through formal treaties, and they saw themselves as allies of the British. The rest varied from county squires to middling states with a population of a few million. Nawanagar came at the bottom of the middle table of princely states and was not big enough to enjoy the status that a princely state like Baroda or Hyderabad enjoyed. It was only in the summer of 1920 that Ranji finally persuaded Edwin Montagu, Secretary of State for India, to grant Nawanagar such a status. A statue of Montagu was erected in Jamnagar, the capital, and King George V was humoured by his playing of some cricket. Ranji knew how well cricket and diplomacy could be made to work.

Ranji did give to India and Indian cricketers the awareness that it was an Indian who had become one of the world's greatest batsmen and this contributed to the growth of Indian cricket. Even today, Neville Cardus's essay on Ranji and Fry putting Yorkshire to the sword is required reading by Indian schoolchildren. Cardus tells the story through Ted Wainwright, the Yorkshire bowler, and while Indian schoolchildren struggle with Wainwright's Yorkshire dialect, there can be no mistaking the strong romantic image he conjures up of an Indian conquering the English cricket field. With India a colony of the British, and Indians made to feel that the British were their superiors in all things, this image of Ranji played an important part in fostering Indian pride and self-respect.

But it was Ranji's example of combining cricket and politics that had the biggest influence on India and its cricket. His fellow princes had eagerly followed his career and noted how cricket had carved Ranji a position he would otherwise not have gained. The Ranji story suggested they could use Indian cricket to further their own political ambitions. The princes were entering a crucial phase in their relationships with the British. Both the British and the princes wanted to maintain the old feudal order but, in the changed climate of the 1920s, this was no longer a simple case of making sure that the Viceroy shot enough tigers. Something more was needed and cricket provided this. It marked the next stage in the development of the game in India.

4

The era of the princes
1920-32

Princely India was a not a natural cricketing nation. Cricket values the individual. It is, probably, the most individualistic of all team games. A major batsman can take charge of an innings, a bowler can bowl a side out cheaply, but at the end of the day there must be teamwork, some element of co-operative endeavour between the eleven players, for a team to perform. Even the great, almost magical feats of cricket like that of Ian Botham at Headingley in 1981 involved other players, the batting of Dilley and then the bowling of Willis. Botham's 149 not out turned the match but without Dilley and Willis England might still not have won.

Princely India was highly individualistic, even idiosyncratic. A prince held complete and total authority in his domain. Unless he grossly misbehaved, or in some other way fell foul of the British, there was little his subjects could do to remove him. Princely rule in India varied enormously: some like Baroda had enlightened rulers who sought to provide a benevolent monarchy, others were despots of the most feudal kind.

The traditional princely sports were polo, pig-sticking and shikar (hunting). They combined adventure with danger, they provided princes a chance to display personal glory. By the time cricket was being taken up by Indians it was heavily laden with Victorian ideals of teamwork, discipline and togetherness, ideals that meant little to an Indian prince. A century before Indian princes started taking to cricket, the English aristocracy had played a major part in converting what had been until then a folk game into a modern sport. The organisation of matches became more elaborate, rules of the game were standardised and professionals were employed to improve skills. The English aristocrats did not just take over a village game, they worked with the grain of the game as it was developing. So while the aristocrats organised great matches between the landed gentry, there were also other games between shopkeepers, craftsmen, the village blacksmith and the village vicar, and these men would be brought into the teams organised by the landed gentry.

The Indian princes had no indigenous Indian pattern on which they could build. In any case the Indian princes would not have much cared for an overall Indian pattern. Each prince saw his domain – however small – as supreme. All he was concerned with was his own rule and his relationship with the paramount power, the British. The rest of India did not matter to him. The princely domains could vary hugely: from the state of Hyderabad which was bigger than France and whose Nizam was one of the richest men in the world – if also the greatest miser – to Bhadwa which had a population of 1,401 and whose ruler had worked as a guard on the railway before he became ruler. Some of these princely states were ancient, like the Hindu state of Rajputana – as modern-day Rajasthan was known; many were the creation of the wars and conquests of the seventeenth and eighteenth centuries that opened the door to British rule. In some cases the governor of a Mughal province capitalised on the anarchy to set up his own kingdom, as with Hyderabad; often a freebooter seized a territory and the British, keen to find allies as they mopped up the rest of India, dignified the freebooter with a title. The brigand became a prince.

The British saw the princes as a cheap but effective means of safeguarding their Indian empire. Their attitude to the princes was enunciated early by two of the great British administrators of India. Mountstuart Elphinstone saw it as a sink to 'receive all the corrupt matter that abounds in India, unless we are willing to taint our own system by the discharge of it'. Thomas Munro saw it as a place where 'the field's open to everyman [meaning every Indian] to raise himself; and hence among them there is a spirit of emulation, of restless enterprise and independence, far preferable to the servility of our Indian subjects'.

A third of India was ruled by Indian princes who were generally allowed to do much as they pleased. In fact the more conservative, even obscurantist, the rulers were, the greater they pleased the political department of the Raj which acted as nanny to the princes. And with the colleges and universities of British India increasingly producing men who used the weapons provided by their English education to question the Raj, the princes became an extremely useful ally. The British knew that in any fight with the Indian nationalists the princes would always support the British. Elsewhere in India, amongst the two-thirds they directly ruled, the British could not stop the flow of history but in the third of India ruled by the princes history was frozen. That part of India remained in the feudal ages.

The princes completed the complicated mosaic that was British rule in India. Only 100,000 Britishers ever lived in India. For them to rule a country of several hundred million they had to have the support of local collaborators. The princes were the most significant of such collaborators, the others were Indians who benefited from British rule, profiting from the stability, justice and the consistent administration which made such a contrast to the capricious Indian rulers who had gone before. These divisions in India posed a problem for a nationalist movement like the Congress which sought to promote a secular, united India. Every move of theirs claiming to represent the real India was checkmated by the British who would argue there had been no united India before the British arrived and that it would disappear once the British left.

But if these presented political problems for the nationalists, they actually encouraged cricket. Before the Raj arrived the Parsees enjoyed no prominence in Indian society. It was the opportunities provided by the British which made the community and helped it to start cricket in India. Now the princes provided the exotic bloom that the sport needed.

Decades later when the princes had been replaced by commercial patrons it became fashionable to decry the princes' efforts: princely cricket was full of intrigue, pomp and selfish ambition. Far from advancing Indian cricket, it set it back. There can be no denying the intrigues, and there is nothing more deadly than princely intrigue. For some two decades Indian cricket was absorbed with the question of finding a prince – any prince – to captain the team and the intrigues that accompanied such a search seriously undermined the game. Yet such an assessment reflects hindsight and the values of another age. Indian cricket might have developed without the princes, but it is doubtful if it would have developed as quickly as it did without their help.

In a country like India, where change almost always comes from the top – in the long history of the country there are few examples of change from the bottom – the lead given by the princes was crucial. They acted as a buffer. Just as the Parsees, who first took to the game, were seen as quasi-foreigners by the rest of the Indians and therefore natural converts to an alien game, the princes had always been exotic. Indians were well aware that their rulers could follow fancy ideas, take up something one minute, drop it the next: capriciousness was the style they came to associate with their Rajahs and Maharajahs. Even Akbar, hailed as one of the great Indian rulers, developed a fancy that he could promote an entirely new religion composed of elements of all the major religions. He spent a lot of time and money promoting it, but it died with him. Another ruler decided that the capital, Delhi, was too far to the north of the country and decided to relocate it to the geographical centre, forcing the citizens on a long, disastrous route march. Before the British arrived a consistent Indian ruler was almost unknown and one reason so many Indians took to the British was that, whatever the drawbacks of their rule and their exploitation of the country, they were always consistent. In a land of inconsistencies this made a big impression. So the princely patronage of cricket could be seen as part of the familiar princely mezzaz, or the mood which could vary from day to day.

However, unlike Akbar's religion, princely patronage, haphazard and unplanned as it was, did manage to give the game a certain image, and spread it to parts of the country it would not otherwise have reached. And by the time the princes withdrew Indian cricket was sufficiently well established for it to flourish on its own.

The first great princely patron was the House of Patiala, and this illustrated all that was both good and bad about such patronage. Patiala was a middling princely state with a population of about 1.5 million and a Sikh ruler in a state dominated by Jat Hindus. Sikh arms had carved out the state in the wars of confusion that followed the collapse of the Mughal Empire and it had a long history of support for the Raj going back to the Indian revolt of 1857 and the Afghan wars. In the 1890s the ruler, Rajendra Singh, began to appreciate the importance of sports as a means of maintaining links with the British and promoting his state. His first sporting foray was to build up one of the most successful polo teams in the country which beat other princely polo teams and also British teams – both of which gave the Maharajah immense pleasure. Such sporting success also built up the reputation of Patiala and this brought great political benefits.

It was after he had satiated his ambitions on the polo field that Rajendra Singh turned to cricket and, almost in the twinkling of an eye, built up an imposing team which included Ranji, Brockwell, the Surrey professional, Hearne the Middlesex bowler, and the outstanding Parsee, Muslim and Hindu cricketers of the time. Prominent among them was Colonel Mistry whom Ranji had described as the Clem Hill of the Parsees. Ranji, then establishing links with the Indian princes in order to further his claims to the Nawanagar throne, was made an officer in the personal bodyguard of the ruler and he much valued Rajendra Singh's financial help. The Patiala team was a fair side by almost any standards. In one match in 1898 the Patiala XI scored 633 for 4 wickets with both Ranji and Mistry scoring more than 250. However, Rajendra Singh died in 1900 when he was twenty-eight, affected, it would seem, by a fall from a horse while playing polo. But he had established the tradition of princely cricket patronage and the style of princely play. The princes were expected to spare no expense in bringing the best players from England and Australia if necessary, and when they batted – a prince only ever batted, fielding was something beneath princely dignity – it was always as a slogger. This came to define a whole princely style. Just a week before his death Rajendra Singh scored 21 runs in 8½ minutes against some good Parsee bowling.

It was his son Bhupendra who established Patiala as the great house of cricket. He would have seen little of his father's exploits for he was barely ten when Rajendra Singh died, but he inherited the style. As a batsman he made a princely slog something special. Once playing in Bombay in a charity match he scored 86, hitting only fours and sixes. Off the field he came to define the archetypal Indian prince in both looks and behaviour. A tall, enormous man, with a full beard and a bull-chest, he had the sort of physique that suggested he was about to gallop off to battle. Money was never a barrier to fulfilling his desires – what he desired he always got and he desired nothing so much as women. One of his disaffected subjects once wrote that the Englishman started the day with bacon and eggs, and the Frenchman with coffee and rolls, and 'His Highness with a virgin'. However, a book, *Indictment of Patiala*, published in 1929, alleged that Bhupendra Singh did not care whether the woman was a virgin, married to another man or even unwilling to accede to requests.

The *Indictment* alleged that Bhupendra Singh had, among other things: procured the abduction of innumerable women whose husbands were murdered, imprisoned on false evidence, or compensated from state funds; imprisoned a state official for failing to supply him with nubile hill-girls; made indecent proposals to his young step-mother who was forced to flee to British India; forced his attentions on a twelve-year-old girl who had died as a result; pursued, caught and burnt alive four Rajput girls who had escaped his zenana; raped the daughter of a European minister in his state; and punished recalcitrant women by putting red pepper up their vaginas. The charges, backed by witnesses and running to two hundred pages, caused a great deal of alarm to the Viceroy, Lord Irwin (later the Earl of Halifax), and eventually an inquiry was held by J. Fitzpatrick, Agent to the Governor-General. He explained:

As to all those stories about women, these should be seen in the light of the custom of a bride coming to the house of a ruler to bring either her young girl attendants to serve the double purpose of attending on the Maharani and providing distraction for her husband, and thus preventing second marriages or recourse to public women should the Maharajah be of an amorous or roving disposition . . . His Highness does not deny youthful indiscretions, and is willing to make monetary amends.

Irwin and his advisers felt the report was a 'whitewash' but Bhupendra Singh was too important a prince, who was playing a crucial role in maintaining the Raj, to be removed. The report did nothing to deter the Maharajah's insatiable appetite for females and a year before his death his amorous adventures were still causing problems.

The womanising fitted in neatly with the Maharajah's promotion of cricket. In the grounds of his palace, which also housed three hundred wives and concubines and a scented swimming pool, there was a cricket field, the Bardari Palace Oval, in an area larger than Lord's and with facilities that rivalled the best of country-house cricket available then in England. Elephants were sometimes used to roll the wicket, the pavilion was a very comfortable club house and there would be tents around the ground. A six hit by the Maharajah or anyone else could well disturb the tent containing the Maharajah's three hundred wives and concubines.

Like his father, Bhupendra Singh invited a number of English professionals: Rhodes, Hirst, Leyland, Larwood, Waddington, Kilner and Australians like Frank Tarrant, Bromley and Scaife. All were brought to India to coach and to play for 'the Maharajah of Patiala's XI'. How much coaching they did is doubtful. Bhupendra Singh was a busy man. When not chasing women he had his princely political ambitions and many of the coaches just enjoyed the winter sun and the opportunities for deer or big game shooting. In a sense Patiala, and the other princes who followed his example, played the same part that, in our day, the South Africans have been doing: providing very agreeable winter employment for some English county professionals who might otherwise have struggled to make ends meet in a bleak English winter. Rhodes spent six winters in India in the 1920s and 1930s, always taking a fellow professional with him. The pavilion was a more than adequate living quarter, and the players catered for themselves in the local bazaars and markets. Later Learie Constantine, the West Indian, was a coach in Hyderabad invited by the Nawab Moin-ud-Dowlah. Again it is difficult to tell how much coaching he did, but he became aware of the contrast of India: opulence of the few existing side by side with the grinding poverty of the many. It also made him realise that, contrary to his West Indian experience, not all black men were necessarily poor. Some could be fabulously rich.

In 1911 Bhupendra Singh widened the scope of Indian cricket by organising a tour of England. Unlike the Parsee tours, this was not confined to any one community, although there was, naturally, a distinct Bombay bias. Even then it included some of the great names of the early years of Indian cricket, prominent Parsee cricketers like Meherhomji and Dr Kanga, Hindus like P. Baloo and Jayaram, and the accomplished wicket-keeper K. Seshachari. Colonel Mistry, who had played such a big part in Rajendra Singh's cricket, was now the Maharajah's private secretary.

Some of these players had experience of English conditions but they performed poorly. They won only two of their thirteen matches, beating Leicestershire and Somerset, but they lost to Oxford and Cambridge Universities, and to Staffordshire, a minor county. But on this occasion they came up against the legendary Sydney Barnes who took 14 wickets for 29 runs in the match. Against Gloucestershire there was Gilbert Jessop, at thirty-seven, debating whether to give up cricket. He declined to tour Australia that winter but against the Indians made a whirlwind 79. There were some Indian successes. Meherhomji scored 1,227 runs on the tour and Baloo took 114 wickets at an average of 18.86. But the tour did reveal an early weakness of Indian teams – inability to reproduce abroad the form they often showed at home; there were, however, extenuating circumstances.

Patiala's team had come to England at the height of the season. This was the high noon of the Edwardian era, the long summer that ended with the shots at Sarajevo and the first world war. In this world of summer balls, deb dances and country-house parties it was becoming increasingly common to see a sprinkling of Indian notables. 1911 was the year the Aga Khan first established himself in British society. The Indian princes had watched the Aga's progress with keen interest. He did not have a state, he was not a ruling prince, but through superb public relations and the ability to cultivate the English both in India and particularly in England, he had won a position of prominence that his following or support did not justify. The princes were very keen to develop contacts in London because it meant they could get away from the hated Political Agents. They were the nannies of the Raj, who tried to control the behaviour of the princes in their charge; many of the princes felt they served their own ends and denied them access to the Viceroy in Delhi and to the King and high officials in London. Direct contact in London meant that they could get round the nanny.

So Bhupendra Singh who, unlike the Aga Khan, ruled one of the chief states in the Punjab, decided to combine the cricket tour with socialising and politics. It is very likely that the timing of the tour was not entirely coincidental. 1911 was a crucial year. In the winter of that year King George V and Queen Mary became the first, and only, ruling English monarch to visit India while it was still part of the Empire. The years before that had been marked by the first nationalist agitation in India when many Indians, smarting under what was seen as the imperious, arrogant rule of Lord Curzon, the Viceroy, revolted. The Raj was now constantly looking over its shoulder, fearful of another Indian revolt, and the visit of the King was meant to soothe the Indians, make amends for Curzon's behaviour and start a new chapter.

A splendid durbar was held in Delhi where the King announced that the capital was to be transferred to Delhi. To be in London while plans for this momentous visit were taking place was, obviously, important and Patiala made the most of it. So while the rest of the team practised cricket, the Maharajah and Colonel Mistry went to polo, attended the Trooping of the Colour and had a private audience of the King. Even when the Maharajah did play, in the MCC match, he was summoned from the ground on the last day by the Secretary of State for India and the tea interval was extended to half an hour to enable him to bat. Not that the Maharajah's batting made much difference as the Indians were bowled out for 96 and lost by an innings. Only Mistry, making 78 in a brilliant display of hitting, lived up to his home form. All the socialising soon took its toll, Patiala fell ill and withdrew from the tour, and with him went Colonel Mistry.

As with Ranji's example, Patiala's tour made other princes realise how useful cricket could be in furthering their political aims. Cricket's importance for these middling-level princes grew the next year when the Chamber of Princes was set up to bring all the princes in India under one body. Before that the princes were forbidden by the British to communicate with their fellow princes. Ever since the revolt of 1857 the British had been fearful that the princes might conspire to form another united front and throw them out. So even though one princely house was allied to another through marriage they could not discuss anything except through the 'nanny' political department. But now, in 1912, faced by the much more insistent and very different nationalist struggle the British could no longer impose such restraint. The Chamber of Princes met therefore under the chairmanship of the Viceroy and this allowed the princes to let off steam, mostly against the nannies in the political department. The Chamber had no power, however, and the really powerful states like Hyderabad, Mysore, Travancore and Kashmir ignored it. But for middling states like Patiala and Nawanagar it was ideal and a prince with cricket connections also carried clout in the chamber. Ranji was Chancellor of the Chamber until shortly before his death and Patiala was Chancellor from 1926 to 1930, then again, after Ranji's death, in 1934 and 1935.

Patiala had planned a return tour soon after 1911 but the first world war intervened and it was only after the war that other princes began to follow his example and seek power through cricket patronage. Even before the war Patiala's example had inspired other states but they were very small ones. Thus Cooch Behar, in Bengal, had taken to cricket. Its ruler, Sir Nripendra Narayan, hired two Sussex professionals, George Cox and Joe Vine, and ran three teams: two were based in Calcutta and one in Darjeeling in the foothills of the Himalayas. One of the first Cooch Behar captains was Prince Victor who had been educated at Eton and later returned to England to help develop the Indian Gymkhana which, to this day, is a home from home for many Indian cricketers. Cooch Behar was one-fifth the size of Patiala while Nathore, which was no more than a country estate, recruited some important Bombay players. But these princely states could not sustain their interest. Two rulers of Cooch Behar died in quick succession, a minor came to the throne and the cricket tradition did not revive until the 1930s.

Patiala, despite his financial problems – his extravagance led him to go turban in hand to the government of India for a loan in the autumn of 1929; the Viceroy reluctantly agreed on stringent conditions – was consistent in his support of the game. Three years before this, for instance, in the winter of 1926-27, he had helped to pay for the MCC tour of India.

The actual organising of the tour was one of those happy accidents that make history. Despite the increasingly important role played by the princes, the English in Calcutta still saw themselves as the rulers of the Indian game. They still played mostly amongst themselves and, in terms of development of the game amongst Indians, Calcutta was a long way behind Bombay. In Bombay the Presidency matches, now the Quadrangular Tournament, were firmly established. Madras also had similar Presidency matches but between 1892, which marks the start of first-class cricket in India, and November 1917 there were no first-class matches of any description played in Calcutta. That first match at Eden Gardens on 23-24 November 1917 is worth mentioning, however. It was between the Bengal Governor's XI and the Maharajah of Cooch Behar's XI. The only Indians were playing for the Maharajah's team, which was captained by Prince Victor though the match was dominated by Frank Tarrant. Playing for the Maharajah's team he took 5 for 9 in the first innings, 7 for 26 in the second, the Governor's team being bowled out for 33 and 59. He also made 43 in the Maharajah's team total of 138 which was enough to give the prince a clear innings victory. The match was repeated the next year with a similar innings victory with Tarrant taking 11 wickets and top-scoring with 52. But when, a few days later, in January 1919, the Maharajah's team met M. C. Bird's XI, there was no Tarrant and the team lost by an innings despite a century by Vithal, the first by an Indian at Eden Gardens.

Amazingly, there were no other first-class matches in Calcutta between that day and the winter of 1926; three matches in two years with Indians was considered enough and the Europeans played club matches almost exclusively amongst themselves while the Indians were forced to organise their own poor alternatives. Not only did Calcutta fail to match Bombay, she was far behind Madras, or even Lahore in organising representative first-class matches. Then, suddenly, the Calcutta Cricket Club decided to invite a team from

52

England. There was a certain method to this. Calcutta felt that its cricket, meaning European cricket, was strong and if the old blues and former county cricketers scattered around India were combined then a strong European side could be formed. What the Englishmen in Calcutta wanted was not to spread the game amongst the Indians but to get the Mother Country to recognise how strong English cricket in India was. Yet in the process, and without meaning to, Calcutta gave a boost to Indian cricket.

A. Murray Robertson, an energetic man, circularised the leading European cricket clubs about a MCC tour: how much money would they put up, what dates would suit, etc.? A committee was formed. The original idea was a tour of India in the winter of 1925-26. But this did not come about and the MCC went to the West Indies instead. In the summer of 1926 Robertson, still working on the plans, went to England. Another club representative, Sir William Currie, a prominent Calcutta businessman, was already in England and they approached the MCC. Their timing was remarkable. The Imperial Cricket Conference was meeting, presided over by Lord Harris as President of the MCC. He decided, unilaterally, that Robertson and Currie should be allowed to attend the conference as 'India's representatives'. They attended a meeting at Lord's on 31 May and at The Oval on 28 July. It was an extraordinary, if very Harris-like decision. India had no governing body, the representatives were not even Indian, but it did not matter. Harris, as ever, knew what he was doing. But imperial as this gesture was it did help Indian cricket. The discussion led to the MCC agreeing to send a team to India, and it was to be the most important cricket team, the first representative side, that had yet visited the country.

Harris himself went to see them off at Tilbury, wishing them luck with the toss, the weather and 'umpires' decisions', and warning, 'Do not take off your topee when out in the field and never eat oysters up-country'.

The team set the pattern for such touring teams from England: the man who had captained England in the summer, and several leading players, were absent. A. W. Carr had regained the Ashes in 1926 but did not come and was replaced by A. E. R. Gilligan who had led the MCC tour to Australia in 1924-25 when England, still recovering from the war, had lost 4-1. Hobbs, Sutcliffe, Woolley and Kilner all declined the invitation. Fred Root accepted but was told by his county, Worcestershire, that he should rest. India had to wait fifty years, the 1976-77 tour, to see a *reigning* England captain (Greig) lead the first full-strength England team to India. Gilligan, on arrival, tried to mollify the Indians by saying this was the strongest team the MCC could get together. All the players had played first-class cricket in the 1926 season and, despite the rejections, there were some very good players including Tate, Astill, Andrew Sandham, Wyatt and the burly Somerset hitter Earle. Gilligan, with his Sussex connections bringing echoes of Ranji (and Duleep had begun to play for Sussex too) was personally very welcome and, in any case, this was the first representative side to tour India.

Gilligan had come with just thirteen players and felt that playing three-day matches would be rather a strain. Only eight of the 34 games played were three-day matches, the rest two-day or one-day. The status of the matches, in one of those characteristic cricket controversies, was debated for nearly a decade in *The Cricketer*. It was not until the 1937 *Cricketer Spring Annual* that a definite ruling was given and then it was accepted that 26 of the 34 matches Gilligan's team played were first-class.

The status of one match was never in doubt. This was the two-day match against the Hindus in Bombay. Gilligan's team had cut a swathe through northern and western India. They came to Bombay unbeaten, having won three matches and so dominated the drawn games that no Indian batsman had scored a century against them. For most of them the pace, swing and swerve of Maurice Tate had been quite devastating. The Hindus were reasonably confident. The Quadrangular Tournament had just finished and, in a quite sensational final, the Hindus had won a match that looked lost: the Europeans requiring 117 to win had failed by a couple of runs.

But, as ever with Indian teams, there were pre-match selection problems. Ramaswami, a Cambridge blue – but for tennis, not cricket – had been selected to play. A couple of weeks before this match he had impressed critics with his batting against R. J. O. Meyer, the Cambridge blue (and later founder of Millfield School) who had made a sensational impact on India. In the final of the Quadrangular Meyer, who had literally walked off the boat from England and into the match, had been virtually unplayable, swinging the ball both ways and also bowling off-spinners. In this match Ramaswami had hit him off his length, scoring a very quick hundred.

Ramaswami was unknown to most of the Hindu players and his selection did not go down well with the Hindu captain, Vithal. On the morning of the match, as Ramaswami was changing, he saw two players coming towards him. 'C. K. Nayudu and L. P. Jai, whom I had never seen before, approached me and asked me if I was C. Ramaswami from Madras. When I told them yes, they told me Vithal will soon be approaching me and asking me to stand down from the team on the plea that I might be tired after a long journey (a two-day train trip from Madras) because he was anxious to take another player called Mahale, of Bombay. They advised me not to give in and to say

54

that, if the selection committee wanted me to stand down, I shall do so.'

Just as Nayudu had warned, ten minutes before the match, Vithal asked Ramaswami to stand down. 'I promptly replied that I shall be pleased to stand down if the selection committee asked me to do so. He was not bold enough to approach the selection committee and I played the match.' Ramaswami's selection did not make any difference to the match. He only made 1, but it illustrated the sort of petty, almost senseless, intrigue that dominated and can still disfigure Indian cricket.

A 25,000-crowd had gathered to watch the match – in a city whose population then was about a million – and they knew little about such intrigue. In any case they were soon riveted by the hitting of Guy Earle. In ninety minutes he scored 130, hitting eight sixes and eleven fours. One of his sixes broke a glass pane in the Gymkhana pavilion, another hit a tree which led the free-seating spectators, who had perched on it, to make a very quick, undignified exit. MCC ended the day on 363 and early the next day they seemed to have the match well under control with the Hindus 84 for 3. This was the cue for Nayudu to walk in.

Cottari Kanakaiya Nayudu was reared for cricket. His father and uncle were contemporaries of Ranji and, as a schoolboy cricketer in Nagpur, he had shown immense promise, captaining the Modi Cricket Club in the city while still at school. He had been a favourite of the Bombay crowd – he was popularly known as C.K. (Indians rarely use or know first names, see Appendix F) – ever since he made his debut at twenty-one for the Hindus in the Quadrangular Tournament of 1916. In that match he had been played as an opening bowler, taking 4 for 97, including the wicket of Greig whose dismissal had led to some ill-feeling between the Europeans and the Hindus. Nayudu came in to bat at no. 9, with the Hindus at 79 for 7 reeling against Tarrant. The first three balls he played defensively, the fourth he hit for a six. That was his first scoring shot in first-class cricket and established his reputation as a batsman always ready to hit the ball. His scores in that first match look modest, 27 and 10, but stood out from the other Hindu performances. There were seven Hindu ducks in the match – and the way Nayudu had coped with Tarrant suggested that the promise he had shown as a schoolboy was likely to be fulfilled.

The following year Nayudu was batting much higher in the order and, while his bowling always remained useful – he was a genuine all-rounder – it was his batting that the crowds came to see. A tall, erect player with an almost military bearing, his very approach to the wicket made crowds anticipate a huge score. Between 1916 and 1939 Nayudu's batting quite dominated the Tournament. In 52 innings he scored 2,156 runs at an average of 45.87 (in contrast his 38 wickets averaged 31). Every year, whether the Hindus won or not Nayudu was usually the top scorer. Opposition bowlers knew they had to get Nayudu out if they wanted to beat the Hindus. He top-scored in the 1917 final against the Parsees, in the 1920 final his 121 helped the Hindus score 428, their highest score till then. In 1921 he failed, but then every Indian cricketer failed. The Europeans, thanks to Patiala's importing of English players, had C. B. Fry, Hirst and Rhodes. Hirst was fifty, Rhodes forty-four, but they were still too good for the Indians, who had never seen anything like them. Against the Hindus Rhodes scored 156 and took 7 for 26 in the first innings, Hirst took 6 for 33 in the second. The Europeans won by an innings and 108 runs. Nayudu made 3 and 1, caught off Rhodes in the first, bowled by Hirst in the second innings. For good measure Rhodes and Hirst beat the Parsees by an even bigger margin: an innings and 297 runs, with Rhodes scoring 183 and taking 11 for 59 in the match, Hirst scoring 62 and taking 3 for 42.

This was about the only time that Nayudu failed, and in 1923, with Hirst and Rhodes no longer assisting the Europeans, Nayudu's hitting helped the Hindus to win the final. The Hindus won again in 1925 and 1926, though Nayudu compared to previous years had rather a lean time. But he was now more than just a Hindu batsman. He was established as the first great Indian player. Before him Parsees had had great cricketers and Hindus and Muslims their own favourites, but Nayudu was becoming the first player all Indians could acknowledge. There was an Indian dimension to him that his contemporaries just did not have. They all came from a particular region and were identified by that region. Nayudu was a south Indian, his mother-tongue was Telgu – a southern language – but he had been born in Nagpur in central India and played almost all his cricket there. In 1923 Nayudu was invited to Indore, also in central India, by the ruler of Holkar who made him a captain in his army and effectively asked him to take charge of all games.

So, as Nayudu now came out to bat, it was as if he was batting for India, although there was as yet no Indian team. He had faced Gilligan's sides in previous matches making 15 and 0 and, like other Indian batsmen, found difficulty playing Tate. But such failures did not worry Nayudu. He had an almost messianic faith in cricket, believing that it could be traced back to ancient Aryan scriptures. He had educated himself to bear physical pain. Once, many years later in a Ranji Trophy match, he was struck on the mouth by a ball which broke two front teeth. He refused medical assistance, brushed the teeth off the wicket with his bat – lest they cause any deviation – and was very upset when the bowler eased up on delivering the next ball. In 1936 G. O. Allen was to discover how brave Nayudu could be in the face of hostile bouncers. Nayudu could also swear like a trooper, and he had a fierce belief in his own judgement.

Nayudu began quietly – quietly that is for him – with a two as his first scoring shot. His next scoring shot was a six on to the roof of the pavilion. Stuart Boyes, the Hampshire slow left-armer, was able both to spin and lift the ball – he had already had the captain Vithal caught by Tate – but every time he flighted one up to Nayudu he hit it for a four or a six. He twice hit sixes into the tent and his 33 included three sixes and three fours when he made his first and only mistake. At the beginning of the innings he had had to face Tate, but Tate had been replaced by William Astill, the Leicestershire all-rounder. A considerable cricketer of the 1920s and 1930s – Astill did the double of 1,000 runs and 100 wickets nine times – he could bowl both slow and medium pace. Now, the fifth bowler used by Chichester-Constable, who was captaining the side in place of Gilligan, he tempted Nayudu with a slower ball. Nayudu went for a hit, miscued, the ball went high in the air but, with the sun in his eyes, Astill dropped the catch.

Astill paid dearly for this mistake. So far all of Nayudu's sixes had come off Boyes, now the fourth, fifth, sixth and seventh sixes came off Astill, the last two off successive balls. One more four and a single brought Nayudu his century in just 65 minutes. At the other end Tate had returned and was being treated somewhat gently – he was only being hit for fours. Tate was replaced by Wyatt who bowled a maiden, almost sensational in this mayhem. Wyatt was made to pay for such audacity in the next couple of overs. In the next over he was hit for a four and a six – Nayudu's eighth of the innings. The following Wyatt over was the most sensational of the innings. Nayudu hit a six on to the roof of the Gymkhana, his ninth, repeated the stroke the next ball, the ball after that was smashed to the scoreboard for four, there was a two to leg, then another four – 22 runs in one over. Nayudu was now the highest scorer in the match. Mercer, who had opened the bowling, was brought back but conceded 14 runs in an over: his fifth ball was hit for a six, Nayudu's eleventh.

Bowling changes were coming fast and furious. Mercer was replaced by Boyes and he kept it tight – Nayudu hitting two successive threes. Geary, the other opening bowler, was brought back and at last with his score on 153 Nayudu, going for another big hit, skied the ball to Boyes at deep mid-off. Nayudu had begun batting at 12.17. He was out at 3.13. In all, he had batted 116 minutes for his 153. In those days scorers did not keep a count of balls but his scoring strokes show that he took 16 scoring strokes to reach his 50 with four sixes and five fours; 17 strokes to reach his second 50, with three sixes and five fours; and 16 scoring strokes for his final 50 with four sixes and four fours. In all, 49 scoring strokes, with eleven sixes and fourteen fours providing 122 of his 153 runs. Nayudu had established a world record for the number of sixes in a match. In 1934 C. J. Barnett of Gloucestershire equalled Nayudu's record but it was not broken until John Reid hit fifteen sixes in his 296 for Wellington in the 1962-63 New Zealand season.

This was, of course, the stuff of legend and the rest of the match – which ended in a draw – meant little. All of Bombay and as much of India as had taken to cricket could talk of little else. Earle's eight sixes had delighted them, Nayudu's eleven had them in raptures. The next day a cartoon appeared showing a group of spectators sheltering from the bombardment on the ledge of the Rajabai clocktower of the university, a great landmark in the city – and almost half a mile away from the Bombay Gymkhana. The students were saying. 'Don't hit us, C.K., we are not playing.' It would be easy to picture this innings as mindless slogging. In fact Nayudu was selective and, if his batting had a touch of Jessop, there was nothing crude about it. Vijay Merchant, watching the match as a fifteen-year-old, was enthralled. He regarded it then and later as the best innings he ever saw.

It is in some ways odd that we should remember Nayudu in terms of statistics because he never cared for them. Writing the Foreword to the inaugural issue of *Indian Cricket* in 1946 he said,

Our age is an age of business and cricket has not escaped the fatal touch of commercialism. There is a tendency to regard statistics as the best indication of a player's ability. This has led to the emergence of a school of stonewallers. Cricket must be played in harmony with its inherent genius, with wild and free abandon. Let our players attack the bowlers and provide spectators with a feast of strokeplay. If cricket like life is full of uncertainties, why make it a dull affair?

It summed up the man and his philosophy.

But perhaps its greatest impact was that it had broken the thrall of the white man, the natural assumption that, in any contest between Indian and Englishman, be it in sport or in war, the Englishman would always win. Indian cricket had grown sufficiently strong for cricketers no longer to fear the local English but whenever English teams or players arrived from England it was different. They seemed to carry all the authority, the power, the magic that had enabled a handful of Englishmen to rule millions of Indians. And, as against Rhodes, Hirst and Tarrant, Indians had just crumbled. Nayudu's innings that day, for the first time, made the Indians, whatever their religion, feel that there was no special magic in English cricket.

Today, in the 1990s, such a claim may seem far-fetched. But

even as late as the 1930s, India, even all of Asia, was in the thrall of the European powers. A handful of Europeans ruled the greatest continent on earth with its millions of people, and their subjects obeyed them because they believed that the European was superior. It was the second world war, and the early Japanese defeats of most of the European powers in Asia, which broke the European spell and while Nayudu's was a very small effort in that direction, in the world of cricket it started the process.

Gilligan himself was impressed by Nayudu's 'polished batting', but Gilligan was even more impressed with the general cricket standard when on 16, 17, 18 December the MCC side met an All-India team in Bombay. MCC scored 362, All-India 437, led by an innings of 148 by Deodhar who only got into the side at the last minute because Vithal had been injured. When stumps were drawn on the third day MCC were only 22 runs ahead with five wickets left. Gilligan's tour also improved relations between the Indians and the English, as the visitors behaved with a naturalness that their countrymen, living in India for so long, seemed to have lost. Certainly their behaviour was far removed from the attitudes that had characterised Cecil Headlam and the Oxford Authentics. No 'obese, black gentleman' was 'capsized' for failing to produce railway tickets quickly.

Despite this, there was an incident which showed how difficult Indian-English relations could be. When the combined Hindus and Muslims team met the MCC a week later, also at Bombay, the English believed that Nayudu had been bowled when, in fact, the ball had rebounded off the wicket-keeper's pads on to the stumps. Nayudu was ready to walk off when his partner, Vithal, asked him to check with the umpire, a Parsee named Warden who had been an outstanding left-arm bowler. Warden ruled Nayudu not out and that, recalls Professor Deodhar, did not go down well with the English who 'created an unusual row in the dressing-room and also at the lunch-table, sitting separately by themselves'. Perhaps Professor Deodhar, sensitive to the racial aloofness that had been such a marked feature of his cricket involvement with the English, was a bit too ready to believe Gilligan's team displayed the same characteristics. Other Indians, however, recall Gilligan's role as a cricket ambassador keen to set Indian cricket right. Gilligan took seriously the MCC's role of cricket missionaries and, as he went round the country, he advised the Indians to form a proper organisation. Calcutta sought to convince Gilligan that the only worthwhile cricket in India was that played by Englishmen. In Calcutta an All-India XI in which there were seven Europeans played Gilligan's team and this after a match against a genuine All-India XI in Bombay had proved the strength of Indian cricket. By the end of the tour Gilligan had seen enough to convince him that Indian cricket was thriving but that it needed to have a proper Board of Control to run the game.

The crucial meeting took place in February 1927, when Gilligan's team played a three-day match against Northern India in Delhi. One evening Gilligan, Anthony De Mello, Maharajah Bhupendra Singh, and Grant Govan, an English businessman who employed De Mello, met in the Roshanara Club. The locals had been thinking of forming a board but it was Gilligan's enthusiasm that, De Mello wrote, 'was of the greatest encouragement. We felt that if a man so cricket-wise as Gilligan considered Indian cricket had reached a stage in its development where it could challenge the world then we had certainly achieved something. Gilligan promised to state our case when he returned to Lord's.'

But where would such a Board be based? Who would control it? Patiala wanted the Board to have its headquarters in Delhi which would be quite near his princely state. Bombay, the centre of Indian cricket, was determined that Calcutta should not be the headquarters. Calcutta had organised the MCC tour but its cricket was European and it did not have any 'cosmopolitan claims'. Interestingly, it was an Englishman, J. S. Spenser, Secretary of the Bombay Gymkhana, who manoeuvred feverishly against Calcutta. He wrote an open letter, addressed to the Governor of Bombay, and, as was the style of the English in India, did not sign his name but used a pseudonym: 'Urbs Prima in cricket', which was meant to signify Bombay. Everyone in the know realised it was Spenser, and his bile against Calcutta was revealed in a private letter he wrote to the secretary of the Parsee Gymkhana:

Do not let the establishment of this Board pass into the insolent hands of Calcutta. The Indian Gymkhanas must oppose if any move is made by Calcutta in this matter. Remember how Vithal, Naidau [sic] and Jamsedji were insulted in Calcutta during the MCC match. Let not Bombay come under the thumb of Calcutta in matters of cricket. The best way is for Bombay to act immediately. All the Indian Gymkhanas must combine and do something in consultation with Bombay Gymkhana.

Spenser, by trying to rope in the Governor of Bombay, was cleverly seeking to exploit the city's position as the centre of Indian cricket. All he succeeded in doing, however, was to delay the emergence of the Board. The influential Parsee industrialist Dorab Tata intervened to denounce Spenser as irresponsible and his remarks as ill-conceived. The Parsees circularised the various associations and clubs about the formation of the Board and the slow efforts to bring all the groups

60

together began. There followed further meetings at the Roshanara Club and in December 1928, nearly two years after Gilligan had first urged the Indians to form a Board, a Board was finally set up. Perhaps in a country of the size and complexity of India that was not too long a delay, but had the Indians acted more quickly then it is very possible that the course of cricket could have been different.

Grant Govan and Anthony De Mello, who became the first President and Secretary of the Board, had journeyed to and from England in the summer of 1928 and produced a plan for a tour by South Africa to India in 1929 and India to England in 1931. Lord Harris, it would appear, had blessed these tours. But when they returned they found that the Board was still far from ready to be launched. By the time India was admitted to the Imperial Cricket Conference in 1929, the impetus had gone; ideas of the South African tour that might have changed the face of cricket had evaporated. And the political climate in India too was changing.

The year 1930 saw the start of Gandhi's great civil disobedience movement when, with 78 chosen followers he marched from his ashram to Dandi on the Gujerat seafront to break the British imposed ban on producing salt. It was one of the most brilliantly designed political campaigns of history. The long march built up public attention both in India and abroad. Salt was a commodity so basic that every Indian, however poor, used it. The fact that the government banned the people from producing it was an example of Raj repression that the poorest of Indians could understand. In an age before television, and when most Indians had still not been introduced to the cinema, Gandhi used his long march to focus newspaper attention, slowly developing interest like the plot of a long novel, as he went through the Indian villages speaking of the inequity of British rule. As he reached the sea and produced the first salt from the sea the movement took off with electrifying force.

Cricket was, inevitably, affected. No Quadrangular tournaments were held between 1930–34 and there was no question of an England team visiting India in the winter of 1930. For a time it seemed that there could be a negotiated settlement as the Viceroy, Lord Irwin, met Gandhi. But in 1932 with a new Viceroy, Willingdon, replacing Irwin's softly, softly approach with a tough, 'jail 'em, flog 'em, fine 'em, shoot 'em' policy, Gandhi was jailed, there were mass arrests, and an attempt made to break the back of the nationalist movement. The Quadrangulars remained suspended, nationalist Hindus refused to have anything to do with cricket, and Vijay Merchant, who had been emerging as a major batsman, and several other Hindu players, were asked not to go for the trials to select the team to tour England in

1932. Merchant had just made his first first-class hundred and was a virtual certainty for the team.

So it happened that, against the background of the premier domestic tournament suspended and some of its promising players not available, India embarked on its first great cricket adventure: the first Test match tour of England.

5

In search of a leader
1932-34

It is not the least of Indian cricketing ironies that the British rulers whom the Indians, at least Nationalist Indians, found the most obdurate, were the ones who had the greatest influence on Indian cricket. Lord Harris may have been a political reactionary but his influence on Indian cricket was undeniable. Now, in December 1931, the Marquess of Willingdon – who was 'becoming a sort of Mussolini in India' as he described himself to Sir Samuel Hoare, Secretary of State for India – began to play a crucial role in promoting Indian cricket both in India and abroad.

Of all the Raj rulers Willingdon had, probably, the longest involvement with Indian cricket. It started when he was Governor of Bombay between 1913-18, continued when he was Governor of Madras, 1919-24, and reached its most significant moment when he returned as Viceroy in 1931. A goodish cricketer himself – he played for Cambridge, Sussex and MCC, later becoming its President – he saw cricket as a link between the English and the Indians. As Governor of Bombay he organised cricket matches, playing in some but also, crucially, picking sides which were 'mixed', including both English and Indian players. Willingdon distrusted the 'clever Hindus', the Brahmins and the Banians, 'the cleverest people in the world', but he was also repelled by the racial apartheid the English practised in India. The Willingdon Sports Club in Bombay, and the Willingdon Club in Madras, unlike the English clubs, were open to all.

Willingdon returned to India to find that Indian cricket needed a leader. Delhi was no stranger to power struggles, the monuments in the city testified to the deadly rivalry waged by claimants to the throne of India. This time the prize was different, and nobody was likely to be killed, but the struggle was just as intense, perhaps even richer in intrigue. Just as Robert Clive had found himself in the role of kingmaker as Mughal authority collapsed in the eighteenth century, so circumstances may have made Willingdon a dabbler in Indian cricket politics; but the zeal with which he took it up showed he could be as adroit as any Mughal kingmaker.

Ranjitsinhji would have been the natural choice as leader of Indian

63

cricket, but he wanted nothing to do with it. Indeed he even forbade his nephew, Duleepsinhji, to play for India. This, even before Willingdon arrived, had already led to a great deal of bitterness. As De Mello and Govan were trying to form the Indian Board of Control a struggle was going on over Duleep. When Ranji had played for England there was no Indian cricket. Now Indian cricket was about to emerge on the world stage, so who should Duleep play for? Ranji made it very clear: 'He ought to play for England, because he has learned all his cricket there. Anyway there is no top-class cricket to be had in India.' A. W. Carr and Pelham Warner were not convinced he should play for England and Duleep found himself being pulled in different directions: by a strong, determined uncle whom he worshipped; by the English; and by the Indians. De Mello and Govan tried to persuade him to play for India, even lead India into Tests, but he opted for England, for whom he played twelve times between 1929 and 1931. However, the struggle left him a bitter man and, after he had left cricket, he vented his feelings, denouncing Govan as a man 'who had never played in any good cricket' and De Mello as one 'who thinks he is a bowler but has never found anyone to agree with him on that point. These gentlemen and a few like them wish to pass rules which would force me to let them run my cricket career or retire from the game.'

Duleep was being unduly harsh. The Duleep option De Mello pursued was an obvious one – he was then one of the best batsmen in the world – but it would also have helped relieve other pressures. There was the real danger that, like the West Indies, India would have to accept a white man as captain, although before the Indian Board was properly set up it had been decided that Englishmen living in India could not play for India. Even though the majority of the delegates who took this decision were English, unlike with the West Indies or South Africa they did not see India as their home. But when India was admitted to the Imperial Cricket Conference in 1929 the English put it to De Mello that, perhaps, an Englishman *should* captain India? Who else could control the various religious and ethnic groups? The candidate they had in mind was Douglas Jardine, born in Bombay and with strong connections with the local English. It is interesting to note that Jardine, the third generation of a family which had long worked in India, only came back to England because of the family principle that every third generation should go back home so as not to be totally absorbed by India. In a sense, therefore, the British desire to maintain their distance from India, and not consider it as a permanent home, meant that India avoided the situation which the West Indies, and now South Africa, face.

A Duleep captaincy would have cut through all that, but he refused even the chance to captain the Hindus in the Quadrangular Tournament of 1928. He did play in that match and, by all accounts, played the first reverse sweep, which so astonished the Parsee bowler Kapadia that he appealed to the umpire – surely this is an unfair method and he is out? The umpire dismissed the appeal. But beyond throwing such crumbs Duleep was not prepared to do any more for India.

So with Duleep not prepared to play for India and Ranji not prepared to play the role which Lord Harris and later Sir Pelham Warner played in English cricket, Indian cricket administration desperately sought a leader and it developed into a power struggle between the princes. Patiala wanted to lead and he had, of course, played a big part in helping form the Cricket Board, but Willingdon could not accept Patiala. Not only was he a fool, thought Willingdon, but an 'overgrown puppy' who had never grown up and was 'terribly amenable to flattery and hates being told the truth'. He had just survived the sexual scandals alleged in the *Indictment* and while this was not common knowledge it gave Willingdon a hold over him. This not only meant there was no obvious leader but was just the situation for a rival prince to intrigue his way into the vacant cricket leadership of India. Patiala had made a rod for his own back. Other princes had followed his example and taken to cricket and it is from their ranks that a challenger rose.

It could not have been a more unlikely challenger from a more unexpected quarter. The Maharajkumar of Vizianagram was not even a ruling prince. The name came from a princely state in the south but a quarrel with a nephew had forced him to leave it and he lived on family estates near Benares in the north. In a land where titles were important, Maharajkumar, meaning son of a prince, suggested someone connected with royalty but never likely to rule. In English terms he was, at best, a duke; in India he was, strictly speaking, no more than a zamindar, a member of the landed gentry. But what he lacked in princely clout he made up in tenacity and an unrivalled capacity for intrigue.

Vizzy, as he popularly became known, had taken to cricket in the wake of Patiala along with other, mainly minor princes. In Hyderabad the Nizam, the most important prince in the land who bore the title His Exalted Highness and Faithful Ally of the British, did not have to bother with cricket to ingratiate himself with the English. But two jagirdars in his kingdom, country squires, sponsored cricket tournaments. Vizzy, however, did such things in a style and a manner that were completely different. When political problems led to the cancellation of the 1930-31 tour of India, Vizzy organised a team of his own which toured India and Ceylon. 'The cancellation of the MCC tour,' said Vizzy, 'gave the greatest disappointment to Indian cricketers and I was fired with a passion to devise ways and means to compensate

India.' The Maharajkumar of Vizianagram's XI became a substitute touring team, composed of the best of Indian players and two of the greatest names in cricket: Jack Hobbs and Herbert Sutcliffe.

This is where the genius of Vizzy as a cricket organiser emerged. Another prince might have managed to get together the best Indian players, like the established Nayudu or the rising star Mushtaq Ali who, as a schoolboy, was taken to Benares by Vizzy and trained there. But to get Hobbs and Sutcliffe, the more so as they had refused to tour India with Gilligan, was a coup. Vizzy was nothing if not persistent. He visited Hobbs' Fleet Street sports shop often during the summer of 1930 and finally persuaded him to come. How Vizzy managed to do so has baffled even Hobbs' biographers – he had refused five previous invitations to travel on such trips outside England – but perhaps the fact that Vizzy had invited Hobbs' wife as well and secured Sutcliffe, who was left out of Percy Chapman's 1930-31 tour of South Africa, tipped the balance. Mrs Hobbs did not much care for India and Hobbs would not play on Sundays, which meant that Vizzy had to rearrange the tour. When Sutcliffe's illness forced Hobbs to play in one match that featured Sunday play, against the Madras Presidency at Chepauk, Vizzy agreed he would take no part in Sunday's proceedings. He did not field that day and, when it was his turn to bat, he was absent. But all this was a small price to pay to get one of the legends of the game. Vizzy also tried to get Donald Bradman, who had made such a sensational impact on cricket during the 1930 tour of England, but he refused. Vizzy had to be content with a film showing Bradman batting.

This was very far from an exhibition tour. A few matches were one-day exhibition matches in the first of which, on Vizzy's own private pitch at Benares – with a wicket of navy blue matting, the white building of the palace and the sea-green of the screens providing the ideal background – Hobbs scored a hundred. Hobbs and Sutcliffe put on 186, with Sutcliffe making 93. Their batting enchanted the Indians although they could not have been impressed by the pair's running between wickets. Where was the legendary understanding? In the first innings Sutcliffe was run out. Hobbs was involved in two more run-outs in Delhi. In the first innings Mushtaq Ali, batting with him, was run out, in the second Hobbs, batting with Vizzy, was run out. The Delhi match showed how competitive some of the matches were. Vizzy's team played a Rest of India XI captained by another prince, Gyanashyamsinhji of Limbdi. Hobbs made 30 in the first innings before being lbw to De Mello – who also had Sutcliffe caught for 7 and did a great jig of joy. Hobbs said later, 'In county cricket I have often scored a century more easily than the 30 I have scored today.'

It is possible that Hobbs was being the polite visitor but this tour showed that India had many fine players. Hobbs and Sutcliffe were particularly impressed with the Rest of India's opening bowler, Amar Singh, and while he only took two wickets in the match, bowling Sutcliffe in the second innings, within a few months when India made her Test debut he would stamp himself as one of the finest medium-fast bowlers in the world.

Vizzy's team won five of their six first-class matches in India. Overall, and taking other matches into account, they won 17 out of their 18 matches. Hobbs and Sutcliffe did have some success. They put on 122 for the first wicket in the Delhi match but, apart from a 92-run stand in Madras, they only showed occasional glimpses of their great ability. Their opening stands rarely went beyond the 20s and in the six first-class matches on tour Hobbs scored: 30, 81, 14, 36, 10, 77, 12, 11, 11. Sutcliffe scored: 7, 69, 6, 62 not out, 17, 40, 165, 23.

Hobbs was lbw three times on the tour, Sutcliffe once, and when both of them were lbw in the final of the Moin-ud-Dowlah tournament – Sutcliffe lbw to Amar Singh, which meant four of the first five in Vizzy's team had fallen in this way – Vizzy was furious. Whether Hobbs and Sutcliffe were unhappy with the decisions we do not know, but on the morning of the second day, a Saturday, Vizzy lodged a complaint about the umpiring. It was rejected by the tournament committee. Vizzy was mollified by the fact that that day Nayudu, 69 not out overnight, went on to make a hundred. He also took seven wickets in the match, and Vizzy's team won by nine wickets.

This was, perhaps, the only sour note on the tour. Hobbs and Sutcliffe were richly rewarded, the Indian players, keen to protect their amateur status, did not receive money but accepted gifts: blazers encrusted with gold buttons; silver statuettes of batsmen; trophies; and a cash prize. Vizzy's generous touch appears to have affected Hobbs, for when Mushtaq Ali, then just making his mark as a *bowler*, took eleven wickets in one match, Hobbs presented him with a pair of silver hair-brushes.

If Vizzy had been content with being such a cricket sponsor, like Sir Horace Mann in the eighteenth century, or Sir Julien Cahn in the twentieth, his name would be one of the most revered in Indian cricket. But he was consumed with the ambition to be a great cricketer. This, in a man capable of being a Test cricketer, would have been a considerable virtue, but for Vizzy, who was no more than an ordinary club cricketer, it was a fantasy which only his position, money and India's peculiar cricketing circumstances could turn into reality. The tour had given a clue to his ambitions. For much of it he liked to bat at no. 3, just after Hobbs and Sutcliffe, and a ridiculously high position in a side containing such established batsmen as Nayudu, Deodhar and the highly promising Naoomal. The fact that he was with Sutcliffe when the winning hit was made in Calcutta – he scored 10 – gave him immense pleasure. In the final of the Moin-ud-Dowlah tournament, the last match on the Indian part of the tour, Vizzy dropped himself down to no. 7 but scored 71, his only substantial innings of the tour, sharing a crucial partnership with Nayudu that effectively won his team the match. That apart, his batting ability in a team made up of some of the best Indian batsmen of the time, hardly justified such a position. But if a man cannot sponsor a tour and bat where he likes what is the good of sponsoring? At the end of the tour, Hobbs, in one of those off-the-cuff remarks to reporters as he was boarding the ship for England, said Vizzy would make a good All-India captain. Before this nobody had envisaged such a role for him, and even now it was not a serious proposition, but with this casual remark the seed had been planted.

Certainly Vizzy's organisation of the tour had given him a standing in Indian cricket second only to Patiala. And with Patiala out of favour with Willingdon, Vizzy had the inside track all to himself. A frequent visitor to the Viceregal Lodge he also offered to pay 50,000 rupees to the Board – of this 40,000 rupees was for the English tour. Even at this stage it is not clear whether Vizzy thought the money could buy him the captaincy. But his money provided the platform for the Vizzy-Willingdon axis to operate, while there was talk, from Bengal and Assam, of a European being asked to lead India. Calcutta had always said that Indians were not much good at cricket, nor could one lead a national side, and if India's first Test team were led by an Englishman then this would provide symbolic proof of the wider political thesis now being vigorously preached by Willingdon – that Indians could only be welded together into a team when an Englishman was put in charge. Politically England could not leave India, otherwise it would collapse into chaos, so a cricket team was only possible with an English captain. As in politics, so in cricket.

Patiala may not have been an Indian patriot but he sensed the dangers and, in November 1931 at the annual meeting of the Board, came up with an offer they could not refuse. The trials to pick the team should be staged at Patiala and he would bear all the expenses for a whole month. Vizzy's offer was swept away. Willingdon grumbled but could not stop it becoming Patiala's show. No Europeans were invited among the fifty players called for the trial and soon the Board found that, despite having appointed a selection committee, it was Patiala who made all the choices. Tarrant hovered round and Duleep and the Nawab of Pataudi who, like Duleep, had established himself in English cricket, also appeared to join the selection committee.

The team that was announced bore the stamp of Patiala. He was himself captain, Prince Gyanashyamsinhji of Limbdi was deputy captain and Vizzy was offered the novel post of deputy vice-captain.

The commoners provided the real players like Nayudu, Amar Singh, Nissar, the burly fast bowler, and Wazir Ali, the elegant batsman, but there were two Sikhs, Jogendra, who was on the Maharajah's personal staff, and Lall Singh, who had been born in Malaya. He must be the most unusual player ever to play for India. Nobody is sure quite where he was born – near Kuala Lumpur is the closest description. He was a brilliant fieldsman, played in one Test, then disappeared from Indian cricket in much the same way as he had arrived. So exotic was he that there were stories of his running a nightclub in Paris. The truth was more prosaic. He lived out his life as a groundsman in Kuala Lumpur where he died in 1985.

The one surprise was the omission of the Nawab of Pataudi. He had skippered one of the final trial teams and then opted out. Like Banquo's ghost Pataudi would cast a shadow over Indian cricket for some years – often mooted as a captain before the tour only to make his excuses when the team was announced. Vizzy, pleading 'reasons of state' also refused to tour. Reason of hurt pride was more like it: the man who wanted to be captain was now third in line. Two weeks after the touring team was announced Patiala, whose announcement as captain was a holding operation, resigned and Porbander, ruler of the small state of Kathiawar, took over. Porbander was the brother-in-law of Limbdi, and no cricketer, but his Kathiawar side had had two of India's best fast bowlers: Amar Singh and Ramji.

So in mid-April 1932 the Indians arrived in England captained by a prince, who could not play, and managed by an Englishman who had served in the Indian army. The Maharajah of Porbander had no illusions about his cricketing abilities. Porbander played in the first four matches making 0, 2, 0, 2, 2. He did not play again on the tour and had a first-class average of 0.66. He was said to be the only first-class cricketer in England to have more Rolls-Royces than runs. The press grew critical of Porbander's batting and an announcement was made that he was still suffering from the 'effects of malaria'. From now on all that England would hear from him were his speeches; his bat, never very resonant, made no sound. The Prince of Limbdi, who was a fair cricketer and who had captained the Rest of India side against Vizzy's team, making 25 and 2, took over. In his first match against Oxford University he scored 2 but he avoided the fate of Porbander and in 17 innings scored 154 runs with an average of 9.62.

C. K. Nayudu, on any proper assessment, should have been captain. Nayudu had prepared meticulously for this English trip. Like all other Indian cricketers he had been told how different cricket in England was: the softer light, the uncovered wickets open to elements that could produce four different seasons in one day, the movement that the seamers got and the turn the spinners could extract. So he had spent the summer of 1931 playing for Indian Gymkhana at Osterley, gauging the conditions. The benefit of his season with Indian Gymkhana was immediately apparent. Unlike his colleagues he was noticeably more comfortable on the softer English wickets. Nayudu's game was always based on the drive, driving in front of the wicket and on either side of it. And he adapted to the English conditions and the extra swing by delaying the decision to drive till the last second, something that puzzled *Wisden* but proved useful. For a tall man he was a very good cutter: pictures show him making what looks like an outlandish, even exaggerated late cut but that could be very effective. Nayudu had come to England with the reputation of being an Indian Bradman. His high scores and his ability to hit the ball hard perhaps suggested this otherwise dubious comparison.

But apart from the temperamental differences which Cardus noted – Bradman was steely, flawless; Nayudu with the bat volatile, sensitive – Nayudu could never convey the certainty that Bradman did and there was one major technical difference. Nayudu, like most Indian batsmen of that generation, was prepared to lift the ball and did it often and very profitably. Bradman never lifted the ball.

Nayudu began just as badly as Porbander and Limbdi – scores of 3 and 2 in his first two innings – but then came a 67 against Sussex, for whom Duleep scored 7, and after that Nayudu was the mainstay of the Indian batting. In a remarkable feat of endurance he played in all twenty-six first-class matches – he missed only two of the thirty-six matches that took place (two other matches were abandoned without a ball being bowled). He did not have a break from cricket between 29 April and 29 June when India played Oxfordshire. But that and the match against Sir Julien Cahn's XI were the only ones Nayudu missed. This, for a man aged thirty-seven, was quite extraordinary. He even had time to play against his old club, Indian Gymkhana, and scored 104 in 100 minutes, with three sixes and twelve fours.

Nothing in Indian cricket could have prepared him for such physical exertion. India did not even have a regular domestic championship and first-class cricket there was never played for more than a few weeks spread over several months. Indians just did not play six-days-a-week cricket – nor do they now. Nayudu's colleagues, who had nothing like his workload, suffered. Nazir Ali and Palia broke down while fielding during the Test, Amar Singh and Lall Singh were also affected and towards the end of the tour many other players were also feeling the strain. In speech after speech Porbander explained that the programme was rather too heavy and his players were just not used to such continuous cricket. Only Nayudu did not complain. He relished the hard work.

It is possible that, had Nayudu not taken on such a heavy burden, he might have made an even bigger impact. Given his burden his achievements are remarkable. In first-class matches he scored 1,618 runs at an average of 40.45, in all matches he scored 1,842 runs at an average of 37.59. He headed the tour batting averages for both first-class and all matches, and was fifth in the bowling averages with 65 wickets at 25.53 in first-class matches and 79 wickets at an average of 24.65 in all matches. He reserved some of his best performances for the showpiece occasions. In late May the Indians came to Lord's to play the MCC, then a match just short of Test status. It had been a cold, wet, cheerless May but 12,000 people turned up to watch the Indians on the Saturday. The MCC chose ten amateurs, led by Jardine and including Chapman, Jupp and Peebles, with Bowes the only professional. Lord's looked as forbidding as it had ever done with overcast skies threatening rain, and Nayudu came in to bat with the Indians in serious danger of being blown away: one opener, Navle, was out, the other opener, Wazir Ali, had been forced to retire after being hit by a bouncer from Bowes.

Neither Bowes' bowling, liberally sprinkling bouncers, nor the conditions worried Nayudu. In between stoppages for bad light and chances – he should have been stumped and there were two difficult slip catches that went down – he made 118 not out in three-and-a-half hours with a pulled six and twelve fours. The rain interruptions made a draw inevitable, but when MCC batted Nayudu showed he was no mean bowler, taking 4 for 31 including Jardine's wicket.

In that match, the first time the Indians were playing at Lord's, Limbdi had captained, batting no. 8 and making 11. But when the Indians returned a month later for their inaugural Test Limbdi, in making a hundred against Eastern Counties, had sustained a back injury and it was clear that Nayudu would have to lead the side. Nobody doubted his leadership qualities, only his lack of royal pedigree. He served a royal but was not a royal. He had captained India already on the tour, guiding them to their first victory over a county side. But a Test match, and the first-ever Test India would play, was somewhat different. Not all the Indian players were prepared to accept Porbander's decision that Nayudu should captain. India was full of reports that, deprived of princely leadership, the Indians had fallen out amongst themselves; there were stories of late nights and drunkenness and of how Nayudu was an unbending leader favouring his own band of players. A player like Wazir Ali, who was almost as experienced as Nayudu and had always seen himself as Patiala's favourite, particularly resented the promotion. If a prince captained the side, fine, but if a commoner was to be captain why could he not do it?

At 4am on the morning of the Test match a group of players

knocked on the door of Porbander, and woke him to say that they would not play unless Nayudu was demoted. Cables flew backwards and forwards between England and India until the matter was resolved by a directive from Patiala himself: Nayudu was captain and the other players had to play under him.

The match, a three-day Test, began on Saturday 25 June 1932 and attracted 24,000 spectators to Lord's on a fine day. India had lost only once to the counties and a fair sprinkling of Indians had come to Lord's. Neville Cardus could not believe that 'so many Indians lived in London; and the silent grace of the women, in their long flowing robes [he meant saris], light as air, moving with the unconcerned beauty of nature! Some of the painted English women appeared by contrast pathetically ineffectual. The scene and the occasion were curiously moving; the crowd actually seemed to be wanting the Indians to win!'

But not even the Indians in the crowd could have anticipated the England start. Jardine won the toss and chose to bat on what was a good hard wicket with a bit of 'bone', enough, thought Cardus, to keep a lazy batsman alive but nothing to worry batsmen of class. And this English batting was full of class. Hobbs had retired from Test cricket but England's batting line-up read: Sutcliffe, Holmes, Woolley, Hammond, Jardine, Paynter, Ames. The attack was possibly a bit weak but there were two leg-spinners in Robins and Brown, and Bowes and Voce spearheaded the attack. The previous week Holmes and Sutcliffe had set up their world record for the first wicket: 555. How many would they get against the Indians?

They had reached 8 when Nissar began his second over. With his first ball he bowled Sutcliffe for three with a yorker, with his last he bowled Holmes for six, the off stump cartwheeling in the air. The Indians, wrote Cardus, gathered round the broken wicket like sightseers at a celebrated ruin. Then Woolley decided to go for a second run even as Lall Singh, the fielder, was picking up the ball. Lall Singh with his colourful turban was a great favourite with the crowd – some of the English thought his beard gave him a boyish, even a girlish, look. All Lall Singh had to do was throw straight and Woolley was run out for 9. There had been twenty minutes' play, England were 19 for 3. Cardus had the feeling that 'on every side you could get the sense of white teeth flashing in triumphant smiles as the English wickets collapsed'.

It was Indian pace that had done it and the English batsmen were clearly surprised by the Indian opening attack. Nobody watching the Indians that day could have foreseen that in little more than two decades India would be known as the land of spinners where opening bowlers only came to take the shine off the ball. In this opening Test there was so little Indian spin that seventeen of the eighteen English wickets that fell went to seamers or quick bowlers.

In contrast to the opening attacks India would field in years to come, Nissar and Amar Singh were as genuine a pair of opening bowlers as any country has ever produced. Nissar, a tall, strapping, six-foot Punjabi was the quicker of the two: he looked like a fast bowler and bowled like one with the ability to swing the ball both ways and with a devastating breakback of the type that accounted for both Holmes and Sutcliffe. Nissar finished with 5 for 93 but in many ways the deeper impression was made by Amar Singh.

Amar Singh, whom Ranji had spotted – he was later employed by Nawanagar – had rather a shambolic approach to the wicket but once there showed an uncanny ability to swing and cut the ball. When he arrived in England he was astonished to discover how much movement he could obtain in the heavier English atmosphere. *Wisden* noted that he could 'curl in the air either from leg or off' and was 'causing [the ball] to come off the pitch at a tremendous pace'. It was this pace off the wicket which disconcerted batsmen, and it proved too much for Hammond in the first innings who was bowled for 35, with the score 101 for 4. Amar Singh, he said later, 'came off the pitch like the crack of doom'. Some critics rated Amar Singh as one of the finest bowlers seen in England since the war. Pelham Warner thought he would easily make a World XI and was probably as good as Sydney Barnes.

England recovered through Jardine, helped by Ames. Ames should have been stumped first ball and went on to make 65. But bowling out England in four hours for 259 was very creditable. On the Monday, when King George V arrived to meet the cricketers, India looked in a fairly sound position. Nayudu and Wazir Ali, their two best players, were at the wicket and the score was just over 100 for the loss of two wickets. But Nayudu had badly damaged his hand in trying to catch Ames and he found it very difficult to hook or cut Bowes who, in a preview of what the Australians were to receive that winter, persistently bowled short. The day before the Test, *The Times* had warned that, if Bowes bowled short, Nayudu would smash the Tavern with his hooks. On 40 Nayudu did try to hook Voce but with his damaged hand could only top-edge it to Robins at short-leg. Even then India lunched on 153 for 4 and seemed right in the game; but, as was to happen in so many subsequent matches, particularly in England, there was the first of Indian Test batting collapses: the last six wickets fell in an hour for 36 runs.

Amar Singh, thought *Wisden*, bowled 'even better than before' in the second innings and England, at 67 for 4, were not that far ahead. But in what proved to be the turning-point of the match Jardine helped by Paynter, Robins and Brown took England to 275. Jardine then declared, at 12 noon on the third day, setting India 346 runs to win. It was not an easy target but the Indians should have managed to hold out to draw the match. But by now they were demoralised. The pitch was worn, several of the players were injured, and Palia, who could barely walk to the wicket, batted at no. 11. Even so, Navle and Naoomal put on 41 for the first wicket but then came another collapse. The score was 108 for 7 before Amar Singh, coming in at no. 9, hit 51, putting on 74 in forty minutes with Lall Singh.

Nayudu accepted that England had completely outplayed India in all departments, although much was due to Jardine who had made 164 for once out. But, Nayudu felt, with a bit of luck, 'the holding of an easy catch or the more determined effort to run out a batsman, and better physical fitness might just have turned the tables in our favour'.

The chances of that would undoubtedly have been increased had Duleep and the Nawab of Pataudi, then playing in England, played for India. Their class would have given India the batting depth and resilience they needed. As it was England missed Duleep, indeed Cardus, unhappy about England's batting – Hammond unable to score heavily, Woolley a mixture of short runs and cross-bat slashes – felt that no England team was complete without Duleep. Of course the Indians were not to know – nor was anybody – what a season of triumph and tragedy this would be for Duleep. At the end of it he was fifth in the averages with 1,633 runs at an average of 52.67. But those figures conceal that he did not play after mid-August. At that stage, led by Duleep's batting, Sussex were 19 points behind Yorkshire with a game in hand. But Duleep was already an ill man, his doctors forbade him to go on, although Ranji cabled from Aix-les-Bains that he should continue. He may not have wanted Duleep to play for India, but he was desperately keen that he should complete his matches for Sussex. It proved too much for the frail Duleep. He was barely able to complete his innings of 90 against Somerset, when Sussex won by ten wickets, for already he was haemorrhaging. He left to go to a sanatorium and never played again. So as the Indians made their Test debut, the man who might have been their finest player was forced to leave cricket.

Before the Test the Indians had been worried about their bowling and confident about their batting. The Test had shown they had a fine attack, if mostly pace, but that it was the batting which required some steel. Even here there was a contrast to the way in which Indian batting developed later. Although Voce and Bowes took eleven wickets, the Indians had looked most comfortable against pace and all at sea against spin, particularly leg-spin. How this picture would change over the years! Yet compared with the record of other Test debutants theirs had not been a bad performance. The West Indies lost five of their first six Tests in England in 1928 and 1933, by an innings. The Indians, whose history had inured them to defeat, had much more to celebrate. Cardus's poetic image as England were reduced to 19 for 3 on the first morning was much quoted: 'In my mind's eyes I saw the news flashing over the air to far-flung places in India, Punjab and Karachi and Kuala Lumpur [which of course was not in India] to dusky men in the hills, to the bazaars of the East, to Gandhi himself and to Gunga Din.'

Gunga Din may not have cared for cricket and Gandhi, certainly, did not, but the Indians could take comfort that they had made a game of their first Test. This satisfaction turned to pleasure the following spring with the arrival of the 1933 *Wisden* which chose Nayudu as one of its 'Five Cricketers of the Year'. A colonial society can never be sure that its judgements are right unless the Mother Country confirms them. The accolade to Nayudu seemed to make Indians believe that their cricket had 'arrived'. *Wisden*'s words were endlessly quoted and requoted in newspapers and magazines across the land. From now on every Indian cricketer would see it as the summit of his achievement to be chosen as one of *Wisden*'s Five Cricketers of the Year.

But within days of the end of the Lord's Test the poison of Indian life – suspicion and distrust – was at work. If hypocrisy is the great English disease, then suspicion must be the Indian one. A story is told of an Indian businessman exporting crabs to the United States. One day he is contacted by his US agent and asked, 'Why do you send the crabs in an open container?' Why, retorts the Indian, have any gone missing? 'No', assures the American, 'but we are just surprised. Surely it would be safer to seal them in a box?' The Indian replies, 'Don't worry, these are Indian crabs. If one tries to get out of the box the others will pull him down.'

So it was with Nayudu. The Lord's Test had won him praise from English critics for his leadership. The leadership had been thrust on him and he had responded magnificently. But for the other 'cricketing crabs' this was too much. Two days after the Test finished, on 30 June 1932, a member of the team wrote to Berry Sarbadhikary, then making his mark as a cricket journalist in Calcutta: 'We should have won the Test but C.K.'s leadership was poor . . . He made all sorts of mistakes and his favourite wicket-keeper Navle let us down badly . . . Few except his own men seem to like C.K. and from the day he has been allowed to captain the team, he has become so stiff-necked that he does not even wish some of us [good morning] . . . with a better man as captain we could have done better . . . I can name at least two who are more fitted to be captain than C.K.'

In a vast land like India, more of a sub-continent than a country, and with tremendous economic and regional differences, it would have been naive to expect all Indians suddenly to sink their differences once they got on to the cricket field. Despite Gandhi, and the Congress movement, they could not quite do that even on the political field and were always open to jibes from the British that it was only *their* presence that kept the Indians united. But these cricket cabals were something much worse. There was no policy or ideology involved. It was personal jealousy.

The Vizzy-Patiala battle coloured this jealousy, but the splits after the Test involved players who, little more than a year ago, had played together for Vizzy's substitute MCC team. The pro-Nayudu and anti-Nayudu factions were, probably, formed on that tour. It is too Machiavellian to suggest that Vizzy actually encouraged such a split. More likely they developed in a very Indian way: by trying to catch the Maharajkumar's attention. In a feudal society like India those who had the ruler's ear, whether he be an Indian prince or a British Viceroy, stood to gain. During the tour Vizzy, who had used Nayudu as his captaincy amanuensis, showered him, and some other players, with generous gifts. The others were also rewarded, but less handsomely, so it became a case of a small group in the team becoming known as Vizzy's favourites and others not so fortunate thinking they were outcasts. Nayudu was in the favourite group, and among the outcasts were two sets of brothers, Wazir and Nazir Ali, and Amar Singh and Ramji.

To an extent Nayudu and Wazir Ali were natural rivals. Wazir, like Nayudu, was a powerful right-hand bat who could play some very elegant strokes, including a charming cover-drive, and he was also a more than useful medium-pace change bowler. Like Nayudu he played in only seven Tests, all against England, and did not have the opportunity to demonstrate his class or his ability to its full extent. What set the two men apart was that Wazir, eight years younger than Nayudu, did not possess the older man's determination or his obsession with the game. Nayudu was, undoubtedly, the greater cricketer, and he left a deeper impression on the game, for he was active in Indian cricket as a player and administrator almost until his death in 1967, by which time the modern era of Indian cricket was well and truly launched. His last match was a festival game in Nagpur in 1963, when he was less than a week from his sixty-eighth birthday and was playing with cricketers whose fathers had been his juniors when he was in his prime. Wazir, in contrast, died at the age of forty-six after an operation for appendicitis just three years after Pakistan was created, and he had little chance to impose his personality on the post-war game in that country.

But in the 1930s all this was in the future, and Wazir Ali was a good stalking horse for the anti-Nayudu camp. Was he not a Muslim, one of the many great Muslim cricketers being produced by the Punjab? Should he not have the same right to be captain of India as the Hindu Nayudu? In fact the divisions were not, strictly speaking, on religious lines. Even the so-called Nayudu group was not all Hindu as it was supposed to include a Muslim, Ghulam Mahomed, and a Parsee, Palia, while the anti-Nayudu faction included Hindus like Amar Singh and Parsees like Colah and Marshall.

Indeed Nayudu's rift with Amar Singh was a classic of its kind. We cannot be sure when it began. It is possible that the 'needle' which crept in during Vizzy's tour, when Nayudu and Amar Singh played in opposite teams, had something to do with it. Hobbs observed this 'needle' and wondered if it was good for Indian cricket. But in England it seems to have started with a fact as trivial as that Nayudu never seemed to have much faith in Amar Singh's batting. To be fair Amar did not do much as a batsman in the early part of the tour; his highest score was 8. But ten days before the Lord's Test, against Lancashire at Liverpool, Amar Singh revealed himself to be a hitter of high class. Coming in at no. 10 he made 131 not out, putting on 125 in eighty minutes with Jehangir Khan for the ninth wicket and then 94 for the tenth with Nissar. A couple of days after this innings Ranji, when asked about Amar Singh the batsman, said, 'Oh, he's no good. He plays for my team in Jamnagar. He can't bat so we put him in last.' Nayudu was, probably, influenced by this view and in the second innings of the Lord's Test, even though the team was racked by injuries, Amar Singh still went in low, at no. 9. Cardus thought that had he gone in earlier he might have attacked Robins more successfully. It is easy to say that with hindsight but it probably sowed the seeds of discord.

Even otherwise the two players were growing apart. Nayudu was already the great star of Indian cricket when Amar Singh, wearing a black fur cap, khaki trousers and black leather shoes, had come on to the field along with his older brother Ramji. At that time Amar looked up to C.K. But now Amar, something of a star in his own right, wanted respect from C.K. who continued to treat him as he had always done. Their temperamental differences hardly helped. Nayudu was part of the generation of Indians who had taken to heart the British stereotype of Indians as a shifty, excitable, emotional race. The ideal Raj ruler, the ones held up as models to the Indians, was an aloof, reserved, erect figure. He would have no time for frivolity. Dedication and hard work were all. Nayudu combined a certain brahminical pedantry and attention to detail with a Victorian high-mindedness and stiff upper lip. Emotions, like children, were never to be freely displayed. Even in his sixties he practised at the game and kept up a punishing schedule of hard physical exercise. In that sense Nayudu was like Jardine, driving his body hard, learning from a young age to bear pain and neither asking nor giving quarter.

The difference with Jardine was that, while his batting reflected his personality, Nayudu at the crease offered a complete contrast. As a batsman Nayudu was one of the great entertainers of the game, and no batsman in Indian cricket is more associated with hitting sixes. In cricket history those who hit sixes are always cavaliers, a Jessop, a Miller, a Constantine. Nayudu's 32 sixes on the 1932 tour ranks only behind Constantine's 37 on the 1928 tour, as the most sixes hit in an English season by a touring batsman. A six is at once an expression of a batsman's command – however temporary – and an act of defiance. If a duel between a batsman and bowler is a novel, then a six hit can conclude one chapter. Nayudu could be so destructive with sixes that he threatened often to write the bowler out of the novel.

But this partiality for sixes did not carry over into a cavalier life-style. Off the field Nayudu was a disciplinarian of the old school. Before the first Test he had threatened to discipline players who had been found drunk or kept late hours. The row led to fist fights and abuse of Nayudu. It is not known whether Amar Singh was one of the players so disciplined but he was a simple, easy-going person and found Nayudu's ways increasingly irksome. A little more than a year after the Lord's Test Amar Singh was saying publicly that he could not play with Nayudu. Amar wanted to enjoy his game and entertain the spectators; he felt that Nayudu wanted to win at all costs and had made the game into a killjoy pursuit.

By the end of the 1932 tour these differences were open. Amar Singh could hardly bear to speak to Nayudu; if Nayudu threw the ball to him in the field then more often than not he dropped it. Nayudu had also upset Amar's opening partner, Nissar. The story went that, after taking 5 for 93 in the England first innings, he had been rebuked by Nayudu for slack fielding. Whether such slights were real or imaginary it is difficult to tell, but instead of building on their Lord's Test showing, the Indians showed wildly fluctuating form thereafter. Against Yorkshire they were one run behind on the first innings but were bowled out for 66 in their second by Macaulay, who took 8 for 21. Of that total 52 runs came from Nazir Ali, Wazir's brother. He hit three sixes and five fours, the next highest scorer was 'Extras' with 5, and no other batsman made more than 3. There were four ducks and Nayudu himself made 2. Yet this was almost the same side that had played in the Lord's Test.

There were some notable victories, however, particularly against Glamorgan in a match where rain had removed almost a day and a half's play, and against Warwickshire when the Indians came splendidly from behind. But generally there was too much inconsistency, too much the feeling that the team was not pulling together. On the ship home Colah, a Parsee, threatened to throw Nayudu overboard, and the rifts found dramatic public expression when the team returned to India.

Delhi now had a new cricket ground, Feroz Shah Kotla on the borders between Mughal Delhi and the Delhi which Edward Lutyens had created for the Raj. Vizzy donated an impressive pavilion named, of course, after Lord Willingdon, and a match was organised to honour the occasion: The Rest of India under Vizzy versus the 1932 touring team. As Nayudu went out to bat, Vizzy lined up his team and applauded Nayudu all the way to the wicket. Vizzy was capable of such grandstand gestures and they often served some deep purpose. But on this occasion he was, probably, trying to pay a sincere tribute to all that Nayudu had done in England. But as Nayudu was being applauded, members of his own team, sitting in the pavilion, responded with boos, hoots, cat-calls, even obscenities and curses and one player, prominently wearing his Indian blazer, shouted out: 'What a shame, this is an insult to Porbander'.

Just when it seemed that a commoner might have established his claim to lead India, the ground was cut from under his feet. Just then, as it happened, the whole princely world in India was again in ferment. And Patiala, who had been feeling increasingly embittered about the role being played by Willingdon, had a chance to exercise leadership amongst the Indian princes. A few months after the match – which the touring team won easily with Amar Singh taking 12 for 56 and Vizzy making a 'pair' – Patiala was once again elected Chancellor of the Chamber of Princes.

It could not have been a more crucial time for princely India. Willingdon had crushed Gandhi's civil disobedience movement with some of the harshest measures the British ever used in India, and now, after three round-table conferences in London – only the second of which was attended by Gandhi – the British were ready to engineer another solution for India. This still fell far short of what Gandhi and the Nationalists were demanding – complete independence – but as the British had no intention of leaving India, it meant that the princes had a new and important role.

The British solution involved the princes joining together with British India in a federation. But the plans gave the princes a veto: without them the federation could not come into being. So, egged on by Churchill and other Empire die-hards, the princes stoutly resisted even this slight concession to Indian opinion. They were from India but not part of India, the Nationalist struggle was none of their concern.

This was the view which Ranji, as Chancellor of the Chamber of Princes, argued both in England and in India, and it was while he was again arguing this that he fell out with Willingdon. A few days later he was dead. Writers on Ranji have suggested since that he had vast political differences with Willingdon and one has even claimed that Ranji fell out with Willingdon because he wanted independence for India sooner than the British were prepared to grant it. This is absurd. Ranji, like all the Indian princes, did not think in terms of Indian independence. The struggle of Gandhi and the Nationalist movement was a world far removed from them – it could have taken place on the other side of the moon for all they cared. They were concerned with their own state and keen to maintain its power and prestige.

It was the vacancy left by Ranji's death as Chancellor that was filled by Patiala. Willingdon did not like it. 'I am sorry,' he wrote to the Secretary of State for India, 'to have Patiala as Chancellor of the Chamber of Princes. Such a stupid man.' In 1935, when Patiala was re-elected, Willingdon was still not reconciled. 'Patiala is the most unreliable man I know. Either a great fool, or the slipperiest customer that ever existed . . . the Chamber of Princes under Patiala is fast becoming a decrepit organ.'

Willingdon's hostility to Patiala coincided with a waning of the latter's cricket power. He had been the kingmaker of the 1932 tour but in the winter of 1933-34 he was pushed to the sidelines. Whether Willingdon turned the cricket authorities against Patiala is not known but certainly, after the 1932 tour, as the acrimony with the Viceroy developed, Patalia found himself cold-shouldered by the organisation he had done so much to create and nourish. The emergency Board of Control meeting in Delhi on 1 May 1933 showed that the associations which had once survived only because of his generosity were now turning against him. Mainly run by British expatriates living in India they divided the Board up into three zones: East, North and West. Each zone would nominate a selector. East and North both nominated an Englishman: Alec Hosie, who, on leave in England, played for Hampshire, represented East Zone; the North chose E. L. West; only the West Zone's selectoral representative was an Indian, the grand old Parsee cricketer, H. D. Kanga. Kanga feared being outvoted by the Englishmen but Bombay, which could not afford to be left out, insisted that he accept the job.

So India prepared to welcome its first Test tour by the MCC in 1933-34 with two out of their three selectors Englishmen and utter confusion about who would be captain or indeed where the three Tests that were scheduled would be played. Patiala's money was no longer available. Indian Test matches are given to associations provided they can guarantee the Board a certain sum of money. Bombay was rich enough to do that, but not Calcutta or Madras. For a time it seemed a Test would be played in Secunderabad, the twin city of Hyderabad,

80

where the Nawab Moin-ud-Dowlah was prepared to put up a large sum of money. This aroused Calcutta and Madras to find the money and so Bombay, Calcutta and Madras were decided on as the venues for the first-ever Tests to be played in India.

Collecting gate money was an historical problem in India, and there was the added complication of the strength of the MCC team. Would it be the full-strength England side? This has been a perennial debate in India before every England tour. For days and weeks before the team is announced there is intense speculation about the players who might tour and, if the team falls substantially below the standards expected, there are protests that the Indians have been 'badly treated'. In the autumn of 1933, as the MCC announced that Douglas Jardine was to lead the side but that it would not include Hammond, Sutcliffe, Leyland, Paynter, Wyatt, Larwood, Voce, Allen – who had been pressed by Lord Hawke to go but declined – or Ames, a telegram arrived at Lord's which said, 'Selection of such a team a disgusting insult to India. Would recommend tour be cancelled unless more stars added. Indian Board of Control.' Lord's, recovering from Jardine's 1932-33 'body-line' tour which had threatened to ruin cricket relations with Australia – the 1934 Australian tour was still in the balance when the team for India left – felt a frisson of fear. Was this another crisis? But it turned out that the telegram was the work of a clerk in the Indian telegraph office. At least the Indians consoled themselves that Jardine, the controversial captain, was to bring the team to India. If it did not have the best that England had to offer it was still quite a strong one with the spin led by Verity and the pace in the hands of Morris Nichols of Essex and E. W. 'Nobby' Clark, the Northamptonshire left-armer.

If all this worried C. K. Nayudu he did not show it. His initial parley with Jardine was as if, like in 1932, he would go out to toss with him when the Tests began. While Jardine and his team were still on the high seas Nayudu sent a cable, 'Wait till I meet you'. He met the tourists in a two-day match in Lahore playing for the Punjab Governor's XI. (The tour was a mixture of two-day, three-day and four-day matches – the Tests being of four days. Debate about the first-class status of some of the matches has only recently been resolved.) The match may not have been first-class but Nayudu landed an important psychological blow by scoring a hundred.

Before that, easy English victories had bred the familiar fear among the Indians: that Englishmen just arrived in India must be superior to the Indians. The fast bowling of Clark and Nichols and the spin of Verity and C. S. 'Father' Marriott, a right-arm leg-spinner, had done much to encourage that feeling. Nayudu's century arrested it. Young Indian batsmen felt emboldened and, when Nayudu did not play in certain of the preliminary matches – he played in so many of them that Jardine referred to these games as Nayudu's flying circus – the Indians tended to collapse. All this must have helped Nayudu's chances of the captaincy and he knew that the chairman of the selectors, Alec Hosie, wanted him as captain.

But Patiala was still not out of it. Not that he wanted the captaincy for himself but his second son, who had already been proclaimed his heir, the Yuvraj, was showing signs of becoming a genuine cricketer. He had been coached by some of the best: Leyland, Waddington, George Brown, Roy Kilner, and Frank Tarrant. If he were to turn into a major batsman then, with his princely rank, he would be the automatic choice as captain.

Yuvraj had made 49 in the match when Nayudu made his century, Nayudu visibly helping the young prince. But for the Maharajah this was only a way to regain his cricket position. As the MCC tour progressed through northern India they were slowly drawn into the Patiala sphere of influence. At Amritsar he had donated the pavilion, which was named after him, and got Frank Tarrant to lay down a turf wicket, and Tarrant and his eighteen-year-old son umpired. Yuvraj did not disappoint his father. He took the score from 12 for 3 to 130, making 66. His partner in the stand was another youngster, Lala Amarnath, who made 109 and for the first time suggested that he was going to be a major batting talent. The Maharajah himself batted, making 22 run out, and altogether the Patiala influence lay heavily over the match. At one stage, when one of the umpires left the field, the game continued and one run was scored.

The next match against Patiala's XI was of four days, the only match outside Tests to be of such duration. It showed the Maharajah in all his pomp and circumstance. One day, play ended at lunch-time to allow for a shoot in the Simla Hills, on another occasion after a banquet lasting till the early hours of the morning, the English were aroused at seven o'clock for a deer hunt to be followed by cricket. Not surprisingly, when the Yuvraj was caught at square-leg the fielder claimed it was not a catch, and next ball the Yuvraj was dropped in the slips. Perhaps this too was a tactical drop. Patiala's lavish hospitality came as a welcome relief after many tough days of touring. Most of the English team knew little or nothing about India. There were long train journeys involved – often of three or four days' duration. They travelled first-class which provided great comfort but W. H. V. 'Hopper' Levett, the Kent wicket-keeper, recalls: 'We would arrive somewhere and be met by our hosts who would bring their bearers with them. Each of us would get a bearer. Then we would be taken to our hosts' home, have breakfast and immediately there would be cricket – after four days on the train.'

After this Patiala was more like the east of fantasy. Levett has a memory of a 'great pavilion at Patiala and all his wives were brought to the match in buses. They watched the cricket through purdah above this lovely pavilion. The colours were wonderful. Indians liked their colours. They walked about in white, green and red turbans, lots of fuss and pomp. The English in the colonial service had a good life, they had done well and treated us well. But Patiala was something else. Dancing girls? Oh yes, they were at our behest if required. That was part of the set-up in India, part of the hospitality.'

Patiala's magic worked even on Jardine who, on the Australian tour, had given the impression that he was a desiccated, unbending man who would not be side-tracked from his mission of winning. But in the next match in Delhi, much to the fury of Willingdon and despite the pleas of Lady Willingdon, Patiala played for MCC. But then Jardine played cricket by his own rules. In the match against the Viceroy's XI Jardine actually got an apology from the Viceroy about rolling the pitch for twenty minutes, much more than the statutory time allowed. The idea of the Viceroy apologising drove the local English almost to apoplexy, but Jardine was insistent. 'I wouldn't have gone on to the field without it, even if the King of England was playing against me.'

Yet despite the battles that Patiala was winning, when it came to the Tests Nayudu was appointed captain. The team for the first Test in Bombay showed five changes from the 1932 Lord's Test. Jehangir Khan, studying in Cambridge, and Naoomal were not available, Lall Singh was now ineligible – which meant that Patiala, the ruler of Sikhs, was not there to back him – and Nazir Ali and Palia were dropped. In their places came V. M. Merchant, Amarnath, L. P. Jai, Jamshedji and Ramji. It was a curious choice. Jamshedji, at 41 years and 27 days, is the oldest Indian to have made his Test debut. If he was not good enough in 1932, why was he good enough now? Ramji, ten years older than his brother Amar Singh (the family name Ladha is never used in relation to these two cricketers), probably should have gone to England in 1932. A man of massive physique he had a simple, almost a childlike disposition: he believed in hurling the cricket ball as fast as he could and for a few overs was very fast. On Gilligan's tour he had bowled so fast and menacingly, particularly on the mat at Ajmer, that Gilligan had asked the Rajputana captain to take him off so as to prevent further injury to his batsmen. He had also, fed up with his lbw appeals being turned down, once bowled a bouncer at the Maharajah of Patiala, and laid the great man out. He then hurriedly left the state never to return. If this showed a difficult, volatile character, then that may explain why he was left out. Merchant and Jai would probably have gone on the 1932 tour had their political convictions not kept them out, while Amarnath was a genuine find – a youngster of rare batting promise.

The selection met with a hostile reaction. There were now several discernible groups in the Indian cricket scene. And each of these groups had its own favourite players. Their exclusion meant, they argued, that 'groupism' was rampant. Soon that word would become as much a swear word in Indian life as words like racist and fascist are in the modern West. Patiala's was the major group but, everywhere you looked, there seemed to be a group with its own special clutch of players. There was the princely state of Kathiawar which had given the MCC a bad fright in a match that became known as the battle of Rajkot. In Bombay there were Hindus who, though divided amongst themselves, did not like the idea that an Indian Test team should be chosen by a selection committee where two of the three members were Englishmen. They were further incensed that, for the first Test staged in India, both the umpires should be Europeans – Frank Tarrant and Bill Hitch. But Jardine, whose preparations for this tour were as meticulous as ever, had decided early on that Indian umpires could not be trusted. There were some good ones around but he would not have them.

It was against this background that India played its first Test on home soil from 15-18 December 1933. For this match the Indian players were allowed into the clubhouse of the Bombay Gymkhana, and temporary stands were erected round the ground. These were reserved sections for the various gymkhanas that made up Bombay cricket. Each spectator had a comfortable seat and, with the Governor of Bombay declaring the first day, a Friday, a holiday, and cutting the working hours on the Saturday, a huge crowd gathered. Some 100,000 people watched the four days of the Test.

For this first Test there was an intimacy between the players and spectators that was never again to be repeated. Only a rope separated the crowd from the playing area; half an hour before play crowds were still gathered on the Gymkhana ground and they watched Nayudu and Jardine toss, the wickets being pitched and the practice of the players. It was only at 10.45, fifteen minutes before the start, that the crowd began to vacate the playing area to allow play to start promptly at 11am. Later, as cricket moved from open grounds like Bombay Gymkhana to concrete stadiums, such intimacy was impossible.

For the first two days the crowd – which knew nothing of the back-stage intrigues – had little Indian success to cheer. England were clearly dominant. Morris Nichols walked back to his run-up with the rollicking gait of a sailor but there was nothing funny about his bowling. He played for England mostly abroad: in New Zealand, in India, and despite the heat he was clearly in his element. The Indians of that generation were used to pace but still found Nichols difficult. Verity was just as much of a problem and, on a good batting wicket, they made just 219. It was all promise, no real substance: Amarnath 38, Wazir Ali 36, Colah 31, and Nayudu 28. Batsmen did the hard work of reaching their 20s and 30s and then got out.

The way to play a big innings was demonstrated by Bryan Valentine who was making his Test debut. Coming in at no. 6, with England 164 for 4, he made 136 and saw England to 438. India could only speculate on the might-have-beens. India had three genuine fast bowlers, Nissar, Ramji, Amar Singh – something rare in Indian Test history. Nissar bowled Mitchell, also making his debut, for 5, and for about half an hour at the start of the England innings produced such pace that Walters edged him in and out of short-leg's hands and there were a couple of other chances. Had they been taken the course of the innings and the match might have been very different. They were not, and Nissar toiled for 33.5 overs, taking 5 for 90.

India's cause looked lost when Nobby Clark, a tall fair-haired left-armer who was so much the ideal bowler that he had featured in a Worthington beer advertisement, had one of his 'on' days and removed both openers for 21.

It was at this stage that Nayudu joined Amarnath. The story goes that Nayudu went up to Amarnath and whispered something in his ear. Amarnath had never lacked confidence. If anything, he had too much of it. What he had never yet shown was a big match temperament. He could play brilliantly, take any bowling apart, but could he do so in a Test where his side faced a possible innings defeat and in front of a packed crowd? Nayudu's words probably convinced him he could and, as if possessed by a mysterious power – that is how he saw it afterwards – he started playing some brilliant shots. In 78 minutes he scored 83, then slowed down to reach his century in 117 minutes.

It was the first century by an Indian in a Test, and even Nayudu, always so calm and so collected, was overwhelmed. As they completed the single for Amarnath to reach his century, he went down the wicket to offer him congratulations. The ball was not dead and Elliott, the wicket-keeper, who had the ball in his hands could have run Nayudu out. But just as he was about to remove the bails he glanced at Jardine who shook his head and a major incident was averted. By now crowds were swarming on to the pitch, Amarnath was engulfed with spectators, garlanded and congratulated while the band played 'God save the King'. As the day's play ended, with Amarnath 102 not out, India 169 for 2, women tore off their jewellery to present it to him, Maharajahs made gifts of money, and India hailed a hero.

The next day the crowd were still too full of Amarnath's heroics to notice the shambles the Indians made of the rest of their innings. After Amarnath and Nayudu had taken the score to 207, Nayudu was out for 67, a run later Amarnath was brilliantly caught by Nichols, off a full-blooded hook shot, for 118. After that, in one of those dramatic batting collapses that India specialise in, they subsided to 258, the last eight wickets falling for 51. Only Merchant with 30 kept his head. England, requiring 40 runs, won by nine wickets.

This was all overlooked in the euphoria over Amarnath's achievement. This will be a recurring theme in the story of Indian cricket: the team fails but the individual covers himself with glory. In years to come this would often provide India solace amidst great, shattering, defeats. Amarnath had restored pride, faith that Indians could bat against the might of the English sahib. Had he not hooked Nichols and Clark, gone down the wicket to Verity, the mighty Verity, who took just 1 for 50 in the second innings? If only luck favoured the Indians, if only they could unite, they would be England's equal.

The first Test set the pattern for the series. On the field India were constantly struggling to contain England but there was always some heroic rearguard action by a couple of Indian players that redeemed the collective failure. Off the field the rancour and bitterness increased. In Calcutta, in the second Test, the hero was Dilawar Hussain . . . Ramaswami has left us an unforgettable picture of the man:

He was a tall and bulky person with a prominent stomach and he invariably played with a clean shaven head without any hat or cap or any kind of head gear. He always wore very loose pants (of the type favoured by northern Indians) and after batting for a while or keeping wicket for sometime his shirt will be hanging out of his trousers and somebody must tuck it in, now and then. He had a rather ugly and uncouth stance at the wicket as he held his bat very low and bent his body forward so much that his head was practically in line with the top of the wickets. Those who watched him batting from the on side could only see his prominent hind portion of the body sticking up while the head, bat and the rest of Dilawar Hussain were hardly visible. However, he had a very sound defence and so it was very difficult to get him out. He was the most selfish batsman I had ever seen as he always tried to have most of the strike and whenever he made a stroke he would run as fast as he could and try and take two runs even if it was risky to run more than one. If, on the other hand, the other batsman made a stroke for which there were two easy runs, he would run only one, so much so many batsmen got run out whenever he was batting with them.

Dilawar's moment came after England, coping well with a green Calcutta wicket – which in those days and for some years afterwards was the best wicket for pace bowlers in India – had made 403. Dilawar was in the side as wicket-keeper but the Indian theory was that wicket-keepers made good openers because having to watch the ball all the time meant they got their eye in. In this case it did not work. Dilawar was dogged and Nichols, unable to get past his defence, let fly with a bouncer which hit him on the side of the head. Dilawar crumpled to the ground and when Nayudu came on to the field to help him he started weeping, 'I am ruined, I am ruined'. But he came back with a bandage over the lump on his head, was hit again by Clark on the thumb, went off again but eventually returned to top-score with 59 in a total of 247. India just failed to avoid the follow-on and Dilawar, this time batting at no. 7, was again the top scorer with 57. It was just enough to deny England victory.

Calcutta had provided India's first draw and in Madras, for the first time in the series, India were on top through some magnificent bowling by Amar Singh. He had shown little interest in the series. In Bombay he had played in tennis shoes and often slipped while fielding. His lack of interest was reflected in his figures so far in the series: six wickets for 241 runs, though this really represented bowling in little more than two full England innings. But now in Madras he showed that, when the mood seized him, or he felt he could play under Nayudu's captaincy, he was a great bowler. With the new ball on a lush, green wicket he was not very effective, England made 111 for the first wicket and then reached 167 for 2. But between lunch and tea with the old ball he swung and cut it so well that many an English batsman thought of Hammond's remark: 'He comes off the wicket like the crack of doom.' Five wickets fell for 41 runs, and from 167 for 2, England were 208 for 7. But Jardine found an ideal partner in Verity. Jardine made 65, Verity 42 and England recovered to 335. Amar Singh finished with 7 for 86. Never again would he bowl as well. The next day on a wicket providing turn Verity was virtually unplayable and India were shot out for 145, no batsman making more than 30 and Verity taking 7 for 49. As he came off the field he was asked what he would like, a drink, perhaps? No, he said, he would quite like a biscuit or two. India were left 451 to get in the final innings but this was always going to be too much. With a wicket worn at one end it did not bear thinking what Verity would do.

But the Indians were becoming rather good at prolonging hopeless causes. Verity could only manage 4 for 104, with one of the wickets that of a genuine tail-ender. It was James Langridge who did the real damage with 5 for 63. Yuvraj, on his Test debut, made 60, using his reach and height to play the spinners while Amarnath played one of those innings which leave a deeper impression on the memory than on the scorebook. He made 26 not out, using his feet brilliantly to cope with two of the world's best left-arm spinners on a bad wicket. India's

249 meant a defeat by 202 runs and 2-0 defeat in the series but it also demonstrated what might be achieved.

However, given the committee room intrigue it was amazing that India managed to field eleven players at all. Before the Calcutta Test there had been something like a plot to get rid of Nayudu as captain. The Indian players were staying in the Great Eastern Hotel – the English players stayed with the local English, Jardine stayed with the Governor. Nazir Ali, who had been dropped for the Bombay Test and was twelfth man in Calcutta, suggested to Dilawar Hussain and Nissar that, as Nayudu was still being preferred over his brother, Wazir, the Test should be boycotted. Wazir had no great love for Nayudu but refused to be part of this shabby conspiracy. After the selection for the Test was announced head-counting started to determine which region had been 'victimised'. Calcutta, furious that the local Englishman, Hosie, 'prejudiced against Bengal', had not selected a Bengali, virtually boycotted the Test. Today Calcutta's Eden Gardens is always guaranteed a sell-out. For that inaugural Test very few attended.

The Madras Test selection was also subjected to the Indian regional test. Which group had benefited? Which region had more players? Bombay had only one representative, Vijay Merchant, Patiala had five and, including the umpire, Frank Tarrant, six – until Jardine objected to Tarrant and had him changed. Nazir was chosen for this Test but, in the first innings, when his bowling supplementing Amar Singh's could have made a big difference for India, he pleaded a groin injury and did not bowl. Nayudu had to open the bowling himself. In the second Nazir had recovered so well that he delivered 23 overs and became the most successful bowler with 4 for 83. Was this, as some alleged, his revenge on Nayudu or just one of those cricket things? Clearly Nayudu could not get the best out of his team.

And like all losing captains Nayudu was now being subjected to criticism, particularly from ex-cricketers. Pavri wrote, 'Major C. K. Nayudu was, undoubtedly, the best all-round cricketer and the best available captain but not an ideal one as he was not able to control the men under his command and there was no co-operation between him and the players. There was also a lack of teamwork and the "team spirit" was absent altogether . . . it seemed Major Nayudu was obsessed with self-importance, which leads to narrow-mindedness and is fatal to success.'

There followed a list of detailed complaints: field-placing, should a left-armer require a long-on, except against a slogger? Should Amarnath be batting higher? Why did Nayudu keep his bowlers on for so long – sometimes two hours at a stretch? Did he not realise a change was usually successful? Pavri conceded that 'Major Nayudu was greatly handicapped because he did not know his men. It was not his fault, because the Indian players were selected from different provinces and they had not the opportunity of playing together.'

For many of the players the first time they met each other was just before a Test and often their only common language was English, as each of the players spoke a different Indian language. This was a breeding ground for intrigue but there was another factor: the Indian inability to rise above their own narrow concerns. Jardine had taught the Indians many lessons: his professionalism, the hard way he played his cricket – if a batsman was hit as Merchant once was he showed no mercy and did not take the fast bowler off – but the most important point was missed.

Jardine's team also reflected different groups. There were amateurs and professionals. Even amongst amateurs there were those who had come from universities and those who, like 'Hopper' Levett, were farmers' boys and felt left out. Levett recalled to me how he had become alienated from Jardine:

> Jardine didn't make life very easy for me. If I had been to a university and got a blue he would probably have treated me differently. I had not been to Eton or Harrow. I rather felt he was a snob, one of those old la-di-dah, aloof men who preferred people who had been to university. I wouldn't have cared to play a lot of cricket under him. I wouldn't have enjoyed my cricket. He wasn't my cup of tea. After the war at The Oval during Test matches on a couple of occasions when I was there he came to me. No-one else seemed to want to know much of him, he asked me if I would come and sit at the top of the stands and talk with him. I always felt he thought he had done me wrong in India. It was his way of saying sorry.

In theory this criticism is not very different to what Amar Singh felt about Nayudu. But such feelings did not stop Levett pulling together as a member of the team and contributing his bit to its success. The Indians, somehow, could not do that.

Only once did Jardine relax. This was when, between the Calcutta and Madras Tests, the MCC played Vizzy's XI at Benares. The Test in Calcutta had just finished, there was a long overnight journey from Calcutta and less than three hours after arriving in Benares they were playing the match. Even then they might have won but at a crucial stage, recalls Levett, 'When Nobby Clark was going through their side, Jardine took him off to give them a chance, a couple of chaps got going and in the end we just lost the match.' Vizzy's team won by 14 runs. It was the only defeat Jardine's team suffered on the tour. Jardine, probably, did not lose much sleep over it, but it was a victory that had important consequences for Indian cricket. Nayudu, after four Tests as captain and three defeats, was now out of it. Vizzy never failed to remind everyone how he was the only Indian leader who had humbled Jardine. The story became almost as much of an Indian legend as Archie MacLaren's defeat of Warwick Armstrong's side in 1921 was an English one. That was Armstrong's only defeat of that tour. But the defeat was not meant to make MacLaren captain of England. It mainly served to make Neville Cardus, the only major journalist to witness it, into a famous cricket writer. But for Vizzy, with his desperate ambition to lead his country, the victory against Jardine's team was to serve a more sinister purpose. Indian cricket was to pay a high price for Jardine's uncharacteristic moment of generosity.

6

Vizzy
1934-36

Jardine's tour had shown that Indian cricket still had far to go – although in one of those statements that usually do more harm than good, at the final dinner in Bombay, he predicted that India would be top of world cricket in ten years. He was, probably, being kind but many people in India believed him and when, more than ten years later, Indian cricket was far from top of the world, they felt cheated. It was the players who suffered from the resulting disillusionment.

Jardine's visit had, however, put the Maharajah of Patiala back on top of the Indian cricket world. His son, the Yuvraj, had shown himself to be a promising bat and his 60 against Verity on a turning Madras pitch had strengthened his case for being captain. Also the Maharajah was once again playing his favourite role as benefactor. Against Jardine Indian batsmen had been short of runs; at the end of the tour Indian cricket was once again short of money. The MCC tour had made a profit of just 3,000 rupees (£231, at the contemporary rate of exchange). Apart from a few centres, cricket did not always attract crowds and when it did there was the cost of staging a match, enclosing grounds, and meeting hotel and travelling expenses. Patiala was always ready to provide money.

Patiala's first gesture was to donate the trophy for the national championship of India. As so often in Indian history cricket development had come from the top down, not from the bottom up. India had played four Tests, was planning several more, yet there was no national cricket championship along the lines of the English County Championship. In this instance Indian cricket was following the Australian example where the Sheffield Shield started some years after Australia had played Test cricket. The plan for the national championships had been made by Anthony De Mello. He had commissioned an artist to sketch out a trophy, a Grecian urn two feet high with a lid, the handle of which represented Father Time. The Board, now more under Patiala's control than ever before – as always happened when it was short of funds – was meeting in Simla, the hill station the Raj had built and which had seen so many Patiala triumphs, both on the polo fields and in the boudoirs.

De Mello was explaining how the championship would work and was showing the artist's sketch to the meeting when, half-way through the speech, Patiala sprang up. De Mello recorded what happened in suitably melodramatic tones: 'The pine-scented air appeared to be immediately electrified. In deep tones charged with emotion, His Highness claimed the honour and the privilege of perpetuating the name of the great Ranji, who had prematurely departed this life only the year before. He offered straightaway to present a gold cup of the magnificent design submitted by me and valued at £500 to be called the Ranji Trophy.'

The news was enthusiastically received. Everyone there was now the Maharajah's fervent supporter. But in the way these things are often done in India this news was not immediately released. The Board members came down from the hills and nobody knew that India had got a national championship. True there had been opposition from Bengal – dominated by Englishmen – to the very idea, but the real reason was more Machiavellian. Patiala's old cricketing enemy Vizzy was at work. Without it ever being said publicly, it was being put about that, perhaps, Ranji's was not the name that deserved to be commemorated. After all, what had he done for Indian cricket? Vizzy was aware of the rift between Willingdon and Ranji that had marked his dying days and he assiduously worked on this. Ranji was more of an English cricketer as he, himself, had said. Surely a more appropriate name on the trophy would be that of Willingdon who had, probably, spent more time in India and done more for Indian cricket than Ranji?

Vizzy had even got a trophy made in England of chiselled gold from a design by Lady Willingdon, and at an emergency meeting of the Board held in Delhi on 26 October it was decided to accept this in place of the Ranji Trophy. A month later the *Times of India* carried a picture of the trophy, calling it the Willingdon Trophy for the Cricket Championship of India. By this time the first two matches of the Ranji Trophy had already taken place, even if the start was a bit limp. In the first on 4 November 1934 Madras beat Mysore in a day. Madras made 130, Mysore 48 and 59. Heavy overnight rain had affected the pitch and Mysore had been confounded by the left-arm pace of Ramsingh, who took 11 for 35. Both teams were captained by Englishmen, Madras by C. P. Johnstone, Mysore by Major M. S. Teversham, but most of the players were Indians. The sponsors for the match were badly affected by such an early finish and Commercial Union lost 2,200 rupees (then, £169).

Vizzy and Patiala still had their own teams and, even as the national championships were getting under way, their two teams were fighting it out in the Moin-ud-Dowlah Cup. Vizzy's team was the Freelooters, Patiala's the Retrievers. The two princes had scoured the land for the best cricketers and Vizzy had also obtained Learie Constantine. The teams met in the final and a crowd of 15,000 turned up at Secunderabad Gymkhana to watch it. Vizzy himself did not take part, a very minor prince, the Rajkumar of Alirajpur, deputised for him but he was desperately keen to win. In the middle of the final he sent Constantine a telegram promising him a certain number of pounds for every run scored and every wicket taken. Constantine did not make many runs – 12 and 1 – but he took six wickets for 72 in the first innings and 2 for 69 in the second. He had the reputation of being a fearsome fast bowler and on a lively matting wicket was quite a handful for the Patiala batsmen. Some of them backed away from his short-pitched deliveries but in the second innings Amarnath took up the challenge, repeatedly hooking his bouncers. Constantine had poor support from his fielders and with Amarnath scoring 104 not out, the Retrievers won by three wickets. First round to Patiala.

So amidst much confusion as to what the championship was called – with newspapers critical of the 'insult' to Ranji – and fairly open rivalry between Vizzy and Patiala the championship continued. Fifteen teams competed in the inaugural championship based on a zonal knock-out system. Some of the cricket was poor, it did not attract great crowds – but then India's national championships have not always been a great crowd-puller – and quite a few of the results were astounding. Delhi scored only 37 and 92 against United Provinces. Southern Punjab, the pre-tournament favourites with a team including Amarnath, Yuvraj, Nissar, and Nazir, lost the North Zone final after being all out for 22. Bombay travelled to Poona to play Maharashtra to find there were no dressing-room facilities and the players had to change by the side of the field in full public view. They also had a three-mile bus journey for their lunch. Only in the West Zone final between Bombay and Western India was there a good crowd but then the public were admitted free.

The curious thing was, Bombay crowds would turn up in large numbers and pay to watch the Quadrangular Tournament. That year the Quadrangular was staged for the first time in five years, having been suspended since 1930-31. Maybe this increased the public appetite, but it also showed that India's greatest cricket centre valued good, competitive cricket between teams packed with stars it knew and recognised. The early cricket in the tournament was one-sided but, in the final, the Hindus met the Muslims to produce a classic match. It was cricket as theatre: two great players pitted against each other: Nayudu versus Nissar. That year few played Nissar with any confidence except Nayudu. Nissar had run through the cream of Hindu batting: Navle, Naoomal, Merchant, Amarnath, Yuvraj, Jai, for just 63. But Nayudu had his measure, making 74 out of 117. To disrupt Nissar he would start walking down the wicket even as Nissar was running up; if Nissar hit him he showed no pain. Nayudu's good work was undone in the second innings when the Hindus collapsed to lose by 91 but the match generated great excitement and wonderful crowds. The national championship, where teams of unknowns were facing each other, just did not excite the same interest.

Even when Bombay got to the final the crowds refused to come. The final, on 9, 10, 11 March 1935, was against Northern India which did not have any recognised stars. The divisions within Bombay cricket may not have helped. Captaining Bombay had already proved a problem. In the match against Maharashtra, Jai, the captain, failed to turn up and the team was captained by Contractor who was originally the twelfth man. Before the final there was intense speculation about whether Vajifdar, the Parsee, would play under the Hindu Jai. They had disagreed over a couple of selections. In the end he did, scoring 71 and taking 8 for 40. Merchant, who had hit a great century against Amar Singh in the zonal final, now scored another 120, and Bombay won by 208 runs. But the crowd was the smallest to attend a first-class match at the Bombay Gymkhana.

There was another twist to the final. At the end of it Bombay did not receive the trophy. For that they had to travel to Delhi, a week later, to play a festival match against the Cricket Club of India. The Viceroy would present the trophy at the end of this match. This was a depressingly anti-climactic match for the first winners of the national trophy. Jai, the man who had led them to the triumph, withdrew at the last minute and his old rival Vajifdar captained. Bombay were so devastated by Nissar, who took 5 for 17, and the batting of Amarnath who made 110 and Palia who made 137, that only joke bowling in the second innings prolonged the game until the third afternoon in order to allow Willingdon to come and present the trophy. Now came the twist to the story, like the final clue in a crime thriller. The trophy that Willingdon presented was not the one named after him and donated by Vizzy, but the Ranji trophy which Patiala had gifted. The Willingdon trophy did not disappear, however. It would feature in a devastating postscript to this thriller.

We shall never know what caused the switch. In that typical Indian way no explanation was ever provided. It has been assumed that the Board, realising they could not manage without Patiala's money, decided to side with him. Whatever it was, this marked the high point of his control of Indian cricket. His enemy Willingdon had been made to present the trophy that he had donated. The Board of Control, with more Indian delegates and fewer English ones, was now more for Patiala than before and he was also made President of the Cricket Club of India.

The Cricket Club of India had been formed during Jardine's visit and was meant to become the MCC of India: to promote the game and make it popular throughout the land. The idea was that it would organise the provincial championships, spread the game to schools and colleges, and arrange for coaching, while the Board would act as a supervisory body arranging foreign tours and speaking for Indian cricket. To make it feel more like MCC it was increasingly referred to as CCI.

Originally, it had been thought that CCI would have its head-quarters in Delhi which is where the Board's headquarters were. But Delhi could not be enthused for cricket. In the winter of 1934 Vizzy had organised a match in Delhi between CCI and University Occasionals. Vizzy's big name professional was Constantine and the occasion produced an enthralling match with a neat 'con' by Nayudu. He joined Constantine at a delicate stage of the game. Constantine, who appeared not to be aware who Nayudu was, reassured the Indian that he would take care of Nissar. For a few overs Nayudu carried on with the deception and allowed himself to be protected by Constantine. Then he decided enough was enough and took on Nissar and, while an amazed Constantine looked on, he hooked, cut and drove him. But despite all this and free admission only 1,000 people watched the game.

So the home for CCI had to be Bombay. The city was then in the middle of its great reclamation work, a process that con-tinues even to this day. Originally seven separate fishing islands, centuries of rotten fish and fallen palm trees had formed creeks which had joined the islands together. The British accelerated this and started a process which is almost the reverse of Venice. While Venice has been slowly losing the fight against the Adriatic, Bombay has slowly been winning the fight against the Arabian sea, reclaiming land and building on it. In modern times there have been two major reclamation projects. One came in the late 1960s and has made parts of Bombay look like Manhattan, ruining its old charm. The mid-1930s saw the first great reclamation project and it was one such piece of reclaimed land, known as sub-block no. 2 of the Backbay Reclama-tion Scheme, which the CCI wanted. The land was being reclaimed by the government and there was a lot of haggling about the price. In the end De Mello went to see the Governor, Lord Brabourne, in his summer residence at Ganeskhind near Poona (now Pune) and offered him an historic choice. 'Your Excellency, which would you prefer to accept from sportsmen, money for your government or immortality for yourself.' Brabourne preferred immortality and 90,000 square yards of land at £1 per square yard was presented to the CCI. Brabourne was very nearly giving the land away, for it was then costing the government about ten times that much to reclaim the land. Today that parcel of land

95

is almost priceless. South Bombay is so congested that flat prices there compare with Park Lane in London.

If De Mello's persuasiveness had charmed the Governor then Patiala's clout as President of CCI was to prove the major factor in the development of the ground. He was also organising a tour by the Australians in the winter of 1935-36. He offered to bear all the expenses and sent Frank Tarrant to Australia to gather up a team. As the Australians were sending an official team to South Africa that winter, Tarrant had enormous problems obtaining players. The Australian Board was particularly unhelpful: Woodfull, Ponsford and Kippax were banned, although they had all retired from first-class cricket, and the task took Tarrant six months. As often in such things there was an element of comic-opera about it. Tarrant, trying desperately to secure players, asked a friend about a player whom he remembered from ten years before. Tarrant meant a player called H. O. Rock. His friend thought he meant Wendell Bill and he got into the team. Initially the Indian press reported he was Wenderbill, then it became two players Wendell, a white Australian, and Bill an aboriginal fast bowler. In the end he turned out to be O. W. Bill, rather an elegant opening bat.

The side Tarrant got together was far from being a representative Australian team. The team was known as the Maharajah of Patiala's Australians and was an amazing mix of old players, long retired from Test cricket, and young players some of whom never had and never would play first-class cricket. It was captained by Ryder who was 46, included Macartney 49, Ironmonger 48, Oxenham 44, Love and Hendry, both 40. Ryder had last played for Australia in the series against England in 1928-29 when he was captain; Macartney, known as the 'Governor-General', had last played in 1926; Hendry in 1928-29; 'Dainty' Ironmonger in 1931-32. The younger members of the team included also some Sheffield Shield players, but the Indian Board, eager to get some practice before the tour to England in 1936, could not sniff even at such a collection. In any case the Maharajah of Patiala's hold on Indian cricket seemed so absolute that it brooked no challenge – or so it seemed.

Given all that, the tourists did not perform badly. They won the first two 'Tests' by wide margins: nine wickets and eight wickets. But then India came back in the last two games to square the series. But these bald results meant nothing. For behind them lay some of the most ignominious machinations ever seen in Indian cricket, or any cricket for that matter.

Vizzy had lost the battle with Patiala but he meant to win the war. His sights were now set on the captaincy of the 1936 team to England and, in the winter of 1935-36, as Patiala's Australians went round the country, Vizzy fought hard to regain the ground he had lost to Patiala.

The first moves did not suggest Vizzy would succeed or even that he was a contender in the captaincy stakes. At a meeting of the Board of Control in Bombay on 11 August 1935, which finalised the Australian tour, a selection committee of Duleep, the Nawab of Pataudi and Dr Kanga was appointed. Colonel Mistry, Patiala's former ADC, was made manager of the 1936 England tour. But Vizzy, mixing cricket with intrigue in that special way of his, quickly showed what he was about. In October 1935, just before Patiala's Australians arrived, Vizzy organised a Silver Jubilee cricket festival in Delhi.

The timing and the nature of the tournament were important. The Silver Jubilee was that of King George V. In the summer Patiala had been in London to attend the celebrations. Vizzy had stayed at home and plotted, the cricket festival was his answer. The winners of the Silver Jubilee Festival would receive the Willingdon trophy. Despite the superb arrangements: free admission and the supply of iced rose water for drinking, only about 300 people turned up to watch. But for Vizzy it was not the masses that mattered but power in the committee rooms and influence with the Viceroy. His team of all talents – he raided some star members of the Patiala side – was far too strong and beat both Patiala's XI and the Nawab of Bhopal's XI to enable Vizzy proudly to hold up the trophy presented by his friend Willingdon. What most people missed at the time was the inclusion of a player who batted no. 8 in the first match, no. 6 in the second and did not play a very crucial role in either. But it was his position that was crucial. He was Captain R. J. Brittain-Jones, the Viceroy's former ADC and now the Comptroller of the Household. It was a name that Indian cricket would come to know well and dread, and very much part of the coalition that Vizzy was building.

An interesting visitor to the tournament was the Nawab of Pataudi. He did not play in the tournament but he practised hard at the nets, watched the other players – as you would expect a selector to do – and talked about the tour to England. There was even talk of selecting hotels for the team to stay. Pataudi was now a serious candidate to captain India and everyone agreed he would be a great catch. He had been a candidate in 1932 but now, if anything, his reputation was higher. After his disappearing act of 1932 he had played for England, scored a century against the Australians and had a very successful season for Worcestershire in 1934. Since then he had not played first-class cricket due to 'nerve strain', but there was no doubting his class. India was still firmly in the colonial era and a man who had played most of his cricket in England, scored a hundred in his first Test against Australia, had to be superior to anything home-grown.

As captain he would also have the advantage of rising above the divisions and camps that divided Indian cricket. On 29 October 1935 a full meeting of the Board appointed him captain for the England tour. Forward planning is one thing but with the tour more than six months away this was carrying things a bit too far. It suggested intrigue, but the Board reassured critics that this would give Pataudi ample time to study the form during the winter and pick more or less his own side for England – based purely on merit. The more crucial decision came later on during the same meeting when Duleep, who was still in a nursing home in England, was replaced as a selector by Vizzy.

The choice of Pataudi had not been unanimous. Nayudu had stood against him, getting only four votes, and doing his own cause no good. There was muttering about 'that man', the feeling that Nayudu was so hell-bent on glory that he would even stand against a candidate like Pataudi, so clearly superior to anyone else around. It sullied Nayudu's reputation that bit more, and this suited Vizzy. In the winter of 1932 he had given the man a standing ovation. Now, although Nayudu had helped him win the Silver Jubilee trophy, there had been a row during the tournament and the two men had fallen out. Interestingly, Patiala himself had voted for Pataudi as captain. It was only later that he was to realise Vizzy's game and how shrewdly he had played it.

Vizzy's next move seemed bizarre. He actually promoted Patiala's son, the Yuvraj. Just before the first 'Test' in Bombay against the Australians, Pataudi announced he was not fit to play. So the selection committee of Pataudi, Vizzy and Dr Kanga appointed the Yuvraj as captain. This did not mean, the selectors claimed, that the Yuvraj would be captain in England. Pataudi would be fit for that, but the selectors were trying out possible vice-captains for the tour. A few days later Dr Kanga resigned, back-dating his resignation and denouncing princely interference.

This was a Vizzy masterstroke. The Yuvraj was immensely unpopular in Bombay. The previous year he had captained the Hindus in preference to the Bombay hero, C. K. Nayudu, and had been booed and jeered by the crowd. Before the 'Test' there was public speculation that several players might not play if Yuvraj captained, but Nayudu pledged his public support. But this could not save the Yuvraj or India. He was booed and jeered every time he fielded. He set no example on the field – the Indians fielded very badly – or with the bat. Yuvraj made 40 with five sixes but there was a suspicion that Patiala, through Tarrant, had fixed this innings, arranging for the young man to have a few half-volleys and full tosses at the beginning of the innings. Indian batsmen followed his example, treating the match like a one-day romp, and lost heavily.

As if on cue the next match was against Vizzy's team. Just as he had done with Jardine's side, Vizzy stopped the all-conquering march of the Australians. The match ended in a draw but his team led the

Australians on the first innings and Vizzy made 40, with most of his runs coming against Oxenham. A right-arm medium-pacer who could also flight the ball, Oxenham had been made out to be a demon by the other Indian batsmen. The joke in India was that Oxenham was so deadly because being a combination of ox and ham he was distasteful to both Hindus and Muslims. Vizzy's showing against him suggested the obvious comparison: Vizzy was a leader of men, Yuvraj was not.

So, of course, was Nayudu. The Central Indian team led by him did very well against the Australians. It made the Australians follow-on before they drew. But a trap was waiting for Nayudu in the second 'Test' in Calcutta. Pataudi again withdrew and Nayudu was appointed captain. His relationship with Amar Singh was at such a low ebb that this meant one of India's main bowlers would not play. Amar said he was ill, the doctors said he was fit, Amar still did not play. Calcutta was full of cliques and groups, all seeking to undermine Nayudu. Mushtaq Ali recalls that, on the eve of the match, he and another player were invited to a party which 'included items which were likely to rob us of our efficiency on the field the next day', a quaint expression which, probably, means drink. In the previous year when Nayudu had been dismissed in the Calcutta Test against England a couple of members of the 1932 team had stood up and congratulated each other. Now the politics were more discreet but far more devastating. India made 48 and 127, Australia 99 and 80 for 2. Nayudu was never again to captain India.

In the third 'Test' at Lahore, with Pataudi still unfit, Wazir Ali captained. Nayudu did not play and Wazir went to his grave nursing a deep grievance against Nayudu. Wazir had often played under him, but when it was his turn to skipper, Nayudu could not face it. Though Nayudu could play the feudal lord as well, in this case he had told Vizzy before the Test that he was not available. For a man who lived and breathed cricket he was just sick of Indian cricket. The captaincy revived Wazir's batting – he was the highest scorer in both innings – Oxenham fell ill, bowled only seven overs, and India won.

For the final Test in Madras, Nayudu was actually dropped for disciplinary reasons. India again won but not even the most fervent Indian supporter could believe it meant anything. The Australians had played 24 matches in thirteen weeks, the long cross-country journeys had exhausted them, Oxenham did not play and they had to include their baggage man, Joe Davis, to make up a side.

More crucial was their defeat, just before the 'Test' in Secunderabad at the hands of Moin-ud-Dowlah's XI by an innings. Vizzy captained the victors. In the weeks leading up to this match the sordid story of the 1932 tour, how players had refused to play for Nayudu, surfaced in the press. The present troubles were traced back to the Lord's Test and there was demand for a man who could unite the team and get the best out of all the players. Who better than Vizzy?

So far Vizzy had played the coy bride. No, he could not possibly tour England, he had to go to Europe to have an operation. But once his team had defeated the Australians it began to emerge he might be available. All the other possible rivals had been eliminated, in particular the dangerous Nayudu. Now only the little matter of Pataudi needed to be dealt with. In the middle of February 1936, Pataudi announced that he could not possibly tour England, he was not fit. Later he confided to friends that he had to withdraw for 'reason of state'. Pataudi never disclosed his real reasons but a hint was given several years later when he wrote that, in 1932 and 1936, the job of leading an Indian side meant trying to 'please each community, each province and association and the rich patrons of the game. By the time we please all of them, we shall have succeeded in ruining the team and we shall then start thinking of the people who will sit on the Inquiry Committee at the end of the season.' Patiala withdrew the Yuvraj's candidacy. This left two candidates: Vizzy and C. K. Nayudu. Patiala, a bit late in the day, supported Nayudu but Vizzy had the votes sewn up. He won 10-5.

It is only with hindsight that we can see how well Vizzy had planned the whole campaign. Had he stood against Nayudu in 1935 he would have stood no chance. Then Pataudi had come in handy to eliminate Nayudu. Now with Nayudu destroyed in the machinations of the Australian visit, Vizzy had his chance. Patiala, realising how he had been duped, withdrew the invitation he had extended to the Indian side to spend a month at Patiala before embarking on the tour of England. He had spent the money, Vizzy had walked away with the spoils.

But then Vizzy's campaign for the captaincy of India bore the stamp of an American presidential campaign. He had journeyed up and down the country gathering votes. Associations that voted for him were promised special consideration when it came to the choice of players for the tour. And you could almost tick the players' names against the associations that had supported Vizzy. Madras got two players; one of them, C. S. Ramaswami, was forty and by his own admission bulky and slow. His batting had deteriorated and, as he confessed later, 'I was selected for reasons other than cricketing ability.' The manager was Brittain-Jones, the earlier selection of Colonel Mistry when Patiala still seemed in control having been forgotten. Brittain-Jones was the Viceroy's man and now Vizzy's choice of him as a player in his team for the Silver Jubilee began to make sense. A year earlier an assistant manager, a Mr Bhattacherjee, had been selected but he was dropped and a S. M. Hadi of Hyderabad was chosen as treasurer. Hyderabad was one of the associations that had voted for Vizzy.

Vizzy was not only captain but he was almost the sole selector for the side. On the morning of the selection committee meeting, Pataudi, the other selector, left Delhi leaving his selections in a sealed envelope. They were said to be different, in what way we shall never know. His father-in-law to be, the Nawab of Bhopal, was another selector but, apparently, played no part.

In fairness to Vizzy the nineteen players selected, barring one or two choices, were about the best going. India then had no more than about forty or fifty first-class cricketers so the available pool was not great. But what made it worse was that Vizzy kept adding to the team. Dilawar Hussain and Jehangir Khan joined after completing their term at Cambridge; C. S. Nayudu flew out a bit later; and Amar Singh was released by his club Colne to play a few matches.

This was not so much a cricket team as a prince's entourage. Vizzy, not really a prince but more of a country squire, was realising through his cricket team his deepest fantasies. He arrived in England with thirty-six items of personal luggage and two servants. There was no vice-captain on the tour, no selection committee. Vizzy was supreme, with Brittain-Jones to assist him. He was required to listen to no-one and he did not intend to.

Vizzy did his best to make himself out to be a better batsman than he was. His average in the three Tests was 8.25, but on the tour he scored 600 runs at an average of 16.25, which was not far behind such recognised batsmen as Palia and higher than Jehangir Khan who was a genuine Test all-rounder. But the trick here, as one English county captain explained, was generous gifts. He himself had been presented with a gold watch before the match began and bowled a few long-hops and half-volleys but, obviously, could not go on like that.

It was at this social level, with Vizzy playing the Indian prince, that the tour was a great success. There were luncheons at the House of Commons with Stanley Baldwin, the Prime Minister, the team was presented to the King at Buckingham Palace with all of the players dressed in dark lounge suits and light blue turbans. This was due to the fact that the King, Edward VIII, was in mourning but it made the team look like Vizzy's retinue. It was at a lunch given by the Royal Empire Society at the Hotel Victoria that Lord Hailsham, the Lord Chancellor, coined the nickname Vizzy. It was easier for the English, though it did not immediately catch on and *Wisden* referred to him as the Kumar. But eventually 'Vizzy' stuck and it started a trend for Indian players on English tours, like Chandrasekhar later going home with a new name 'Chandra'. The inability of English tongues to cope with Indian names has continued to produce new names that the Indians then adopted themselves.

Between the first and second Tests Vizzy acquired the title he coveted. He was knighted and became Sir Gajapatairaj Vijaya Ananda, the Maharajkumar of Vizianagram. Vijaya stood for victory, Ananda for happiness, although there was little of either on the tour. While Vizzy was at the Palace, Nayudu got a chance to captain the side and led India to the first victory over a county side that summer. At Aigburth, Lancashire were beaten for the first time since 1909. Lancashire had been set 199 to win and Indian dressing-room gossip was that Vizzy, determined to deprive Nayudu of the honour, had sent a cable to Nissar to bowl only full tosses in the Lancashire second innings. Nissar bowled two overs, conceded 10 runs, Nayudu took him off, and he and Jehangir Khan bowled India to victory, Lancashire collapsing for 114. India beat only one other county, Hampshire, on the entire tour. This was under Vizzy's captaincy but it was desperately close – a victory by two runs.

Vizzy's best captaincy in India had come when he had used Nayudu. Now the two were hardly on speaking terms. Fairly early on in the tour there was a Vizzy party and a Nayudu party, and anyone who was with Nayudu was cut dead. Those in the Vizzy party received all sorts of favours including a trip to Paris and they could curry favour with Vizzy by insulting Nayudu. Baqa Jilani did that before the Oval Test: coming down to breakfast one day he insulted Nayudu and was rewarded with his first cap.

Sir John Beaumont, Chief Justice of the Bombay High Court, who headed the committee which was later set up by the Board to inquire into the tour, found Vizzy guilty but also blamed Nayudu. He had held himself 'aloof from the team' and failed to offer any support to the captain. But Vizzy had 'formed his own party' and not treated 'all members of the team with strict impartiality. This destroyed any chance there might have been of healing the existing dissensions.' Vizzy, said the committee, had shown 'very faulty' captaincy on the field; 'he did not understand the placing of the field or the changing of the bowling and never maintained any regular order in the batting'.

It was this last habit that was to lead to the most sensational event of the tour. Ten days before the first Test, in the middle of June, the Indians were playing the Minor Counties. They had had a miserable May, rain and defeat chasing them around England. They had lost seven of the twelve matches, including a defeat by Durham when Vizzy underestimated Durham's ability to score quickly. Again it was spin that was mainly causing the Indians problems, both the leg-spin of Jim Sims and Walter Robins and off-spin, except against Yorkshire when the quick bowling of Bowes and Smailes did the damage.

102

For the Minor Counties match, at Lord's, the sun shone and the problems seemed to ease. The match produced the first victory of the tour by an innings and 74 runs, Amar Singh took 9 for 64, Merchant made 95, Mushtaq Ali 135. But the victory was won at a very heavy price. During the Indian innings Merchant and Mushtaq had a long stand for the third wicket. They put on 215 in 140 minutes. The stand started on Wednesday evening, then, due to rain which meant play did not restart till 3.30 on Thursday, continued for a bit on Thursday evening. Amarnath was the next man in and champing at the bit in his desire to get at the bowling. He was clearly the batsman in form having scored 591 in 19 innings and taken 32 wickets at 21 runs per wicket. But since the match against Essex, a couple of weeks previously, when he had scored a century in each innings, his batting had slumped and he wanted to regain form. Clearly, Minor Counties provided the opportunity but after sitting padded up for the better part of two days he was told by Vizzy he was not going in next if either Merchant or Mushtaq got out. Other batsmen needed practice and Amar Singh, C. S. Nayudu, and Wazir Ali were sent in ahead of him. Amarnath went in at no. 7 but, with only a few minutes left, he could only make 1 not out. When he came back he flung his bat and pads down and, in choice Punjabi, abused Vizzy, claiming he had never been treated like this before. When Hadi, the treasurer, came in to ask when the players would like their massage, Amarnath abused him as well.

There had been an altercation with Vizzy in an earlier match, at Leicester, when Amarnath was unhappy about the field placings and had thrown the ball down. Amarnath was an impetuous young man, on his first tour outside his country. So far he was the best performer in a dismal tour and this may have gone to his head. Ramaswami had noticed even before this how he kept himself just that bit aloof from the rest of the team, as if to suggest he was indispensable. Fame had come to him suddenly, quickly. Before his discovery on Jardine's visit and his great century in Bombay he had been unknown. In the last couple of years he had become a great Indian hero. But he was a rough diamond. The vivacity and charm of his cricket were not matched by his manners which were those of a simple farmer's boy from the Punjab. Amarnath's cricket was instinctive, it did not have time for nuance, or the finesse of diplomatic skills. If he was angry he showed it, no matter what the circumstances.

But this time he had chosen the wrong circumstances. Below the Indian dressing-room were sitting some of the elderly MCC members including, possibly, Willingdon. It did not go down too well with them. It was Hadi, suffering from the rough end of Amarnath's tongue, who complained to Vizzy and Brittain-Jones and they very quickly decided that enough was enough and that Amarnath should be sent home. The match with the Minor Counties finished at 3pm on Friday. At 6pm that Friday Amarnath was told to pack his bags and catch the boat train the next morning. How much of this was Vizzy's decision, how much Brittain-Jones', or perhaps even Willingdon's, we shall never know. Indians believed that Vizzy was more the tool of the two Britons. On Monday 22 June at a dinner for the Indians, during the next match against Surrey, Willingdon claimed full knowledge and said, 'The manager was justified in taking the action against that particular player.' It seemed extraordinarily harsh but Brittain-Jones had decided that an example had to be set.

That Friday night Amarnath approached C. K. Nayudu, Wazir Ali and Nissar to plead with Vizzy. About midnight Ramaswami was woken up and asked to accompany them. Vizzy was at first reluctant to do anything but the players refused to leave his room until he agreed and eventually he did agree. However, he cautioned, the matter was in the hands of Brittain-Jones but he was prepared to intercede. A letter of apology was drafted which Amarnath agreed to sign and give to Vizzy. Next morning Amarnath was summoned to Vizzy's room. Brittain-Jones was present and Amarnath was told the decision could not be changed. It was what the Indians knew as the iron law of British rule. It was possible to change the hakim (magistrate, giver of order) but never the hukum, the order. To do so would be to lose face and undermine the basis on which the Raj was constructed.

So far the tour had been allowed a sort of indulgent grace. The Town Clerk of Gravesend had complimented the Indians on how well they spoke English. The *Observer* had thought that, as essentially club cricketers, Indians brought a touch of holiday atmosphere at a time when English cricketers made the game seem such a 'painful duty'. Another paper summed up how the English probably saw the 1936 Indians. 'The Indians' main attraction was indeed their novelty, successful or unsuccessful they are certain to brighten the season. For when a stranger of a different nationality, whose name you cannot pronounce, comes out of the pavilion and walks with a certain lithe grace to the wicket, you at once feel an interest in him. He may not proceed to play particularly distinctive cricket, his skill may be below that of many of our own batsmen, but everything about him is new to us. We search for points of individuality. That is one reason why the Indians are an attraction.'

After the Amarnath episode they were a sensation, though not in the way the Indians would have wanted. Before the tour began the players had been warned they must not speak to the press, not even about the weather. Now the press was as full of Indian dissensions as the Indian press had ever been. Even with Amarnath back in India

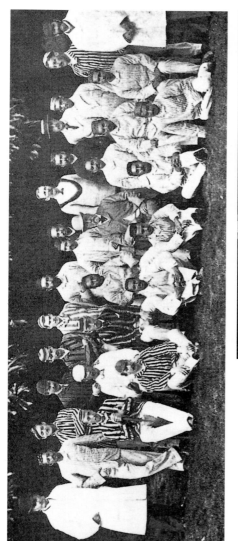

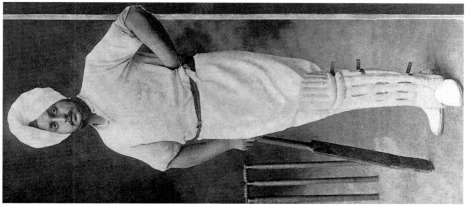

Above: 1886. Prince Christian Victor's team play the Parsees, the first Indian cricket team to tour England (*MCC*).
Left: Bhupendra Singh, Maharajah of Patiala, who both shaped and distorted Indian cricket (*Roger Mann*).
Right: All-India v Oxford University, 1911 (*MCC*).

Left: Lord Harris, Governor of Bombay 1890–94, encouraged the Parsees and Indian cricket, but doubted the Indians would ever have a side of county standard (*MCC*). *Centre:* K.S. Ranjitsinhji – 'Ranji' – a central figure in the 'golden age' of English cricket, but who did little to help Indian cricket (*All-Sport*). *Right:* K.S. Duleepsinhji – 'Duleep' – torn between the pressures exerted by Ranji, his uncle, and the Indians seeking to organise their cricket (*Hulton-Deutsch Collection*).

The MCC team, 1926–27. In the front row, Patiala, who financed the tour, and Arthur Gilligan, the captain, who recommended the Indians to form a cricket board *(MCC)*.

The Indian touring party of 1932, the first to play a Test match in England. The Maharajah of Porbander (*centre*) was the only touring captain reputed to have more Rolls-Royces than runs *(MCC)*.

Lord's, June 1932, India's first Test match. Jardine facing Amar Singh *(Roger Mann)*.

Left: Amar Singh (*Roger Mann*). *Right:* Mohammed Nissar. Amar Singh and Nissar were probably India's best ever pair of opening bowlers *(Hulton-Deutsch)*.

C.K. Nayudu *(left)* and L. Amarnath, at the first Test in Bombay, 1933–34, where Amarnath scored India's first Test century in his first Test. They put on 186 for the third wicket out of a total of 258. Note the solar topees worn by the Englishmen in the background as recommended by Lord Harris *(Hulton-Deutsch)*.

Guarding the pitch in Calcutta, 1934. See also the advertisement for Dunlop tyres *(Roger Mann)*.

MCC v the Nawab of Moin-ud-Dowlah's XI, Secunderabad, 1934. Jardine is absent, and MCC is captained by C.F. Walters *(Roger Mann)*.

Above left: 'Vizzy' – the Maharajkumar of Vizianagram – was given his nickname in England. Here he looks as owlish as an Indian Billy Bunter, but *below* he is leading his team, the Indian touring party of 1936, specially turbaned, to be presented at Buckingham Palace. *(Roger Mann). Above right:* Amarnath looking forlorn, as though anticipating being sent home *(Hulton-Deutsch)*.

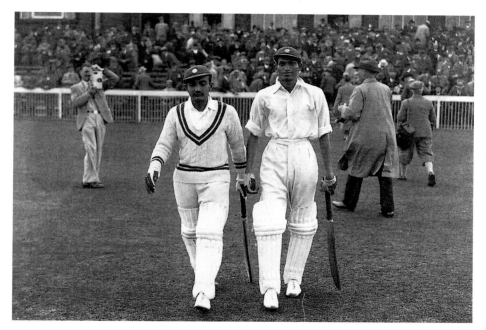

Merchant *(left)* and Mushtaq Ali walk out to open the batting at Old Trafford, 1936. They put on 203 in the second innings, a record for India against England that stood for over forty years. Yet as they walked out Mushtaq told Merchant that Vizzy had ordered him to run Merchant out *(Hulton-Deutsch)*.

The England and India teams at The Oval, 1936. This was C.K. Nayudu's last Test – here he is separated from Vizzy by the England captain, G.O. Allen *(MCC)*.

Above: 'All-India' in England 1946, the last team to be so called. *Below:* the Nawab of Pataudi, sr, and Walter Hammond, old comrades of the 'bodyline' tour of 1932–33 but now opposing captains, inspect the pitch at The Oval where rain only allowed India to make 331 and England 95 for 3 *(Hulton-Deutsch).*

the affair refused to die down. There was a plan to send him back and initially Vizzy and Brittain-Jones agreed, provided Amarnath made a full apology. But then, it seems, Willingdon or India Office or someone high up intervened and just before the second Test Vizzy announced that Amarnath was not coming back. By then the press had long forsaken talk about the novelty of the Indians and was carrying reports about how the rest of the team felt. There were reports that players had signed a statement against Amarnath, there were reports of senior players asserting, albeit tongue-in-cheek, that there were no dissensions in the team.

Then, just before the first Test there was a four-point demand from the senior players: C.K., or Wazir, should be made vice-captain, Vizzy should consult the team regarding selection and tactics, senior players should be respected and no player should receive preferential treatment. They were very reasonable demands although it showed what a hot-house atmosphere the Indian team operated in. For instance, the lack of respect for the senior players involved Jai not being 'given a seat when the team was photographed at Warwickshire'.

This was hardly the best preparation for Test cricket. But amazingly in the first Test at Lord's India held her own for much of the match. At the end of the first innings India actually led England 147 to 134. This was the first time in Tests that India had secured a first-innings lead. It was to be July 1971, again at Lord's, before India once again led England in a Test in England.

G. O. Allen, captaining England for the first time, put India in and after a good start on a wicket drying from overnight rain there was an amazing collapse. From 62 for no loss, the Indians went to 147 all out, Allen taking 5 for 35. England were batting by 3.15 on the Saturday, which was the traditional opening day for Tests.

It was then that Amar Singh showed what a fine bowler he still was. *Wisden* wrote, 'Well as Allen bowled, his work was outclassed by that of Amar Singh who, when England went in on an improved wicket, maintained a superb length and swung the ball either way'. In his first nine overs he took 4 for 13, Mitchell, Gimblett, Turnbull, Wyatt. Nissar bowled Hardstaff, and England were 41 for 5. Only Leyland with 60 kept England in the game. Amar Singh finished with 6 for 35 in 25.1 overs.

Again India had the worst of the batting conditions. Rain on Monday meant there was no play till 2.15 and blankets were used to dry the pitch – the first time such artificial means had been used in Test matches in England. England lost their last three wickets in 19 balls for 2 runs, India finding the ball kicking up and rising at different heights lost four wickets for 28 runs and were 80 for 7 by the close. Rain on Tuesday meant there was no play till 3.15, but by 5.40 England had won. India were all out for 93, England making the 108 for the loss of 1 wicket. Again Amar Singh was the main threat but that old Indian failing, dropped catches, intervened; even so, given that not even two full days' play was possible it was not a good Indian performance. What was really depressing was that not one Indian batsman showed any real steel. Yet considering all that had preceded the Test that was, perhaps, no surprise.

The second Test threatened to be like the first. India made 203, finding Verity, who had not bowled well at Lord's, a problem. England's reply was all Hammond, who had missed the first Test. His 167 was a quite superb innings: eight fours in his first 50 runs, 100 out of 138 in a hundred minutes. Against such an onslaught on a good wicket the Indian bowlers did well to stick to their task, both Nissar and Amar Singh conceding centuries, and England declaring at 571 for 8. India faced a deficit of 368 and since, at that stage, India had never scored more than 258 in any Test innings, it seemed all over.

Then, for the first time on the tour, the Indians showed that some of their players had both courage and skill. It came from an unusual combination of Vijay Merchant and Mushtaq Ali. No two batsmen could be more different. Mushtaq was the great cavalier of Indian cricket, Merchant the eternal roundhead. They provided the perfect opening contrast, one always ready to hit the ball; the other watchful, weighing every situation carefully. Although India has produced its quota of stodgy openers such contrasting pairs are not unknown. In recent years Gavaskar and Srikkanth, the one methodical, the other a cavalier have been very much in the Merchant-Mushtaq Ali tradition. This innings established them as openers, indeed provided India – in her sixth Test – with the first pair of capable Test openers. Before this in five Tests there had been six different opening pairs, although once this had been due to injury, and they had made: 39 and 41; 44 and 9; 12 and 0; 15 and 16; 62 and 0.

Mushtaq opened with Merchant because Hindlekar's injury – he had opened with Merchant at Lord's – meant that India lost both an opener and a wicket-keeper. Neither Mushtaq nor Merchant were born openers. Mushtaq was originally in the side as a left-arm bowler – that is how he made his debut against Jardine's team and had earlier impressed Hobbs. Merchant, also making his debut on Jardine's tour, had batted at no. 6.

Mushtaq was not quite as much of an untutored, natural cricketer as Indian legend would later make him out to be. He came from a family with a sporting tradition. In Indore where he was born he lived near C. K. Nayudu, and C.K.'s younger brother, C.S., became a very good friend. This quickly drew him into the Nayudu circle which provided a good class of cricket, hard discipline and stern advice. Later there was

106

coaching from a Mr Salter, an Oxford blue, and the patronage of Vizzy. But what Mushtaq retained was that sense of carefree, instinctive cricket which the Indian maidan generates. Like so many Indians he first played cricket on a maidan, that open space of ground which bore more resemblance to the surface of the moon, rugged, pock-marked rather than a proper cricket pitch. His early cricket was played with a bat bought from a junk shop and a cork ball. His first strokes were improvised and it was this air of maidan cricket, with its charm and unpredictability, that he brought to Test cricket.

This innings exemplified that. Allen thought Mushtaq had a weakness outside the off-stump and directed his attack there. Mushtaq pulled him for fours to leg. It was not orthodox but to the Indians watching the game typical of Mushtaq and quite delectable. 25 runs came in twenty minutes, the 50 in three-quarters of an hour. Soon Mushtaq was doing what he liked doing best: walking out to fast bowlers as they ran up to bowl. In future years this would become his speciality and, in India, every time he did it the crowd would roar. At Old Trafford they were just stunned. Allen, on his day, could be as fast as Larwood, yet here was Mushtaq Ali walking out to him. Once he was beaten, missed the ball by a yard and might well have been stumped: if he had been stumped off England's quickest bowler it would have been quite a feat but very like Mushtaq. Two on-drives off Verity took India to 100 in eighty minutes and Mushtaq to his 50. True, as *Wisden* said, England bowled an 'unusual number of full pitches' but then Mushtaq's footwork had often made them into full tosses.

As Mushtaq moved to his nineties, Hammond came up to him and said, 'My boy, be steady, get your hundred'. Mushtaq got his hundred just before the close with the Indians 190 for no wicket, Mushtaq 106, Merchant 79. The ground rose to him and Cardus was in ecstasy. 'There was suppleness and a loose, easy grace which concealed power, as the feline silkiness conceals the strength of some jungle beauty of gleaming eyes and sharp fangs.' The English were fulsome in their praise, led by Fry, Pelham Warner, Hobbs, and Jardine. Mushtaq Ali was overwhelmed. But what touched him was the gesture of the gateman who presented him with a sixpence. He had made two similar presentations to Duleep and to Bradman. But then it had been a record-breaking day. Between them England and India had made 588 runs for the loss of six wickets – it remains the highest number of runs scored in a day of Test cricket.

To Mushtaq such records did not much matter. His was the delight of the small boy who had got something he could never imagine possessing. The next morning, as they went out to bat, Merchant, more meticulous, more studious, reminded Mushtaq that the then world record for the first wicket, 323 between Hobbs and Rhodes, was only another 134 runs away. Mushtaq promised to be careful. There had been overnight rain and, on uncovered wickets, Verity and Robins were soon extracting life. The pair added another 13 to reach 203, exactly equal to the whole Indian score in the first innings. But Mushtaq could not resist the drive and was caught and bowled by Robins for 112. The stand had lasted just two and a half hours.

After Mushtaq everything was a bit anti-climactic. Merchant carried on in his more measured way, off-driving and late-cutting as and when the opportunity arose. In his nineties, for the first time he was flustered: dropped by Hammond at slip on 91, he spent an hour over 12 runs before reaching his hundred. When Hammond got him lbw with a full toss he had made 114 in four-and-a-quarter hours and he had been the ideal counterpart to Mushtaq. Ramaswami, Nayudu, Amar Singh saw to it that India did not squander the position these two had built and, when bad light intervened, India were 390 for 5 wickets, 22 runs ahead.

Yet the Merchant-Mushtaq partnership might never have got going had Mushtaq not disobeyed Vizzy. On the tour Merchant was very much his own man and he had annoyed Vizzy by suggesting he should step down as captain. Just before the second innings Vizzy instructed Mushtaq to run out Merchant. Mushtaq had been run out in the first innings but that was a freak accident. As the pair went out to open the second innings, Mushtaq spilled the beans. Merchant said, 'Just you try', they both laughed and forgot about it.

Merchant and Mushtaq also played well in the third Test at The Oval, putting on 81 and 64 in the two Indian innings, but their efforts were overshadowed by a quite majestic 217 by Hammond. At Old Trafford when Hammond had returned to Test cricket after ill-health, Howard Marshall had told BBC radio listeners of Hammond entering 'his kingdom again, fit and confident, master of himself and the occasion'. This was even more so at The Oval. He had his early problems against his old foe, Amar Singh, when on 3 Nayudu at short square-leg was unable to hold on to a low catch. Then on 96 Wazir Ali dropped a much easier chance at deep square-leg although he, probably, had the sun in his eyes. Hammond was finally bowled by Nissar.

This led to an amazing England collapse when from 422 for 3, England went to 468 for 8 with Nissar taking four wickets in nine overs for 46 runs. He finished with 5 for 120, the third time in six Tests that he had taken five wickets in an innings. The only other crumb of comfort for the Indians came in the second innings when Nayudu averted an innings defeat.

The old man – he was in his forty-first year – had played nothing like as well as he could. In five previous Test innings on that tour he had made 1, 3, 16, 34, and 5. Three times he had fallen to Allen, once to the new experimental lbw law which the Indians had been pressurised to accept. He came in to bat with India still requiring 90 to make England bat again. In the first innings he had batted no. 4, but Vizzy had changed the order and he was now at no. 6.

Once again Allen was bowling. Nayudu liked to knock a bowler off his length and his style – which Mushtaq must have copied – was to walk out of his crease as the bowler ran up to bowl, as if he was playing a spinner. Allen saw this, dropped it short and Nayudu was hit on the chest. It was a painful blow and for a time he struggled to breathe. Hammond, Verity and Dilawar gathered round him, somebody rubbed his chest, he had some water. But Nayudu did not believe in showing his opponents how hurt he was. Some of his best innings were played after he had been hit. There was no question of retiring. The next ball, he again walked out to Allen, it was another bouncer but this time Nayudu hooked him for four.

Allen continued to bowl bouncers and Nayudu continued to hook. Nayudu had made 81 when Allen finally pitched one up and bowled him. His innings was nowhere large enough to save India but the innings defeat was averted. England had to make 64 and got it for the loss of one wicket. The 81 meant Nayudu also reached his 1,000 runs for the tour. Though he was not to know it then, it was his farewell to Test cricket and to England. In the shambles of the tour his bravery at The Oval shone brightly.

But this was small comfort. The tour had been a cricketing and financial loss. *Wisden* was polite, the tour was 'disappointing', it wrote. In India critics were more scathing. Many felt that, instead of furthering Indian cricket, it had taken it back. Some thought cricket itself was bad for the country. A motion to this effect was passed in a students' union debate. In years to come India would have worse tours: 5-0 defeats in England and the West Indies, but this tour produced a sense of waste, a feeling of wantonness that was quite unique. India, it was felt, had sent its greatest ever team to England: Merchant, Mushtaq, Amarnath, Jai, Nayudu, Wazir Ali as batsmen, Amar Singh and Nissar as opening bowlers, Jehangir Khan as all-rounder, Hindlekar, whom *Wisden* considered was not far behind Duckworth, as wicket-keeper, yet they had nothing to show but defeats and dissensions.

The dissensions in cricket had their historical parallels in India's past: Rajput kings fighting each other and letting the Muslim invaders gain a foothold, later Hindu and Muslim kings fighting each other and allowing the British to take over. It seemed that, neither on the cricket field nor in politics, could India unite and this deepened the gloom. The bitterness of the tour resurfaced when the report of the

Beaumont Inquiry came out. Vizzy had flown back ahead of his team to try and thwart the committee being set up but failed. He withdrew from cricket – though only for a time. Nayudu remained a major player in Indian domestic cricket and, as if to make up for what the princes had done to him, in years to come Indian cricket showered him with honours. But he played no further part in international cricket.

An era was ending. The first turbulent phase of princes and commoners was over; a new one was about to begin.

7

The Merchant era begins
1937-40

The 1936 tour had produced one new star, Vijay Madhavji Merchant. Merchant had arrived on the tour bearing the badge, 'the soundest batsman in India', pinned on him at the end of the 1933-34 tour by Douglas Jardine. For a lesser cricketer such advance billing might well have turned out to be a curse, not so much a badge of honour but a gag to throttle him. But by the end of the tour that was the least of the compliments being showered on Merchant. He was now being hailed as India's best batsman.

Wisden named Merchant as one of its Five Cricketers of the Year, the second Indian, after Nayudu, to be so honoured. The recognition meant a great deal to Merchant who, years later, wrote, 'How much that meant to me few will ever realise.' To be named as one of *Wisden*'s five cricketers of the year has always been a great honour in India – partly because there is no equivalent – and the tour marked the start of what may be called the Merchant era in Indian cricket. While other players contributed to it, for the next fifteen years it was Vijay Merchant who dominated it. His was not as great a dominance over the game as Donald Bradman exercised in Australia, nor, except when he was briefly a selector, was he quite the *eminence grise* that G. O. Allen has been in English cricket. But he set the style, the standards, he influenced the batsmen, the way Indian cricket conducted itself, the manner in which the players approached the game. It was always 'Merchant says', or 'Merchant thinks, or feels'. He was also the first major Indian cricketer to emerge without either English or princely help. His emergence marked not only a dramatic shift away from the traditional promoters of the game; he represented the new class that was beginning to dominate Indian life.

The great cricketers who had represented India so far: Nayudu, Amar Singh, Amarnath, Wazir Ali, Mushtaq Ali, were all either brought up by princes or employed by them. Merchant was, in a way, a prince in his own right but of a different kind: a business prince. Among Indian Test cricketers he is the only one whose occupation reads: industrialist. His family owned cotton mills in Bombay and was part of the powerful Gujerati clan that was increasingly beginning to dominate Bombay's business world, and to take over from the Parsees who had done so much to build Bombay. Gujerat, the Western Indian region adjoining Bombay, is the home of the Patels, so well known in England as shrewd businessmen, indeed business is said to run in their blood. In a region of numerous castes and sub-castes – Merchant himself was from the Bhatia sub-caste – everyone seems to know how to make money.

As in business, so in cricket. If India had made its Test debut in 1911 and not 1932, the team would have been composed of a substantial number of Parsees. The Parsee dominance of cricket had been matched by their dominance of Indian industries, many of which they had pioneered. Now other Indian communities were supplanting them, of which Merchant's Gujerati community was the most intriguing.

Drawn from the same stock as Gandhi, Bombay's Gujerati businessmen financed the Mahatma heavily. They were part of a number of Indians who increasingly resented the stranglehold the British had on Indian business. As it happens, this stranglehold was most evident in Calcutta but there the Bengalis, more given to poetry than money, could make no challenge. In Bombay the businessmen shrewdly sensed that, once the British left – and they would have to leave sometime – there would be rich business pickings. So they financed Gandhi who, despite his frugal style, confessed that he had an insatiable need for money, and they remained on very friendly terms with the right-wing of the Congress Party.

Bombay, already the financial capital of India, was the centre of this business activity and the Mahatma's great struggles against the British always had a big influence there. Inevitably they affected cricket: the Quadrangulars, for example, were not held for four years, and Merchant was deprived of some rich cricket years. Born in 1911, he could not but be affected by the growing nationalistic atmosphere. How much of a nationalist in the Congress' sense he was remains debatable, but he stayed away from the trials to select the 1932 team. *Wisden*, in its profile, explained this was due to 'personal reasons'. Perhaps there was an element of nationalism as well. However, in 1936/37 any admission by *Wisden* that it was honouring an Indian nationalist who supported Gandhi may have been impossible. In any case Merchant was not a strident, jingoistic nationalist, although when required he spoke, as during the 1946 tour when deputising for the Nawab of Pataudi, and told the MCC that it must not believe that an exchange of cricketers would bring the two countries together. Only independence could do that. But like Gandhi, Merchant could see the good in British rule and cricket was part of what he wanted to retain.

Some of this confidence came from his settled, secure, rich background. But there was nothing in this background to suggest that he would be a great cricketer. His father had played the game but an injury, which almost led to a leg being amputated, forced him to retire. If his father exercised much influence on him this was never very evident. Perhaps he was lucky that he went to Bombay's Bharda school which was – and remains – a great nursery of cricket in that city, and there was some coaching there. It is also a Parsee school and Merchant benefited from its greater cricket awareness. But otherwise Merchant was very much a self-taught cricketer. It is said in India that the sharpness of the Gujerati business mind lies in the ability to plan, study the market and the opposition carefully, and then make the move. Merchant brought this art to cricket. Indian cricketers before him were generally instinctive cricketers. Nayudu could present a violent contrast between his batting, which was often so impulsive, and his personality, which was so stern and demanding. Off the field he was like a headmaster; with a bat he could be a D'Artagnan. Merchant the cricketer was very like the man: thoughtful, measured, composed.

If his batting was at times too pedantic then that was the nature of the man. Indeed that leads one to the most curious aspect of Merchant. He played his entire cricket career under a false name, like an actor who might assume another name when he goes into films, except that in his case, he did not assume the name, it was forced upon him. His family name was Thackersey and, as he explained in an interview with Richard Cashman, to whose *Patrons, Players and the Crowd* he wrote a Foreword, he got so involved in explaining to the Principal of Bharda, an Englishman, the intricacies of Gujerati family names that the Principal decided to give him a new surname. Merchant had listed his father's occupation as a merchant, meaning businessman, and the Englishman decided that this would do as a surname. There was an Indian precedent for this. Most of the Parsee surnames like Doctor, or Engineer, or Contractor, arose from their ancestral occupations. So one of the world's greatest batsmen played cricket under a name that was not his own. It was as if Hobbs had played his cricket under the name of 'Groundsman' since his father was once a groundsman.

But charming though this story is, it does not seem to be quite true. There was never a Principal of Bharda High School who was an Englishman. The Principal when Merchant was admitted was a Parsee named K. B. Marzban. When he asked the boy about his surname or family name, young Vijay appears to have become confused and could not give a coherent answer. So Mr Marzban decided to call him Merchant. Later, when Merchant had become well known, his younger brother Uday and his sister used the name too when playing cricket or tennis.

113

Merchant's ability to study cricket and benefit from it was brilliantly illustrated during the 1936 tour. After his Old Trafford innings of 114, and the opening stand of 203 with Mushtaq Ali, Cardus had called Merchant India's good European: he could easily be England's opening batsman. But Merchant was not a natural opening bat. He became one during that tour. In his first seven innings, when he made 366 runs, he batted either at no. 3 or no. 5; then he broke a finger, missed three weeks' cricket, and returned to find that Vizzy needed an opener. After that only once did he bat no. 3 and, while Vizzy permutated the openers from Hindlekar, Wazir, Dilawar, Mushtaq, Jai and even Jehangir Khan, Merchant was almost always their partner. Nearly 1,300 of his 1,745 runs – 600 more than anyone else in the side – were scored from this position. Merchant had never opened in India. Even had he done so, opening in England, where the ball moves about a great deal, was an entirely different proposition. But to do so suddenly and successfully shows how sound his technique was and how he could easily adjust to cope with the extra responsibility. Over the years other Indian batsmen, including some great ones like Hazare, were asked to make the switch. In 1946 the Nawab of Pataudi, as captain, thinking Hazare had a technique similar to Merchant's, got him to open. He made a duck, hated the idea and the experiment was abandoned. Hazare returned to his customary no. 4 position and in this position, of course, he sometimes even had to go in and face the ball when it was still new. Being forced to face the new ball was one thing, but opening the innings was another, and psychologically he could not contemplate it.

But then Merchant had prepared himself meticulously for the England tour. Like all Indian batsmen of his generation Merchant was brought up to believe that the conditions a batsman would face in England would be nothing like those he encountered in India. The ball would move, it would swing not merely for a few overs but throughout a day's play. In India a ball swings as long as it retains its shine. Once the shine goes it hardly ever deviates. But where in India could Merchant hope to duplicate English conditions? Answer: early in the morning in Bombay. The misty early morning sea atmosphere would make the ball swing and the dew on the wicket would make it seam and skid. So every morning, with the dew still glistening on the grass, Merchant was up early practising against the best, and fastest, of Indian bowlers in open-air nets. Round about him Indians would be taking their constitutionals, or 'morning walk', while Merchant was practising his forward defensive stroke, making sure his technique could measure up to the moving ball.

In his garden in Bombay he built a concrete pitch and, whenever Amar Singh came to Bombay, he stayed with him and bowled to him for hours on the concrete. On the 1936 tour he persuaded Jack Hobbs to watch him bat against Amar Singh in the nets, watching the position of his feet, head, wrists. Others in Indian cricket relied on their ability, Merchant nursed his.

This zeal, this dedication, never left Merchant. Even when he was in his forties, and about to retire from first-class cricket, Vijay Merchant practising on the early-morning dew-affected wickets of Bombay was a feature of Bombay life. This sense of perfection remained a part of Merchant. After he retired he became a commentator, and there was no attempt on his part to copy John Arlott that so obsessed other Indian commentators. In their cases it produced comical results; Merchant's style was simple, straightforward and always a very detailed description of the play: where the ball had pitched, how it had behaved, where exactly it had been played. The modern Radio 3 commentators, with their cream cakes and red buses, would have thoroughly confused him.

Hardly surprising, then, that he so easily converted himself from middle-order batsman to opener; but that was not the only outstanding feature of his batting on the 1936 tour. The other was his sheer stamina. In this he was the equal of Nayudu. Merchant did not have as long a first-class career as Nayudu and towards the end of his career he was dogged by cruel injuries, but his sheer consistency was extraordinary. If the practice on the dew-covered early-morning Bombay wickets had prepared him for swing and seam, nothing could have prepared him for six-days-a-week cricket. Like all other Indian cricketers Merchant played weekend club cricket which in Bombay was concentrated in the winter months – it has since become almost all the year round – and a few first-class matches. But these in any year were rarely more than half a dozen. Between 1929-30 and 1934-35 Merchant, on average, played four or five first-class matches a year. When the Quadrangular Tournament was suspended he hardly played any at all. He had no first-class cricket during the 1930-31 season and in 1932-33 only a couple of matches in the Moin-ud-Dowlah Tournament. By the time he came on the tour of England, after six seasons in first-class cricket, he had played a total of 24 first-class matches. In five months in 1936, between 2 May and 15 September, he nearly doubled that figure, playing 23 first-class matches. Other Indian cricketers could tell of similar experiences – club cricketers all their lives in India suddenly becoming full-time professionals on an English tour. What set Merchant apart is that this did not affect his performance, it only enhanced it. Before he came on the English tour his career figures after 24 matches were: 1,778 runs at an average of 52.59. By the end of the tour he had nearly doubled the runs to 3,523 and his career average was 51.80. It would never again fall below 50 and would slowly rise to the heights which make him second only to Bradman in all first-class cricket. Bradman from 338 innings scored 28,067 first-class runs at an average of 95.14. Merchant from 229 innings scored 13,248 runs at an average of 71.22. We can only speculate what his figures would have been had Merchant had the amount of cricket that his contemporaries in England or Australia enjoyed.

Other players might have returned from a tour as gruelling and morale-sapping as the 1936 one exhausted, but Merchant seemed determined to scale new heights. As in previous seasons there were only a handful of matches: four in all. But in each of them he scored a century, making an aggregate of 614 runs in eight innings for the astounding average of 130. But this was still not enough to retain the Ranji Trophy for Bombay.

Bombay met Nawanagar in the first round, but although Merchant scored a century, Nawanagar took the first-innings lead, won the match on that basis and went on to win the Ranji Trophy. That was the first year they had entered the competition and it was part of the new cricketing policy of Ranji's successor, Digvijayasinhji, the new Jam Saheb. Unlike Ranji, Digvijayasinhji cared passionately for Indian cricket. He now had his brother Duleep to help him, imported Bert Wensley, the old Sussex professional, as captain and built around him a team composed of some of the best players in India. Like Vizzy, but without his flamboyance, unpredictability or deadly ambition, Ranji's successor busily accumulated players: Amar Singh; Abdul Aziz, the wicket-keeper from Sind and father of the Test cricketer, Salim Durani; and an opening bowler from Lahore called Mubarak Ali. Duleep, of course, could never again play but he had spotted a nineteen-year-old schoolboy called Mulvantrai Himatlal Mankad. His school chums called him 'Vinoo', he batted no. 11 and bowled medium pace. Duleep, in the way great cricketers have, quickly recognised his potential. His weakness on the leg stump was eradicated by intensive practice and he was made to open the innings. Wensley concentrated on his bowling, developing the youngster into both an opening bat and a marvellous slow left-arm bowler. So the man who was to become the first great Indian all-rounder – arguably India's greatest ever – took shape under Sussex tutelage.

Mankad, like Merchant, was Gujerati, from Kathiawar. He was born in the Gujerati heartland of Jamnagar. But while Merchant represented the upper-crust Gujerati businessman of Western India, Mankad was part of the developing urban middle class – his father was employed as a doctor by the government. Mankad's success in cricket meant that he did not even pass the matriculation which has the same popular standing as 'O-Levels' have had in England. In India, matriculation forms the great divide and Indians, who can be very class-conscious, can almost spit out the words 'non-matriculate' as if to say the person is beyond the pale. In Mankad's case being a non-matriculate did not matter. Once he had been taken up by Duleep and Wensley, school mattered little. He was on his way to become the first of the truly professional players to be produced by India.

In Nawanagar's first match Mankad made 86, and took 3 for 23 with his left-arm spinners. He did not do much in the match against Bombay which was dominated by Amar Singh who took 8 for 62, bowling out Bombay for 174 with Merchant run out for 32. But in the final, against Bengal, Mankad made 185 runs, 100 of them in fours, in just over five hours. Nawanagar made 424 and Bengal was always fighting a losing battle.

The Nawanagar victory brought immediate rewards to Digvijaya-sinhji, who was elected President of the Board in June 1937. Vizzy's disgrace, and the cricket Board's penury, meant that Patiala was now back at the helm, and it was Patiala's support that secured the Presidentship for Digvijayasinhji. But Patiala was now a dying man although, even to the end, his amorous exploits had not ceased. That year he was threatened with exposure in the press by an Anglo-Indian husband who claimed the Maharajah had stolen his wife. Sir Edward Wakefield, secretary to the Agent to the Governor-General, had to deal with the matter and suggested a financial compromise. But the husband wanted the seducer punished. This, for a Maharajah, was impossible: his own courts could not try him. However the resourceful Wakefield suggested that, perhaps, the Maharajah could be made to pay a sort of fine: 10,000 rupees (then £769) shall we say? No, not of course to buy you off but to punish the man who has done you wrong. The husband's anger cooled and that was the last heard of the matter.

Soon after that Patiala performed his last great public cricket function when, in what was to be his greatest gift to Indian cricket, he opened the Brabourne Stadium. The immortality that De Mello had promised Brabourne was now being realised. Brabourne himself was no longer Governor – he had moved to Calcutta – but sub-block no. 2 was now a marvellous stadium. The cricket ground covered 40,000 square yards with covered accommodation for 35,000 spectators. There was a three-storeyed stucco pavilion coloured light blue, dark blue and gold which included rooms overlooking the square where the players could stay. A batsman could keep his dressing-gown on until just before he was due to bat and then discard it, pick up his bat and walk down the steps to the wicket! Frank Worrell claimed this was the aspect of Brabourne Stadium he most enjoyed. After his innings the batsman could go for a quick dip in the pool or play a vigorous game of tennis.

But the new stadium did mean that the intimacy of the Bombay Gymkhana was lost and if the players and members in the club house had the luxuries, some of the spectators were accommodated quite roughly. The crowds were completely segregated. The cheapest seats, to the right of the pavilion, were known as the East Stand. Here the spectators sat on hard concrete floors caged away from the cricket by wire fencing. As you went round the stadium in an anti-clockwise direction, so the amenities increased. The North Stand, opposite the pavilion, was reasonably comfortable, then came the stand for the various clubs to the left of the pavilion. But apart from the club-house end which was open, all the other spectators in the other stands sat behind high wire fencing with each stand walled off from the next. Unlike in England, you could not walk right round the ground. Every section was segregated and, in time, the popular East Stand with its overcrowding, its noise, its enthusiasm would generate its own legends and the stadium would be the model for others of its kind on the sub-continent.

Patiala had instructed Frank Tarrant to prepare a good turf wicket and, through the summer of 1936 while India struggled in England, Tarrant tried to keep the Bombay monsoon at bay and fulfil his master's wishes. On 7 December 1937 everything was ready. Patiala appeared in all-white sherwani and churidar – the traditional northern Indian dress; Sir Roger Lumley, the Bombay Governor, in a topee, looked imperial; his wife, in a polka-dotted dress and a large, wide-brimmed hat, seemed as though she feared (or hoped for?) a Patiala pass; all were profusely garlanded, playing a part which had been carefully scripted. After the speeches a match between the Cricket Club of India and Lord Tennyson's team began.

This was another one of those curious teams which the Indian Board imported in order to make up for its failure to obtain a proper Test side. They had, it seems, invited the West Indians and even the South Africans, to no avail. Tennyson, a Regency figure, was famous for his heroics with a broken hand against Gregory and Macdonald. But he had last played Test cricket for England in the 1920s, and gave up the Hampshire captaincy in 1933. After his retirement he specialised in being a cricket ambassador, taking teams to West Indies, South Africa and now India. Tennyson had come to India more for the thrill of savouring the jewel in the crown than for playing serious cricket. The style of the tour was set when Tennyson went to Nawanagar on a panther shoot with the Jam Saheb and shot a goat instead.

His team, as such teams go, was not a bad one. It included James Langridge, Stan Worthington, Bill Edrich, Joe Hardstaff, Yardley, Wellard, Gover, Peebles, G. H. Pope, Gibb, T. P. B. (Peter) Smith and J. H. Parks, a fairly strong England second XI, a mixture of players who had played for England and those who might. Like the 'crock'

Australian side of 1935-36 – they had a slightly worse record – they played four unofficial 'Tests' against India. Merchant was appointed captain for all four. He had kept out of the cliques that infested Indian cricket and, with Colonel Mistry as selector, it seemed as if he would have some freedom to choose his own team. But not even Merchant could completely overcome the residue of the years of bitterness and infighting. He soon found he could not make as clean a break with the past as he would have liked.

At twenty-six Merchant already had a mature cricketing brain, but he still felt he could do with the advice of senior players. In his years in Bombay cricket he had much valued the guidance of Jai, but in the first 'Test' Jai appeared strangely reluctant to help him. Perhaps he resented the younger man's elevation. The result was that India played poorly and lost by nine wickets. Nayudu, who had been on a world tour, was available for the second 'Test' in Bombay and Merchant wanted him, but would Nayudu, a senior player, a former captain, play under Merchant, almost fifteen years his junior? Nayudu agreed and he was among the fourteen players selected.

However, almost anything connected with Nayudu was now high drama. Soon after he arrived in Bombay he was asked to report to a 'certain personage's' address in the city. His biographer does not say who this personage was but we may assume it was Patiala. He was grilled about the 1936 tour and then dismissed. On the morning of the match Nayudu woke up, picked up the newspapers and learnt that he was not in the chosen XI. His place had been taken by Mohamed Saeed, a Patiala player who had done rather well for CCI in the inaugural match of the Brabourne Stadium against Lord Tennyson's team. Saeed was not even in the original fourteen and his achievements will not long detain us. But he had served his purpose in assassinating Nayudu's representative cricket career. Long after the princes and kings had gone, Nayudu continued to play but he never took the field with an Indian team.

Bombay, where Nayudu was such a hero, did not take kindly to this last, almost gratuitous, act of princely diktat. Nor was its humour helped by India losing the Bombay 'Test' by six wickets. Feelings came to the surface when a C. K. Nayudu XII played a Deodhar XII at the Hindu Gymkhana. That year a dispute about allocation of seats had led to the Hindus withdrawing from the Quadrangular Tournament, so this match attracted great crowds. On Christmas Day Nayudu showed how to cope with the new wonder boy Mankad, making 89 not out, but, at the end of the day's play when, despite repeated requests, he failed to emerge from the club house to accept the crowd's greetings, the mob went berserk, invaded the gymkhana, and wrecked it.

This must have worried the authorities for, during the next 'Test'

119

in Calcutta, it was announced that a fifth Test would be played in Bombay with Nayudu as captain. Yet even this was not enough to cool tempers. In the first week of January, just before the annual Europeans versus Indians match in Madras, where the fourth 'Test' was due to take place later in the month, there were the first of the characteristic Indian cricket protests. Demonstrators took to the streets carrying placards 'No Nayudu, no Test'. Over the years other players whom the crowd felt had been badly treated would also provoke such a response. Nayudu was the first. The authorities, worried about the boycott, did invite Nayudu to play but, by now fed up with the machinations, he did not even bother to reply to the invitation.

Meanwhile the announcement that a fifth 'Test' was due to take place had infuriated Digvijayasinhji. He was President of the Board but knew nothing about it. He issued a statement saying that the match would not be played, but the cricket associations which made up the Board insisted it should be played, so he resigned. There followed conflicting statements, counter-statements and mysterious resignations and withdrawals. Yuvraj, who had been selected for Calcutta, did not turn out and never played again. As it happens, India won the third and fourth 'Tests', so that the fifth match was a decider. But with no Nayudu, and with disputes over seat allocations still continuing, only 5,000 spectators, out of the Brabourne's 35,000 capacity, attended. India, after bowling out Tennyson's XI for 130, let the game slip away and lost by 156 runs.

All these comings and goings must have affected Merchant. If his captaincy was always shrewd and able, his batting suffered. For the only time in his career he had a prolonged run of bad scores. He failed to score a century in the season, and passed 50 only three times. He even got out 'hit wicket b Gover', the only time in his career he was out in such a fashion. This was in the match which inaugurated the stadium. In the 'Tests' he was a failure: 5, 15, 6, 1, 19, 9, 19, 17, 7 – altogether 98 runs in nine innings. Never again would he fare so badly. The failures made him question the idea of opening and after the first two matches he went back down to the middle order but did no better. His season's average of 23.50 was the lowest he recorded in any season when he played in a reasonable number of matches (there were odd seasons where he played only one or two matches but for that reason they are not significant).

With Merchant so out of form, India had to rely on Mankad, who confirmed that the promise he had shown in the Ranji Trophy was not a fluke. He headed the batting and the bowling averages of both sides: 62.66 with the bat, 14.53 with the ball, and India's two victories in Calcutta and Madras were built around his efforts. Tennyson was amazed that he was only just twenty, and at the end of the series was ready to place him in a mythical World XI. In India where foreign praise, particularly from an English lord, is greatly valued, much was made of this accolade.

But in many ways the crucial quality of Mankad was not so much his batting, invaluable as it was, as his bowling. He was that rare thing in India then: a left-arm spinner. India never had had quite such a high-class left-arm spinner. Mushtaq Ali had impressed Hobbs, Jamshedji had played against Jardine's team, and even earlier there were Baloo and Warden. Now with Mankad India had a bowler who undoubtedly could rank with the very best in the world. Yet Mankad had started his schoolboy cricket career as a fast-medium bowler trying to imitate the great heroes of Indian youth: Amar Singh and Nissar. It was Wensley who realised that Mankad's short stocky build would never allow him to be a fast bowler. Over long sessions in Jamnagar he taught him the art of flight, variation of pace and spin and advised him to discard the off-break. They might, said Wensley, make him lose his grip and action, far better to concentrate on the leg-breaks, the natural break. So the leg-break delivered with a slight round-arm action became his stock ball to the right-hander and for variation there was a faster ball which went with the arm and, even when the batsmen were prepared for it, they often could not detect it. This was the ball that brought Mankad a great many of his wickets.

But if this marked a great advance there was also a loss. Wensley's shrewdness undoubtedly made Mankad, but the fact that a bowler who wanted to bowl fast was converted into a left-arm spinner showed a distinct trend in Indian cricket. Yet another phase of Indian cricket was ending. Tennyson's tour marked the end of the greatest decade of pace India has known. Today it is hard to imagine, despite the advent of Kapil Dev and others, that India ever had pace bowlers. Yet between 1926–27 and the visit of Gilligan's side, and 1936–37 and Tennyson bringing another English side, it was Indian pace that dominated the bowling. Nissar and Amar Singh regularly opened the bowling, there was Amar Singh's brother Ramji who, for a few overs, could be quicker than Nissar, and Jehangir Khan. Had India made her Test debut in the 1920s, the number of pace bowlers to get Test recognition might have been higher. Every Indian side had two or three genuine opening bowlers, not merely the Solkars and Abid Alis whose job was mainly to take the shine off the ball so that the spinners could come on. If anything, it was spin that India then lacked. Their batsmen showed good technique against pace and, as both the 1932 and 1936 tours demonstrated, spinners caused the greater problems. Critics like Cardus noted how uncomfortable the Indians were against the turning ball, particularly the leg-break. Pace hardly worried them.

Mankad's conversion from a fast-medium bowler into a spinner marks the beginning of the great era of Indian spin. By the time Mankad was established young bowlers wanted to be like him and Amar Singh became a distant memory. In time this was to bring India great victories but in the folk memory of Indian cricket the yearning for the age of Amar Singh and Nissar has never ceased. 'Oh my Amar and my Nissar' is even today as longingly uttered as 'Oh my Hornby and my Barlow' ever was in Lancashire. Nostalgia adds golden ribbons to memory and Nissar and Amar Singh are usually portrayed as world-beaters. They were not quite that, yet their achievements were extraordinary. They only played together in six Tests, Nissar missing the Madras Test of 1933–34. Their Test career figures read:

Nissar: Balls, 1,211; Runs, 707; Wickets, 25; Average, 28.28
Amar Singh: Balls, 2,182; Runs, 858; Wickets, 28; Average, 30.64.

All these Tests were against England, then one of the best batting sides in the world. Despite this, Nissar took five wickets in an innings three times in six Tests, and Amar Singh twice in seven Tests. Just as a century stamps a batsman's command so does taking five wickets in an innings establish a bowler's dominance. That Nissar and Amar Singh did it so frequently in their short careers shows how they could dominate a batting side. If India had no success to show for their efforts, it was partly because they suffered from poor fielding and also because their batsmen, time and again, squandered the positions Nissar and Amar Singh had created. These positions were created despite the fact that they were both the shock and the stock bowlers of India. Just as in later years the spinners were expected to take all ten wickets, so in the era of pace Nissar and Amar Singh were expected both to take wickets and contain if necessary.

The inaugural Test at Lord's in 1932 set the pattern. The match figures of the two bowlers were Nissar: 44-8-135-6 (5 for 93 in the first innings), Amar: 72.1-23-159-4. Between them the two bowled 116.1 overs. India used five other bowlers in the two innings and they delivered 99 overs between them. The spinners bowled just eighteen overs. In India in 1933–34 this pattern of hard work and wickets continued. The spinners bowled a bit more but India did not have class spinners and Nissar and Amar Singh dominated the bowling. In the heat of Bombay, in the first Test, Nissar bowled 33.5 overs, taking 5 for 90. In Calcutta, while England made 403, Amar Singh bowled 54.5 overs, taking 4 for 106. In Madras during England's 335, Amar Singh bowled 44.4 overs to gain his best-ever Test figures of 7 for 86. The longer an innings went on the longer the pair were expected to bowl. At Old Trafford in 1936 when England made 571 for 8 declared, Nissar bowled 28 overs, taking 2 for 125, Amar Singh 41 overs, 2 for 121. Two weeks later at The Oval, while Hammond hit 217, Nissar bowled 26 overs, taking 5 for 120, Amar Singh 39 overs, with 2 wickets for 102.

In contrast, apart from Bowes who bowled 30 overs in the first innings of the 1932 Test, no English fast bowler had to carry such a burden. England's was a much more evenly balanced bowling attack with the workload shared by the pace men and the spinners. Partly this was forced on India. England had top-class spinners like Verity, Robins and Sims to do much of the work. India had to rely on their two class fast bowlers.

Mankad did reduce their workload but, despite his arrival, Nissar and Amar Singh continued to bowl a disproportionate number of overs, Amar Singh in particular bowling prodigiously during Tennyson's tour. By the end of the series he was just behind Mankad in the averages, with 36 wickets at 16.66.

What nobody then knew was that this would be the last series in which Nissar and Amar Singh would play. Within two years Amar Singh, not yet thirty, was dead from pneumonia and, while Nissar lived to see the era of spin firmly established, he never played again for India. The 1939–45 war meant that India would have no further opportunities to tour. This sudden end to what had been the country's greatest opening pair has undoubtedly increased the nostalgia and, for all the success that spin has brought India, and continues to bring, there remains a feeling of loss – something that ended unnaturally, before its time. Indians accept that this loss, far too early in their Test history, was largely due to the fates but this does not stop them railing against its cruelty. Only when another pair like Nissar and Amar Singh emerges, will Indian cricket feel that the loss has been made up.

Tennyson's visit rang down another curtain. Within a few weeks of the end of the tour Patiala, who had said when the Brabourne Stadium was opened, 'Now I can die happy' did die. His three hundred wives and concubines rent their clothes, tore off their jewels, bashed their heads against the wall in a theatrical show of grief which suggested they were aware of the sad fate that mistresses of dead kings have to suffer. Indian cricket had suffered through the capriciousness of the Maharajah, but it also knew that it had benefited from his generosity and showed a more decorous, if still grieving, response.

The departure of the greatest princely patron that Indian cricket had seen marked the end of the age of the Maharajahs as well as the end of the dominance of pace. Indian cricket, in more ways than one, would from now on acquire a slower tempo.

If this made no impression on world cricket it was because Tennyson's tour also started India's long isolation from world cricket. All international cricket would cease once the second world war started, but whereas elsewhere the 1938–39 years were a halcyon period to which cricketers would look back, they saw India forced back on her own resources. The winter of 1938–39 did not see any visitors even though India was a long-distance bystander to the momentous political events taking place in Europe and elsewhere. As ever Indian newspapers reported English cricket fairly thoroughly, but Indians could only follow from afar the feat of Len Hutton in becoming the world's highest Test run-getter with a score of 364, passing Bradman's 334 made at Leeds in 1930.

Merchant, in his own way, was beginning to show a similar appetite. The 1938–39 season saw him recover all his old batting form. There were only three first-class games for him that season but he scored 334 runs and, with a highest score of 143 not out, his season's average was also 334.

That innings of Merchant's came in the Ranji Trophy match against Baroda in a total of 441. Baroda replied quite strongly and two minutes before the end of the match were 326 for 9. If they had held out, the match would have been replayed, but the last wicket fell and Bombay won on the first innings. However, in the next match, Bombay was surprisingly beaten by Sind, again on the first innings, despite 120 by Merchant. The championship was now wide open, and Bengal won it with one of the strongest sides it has ever fielded. There was quite a strong English element in the side: T. C. Longfield, the all-rounder, as captain (and later father-in-law of Ted Dexter) and Hitch, the Surrey and England fast bowler, as coach. Much to the surprise of most people, and probably themselves, they beat Southern Punjab, including Amarnath, in the final, and that by the comfortable margin of 178 runs. It remains Bengal's only victory in the Ranji Trophy.

So at the end of the first five years of the national championships there had been four different winners: Bombay (twice) and Nawanagar, both from the West Zone, Hyderabad (South) and Bengal (East). But if this spread suggested cricketing depth then this was illusory. For at this stage, outside the city of Bombay, the strongest cricketing talent was in the north. But as the defeat of Southern Punjab showed, its cricketers could not quite pull it off in the major domestic championships, partly because not all its players played in the tournament. In 1938–39 Nissar had played a big part in Southern Punjab getting to the final, but this was the first time in three years he had taken part in the Ranji Trophy.

Just as the top players stayed away, so did the crowds. In 1937–38 when the Ranji finals produced the shock win of Hyderabad, with no great names, beating star-studded Nawanagar, only a handful of people turned up at the Brabourne Stadium to watch the final. It would not have cost anything to watch, for admission was free, but even the prospect of seeing Amar Singh and Mankad did not stir the crowds. It was not felt to be competitive enough. One reason for this was that

124

many of these teams were artificial. Nawanagar represented a princely state which meant nothing outside the state and, even within it, was seen as one of the toys the prince played with. There was nothing to compare with the county loyalties of England or the island loyalties of the West Indies.

All this was very different to the Quadrangular which, with the addition of the Rest (meaning Catholics, Jews and Anglo-Indians, the word used to denote mixed Indian and English), was now the Pentangular. The change of name and a new team had only increased its popularity and no player wanted to miss this tournament. Here there were such loyalties, albeit religious ones, and players were fired up by the crowds that turned up in huge numbers. In November 1938, when the Hindus played the Rest in the Pentangular, the stadium was bursting long before 11am, with queues snaking all round it and the adjoining houses. Such public expectations created the right response amongst the players. In this match Amarnath made 241 which, at that time, was a record for this tournament. As the Ranji Trophy acquired an identity and status it did begin to attract crowds but it never rivalled the fervour of the Quadrangular and Pentangular.

It was the war years that were to give the Ranji Trophy its biggest fillip and make it a truly national championship with thousands of spectators attracted to it.

8

War-and the golden age of batting

On 3 September 1939, Indians were told by Lord Linlithgow, the Viceroy, that they were at war with Germany. Not one Indian in a million, probably, knew where Germany was or what could have caused India to go to war with that country. But Linlithgow, as the representative of the King-Emperor, was doing his patriotic – English – duty. England was at war and India, being her colony, was also at war. Within hours of the Prime Minister, Neville Chamberlain's broadcast Lord Linlithgow, without consulting a single Indian, had plunged 400 million Indians into a war they did not understand or even know much about.

Indians, even those like Nehru sympathetic to the British cause, were outraged and the decision further widened the gap between the Raj and the Congress. There were, of course, Indians who fought with the British, but others saw this as India's great opportunity and tried to use German and Japanese help to get rid of the Raj. For the majority, however, the war provided a vicarious thrill. Physically the war hardly touched India except the north-eastern corner and that, too, only in 1944 when the Japanese invaded Assam. There were lots of scares but, along with continental America, India was one of the largest land masses to avoid any fighting. The war in England meant suffering and privation, rationing and shortages. In India, too, there was suffering and the Bengal famine killed millions. But for the well-off and the privileged life could be very different. One British officer, arriving in India from a rationed England, was amazed to find he could drive to the hill station of Nilgiris in south India using up a gallon of petrol every sixteen miles.

So, in this oasis of calm, in a world gone mad, cricket prospered. In a sense India was not different from Australia, or South Africa, or the West Indies, or New Zealand – the other major cricketing countries which did not see much physical action during the war. But while in those countries cricket took a back seat – the Sheffield Shield was suspended in Australia – in India the war years were boom years for cricket, if not in terms of people watching, at least in terms of batting. Cricket is essentially a batsman's game. No bowler, apart

126

from Drake, has ever been knighted, jests Alec Bedser; but behind the jest lies a grim cricketing truth. The structure of the game is such that its great deeds are batting deeds. The first 'golden age' of cricket from 1895 to 1914 was a batting age: Grace, Ranji, Fry, Trumper dominate that era. The bowlers are there and they have their share of honour, but only after the batsmen have taken their bow. The second golden age, from 1919 to 1939, if we follow Gerald Howat's classification, was also a batting age: Bradman, Hammond, Duleep, Hutton. Again, there were great bowlers. One of them, Larwood, very nearly stopped the golden age in its tracks when he made Bradman the batsman seem humanly fallible. But Larwood is one of the villains of the story, the heroes are the batsmen.

Now, as the world turned to war and destruction, the Indian batsmen turned to runs. Within months of Hitler devastating Poland, new batting records were being set in India. By the time the 'phoney' war in the West had begun Indian batsmen were in full flow. In the match against the Europeans the Hindus totalled 591, the highest ever in the tournament. Mankad made 133, Merchant made 192 before he was bowled. Merchant had already made 140 in the season's first match for Bombay and by the end of the season he had scored 456 runs at an average of 114. He was now captain of Bombay and it seemed his 140 would see Bombay to victory over Nawanagar. Chasing 387, Bombay were 341 for 6 with Merchant and his brother Uday, who scored 94, adding 143 for the fourth wicket. But then Amar Singh and Mankad, in a great spell, took the last four wickets for 10 runs and Nawanagar had the precious first-innings lead. But despite some great performances by Amar Singh – in the next match he scored 113 not out in 88 minutes, with one six and 17 fours, to become the first player to score 1,000 runs and take 100 wickets in the championship – this was not to be Nawanagar's year.

There was to be a new name on the trophy and the winners created yet more batting records. Maharashtra had been the tournament's rabbits. They had never won a single match in the championships. This was particularly galling to their captain, D. B. Deodhar. Though he never played Test cricket, something he always regretted, in India he has occupied a position not far below that of Nayudu. Indians respect age, the old can sometimes become the old men of the mountain, so crushing can be their weight on the young, but in cricket Deodhar has always been held in high affection and it became a cliché to refer to Nayudu and Deodhar as the two grand old men of Indian cricket. Some of his attitude to life can be gauged from the introduction he wrote, in 1989 at the age of ninety-seven, to a book about Nayudu. It is a typical cricket introduction from someone who was Nayudu's contemporary and played a lot of his cricket with him. If

127

he moans about the lack of cricket opportunity in his youth (by the time India came to Test cricket Deodhar was forty-two and just missed it) that is understandable. What is revealing is his rebuke to Nayudu for being a 'chain-smoker'. Otherwise, Deodhar writes, Nayudu would not have suffered 'his early death at the age of seventy-two'.

This belief in a 'disciplined life' went with a strong sense of nationalism. Not so much Indian nationalism as Maratta nationalism. Having grown up in Poona, Deodhar was full of the folklore that this nationalism had inspired when the Marattas were the supreme power in India fighting the Mughals and dictating terms to the British. Then Poona was the great city in India and Bombay little more than a fishing village. The British had reversed the process. Bombay had become the great city by the sea, Poona was a small town 120 miles away in the hills by a slow four- or five-hour tortuous rail or road journey. Deodhar felt this deeply, particularly when he came down to Bombay to participate in the Quadrangular Tournaments. Though, as a Hindu, his common cause was with them, the Hindus who ran Bombay's Hindu Gymkhana treated him with disdain. In 1934 Deodhar, who had captained the Hindus capably in the first match, was dropped from the second and the Yuvraj was made captain. This was no doubt a deal with the Maharajah of Patiala but, as it happened, it backfired and made the Yuvraj very unpopular. But it did little to endear Bombay to Deodhar.

At this stage the Presidency of Bombay included Bombay city, Poona and several other cricketing centres. In the Ranji Trophy there should have been just one team from Bombay Presidency, for this was how the association joined the national body. But Gujerat and Maharashtra were keen to get away from the stifling dominance of Bombay city and left to form their own association. So Bombay, in effect, represented only the city. Deodhar organised Maharashtra's cricket from Poona and at first he had no success. There was little money and not much experienced talent. But in 1939, on a visit to Bombay during the Pentangular Tournament, Deodhar met up with an experienced cricketer who could provide the counterweight to the mainly young college students he had been recruiting for his team. That cricketer was Vijay Samuel Hazare, then aged twenty-four and desperate for a change. He was like a man at a street corner hoping his luck would change. At that moment Deodhar walked round the corner and made an irresistible offer.

Most Indian Christians are Roman Catholics converted by the Portuguese in Goa, but there are not a few Protestants and Hazare was one of them. A Christian Maharashtrian, he had played his early cricket in Maharashtra and he had even represented them in their first Ranji Trophy match in February 1935 when they lost narrowly to Bombay. But then, like so many other Indian cricketers of his generation, he

128

took the princely shilling. His employer was the Maharajah of Dewas, Senior, the ruler of another princely state with a fifteen-gun salute and a population of 83,000. Dewas, the subject of E. M. Forster's *The Hill of Devi*, was a state so full of intrigue that it made Ranji's problems in Nawanagar look simple. Hazare's employer, Vikram Singh, narrowly escaped being poisoned by his own father. It seems that the father, who was then the ruler, wanted to seduce Vikram's wife, his own daughter-in-law. He failed, she was driven out of the state, and he then denounced his son Vikram as an illegitimate child.

In the end the father, having run the Treasury dry, decamped to Pondicherry which, being a French possession, was outside British control. Then Vikram Singh became the ruler, and one of his first acts was to take Hazare on to his staff. Vikram Singh was very keen on cricket but his brother-in-law, the Raja of Jath, was even keener. He imported Clarrie Grimmett to teach him to bowl wrist spin and improve his batting and Vikram Singh asked Hazare to try and help the Raja. Perhaps he too could pick up a few hints about the leg-break which was then still a developing art in India?

Grimmett quickly saw that Hazare would never become a leg-spinner. His medium-pace trundling was good enough as far as it went. As a medium-pace change bowler he had already played for India against Tennyson's side. In the match before the first and final 'Test' he had taken 6 for 54 and this had gained him selection. In the Test itself Hazare batted no. 9 and the only memorable thing about his batting was that, while he was at the crease, an earthquake shook the ground and so frightened the English fielders that they were convinced the world was coming to an end.

Nor did Grimmett change Hazare's batting stance which was not very attractive to look at: hands apart, bat tucked in between the pads. Once in motion, however, Hazare soon came out of his ugly duckling shell to look a swan. What Grimmett did teach Hazare, as they practised with a tennis ball, was patience and judgement. Bowling from a distance of some ten or twelve yards, rather than the twenty-two yards of proper cricket, he would shout out instructions with every ball. Grimmett also watched over Hazare as he played club cricket. They often played in the same team and after every match there was a post-mortem. If Grimmett's influence on Hazare was not as dramatic as Wensley's on Mankad, it was still decisive.

Grimmett had broadened Hazare's cricketing horizons and these were further extended on a private tour of England in 1938. He saw the best of Australian and English batting, including Bradman, McCabe, Hammond, Brown and Hutton. Hazare returned to India a restive man, which increased, for the outbreak of war meant that the 1939-40 England tour to India would be cancelled, and, as long as it lasted, there would be no international contests – always the quickest way to wider recognition in India. Another season in Central India seemed too dreadful to contemplate. Deodhar's suggestion of a return to Maharashtra came at just the right time and Hazare accepted with alacrity.

In the first match Hazare was still the bowler who batted a bit. Playing at the Poona Club on a good batting wicket, Hazare made 40, but there were centuries from Deodhar's youngsters: the left-handed Khandu Rangnekar and Sohoni. Deodhar, himself, at the age of forty-six, made 157 and Maharashtra made 543 for 8 declared – the highest score in the championship at that stage. Hazare took 7 for 94 and Western India, who had beaten Maharashtra three times in the last five years, were conquered. At last Maharashtra had won a Ranji Trophy match, after five years of trying.

A side denied victory for that long can either go mad or scale new heights. Having set one record the dam of Maharashtrian brilliance now burst. The next match, in January 1940, also at Poona Club, was against Baroda who included C. S. Nayudu, C.K.'s younger brother. He was developing into one of India's first dangerous leg-spinners for, in the previous match, he had taken thirteen wickets. Baroda made 303 and this seemed a good enough total against which C. S. Nayudu could practise his arts, but by the end of the second day Maharashtra had passed the score and Hazare was 165 not out. The next day was one of those days Hazare would long remember: a crisp winter's day that can make Poona such a delightful place. A bit of a breeze to suggest a sweater would not be out of place but bright, warm and sunny – very like a good, mild English summer's day. Deodhar had told him to attack and by lunch Hazare had passed 200. Ahead was Wazir Ali's 222, then a Ranji Trophy record, and beyond that Amarnath's 241, an all-comer's Indian record. It was over lunch that Baroda's skipper sportingly suggested to Hazare that perhaps he ought to go for these records.

Once these records were broken, others beckoned. Hazare and the no. 10 batsman, Nagarwalla, no mean batsman himself, put on 245 for the ninth wicket – an Indian record. When Nagarwalla was out for 98, Hazare was on 283. He now found another partner in the no. 11 batsman, Patwardhan, who showed just the right temperament, and at last, on the third day, Maharashtra declared with their score on 650 for 9. Hazare had made 316 not out, becoming the first Indian to score a triple hundred. Duleep had scored one, but that was in England playing for Sussex. Hazare had batted in all for seven hours and his last 151 had come at a run a minute. Grimmett's lessons of patience had paid off.

The semi-final was again at Poona, against Southern Punjab led by Wazir Ali. Immediately the match became the sort of contest that cricketers love. Hazare versus Wazir Ali. Could the latter retrieve his record? He could not, but his team made 429. Maharashtra were in some danger at 150 for 4, but were rallied by Hazare and Rangnekar. Rangnekar made 87, Hazare 155. The final was also at the Poona Club and, after United Provinces had been dismissed for 237, Maharashtra made 581, Hazare a mere 53. Palia, the UP captain, who had looked so elegant but not made many runs on the 1932 tour, now played one of his finest innings. In just over five and a half hours he scored 216. Maharashtra had to bat again to win the match by ten wickets. By the end of the season Hazare had out-Merchanted Merchant, having in five innings scored 619 runs with an average of 154.75. This was still the era of Merchant, but now he had a rival. For the next decade the two matched each other – at times run for run, stroke for stroke. With both of them named Vijay, meaning victory, it became popularly known as the age of the two Vs.

Cricket has provided many such duels. But generally one master batsman has been in his prime when another has emerged – perhaps the most remarkable example being that of Ponsford and Bradman. Ponsford's records were a spur for Bradman. To an extent the relationship between Merchant and Hazare was similar, except that Merchant – the older player – was more like Bradman, Hazare something of a Ponsford. Also they were more nearly contemporaries and rivals in a sense that Bradman and Ponsford were not – in a few years both would be candidates for the captaincy of India. Their emergence also established a run-making era that has gone largely unnoticed in the rest of the cricket world. The conventional histories, written from an English perspective, see the timeless Test in Durban in 1939 as the end of the great run-scoring feasts. But Hazare and Merchant – and the batsmen they inspired – continued this tradition, and within a few years Worrell, Weekes and Walcott in the West Indies began to carry on the great era of run-making.

The 1940-41 season was to see the two Vs in almost head-to-head confrontation. On 15 November, again at the Poona Club ground, a three-day match between Bombay and Maharashtra started in the first round of the championship. Just a month before that, in a speech at the Hindu Gymkhana ground, Merchant had warned Bombay that it needed discipline and a new sense of purpose and dedication if it was to become the great king of Indian cricket. Bombay suffered from apathy and complacency, the two greatest crimes in Merchant's book. It neglected schools cricket at its own peril, Merchant warned. A month was not enough to reclaim all this lost ground, but before the season began Bombay had recruited Rangnekar, who had been born in the then outer suburb of Thana.

Maharashtra batted first. If in the previous seasons his youngsters had set the trend, now Deodhar himself did. He scored 246, adding 155 with Hazare. Maharashtra passed their own previous highest total, scoring 675 runs. Bombay began disastrously: Hindlekar was out without a run on the board. Merchant made the sort of century that Indians now accepted as commonplace for him, but on 109 he was bowled by Hazare. Everything depended on Rangnekar. Against his old team he now scored runs with great relish: his century, then his double-century, 202 in just 265 minutes. But as he reached his double-century an admirer, overcome with emotion, rushed on and kissed him on the cheeks. In the strict puritanical tradition in which Indian cricket was then played such things were just not done. Though Rangnekar was kissed by a man and Indians could be exuberant in garlanding their heroes, such distinctive acts were uncommon. Hazare feels this embarrassed Rangnekar and upset his concentration. Also, batting with wet gloves, he decided to wait until the end of the over to change. Off the next ball his bat slipped, he spooned up a catch and was out. Even then Bombay got to within 25 of Maharashtra's total, 650; so titanic had been the struggle that the match scheduled to last three days was extended to a fourth to produce a result.

Anything after this was bound to be an anti-climax, but there was a question mark over Maharashtra. All their successes had come at Poona. How would they fare when they were drawn away from home? The next match was against Gujerat on the matting of Ahmedabad. Maharashtra won by making 518, Hazare 117 and Sohoni 134. The Zonal final, also on matting at Rajkot against Western India, saw another huge Maharashtra score. Western India made 459 and Maharashtra replied with 459 for 3, with Sohoni 218 not out and Hazare 164. The pair put on 342 for the fourth wicket – then a record Indian partnership for any wicket.

Maharashtra seemed capable of setting a record in one match only to better it in the next. This is just what it did in the semi-final. Sohoni, for a change, did not score a century, but three other Maharashtrian batsmen did, including 196 from Deodhar. Maharashtra now scored 798 against Northern India and, while they too had a century-maker, Ram Parkash who scored 209 not out, their total of 442 was nowhere near enough. The final at Madras, described in those days as having a sporting wicket – which meant that bowlers had a chance – saw something more like a normal cricket match. Madras made 145 and Hazare, with 137 in a score of 284, rescued Maharashtra. Madras made 347 in their second innings, but helped by dropped catches Sohoni made 144 and Maharashtra, on a crumbling wicket, won by six wickets.

In many ways Sohoni had eclipsed both Hazare and Merchant that season. He was talked about as the cricketer with film star looks – he was tall, fair-skinned and light-eyed. This was the first time a cricketer had been so likened and it showed the growing influence of the cinema in India. He was undoubtedly the batsman of the season (he was a bowler too) with an aggregate of 655 and a Merchant-like average of 131. But although Sohoni's looks continued to attract attention he never scaled such heights again. The real confrontation remained between Merchant and Hazare. Hazare had made 565 runs against Merchant's 246, but then Merchant had only two first-class innings in the whole season. Apart from his 109 against Maharashtra he made 137 against the touring Ceylon team. The Hindus had again withdrawn from the Pentangular and Merchant could only sit and watch while his rival Hazare, playing for the Rest, scored 182 against the Europeans. If Merchant was not to see him disappear over the horizon he had to secure more first-class matches for himself and this meant Bombay going further than the first round of the Ranji Trophy.

As if on cue the 1941-42 season provided Merchant with about as much first-class cricket as Indian domestic cricket was then capable of providing. But luck seemed to be against him. In the first match Bombay met Western India at Bombay and he was run out for 12, his lowest score for almost two years. Even without him Bombay made 462 with a young college boy, K. C. Ibrahim, scoring 230 not out. Western India made 95 and, following-on, 167 for 5. They were well beaten, if only on the first innings.

Bombay had got into the second round after many years and now Merchant revelled in the opportunities. At the end of November he scored 170 not out in 462 for 8 declared against Nawanagar. In December there was the Pentangular match against the Muslims and Merchant scored 243 not out in a score of 443 for 6 declared. A few days later, in the final against the Parsees, he scored 221 out of 474. This was the first time he was out in three innings and those three innings had totalled 634 runs for once out, a record in first-class cricket at that time and beaten only by K. C. Ibrahim some years later. Barely was the Pentangular final over than there was the Ranji Trophy match against Sind when Merchant scored 153 and Bombay 405, winning, as ever, on the first innings. In the semi-finals at Lahore Merchant had his only poor scores of the season: 25 and 48 not out, but Bombay won a relatively low-scoring match, and then in the final Merchant made 60. In a strong all-round Bombay effort, with Ibrahim making 117, the side totalled 506 for 9 declared for an easy victory. Merchant in seven innings had made 932 runs with a staggering average of 233. He had hit 787 in four successive innings and had come almost as near as any batsman in the history of the game to the never-performed feat of three consecutive double-centuries. Even so he remains the only player to have made four consecutive scores of 150 or more.

Hazare was eclipsed – at least for this season. He had left Maharashtra to move to Baroda. Cricket was all very well but Poona just did not offer him the job security he needed, while the Maharajah of Baroda was at last turning to cricket – one of the few large princely states to do so. With Hazare's departure, followed by yet more defections, Maharashtra collapsed. Having hit all the high notes for two years, Maharashtra now hit one of the lowest of low notes. They vanished as quickly as they had come and in the first round they lost to Nawanagar, with Shute Banerjee taking 8 for 25 and bowling them out for 39. Baroda, Hazare's new team, did not fare too well and Hazare had only one century in the Pentangular. Even on his lucky Poona ground in a festival match he was bowled for 25 by Amarnath. But the duel with Merchant was not over.

The Hazare-Merchant cricketing rivalry could now be pictured as reflecting other Indian rivalries. Indian newspapers loved to play around these themes. There was the Bombay man versus the Baroda batsman, the Gujerati Merchant versus the Maharashtrian Hazare. Overtly nobody referred to their religious difference: Hindu versus Christian. Indeed it is debatable how many Indians appreciated that Hazare was a Christian for Vijay is not a common Christian name. At one stage he had been invited by the Hindu Gymkhana to play for the Hindus in the Pentangular. In 1941-42 Merchant and Hazare did not confront each other in the Ranji Trophy, which could be such a capricious tournament, but the following year was to provide one of cricket's cruellest tricks and Merchant his worst season.

The year 1942 was an historic one in Indian politics. On 9 August, on the sandy beaches of Chowpatty, along Bombay's seafront, Mahatma Gandhi, addressing India's greatest political rally, told the British to quit India. There had been attempts to negotiate but they had now failed, and Gandhi launched what was to be his last struggle to get rid of the Raj. It put the Congress on a dangerous collision course with the British government. Gandhi was arrested and the awesome Raj machinery was employed to crush the Congress, even more so than in 1932 when Willingdon had cheerfully played Mussolini. Bombay was caught in the middle of it, the Pentangular was cancelled and Bombay dropped out of the Ranji Trophy which saw six other Indian teams withdraw: from the north, from the west, from the south and from the north-west. This Congress versus Raj battle came in the midst of a worsening war situation. For the first and only time India felt it was going to be physically dragged into the conflict. The Japanese had swept the British out of south-east Asia and had reached India's north-eastern borders. The British had to beat an ignominious retreat, the first time the Indians had seen the British fall since Clive had won the Battle of Plassey. It made the Indians realise that, contrary to Raj propaganda, the British were not invincible. Early in 1942 a couple of Japanese bombing raids over Madras threw the city into panic, leading to a mass evacuation and the virtual suspension of all cricket there for a year. If the Japanese could strike that far south, where might their carriers strike next? For most Indians, in fact, 1942 marked the beginning of war.

So while Merchant concentrated on the family business – driving daily on his way to work past the Chowpatty beach where Gandhi had made his historic call – Hazare was busy on the cricket field. Hazare was now a captain in the Baroda state army and he played with what were very solid military virtues. He made more runs than anyone else, 398, but there was no century in the season. In the final he reached 97 before he was bowled. Otherwise there was very steady scoring: 32, 44 not out, 73, 81. The runs Hazare made and the wickets he took, once a wicket with his last ball to win a match, played a supporting role to C. S. Nayudu's spin which effectively won Baroda the Ranji Trophy for the first time. Nayudu became the first bowler in the championship to take 40 wickets in the season at a stunning average of 12.85 and this in a season of only four first-class matches. In every match Nayudu seemed to take ten or more wickets: 12 for 56 against Rajputana, 11 for 81 against Hyderabad, 10 for 173 against Western India. In 1932 Cardus had moaned that India could not play leg-spin. Now Nayudu's leg-spin was proving impossible for other Indian batsmen.

Nayudu, whose cricket was nurtured by his older brother C.K., was a very unusual bowler. Ramaswami has left us a vivid picture: 'C.S. bent his body so low while delivering the ball that his head was almost on a level with the top of the stumps. He stretched his arm fully and threw his body-weight into his delivery so that the ball came off the pitch very quick. He also spun the ball extremely well but unfortunately his length and direction were not always controlled. Probably because of this unpredictability C.S. got quite a number of wickets. The batsman did not seem to know when C.S. was going to produce "the unplayable ball".'

It was March 1943, more than a year after he had played his previous first-class match, when Merchant at last got a chance to play. There had been famine in Bijapur, a cyclone in Bengal and a match in aid of the two relief funds was played at the Brabourne Stadium. It was a worthy cause and nearly everybody made runs on a slow, flat batting wicket. The combined first innings scores of the two sides set a world record: 1,376. Only Merchant missed out: in the first innings he was out for 1, bowled by Mankad; in the second he was out for 6 – bowled by Hazare. And who should make runs for the opposition? Why, Hazare, who scored 250. He and Gul Mohammed put on 302, the partnership showing their contrasting styles: Gul Mohammed ever keen to attack the bowling, sometimes recklessly, Hazare always ready to wait for the bad ball. This was Hazare's first double-century at the Brabourne Stadium and, with Merchant failing, it was the young K. C. Ibrahim who matched him by also scoring 250 before Hazare caught him. In that year Merchant had just two first-class innings, scored 7 runs, averaging 3.50 for the season!

But such twists of fortune did not worry Merchant overmuch. He displayed that marvellous Hindu phlegm which, while different from the English variety, is just as strong. Treat joy and sorrow in the same way, the Hindu god Krishna had advised Arjun on the battlefield of Kurukshetura. Merchant, instinctively, believed this. The odd bad season had always been followed by a glorious one and he knew that if he was patient a good season would come along. But even he must have felt just a little nervous as the 1943-44 season began. There were now insistent voices being raised in Indian cricket against the Pentangular. As the forces of religious reaction grew stronger, it seemed insane to focus religious difference by having a week in which different religious communities played cricket against each other. Surely, argued the critics, the very existence of such a tournament sharpened religious differences? In fact the matches rarely caused problems and despite the objections the Pentangular returned that year and in the first match, against the Europeans, Merchant made 62. This would have been seen as a welcome return to form by any other batsman but not for Merchant. His 62 came in a total of 515 for 7 declared – too much for the Europeans – and while he was 'failing' Hazare was making one of his cherished records.

The Rest were playing the Muslims and, as so often, it became a case of Hazare versus the Muslims. The Muslims made 350, the Rest lost four wickets before Hazare found a partner, first Arolkar, then his own brother Vivek. While they basically kept their end intact, Hazare made the runs. For much of the time he faced the leg-spin of Amir Elahi, whose variations and turn had often posed problems for Hazare. But the 250 he had scored the previous season, also at Bombay, was also against Elahi, and this had given Hazare the confidence to face his old enemy. When finally Elahi had him caught and bowled, Hazare had made 248 in a score of 395. The first innings lead this gave the Rest meant they had beaten the Muslims and, of course, Hazare had now broken Merchant's record of 243 not out set in November 1941.

Merchant's response to such challenges usually came swiftly. Within a week the Hindus met the Rest in the final. The Hindus batted first and there could be no doubting Merchant's determination to snatch back his record. For a year he had little luck in his cricket, but now he found some. On 30 he was dropped, on 87 he was dropped again – neither very difficult chances – but he rarely gave so many chances in an entire season. Now that he had effectively three starts for the innings the Rest could not hope to hold him back. Shortly before tea on the second day, after batting five minutes short of seven hours, he reached 250. Immediately he declared the innings closed. The Hindus were 518 for 8 and that should have seen the Rest and Hazare off.

Merchant had shrewdly noted that Hazare had bowled nearly fifty overs of medium-pace in quite intense heat – indeed he had been the most successful bowler with three wickets – and would be dog-tired by the time the declaration came. So it proved. Hazare still made runs, but only 59 and the others collapsed for 133. They were forced to follow-on. In no time they were 60 for 5 with Hazare, himself, looking edgy and even Arolkar, who had supported Hazare in the previous match, was out. Even if Hazare stayed, who could stay with him? But now began what must be one of the most remarkable partnerships in first-class cricket. Vivek Hazare was a moderate batsman, but on a good wicket he could defend and this is what he proceeded to do. By the end of the fourth day's play the Hazare brothers were still together, with Vijay Hazare just past his century.

Few turned up at the Brabourne Stadium for the final day's play. Yes, there would be further resistance from Vijay Hazare but surely the cause was lost? But with Vivek presenting the deadest of bats Vijay kept on. He reached 150, then 200, then 250. He had now equalled Merchant's record. There was no radio commentary for this match but Bombay's bush telegraph was spreading the word and crowds began trickling in all morning. It was very nearly full when Hazare went past Merchant's record. The two brothers had put on 300 when Vivek was finally out. In five and a half hours he had made 21. Hazare could not find another partner as reliable as Vivek and by the time he reached 295, nine wickets were down. His side not only faced an innings defeat, but he, himself, might miss 300 runs. All day he had played the bowling, particularly the spin bowling of Sarwate, with care, waiting for the bad ball. Now Hazare did something quite out of character. He hit a six. He had never hit a six before at the Brabourne Stadium, he rarely lifted the ball, but now, driven by the ambition to score 300, he played a shot quite outside his usual style.

Tiredness rather than anything else finally caught up with him. After six hours and forty minutes he hit a hard caught and bowled back to the bowler. Hazare had made 309 out of a total of 387: nearly eighty per cent of his side's score. For many years it would remain the most remarkable statistic in first-class cricket.

It was not enough to prevent the innings defeat but for the crowd this did not matter. As Hazare walked off, they surged on to the field and formed a huge throng in front of the CCI pavilion, insistently chanting his name. A crowd like that in India could easily turn nasty. If Hazare did not come out and acknowledge their greetings there might be a stampede and the pavilion damaged. There were a number of ladies present and there were fears for their safety. Hazare had quickly vanished into the pavilion and, with the crowd insistently shouting his name, the situation was tense. Now Merchant showed another facet of his personality: his touch for public relations, always shrewder than that of his contemporaries. He fetched Hazare and persuaded him to appear on the balcony: say a few words, say something, say anything. Hazare, exhausted, nervous about speaking in public, could not think of anything to say. Merchant prompted him: say thank you, say how pleased and grateful you are for their good wishes, remind them that in a week Bombay will meet Baroda in the Ranji Trophy at the same ground. They would have a chance to see many of the same players in action again. Hazare followed the script, the crowd was satisfied and it provided quite a touching moment. Two record-breaking batsmen, one the new record holder, the other the previous one, helping each other out.

The Ranji Trophy match which Hazare advertised saw Merchant make 141. Hazare too scored a century for Baroda but there was little support from the others. Baroda's 297 in reply to Bombay's 487 meant that the match was lost on the first innings. Cricket followers, however, could not help wondering: when will Merchant reply to Hazare's score? The answer came at the end of December when Bombay played Maharashtra. Merchant was batting no. 5, allowing youngsters like Ibrahim their head at the top of the order. Just after lunch Bombay were 90 for 5. At the end of the day's play the score was 308 for 5 with Merchant on 119 and Rusi Modi, a nineteen-year-old youngster just coming into the side, 101. When the pair were eventually parted, with Modi making 163, they had put on 371 for the sixth wicket – which is still an Indian record. Merchant found another reliable partner for the eighth wicket in Cooper and, by tea on the second day, he was 240 not out. In India a day's play was five and a half hours, with the last session, the tea session, the shortest of the three with only an hour and a half's play. The next landmark for Merchant was Hazare's Ranji Trophy record of 316, but as he sat drinking his tea he wondered if there was enough time. Merchant, ever cautious, thought there would not be. He was feeling tired and he decided he would play out the post-tea session and leave further records for the morning of the third day. But his team-mates thought he should try to get the record the same evening because, even if he was tired, so were the bowlers. Merchant drank his tea, said nothing but, once play restarted, he was busy accumulating runs. Twenty minutes before the close Merchant reached his 300. Ten minutes before the end of play, scoring mostly singles, he passed Hazare's 316 not out. The next morning Merchant just carried on and he was still there, 359 not out, when Bombay were all out for 735.

This innings showed the best and the worst of Merchant. His ability to score runs, and score a huge amount of runs, was never in doubt, but even when he was totally in command as on the second day, with just the tea session remaining, he could never think of totally dominating the bowling. He still thought in terms of safely accumulating runs. Merchant often dominated bowlers but he seldom destroyed them. In this innings Maharashtra's bowlers who had looked so good on paper, Shinde, Mankad and Phadkar, had all been vanquished. Maharashtra collapsed to 298, half an hour after the start of the fourth day's play, and since the first-innings lead was all that mattered, it made little sense to carry on with the match. In the context of what was happening in India then this hardly mattered. Merchant had established a record and put Hazare in the shade.

As it happened, Merchant did not have many more opportunities that season to score runs. In the next match against Western India he made 53 and Bombay lost. Merchant had one more match, playing for the Rest of India against Western India, who went on to win the Ranji Trophy championship, but after less than an hour on the field he injured himself attempting a catch and did not bat. In just five innings he had scored 865 and had one of his familiar averages: 288.33. Hazare was also playing in the match and, while Merchant nursed his injury, he got into the runs. He made 233 in the first innings, 87 in the second. In just six innings that season he had made: 248, 59, 309, 101, 223 and 87. This was the first time any Indian had scored 1,000 runs in a season. Given how short an Indian season is, it was – and to an extent still is – a quite remarkable achievement. This was a record which not even Merchant had performed. Still Hazare could not help feeling that, if the Indian domestic season were not so peculiar and did not curb opportunities for first-class cricket the moment your team lost, he might have made more runs. That season he felt in such form that he could have scored many more runs.

The season marked a certain divide in Indian cricket. It was the end of the first decade of the Ranji Trophy, and the ten years since Madras had beaten Mysore in a day to start the competition showed how much Indian cricket had changed. For much of the first decade the quick bowlers had dominated the competition. Amar Singh was the first Indian to take 100 wickets and score 1,000 runs which counted as a Ranji double. But now spinners such as Nayudu, Sarwate, Elahi, Shinde and even Tarapore were coming into the game. Indian cricket, from being a theatre of pace, at times raw pace against exuberant batting – measured in sixes and fours – was becoming measured batting against wily spin. This is now the accepted image of Indian cricket: mention Indian cricket and we conjure up a picture of a hot, dusty land, spinners wheeling away hour after hour, and batsmen with monumental patience carefully building their innings. But this transformation only started taking place in the early 1940s. Indeed it was the Hazare-Merchant batting duels that contributed greatly to the transformation and confirmed it.

Inevitably with such prolific scoring they changed the nature of Indian batting. It was not merely that they had answered Lord Harris' jibe that Indians would never be the equal of Englishmen because they could never be as patient. In the batting of Merchant and Hazare patience was often its own reward. The impatient method of the early Parsee batsmen was now not even a dim memory, even the exuberance that C. K. Nayudu brought to his batting was being forgotten. This exuberance had been transmitted to Mushtaq Ali and could be seen in batsmen such as Khandu Rangnekar and Gul Mohammed, but now a new generation was coming to believe, like Merchant, that defence, a solid defence allied to an impregnable technique, was the key to batting. At some stage during his record-breaking feats Merchant discarded the hook and the lofted shot. In his early career, like all Indian batsmen of the 1920s and 1930s, he had not been unafraid to loft the ball into the vacant outfield. But then he read that Bradman never lofted the ball. In the 1933 Bombay Test he had been struck a glancing blow on his chin by an English fast bowler, and immediately discarded the hook – a shot which cannot always be controlled – and kept the ball down, always down. Other Indian batsmen followed Merchant, and the lofted shot, which had been such a feature of Indian cricket, disappeared. For more than twenty-five years the Bombay crowds never saw the ball being lofted, but after it returned, influenced by the younger Pataudi, it did, quite suddenly, win a Test match for India at Bombay in October 1964 – the scene of so much of Merchant's great batting and, with a nice touch of irony, while Merchant was commentating.

Hazare was not quite as defensive as Merchant. The cover-drive, always a flowing cricket stroke, was his great stroke, along with his on-drive. But both men could score runs very quickly. They were to demonstrate this early in the 1944-45 season when a match between CCI and an English Services XI was held in Bombay. There were a number of English cricketers in India then: Jardine, Hardstaff, Compton and Reg Simpson – who at the age of twenty-four had made his first-class debut in this match. Simpson, an RAF pilot, first stationed in Murraypore and then Palam near Delhi, had never thought of playing first-class cricket, but India gave him such a taste for it that when he returned to England he decided to become a first-class cricketer. The match, in contrast to other wartime cricket in India, was more like the wartime cricket in England where the accent was on fun rather than on any serious competitive interest, and Merchant and Hazare showed they could join in as well.

For almost the first time since their great rivalry began they batted together: matching each other stroke for stroke, run for run. 382 runs came in the fourth-wicket partnership, Hazare making 200 not out and Merchant retiring after reaching 201. He later regretted the retirement because he was told that it would count not as a not-out innings but as retired out which would spoil his average. The important point, however, is that the man who, after making 240 not out by tea-time, thinks in terms of batting for the next day instead of going for 300, now nearly hit a century before lunch. His footwork and timing quite dazzled Denis Compton. Hazare, in fact, did score more than 100 runs between the start of play and lunch as he went from his overnight 50 to 163 at lunch – adding 113. It showed that, when the mood struck them, they could tear an attack apart, but not in serious competitive cricket.

The 1944-45 season was to demonstrate this yet again and reveal the influence the Merchant-Hazare school of batting was having on the young players. Rusi Modi was now showing almost the same appetite for runs and the same patience. In the previous season Modi had made his debut and scored 200, 168 and 128, and shared in the record sixth-wicket partnership of 371 with Merchant. But in 1944-45 he overshadowed both Merchant and Hazare. Indian newspapers, which had so long been talking of the two Vs, began talking of the two Ms: Merchant and Modi. Just twenty and still a college student Modi matched Merchant run for run. In the opening match he made 160 against Sind and a 205-run stand with Merchant who made 84. In the next match Modi made 210, Merchant 217 and they shared 373 for the third wicket which is also still an Indian record. Against Baroda Merchant was out first ball – yes, caught off Hazare's bowling – but Modi made 245 not out and held the Bombay innings together. Bombay won by seven wickets.

In the semi-final Merchant was run out for 15 but Modi made 113 and, helped by Uday Merchant scoring 183, Bombay made 620. Bombay won by ten wickets. This meant the final would be against Holkar, led by C. K. Nayudu. Nayudu had led Central India in the early years of the Ranji Trophy, but in 1941 Holkar, the princely state Nayudu had so long served, had taken over from Central India and over the years Nayudu had been slowly building his side. It included many of the players he had brought into cricket: his brother C.S.; Mushtaq Ali, who had wandered about India in search of jobs in cricket before being persuaded by Nayudu to return to Holkar; and, through the accident of war, Denis Compton. Compton was training at Mhow, fourteen miles from Indore, and special permission was sought from the Indian Board to enable him to play. Compton was on his way back to England and this was like a bit of holiday relief before he returned.

The final should have been played on the coir matting wicket at Indore. But Bombay requested that the final be at the Brabourne Stadium and Nayudu agreed. There were stories that Nayudu had been persuaded by Bombay's Hindu Gymkhana who dangled the bait of a benefit match. One can hardly blame Nayudu for being tempted. He knew how unpredictable cricket could be. When the previous Maharajah of Holkar had died, Nayudu found that he was out of the state service and out of cricket full-time. It was the new Maharajah who had revived cricket and provided him with the opportunity. Before the final a benefit match, described as a match to celebrate Nayudu's fiftieth birthday, was held at the CCI. In any case it was just as well that the final was played at Bombay. No other ground but the Brabourne Stadium could have provided a setting for such an epic match.

Bombay batted first and Merchant was the only failure – his 4 was the lowest score in the innings. Everyone else made runs, and Modi 98, in a total of 462. Holkar, led by Mushtaq Ali who made 109, replied with 360. This meant that if the match was drawn, Bombay would win the trophy on the first-innings lead. Bombay batted as though they would be quite happy with that. That year in the Ranji Trophy Merchant had either failed or scored 200. So after the first-innings failure there had to be a double-century from Merchant and a 278 duly followed. It was a monumental innings: eight hours and five minutes, a stand of 226 for the third wicket with Rusi Modi who scored 151, a 246-run stand for the fourth wicket with Cooper who made 104. During the innings Merchant reached his 1,000 runs for the season and the double-century meant he was the only player to score four double-centuries in a season outside England in his home country – there had been a 221 earlier in the season against the Parsees. Merchant was finally caught off C. S. Nayudu and Bombay were all out for 764. Over all they had not been slow: Bombay had batted at more than a run a minute and the whole innings had taken 670 minutes. Only once in cricket history has the second innings of a side been larger – that was by New South Wales with 770 against South Australia in 1920-21. One Holkar player knew the pain of Bombay batting very well. This was C. S. Nayudu, who in the first innings had bowled: 64.5-10-153-6. In the second innings his analysis was: 88-15-275-5. Never could a five-wicket haul have tasted sweeter!

So Holkar, Mushtaq Ali and Denis Compton were left to make a mere 867 to win. Holkar lost wickets early and the burden fell on Mushtaq and Compton. Mushtaq was not a man for huge scores. A

142

quick fifty, a quick hundred was his limit. In India Compton had shown that his pre-war billing as a great batsman was not exaggerated. His 81 in the semi-final on a rain-affected Chepauk wicket had been crucial in getting Holkar to the final. But could two such free-scoring batsmen make the double-, possibly treble-centuries, required. Their incentive was the money offered by an Indore merchant: fifty rupees for every run made after a batsman scored a hundred.

The pair swiftly put on a double-century with Mushtaq becoming the fourth Indian to score a century in each innings of a match. As he did so Denis walked down the wicket and advised caution: 'We can still win this match.' But Mushtaq could never restrain himself and he was caught on 139. This did not deter Compton. Unfortunately, he could not find another Holkar batsman to stay with him. All he wanted was someone to block and he would score the runs. This is just what happened with Rawal, the no. 11, who scored 11, but helped Compton add 109 for the last wicket. When Rawal was out, Compton was 249 not out. Holkar were still beaten by 377 runs. The innings ended on a sour note for, as Compton came off the field, he found that the businessman had vanished, leaving a note saying he had been called away, but no money.

The final, played over six days without a rest day, had produced 2,078 runs, and 694.5 overs in thirty-three hours of play. Every ball of every hour had been relayed by All-India Radio (AIR), then being fashioned in the image of the BBC. Throughout, there was only one commentator: the Parsee A. F. S. Talyarkhan. The first cricket commentator in India, he did not believe in sharing the microphone with anybody – not for him the radio commentary team that is now fashionable. He wanted to do the whole job himself and when AIR insisted on having a team he left in a huff, never to commentate again, except for one Test almost five years later. But if this seems selfish he was also a man of fierce determination with a quite superb ability at describing the game. Even before the war his commentaries were famous, conveying an image of the game, its characters and players far and wide in India. During the war his broadcasts of such matches were to spread the popularity of the game even wider and by the time the war ended his voice had made the game familiar to many who had never watched cricket. Hazare, Merchant, Modi, Mushtaq, even Compton, were now known to many.

But what the Indians did not know and could not tell was how good their game was compared with the rest of the world. On April Fool's Day 1945 they had a chance. Merchant led a team to Ceylon. It suggested that, perhaps, the Indians were living in a fool's paradise. The wet, under-prepared Ceylonese wickets were a world removed from Brabourne Stadium, and Merchant and Hazare looked human.

Merchant was run out for 36, which meant his season's total was 1,323, while Hazare with 70 top-scored with Amarnath. The match was more of a triumph for Mankad. In the war years he had been overshadowed by Merchant and Hazare, but now he took 8 for 35 and gave the Indians a first-innings lead in a drawn match. The Indians knew, however, that any real test of their ability would have to wait until they met more formidable opposition once the war was over.

9

The search for clean shirts
1945-47

Indian cricket should have emerged from the war more confident than cricket anywhere else in the world: strong, vibrant, ready to take on any of the established powers. The old Indian failing had been the inconsistency of the batting and the lack of top-class spinners. But now with Merchant and Hazare the batting was as solid as it would ever be and there was a whole generation of spinners. The south, which in the past had produced few cricketers of national importance and at that mainly batsmen, now had a quality off-spinner in Ghulam Ahmed. Just before the tour to Ceylon in a match against the Madras Governor's XI he had even had the great man out for a cheap score: Merchant, c Johnstone b Ghulam Ahmed, 27.

Also the old Indian question about captaincy appeared to have been resolved. Merchant led the team against Ceylon and in the winter of 1945 he was appointed captain of the Indian team to play an Australian Services side. India had tried to persuade the MCC to tour but England, devastated by war, could not contemplate such a tour so soon. So the Australian Services side, led by Lindsay Hassett, which had played a series of five 'Victory Tests' in England in the summer of 1945 was persuaded to return home via India. If the Maharajah of Patiala's Australians in 1935-36 were the old 'crocks' this was very much a new breed of Australian. Only Hassett had played Test cricket but there were some very promising players, including Cec Pepper, Stan Sismey, Bob Cristofani, Keith Carmody, Jack Pettiford, and above all Keith Miller who was then on the threshold of his explosive international career. They had also drawn the Victory Test series, 2-2, against an England team which – Compton apart, because he was still in India – was nearly as good a side as England could muster.

But for India most of these Australian names were total unknowns and, before the first of the three 'Tests', at Bombay, India oozed confidence. There was some doubt whether Hassett or Cristofani would play and Talyarkhan wrote that he hoped they would. 'If so what might have been a rout will be merely a debacle.' Indian optimism was soon exploded. The Australians made 451, India followed-on, and saved the match only through a last-wicket stand.

What was worse, one of those all-too familiar Indian 'things' had happened. Mushtaq Ali had been in superb form in the early matches and he was chosen for the first 'Test'. He was so feared by the Australians that Hassett, humorously trying to give him a complex, described him as India's 'ugly first-class batsman'. It caused a furore and Hassett went round India explaining that the emphasis was on first-class not on ugly. Mushtaq Ali, of course, was selected for the Bombay Test but just before the match he fell ill and wrote to the Board. The letter went missing and it was only on the morning of the match that the Indians woke up to discover that there was no Mushtaq Ali. There were rumours that he had missed the train to Bombay, that he was seen during the match in the Muslim quarters of the city. The Indian selectors, with Duleep now chairman, retaliated by sacking him for the second Test in Calcutta. Mushtaq protested his innocence and Calcutta, where he was always a great favourite, took up his cause.

Calcutta was then in a near revolutionary state – the rest of India would follow in a few months. Just as the war had seen India, at least after the Congress had been crushed in 1942, as one of the most peaceful places on earth, at the end of the war all the pent-up political feelings burst forth. The match preceding the Calcutta 'Test', between East Zone and the Australians, took place amidst a political riot with troops firing on students. Such was the state of confusion in the city that the players knew little about this. They only became aware when students interrupted the match and demanded a minute's silence for the student dead. The news of Mushtaq Ali's expulsion led to another demonstration – this time by students demanding 'No Mushtaq, no Test'. Duleep was manhandled and Mushtaq was eventually drafted back in.

All this upset the Indians much more than the Australians, who knew India was a strange land where anything could happen. They also drew strength from their shared experiences in the war and their living and playing together as a team. As the home side the Indians only came together on the morning of the match. If the match was being played in their home town they lived at home and could not easily avoid the troubles around them. The Indian team arrived at Calcutta's Howrah station on what the locals call a 'bandh', a strike that had brought the whole city to a grinding halt. There was no transport available and they had to walk the two and a half miles from the station to the hotel. Given all this the Indian performance was probably not all that bad. India trailed the Australian Services in the first innings by 78 but then Merchant, for the first time in the series, showed his form. He had found Cec Pepper's flipper a problem: Pepper had him lbw in the second innings at Bombay. But now Pepper, who had taken 4 for

120, was tamed. When India declared at 350 for 4 Merchant was 155 not out.

Two weeks later the caravan moved to Madras and at last the Indian batting showed the power and mastery it had been displaying in domestic cricket during the war. Merchant failed, lbw once again to Pepper for 11, but Amarnath made 113 and Modi 203 – the first Indian to score a double-century in a representative match. Australia crumbled to the pace of Banerjee and the spin of Sarwate and India were left 92 to win. Even then there were a few hiccoughs. Whitington, a batsman, had only come on to bowl because Hassett wanted a quick finish. But as if affected by nerves Merchant was run out for 35. Hazare was caught and bowled by Whitington for a duck, his first duck in a decade. Eventually Modi snicked a four and India had won its first representative series.

But the victory raised more questions than it answered. It was not so much that India did not know whether this victory against a team that only contained one established Test player meant anything: Indians have a constant need to measure themselves against foreign opposition. The long period of colonial rule had left them with little confidence in their own ability, their own assessment. The Australian visit also seemed to suggest doubts about Merchant's captaincy.

There was his noted defensiveness, a disinclination to take risks. This was in marked contrast to his Bombay mentor, L. P. Jai, a dashing, stylish batsman and an aggressive captain. Merchant's more calculating style of captaincy, weighing everything before deciding, was to set the standard for subsequent Bombay captains. Their first priority was to avoid defeat. Only when that was secure would they chase victory. But Merchant sometimes saw defeat where there was none and this led him to absurd decisions. In the first 'Test' at Bombay, by the time India were bowled out, Australia were left 113 to get in 20 minutes. Merchant instructed his bowlers to bowl wide of the stumps and when the match ended Duleep, furious with rage, shouted at him, 'Merchant, you have brought shame upon Indian cricket.' Hazare has since said that it was Amarnath who suggested the idea but, even if that was so, Merchant had shown a tendency to panic into defence at the first hint he might lose.

Then there was his bowling of Mankad. Somehow he never seemed to use him properly. When Mankad played for the Hindus under Merchant he never seemed to get a bowl. In the 1943 final he had two overs, in the 1944 final one over. Yet against Ceylon and against the Australians he had shown that he was India's best left-arm spinner, a potential match-winner. He had only been rediscovered as a bowler in Ceylon when, with Amarnath deputising for an injured Merchant, he came on to bowl and proved what a mystery he could be for most batsmen. Probably Merchant saw Mankad as a matting-wicket bowler, but then by not giving him a chance on turf he did not help him.

But perhaps the largest question asked about Merchant was to what end were his great scores? His domination of the domestic batting since his return from the tour of England in 1936 could scarcely have been more complete. In eleven seasons he had only thrice averaged below 100. One of those seasons was 1945-46 when he averaged 84 with an aggregate of 840 runs. Yet during this period Bombay, under his captaincy, won the Ranji Trophy only twice. Personal glory had not translated into corporate victory. What was even more disturbing, these high scores often resulted in drawn matches. With matches decided on the first-innings lead, the tactical thinking needed to win a match outright was not being developed. But in Tests it would not matter who had the first-innings lead and any obsession with first-innings lead could result in tactics which, at Test level, might prove counter-productive. This, of course, was not all Merchant's fault. It was a general Indian problem and, to an extent, remains an Indian problem. But Merchant's huge scores exaggerated this and seemed to convert what should have been a two-innings match into a fight for a first-innings lead with its narrow, defensive implications.

This was illustrated in the Ranji Trophy match against Baroda in the 1945-46 season. Bombay took over two full days in a four-day match to score 645. Merchant was finally out for 171, stumped off Elahi. Nimbalkar, the Baroda skipper, knew he could not win or even better Bombay on the first innings. He told his batsmen to make sure they did not lose their wickets. At the end of the fourth day they were 465 for 6, so the match had to be decided on the spin of the coin. A few days later, in a committee room far from the field of play, a coin was spun. Baroda called correctly and Bombay were out of the Trophy. In contrast Holkar, who won the Ranji Trophy for the first time, won all their matches outright: often by an innings. C. K. Nayudu, at fifty-four, provided he had players who believed in him, could still be a formidable leader. Indeed the Holkar team he had built up was now showing itself to be the best team in India and this victory in the Ranji Trophy started a period of awesome consistency in the domestic tournament. For the next half a dozen years Holkar would either win the Trophy or be the team to beat.

Nayudu, of course, was no longer in the running as a Test leader. But another voice from the past had begun to be heard again in the land. When the Nawab of Pataudi had left his selections for the 1936 team in a sealed envelope, he then caught a train from Delhi almost like a character from a 'Wild West' movie. Now the man who had walked away into the sunset returned, as if this was a sequel to an earlier movie. To an extent it was. On 10 January 1946 Pataudi reappeared in Delhi on a cricket field, opening the innings for Southern Punjab against Delhi.

He made 7. Southern Punjab won and were only stopped in the next round by Baroda's luck with the coin. This time the match ended in a tie and Baroda again called correctly.

But in a sense the results did not matter. What mattered was that Pataudi was back. In the Southern Punjab match he had batted with the Maharajah of Patiala, the former Yuvraj, now of course a fully fledged ruler. So could one of these princes be captain of India? If Pataudi, who was such an illustrious batsman, was available, then with his English experience he would be invaluable, so ran the argument. That Pataudi had hardly played serious first-class cricket for ten years, since 1935, and his great moment of glory, a century against Australia, was now a dim memory from 1932, seemed not to matter.

The politicking had been going on for some time, and clues to this had been available in that Bombay-Holkar match in March 1945 when Merchant had a clash about umpiring with Dr Subbaroyan, a prominent Congress politician and also President of the Board. Subbaroyan, upset about a couple of lbw decisions, decided to intervene directly with the umpires. Merchant was furious and ordered him out of the Bombay dressing-room.

Just under ten months after this incident the Board met for its annual meeting in the Connemara Hotel in Madras. It has become known as the Madhatter's Tea Party. Bombay went into the meeting confident it would win. It wanted Homi Contractor to manage the tour, with Merchant as captain. Within a few hours it realised how carefully its opponents had prepared for this moment. Instead of Contractor, Pankaj Gupta, more noted for his experience in running hockey, was appointed manager. Then Duleep found he was voted out from the Selection Committee. Subbaroyan, Nayudu, Deodhar, even De Mello, got more votes than the man who was then India's greatest living cricketer. This so upset C. P. Johnstone, the Madras delegate and the only Englishman present, that he vowed never to attend another Board meeting. Pataudi and Merchant were proposed for the captaincy and Pataudi won by ten votes to eight.

In the days that followed the press was full of reports of how the coup had been organised, who would now divide the spoils. But Pataudi was unperturbed. 'It will do no harm if a lot of dirty linen is washed in public. At least it will enable us to go to England in clean shirts.' The Nawab's motives are not at all clear. In 1941-42, as we have seen, he had explained his refusal to play for India in 1932 and 1936, by saying that selection would have meant trying to please everyone: 'each community, each province and association, and the rich patrons of the game'. His real reason may have had more to do with politics.

Just as the cricket politicking was going on at Madras, the Chamber of Princes was meeting in Delhi with the Nawab of Bhopal, Pataudi's father-in-law, as the Chancellor. The princes were now increasingly concerned about what would happen should the Raj leave India. The Labour government in England seemed to be coming round to the view that, faced by an India where there was an almost revolutionary fervour – in early 1946 the Navy mutinied in Bombay – India could not be held. But the divide and rule policies the British had followed for over two centuries were not easy to unscramble. With the negotiations entering a crucial phase Bhopal was arguing for dominion status for the princely states, and at this stage a prince, his own son-in-law, as captain of the Indian team in England, could prove immensely valuable. Two months before the Indians left for England the Prime Minister, Attlee, sent a Cabinet Mission to India to try to sort out the independence issue.

Whether the Nawab of Pataudi played a part in the political process remains doubtful, but certainly an Indian team led by a prince seemed preferable to a team led by a merchant. The team Pataudi took to England was a reasonably strong side but there were some promising individuals who had been left behind. Pataudi, himself, had wanted Ghulam Ahmed but could not convince the selectors. He felt that, had Ghulam Ahmed come, he would have taken 150 wickets. Amir Elahi, the leg-spinner Compton rated so highly, and two of the most promising fast-medium bowlers, Dattu Phadkar and Fazal Mahmood (who later became a spearhead of the Pakistan attack), were left behind. It is possible that even with these players the tour results would not have been much different but the players would have developed quicker.

It was a wet summer and the Indians not only suffered from the cold and the rain but also lack of food. In rationed England the vegetarians in the party found it particularly difficult and finally appeals had to be made to secure the right food for some of the players. Pataudi, himself, did not enjoy the best of health. He was thirty-six, had last played in England at the end of July 1938 and as *Wisden* wrote was 'but a shadow of the Pataudi England knew so well'. While he was third in the tour average with 981 runs at 46.71, he found top-flight cricket difficult. In five Test innings he made 55 runs at an average of 11. He was always liable to strains, which caused him to retire from the field on a number of occasions and kept him out of a few matches. Like Vizzy he never seemed able to settle on a batting order and 'was too conservative in employment of his attack'. His captaincy was at its worst in the second Test at Old Trafford when he asked England to bat, saw them score 294, then, when India had put on 124 for the first wicket, disastrously changed the batting order. Abdul Hafeez Kardar and Mankad were promoted, they both failed, and India never really recovered.

The reasons Pataudi gave on that occasion were that he feared his batsmen may not have coped with batting on soft wickets. Heavy rain meant that the Old Trafford Test did not start till 2.15pm. Perhaps the inconsistency of Pataudi's approach reflected the inconsistency of India's batting. On plumb, hard wickets, the Indian batsmen were masters. On a green wicket responsive to seam bowling and where there was also some swing, they looked like novices. Nothing illustrated this better than two amazing matches at the end of July when India first played Sussex, then travelled on to Taunton to play Somerset. Against Sussex on a rare warm Saturday, a hard Hove wicket and fast outfield India batted as if this was the Brabourne Stadium. Averaging 90 runs an hour they made 533 for 3 wickets declared, Mankad, Pataudi, Amarnath all scoring hundreds, and Merchant a double-hundred. India won by nine wickets, went down to Taunton and there batted on another hard, true pitch. But this was a cloudy day, the Somerset bowlers could swing the ball in the air. Merchant was out first ball and India were bowled out for 64.

Sometimes the batting could flower in the most unexpected circumstances. Against Surrey in early May, India were 205 for 9 when the no. 11 batsman, Shute Banerjee, joined Chandu Sarwate, the no. 10 who was on 0. As Banerjee walked out the groundsman, as was the custom, accompanied him to ask the Surrey skipper what roller he would like, expecting that he would have to roll the wicket for the Surrey innings in a few minutes' time. It was another three hours and ten minutes before he had the chance to roll the wicket.

Banerjee and Sarwate both scored centuries, Sarwate 124 not out, Banerjee 121 – something no no. 10 and no. 11 had done in the same innings – and they put on 249 runs, looking in not the slightest trouble against an attack of Gover, the Bedser twins, Watts and Parker. Alec Bedser, who had taken five wickets for not much before Banerjee walked in, ended up with 5 for 135. Banerjee finished the tour with a slightly better batting average than Sohoni but, despite being the fastest of the quick bowlers, he did not take enough wickets to force his way into the Test side.

This meant that, in all three Tests, the bowling was opened by Amarnath with either Hazare or Sohoni. None of them was remotely quick. Amarnath bowled with a shuffling run of three paces, off what looked like the wrong foot, but brought to his bowling an almost demonic energy. It was not the pace of Nissar or Amar Singh but it was surprisingly effective. At Lord's in the first Test, after India had been bowled out for 200 on a wicket affected by rain, Amarnath removed the first four English batsmen: Hutton, Washbrook, Compton bowled for a duck, and Hammond for 33. Gibb, never comfortable, stayed with Hardstaff who made 205 not out and the game went away from India. Amarnath finished with 5 for 118 in his first Test since March 1934, the delay being due to the 1936 rumpus. But he could not match Bedser who, in his first Test, was irresistible. In the first innings he had taken 7 for 49, in the second he took 4 for 96, match figures of 11 for 145 to ensure an easy England win by ten wickets.

Amarnath again took five wickets at Old Trafford: Compton, Hammond, Hardstaff, Ikin and Bedser – 5 for 96. In his first 13 overs he conceded 17 runs and at one stage he had figures of 13-4-19-3. Helped by Mankad, who took the other five wickets for 101 runs, England were bowled out for 294. Then came the disastrous switch in the order by Pataudi; India collapsed to 170 and, on the final day, the last-wicket pair of Hindlekar and Sohoni had to bat for 13 minutes to gain a draw. India, set 278 to win, were hanging on for dear life at 152 for 9 when the Test ended.

The last Test was virtually a wash-out. Play started at five o'clock on the first day – it then used to be a Saturday – only because about 10,000 people had gathered outside The Oval. There was no play after lunchtime on Tuesday. Only the Indian innings was completed but in that time the reputation of one Indian, Merchant, was reconfirmed and that of another, Mankad, established. Opening the innings Merchant made 128 in quite masterly fashion, says *Wisden*, in five and a quarter hours. The usual Merchant virtues were there: concentration, 'late cuts and pulls', total absorption. Hammond frequently changed the bowlers to try and disturb Merchant, but eventually he fell to one of the most amazing run-outs in cricket history. He started for a short run, Mankad sent him back and Compton running behind the bowler at mid-on kicked the ball on to the stumps in a style that belonged more to Highbury than The Oval!

That innings meant that Merchant easily topped the Test averages. In five innings he had made 245 runs, averaging 49. Almost inevitably he topped the tour averages with 2,385 runs at an average of 74.53. He had become the first Indian to score 2,000 runs on a tour. *Wisden* wrote, 'No praise can be too high for Merchant who, on any reckoning, must be counted one of the world's greatest batsmen. Merchant gave of his best in every situation, showing a degree of concentration and determination, especially on a big occasion such as a Test match, more developed and controlled than any batting of his team-mates . . . his cutting, both square and late, touched the height of brilliance; he hooked, drove and played the ball off his legs with a masterly certainty and, with all his triumphs, remained a charming, unassuming man and a studious captain whenever Pataudi was absent.'

This last was, perhaps, the most interesting observation. Pataudi's selection as captain had prompted suggestions that Merchant might not tour. Bombay, itself, was in revolt and just before the tour began the *Times of India* even advised Bombay to break from the Indian Board and declare independence. But Merchant hid his disappointment at not leading India because, as he liked to put it, he was a 'disciplined soldier of cricket. I have grown up in an atmosphere of cricket which places the game before the self.' It is possible that Merchant benefited from the fact that he was not captain. As captain of Bombay his batting was not affected but as captain of India it might well have been.

Unlike some of his contemporaries Merchant had the ability to shut himself away from the world. R. S. Whitington, on the Australian Services tour in India, had noticed how at lunch and tea intervals Merchant could divorce himself completely from the cricket, chatting amicably about everything under the sun. Now on this tour he cocooned himself in his batting. This was a great challenge, greater than the 1936 tour. Merchant was a strict vegetarian and did not even eat eggs. Pataudi had warned his team not to patronise the few Indian restaurants that existed then in England. They used a type of oil that Pataudi distrusted. Merchant lost a stone in weight but with a woollen muffler round his neck and three sweaters he just carried on.

His colleagues could not cope with the privations of food, the constant changes in weather, the constant travelling. Used to playing half a dozen first-class matches in good light and warm, sultry conditions they found six-days-a-week cricket with long coach journeys exhausting. Merchant alone seemed unaffected. There were the odd failures, particularly against Yorkshire when in three innings he made 2, 18 and 7. And when he was out first ball to Andrews of Somerset, Andrews did not realise he had got Merchant's wicket. After a few more Indian wickets had gone, he asked, 'When do we see Merchant?'

But otherwise Merchant, whatever the conditions, made runs. The true nature of a great batsman is that he makes runs when others fail. Merchant showed this in Leicester, for instance. He faced cold, bad light, rainstorms and a wicket of different paces but made 111 not out in a total of 198 when no other batsman made 30. His first 50 came in 75 minutes which, given the conditions, was remarkable. In the second innings he made 57 not out, out of 107; nobody else made more than 16. Only one other batsman in the entire match on either side made more than 30.

It was the Lancashire match which showed his ability to dominate an innings. In the first match at Liverpool his 93 not out, along with Pataudi's 80 not out, had seen India to an eight-wicket victory. In the return match at Old Trafford, Lancashire made 406: Washbrook 108, Ikin 139, Place 46, Wharton 73. India replied with 456 for 8 of which Merchant made 242 not out. No other Indian batsman reached 50. In eight hours and ten minutes, says *Wisden*, he scarcely played a false stroke. If this was not devastatingly quick he also showed England how quickly he could bat when in the Sussex match he scored 205, out of 314, in just three and a half hours.

Merchant's batting did answer one question which Indians had been asking: who was the greater of the two – Vijay Merchant or Vijay Hazare. Vijay Hazare was second in the averages but some way behind: 1,344 runs at 49.77. And in the Tests his highest score was 44 at an average of 24.60. The comparison is not entirely fair because Hazare was a genuine all-rounder. He bowled 604 overs on the tour and was second in the bowling averages with 56 wickets at 24.75. This must have affected his batting though he himself felt he had not adapted quickly enough to the English wickets. As a batsman he liked to get on the front foot, whereas the slow, green wickets of 1946 demanded more back play. When he found a wicket where he could get on to the front foot and play his flowing, lovely drives, he could be irresistible.

Against Yorkshire at Bradford on a wet wicket he found Booth quite difficult: out for 29 and 18 in a sorry Indian batting display. But in the return match on a hard, fast wicket at Bramall Lane, in front of a packed Yorkshire crowd, Hazare was back at his Indian best. He made 244 not out in six and a half hours. He offered one chance, but that was after he had made 232. Pataudi batted with him towards the end of the innings, making 51 not out, and waited till Hazare had gone past Merchant's 242 not out against Lancashire before declaring. The story went that the Nawab wanted to make sure that Hazare had at least one batting honour Merchant could not take away: the highest score of the tour.

To an extent Hazare could feel deprived by the war. Had the 1940 tour of England taken place he would have come on an English tour at the age of twenty-five, just coming into his prime. Now he was thirty-one, less able to take the strain of such a relentless tour. This was also true of Amarnath, who was thirty-five, and had an even bigger share of the bowling: 782 overs, more than twice as many as the other pure bowlers in the side like Shinde, C. S. Nayudu and Banerjee. Amarnath also was unfortunate in that an injury in the first match affected his batting confidence and he only showed his great batting form spasmodically. He came nowhere near performing the double that he would so dearly have loved to do.

The double is, of course, the proof of an all-rounder's true worth. Not many tourists do or did the double. Nor was the wet summer of 1946 a great one for English doubles. Only one Englishman did it: the Worcestershire player, Dick Howorth. This shows that Mankad's achievement in becoming the first Indian (and the last tourist) to do so is astounding. It almost immediately put him in the select company of cricketers like Constantine who was the last visiting player to do the double, in 1928. Mankad, at twenty-nine, was not all that much younger than Hazare but he was in peak condition and thrived on the

154

hard work. *Wisden*'s comment that 'few men have accomplished finer deeds on their first first-class cricket tour to England', can hardly be bettered. He was 'seldom collared', bowling 1,160.1 overs and taking 129 wickets at an average of 20.76. He bowled 380 more overs than any other bowler, taking twice as many wickets as Amarnath or Hazare, the next most successful bowlers. Mixing flight, guile and pace his stock ball was the leg-break spun hard with his fingers and his wicket-taking ball the faster one that went with the arm. *Wisden* noted that, had the Indian catching been anything like adequate, he would, probably, have got another forty or even fifty wickets.

When, at the Oval Test, he had Hutton lbw for 25 and Washbrook caught for 17, Arthur Gilligan, watching this new generation of Indian bowlers, was in raptures. The best left-hander he had ever seen, said Gilligan. Best? Better than Rhodes, Blythe, Verity? Yes, said Gilligan, better than them. Perhaps Mankad lacked the 'devil' of those great bowlers on sticky wickets. In India rain-affected wickets were unknown and, brought up on firm hard wickets where he had to work hard to get batsmen out, he did not always exploit a bad wicket as effectively as he might, except against the MCC when, after rain had made the wicket difficult, Mankad took 7 for 37 and India won by an innings.

As a batsman, Mankad felt the capricious Pataudi batting order to the full: sometimes he batted no. 1, sometimes no. 9. But this did not seem to affect him. It allowed him scope to display his versatility. He scored three hundreds – 132 against Yorkshire, 109 against Middlesex, 105 against Sussex – shared in seven century stands and some of them were the biggest on the tour: 293 with Merchant for the first against Sussex, 322 with Hazare for the fourth against Yorkshire, 227 unfinished with Hazare for the sixth, against Middlesex, and 110 with Merchant for the eighth, against Lancashire. His season's tally was 1,120 runs at an average of 28.00.

Mankad was clearly the future of Indian cricket but what about Merchant? Could he become captain? Pataudi had indicated he might want to take India to Australia. Despite the loss at Lord's India's overall tour record was not bad: played 29, won 11, lost 4, drawn 14 was the best ever and was to remain so until 1986. So was Merchant destined never to captain India in a proper Test series? The general assumption was that Merchant would soon inherit his rightful place but as events were to prove the English tour was almost his farewell to Test cricket.

At thirty-six he had put his body through a most strenuous exercise. In 1936 as a young man of twenty-six it could cope with the sudden doubling of first-class matches within a space of five months. At thirty-six, after years of averaging five first-class matches per season, he had suddenly played twenty-six matches in five months. Could the body take the strain? Hazare later came to the conclusion that his rival had asked too much from his body on that tour. Even if this was not true events in India soon conspired to make it seem like that.

10

A new age
1947-49

At midnight on 15 August 1947, the Union Jack was lowered from the ramparts of Delhi's Red Fort, the Indian tricolour hoisted, and Jawaharlal Nehru, India's first prime minister, spoke of his country keeping its tryst with destiny. India was free after two hundred years of British rule. But for many Indians the joy and sheer elation of the moment was dimmed by the partition of the country into India and Pakistan.

The shock of it was all the greater because, until it happened, nobody thought it would happen – but then not many people could convince themselves that the British would leave – and when Partition came it produced one of the century's most violent moments. The Punjab had been partitioned between Pakistan and India. Hindus trapped in what was a Muslim country sought to flee to India, Muslims from India sought to flee to Pakistan. Punjab, which over the centuries had seen huge armies marching back and forth fighting the great battles that decided the destiny of India, now saw millions dragging themselves across its hot, dusty plains in search of peace and security. The violence and the carnage this produced were almost as great as any war.

Through September of 1947 some ten million people were on the move in the Punjab in one of the greatest exchanges of population known in human history. Half a million or perhaps even a million never reached their sanctuary. Nobody even now knows how many were killed. Hindus and Muslims who had lived side by side for decades now fell on each other with medieval ferocity. As Hindus arrived from Pakistan with dreadful stories of massacre at the hands of the Muslims, Hindus in India fell upon Muslims. The savage within us that is held back by the thin veneer of civilisation, as John Buchan had written, now broke free.

Cricket, part of that thin veneer of civilisation, was an irrelevance in such a context. India lost cricketers like Fazal Mahmood, Amir Elahi and the young Hanif Mohammad who, born in Junnagadh in India, took the train to Pakistan. But horrific as the carnage was in Punjab, life in its strange way continued. Apart from Delhi in the

157

north and Calcutta in the east, where Hindu and Sikh refugees came pouring in, in most other parts of India the Punjab horrors came in the shape of newspaper headlines and chilling radio news but there was little direct physical impact. Except that communal cricket was now considered an anathema. In fact even a year before that, in the winter of 1946, communal cricket had effectively disappeared.

The great matches between Hindus, Muslims, Parsees and the Rest which had nurtured Bombay and Indian cricket were now seen as an ugly manifestation of communalism in sport. Politics was dividing along religious lines. Cricket could only perpetuate these divisions by having a team of Hindus playing against a team of Muslims. Gandhi, who took no interest in cricket whatsoever, although he was a contemporary of Ranji and came from the same part of the world, had pronounced that he was opposed to communalism in sport. For some years now there had been agitation to stop these games. Initially Bombay had seen it as a move directed against its cricket, but in the end had to give way.

The summer of 1946 – even as the Indian team was on tour in England – provided a foretaste of the religious frenzy that was to sweep Punjab a year later: carnage in Calcutta, riots in Bombay. De Mello, Secretary of the Board and soon to become its President, vividly described to the Board scenes he had witnessed and in the winter of 1946 the Pentangular became not a contest between different religious communities but mixed teams from all religions organised in the names of the Presidents of the five communal gymkhanas. Merchant played for Dr C. R. Pereira's XI – the doctor himself being a Christian – against an XI playing under the name of Sir Homi Mehta, one of the city's leading Parsees.

Of course, such matches could not quite recapture the fervour and the enthusiasm of the real Pentangular matches although, in Merchant's case, it produced a unique performance. He made 142, the first of his two centuries that season – an under-average one for him with 469 runs at 46.90 – and took a hat-trick. None of the batsmen was of the top order but it remains the only instance of this feat being performed in domestic cricket outside England. Apart from his early days Merchant had hardly bowled his medium-pacers – in his first-class career he bowled a total of 847 overs, taking 65 wickets – but this season he seemed determined to prove himself as all-round cricketer. He not only took wickets but, in the match against Baroda, took two brilliant catches, one to remove Hazare. Merchant was always a safe rather than a flashy fieldsman. These two catches considerably surprised the batsmen and even Merchant's own team.

They were not quite enough to win the match, however. Merchant made 33 in a score of 269 but Hazare made up for his batting by taking 6 for 88 and giving Baroda the vital first-innings lead. Merchant's all-round effort quite paled in comparison with Hazare's who virtually won the Ranji Trophy for Baroda. In every match he did something either with the bat or the ball, in some he proved himself to be a genuine all-rounder, opening the bowling to skittle the opposition, then knocking off the runs himself. In only four Ranji Trophy matches he took 38 wickets at 19.30, and made 561 runs at an average of 80.14. More than half those runs came in the final, which was to provide one of the greatest feats of all-round skill India has ever seen.

The final was against Holkar, this time on the matting of Baroda. Hazare took 6 for 85 with medium-pace cutters to bowl out Holkar for just over 200. Baroda were 91 for 3 when Gul Mohammed joined Hazare. There could be no greater contrast. The batsman who often made the heart leap into one's mouth joined the batsman who rarely made the heart flutter. Mr Chance and Mr Dependable.

As so often in this era the deeds of other Indian batsmen were a spur. Earlier in the season Amarnath and Modi had put on 410, which was the record for any Indian wicket. Once their partnership had begun to blossom Hazare made this his target. Gul Mohammed led the way as he always tried to do. 410 came and went, the pair still went on. They passed 500. Now there was another target. The previous year at Port of Spain Frank Worrell and Clyde Walcott had set up a world record for any wicket: 574. So Hazare, having passed Amarnath and Modi's record, now readjusted his sights. After nearly two full days they passed that too. The partnership had reached 577 and the Baroda total was 668 for 3 when a wicket fell. Gul Mohammed was out for 319.

Hazare was yet to reach his triple-century. It would have been the third of his career but he was out for 288. Gul Mohammed had taken seven minutes short of nine hours for his 319, Hazare had batted for ten and a half hours for his 288. This was one Hazare record no-one would break. It remains the highest partnership for any wicket anywhere in the world. The rest of the match was forgotten in the euphoria. Baroda reached 784 and Holkar collapsed in the second innings.

So, as India prepared for the first tour to a country other than England, everything seemed right in the Indian cricket garden. Hazare and Merchant in their familiar rivalry. Despite the rising political and religious passions the Indian Board, excited by the prospects of the tour, prepared as if nothing would disturb cricket. With the Indian tour to Australia coinciding with the 1947-48 domestic season it was decided that selection would be made on the basis of the 1946-47 season which concluded nearly six months before India was due to leave for Australia. Long before 15 August 1947 the team to tour had been selected. De Mello, now President of the Board, spoke of the team selection displaying the whole map of India, a remark which was meant to counter the familiar criticisms of regional bias. But on 15 August the map itself had been redrawn. Half of Punjab, the half that had produced some of the great bowlers like Nissar, was now gone and Fazal Mahmood, who should have gone to England and had been selected for Australia, withdrew. Overnight an Indian cricketer had become a foreign national.

There followed those withdrawals and rumours of withdrawals that always seem to plague the preliminaries of an Indian tour. Merchant reported a mysterious groin strain and there was something possibly wrong with his stomach. Had he perhaps over-exerted himself on the English tour? It did not seem serious enough but Merchant, at last given the chance of captaining India on an official tour, withdrew. So did Modi, and there was a very peculiar business with Mushtaq Ali.

He was fit and raring to go, and Merchant's withdrawal meant Amarnath as captain and Mushtaq Ali as vice-captain. But just before the team was due to leave Mushtaq's elder brother died. In Indian families, as in Mushtaq's case, most people live in joint families. Mushtaq from being the younger brother was now head of an extended family which included his own and that of his brother. He telegraphed De Mello that he could not go.

Since Mushtaq had gone AWOL in the Board's view once before, no doubt the Board was wary of him. Perhaps there were others who saw an opportunity to 'push' (the word the Indians themselves use) their particular candidate. In any event when, a few weeks later, after the period of mourning was over, Mushtaq was persuaded by the Maharajah of Holkar to go on the tour he found that the Indian Board did not want him. Vice-captain one minute, nonentity the next. The team had not yet left Calcutta for their long flight to Australia, and the Maharajah was prepared to meet his travelling expenses. But when he telegraphed the Board De Mello replied that a replacement had been found and it was too late. Mushtaq was convinced he had been another victim of India's perennial cricket plots.

If so, it was a short-sighted policy on De Mello's part. Without Merchant and Mushtaq Ali, India went on the tour without a recognised opening pair. Mankad opened with Chandu Sarwate. In England Sarwate had usually batted no. 10, scoring from there that century against Surrey, and while he did open for his state, the task of facing Bradman's Australians – Lindwall, Miller, Toshack and Johnston – was too great for him. In the five Tests Mankad and Sarwate's opening partnerships were: 0, 14; 2, 17; 124, 10; 6, 0; 3, 0. In contrast Merchant and Mushtaq Ali's opening stands in Test cricket – all against England – had been: 18, 203; 81, 64 (in 1936) and then 124, 0; 94 (in 1946).

So without a good start India were always struggling. Even with

Merchant, Mushtaq Ali and Modi, Bradman's Australians, arguably one of the greatest ever Test sides, would probably have proved too strong. But at least they might have made it a more equal contest. Without them India were thoroughly outclassed. For the first time they played a five-Test series, each Test lasting five days. Often they looked beaten at the end of the first day, and they lost three Tests by an innings and one by 233 runs.

The Indian team needed everyone to play to the top of their form. They needed luck. They had neither. Bradman won the toss in four of the five Tests and in two of the matches India had the worst of the batting conditions. In the first Test India was caught on a Brisbane 'sticky': heavy rain which saturated the pitch followed by hot sun. Australia had won the toss, batted in the most beautiful conditions and Bradman made 185. India batted on an uncovered wicket where the ball did 'all manner of unexpected tricks' as *Wisden* put it; one would skid through, the next one would pop, and they were bowled out for 58 and 98. In the third Test at Melbourne India were comfortably placed when overnight rain changed the nature of the pitch and caused a collapse. Amarnath declared, hoping to catch Australia on a bad wicket. Bradman sent in Dooland and Johnson, no. 9 and no. 10, to open and when the wicket improved came in himself to make another century. Another heavy Indian defeat.

But in one Test Amarnath won the toss, batted first and the Australians showed that they found uncovered rain-affected wickets just as difficult. Hazare, like Toshack, could be very effective with his medium-pace bowling. He took 4 for 29 and Bradman made 13, the only innings when he did not score a hundred, except for the fifth Test when he retired hurt at 57. Australia were bowled out for 107 but rain ruined any chance of a result.

This Test showed that the Indians were not as bad as the results suggested. Outside the Tests they had their moments, particularly just before the series began in Sydney when, against an Australian XI which was almost the Test team, they won by 47 runs. Bradman made his hundredth hundred in this game but the match belonged to Mankad who took 8 for 84 in the second innings and the Australians, set 252, lost by 47 runs.

Then there was Amarnath's batting. In the first match he made 0, but then there was 144 against South Australia, 228 not out against Victoria, 172 against Queensland, 171 against Tasmania: 1,162 runs on the tour at 58.10 and he easily headed the averages. But only 140 of those runs came in the Tests where his highest score was 46 and his average just 14. Harvey fielded in the covers that day in Melbourne when Amarnath tore apart the Victoria attack of Johnston, Johnson, Loxton and Ring. Probably the best cover-point in the world then, Harvey could not get anywhere near Amarnath's fours and remains convinced that it was the best cover-driving he has ever seen. Amarnath's 228 took just six and a half hours. But in Tests he just could not perform, perhaps another case of an Indian captain finding the task of leadership too daunting.

So India were left in the familiar position of consoling herself with individual achievements. Mankad carried on from where he had ended the English tour. Once again he was the bowling workhorse and the leading wicket-taker. He headed the tour bowling with 61 wickets, twice as many as Amarnath – next in the averages – and bowled 494.3 overs, 200 more overs than Amarnath. If his bowling in the Tests was more expensive, 12 wickets at 52.50, it just showed the mastery of the Australian batsmen. In the Tests his batting was more significant and for this he was indebted to Lindwall. In his first four innings Mankad had made 0, 7, 5, 5, thrice bowled by Lindwall, once caught by Tallon off Lindwall. Finally Mankad went up to Lindwall and asked him what was wrong. 'You bring your bat down much too late on the yorker,' Lindwall told him.

After that Mankad, ever a good learner, watched for the fearful Lindwall yorker. In the next Test he made 116, the first century by an Indian in Tests in Australia. His subsequent scores were: 13, 49, 0, 111, 0. The two noughts he made were also against Lindwall but both times he fell to the out-swinger and was caught by Tallon. Whenever he managed to escape the early Lindwall yorkers and out-swingers he scored runs.

Mankad's achievements were overshadowed by Hazare, though his moment of batting glory came on two successive days. In England Hazare had not been quite able to produce the full mastery of his Indian form. Neither did he in Australia. And for some time he seemed to follow Amarnath. Like him in the first match he had scored a duck, both falling to the googly bowler Herbert, and like him he only appeared capable of scoring outside the Tests: 95 against South Australia, 83 against Victoria, 142 against New South Wales, 115 against Tasmania. On the tour he was second to Amarnath with 1,056 runs at an average of 48.

But in the Tests he could not get going. His first six innings were: 10, 18, 16, 13 not out, 17, 10. He had been so keen to impress his guru Grimmett but he kept finding ways of getting out, even (like Amarnath) falling to Barnes who was hardly a regular bowler.

Then in the fourth Test at Adelaide Hazare at last found his form. It could not have been in more depressing circumstances. Australia had made 674: Bradman 201, Hassett 198 not out, Barnes 112. It was the biggest total for any Test match in Australia. Hazare came in to bat on the third day when India were 69 for 3. For the first time in the Tests Amarnath was making runs, but on 46 he was caught by Bradman off Johnson and Gul Mohammed his partner in the great stand against Holkar walked in. If ever a pair needed to replay their act this was the occasion. The conditions could not have been more like in India but Gul was never a batsman who could restrain himself and he was stumped off Johnson for 4 – Gul Mohammed never showed his Indian form, making just 130 runs in 10 innings for an average of 13 – and it seemed Hazare just would not find a partner. It was only after half the side was out for 133 that Hazare did find a partner: Dattu Phadkar. Although Phadkar had begun the tour more as an opening bowler than as a batsman – in the first match of the tour he had batted no. 10 – it was his batting that surprised the Australians. Just over a month before this in his first Test Phadkar, coming in at no. 8, had made 51. In the next Test he was promoted to no. 6 and made 55 not out. Now he was determined and aggressive enough to hook Lindwall's and Miller's bouncers. He and Hazare put on 188. Throughout the third day they batted, Hazare making 108, Phadkar 77. India were 308 for 5 at the close. Next morning Hazare was finally lbw for 116 and the innings virtually collapsed with him. Amidst the flurry of wickets Phadkar, in near desperation, reached his century. He was finally out for 123, the total being 381.

This was not enough to save the follow-on and, no sooner had the innings started, than Hazare was back in the middle. India were 0 for 2, both Mankad and Amarnath falling to Lindwall. At 33 Sarwate went and Hazare was joined again by Gul Mohammed. This time Gul Mohammed was a bit more patient. When the score reached 99, Bradman brought on Barnes. In his Test career Barnes only ever took four wickets, each at 54.50. Three of them were in this series and Gul Mohammed was the third victim when he was bowled for 34. The pair who held the world record for the highest number of runs for any wicket, 577, had put on six runs in the first innings and 66 in the second. Of such inconsistencies is Indian batting made. Phadkar made only 14, but at 139 for 6 Hazare found another reliable partner: his Baroda colleague, Hemu Adhikari. They put on 132, with Hazare making most of the runs. At the end of the fourth day Hazare was again not out: 102 out of 174 for 6. Adhikari stayed with him till the score reached 271, Adhikari making 51 in a stand of 132. Almost immediately Kischenchand, Rangnekar and Rangachari were dismissed by Lindwall – none of them scoring. Hazare was last out, bowled by Lindwall. But he had made 145 out of 277.

Only one other Indian, Adhikari, had passed 50. There had been five ducks in the innings and one 0 not out. In two days' batting the rest of the Indian side, Phadkar and Adhikari apart, had made 207 runs in two innings. Hazare had made 261 on his own. By any measure Hazare's was a great achievement. Given how little support he received it was quite astounding. It was also the first truly international cricket achievement by an Indian. Before that Indian cricketers had made their mark with both bat and ball but they were good rather than great events. There was something epic about this achievement. Hazare had moved into a very select company of batsmen who had made two centuries in a Test match: Headley, Sutcliffe, Bardsley, Hammond, Compton and Bradman himself, who had done it in the Test immediately preceding this one. Since Hazare, many others have performed this feat and the list is steadily growing but in the 1940s only half a dozen or so batsmen had done so and suddenly Hazare was a member of an exclusive club.

The one problem was that the praise that was lavished on Hazare by Bradman, by Duleep, even by Robert Menzies, the Prime Minister of Australia, obscured the wretchedness of the overall Indian performance. And consoling as it was it helped India shut out the pain of the Australian tour by thinking of Hazare's epic innings. The whole tour became just a case of Hazare scoring a hundred in each innings. In years to come it set a precedent. Indians would come back from a wretched overseas tour blocking any memory of the defeat and the humiliations by concentrating on the odd moments of individual glory. That, in itself, is not surprising. Defeats can only be sustained by the hope of individual promise but it meant that the fundamental problems which had caused the defeats in the first place were, at times, obscured.

Perhaps there is some virtue in such an attitude. It had enabled the Hindus to survive as a nation for almost 5,000 years despite appalling defeats and now, for the winter of 1948-49, India looked forward in surprisingly good heart to the visit of the West Indies. In the first fifteen years of international cricket, albeit interrupted by war, India had played ten Tests, all against England. Now in the space of two years India would have doubled that number, playing five each against Australia and the West Indies. Merchant was still *hors de combat* with his mysterious ailment and, despite the defeats in Australia, there were no realistic challengers to Amarnath as captain.

The West Indies were a totally unknown quantity for India. Nor were they then as powerful as they have since become, but while India was being thrashed in Australia the West Indies were beating an England team led by G. O. Allen. There were only two West Indian names that meant anything to Indians: Headley and Constantine. Constantine had retired but Headley was still playing and the Indians insisted he tour. They feared that without him the gates might be affected.

They need not have worried. Although Headley played only in

the first Test huge crowds watched each Test and even the zonal matches. The withdrawal of the British, far from affecting cricket, seemed to have increased its popularity. The Congress Raj had effectively taken over from the British Raj, and cricket was now part of the Indian scene. If anything it was more important. This was partly due to the Gandhi philosophy which sought to discriminate between the evil of imperialism and the good that the Raj wrought, but also because Pandit Nehru was more aware of cricket than Gandhi. He had not distinguished himself at the game while at Harrow, nor at Cambridge, but he had played it and begun to appreciate it. In his long fight against the British his love for Harrow actually deepened. When he was jailed by the British, as he often was, he used to stick pictures of Harrow on the prison walls and sing the school songs. Now as independent India's first prime minister – who was increasingly referred to as the country's first English prime minister – he became an active patron and supporter of the game; and he used regularly to turn out for the annual Parliamentary Match.

It was largely due to Nehru that Delhi, which had never before staged a Test or representative match, now hosted the first Test between India and the West Indies. Since this was the first Test which independent India would play at home, he considered it vital to play it in the capital. Other politicians followed Nehru's lead and this too was crucial for cricket's development. Even without it cricket might have developed but it is interesting to contrast cricket with hockey.

Here was another British game, successfully taken up by the Indians. Indeed India were world champions in hockey and enjoying one of the longest win sequences in sport. They won the Olympic Crown – which in those days was the only international competition – in 1928 and did not lose a hockey match in the Olympics till 1960. Cricket, in contrast, produced heartache. Yet while hockey is played and followed all over the country (though it is especially strong in the Punjab), it remains a sport ranked much below cricket. Unlike with cricket Nehru did nothing to encourage it.

The crowds came to the 1948-49 series despite India's uneven performances. In the first two Tests West Indies made huge scores, India followed-on, and then saved the match with some ease. The third match – also a draw – was the first in which the West Indians had to bat a second time. Headley in his only Test innings made 2, but West Indies now had a new champion in Everton Weekes. Weekes had scored a century in his last Test against England in Jamaica in March 1948. In his first four Test innings in India he scored 128, 194, 162, 101 and that record of five consecutive Test hundreds still stands. In his fifth innings, during the fourth Test in Madras, he was run out controversially for 90.

That, as it happened, was the one Test which the West Indies won. In the three previous Tests they had huge scores but could not bowl the Indians out twice. Neither side had great fast bowlers, nor were the spinners of either side match-winning bowlers. India acquired a reputation for collapsing in the first innings but for batting strongly in the second, which made Vallabhai Patel, the Deputy Prime Minister, say that India should play her second innings first. They seemed to follow his advice in Madras by making 245 runs in the first and only 144 in the second. The problem was that the West Indians, in their only innings, made 582 when Amarnath, unable to dislodge the openers, instructed Phadkar to bowl bouncers. The tactics backfired. The West Indians, instinctive hookers, fell for the bouncers and Phadkar got seven wickets, though for 159, but when the West Indians retaliated the Indians had no answer.

Defeat can sometimes be a spur and the Indians still believed they could beat the West Indians. In the final Test at Bombay – the second Test at Brabourne Stadium that season – the Indian bowlers suddenly struck form. The previous Bombay Test had seen the West Indians make 629. Now, for the first time in the series they were bowled out for less than 300: only 286. India, in turn, were bowled out for 193. West Indies led by 93. But then the Indian bowlers, with Shute Banerjee, the Bengali fast bowler on his Test debut, taking 4 for 54, repeated their feat and for the first time in the series the West Indians were bowled out twice in the match. India were left to make 361 to win in 395 minutes.

In theory that was a difficult fourth-innings total to make. But the wicket had improved as the match went on and India had shown, in the Calcutta Test, that large targets did not worry them. There they had been set 431 to win and had easily saved the game with 325 for 3. India needed a good start this time, but Mushtaq Ali, the century-maker of Calcutta, went for 6, Ibrahim, his partner, for 1. Amarnath, furious, promoted himself in the order and played a little gem of an innings, just 39, but it took the sting from the West Indian attack. However, just before the close he was out, there was no nightwatchman and Hazare had to go out to join Modi. India finished the fourth day on 90 for 3. It was really 90 for 4 as the wicket-keeper, Probir Sen, by no means a bad batsman, was injured. The West Indians reckoned that the Indians could not possibly score 271 in 300 minutes on the last day.

But by lunch on the fifth day the West Indians were revising their opinions and beginning to feel nervous. Modi and Hazare were still together. They had scored 85 runs and the target looked ever closer. Over lunch Stollmeyer, who because of leg strain was resting in the pavilion, warned Goddard not to take the new ball until the partnership had broken. The rate of scoring increased after lunch. India were well over 200 for 3 when Gomez, the vice-captain, took matters in hand. The captain, Goddard, was no great strategist or tactician. He had to be pushed into a course of action, and Gomez, prompted by Headley, advised Goddard to bring back Jones and Gomez himself and use leg-theory.

Gomez recalls, 'It looked as if the rate of scoring was getting out of hand. So we decided to pack the leg-side field. There were two men behind square, there was one on the deep backward boundary, a mid-on, mid-wicket and one more on the leg side, six in all on the leg side, just three on the off side with a cover very short to stop the single. We bowled so that the batsmen could not drive, we bowled across the batsmen going down the leg stump. It was negative tactics but we were quite entitled to use negative tactics. It was within the Laws.'

And so was 'body-line' when it was tried out by Jardine. Today both body-line and the field which Gomez persuaded Goddard to set would be ruled illegal as there are fielding restrictions on the leg side. The Indians had never seen anything like this. Suddenly the runs dried up. Hazare thought of taking guard outside the leg stump to try to counterattack. Modi, after an excellent 86, fell trying to speed up the scoring.

Still the Indians would not give up the chase. Hazare and Phadkar came together and Hazare reached his century. Not even Gomez's negative tactics would work, it seemed, but on 122 Hazare was hit by a short ball from Prior Jones. He could barely stand, but Phadkar, instead of sparing him, called him for a quick single. When, a few balls later, he had to face Jones again he was bowled. At tea, with a further ninety minutes' play possible, India needed 72 to win with four wickets in hand.

The Indians had never come so close to victory in a Test match. Bombay was agog with excitement. The crowds anxiously debated the possibilities. If somebody stayed with Phadkar, then it would be all right. Adhikari was a major batsman, surely he could provide the support? But soon after tea, Adhikari went for 8. Shute Banerjee had done nothing with the bat since his century against Surrey in 1946, but he could bat and now he hit a six before falling to Jones. Two more wickets to fall – in effect one as Sen was unlikely to bat – and 40 runs to win.

Ghulam Ahmed came to join Phadkar. He was not much of a batsman, and was to play many more Tests and finish up with a batting average of 8.92. But now all that was required was that he stay with Phadkar. And he did, occasionally scoring a few runs himself but leaving most of it to Phadkar.

With fifteen minutes left 21 runs were wanted. The West Indies were now desperate. Even their negative tactics had not worked. The Laws permitted one drinks interval in every session. So with only fifteen minutes of the match remaining Goddard asked for drinks. A few minutes saved. They had dominated India for so long in the series that the thought of defeat seemed almost physically difficult to bear. They kept within the letter of the Laws but violated its spirit in order to deny the Indians victory. What possible method could they use to thwart the Indians? Walcott thought of one. He was keeping wicket and when the ball went down to the fine-leg boundary he waddled after it to retrieve it and give it back to the bowler.

Even then with two possible overs remaining India required 11 runs to win. As Jones bowled, Stollmeyer recorded it in his diary. First ball down the leg side, no stroke possible. Second ball short on the leg stump, Phadkar steps back and hits through the covers for four. Third ball on the pads again, pushed for a single, fourth ball another push to the on, a single possible but not taken. Fifth ball a bouncer, way over batsman's head. India now needed 6 runs to win from the last ball and one more over as the clock showed another minute and a half to go. But the sixth ball was never bowled. Nor another over.

In the excitement Joshi, the umpire, had miscounted and called over. With that he removed the bails and ended the Test. West Indian negative tactics and Indian incompetence had conspired to prevent an Indian victory. There is no guarantee India would have won but they had the momentum as the desperate West Indians realised. Goddard and Walcott left the field to boos, cat-calls and jeers.

After such glorious cricket from the West Indians this last Test of the series left a sour taste. The Bombay crowd never forgave Walcott. It is interesting that, even today, Gomez expresses no regrets for it. 'You don't carry on and get clobbered just because you think it is sporting,' he told me. 'You are playing Test cricket. It is a serious thing.'

This was the one thing the Indians had to learn from the West Indians and other Test-playing countries. The West Indians also taught them how to play the imperial visitors. The imperial attitude is revealed in Jeffrey Stollmeyer's book *Everything Under the Sun*. Forget that he is West Indian and he reads like a Raj visitor, a latterday Cecil Headlam surveying Indian society. There are no tirades against babus, though there is much fun at the expense of babu English, and the viciousness with which the post office at Patiala is described would have met with the Headlam approval. All the Indian servants assigned to the West Indian cricketers turn out to be either crooks or idiots. Stollmeyer also strongly implies that the Indian Board cheated the West Indies Board about the tour, promising them a share of the profits, then despite vast crowds, sending a cheque for £10. The hotels may have

V.M. Merchant. The portrait shows him more as the business man than as the great cricketer he was *(Roger Mann)*.
Below: In his 128 in The Oval Test of 1946, and warmly wrapped up against the cold, he plays his favourite shot, the late cut. He was finally run out by Compton's quick footwork *(Hulton-Deutsch)*.

'Vinoo' Mankad. *Above left:* The first of India's great spinners, he was the last tourist to England to do the 'double' *(Roger Mann)*. *Above right:* In 1952 he was called into the Indian side after the Headingley débâcle and responded by making 256 runs as opener and bowling 97 overs for 5 wickets *(Hulton-Deutsch)*. *Below:* Worcester, 1946. The picture, though blurred, shows Mankad's bowling style perfectly *(Roger Mann)*.

V.S. Hazare, One of India's great batsmen, he led India in their first Test win in 1951–52, and was the first Indian to score two centuries in one Test. *Below*, he counters a rampant Trueman at The Oval in 1952 – a beleaguered captain whose calm and sound technique could not inspire most of his colleagues to emulate him *(Hulton-Deutsch)*.

Top left: Dattu Phadkar, one of few opening bowlers to emerge in the 1940s, though his batting was often more crucial. *Top right:* Ghulam Ahmed, the off-spinner who became a noted cricket administrator. *Below left:* 'Polly' Umrigar, the great enigma of Indian cricket, an outstanding batsman in India whose abject failure against Trueman in 1952 created the myth of Indian batsmen fearing pace. *Below right:* Hemu Adhikari, a brilliant fieldsman, but more famous for his managerial role in 1971 *(Hulton-Deutsch)*.

Left: Vinoo Mankad and Pankaj Roy shared an opening stand of 413 against New Zealand at Madras in 1955–56 which is still a world Test record *(David Frith)*.

Below left: Vijay Manjrekar who made a century in his first Test in England in 1952, and was rated the best post-war Indian batsman of the pre-Gavaskar era *(Hulton-Deutsch)*.

Below right: 'Bapu' Nadkarni, a 'mean', defensive left-arm spinner who epitomised India's main concern in the 1950s – to avoid defeat *(Hulton-Deutsch)*.

S.P. Gupte. In his classic leg-break bowler's action, the drag of the right foot gave him better balance. Possibly the best post-war leg-spinner, he failed to be a match winner in England in 1959 *(Roger Mann).*

Pullar, c Joshi b Gupte 14 at Old Trafford where Gupte's analysis was 26–6–76–4 *(Hulton-Deutsch).*

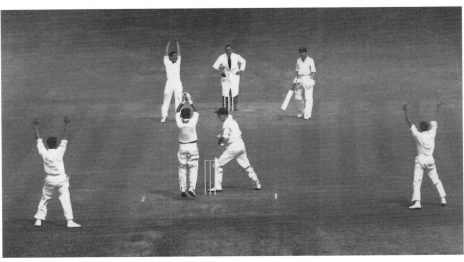

Nari Contractor, a dour left-handed opener, promised a revival when he beat Dexter's 1961–62 team but a few weeks later in Barbados he suffered a head injury and never played Test cricket again *(Hulton-Deutsch)*.

Left: Chandu Borde was a significant figure in the regeneration of Indian cricket after 1958–59. Like Hazare, he found it difficult to impose his personality, and was overshadowed by Pataudi *(The Cricketer)*.

Centre: Dilip Sardesai, a sound middle-order batsman who was made to open, then discarded but, brought back almost as an afterthought, he provided batting steel in 1971 *(The Cricketer)*.

Right: Salim Durani, the darling of Indian cricket crowds whose figures do not convey the magic of his personality *(Indian Cricket)*.

Nawab of Pataudi, jr, pictured in 1961 when captain of Oxford University and just before his eye was injured in a car crash. He became India's captain after Contractor was hurt, the youngest Test captain of any country (*Hulton-Deutsch*).

Below: Pataudi batting for the Indians against Hampshire in 1967. He freed Indian cricket from the dull-dog image of the 1950s although his best innings, as at Headingley that year and later in Melbourne, were often played in adversity (*Patrick Eagar*).

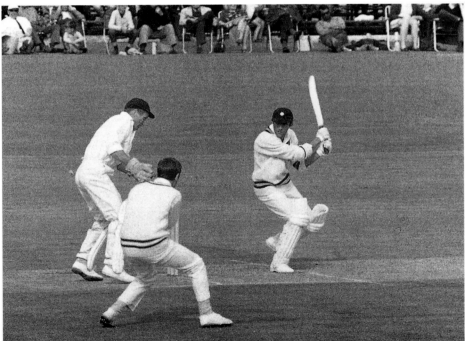

had stylish names but they were 'cold, damp and dirty' (the coldness of hotel rooms in a hot country is somewhat puzzling), but the Stollmeyer wrath is particularly reserved for the travel arrangements. To be fair arrangements were bad, but then the Indian players faced appalling conditions too.

At the time there was little or no passenger air travel in India. Nearly all journeys were by train, mostly long-distance journeys of two or more days. Normally such journeys can be quite comfortable, but with India still recovering from Partition, and a war going on with Pakistan over Kashmir, Indian railways had other priorities. But led by Stollmeyer the West Indian players rebelled against the long train journeys. They virtually refused to tour if there were any more long rail journeys. The Indian Board gave in.

But for the Indian players rail travel was all that was available. The result was that a sort of class system built up. From this time on, while cricket visitors to India had the best of the travel and hotel arrangements – air and the best hotels – Indian cricketers were made to travel by train and stay in the cheaper hotels. Indians, far from enjoying the home advantage, found themselves treated by their own Board like second-class citizens in their own country.

This had an immediate effect as soon as the tour ended. Amarnath asked for more money and fell out with De Mello. The row had been brewing for some time: De Mello listed twenty-three allegations against Amarnath, including claims for extra out-of-pocket expenses, receiving money from the Cricket Association of Bengal, and not being a conscientious captain. At an extraordinary meeting of the Board on 10 April 1949 a resolution was passed suspending Amarnath from domestic and representative cricket in India 'for continuous misbehaviour and breach of discipline'. De Mello was furious that the man he had dragged 'out of the gutter and made captain of India' should now stand up to him. A subsequent Board meeting accepted Amarnath's 'apology' but now the captaincy question had been reopened.

De Mello, who had voted against Merchant in 1946, was now for him. It seemed that after two years out of cricket, he was fit. Merchant had tried hard to be fit for the West Indian tour. Early in the morning he could be seen at the Brabourne Stadium practising. But Merchant was no longer the batsman he had been and regaining the captaincy proved a Pyrrhic victory. MCC were due to tour India in 1949-50 but decided not to send a team. So De Mello contacted George Duckworth, the former England and Lancashire wicket-keeper, and he gathered together a Commonwealth side. It was essentially players prominent in League cricket in Lancashire: the Australians including Livingston as captain, Alley, Pepper, and

Tribe; five Englishmen including G. H. Pope; and two West Indians: Holt and Worrell.

On 11 November 1949, two years and eight months after he was last seen on a first-class cricket field, Merchant led India out against the Commonwealth side in the first unofficial 'Test' at Delhi. It was a most unhappy return. The Commonwealth team made 608 for 8 declared. Merchant, trying to catch Worrell, injured his hand, did not bat, his brother Uday pulled a leg muscle and also did not bat. India with nine men lost by nine wickets. Merchant returned for the second 'Test' in Bombay and played his only two first-class innings of the season: 78 and 94. India, faced with 448, had followed-on but Merchant's innings held the batting together in the second innings and India performed their usual escape act.

However, the hand injury proved much worse than had been feared and, just before the Calcutta 'Test', Merchant announced he was not available. Indeed it became clear he would not play any more first-class cricket that season. With Amarnath also injured, and in any case out of favour, it was now Hazare's turn to be chosen to captain India. This did not go down well with Mushtaq Ali who was much senior to Hazare and recalled that he had originally been appointed vice-captain for the Australian trip in 1947-48.

The rest of the series was Hazare versus Worrell. They both finished with almost identical totals for the series. Hazare in ten innings scored 677 runs at an average of 96.71. Worrell in nine innings scored 684 at an average of 97.71.

Worrell had been unlucky to miss the West Indian visit to India – India would never see him in an official Test – but he more than made up for this in these unofficial Tests. He did not have the awesome power of Weekes, or his murderous certainty, but there was charm. Right from the first innings in the opening match in Delhi Worrell was making runs in such a manner that, more often than not, the spectators would shout 'wah-wah' which in India is an expression that conveys wonder and delight at something artistic. There were two Weekes-like innings – 223 not out at Kanpur and then 161 in the final 'Test' at Madras. Indians may have disliked Walcott but about Worrell they would never hear a bad word.

However Hazare's proved to be the crucial innings. His 175 not out in Calcutta was the basis of India's 422 and a seven-wicket victory. Worrell failed in both innings: 9 and 28. And in the deciding match at Madras, while Worrell dominated the first innings, he was a relative failure in the second. Hazare, consistent in both innings with 77 and 84, saw India to a three-wicket victory. In the end, though, it required Mushtaq Ali, who had injured his hand earlier in the innings, to return and hit the winning boundary.

The Madras crowd was jubilant, and Mushtaq Ali was mobbed. The tour was a commercial success and it had taken cricket to parts of the country that had not seen much big cricket, like Kanpur. But what had it done for Indian cricket? Partly due to injuries, but also to vagaries of selection, there was no consistency. Only five men appeared in all five 'Tests'. Phadkar had further developed as all-rounder. He took the most wickets and was fifth in batting. But Polly Umrigar, who had made his debut against the West Indies, did not appear to have progressed much. A useful medium-pace off-spinner he bowled only 22 overs, and his 276 runs meant a batting average of 39.42

There was still no settled opening pair. In the first three 'Tests' four different pairs were tried. The fourth was Mushtaq Ali and Mankad and this proved durable. The bowling, perhaps, was the bigger problem. Ghulam Ahmed still could not command a regular place in the side, C. S. Nayudu and Sarwate were clearly never going to be match-winners against international opposition. In some sense the most disappointing aspect of the tour was how Indians who did so well in domestic cricket did not translate such deeds into international competition.

In December 1948 a Maharashtra batsman, B. B. Nimbalkar, suddenly hit the most fantastic form. Against Kathiawar he scored 443 not out, almost a run a minute. With Bhandharkar he put on 455 for the second wicket, which was then a world record, in just 300 minutes. Kathiawar had been bowled out for 238 and, by lunch on the fourth day, Maharashtra were 826 for 4. It seemed that another few minutes' batting would see Nimbalkar pass Bradman's 452 not out, which was then the highest individual score in first-class cricket.

But over lunch the Kathiawar captain, a minor prince with a grand title – High Highness the Thakur Sahib of Rajkot – decided he had had about as much as his princely dignity would bear. He said that if Maharashtra declared at lunch he would bat, but if Nimbalkar wanted to carry on batting he would not field. He would rather concede the match. No amount of pleading by the Maharashtrians could budge him and Nimbalkar missed his world record. Bradman's record has since been passed by Hanif Mohammad who made 499 in 1958-59 before he was run out in the last over of the day. Brian Lara has since scored 500 in first-class cricket, but Nimbalkar's 443 not out remains a landmark, the fourth highest score in first-class cricket.

Almost exactly a year later, when the Commonwealth side came to India, Nimbalkar played in the second 'Test' at Bombay. He batted no. 9, made 3 and 12 not out, and did not play again in the series. He kept on playing in the Ranji Trophy and scored 219 for Holkar against Bengal in Calcutta some years later but never played in Tests for India.

171

Nimbalkar's performance once again raised the question of what these high Indian domestic scores meant. That year the Ranji Trophy had been an orgy of run-making. In the semi-final between Bombay and Maharashtra, Bombay made 651 and 714 for 8 declared, Maharashtra 407 and 604 – nine centuries, a world record of 2,376 runs spread over seven days. The final had been another seven-day marathon. Bombay scored 620, Baroda replied with 268. Bombay batted again and scored 361, setting Baroda 714 to win. They made 245. It was after this that the Board decided that the semi-finals and finals should be of five days' duration, a rule which applies even today. To an extent the Board's decision was an attempt to ring down the curtain on the high-scoring era inaugurated by Merchant during the war.

As it was, the visit of the Commonwealth side had left Merchant depressed. His form had been wretched, he had been injured, perhaps he should retire? De Mello persuaded him that, for the good of Indian cricket, he had to stay. True for the winter of 1950-51 he could offer nothing more than another Commonwealth side but there was the visit to England in 1952 and then a tour to the West Indies in 1953. See us through till then, Vijay, and then you can go. De Mello appealed to Merchant's patriotic instincts and Merchant succumbed.

So once again India prepared for a curious season.

The second Commonwealth side to tour India was, if anything, even stronger and better balanced than the MCC side that was then touring Australia. Leslie Ames, who had turned down the chance to tour India with Jardine in 1933-34, had accepted George Duckworth's invitation to be captain. He told me in an interview:

> Duckie asked me whether I would go as captain. I had never been to India. It was my last opportunity to tour. I would never tour with England again because I had given up keeping wicket. George Duckworth chose the side mainly but we collaborated. He would ring me and say, have you seen so and so this season, how good is he? We had a fabulous side. It was not difficult to get the spirit going. We didn't need a great deal of strategy with that side. We were unbeaten. One of the best sides I ever travelled with. We had everything except a really fast bowler, a Lindwall, Larwood, or Statham. But we had Ridgway, the best fast bowler Kent has had since the war.

Old men's memories can sometimes be suspect but Ames is right. Though he himself missed three of the five 'Tests' with a bad attack of lumbago, such was the dominance of Worrell and the Lancashire batsman Ikin that the highest Indian wicket-taker, Mankad, took his

22 wickets at a cost of 34.36 runs each. In only two completed innings did they score below 300. Ames hardly missed the lack of genuine pace and even then, in the first innings at the Brabourne Stadium, Ridgway bowled India out for 82. But Ames admits that was not in the script. 'Something went wrong there, I don't know what.'

For the early part of the tour there was Laker, whose 5 for 88 in the second innings of the Bombay 'Test' after Ridgway had done so well in the first, sealed the Commonwealth win. Then when Laker returned home due to sinus trouble, there was Ramadhin. If he was not quite the wizard he had been in England in the summer of 1950, he was still very effective, taking 15 wickets at 28.86.

India, basically, was Hazare. He was the highest run-getter on either side in the series: 634 runs at an average of 79.25. When he failed, India failed. In Bombay he was one of Ridgway's victims out for a duck; six other Indians made ducks. In the second innings Hazare made 115, Umrigar supported him and India made 393. But India could not make up for the first-innings failure. Over the course of a match Hazare never really failed. In the first 'Test' he had made 144 not out, in the third it was 134, in the fourth 80 and 75, in the fifth 47 and 8. That 8 came in the final innings when India had been set 440 to win – Ames declaring at lunch-time on the fourth day. It was a crucial failure. India made 362 and failed by just 77 runs. A series that might have been drawn 1-1 was lost 2-0.

Yet to an extent Hazare was also the Indian problem. He was, as *Wisden* reported, 'over-cautious'. Runs were never made fast enough to give the bowlers time to bowl out the opposition. One man who could have tipped the scales was Mushtaq Ali. It was clear that the key bowler for the Commonwealth was Ramadhin. His annihilation of England in 1950 had spread a fearsome reputation of a mystery bowler whom it was impossible to 'read'. Before the first 'Test' at Delhi Mushtaq studied Ramadhin closely in the nets and decided the only way to deal with him was to use the feet. In the first innings he was run out, and Ramadhin took 4 for 44. In the second he succeeded in such masterly fashion in converting his spinners into half-volleys that Ramadhin quite lost confidence and finished with 1 for 111. But consistency was never a Mushtaq speciality, he failed in the second 'Test', was dropped for the third, brought back for the fourth and finally used as a middle-order batsman in the fifth 'Test'. He was at his best as an opener who set the agenda for the innings. Although in the fifth match required to prop up the batting, he made an invaluable 80 in the second innings and as long as he was there India looked like winning. His absence from the opening position meant that India never took command and were always struggling to draw level.

Merchant, himself, recognised the failure of the Indian batsmen to score quickly: while visiting teams average between 50 runs and 55 runs an hour in representative matches, he wrote, India have not been able to average more than 35 or 40 runs. Looking back on that season he said in the 1952 *Wisden*, 'Some years ago Indian batsmen threw away their wickets for no reason whatsoever. Now some of them become too slow and simply cannot force the pace when quick scoring is essential. In 1950-51 against the Second Commonwealth team, unenterprising batting prevented India from gaining a single victory.'

Hindsight is a marvellous thing but who was the Indian captain in 1950-51? Why Merchant, of course. Surely as captain he could have ensured that his batsmen score quickly – even Hazare? But he had not and, by the end of the tour, this was not the only criticism being made. Merchant's tactics were also under fire. In the final 'Test' at Kanpur he had put the Commonwealth side in. 'Inserting' the opposition is only now a regular feature of international cricket, then it was seen as something very bold. Merchant thought the rain that had fallen before the match would affect the wicket. It did not. Worrell made 116, the Commonwealth XI 413, and it was India who had to bat last on a wearing wicket. Merchant, himself, with 107, showed how to bat on a last-day wicket. But that had not been enough.

Of course the Indians had once again been their own worst enemies. The Commonwealth team had travelled mostly by air, the Indian players by train. In Kanpur the Commonwealth team had stayed in good private accommodation, the Indians in a shabby guest-house with wretched food and inadequate blankets.

So after two Commonwealth visits meant to prepare India for two back-to-back Test series against England and then a tour to the West Indies, Indian cricket seemed as much at the crossroads as ever. As during the first Commonwealth visit, the second visit had seen no settled Indian side. Nineteen players had been used in the five 'Tests', only five – Hazare, Merchant, Mankad, Phadkar and Umrigar – had played right through the series. Apart from Umrigar, who had improved during the season, the others were established players. During the West Indian visit Ghulam Ahmed's off-spin was seen as supplementing Mankad. Now he did not play a single 'Test' despite a marathon bowling effort against Holkar in the Ranji Trophy. While Nayudu's team made 757, Ghulam bowled 92.3 overs.

Ghulam, as he was to be popularly known in India, remained the great enigma of Indian cricket. In some ways his name suggested it. He should have been known as Ahmed, his surname, but instead it was always Ghulam and he is one of the very few cricketers to be listed in the record books under his first name. Unusually tall for an Indian – certainly for an Indian spinner – he had an easy action, and subtle control of flight and variations of length. He was a bowler who gave the impression he 'thought' batsmen out. But he quickly fell into the trap of Indian cricket politics and played in only twenty-two Tests, never quite achieving the dominance he suggested he might. Essentially a matting-wicket bowler he had to work hard on turf ones but on his good days he could be the equal of Jim Laker. What he, like so many Indian cricketers, lacked was consistency. But then he was never handled consistently, and once he got enmeshed in cricket politics he cut a sorry figure. Few people in Indian cricket could avoid the politics. Merchant was an exception, but he had his own secure income and did not have to worry about 'currying favour'.

Amarnath was another mystery. Whatever had happened to him? He had not played any cricket in India for almost two full seasons. In April 1950, as he left India to travel to England to play in the Lancashire League, he had sounded off against De Mello and used Bradman's memoirs *Farewell to Cricket* to justify his position. De Mello had done him a lot of harm, Amarnath claimed – 'He had tried to drive me out of cricket but without success. One day I feel sure he will come crawling to me begging me to help him once again' – but Bradman had vindicated him.

In *Farewell to Cricket* Bradman had written that he looked back 'on the season with him as my opposite number as one of my most pleasant cricket years'. Amarnath, Bradman said, 'was such a splendid ambassador that it makes it all the more difficult to understand his recent suspension by the Indian Board of Control'. Denied honour at home, Amarnath drew what solace he could from those words of the world's greatest cricketer. They could not bring him back to Test cricket, but a year after Amarnath had spoken on the Bombay sea-front, it was De Mello who faced trouble.

Things were moving in the labyrinth of Indian cricket politics. De Mello had ruled Indian cricket for six years. He had popularised the game, made money for the Board. But where was the success on the field? And he had antagonised Bombay. In the 1950-51 season Bombay had threatened to concede a match rather than play away from home. Eventually they relented, played what turned out to be Merchant's last Ranji Trophy match and lost to Gujerat, with Merchant making 17 and 9. But the Bombay knives were out for De Mello with the *Times of India* denouncing him as 'dictator'.

Also there was another, older, threat. Quietly, almost surreptitiously, Vizzy had returned to Indian cricket as an administrator. He was now a vice-president of the Board. India, quick to forgive, had forgiven 1936. Vizzy had secured a 'Test' for Kanpur even if the Kanpur crowd hardly showed they were ready for 'Test' cricket. After the Indian defeat they had smashed the pavilion and nearly manhandled the players. The regional power barons were flexing their muscles, and thinking of the visit by England to India in 1951-52 and India's tour to England in 1952. It was a time for another throw of the dice, another turn of the roulette wheel.

On 5 August 1951 the Indian Board met in the Imperial Hotel, in the centre of Delhi, which recalls a bygone gracious era with its neatly manicured lawns. But there was nothing gracious about this meeting. This was cut-throat cricket politics. For nine hours the administrators argued, debated, haggled. Some of them, probably, got drunk as well. In the end it was clear that De Mello had lost. A. J. C. Mukerjea, President of the Cricket Association of Bengal, was elected President by 12 votes to 5. De Mello departed on a suitably dramatic note, 'I leave cricket never to return.'

There were contests for various other posts but the crucial one was for captain. Amarnath was still out of the picture and it was now between the two Vijays. Vijay Hazare versus Vijay Merchant. Ever since his century in each innings at Adelaide, Hazare as a player had completely overshadowed Merchant. In three successive Ranji Trophy seasons he had averaged 72.16 (433 runs); 101.50 (609 runs); 80.33 (241 runs). He had been just as successful with the ball: 20 wickets at 18.3; 28 at 16.2; 13 at 16.2. And there was his success in leading India to victory against the first Commonwealth side – having taken over the leadership on Merchant's injury – whereas Merchant had failed against the second. Perhaps all this did not matter and the delegates, like those at an American Presidential convention, were all pledged for their chosen candidate. Hazare won by 12 votes to 5, the same margin as Mukerjea. The party loyalties clearly held.

Neither Hazare nor Merchant knew the voting was taking place. Merchant would have withdrawn had he known. Hazare was playing League cricket in England when he read about it in the papers. Then he suddenly realised that his first Test as captain would be against England in Delhi. It was to prove the best and the worst of times.

11

Victory-then ruin
1951-53

Hindus believe in a circular concept of time. The Hindu golden age was the Ram Rajya when the god Rama took the form of man and came down to earth. This was the age of bliss, happiness, peace, prosperity. Nobody stole, nobody told lies, and India had the perfect government. It was this mythical age that Gandhi sought to recreate. Its destruction led to less fruitful ages each worse than the preceding one right down to the present age, the Kaliyuga, an age of sin, debauchery, destruction and lies. It is said to last 5,000 million years. Then the cycle is repeated and Ram Rajya re-emerges.

In the 1950s Indian cricket went through something similar. It began with India's first Test victory – after twenty-five Tests – but then came such ruin and destruction that for a time it was seriously suggested that India should lose its Test status – Pakistan and New Zealand were also to be demoted – only for the dark ages to pass and Indian cricket to re-emerge stronger and more vibrant than ever. The decade ended as it had begun with a victory. At the end of the decade India beat Australia for the first time, at the beginning India beat England for the first time.

Nobody in India believed that that victory over England on 10 February 1952 in Madras marked the start of a Ram Rajya in cricket. India was well aware that this was very much an England Second XI – and a curious Second XI at that. In the first Test in Delhi England had five new Test caps, amongst them the captain, Nigel Howard, and the vice-captain, Donald Carr. Howard, the Lancashire captain, has the unique distinction of having played for England only as captain – four Tests against India – and never being beaten. If this was bizarre, then perhaps in the second Test when Leadbeater, flown out to replace the injured Rhodes, played for England before he was capped by his county, showed how very second-rate this England team was. No Hutton, no Compton, no Evans, no Bedser, no Laker, no May, and no Brown who had captained England against both South Africa in the summer and Australia the previous winter. The England side included only two of their world-class players: Graveney and Statham, with Shackleton,

177

Tattersall, Robertson, Lowson and Kenyon all no more than excellent county standard.

India should have proved emphatically superior and, for the first couple of days of the Delhi Test, when Shinde with his leg-spin took 6 for 91 and Merchant and Hazare added 211 for the third wicket, it seemed that England would be made to suffer. But that stand had also revealed the Indian weakness. This was the first time in Tests that Hazare and Merchant had batted together for any length of time and it seemed they were batting against each other rather than for India. Merchant made 154, then the highest score made by an Indian in Tests, in seven and a half hours. Hazare immediately went on to pass that by making 164 not out in eight hours 35 minutes. But with the batsmen so much on top only 186 runs came in an entire day for the loss of two wickets, 39 runs in the last 90 minutes. On the third day only 232 runs came in five and a half hours' play.

Hazare blamed Statham and his leg-theory bowling – just one slip and a cordon of seven fielders on the leg side with the attack round the leg stump. And it is possible that Hazare did not go on batting just to pass Merchant's record. But a declaration on the third evening, when England had spent two days in the field, rather than on the fourth morning – after a rest day – might have meant getting a couple of early wickets. But Hazare, who declined Merchant's offer to hit out after reaching his hundred, wanted to make sure and in the process failed. England had to bat out two days and this, on a pitch getting slower by the minute and with the Indians dropping numerous catches, they managed to do with Watkins batting nine hours for 137 not out. Once again Hazare had given the impression that he could not quite seize a game.

At the end of the Test Merchant retired. While fielding in the second innings he made a full-length dive and injured his shoulder. The thought, at forty, of making yet another attempt to recover from injury was too ghastly to contemplate. In any case with Hazare in charge, Merchant could see little chance of either regaining the captaincy or setting up new records. Whatever he did the skipper could always pass. 154 against England was a satisfactory way to bid goodbye. So India's first truly great batsman announced he would not play any more cricket. In eighteen Tests, all against England, he had scored 859 runs at an average of 47.72. Any average over 42 in Tests is a sure sign of class and, while there may have been other peaks for Merchant to conquer, the summits did not look inviting.

Hazare plodded on, unable to impress his personality on the series. A captain has to make things happen and Hazare just could not do that. As a batsman he never collared the bowling, as a skipper he never really took charge. In the next Test in Bombay it took him fifteen minutes to

178

decide whether he should bat or field; in the end he batted and India made 485. In this second Test he hit another century, then was run out. In two innings he had scored 319 runs and an Englishman had yet to get his wicket but this innings ended ignominiously. After his century he hooked a Ridgway bouncer on to his head, was led away to the pavilion but no sooner did he reach the dressing-room than C. K. Nayudu, now chairman of selectors, stormed in and ordered him back on the pitch. His task was to face the fast bowler. Hazare, who had been wearing a thick pith helmet, was more stunned than injured and just made it to the crease before the new batsman could get there.

He carried on with that innings and reached 155 but the episode did immense damage to Hazare. After it Hazare's batting form completely deserted him. He made 6 in the second innings, 2 in the third Test, a pair in the fourth and 20 in the fifth. And it showed that, as captain, he could not even decide when he wanted to bat – he, still, too easily took orders from others. His captaincy touch so deserted him that in the Bombay Test, after making 485 in the first innings, his order to the batsmen to score quickly in the second nearly cost India the match. The third was a dull draw, the fourth saw the Indians, on an under-prepared pitch, beaten in three days by the spin of Hilton and Tattersall. By the time the fifth Test began even this Second XI England side was looking too good for the Indians.

To an extent Hazare was not helped by the selectors. That season Indian selectors seemed to have a fixation with the number five. Every Test saw five changes, two or three of them were players making their Test debuts. By the time of the fifth Test India had had three different wicket-keepers, four sets of openers and four sets of opening bowlers. The one constant player in all this change and change again was Mankad, and he now took virtual charge of the Test.

Wisden wrote: 'Their hero was Mankad who bowled superbly in each innings, taking twelve wickets in the match for 108. His performance of 8 for 55 in the first innings has seldom been bettered in Test cricket when it is considered that the pitch gave him little assistance. Mankad's bowling inspired the whole side, the fielding being far better than in previous matches and the batting possessed a more adventurous spirit, necessary for the occasion. England disappointed badly. There was no real reason for the batting collapse in the first innings which virtually decided the match.'

Mankad had come on to bowl with England 65 for 1 after winning the toss on a good batting wicket. When he delivered the fifth ball of his thirty-ninth over, some hours later, England were all out for 266. Mankad had taken the wickets of Graveney, Robertson, Watkins, Poole, Carr, Hilton, Statham and Ridgway. Four of them were stumped and they told the story of a classic piece of left-arm bowling on a good wicket: endless variations of flight, teasing and testing the batsmen before they were fatally lured forward and then, as four of them were, stumped.

As so often with Mankad he was more dangerous when there was nothing in the wicket to help him. It seemed to be a challenge to him. On a helpful Kanpur wicket he had bowled well but not devastatingly; now on a wicket that suited batsmen he was devastating. In the second innings, after India had batted more enterprisingly than they had done at any other time in the series to gain a lead of 191, Mankad was again in his element, taking 4 for 53, but on a wearing wicket Ghulam Ahmed was just as effective, taking 4 for 77.

It was twenty years since India made her Test debut. A victory coming after such a long time should have been savoured but, *Wisden* noted with some surprise, it was received in a very subdued fashion. With good reason. The Maharajahs may have departed but the caprice they had planted in the heart of Indian cricket still survived. Instead of building on this victory India seemed determined to cast it off.

Within a week of the victory Hazare was appointed to lead India on the tour of England but there was no Amarnath, no Mushtaq Ali – both of whom had played in the Madras Test – and no Mankad. Rarely in cricket history can a team have conjured up such a situation: a victory after 25 Tests and twenty years and in the very next tour no place in the side for the man who had done more than anyone else to achieve that victory. It was a classic Indian cock-up, mostly the result of pride and mismanagement on the part of Indian officials, like Nayudu, and partly a desire by Mankad, very understandably, that as a professional cricketer he should not lose money.

Back in November Mankad had written to the Board about his dilemma. He had had an offer from the Lancashire League club Haslingden worth over £1,000 – very good money in those days – and asked the Board whether they could give him any guarantee of selection for the England tour. That a player like Mankad should have had doubts that he would be chosen showed how volatile Indian selectors could be. He did not want to be in the position, come the summer, of not being in the Indian team and also without a Lancashire League contract. The Board could not give him any such guarantee and decided that if he was not making himself freely available for the whole tour Indian cricket could do without him. Nayudu was supposed to have said that India could produce ten such spinners.

Amarnath and Mushtaq Ali had long fallen out of favour and Mushtaq seemed to have been chosen for the last Test on that old selectorial principle that, if he failed, then his exclusion for the tour could be fully justified. He made 22 and did not make the trip. Amarnath's omission was one of those Indian mysteries that will never

180

be resolved. He had missed the coaching camp at the beginning of the season, so was not considered for the first Test. Then he played in the second and third Tests, was dropped for the fourth and restored in the fifth.

So India arrived in England for her first tour in six years – and a crucial one – without a recognised opening pair, without her match-winning bowler and crucially short of the leavening of experience that youth needs. Hazare, Shinde and Sarwate were the only ones who had toured England before and this made the team dangerously short of English experience in an age when uncovered wickets made an England tour a very difficult proposition. To make matters worse Hazare decided to follow the most absurd policy a touring captain could ever have adopted. He decided that with so many inexperienced youngsters he would play his most experienced side in the first few matches so that the youngsters could learn from watching the 'seniors on both sides in action and pick up a few hints'. The youngsters bored by this called themselves the sight-seeing club and some of them never really got a proper chance. The left-handed Hiralal Gaekwad played in only 9 games, the medium-paced off-spinner Chowdhury in only ten. Umrigar, in contrast, played 25 matches, Hazare himself 27.

India were inviting a fall. And what a fall. In the second innings of the first Test at Headingley, in front of a packed Saturday afternoon crowd, India began their second innings 41 behind. If anything, they were slight favourites. Hazare, who had batted no. 4 in the first innings, was reasonably confident and, suffering from a thigh strain, decided to drop down the order to no. 6. He thought it would give him a bit of rest. He was able to rest for barely 14 balls. In that time India lost four wickets without a run on the board – still the worst start in Test history. When a journalist tried to telephone his newspaper with the story he was rebuked for getting the score wrong: surely it was 4 runs for no wicket?

Hazare came in to find Trueman was on a hat-trick. Hazare drove the first ball he faced from Trueman for four and, with Phadkar, repaired the damage to an extent. They put on 105, Hazare making 56, Phadkar 64. But the moment they were out India fell to 165 all out. This was never enough to avoid defeat but it was the deeper wound Trueman had inflicted on Indian cricket that could never really be healed. Trueman became an ogre India could not cope with, and a whole generation of Indian batsmen were branded as cowards, men who ran away to square-leg at the first sight of a fast bowler. Not all Indian batsmen ran away from Trueman and it is a canard to suggest that.

However, one man did. Polly Umrigar. In the third Test at Old Trafford when Trueman with 8 for 31 routed India in a day – for totals of 58 and 82 – even Hazare found it disturbing that Umrigar backed away to square-leg when he faced Trueman. Physically he looked the best equipped of the Indians to stand up to pace. Here was a man who looked like a mighty batsman: a six-foot tall, well-built Parsee with massive forearms and muscles that bulged as he drove and cut the ball. He could tear attacks to bits. Just before the tour in the Madras Test he had made his first Test century against Statham and Ridgway. On the tour he scored more hundreds than anyone else: five, three of them double-hundreds. Even if we disregard the 229 against Oxford University, there was his 204 against Lancashire where *Wisden* found him 'in his most punishing mood', 204 against Kent, and 137 not out against Yorkshire, even if there was no Trueman then. On the tour he was second in the averages, making 1,688 runs at an average of 48.22. In seven Test innings he made 43 runs at an average of 6.14. He was out to Trueman four times – three times bowled backing away.

So what made him run away from Trueman? Umrigar has never revealed why, and we may have to enter the realms of psychology to get an answer. The most probable explanation is that Trueman cowed him mentally. He looked wild, with a full mane of dark hair, and he acted wild. He swore, four letter words flew as he beat the batsman. This, allied to the conditions, made him devastating. At Old Trafford and at The Oval India batted on wickets made greasy by rain where the ball flew unpredictably. At The Oval they batted just after a thunderstorm had flooded the ground and made it one of the worst pitches they had ever played on. Hazare showed you could survive on such wickets, and the 38 he made out of 98 at The Oval, with the ball alternatively kicking up or skidding through, was a little masterpiece of defensive batting. If a batsman is judged by his play on bad wickets then it was the best Test innings Hazare ever played. He was as proud of it as of any double-hundred.

But only three other colleagues had the temperament to fight in such alien surroundings. One was Dattu Phadkar who did little with the ball but showed courage as a batsman, twice partnering Hazare in futile rescues. Another was Mankad.

Even before the Headingley debacle Hazare had been trying to get Mankad released from Haslingden. Haslingden was prepared to release Mankad but would do so only for the first Test and if the Indian Board paid £300 – £100 to Mankad, £200 to the club – plus a player in exchange. The terms were considered too stiff but, after 0 for 4, obtaining Mankad for the Tests became imperative and negotiations were resumed. The then Glamorgan chairman, Sir Herbert Merrett, made an offer to pay the money but in the end it was the Indian Board that found the £300 as well as the player in exchange. Why Sir Herbert should have intervened is not clear, but the deed was done and Mankad came straight from the Lancashire League cricket to a Test at Lord's.

It provided the one romantic story of the summer for the Indians. Mankad opened the batting and within half an hour of the start had hit the leg-spinner Roly Jenkins over the sight screen for a six. He was the top scorer with 72 in India's first innings of 235. Then while England made 537, Hutton 150, Mankad bowled, and bowled and bowled. At the end of it his figures read: 73-24-196-5.

As soon as the England innings was over Mankad was back on the field opening the batting. On that Saturday he had bowled 31 of the 73 overs, now he batted through the rest of the day, seeing India to 137 for 2. And this was attacking opening batting. India faced a deficit of 302 but the first ball from Jenkins was pulled for a six. On Monday while the Queen, in the first summer of her reign, watched, Mankad put on another display. Hazare was almost a silent partner as he set new Indian landmarks. He passed Hazare's 164 not out to record the highest score by an Indian in Test cricket, the Merchant-Hazare stand of 211 for the third wicket was equalled before, as *Wisden* says, 'exhaustion overtook him and he was yorked' by Laker. He had made 184 out of 270 in four and a half hours.

This should have galvanised his colleagues but they surrendered tamely to Laker and Trueman and with 80 minutes' play left Mankad was back on the field, bowling. England required 77 to win. Mankad rubbed the ball on the ground to take off the shine and bowled 24 overs of such accuracy that at the end of the day England were still 37 short of their target. They had to return on the fifth morning before they could win the match by eight wickets. By the time it ended Mankad had made 256 runs of the 613 his team made and bowled 97 overs. 'His powers of endurance,' wrote *Wisden*, 'seemed inexhaustible.' But with such meagre support they were not enough to save the Indians, even if it did provide them one memory to cherish from a dismal tour.

The other memory to cherish was provided by Vijay Manjrekar.

So many of the young promising batsmen had failed on the tour. The opener Roy who had hit two hundreds against England in India now made five noughts in seven innings, out to Trueman four times, Bedser thrice. His only possible consolation was that his Test average of 7.71 was better than Umrigar's. But Manjrekar was different. Roy came from a middle-class Bengali school, a rare Test player from that region. Manjrekar was from the tough Maharashtrian school of Bombay. Englishmen with flowing locks and flying curses and bouncers did not intimidate him. In the first innings of the Headingley Test he came out to bat when India were 42 for 3. At twenty he was the youngest member of the side and Hazare watched him come out to the middle feeling a little bit sorry for him.

But it was Manjrekar who gave Hazare confidence. He had been in poor form; now, seeing Manjrekar middle the ball, Hazare regained his touch. The pair put on 222 runs for the fourth wicket, still an Indian record, before Hazare was out and then Manjrekar fell for 133. After that the almost inevitable Indian collapse followed but Manjrekar had demonstrated that good technique allied to guts could make this England attack look pedestrian. Some of his colleagues had the technique, most of them did not have the guts.

This innings was to announce Manjrekar as the next major Indian batsman and, while he made only one other double-figure score in the series – but a significant 22 out of 58 at Old Trafford – the promise that he held out in the first innings at Leeds was more than fulfilled. In the next decade and a half, while Indian batting reached the depths of despair, Manjrekar was often the only batsman who combined ability with guts. He could stand up to pace like no other Indian batsman could and he was a beautiful player of spin.

His overall Test average of 39.22 – for 3,209 runs in 55 Tests – places him just outside the '40 club' considered to be the mark of a good Test player, but for over a decade between 1952 and 1964 he was quite clearly the best Indian batsman. No Indian cricketer who played during that period has any doubts on that score. Gupte, who grew up with him, rated him the best; Prasanna, who was coming into the side as Manjrekar was on his way out, also rated him the best. To everyone he was 'Tatt', the nickname he picked up in the Lancashire League. Manjrekar might have made an even greater impact had he – at the height of his dominance – not allowed his weight to get out of control. Once or twice at the beginning of a new series he looked grossly unfit.

Manjrekar's position in Indian cricket might have continued till the late 1960s – he desperately wanted to tour England in 1967 and Australia in 1967-68 – but the selectors felt that a man of thirty-four was too old, overruling Pataudi, the captain, who wanted him in the side. So, just as he had scored his seventh Test century he was dropped – the odd case of a man being forced to retire after making a hundred. The hurt this caused him was never healed and his last days – when he spoke bitterly of his triumphs – were sad and a reflection on Indian cricket.

Manjrekar's batting at Leeds had shown that there were Indian batsmen, as well as Hazare, with the right technique. Hazare's own technique was a model that others could copy but unfortunately he was no teacher, no inspirational leader. He did not have the dash that a Mankad or an Amarnath possessed. He could never make the imaginative leap that could transform his team, the spark that might convert a chance into an opportunity. Throughout this series he never made any attempt to talk to his batsmen, encourage them. That was not his style. The batting failures against Trueman can hardly be blamed on him. He, himself, made 333 runs, averaging 55.50 which, in a summer of such ruinous batting, was remarkable. But even before Trueman struck on that fateful Saturday in Leeds, Hazare had had the chance to seize the match. At the end of the first day, with India 272 for 6, it started raining. Ghulam Ahmed thought the uncovered wickets would be just right for him. But Hazare could not contemplate declaring at such a score. India batted on for 35 minutes on the second day, adding a measly 21 runs, while Laker took 4 wickets in nine balls.

No sooner did England bat than Ghulam removed Hutton, Simpson and Compton. Shinde bowled May and England were 92 for 4. But as the wicket eased Graveney and Watkins, who knew the Indian attack so well from the winter tour, took the game away from India and what might have been a possible Indian victory turned into a rout. But then that generation of Indian captains, like Hazare, first thought of drawing a match. Anything else was a bonus. What they failed to realise is that teams that play for draws more often lose. Defeat was a horrid ogre, *Wisden* wrote, summing up the tour, and in fearing it India made themselves appear much worse than they were.

Two months after the Oval Test the Indians were back in Delhi facing Pakistan. Pakistan had just become a member of the Imperial (now International) Cricket Council and this was their inaugural series. Batsmen in a side which had made 58, 82, and 98 in three previous innings in England might have feared this Test but in the curious way the Indian selectors work the two players dropped were the two who had opened the bowling at The Oval: Phadkar and Divecha. Indian selectors so quick to change sides now seemed reluctant to discard batsmen who had failed. Gul Mohammad and Amarnath came in. The crucial change was the latter one. Amarnath replaced Hazare as captain, with Hazare staying on as a batsman. The two months had seen the usual machinations in the Indian Board, Vizzy was now pulling the strings and, with 1936 a distant memory, Amarnath was now his man.

The Board felt justified about the changes as Amarnath led India to an innings victory in Delhi and then, despite a defeat by a similar margin in Lucknow – India finding the medium pace of Fazal Mahmood on the jute matting wicket unplayable – won the third Test in Bombay by ten wickets. With the other two drawn this meant that Amarnath had led India to her first ever series victory. Yet how much of this was due to Amarnath? The Delhi victory was almost wholly due to Mankad. India made 372 largely due to a last-wicket partnership of 109 between Adhikari and Ghulam Ahmed who scored his one and only Test 50, defying his career Test batting average of 8.72. After

Pakistan had started well, Mankad proved so destructive that he took 8 for 52 in the first innings and 5 for 79 in the second, and Pakistan were beaten with a day to spare.

In the second Test for various reasons Hazare, Mankad and Adhikari did not play. As Pakistan played most of their cricket on matting India, generously, arranged a Test on the mat of Lucknow – the only Test to be played there – and were duly beaten.

For Bombay, Mankad was back and about half an hour before the Test was due to begin Amarnath gathered the team together in his room on the second floor of the CCI. The Brabourne was a great place for batting but, at about this time of the year first thing in the morning, the effect of hot sun on dew often caused the ball to move. Everyone recalled the occasion, almost exactly two years ago, when Ridgway, playing for the Second Commonwealth XI, routed India for 82. Amarnath turned to Mankad and asked in Hindi, 'Arey Vinoo, kya karen?' 'What should we do if we win the toss?' Mankad, who was known for his forthright views and use of colourful language – he could swear in every language and once swore continuously in Hindi for a full two minutes – replied, 'Arey Lala, saley log ko dal tho.' 'Put the bastards in.' Amarnath was shocked. Not by the language, he could be just as colourful, but the idea. In those days the idea of winning the toss and putting the opposition in was almost unknown. This, he cautioned Mankad, would be a 'bombshell' for the press.

Whether Amarnath would have braved the press and taken the gamble we do not know. He did not have a choice. Kardar, the Pakistan captain, won the toss and, with no Mankad to guide him, batted. Amarnath, opening the bowling, found so much movement that he soon set the most attacking of fields. He took 4 for 40, Mankad took 3 for 52 and Pakistan was bowled out for 186. Hazare and Umrigar made centuries, Mankad took another five wickets, 5 for 72, in the second innings and India won by ten wickets. In the process Mankad completed the Test double of 1,000 runs and 100 wickets in only his twenty-third Test. This remained the fastest double in Test history until 1979, when Botham completed it in twenty-one Tests, ironically against India.

If the next two Tests were not as gripping, then one reason was that Mankad was no longer so central a figure. The fourth at Madras was ruined by rain after an Amarnath gamble had backfired. Pakistan scored 240 for 9 but he instructed his bowlers not to take the last wicket. This recoiled so badly that the last wicket put on 104, and when India batted they were struggling at 175 for 6 before the rains came. Finally at Calcutta, Amarnath did put Pakistan in but they easily saved the match and by then Amarnath was a very bitter man. At one stage he threatened not to play in the Calcutta

186

Test and only did so because otherwise Mankad would have taken over.

As usual the Board's politicians had been at work. They met the day before the Madras Test to choose a captain for the West Indies trip but decided not to announce it until just before the final Test. But the news leaked out, a journalist told Amarnath and, at the dinner after the Test, Amarnath himself announced the news, much to the consternation of the Board. He promised to play the last Test under Hazare but with India departing for the West Indies within days of the Calcutta Test, Hazare dropped out. He had to prepare for the tour and Amarnath, unhappy and angry, captained India for the last time. After the end of the Test, at a dinner where the great and good of Indian cricket were gathered, he vented the anger that had been building up. 'I have been taught to play cricket in a bad school. Vizzy will bear me out and since 1936, and since he has become a member of the Board of Control, he has not played cricket. I know he is a responsible man, but he plays other games than cricket on the Board.'

Amarnath was not chosen to go on the West Indian trip. Hazare's vice-captain was Mankad. The man who had excited such visions in November 1933 when he had scored the first ever Test hundred by an Indian was leaving Test cricket, his potential clearly unfulfilled. In 24 Tests he had scored 878 runs, averaging 24.38, and had taken 45 wickets at 32.91. In international cricket such figures belong to the second division. But Indians and others who had seen him play knew he belonged to the first division, to the select pantheon of great Indian cricketers. If the figures were not there to back his claims then he was just another one of those Indian cricketers who left behind memories that were more eloquent than the figures.

So four months after the disaster in England India were again touring – their fourth Test series in eighteen months. Indian cricket never seemed to be able to plan properly. Between 1947 and 1951 the Indians had played ten Tests. Now, between November 1951 and April 1953 they would be playing eighteen Tests. Of course this was not entirely the Board's fault. India was still the junior member of the cricket world and had to accept the crumbs from the big boys' tables. But surely they could plan these tours better? India's last series with Pakistan finished in Calcutta on 15 December 1952. The first match in San Fernando in Trinidad started on 10 January 1953. This, given the arduous journey – flight to London, then banana boat from Southampton – meant that the Indians had barely had time to catch their breath before they were touring a country they had never been to before. The tour followed the Pakistani series so quickly in fact that the players had no time to pack their gear, which followed later.

Nor were matters helped by the usual pre-tour withdrawals. It had been whispered that if a 'certain player' was chosen then certain other players would not tour. So with Amarnath left at home, Sen, Ghulam Ahmed, Gopinath and Kasturirangan withdrew from the team. It meant finding a new wicket-keeper, another batsman, but Ghulam Ahmed as off-spinner who, with twelve wickets, was Mankad's principal ally against Pakistan, was quite irreplaceable.

But this was now all part of the pre-tour comings and goings in India. In any case the Indians knew little about the West Indies and they had no expectations from their team. As long as they avoided the humiliations of England, everybody would be satisfied. Before the team left India Justice Tendolkar, President of the Bombay Cricket Association, consoled the Indians that, while the team was not strong enough to beat the West Indians, perhaps they would manage to play good cricket without bothering about the results. What the Indians did not want was to be surprised by news from the Caribbean. But they were to be surprised – pleasantly surprised. Just when least expected the Indians produced their first respectable overseas showing since they had started playing Tests. For the first time away from home they showed some of the form they so often did at home. For the first time cricketers returned from an overseas visit and were greeted by editorials praising them rather than demanding an inquiry. In Indian cricket history it became known as 'the happy tour'.

12

The age of Gupte
1953-56

In cricket history the Indian tour of the West Indies in the early part of 1953 does not appear very significant. The tour finished on 4 April 1953. Three weeks later the Australians arrived in England to begin one of the most dramatic series since the war. Australia had held the Ashes for nineteen years, since 1934, but this was an Australia without Bradman and in the final Test of the series – after four drawn games – Hutton won back the Ashes with an emphatic victory. In cricket history 1953 will always be associated with that day at The Oval when Compton swept Morris to the square-leg boundary and Hutton stood on the balcony of the pavilion to accept the crowd's cheers.

Yet for both India and the West Indies the 1952-53 tour was very important. Not so much for the results. West Indies won the Barbados Test and that was enough to give them a 1–0 victory in the five-Test series. The Indians never looked like winning a single Test, yet their cricket often surprised and delighted the West Indians and it was their very presence on the cricket field that had the most dramatic and unexpected impact. For it meant that a vital part of the West Indian population – who had been virtually ignored in the white/black divide of the islands – now found their voice.

India approached the tour much as a convalescent might after a long illness. The tour in England had suggested that Trueman's jibe, that Indians could not bat, was true, and in the first Test at Port of Spain, soon after winning the toss, India were 16 for 1. But now India recovered so well that the final score was 417 with the batsman who had been struggling to get into double figures in England, Umrigar, making a century. Umrigar may have been frightened by Trueman but Ramadhin and Valentine – who had demolished England in 1950 – held no such terrors. Ramadhin took 1 for 107, Valentine 2 for 92 as Umrigar made 130. After that Umrigar rarely failed and topped the batting, making 560 runs at an average of 62.22. Not far behind him was Roy. He had hardly scored a run against Trueman, now he was nearly always making runs and in the final Test he made 85 and a grand 150: a total of 383 runs in the series at an average of 47.87. Madhav Apte, making his first tour, was second in the averages with

189

460 runs at 51.11, suggesting India might have found a reliable opener, while Manjrekar, without doing anything extraordinary, confirmed that he was the best of the younger batsmen.

So consistent were these four that Hazare's failure with the bat did not matter -- he averaged 19.40 – and the batting never really failed except on the final day of the Barbados Test when, on a wicket that had badly crumbled and with the ball keeping horribly low, Ramadhin came into his element and took 5 wickets for 26, his only five-wicket haul of the series, and India lost by 142 runs.

Even more than their batting the Indians' fielding surprised the West Indians. West Indians, with their long history of brilliant fieldsmen, are not easily impressed by visiting fielders but even today in the Caribbean this Indian team is talked about as the best fielding side to tour the area. The catching could still be suspect. In the first Test Weekes was missed when he was 19 and went on to make 207. But it was the ground fielding that took the eye. It reached, *Wisden* wrote, 'great heights' and 'there was little doubt that their brilliant out-cricket had much to do with maintaining interest in the tour'.

Fielding in cricket is usually talked of in terms of cover fielding. Cricket memory insists that the great fielders were constantly 'patrolling the covers', a term which has its mock overtones but is more often than not meant seriously. On this tour the Indians did have some of the best fielders in the covers. This was a young man's tour and Gadkari, Ghorpade, Gaekwad, Apte and Umrigar formed a wonderful quintet of fielders, quickly covering the ground, and making flat, hard, accurate returns to the wicket-keeper. Such fielding can never be conveyed in terms of figures but the abiding memory of that tour was of Weekes, Worrell and Walcott hitting the Indian spinners murderously hard into the covers. Four, shouted the crowd as the ball left the bat, only to find an Umrigar or a Gadkari or Apte or Ghorpade or Gaekwad cutting it off. As an eighteen-year-old Ivan Madray from British Guiana, who later played in two Tests, felt he was enjoying a feast:

It was a fantastic fielding side . . . like lightning in the field. They chased the ball to the boundary as if their lives depended on it; picked it up and hurled it in one motion right above the bails. Effortlessly. Cleanly. All day. It was a feast for me; it was like eating a bowl of rice.

The spinner who nearly always seemed to be involved in these exchanges was Subash Gupte. He had made his debut against England in 1951–52 on the unhelpful Calcutta wicket, and then been discarded both for the remaining Tests and the tour that followed. Against Pakistan he was still on probation, bowling just 47 overs in two Tests, and was sent to the West Indies with great trepidation. On the hard, fast, bouncy Caribbean wickets did a leg-spinner who flighted the ball have a chance against the three Ws? They were the best batsmen in the world then, and, playing on their home wickets, surely they would murder him? They never got a chance. Gupte was always a step ahead with his flighted leg-breaks, his top-spinner or his well-disguised googly – not one but two. Gupte flighted and spun the ball so cleverly that few of the West Indies batsmen faced him confidently. In the Tests he took 27 wickets at 29.22, on the tour he took 50 wickets at 23.64, seven less than the rest of the Indian bowlers put together. His twelve wickets against Jamaica earned India its only victory of the tour.

He showed his class in the very first Test when, faced by the three Ws, he did not lose his faith in his own ability. Weekes made 207 before Gupte got him and he finished with 7 for 162 – the wickets of Stollmeyer, Worrell, Weekes, Pairaudeau, Gomez, King, and Valentine.

After that in every Test, barring the second, Gupte was the main Indian bowler. In the third, again in Trinidad, he took 5 for 107, Rae, Walcott and Worrell being his main scalps. In the first innings of the fourth Test he took 4 for 122, and then 5 for 180 in the fifth. There was in Gupte not only the power to express the leg-spinner's rare art but the patience, the ability to wage a war of attrition that a spinner needs to conduct. Quick bowlers by their very nature take wickets in a rush. They are the cricket equivalent of the fast food business. Sometimes it can be very satisfactory, often it is necessary, but it is always quick. The spinner, in contrast, presents a five-course gourmet meal; slowly, patiently he achieves his objective.

What impressed Madray, who was inspired to become a leg-spinner by watching Gupte, was 'his stamina, his intelligence, and his ability to control his emotions', as he said to the authors of *Indo-West Indian Cricket*. 'On a number of occasions when he was hit, he would stroll back slowly, thoughtfully, to his bowling mark, as if nothing had happened. And when you thought he was giving you the leg-break again, he would bowl his beautifully disguised googly or he would toss it up or shift it. He would try everything in one over, a different ball each time. And rarely did he lose control: it is so easy to make mistakes when you are trying so many things. He made few.'

Gupte illustrated this approach in the first Test. At one stage he had taken 1 for 107. It was a flat jute matting wicket, and nothing in the conditions or the hot sun to stop the batsman. But Gupte kept on and in the end he had bowled 66 overs, taken 7 for 162, and the West Indies, massively placed at 409 for 4, had been contained to 438 all out. Gupte kept doing this throughout the series. He could not entirely stop the three Ws scoring runs – but then no bowler at that time could. But he restrained them and often prevented them from running up really huge scores.

In the fourth Test Walcott made 125, West Indies were 302 for 4 and Gupte had not taken a wicket. But then Hazare had Walcott lbw and Gupte swept through the rest of the batting. From 302 for 4 they were 364 all out, Gupte taking four of the last five wickets. In Kingston, Gupte did even better. This time all three Ws made runs: Worrell 207, Weekes 109, and Walcott 118 and on the fourth day West Indies were 543 for 3. But then Gupte, helped by Mankad, caused such devastation that the West Indies were all out for 576, the last six wickets falling for 33 runs. Given the wickets and the power of the three Ws they remain some of the best advertisements of the leg-spinner's art that have ever been seen. In that era, bowling against the best batsmen then in the world, and on their home patch, no other bowler did remotely as well. The three Ws made runs against Gupte but they never collared him. If Gupte had never bowled again this tour was enough to mark him out as a great bowler.

Gupte formed a natural link with Mankad who was the second highest wicket-taker with 15 wickets but at the expensive rate of 53.06. Mankad had briefly paired with Ghulam Ahmed but this new combination, the first real spinning pair in Indian Test history, marked a new trend. For a long time Mankad had been the only world-class spinner, other spinners who bowled alongside him were not in the same class. This was the first in a line of great spinning pairs and soon India came to produce two or at times even three world-class spinners who could operate together.

The contrast with Mankad was not merely that one was a left-armer and the other a right-arm wrist spinner. Mankad was the product of an old, dying school: princely influence and English coaching, Gupte the product of a new, vibrant, very Indian nursery. This was Shivaji Park, the maidan in the congested Maharashtrian heartland of central Bombay. It is here that the great dreams and ambitions of the founder of the eighteenth-century Maratta empire, Shivaji, are kept alive, burnished with the re-telling of the legend and the exploits of the modern-day heroes, and it provides one of the hardest cricketing schools in the country, blending local nationalism with an intense desire to win and succeed. Over the years it has produced some of the great Bombay and Indian cricketers. Gupte, as also Manjrekar, was one of the first products of this nursery. He had started his cricket a few miles up the road from Shivaji Park at Mahim Juveniles – one of those maidan clubs that had no clubhouse but put up a tent on match days – and then moved to Shivaji Park.

Supplementing the maidan cricket at weekends was gully cricket at all hours of the day, every day of the week. Gully cricket is, perhaps, the most evocative part of urban Indian cricket, next only to the maidan in importance. Maidans are broad, open spaces, gullies are little lanes running off busy, main streets where children learn the game by improvising with a tennis ball, bits of wood or any other implement that comes to hand. The gully where Gupte learnt his cricket is now called Sandip Patil gully but this only shows that Indian sporting memory, like that of other nations, can be notoriously unreliable and short. For long before Patil was even conceived – he was born three years after Gupte had proved his class in the West Indies – Gupte was perfecting his art by bowling his leg-breaks to his friend Vijay Manjrekar. One was to prove the first great spinner India produced (if we count Mankad, as we should, as an all-rounder), the other the first major post-war batsman. Their progression through Indian cricket was very similar. They both made their Test debut against England in Calcutta and affirmed, now the princes had all but disappeared as patrons, that India had found new ways to unearth cricket talent.

The West Indies tour had also, quite unexpectedly, unearthed a new cricket constituency for them in Trinidad. Cricket, the island's greatest writer, V. S. Naipaul, has written in *Middle Passage*, provides a hero figure for Trinidadians:

Cricket has always been more than a game in Trinidad. In a society which demanded no skills and offered no rewards to merit, cricket was the only activity which permitted a man to grow to his full stature and to be measured against international standards. Alone on a field, beyond obscuring intrigue, the cricketer's true worth could be seen by all. His race, education, wealth did not matter. We had no scientists, engineers, explorers, soldiers, or poets. The cricketer was our only hero-figure.

For the Indians of Trinidad, the visit of the 1953 Indians seemed to generate the sort of feeling that the sight of returning Roman legions must have produced amongst the colonists of that ancient empire. These were Indians who, as indentured labourers, had been brought to work the sugar plantations of the West Indies, mainly in Trinidad and what was then called British Guiana. Slavery had been abolished, the white-owned sugar plantations required labourers, and Indians, mainly from central and eastern India, were pressganged into service. Many had been tricked by their British recruiters with promises of escaping the poverty of India in a land of plenty across the seas. They arrived to find they were living in the old slave quarters and, while they were not slaves, the life of the indentured labourer was, at times, not much above that of a slave. By the time the Indian cricket team arrived indentured labour had long since vanished and now the second, third or fourth generations were slowly becoming active in business or agriculture. But many Indians retained the customs of the old country, many of them still spoke Hindi, and the memories of a lost land remained. In contrast to the rest of the population they were the odd people of the Caribbean, East Indians in a West Indian setting – a strange community about whom they knew little. Suren Capildeo, just such an East Indian, was then studying at Queen's Royal College.

I was the only Hindu in my class. The other students were mostly white and there were a few blacks. The blacks were what I call Afro-Saxons: English in their outlook, in everything but their skin colour. Indians were seen as people who ate different food, ate with their fingers, wore funny clothes, spoke a funny language, worshipped gods with four arms and a couple of heads. In a society built on Empire and 'God save the Queen' all this was very primitive. The effect of the visit of this, the first, Indian cricket team was to coalesce the Indian community. Before the cricketers arrived all the news that came out of India was bad: famine, riots. We were seen as coming from a country that had all sorts of distressing events. Gandhi was seen as a half-naked fakir. The biggest ideal in this society was to become an Englishman. The black man wanted to be English. We were made to feel ashamed. They didn't think that a people like that could play cricket. The 1953 tour came as a culture shock. Suddenly they found that Indians could play cricket and compete with the West Indians.

For Port of Spain itself, the arrival of the tourists was a great shock. Trinidad, then, was very much an island paradise with Port of Spain, the capital, a town with narrow streets: a rum and calypso society. In this society the Indians scarcely seemed to exist. The sugar plantations their forefathers had worked on were mainly in the south, some way from Port of Spain, and most of the Indians still lived there. They knew little about Port of Spain and Port of Spain knew little about them. The West Indies Board had shrewdly arranged the tourists' first match, a two-day East India XI versus India, at San Fernando in the Indian rural heartland of Trinidad. While the Indian cricketers were immediately warmed by the hospitality, for the locals there was a magic and romance about seeing real Indians from India play. One Trinidadian lady of Indian descent was taken to the match by her father. She sat glued to her seat watching Gupte bowl. It was love at first sight and within a few years they were married.

But the big surprise came when the Indians travelled to Port of Spain for the first Test. East Indians of rural Trinidad, who had never been to their own capital city, travelled down with them. The gates had to be closed on two successive days and 22,000 spectators crammed into the Queen's Park Oval – the largest crowd ever to watch a cricket match in the Caribbean. The West Indies had never seen anything like this. A cricket team, to which nobody had given a ghostly chance against the mighty West Indies, one that the West Indies Board had agreed to receive on sufferance, as it were, had suddenly discovered a cricket constituency for them, one which the Board did not know existed – nor had they done anything to encourage it. If the Trinidadians of Indian descent saw the visit of the Indian team as a chance to rediscover a lost land, for the West Indies Board it made a welcome profit.

And the tour encouraged a whole generation of East Indians in the Caribbean. Just before the visit one of them, Sonny Ramadhin, had made a breakthrough, having played a major part in the West Indies winning a series for the first time in England in 1950. This made the East Indians believe in themselves playing the white man's game. As it happened Ramadhin travelled back to Trinidad from England on the same boat as the Indian team, and the joint arrival was front-page news in the *Trinidad Guardian*. They were heroes for a people who had been denied heroes. As the Indians progressed through the Caribbean they found that East Indians – first suppressed by the whites and soon to be suppressed by the increasingly powerful blacks – discovered more heroes amongst the Indian cricketers.

This was particularly so in British Guiana where the East Indians were in a majority and, for a brief moment, seemed to be ready to take over from the colonial power. But mistakes in political leadership, the ruthless use of terror by the black political leader Forbes Burnham, and the help of America cheated the East Indians of their political prize. All this was in the future. 1953 was a heady time in politics, the Indo-Guyanese were coming into their own and the visit of the 1953 Indian team was part of this process of discovery, the start of a false dawn that was all too cruelly obliterated.

Clem Shiwcharan was a boy of three when the 1953 Indians arrived in Guiana. He was too young to experience the feelings at first hand but was told often enough about the effect the tour had:

The tour by the Indian cricketers in 1953 . . . set Indo-Guiana alight. Among the Indo-Guianese there were still many Hindi-speakers, former indentured labourers, who were born in India. Memories of the old country, dimmed perhaps, still survived. Most Indo-Guianese supported India; and the supreme fielding of the Indian team was a real joy, I was constantly told, coupled with the mastery of the leg-spinner Subhas Gupte, brought much pride . . . Every little Indian boy would play at being Gupte, or Apte or Mankad. My grandfather, who made his maiden trip to Georgetown to see the Test in March 1953, often told a story. An ebullient Hindu priest, of considerable repute, unleashed a string of popular Hindu curse words, punched the air, uncoiled his sacred turban, turned to the crowd and waved it triumphantly. Then, suddenly collecting himself, recoiled with embarrassment, failing to be unobtrusive as he hurriedly assumed old civilities. All this, because the Indian bowler, Ramchand, had bowled Bruce Pairaudeau, the West Indies opening batsman, a white Guianese from Georgetown. . . .

The visit produced joy and mixed feelings: the older Indians who had always wanted to return felt all the more keen, the small minority who had returned and found India wanting were confused and 'for the locally born, the overwhelming majority, images of a more idyllic India, the India of movie stars, solidified'.

For one, in particular, Ivan Madray, it meant a new hero and a new career. Madray was at High School when the Indian team came to Georgetown to play the Test:

Watching the Indians – this was the first Test match I ever saw – observing Gupte as he bowled, the keenness, the neatness of the Indians; it was a privilege to be an Indian watching the first Indian side playing in the West Indies. Although I was born in the West Indies and I should have identified with the West Indies team, I was, at that time, in total sympathy with the Indians. I think that it is true of most Indians in British Guiana in 1953. At Port Mourant [the main Indian area in British Guiana] we were very proud of this Indian side, and it made cricket even more attractive to us. . . . I was filled with joy watching the Indians play. I was filled with sadness leaving that scene of the Test match and returning home. But I became more dedicated to my cricket; I played with a new courage. And I made the pledge to play first-class cricket on that ground. Gupte was my idea of what a leg-spinner should be.

Madray went on to fulfil his fantasy and play for the West Indies. But while his career showed the wretchedness which the West Indian selectors often displayed to those of Indian blood, his boyhood friends Rohan Kanhai and Joe Solomon, both of Indian origin and both from the plantation of Port Mourant, went on to great prominence in cricket through the 1950s and 1960s and provide the West Indies and the world with two of their most brilliant cricketers, in addition to Ramadhin. But that period of West Indies Indian excellence proved an illusion. Never again were the cricketers of Indian origin to exercise such dominance in West Indian cricket. The West Indian team is now wholly black, has been so for some years and cricketers of Indian origin in the Caribbean despair of ever getting selected. But they had enjoyed one brief shining moment and the 1953 Indians had prepared the way.

It is a reflection on modern West Indian society that none of its writers, not even C. L. R. James or Michael Manley, has looked at this interaction between India and the West Indies or examined the feelings of their own Indian-origin population towards cricket. The story they tell of West Indian cricket is in conventional terms: the story of black and white. The Indian element is not seen to be significant, almost as if Indians do not belong to the history of the West Indies.

The Indians returned from the West Indies thankful for a rest. They had never had such concentrated Test cricket as their 18 Tests in 18 months, including two long tours to England and the West Indies. But after the feast came the famine. Like somebody who has overeaten and needs to go on a diet, India now went nearly two years without any Test cricket. The last Test against the West Indies had finished in April 1953, and the next Test was against Pakistan in January 1955. In between there was a third Commonwealth XI tour, but that underlined how India was still not part of the international circuit of regular summer and winter tours.

The Indian Board would have dearly loved to have had an official team to tour India in the winter of 1953–54, which marked the Board's twenty-fifth anniversary, but there was nobody available so George Duckworth assembled yet another Commonwealth side – by common consent the weakest of three to tour India. It was never a settled side. Worrell and Ramadhin left after two 'Tests'; R. T. Simpson returned after the third and there were several other changes. The Indians won the series 2–1, both their victories being by innings.

What this signified it was difficult to say. The Indians maintained a depressing tradition they had set in most home series. Against England in 1951–52 every Test saw five changes, 23 players were used in all. Now the Indian selectors seemed hooked on a new number: 26. Against Pakistan they had used 26 players, against the Commonwealth team another lot of 26 players was used. The treatment of Madhav Apte showed how inconsistent Indian team selection could be. Apte had returned from the West Indies a considerable batsman who, it seemed, would solve India's opening batting problem. He played in the first 'Test', made 30 and never played for India again. So in all too brief a Test career of seven Tests, five of them in the West Indies, he scored 542 runs at an average of 49.27. Characteristically no Indian Board official ever explained why Apte was discarded. Some critics have argued that many of Apte's runs 'came off the edge'; the more probable reason was that he had fallen foul of the regional power games.

The same regional considerations characterised the choice of captain during the series. Hazare played in three 'Tests', but he had given up the captaincy and the Indians just would not decide on a successor. Umrigar captained in the first two matches, won the first and drew the second. Adhikari captained the third and lost it. Ghulam Ahmed the fourth and won. But even this was no guarantee of retaining the job. For the fifth the Indians had a new captain in Phadkar.

The man who had not been captain in the series at all, Mankad – the vice-captain in the West Indies – should have been the logical choice. But while he did not captain at home he did take the team to Pakistan in January 1955. Perhaps the Indian Board was right to have reservations about him for in Pakistan Mankad proved a dismal captain. That fine cricketing brain, the man who was always ready with good, sound cricketing advice for other captains, just could not come to a decision when he was captain. In Indian cricket there has rarely been a better mind, a better tactician than Mankad. He could size up situations expertly. He had only to see a player to judge how good he was, what he should do. He only saw Madhav Apte bat for a few minutes in the nets at Bombay's Elphinstone College and he formed the impression that he had the making of a good opener. Apte was encouraged to open and, but for the vagaries of the Indian selectors, might have become a major Test opener. But now that he had the captaincy thrust on him Mankad seemed to have left his thinking behind. It is possible that Mankad was distracted during his tour when he fell madly in love with a young, beautiful, Pakistani girl. She followed him everywhere, coming to the matches and became very much part of Mankad's life while in Pakistan. Such love affairs are not unknown in cricket but Mankad lost his head, spent rather more time with the girl than his team and his own performance and that of India's cricket suffered. The passion that he normally brought to the game, the enthusiasm and the dedication were siphoned off elsewhere.

With the Pakistani captain, Kardar, desperately keen not to lose, the two teams faced each other like boxers sparring for an opening, and for the first time in Test history all five Tests were drawn. During the series the Indians also had a foretaste of the umpiring problems that can bedevil visitors to Pakistan. In one Test Kardar was run out halfway down the wicket, the picture in the next day's paper showed him stranded in the middle of the wicket with the stumps broken. The umpire ruled that Kardar was in. In the Lahore Test Alimuddin, who headed the Pakistani batting, was caught behind. By then the Indians were becoming cynical about Pakistani umpiring and, when he was given not out, just looked at the umpire and, as Pankaj Roy recalls, 'laughed. Then Alimuddin took a run and was behind the popping crease and the return crease when somebody hit the stumps and in joke asked "How's that?" The umpire gave Alimuddin out. Alimuddin was furious. As he left he abused the umpire, "You give me not out when I am out and give me out when I am not out." '

Only one bowler really enhanced his reputation. That, again, was Gupte. Outside the Tests he was almost unplayable, taking 55 wickets for 16.21. In the Tests he took 21 wickets at 22.61 and this on wickets that, if anything, favoured batsmen even more than in the West Indies. As in the West Indies he showed the ability to cause sudden, sensational collapses and occasionally it seemed he would run through Pakistan. In the second innings of the first Test he took 5 for 17 in six overs, Pakistan going from 122 for 2 to 158 all out. In the Lahore Test Gupte bowled 73.5 overs, 33 maidens and took 5 for 133 and in the fourth Test, at Peshawar, the only Test ever played there, he caused another collapse, taking 5 for 63. But there was never enough support for him, while the Indian batting was experiencing its own collapses against the fast-medium bowling of Khan Mohammed and Fazal, to make the most of his extraordinary gifts.

In two series now Gupte had taken 48 wickets and nobody could doubt his class. The question was: when would he win a series for India? The answer came in the winter of 1955–56 when New Zealand made their first tour of India. It was as complete a bowling triumph as any. Gupte was devastating; and confronted by a country and a diet totally strange to them the New Zealanders capitulated. Their two great players, Sutcliffe and Reid, made runs but most of the rest could make little of Gupte and their plight was illustrated by Petrie, a good, workmanlike wicket-keeper who, opening in the first two Tests, would make a few runs against the Indian opening bowlers, then Gupte would come on and Petrie would be baffled. In four innings as opener he got out to Gupte three times, and the only occasion he got out to an opening bowler, Phadkar, it was Gupte who took the catch.

Gupte came on almost as soon as New Zealand started batting in the first Test and never relaxed his grip. In the first innings he took 7 for 128 and after that in only one Test, the third at Delhi, did he fail to take five wickets in at least one innings. In the second and the fifth Tests, both of which India won by an innings, Gupte showed how destructive high-class leg-spin bowling can be, even on easy-paced wickets. In Bombay, after India made 421, New Zealand were bowled out for 258 and 136, Gupte taking 8 for 128. In the fifth, after India had made 537 for 3 declared on another easy-paced Madras wicket, Gupte took 9 for 145, bowling New Zealand out for 209 and 219. By the end of the series Gupte had taken 34 wickets, two more than all the other Indian bowlers put together, at an average of 19.67.

Much has been made of the fact that New Zealanders had little experience of leg-spin, though there were two leg-spinners in their party; even so this was a quite astonishing display of controlled and accurate performance of the art. Different facets of bowling have their own appeal: the left-armer, the off-spinner, the fast bowler. But no bowling art is more evocative than leg-spin. It seems doomed to failure, at times so unnatural – which explains why Yorkshire distrusts all this 'back-of-the-hand stuff' – yet when it works it presents the most wonderful sight. It is cricket's equivalent of high-wire walking. There is always the possibility that the batsmen will make the bowler look inadequate, but a great leg-spinner can make any batsman look like a fool, playing for the leg-break when it is a googly, and now Gupte was doing that to most of the New Zealand batsmen.

Over the years he had further developed his art, talked to people like Mankad, and learnt how to set his field. So, unless the wicket was turning, he always had his square-leg fine; he was only placed on the boundary square with the wickets when the ball was turning. Gupte always began a spell by bowling line and length. And from the beginning he decided which side of the wicket he would attack: off-side or on-side. Normally he concentrated his attack on the off stump or wide of the off stump. Against West Indians he was particularly careful, given their strength there, not to attack the leg stump. The idea was either to get a stumping or have the batsman caught in the slips, very rarely bowled. If the wicket was turning then Gupte would bowl a lower trajectory, much flatter. On a good wicket he would flight the ball more. He worked on a simple mathematical principle: the slower you are, more spin; more speed, less spin.

In retrospect the New Zealand series marked the high tide of the reign of Gupte. There were still some great achievements to come but he would never again dominate the Indian bowling, or a series, as he did then. Ever since January 1953, when he played in the first Test against the West Indies, he had dominated Indian bowling like no other Indian bowler. In two of the four series he had topped the averages, in all four he had been the leading wicket-taker, well ahead of the other bowlers. In the four series including the unofficial one against the Commonwealth his figures read:

West Indies: 329.3–87–789–27, average 29.22; next highest wicket-taker Mankad, with 345 overs and 15 wickets at an average of 53.06;

Commonwealth: 275.3–67–676–27, average 25.03; next highest wicket-taker Ghulam Ahmed, with 212.5 overs and 23 wickets at an average of 14.30;

Pakistan: 276.5–107–475–21, average 22.61; next highest wicket-taker Mankad, with 263.3 overs and 12 wickets at an average of 33.25;

New Zealand: 356.4–153–669–34, average 19.67; next highest wicket-taker Mankad, with 167.1 overs and 12 wickets at an average of 27.33.

Gupte was now established as the great hero of millions of Indians. In the Bombay Test as he ran in to bowl the volatile, noisy crowds in the East Stands took up the rhythmical chanting b-o-w-l-e-d until the New Zealanders, harassed enough already, complained and Umrigar, the captain, had to go up to the wire-fencing separating the crowd from the players and with folded palms ask them to be quiet. There had been Indian cricket heroes before this but they, with the possible exceptions of Nissar and Amar Singh, had all been batsmen: Nayudu, Merchant, Mushtaq Ali, Hazare. Now for the first time it was a pure bowler and a spinner at that.

Every day on the country's maidans one could see young children wanting to bowl like Gupte. All tried to imitate his action: the short, quick run-up, the chesty action with the right foot dragged at the moment of delivery – Gupte thought that anchoring the foot this way gave him greater control – and the classical mode of delivery with the wrists cocked and the arm high. Few of us who tried to imitate him got it right. Like the batsmen we missed the subtle variations: the lower arm and chesty action for one googly, the high arm for the other. But this did not diminish our ardour. One acquaintance who was called Gupta even started calling himself Gupte to see if some of the magic would rub off. The devotion and the desire to imitate reflected the fact that all Indians knew he was the one great bowler the country had, the only one who could bowl out the opposition. Praise of him by foreigners was cherished and when Tom Graveney forecast he would be a world-beater in England in 1959 this was carefully retold to add to the growing legend. If all else failed Gupte would see India through.

Against New Zealand, Gupte's bowling was backed up by the Indian batting which for a change avoided its usual failures. Only once in the entire series did India make less than 400 in any innings. That was in Calcutta, but India came back so strongly that in the end New Zealand were hanging on for dear life at 74 for 6. Batsmen vied with each other in setting new records. Umrigar became the first to score a double hundred in Tests, 223 in the first and in the process he passed Mankad's then Indian record of 184 set at Lord's. In the next Test Mankad regained the record by making 223 as well. India was now scoring runs like it had never before done but it was in the fifth Test that the high water mark was reached.

The match was played at a new ground in Madras, the Corporation Stadium. India won the toss and for a day and a half New Zealand could not get the opening pair out. Eight hours after the match had started the first Indian wicket fell and that because the two Indians had been told to hit out by their captain. The two Indians were Vinoo Mankad and Pankaj Roy. Mankad made 231, the highest score by an Indian in Tests at that stage, Roy made 173 and the pair put on 413 for the first wicket, passing the then world record of 359 set by Hutton and Washbrook for England against South Africa at Johannesburg in 1948–49. At last an Indian pair had brought to Test cricket the sort of remorseless, relentless run-making that had been so common in domestic cricket during the war. Mankad's Indian record stood for many years but, while that has been broken, the first-wicket record he and Roy established still stands – the only Indian Test batting record.

Yet a more unlikely opening partnership can hardly be imagined. Mankad had opened the innings often enough but then he had batted in almost every other position. It seems as though, every two years or so, an Indian captain or selector would decide that it was time, once again, for Vinoo to open. In the West Indies he had opened in the first innings of a Test, batted no. 9 in the second. In this series, for the first time in almost four years, he was consistently opening. If this was unusual, then his partner's name in the record books must have come as a surprise and not merely to Trueman. Roy's dreadful English experience in 1952 should have ended his Test career. Roy, himself, believed it would. He perhaps benefited from the fact that, as the only viable representative of the East Zone, the regional balancing game worked out in his favour. He recovered slowly from his English trauma, making runs against the West Indies, against Pakistan but against New Zealand, in the first Test, in an Indian score of 498 for 4 declared, he made a duck. And a slow duck at that: when he was out the score was 27, mostly to Mankad. Roy was dropped and then something strange happened, as he himself related:

I took my mother to see Dr Aloke Ghosh, an eye specialist. He used to play for Sporting Union [a strong Calcutta club]. After her checkup I asked him if he would check my eyesight. The doctor was annoyed and asked me not to waste his time – 'You are playing against Test bowlers' – but reluctantly agreed. I found I could not read more than three lines of the eye board. The doctor was very surprised. 'Pankaj,' he said, 'you are short-sighted.' It turned out I had minus one power. I did not want to wear spectacles. I feared that if I was hit I would go blind as the glass would enter my eyes. The doctor asked me how many times I had been hit in the face. I said never. 'So,' he said, 'if you have never been hit, why worry? Take the glasses and if it works well and good.' The glasses were a revelation. Before that Vijay Merchant had asked me how I played the googly. I had said, I play it off the wicket, judging whether it is an off-break or a leg-break. He asked, 'But don't you see the spin in the air as it leaves the hand of the bowler?' I had tried to see the spin but couldn't see it and I thought this was big talk from a great cricketer. When I got the glasses I could see the googly spin as it left the bowler's hand and I apologised to Merchant.

So now Roy, wearing spectacles, started making copious runs in the Ranji Trophy. He was confident he would be back for the Calcutta Test, on his own home ground. He was, and he made a hundred. Then came Madras. At the end of the first day Mankad was 120, Roy had just reached his century. Mankad planned to hit out the next day but at lunch they were still together and it was then they realised that a world record was within their sights. A simple on-side shot secured it. Roy should have got his double-century – he never scored one and his 173 remains his highest score:

Vinoo got his 200 and he told me now, go for your 200. But then I got a chit from the captain [Umrigar]. He said hit every ball. I thought he was going to declare. I got out trying to hit. But even after I got out Umrigar batted on for another 80 minutes. When Vinoo came back he was furious.

Roy himself had not originally been an opening batsman. All his early cricket till the age of twenty-three was played as a no. 3 or no. 4 batsman, even no. 5. But during the trial matches that preceded the MCC tour of 1951–52 he was asked to open with Merchant and made runs. This impressed the selectors and suddenly Roy realised that, at last, he had found a way of forcing his way into the Indian Test team. For months he had not been able to work out how he could break into the solid middle-order. Wherever he looked, from no. 3 to no. 6, there was an established batsman. But Merchant, as opener, did not have a partner and wanted one: 'I knew Mushtaq Ali was not in the good books of the cricket Control Board. I knew there was a vacancy there. It was the only way I could get into the side.' Roy's chance came early on the tour in the tourists' first match against the Universities of India. Roy was captain and went up to C. K. Nayudu, chairman of the selectors, and asked his permission. 'Sir, I would like to open.' 'Why?' asked Nayudu. 'When you played against Holkar and made 172 you came in at no. 5. You are not an opening batsman.' Roy could not very well reveal his naked ambition and said, 'I am very confident because of the trials.' Nayudu replied, 'You are the skipper,' and shrugged his shoulders. Roy opened, made 89 quite brilliantly, putting in the shade the 30 made by Apte and he played in the Test with Merchant.

So a middle-order batsman became an opener and is now in the record books as one half of the partnership that set the world opening stand record. But he remained a middle-order batsman, never really comfortable against the moving ball. Interestingly, he had made a hundred against New Zealand in the Calcutta Test going in at no. 3 which was his ideal position and it is possible that he did his talent a disservice by adopting such an expediency. Yet it is, of course, entirely in keeping with the story of Indian cricket that its only Test batting record should be held by an all-rounder and a man who chose to open only in order to play Test cricket.

Indians rejoiced in the world record but this did not make Roy an Indian hero. The Indians knew that the victory against New Zealand and the large scores meant little against a country that had yet to win a Test match. The phobia of pace which Trueman had implanted had not been completely exorcised and the real test would come when Australia visited India, on their way home from England in 1956.

India should have had the advantage over the Australians who had had a demoralising tour of England, unable to cope with Laker, and lost the only Test they played in Pakistan; but in India the Australians were transformed. They won the three-Test series 2–0, and after the heavy scores against New Zealand, not once did the Indians top 300. Batting failures in both the first and third Tests cost them the match, the pattern being set on the first day of the series when India, on winning the toss, made 117 for 5 in a full day. Occupation of the crease was falsely equated with safety and the Indians never appeared to come to terms with the Australian bowling. Perhaps most galling of all, however, Gupte was overshadowed by an Australian leg-spinner. Benaud took 23 wickets in the series at 16.86. In the first innings of the first Test Benaud took 7 for 72, in the third match in Calcutta he took 11 for 105. On a wicket which took spin India were bowled out for scores of 136 in both innings.

Gupte should have been the Indian match-winner in Calcutta but had his most anonymous match to date. In the first innings he took just one wicket. Nobody scored many runs off him, 35 runs in 23 overs with 1 maiden, but he was not the destroyer India hoped he would be. It was Ghulam Ahmed, at the other end, who did the damage with 7 for 49. In the second innings Gupte was hardly used. He bowled only 7 overs, taking 1 for 24 as Ghulam and Mankad made the Australians struggle for runs. One reason could be that Gupte had finally come up against a batsman, the left-handed Neil Harvey, who used the different angle available to him as a left-hander to take the attack to the leg-spinner. Almost for the first time in his career Gupte was subjected to a concentrated attack. The Australians worked to a plan and Harvey had decided he would never allow Gupte to settle into a groove. This was made most evident in Bombay where Harvey made a magnificent 140.

Gupte's problems against Harvey were aggravated by the fact that he had so little practice against left-handers. India – and Pakistan for that matter – rarely produce top-class left-handed batsmen. In Indian cricket only a few have reached Test standard, notably Contractor, Wadekar and Durani and in the 1990s Kambli and Ganguly. Of these only Contractor was prominent in Indian cricket while Gupte was at his peak and in the 1950s he hardly ever bowled to left-handers in domestic cricket. One can speculate as to why India produces so few left-handers.

One possible reason could be that Indians regard the left hand as the 'dirty' hand. It is the hand they use to clean themselves after a bowel movement – most Indians use water, not toilet paper to clean themselves – and for most Indians using the left hand is considered discourteous. An Indian handing something to another Indian would never use the left hand. When I advanced this as a possible explanation for the lack of left-handers in the first edition of this history, Ramchandra Guha, an Indian writer, poured much ridicule on me for daring to suggest this and had much fun at my expense. However he advanced no explanation as to why Indians have produced so few outstanding left-handed batsmen or why Sachin Tendulkar who is left-handed in almost everything is right-handed as a cricketer. The fact is in cricket Indians tend to frown on left-handers, for whatever reason, and this prejudice was more marked when Gupte was learning his trade.

However, despite the unusual problem presented by Harvey, Gupte was not collared. Even in Bombay, while Australia made 523 for 7 declared, Gupte kept some sort of check: 38–13–115–3, the most successful of the Indan bowlers. But he was under more severe attack than ever before and this, coupled with some atrocious Indian fielding, probably dented the confidence he always had in himself. Gupte was still the best of the Indian bowlers but not quite as supreme as he had been.

13

Blown away
1958-59

Indian cricket ended the 1950s in much the same way as it had started the decade: with a sudden glut of Test matches. Between November 1951 and April 1953 there had been 20 Tests, then 13 between 1953 and 1958. Now, between November 1958 and January 1960, there were to be 15 altogether, five each against West Indies, England and Australia. The Indians would indeed be tested as they never had been before.

The defeat by Australia had already shown that India had some way to go before they could take on the major powers. For all the dominance that Gupte and the other spinners had exercised India still hankered after fast bowlers, the Indian imagination still looked back to the days of Nissar and Amar Singh. Then India answered pace with pace. Indian batsmen were not shamed by foreign pace because India's bowling was led by pace.

Ever since 0 for 4 at Headingley in 1952, Indians had been debating furiously about the need for fast bowlers. Even as Gupte was laying the basis for the great age of spin, Indians agonised about their inability to produce fast bowlers. Merchant used to argue this was due to the fact that Partition had meant the country had lost Western Punjab with its tall, strapping, sturdy men, like Nissar. Others said it was all due to diet. How could Hindus bowl fast when they did not eat beef, drink wine and produce the sort of strong, virile men who can bowl quickly. Indians were largely vegetarian and mockingly referred to their attack as 'non-violent cricket'. Others spoke of the heat of the country, the general attitude of the people, the influence of Gandhi's non-violence movement, in fact every conceivable argument was dredged up to explain this appalling deficiency. And as the age of Gupte meant that even the fast-medium bowlers like Phadkar were gradually being replaced by bowlers who just came on to take the shine off the ball, the despair grew greater. Vizzy, now President of the Board, declared that if he was given ten, tall, sturdy Sikhs he would make sure India had fast bowlers.

In January 1958 Alan Moss, the Middlesex and England fast bowler, arrived to try to unearth some fast bowlers. Moss spent about four

206

months in Bombay and the experiment was a colossal failure. The boys, gathered in Bombay from different parts of the country, did not like the hard, physical regime Moss laid out for them. Moss recalls:

It was disappointing what they sent for me to look at. The boys they gave me were not up to it physically. When I arrived in Bombay there was nothing to do there for some time. I was supposed to go to Calcutta and Madras and elsewhere but I did not move out of Bombay. Eventually I saw about fifty in the 16–20 age group. There was one, the only one who made Test cricket, Desai. He was a good bowler, he had the right attitude. He was quite sharp, deceptive with a whippy action. But his bouncer was suspect, there was a kink in the arm when he delivered it. It was like Loader who also had a suspect bouncer. We had good nets in the middle of the CCI. I was not impressed with the way the boys were treated. Polly [Umrigar] used to come to the nets and he would splay the ball about all over the place, putting the flat bat on them. As long as he could hit them he was the great Polly. I would say to Desai, 'Don't let him treat you like that, let him have one'. And, of course, Desai did have a very deceptive bouncer. Polly would get furious. I would say to Polly, 'Don't come here and smack these boys all over the park. It is not the way to treat them.' I was teaching them to bowl line and length, and what it was all about and understanding matches. I played several matches around Bombay with them. There were a couple of other good ones apart from Desai but nothing came of them.

Some months after a disillusioned Alan Moss had returned home, the West Indians arrived in India in November 1958 clearly in the process of building a new side. They still had a white man as captain, Gerry Alexander, the wicket-keeper from Jamaica, but the three Ws had gone and their places were taken by new, young batsmen: Sobers, Kanhai, Butcher, Solomon, Collie Smith. Some of them had already suggested they were going to be major players and Sobers had broken Hutton's Test record with 365 not out against Pakistan earlier in the year. But in their previous two series against the West Indians the Indians had not encountered any real pace, Ramadhin was still expected to be the principal West Indian bowler and the Indian batsmen slept easy.

They were rudely awakened. Just as, in the eleventh century, Mahmud of Gazni swooped down on the lush, inviting Indian plains from his retreat in Afghanistan to plunder and loot, so in that winter of 1958–59, Wesley Hall and Roy Gilchrist, two young fast bowlers of whom the Indians had only heard rumours, devastated the Indian batsmen. Gazni was a freebooter and a plunderer of the classic medieval type. His raids on India were motivated by plunder, devastation, massacre and desecration. India never recovered and it paved the way for the eventual Muslim conquest of India. Something very similar happened to Indian cricket in those dark months of 1958–59 – the darkest in Indian cricket history.

The medieval Indian world had been quite unprepared for the fury, the rapacity, the greed and the sheer ferociousness of Mahmud of Gazni. Indian batsmen were similarly unprepared for Gilchrist and Hall. Not even Trueman in 1952 was like this. The tactics Trueman had used were devastating but legitimate. Hall and, in particular, Gilchrist seemed to aim at the batsmen, and even the beamer, which should have no place in cricket, was used. One of their early matches was against Baroda where a sad Hazare, who bagged a pair, watched his young batsmen as they feared for their lives. By the end of the match, which the West Indies won easily, Hazare found that 'the Baroda side looked like the patients at the out-patients department of hospital'. This was only the beginning.

The next match was on the matting at Ahmedabad. Roy was playing. 'At lunch I was sitting next to a player who turned to me and asked, "Who is Pankaj Roy?" They had heard of me and of my world record and they set out to make me a target. On the coir matting wicket the ball had a terrific bounce. At times in that match Hall and Gilchrist bowled six bouncers an over.'

So it went on. Not since 1932–33 has a cricket field seen such intimidation. Cricket, a delicate game, was converted into warfare where one side, the Indians, only had pea-shooters, and the other side the latest machine-guns. It was surprising that, in this era, long before the wearing of helmets or other protective gear had been adopted, nobody was killed. In the second Test Hardikar was nearly killed when a beamer grazed his temple and went for four. He batted on bravely to score 13 and 11, bowled by Hall in both innings, and never played Test cricket again. A promising career was cut off even before it was launched. Hall and Gilchrist sometimes bowled bouncers round the wicket to a packed leg-side field. In the first match at Ahmedabad Roy had not got into line but afterwards he did and generally the Indians stood up and took the punishment. Umrigar, for example, not only stood up to the pace attack but headed the Indian Test averages with 335 runs, average 42.12.

In the end there was a reaction but by then the series had been won and the Indians were cowed. The last match of the Indian section of the tour was against North Zone at Amritsar (for some reason the 1960 *Wisden* omitted this match in its report of the tour). Gilchrist bowled yet another beamer and at the end of the match was sent home. Willie Rodriguez, a member of the West Indian team, recalls:

> This was the last match of the tour. Gilchrist had been warned in the first match. He deliberately bowled a beamer. Alexander [who was not playing] heard about it from the team talk and said if he bowled beamers he would not bowl any more. Gerry said he could injure a batsman. Swaranjit Singh was playing in the match. He was upset he hadn't played in the Tests. He had been critical of the bowlers, saying West Indians were slow bowlers. Gilly bowled bouncers at him, but it was a slow wicket, a spinner's wicket – it was the only time on the tour Gibbs got a lot of wickets – and Swaranjit Singh easily hooked them. Then Gilly bowled a beamer. Gerry warned him. Gilly bowled two more. Gerry took him off and decided to send him home. Gerry was a terrific disciplinarian. Gilly had also had other problems and just did not have the intelligence to understand what was going on.

Alexander had had problems with Gilchrist earlier. On the eve of the second Test he had a row with Butcher and walked off saying that he was not going to practise. Alexander called him back, he would not listen and he was dropped. Now Alexander had had enough and Gilchrist went home and never again played for the West Indies. Yet if this sounds drastic enough, questions still remain. If Alexander knew Gilchrist had bowled a beamer in the first match, why did he not take action earlier? In any case he apparently did nothing to stop Gilchrist and Hall bowling, at times, six bouncers in an over. Gilchrist's absence was immediately felt. Much as the Indian part of the tour was a success, in Pakistan without Gilchrist the West Indies lost two of the three Tests.

Questions also need to be asked about West Indian writing on this subject. Gilchrist's humiliation of the Indians had been reported as a resurgence of West Indian cricket. His subsequent fall has been interpreted as a consequence of the racism that scarred so much of West Indian cricket: a much misunderstood man whom a black captain, like Worrell, would have handled but a white man like Alexander could not. But where has there been condemnation about his beamers and bouncers?

Nor does Indian umpiring emerge too well. In any other country the umpires are likely to have raised objections to the number of bouncers and beamers – they surely infringed Law 42 on unfair play. But just as umpire Joshi in 1948 had taken off the bails early with one ball and a minute and a half left, so now none of the umpires raised any objections. The cynical explanation offered by some Indians was that umpires were eager to get Alexander's approval since foreign approval, apart from bolstering their own esteem, could be used as a reference with the Indian authorities. .

The Indian press, mesmerised by India's own dissensions, could not cast a critical eye over the opposition tactics. They had their hands full trying to follow the amazing Byzantine games the cricket authorities were engaged in. Just as the medieval Indian kings had been unable to unite to fight Mahmud Gazni, so Indian cricket and cricketers fought amongst themselves and, in the middle of the devastation, disputed who should be captain. For one Test the captaincy was not decided till about fifteen minutes before the start of play.

The Indian dissensions began even as the West Indies were leaving their islands on the banana boat SS *Golfito* for England and then India. As before all such tours, the Indian 'probables' had been assembled in Bombay, after which the captain and the team would be selected. This was in October. But once the selectors arrived in Bombay, the machinations started. Vizzy was still in charge of the Indian Board, although in 1958 there was another President. However, his quarrel with Amarnath, the man he had sent home for creating a row in the dressing-room at Lord's, had long been patched up and Amarnath was now chairman of selectors. The scope for intrigue was wide. The word was that Amarnath wanted Ghulam Ahmed as captain for this series and for England in 1959 – the two were great friends – while he, himself, would manage the English tour.

However, Ghulam Ahmed was not at the camp at Bombay. But with Amarnath keen to have him it was decided to postpone the selection until the Board President's XI met the West Indies in Ahmedabad. Here Ghulam Ahmed sustained a leg injury while fielding, withdrew from the match but was still elected captain. Two of the selectors, Ramaswami and L. P. Jai, voted against him but with Amarnath's casting vote he got the job.

There was, however, one problem. The first Test was in Bombay and Ghulam Ahmed did not fancy bowling on the Bombay wicket or much like the Bombay crowd. (He felt the crowd were always against him – it is not uncommon for Indian players to develop such phobias about certain Test centres.) In 1955 he played against New Zealand in the first Test at Hyderabad, came to see the Bombay boys off at the station and talked of the next Test in Bombay, but when they arrived in Bombay they discovered that Ghulam had withdrawn because of injury. He did not play in Bombay against Australia in 1956 and two days before the West Indies Test he duly withdrew. When Ghorpade also withdrew, the Bombay-based selector Jai decided to draft in Hardikar and Nadkarni, both of whom were based in Bombay and had been in the reserves. This led to a furious row with Amarnath who argued that any replacements should be discussed with the entire selection

210

committee. Jai, a man of decided views, walked out of the meeting and out of the selection committee. The selection committee was now down to three persons, one of them Dutt Ray who was notorious for his expertise on football. The story went that in the middle of one cricket match, at a particularly tense moment, he had suddenly shouted 'goal'. The tale may be apocryphal but it is widely believed and so, even before a ball was bowled, the Indians had sustained a casualty in the selection committee, and the team took the field without the captain appointed for the series – and with three new Test caps.

Umrigar was now captain and, considering all that had happened, India did quite well. India were fearful of what Sobers, the world record holder for the highest score in Tests, might do. He tried to hook a bouncer from Ghulam Guard – who the Indians thought might provide some pace because he had the build, though not the energy or skill – miscued, the bat flew out of his hands and he was caught and bowled for 25. Gupte still showed he could be master even on a good batting wicket, and on the first day in perfect conditions took 4 wickets for 86. It might have been many more wickets had the Indians not dropped several chances.

With the Indian innings came the Gilchrist and Hall barrage. Both bowlers took a long time to bowl their overs – often starting their run-up from close to the sight-screen. It was to become a familiar sight of the season: a long, accelerating run-up, almost from the sight-screen, often followed by a bouncer, then a slow walk-back. On the first day the Indians had bowled 103 overs in 5½ hours' play; the next day, a Saturday, the West Indians bowled 68 overs in the same time. The Indians struggled but held on. In the final innings India, set 399 to win in 9½ hours, decided to go for a draw and got to it safely. It was not very exciting cricket for in that period the West Indians bowled only 132 overs, just under fourteen per hour. The match ended with a foretaste of the mayhem to come: Hall and Gilchrist bowling a succession of bouncers and lifting deliveries to Hardikar, which almost suggested a long-stop might come in handy.

Ghulam Ahmed was back at Kanpur and for the first day and a half India seemed on the verge of an historic victory. On the first day, on a wicket where jute matting had been laid on almost bare earth, Gupte was nearly unplayable. The West Indies won the toss and batted and by lunch the score was 88 for 6, with Gupte having taken all six wickets for 36 runs. He should have gone on to take all ten but the last man, Gibbs, was dropped by Tamhane, the wicket-keeper, before being bowled by Ranjane. Gupte ended up with 9 for 102, the first Indian to take nine wickets in a Test innings, and the final West Indian total, at 222, was something of a recovery. They might not have reached that but Ghulam Ahmed, for some reason, bowled himself for only ten overs. India replied well, at one stage they were 182 for 2, but then Hall and Taylor (in place of Gilchrist), caused the rest of the side to collapse, also for 222.

It was the second innings debacle, however, that turned the match and the series. West Indies had lost both openers, Holt and Hunte, for 0, but then Kanhai was dropped and Sobers given two 'lives' by the indulgent Indian umpire – not given out lbw, not given out caught behind. Sobers smiled, thinking how generous Indian umpires could be, and went on to make 198 before he was run out. India were set 443 to win. Again India made a good start: 99 for the first wicket by Roy and Contractor. Then came the first of two mistakes by Umrigar. Roy drove Hall to the left of Kanhai, Umrigar called for a run, then sent Roy back. He was wearing shoes with crêpe soles, could not turn quickly enough and Kanhai's throw broke the wicket. But still there was fight in the Indians. Umrigar and Manjrekar saw the Indians to 173 for 2 when Umrigar, eager to get the strike against the occasional bowler Solomon, who had been brought on almost in desperation, called Manjrekar for an impossible run and ran him out. The two self-inflicted wounds were all that the West Indians required and Hall and Taylor ripped through the rest. 173 for 2 became 240 all out – a defeat by 203 runs.

The Kanpur crowd was incensed and the players arrived back at the hotel under police escort. Now there was no holding the West Indians. Kanhai had been Gupte's 'rabbit' in the first two Tests, out to him three times. He was dropped before scoring in the third, Calcutta, Test at short-leg off Surendranath. He finally went to the same bowler but by then had made 256, his first Test century and a truly epic innings. Gupte had 1 for 119 and Kanhai could now toss back the jibe of rabbit. West Indies made 614 for 5 declared, India just managed to score more runs than Kanhai: 124 and 154. It was India's worst defeat in Test history and had this been a boxing match the referee would have stopped the bout long before the end; but he might also have said something about bouncers and beamers.

The Indians were too shell-shocked to do anything. The Test in Calcutta had finished a day and a half early. The selectors met in the evening and gave themselves just fifteen minutes to pick the side for the next match. Ghulam Ahmed offered his resignation but was persuaded to withdraw it. The Indian performances were now provoking national debate, even in the Lok Sabha, the Indian House of Commons. For Calcutta the selectors had brought back Phadkar. He had bowled 43 overs for 173 runs without a wicket. Now they brought back Mankad, who had had one of his familiar contractual disputes with the Board but was now prepared to play.

Four days before the Madras Test Ghulam Ahmed announced he

...ket. The selectors could not agree who should
...asu Patel, an off-spinner from Gujerat,
...gh, an off-spinner and all-rounder from
...meantime Manjrekar, the best Indian
...here was total confusion. Umrigar, who
...Ahmed as captain, wanted a batsman to
...to get Hardikar but he could not get on
...y and the choice developed between Jasu
...en Gupta, a young armed services player
...gainst the West Indies in the first match of
...rd President was a Mr Patel from Gujerat
...asu Patel (no relation but a man from his
...sed to captain the side if Jasu Patel was

...thetic to Umrigar but, with the Board Presi-
...Umrigar felt he had no alternative but to
threaten to resign. ...evening, the eve of the match, there was
a reception by the Madras Cricket Association for both teams and
Umrigar gave a speech as captain, then came back to the hotel and
resigned. Through the night the Board officials tried to persuade him
to withdraw his resignation but Umrigar had had enough. He could
not carry on. At three in the morning Gupte heard what sounded like
crying from the next room:

> Polly and Vinoo were in the room. Polly was crying. It was really
> sentimental stuff. Next morning at the Corporation Stadium with
> about fifteen minutes to go for the match Gerry came up to me
> and asked, 'Subash, who is your captain?' I said, 'We don't need
> captain, it is all communal.' Then the Board officials took Vinoo
> aside and at the back of the dressing-room and the latrines made
> him captain of India.

No team could play properly in such conditions and the Indians
did not. The West Indians made 500, India 222, Alexander did not
enforce the follow-on and India eventually lost by 295 runs. Hall
and Gilchrist added to their awesome repertoire by going round the
wicket to a deeply set leg-side field. Ramchand was one of the
players hit painfully behind the ear.

He was soon to feature in an extraordinary drama after the Test,
which in some ways dwarfed what had gone before. The Test finished
on 26 January which is India's Republic Day, a national holiday when
crowds pour out into the streets to watch the parades. This now
assumed great importance. For the selectors met at the end of the match
and decided that, for the final Test, Ramchand should be captain. He

had led India briefly in the fourth Test when Mankad, suffering from an allergy as a result of some fish he had eaten, could not take the field. Ramchand's boldness in a hopeless cause had impressed and he was appointed for the last Test. An official hurried to tell him, but Ramchand and the other Bombay players had left the hotel worried they might miss the train on a day of parades and traffic jams. The official hurried after them but by the time he got to the station the train had gone.

The selectors decided that there was little point chasing after Ramchand and appointed Adhikari instead. Ramchand did not even make the team for the Delhi Test, nor the touring team to England which was selected just afterwards. India secured a draw in Delhi and for the first time in the series made over 400, with Borde – who had made his debut in the first Test and scored 56 at Madras – coming agonisingly close to making a hundred in each innings: 109 in the first, 96 in the second. In the end the West Indies required only 47 to win but did not have enough time. Borde's batting, and Manjrekar's courage in coming out with a broken arm to try to help him secure his second hundred, lifted the crowds. Desai, testing the West Indians with some bouncers which the West Indians did not relish, made the crowd realise that not only Indians but all batsmen dislike bouncers.

Adhikari, who had scored 63 and 40 and took three wickets, had restored some sanity, but for the England tour there was yet another captain: D. K. Gaekwad who had played only in the Delhi Test, making 6 and 52. He was captain of Baroda which, the previous year, had won the Ranji Trophy, making a dent in Bombay's long sequence. But his choice was so much a surprise even to Gaekwad himself that just before this he had asked Roy whether he should accept a Lancashire League contract. Roy had advised patience. In the event he was captain, Roy was vice-captain, and the team included only four players who had toured England before. No Mankad. No Ramchand.

In the sort of farce that had characterised the Indian selection, Ghulam Ahmed was chosen. His retirement from Test cricket had proved one of the shortest on record. This so incensed Ramaswami – who was also bitterly opposed to Umrigar going – that he resigned. He made public his reasons and this prompted Ghulam Ahmed, for the second time in three months, to retire from Test cricket. This time he stayed retired. An Indian Air Force off-spinner called Muddiah was selected in his place. He had played most of his cricket on matting wickets, and English turf was something of a mystery to him. After the tour he made his Test debut at home against Australia, played a Test against Pakistan a year later but then vanished as mysteriously as he had arrived.

* * *

214

Like India, England too had had a disastrous winter. One of the strongest sides ever to leave England, containing some of the greatest English cricketers: May, Cowdrey, Graveney, Trueman, Statham, Tyson, Laker, Lock, Loader, Bailey, Dexter, had been beaten 4–0 by Australia. But any chance India had of making capital from England's demoralisation vanished on the morning of the first Test at Trent Bridge when, after England were 60 for 3, May made a commanding century. After that India never had a ghost of a chance. To add to India's problems Gaekwad had contracted typhoid between his selection in March and the start of the tour in April and was never fit. He had to miss the Lord's Test, where Roy captained the side. Roy, unhappy at missing the captaincy, proved a good leader but the Indians performed as ever as a set of individuals.

In the Lord's Test under Roy's captaincy India kept themselves in the match for two days and at one stage, with England 80 for 6 in reply to India's 168, it looked as though India could have an advantage. But the problem was that the wickets were being taken mostly by Surendranath and Desai, the opening bowlers, and the man who was supposed to be India's match-winner could not perform effectively. Gupte had played for many years in Lancashire League cricket but the field placings that had worked so well there did not work in the Tests. The Indians did not field very well, he became disheartened if the fielding was not up to standard, and though he took 95 wickets on the tour, in the Test matches he finished with 17 wickets, more than any other Indian bowler, but with an average of 34.64 he never looked like winning a match for India.

India's only real moment of hope came in the fourth Test. With the series decided Cowdrey had taken over from May, who was undergoing an operation, and decided not to enforce the follow-on but to give the crowd some cricket. India were left to make 547 to win. Now, suddenly, for the first time in the series they came alive. India had a new batsman in Abbas Ali Baig, an Indian student studying at Oxford. Baig had scored a century in his first match for the tourists against Middlesex and now he showed a mixture of courage and skill that his colleagues lacked. Despite being hit he made a glorious 112 in this his first Test. His batting seemed to inspire the rest of the side, Contractor made 56 and even Umrigar who, as in 1952, had 'murdered' attacks that were short of Test class but failed in the Tests, started playing as if he really believed in his own batting. At one stage Baig and Umrigar were together when the score was 321 for 5. It seemed as if the impossible could come true, that India might win. But Baig was run out and India collapsed to 376.

In this general disaster, however, the Indians could console themselves that the future might not be so bleak. Baig had emulated Ranji and Amarnath in making a hundred in his first Test. There was talk of Pataudi, the Nawab's son, doing great things for Winchester and Oxford. Maybe English cricket would repay the debt they owed to Ranji and provide batsmen who could revive Indian cricket.

But this lay still sometime in the future. India returned from England and awaited the arrival of the Australians. India expected nothing from the visit of the Australians that winter. They had beaten England 4–0 at home in 1958–59, they had beaten Pakistan in Pakistan in 1959–60, the first time Pakistan had lost a series at home and, when India lost the first Test in Delhi by an innings, the crowd took it badly – throwing bottles and jostling the umpires. A suggestion was even floated that Indians might do better if they played gilli-danda, not cricket! The despair was understandable. India had now lost nine out of their last eleven Test matches.

But for the Australian visit there was a new captain, Gulabrai Ramchand. The man who had caught the train to Bombay and in doing so missed the captaincy boat was now captain after all. The farce in Madras had nearly lost Ramchand to Indian cricket. He was even dropped by the Bombay selectors on some obscure point of discipline and had to apologise before being readmitted. In the trials before the Australians arrived he was sufficiently nervous to ask Roy, one of the captains, to give him 'halwa bowling', meaning bowling he could hit. When Roy put on someone who proved difficult Ramchand complained, but he must still have impressed the selectors. There had been a move to retain Gaekwad but he was still not fully fit and Amarnath, back as chairman of selectors, this time made sure that Ramchand got the job.

Ramchand was an unusual captain. He was a Sindhi, born in Karachi, and since Sind was now part of Pakistan this meant he was a refugee. Most of the Sindhis had settled in Bombay where their business skills were already feared. The saying went that, if you see a tiger and a Sindhi in the jungle, shoot the Sindhi first. Sindhis were not greatly known for sports though Karachi was a cricket centre. Ramchand, however, brought to the game some of the combative, hustling, business skills of the community. He was a useful medium-pace swing and seam bowler, and a hard-hitting lower-order batsman who was never afraid to strike the ball.

He keenly felt the way the Indian Board treated its own players. 'The tourists stayed in better hotels, Indian cricketers always stayed in inferior hotels,' he recalls. 'Both teams would travel in a train to a match. The visitors would travel in air-conditioned comfort, we would travel in ordinary first-class. This happened during the West Indies tour. We were both on the same train and I complained to the President. He said this was a Board decision. Sometimes the visitors flew, we travelled by train. We were made to feel inferior in our own country. I felt terrible about it.'

This steeled his determination to win and in the second Test, shrewdly prompted by Amarnath, they conjured up a most unexpected victory. Jasu Patel, whose inclusion in the fifteen for the Test was a surprise even to himself, was on the morning of the match called into the side. There was a new turf wicket at Kanpur and Amarnath shrewdly guessed that the off-spinner who, because of a wrist injury, had a jerky action – which some thought suspect – might be useful. Patel was not a classical off-spinner. He did not spin the ball, instead he bowled with the seam and could cut the ball. His ideal bowling surface was matting but the newly-laid turf was soft on top and Amarnath thought it might suit him

The plan worked like a charm. India batted poorly, making 152, and Australia were 71 without loss when Patel persuaded Ramchand to let him switch ends so that he could pitch in Davidson's footmarks. He had Stevens caught and bowled and took eight more Australian wickets for 24 runs to finish with 9 for 69, the best bowling analysis ever by an Indian in a Test innings. Australia had a lead of 67, but India batted much better in the second innings and Australia were set 225 to win. On this wicket Ramchand thought any target over 200 would be a problem. This time Patel had support from Umrigar (who bowled off-spin at a brisk pace), taking 4 for 27 in 25 overs. Patel's 5 wickets for 55 gave him the best match figures by an Indian in a Test: 14 for 124 runs. Australia had been beaten by 119 runs.

It was too much to expect India, or Patel, to repeat the trick. Australia were the superior side and, after the draw at Bombay, Australia won the fourth Test at Madras to win the series. Patel was inclined to rest on his laurels. He did not play in Bombay, where India drew, returned for Madras and Calcutta but was never again as effective. Patel was truly the one-Test bowler. He only ever played seven Tests, and of his 29 Test wickets, 14 came in that one match. He had been in and out of Indian cricket before this series; now that he had done his great deed he vanished. The Calcutta Test was his last. It was as if the genie had told Indian cricket, 'You can have one wish.' That wish was to have a match-winner at Kanpur and, once the wish had been granted, the genie and the magician he brought with him had vanished.

Patel's magical act had, with superb timing, come two days before Christmas 1959 and even in this predominantly non-Christian country that Christmas was an occasion for special joy. This was India's first victory over Australia, an Australia that could claim to be the champions of the world. After the disasters which the 1950s had brought, at least the decade could now be seen out in some hope and comfort. The 1960s could be welcomed without too great a hangover.

14

The new breed
1960-62

The 1960s began in Indian cricket with Abbas Ali Baig being kissed by a girl in the Brabourne Stadium. He had just completed his second fifty in a Test against Australia and the sheer audacity of the act – it was a demure, proper kiss, a light peck on the cheek – drew gasps of wonder. Merchant was commentating at the time and remarked that, for all the runs he had scored at Brabourne (they were 5,060 runs at an average of 105.41) no girl had ever kissed him. This was part of some bet but, more interesting, was the spotlight it threw on the wide appeal of cricket in India. The girl had come out, not from the popular East Stands which normally produced the spectators who invaded the ground when batsmen scored a hundred – but from the more respectable North Stand.

Bombay, as Indians saw it, was a 'fast' city. You expected a girl from Bombay to do something like that. At just about the time she was clambering over the fence to peck Baig on the cheek the great film stars of the Hindi screen – like Raj Kapoor, Dilip Kumar, Pran, and others – were in the CCI pavilion trying to persuade Ramchand to declare. Baig's second fifty had made the game safe for India and the crowds in the East Stand and the North Stand had taken up the chant, 'Declare, declare, declare'. Raj Kapoor, aware of his role as the popular man's hero, took up their cause and was 'pushing me to declare in the middle of the over', recalls Ramchand. 'I said, let's wait till the end of the over.' Ramchand gave the Australians twenty-five minutes in which to make 129 and it ended in farce. Roy opened the bowling, Meckiff opened the batting but the crowds loved it. Test matches in India were now tamasha, a fiesta, a spectacle.

The Raj Kapoor influence on Ramchand was not entirely coincidental. Bombay was the great film capital of India, on its way to becoming 'Bollywood', as the Indian Hollywood is known, making more films than the declining Hollywood of California. Cricket was becoming part of this 'filmi' culture, as Indians put it, and this Test saw the first manifestation in Bombay of what Indians would call cricket fever. For days before a Test match there would be a rising tide of interest, speculation, demand for tickets, publicity surrounding the

Test, then, the moment it ceased, cricket would almost vanish from the public consciousness. This is how Indians also reacted to the release of a new Hindi film. It was cricket as tamasha-spectacle. The demand for tickets was such that all-night queues for seats were very common. For days before a Test match the buildings and houses round CCI would have solid lines of people, queueing, and often sleeping, to get tickets. Such was the demand that the authorities no longer sold daily tickets but 'season tickets', meaning a ticket covering all five days. Normally a family would buy one season ticket for the Test match and each member of the family would be allocated a day. So even if the last day was meaningless in playing terms, it would invariably produce a 'house full' (another favourite Indian expression borrowed from the cinema).

Those who could not get a season ticket clustered around the radio. The roadside pan (betel nut) and bidi (Indian cigarette) stalls all had radios tuned to the commentaries and crowds gathered round them chewing pan, smoking the odd cigarette, vigorously discussing the cricket. Some popular restaurants even put up notice boards displaying the score. During a Test match urban India seemed to be one great fair with everyone involved with cricket. It was now more than a decade since the British had left and the industrialisation that Nehru had embarked on was changing the landscape of urban India. Prosperity was coming to the cities, people were pouring in from the impoverished villages to look for work, and for security, and for these masses cricket was an ideal game – five days of guaranteed entertainment, a release from the rigours of daily living. Just as Indian films offered an escape, so did Indian cricket.

And cricket was gaining a new constituency. Women, in increasing numbers, were being drawn to the game. All-India Radio had started supplementing the English radio commentaries with ones in Indian languages: Hindi, Bengali, even Maratti, and these were drawing in the housewives. It was about this time that my two aunts in Calcutta, attracted by the Bengali radio commentary, got hooked on cricket. They had taken no interest in the game hitherto and knew little about it, but the highly flowery Bengali radio commentary enchanted them and soon they were eagerly following their new-found heroes.

Baig was one such hero, although his studies at Oxford meant that he did not play after Bombay. The Bombay Test had also introduced two other players who were soon to become even greater heroes. They seemed to bring to Indian cricket a certain spontaneity that had been missing for much of the dull, dreary 1950s. One was Salim Durani, although he did not come into prominence until the series against England in 1961–62. The other was Budhi Kunderan, a largely untutored wicket-keeper batsman who overcame his father's objections in order to play cricket. This was a case of natural talent harnessed to the game through luck and chance. He was lucky to be living near the Azad Maidan which brought him under the influence of Fort Vijay Cricket Club, Merchant's maidan club, and his school was also Merchant's old school, Bharda, the great nursery for cricket in Bombay. In his first school match, playing in borrowed whites and borrowed equipment, Kunderan scored a double-hundred. He was soon playing with Merchant and then, finding the Bombay team difficult to break into, was picked up by the Railways. It was while playing in a Railways match that he caught the eye of Amarnath, who was coach to Railways.

Kunderan was called up for the trials before the Australian tour began, had been twelfth man in the first two Tests, and in Bombay he got his chance. He had yet to play in a first-class match, yet to play in the Ranji Trophy. It was like a dream story. Like all Indian players who had a home in Bombay, during the Test Kunderan lived in his modest house in the Fort area, travelled in the morning to the Test and, in front of 40,000 people, made his first-class debut. In Bombay he did nothing extraordinary but, in the next Test at Madras, when India began their reply to the Australian score, Kunderan recalls:

We fielded for a day and a half. Nari Contractor was our regular opening batsman but he fell ill. Ramchand asked me to open with Roy. I had nothing to lose. As a youngster you don't feel sort of nervous. You don't have nerves. You just play your cricket, you just enjoy it. There was no pressure, no tension. I did pretty well behind the wickets in the first innings, I was quite confident. First over Pankaj played a maiden from Alan Davidson. Then I had to face Meckiff. I had never faced a bowler of that calibre in my life before in club cricket or any other cricket that I had played. So he bowled and I played my normal club cricket as if I was playing in the Kanga League, as if there were only ten overs to go and I had to score fifty-odd runs. I got 14 runs in the first over off Ian Meckiff. Suddenly the whole crowd started screaming. The Australians were looking at me. I was so young, so naive, I did not even know what the cursing was all about. But they were cursing me. I was slashing outside the off-stump, over the slips for four, over the covers for four. I couldn't understand what they were saying. But they were abusing me. They had probably never seen anyone bat like that, either an opening batsman or any batsman. Roy, at the other end, kept saying, 'Be careful, be careful, don't keep chasing the ball.' As a youngster anything you see outside the off-stump you must hit. Nothing like leave the ball early on as a regular opener would do. I was a stroke player. I just played my shots and luck was with me. At the end of the day an Australian commentator came up and said, 'Budhi, do you realise you are playing a Test match, or did you think this was maidan cricket?'

As it happened, at the end of that day it was Roy who was out for 1, Kunderan not out 30 and he went on to make 71 out of the Indian total of 149. Although India lost, Kunderan's style captured the imagination of Indians. It seemed to answer English critics who had labelled the team the 'dull dogs of cricket'. To call somebody a dog is a great insult in India and the description had been greatly resented. Not since Mushtaq Ali had India produced an attacking opening batsman and, while Kunderan was soon sucked into the roulette wheel of Indian team selection, in for one match, out for two, and the ingrained defensiveness of the 1950s was still to be removed from the system, he had made a start. His was the first blow against the 1950s ethos that made it seem as if India always played for a draw and saw a draw as a substitute for a win.

For over a year Kunderan's Madras effort seemed an aberration. In the very next Test Jaisimha, also a brilliant stroke-player, played one of the dullest innings on record as India ground out a draw. It seemed as if the Indians would never be able to escape the crippling ethos of the 1950s; and when Ramchand retired at the end of the Australian visit, his successor, Contractor, was even more defensive. A good technical cricketer, his approach to the game was very much that of a 1950s man: first make sure we don't lose, if victory comes well and good but don't strive for it. Against Pakistan in 1960–61 all five Tests were drawn. Neither team could afford to lose, although the Indians nearly won the last Test in Delhi. When they ran out of time they needed 57 runs with ten wickets in hand after making Pakistan follow-on. The only significant pointer on the tour was that Hanif Mohammad did not relish Ramakant Desai's bowling and backed away from the bouncer. To add to the misery, the visit seemed to have snuffed out the great bright star of the Australian visit. Baig suffered the vicissitudes of professional sport. He went from hero to villain in the space of three matches. The man around whom the next generation of Indian batting was to be built had a miserable series. In five innings in three Tests he made 34 runs, highest score 19, averaging 8.50. Baig is a Muslim, and the fantastic allegation was made that Baig had failed deliberately to help his co-religionists from Pakistan. This was monstrously untrue, but he received poison-pen letters, was dropped and only played two more Tests, six years later, against the West Indies. Now no girl jumped barricades to kiss him and another fine talent had been lost.

To add to the Indian sorrows, on 1 July 1961, just days before the Varsity match between Oxford and Cambridge, the Nawab of Pataudi

221

was in a car crash. A car driven by an Oxford team-mate collided with another and a splinter of windscreen entered Pataudi's right eye. The lens of the eye was destroyed and the whole eye shifted slightly out of alignment. In 1960 he had emulated his father by scoring a century against Cambridge, as a Freshman. In 1961, up to the time of the accident, he had made 1,216 runs at an average of 55.27. He seemed certain to surpass his father's record of 1,307 in a season. *Wisden* was in raptures about his batting, unorthodox but so 'dazzling', then came the crash and it seemed that yet another potentially great cricketer would be lost to Indian cricket.

It was in this climate of a sense of loss that Ted Dexter brought another England side to India in November 1961, again missing some of the great players – no Cowdrey, Statham or Trueman – and India seemed unable to get out of its defensive groove. In the first Test, which England dominated, India were left 295 to win at 72 runs an hour. It was not an unreasonable target but the Indians were so used to defensive cricket that the papers saw it as an unrealistic target and Contractor made no effort to get the runs.

The second Test of this series provided a last hurrah for Gupte. He had missed the Australian visit, and lost his enthusiasm for the game. He went to the West Indies and then returned to be in and out of the team against Pakistan. But now on another easy wicket he showed he had not lost his ability to confuse and destroy good batsmen with his flighted leg-breaks. India took eleven hours and forty minutes to make 467 for 8 declared, then Gupte took 5 for 90 – all first five batsmen – and for the first time against India, England were made to follow-on. Mike Smith, who had scored so heavily against Gupte in 1959, often cross-batting him, now could make nothing of him and collected a pair: caught and bowled, and lbw. England saved the match mainly through a very slow hundred by Barrington, and centuries also from Pullar and Dexter, but it seemed that dull attritional play would be a feature of the series. In the third Delhi Test India made 466, England, before the rain came, 256 for 3, with Barrington making 100 runs in 5½ hours.

But the Test is noteworthy because of a bizarre incident which ended Gupte's career. He recalls:

For the Delhi Test we were staying at the Imperial Hotel (in Connaught Circus in the heart of the city). Kripal Singh was my room-mate. He tried to make a date with a receptionist at the hotel. She complained to the Indian manager, an Army man, saying she didn't expect Indian cricketers to behave in this way.

222

She traced the call to our room, Room no. 7. When the match was abandoned, Kripal had to go to Madras and I helped him pack. I was heading for Bombay with Polly and the other Bombay boys and I went to Polly's room. He said, 'You have been behaving badly. Go and see Nari.' I went and Nari Contractor told me about the complaint. This was the first I knew about this. I rushed out and, taking Ramakant Desai with me, headed for the airport. As we were going I was praying Kripal's flight would be delayed. I cornered Kripal at the newspaper stand. He said, 'You had nothing to do with it.' I saw Mr Chidambaram [the Board President] having breakfast at the airport and told him, 'Your culprit is confessing.' He said we will talk on the plane. They suspended both Kripal and me. An enquiry meeting was to be held in Calcutta, it was not. It was held in Madras, just before the team to the West Indies was to be announced. I went for it and, after I had explained what had happened, Mr Ghose the Board Secretary asked me, 'Did you try and stop Kripal making the call?' I said, 'He is a big man. How can I stop him?' Nothing had happened. Kripal had not raped the girl or assaulted her, he just asked her out for a drink. At the end of the enquiry, I was staying with friends in Madras, Nari came to the house. He said, 'Prepare yourself for a shock. The Board President has told the selectors not to pick you for the tour.' My father thought of suing Kripal but he had no money. I felt bitter. I would have liked to have played against the West Indies, make it my last trip.

Gupte did not play again. He was now married to the girl he had met at the San Fernando match all those years ago and emigrated to the West Indies and settled there, feeling it was the best thing that could have happened to him. So India's first great spinner – if we classify Mankad as an all-rounder – ended his career because he happened to share a room with a man who wanted a drink with a girl. Only in India could it have happened. On the field he had bowed out in the same style as he had announced his arrival, and his final figures of 149 wickets, at an average of 29.55, in a career that covered thirty-six Tests are very impressive for a leg-spinner. But what is most impressive is that on twelve occasions in those 36 tests he took five or more wickets in an innings. That is a sure measure of a bowler's command and in this respect he was not overshadowed either by his contemporaries or by the great spinners who followed him. Gupte bowled at a time when he had sporadic support at the other end, mainly Mankad, sometimes Ghulam Ahmed, on a few occasions Jasu Patel. He knew it was he who had to bowl out sides, and it is remarkable how often he did so, as the following comparative list shows:

	Balls	Wickets	Times 5 wickets in an innings
Mankad	14,686	162	8
Ghulam Ahmed	5,650	68	4
Bedi	21,364	266	14
Chandrasekhar	15,963	242	16
Prasanna	14,353	189	10
Venkataraghavan	14,877	156	3
Gupte	11,284	149	12

His figures also compare well against his international contemporaries:

Laker	12,027	193	9
Lock	13,147	174	9
Ramadhin	13,939	158	10
Valentine	12,953	139	8
Benaud	19,108	248	16

Gupte's dismissal meant that India's spin attack in three years had completely changed character and complexion. Just before the West Indian visit of 1958–59 it consisted of Gupte, Ghulam Ahmed, Mankad, with Gupte the dominant partner. A leg-spinner led the attack, an off-spinner and a left-armer supported. Now the main spinners were to be two left-armers supported by a leg-spinner. Borde was the leg-spinner, Salim Durani and Nadkarni the left-armers.

In contrast to the Gupte era all three spinners were also genuine all-rounders, indeed Borde was more a batsman who was also a useful bowler. In latter years, after he suffered shoulder trouble, he became solely a batsman. He was not in Gupte's class as a leg-spinner, he did not spin the ball but rolled it. Nadkarni, too, was not a great spinner. His forte was his accuracy. He kept a nagging line, bowled just short of a length which batsmen found almost impossible to hit. Nadkarni once bowled 21 successive maiden overs, and batsmen generally got out when they lost patience. Manjrekar once joked that 'the only time Nadkarni turned the ball it was declared a national holiday'. He had been nicknamed Bapu, the name given to Gandhi – it means 'father' – but this did not refer to his bowling but to his underwear. Like Gandhi he did not wear conventional western-style underwear but a longoit, a long, kite-shaped piece of cloth with a prominent V at the back which has to be draped round the body every time it is worn. Whenever, in

224

the dressing-room, Nadkarni changed the Indian players used to stop whatever they were doing to watch him draping the cloth around him.

In complete contrast was the third spinner, Salim Durani. He could turn the ball and turn it at speed, and he specialised in yorkers which often obtained important wickets. He had made his debut at the same time as Kunderan in Bombay against Australia, batting at no. 10 and making 18, and bowling just one over in the joke second innings. It was a mystery why he was played at all, and no debut could have been more anonymous. In the excitement over Baig nobody noticed him. Indeed he only reappeared, against Dexter's English side, two years later.

He played as a batsman. In England's 500 for 8 declared he did not bowl at all but he made 71, the highest Indian score, and put on 142 crucial runs with Borde. This was their first partnership together but soon it became almost a habit for these two, usually batting in the lower middle order, to prop up the innings after the top batsmen had failed; and when they were not batting together, they were often bowling together. In the fourth Test at Calcutta their batting made sure that India reached 380. It was now that Durani the bowler emerged. In Gupte's absence he was the first-choice spinner, and began to show how he had benefited from the coaching he had been receiving from Mankad. Earlier that year, in the Ranji Trophy final, he had taken 6 for 99 against Bombay, not enough to stop Bombay winning the Trophy yet again, but good enough to make people sit up and take notice. Now in Calcutta he took 5 for 47, Borde 4 for 65, and England were bowled out for 212. When India batted again Borde made runs, and when England went in Durani took three more wickets. India won by 187 runs.

The final Test saw more triumphs for Borde, Durani, and Nadkarni who had not played in Calcutta. Durani took ten wickets, Borde five, Nadkarni made 63, adding 101 for the eighth wicket with Engineer who had replaced Kunderan as wicket-keeper but batted in the same adventurous style: he took 16 in one over from Knight.

If these players who, apart from Nadkarni – very much a 1950s man – represented the new stream the main difference was the arrival of the Nawab of Pataudi. Despite his accident, he found that he could bat. Within months of his injury, experimentally but determinedly, he was back on the cricket field and playing his first match for the President's XI against Dexter's side in November. Batting at times with his right eye closed, he scored 70 in a thrilling game. He also captained the side and showed an imaginative touch, twice declaring – rare in Indian cricket then – to try and get a result. He made a quiet debut in the Delhi Test, 64 and 32 in Calcutta and 103 and 10 in Madras. It was in Madras that he began to change the way in which India batted. For almost twenty-five years Indian players, following Merchant, had hardly ever lifted the ball. Now Pataudi lifted the ball deliberately, intentionally, successfully. On the first day India made 296 for 7 which in five and a half hours was good going, and for India sensational. At one stage Pataudi and Contractor, who could be so stodgy, added 82 in an hour, and Pataudi eventually made his 103 in just two hours and 35 minutes. India made 428 in seven hours and 50 minutes. In Kanpur, the Test before Pataudi arrived, India had made 467 for 8 in eleven hours and 40 minutes.

India won the Madras Test convincingly, by 128 runs, a second successive Test victory and the first series victory against England. True, this was not England's full side, but, as Indians saw it, that would teach England not to treat India so contemptuously. Victory can make all things seem possible and so uplifting was the contribution of the new players, in particular Pataudi, that even Contractor, who had been a very 1950s-style captain in the first Test, now seemed imaginative.

Alas, within a matter of weeks this had turned to dust. Immediately the England series was over the Indians left for the Caribbean to meet perhaps the best all-round side the West Indies have ever had, wonderfully led by Frank Worrell. The Indian Board allowed its players far too little time to prepare for the trip. One moment they were freezing in London and New York, the next they were basking in the hot sun of Trinidad. The first two Tests were quickly lost.

Then came the colony game against Barbados. In their ranks was a bowler called Charlie Griffith. Griffith was said to be a gentle man off the field but quite different once he had the ball in his hand. The Indians had been warned about him. Kunderan recalls, 'We all thought he had a doubtful action. Frank Worrell had told us there is a bowler in Barbados who is really quick. We had heard he had played against the MCC and a couple of the MCC boys went to hospital.'

Contractor opened the innings as usual and got behind the line to play a lifting delivery from Griffith. He probably wanted to fend it away, but, according to *Wisden*, 'could not judge the height to which it would fly, bent back from the waist in a desperate, split-second attempt to avoid it and was hit just above the right ear'. Kunderan, who was not playing in the match, was in the dressing-room:

> We could hear the sound in the dressing-room. Nari just stood up and thought nothing of it. We thought he was all right. But after a while he was very uneasy and he wanted to come in. The next person to go in was Manjrekar. The very first ball from Griffith flew up, brushed his nose, the keeper fumbled, the ball flew to the

slips and the slip fielder got injured. So, suddenly, everyone started noticing Charlie Griffith. But in the meantime Nari, who was in the dressing-room having a rest, suddenly started screaming. He was taken to hospital for an X-ray. At the end of the day we heard he would have to be operated on. We all went to the hospital that night. We were told he was going to be operated on. Ghulam Ahmed [the manager] was very nervous. The whole team was at the hospital that night. Charlie Griffith was there too, he was in tears. Frank Worrell donated blood. The tension of waiting got to everyone.

Contractor survived the operation, an iron plate was inserted in his skull and he even played cricket again, but not Test cricket. The story was put about that he had ducked – when, of course he had not – but the incident generated such odd memories that when Contractor was hit Peter Lashley fielding at short-leg even felt like appealing for lbw. In the second innings Griffith was no-balled for throwing, while Manjrekar in one of the bravest displays seen on a cricket field scored 100 not out.

The innings showed that the Indians did not lack courage as long as the game was legitimate. But the Contractor incident was just too demoralising to cope with. Cricket could be a violent game but it was not meant to kill people and the Indians, already playing below their best, could not recover. While Pataudi, as vice-captain, took over the captaincy, they now lost the remaining three Tests as well. So was this 1959 all over again? Not quite. India had returned from England depressed. They had not only been beaten, they had played depressing cricket, boring, slow cricket which had given them that insulting tag of being the dull dogs of the game. Apart from Baig there had seemed nothing then to cheer Indian cricket.

In contrast the younger players now returned from the West Indies all suggesting that in the ruins there was the prospect, the real prospect, of a brighter future. No one suggested this more than Durani. He was the leading wicket-taker with 17 wickets and third in the batting averages with 259 runs at 28.77. But more than these figures, what he did was define a new style in Indian cricket. This was not 1952 when, as *Wisden* said, 'defeat was the horrid ogre in their path, and to ward it off they retired into a cave, pulled a massive rock over the entrance and attempted to defy all efforts to dislodge them'. Nor 1959 when India took six and a quarter hours to score 206 runs with Roy and Contractor defending dourly. The 1962 Indians were aggressive, India might get beaten but in the process there would be some colourful, entertaining cricket. The memory would be of Indians playing some fine shots, even some fine innings before being defeated by a superior side.

One innings does not make a cricket summer but in a game of quickly changing moods, where one over or one innings can be so crucial, Durani played a grand innings that made the Indians forget some of the terrible things that had happened. Long after the tour was over, and Contractor was well enough to pick up a cricket bat again, Indians were still talking of Durani's 104 against Hall in the fourth Test in Trinidad. Durani had batted no. 9 in the first innings and made 12. India made 197 and crumpled to Hall who in nine overs took 5 for 20. In the second innings, following-on, Durani was promoted to no. 3 and decided to take the battle to Hall.

In a situation like this the Indian batsman of the 1950s would have defended dourly, hoping to occupy the crease and buy time. Durani's defence was to drive the fastest bowler in the world straight past him for four and when Hall bowled the bouncer he hooked. It is amazing how often in cricket one man can change the mood of a team. Durani did it so completely that every Indian batsman wanted to bat, every one wanted to play strokes. Even Umrigar, who had only twice reached 50 in the series, now attacked boldly, making 172 not out of 230 in 248 minutes. It was never enough to save the match but Durani had made the Indians realise that Hall and the other West Indian fast bowlers were not ogres who could not be tackled.

Even before this innings Durani was well known. The victories against England in Calcutta and Madras had made him very popular. Now he acquired a romantic glow as easily the most debonair and dashing of the new breed of players. He was simply 'Salim'. Other cricketers were known by their surnames, many of the first names of cricketers were often not even known. M. L. Jaisimha's first name remained a mystery to most Indians for all his cricketing life. It is Motganhalli. But Durani was now 'Salim' to everyone. The name had a special romance about it. It was the name of the Mughal Emperor Akbar's son who later became Emperor Jehangir and was famous for his love of beautiful women. Just as Durani was making his mark in cricket, *Mughal-i-Azam*, a very famous Hindi film, was released which made the Mughal Salim's love-life into a great story of romance amidst imperial pomp and splendour.

For a long time Durani was suspected of having Pathan blood. In truth he had Afghan blood, and is the only Test cricketer to be born in Kabul. This increased his romantic appeal. The Afghans may have spawned freebooters and brigands who raided India, but they were also reputed to be great lovers, always ready to take up a challenge. Durani's cricket suggested that he too would always accept the challenge.

His century at Trinidad showed how well he could do so and, after that, he became even more of a hero. In India the word 'hero' can often be used in an ironic sense. Even Indians who do not know English use it, copying Hindi films, to denote someone who puts on airs which his performances do not justify. Durani looked like a Hindi film star with his long, black hair, his tall figure which, over the years, gave just the slightest suggestion of rotundity that Indians like in their leading men and that casual air, the hand perpetually tossing back the hair from the eyes, which hinted at a certain appealing vulnerability. But in Durani's case the use of the word 'hero' was meant as a tribute and after his Test career he went on to act in films.

Unfortunately, unlike the heroes of Hindi films, Durani did not get all that he wanted. He was very much part of the new shape in Indian cricket in the early 1960s, but his century in his tenth Test was his only one. He played nineteen more Test matches and his final figures of 1,202 runs at 25.04 and 75 wickets at 35.42 did no justice to his ability. But then Salim had not won the girl he loved and, although he went on to become Mughal Emperor, there was always a vacuum in his life. So it was with Salim Durani.

15

The rise of a tiger
1963-68

The Nawab of Pataudi's reign in Indian cricket lasted from 1962 to 1975, interrupted for three years by a man whom many Indians still consider a pretender who should never have been allowed near the crown. By the time Pataudi finally left Indian cricket he had lost his princely title and acquired a new name, Mansur Ali Khan, so becoming one of the few cricketers who started his career under one name but finished it under another. But for Indian cricket followers he will always be 'Tiger', the nickname which was given to him by his father and which is also the title of his autobiography.

It seemed so appropriate for a man who was, and is still, seen as the great redeemer of Indian cricket, rescuing it from the woeful, defensive 1950s, and giving it new life and a new definition. By international standards perhaps Pataudi's long reign is not impressive, but in India it does not matter how many Test matches he won or lost, what stands out is the way he changed the game. To a nation that for twenty years regarded a draw as a victory and whose cricket had a certain predictability, he brought the prospect of victory, often unexpected victories, and his captaincy had an element of daring, at times maddeningly unpredictable, so that even when India failed the impression was of having attempted the impossible. Pataudi's teams were often infuriating, never boring. Indian cricket has achieved a lot more since Pataudi left but he is still the biggest name. More than fifteen years after he had retired his cricket exploits are still potent enough to sell commercial products like suits, clothes, and household goods. Outside of Indian films nobody else in India has had such an appeal but then Pataudi's story could almost have come straight out of the movies. Like the most popular of Hindi films it had romance, tragedy, a convoluted story-line and, in the end, the restoration of the hero to his rightful place.

A Pataudi at the helm of Indian cricket was for Indians intensely romantic: the son succeeding the father. So much of Indian life runs in families: businessmen's sons succeed to the business, in politics the Nehru family made the Prime Ministership of the world's largest democracy almost a private family preserve for many years. India may be a democratic country but at heart it is still a feudal one and Pataudi captaining India was like an old family heirloom being returned to its rightful owner. Then there was the added romance that he was a Nawab. Hindu-Muslim relations, particularly since Partition, have been distant and often distrustful; but Pataudi recalled the great Muslim kings who were capable of daring exploits, of building world-famous monuments, and whose kingship elevated the country. To this romance was added tragedy, the spice that is a vital ingredient in Hindi films. Such films always feature a sudden tragedy, a road accident, a drowning, a freak storm. In Pataudi's case, of course, at the height of his powers he had lost an eye.

He succeeded to the captaincy in very tragic circumstances. When he was made vice-captain to Contractor on the West Indies trip it was seen as a move for the future. Contractor was expected to remain captain for some years and Pataudi, it was hoped, would learn under his tutelage and in time be ready to take over. India, like other nations, would groom people for captaincy. But Pataudi had had to take over the leadership for the third Test against the West Indies in 1961–62 at the age of twenty-one, the youngest ever Test captain. After that, tragedy in some form always seemed to be associated with Pataudi and some of his great, epic innings were played against a background of injury and cricketing calamity. He always seemed to be acting out a Greek tragedy. Once he sought to rescue India on one leg, on another occasion two of his team-mates were injured as he played one of his best Test innings. But then all this was part of the spell that Pataudi cast over Indian cricket, the magic that made the legend.

There did not seem anything very magical in the winter of 1963 when Pataudi formally took over from Contractor. India had had a year's respite from international cricket and in this time the Indian Board, appalled by the 5–0 defeat by the West Indies, tried an eight-ball over experiment in the Ranji Trophy and imported four West Indians: Gilchrist, King, Stayers and Watson. They were to play in the domestic competition in the hope that they would give the Indians practice against quick bowling. But they had been allocated to the stronger teams, and this meant that the best players, who could have done with the practice, rarely played against them and the stronger teams grew even stronger. It was a good holiday for the four West Indians, but it did nothing for Indian cricket and Bombay, as ever, won the Ranji Trophy. However, the Board did start a useful zonal competition called the Duleep Trophy and this both produced good cricket and attracted crowds.

The visitors in 1963–64 were, again, England led by Mike Smith but still missing some key players. It was by no means sure that Pataudi would captain India. He got the job on the casting vote of the chairman and this, clearly, weighed him down. Pataudi, who had shown dashes of a more imaginative captaincy earlier, seemed unable to break out of the ultra-defensive groove of his predecessors. In the first four Tests there was nothing to choose between Tiger and the 1950s men. India should have won the first two Tests when the English team was so stricken by injury and illness that in one match Kripal Singh fielded almost as a permanent substitute for them. In the second at Bombay England really had only ten men (with Mickey Stewart absent ill): two specialist batsmen, two wicket-keepers, four quick bowlers and two spinners, yet Pataudi still refused to set any sort of challenge, with Jaisimha batting almost four hours for his 66 in the second innings.

Yet Pataudi had batsmen like Kunderan who, on the first day of the series, opening the batting, scored 170 in five and a half hours. Kunderan only knew on the morning of the match that he was playing. Engineer was the first choice, the wicket-keeping job seemed to alternate between the two, and he was keen to play despite an injury to the small finger of his right hand. Kunderan fielded and bowled during practice but did not bat. When he was told he was playing, for the first time in four days he had a net. He must have been out four or five times in the net, but he still retained that instinctive, club cricket approach to Test cricket. The first ball he faced in the match was short, outside the off stump, he square-cut it for four, felt good, and was on his way.

There was also Hanumant Singh whose century on his debut in the fourth Test at Delhi was the most brilliant innings played on either side. But Pataudi relied on Nadkarni who, in the first Test, bowled 21 successive maidens, mostly to Barrington. India also dropped catches in this innings and it seemed as if Pataudi, who had started the series in poor batting form, was afraid to make mistakes. He did not want to give the selectors any chance to gun him down. He knew his captaincy was balanced on a knife-edge. In Calcutta it was even suggested he should have an eye test, an idea he contemptuously rejected. At that stage he had made 0 and 18, 10 and 0, 2 and 31. In the second innings at Delhi, after 13 in the first innings, he made 203 not out, the highest score by an Indian against England at that stage. His second hundred was against exhibition bowling with Mike Smith bowling thirteen overs, but this was the first major innings he had played as captain and it gave him tremendous confidence.

In the last Test at Kanpur he won the toss and on a blameless wicket, prepared by the same groundsman who was responsible for the Delhi wicket, he put England in. This was the first time that Indians experienced one of those Pataudi decisions which were so unpredictable that not even Pataudi could give a rational explanation. Pataudi had put England in and he opened with Jaisimha and Durani, hardly the quickest attack in Test history. It was just that, after four draws, he felt it was time to try something different. At the end of the first day, with England well placed at 271 for 2, Smith offered Pataudi an even more exciting choice. Like two county captains discussing how to get a result in a championship match he offered to declare if India would reciprocate and make a match of it. Pataudi was not that powerful or that bold yet to take such a gamble. He told Smith he would consult the Indian Board. The selectors were horrified and England batted on and made 559, and India, at its defensive worst, almost gave the match away, being bowled out for 266 with only Nadkarni at no. 9 showing how runs could be made. When India followed-on he was promoted to no. 3, made 122 not out, and India saved the match easily. So once again all five Tests had been drawn. Had India lost the match Pataudi would almost certainly have lost the captaincy. Now, having secured a draw, his eccentric decision to field first seemed to give him extra prestige. He had dared, just a bit, and had not failed.

It was only later that year when Bobby Simpson's Australians, on their way back from their English tour, stopped over in India for a three-Test series that Pataudi's captaincy took flight. This was the third visit by the Australians in nine years. On their two previous visits they had played eight Tests, won four, and also won both series comfortably. But despite their batsmen and their bowlers proving vastly superior to the Indians they were always the most eagerly awaited of cricket visitors.

Outside cricket, Indians knew little about Australia. But when it came to cricket Indians adored Australians. In those days All-India Radio did not allow commercial advertisements – India still had practically no television – and Radio Ceylon made the most of this opportunity. Using powerful transmitters it broadcast popular Hindi film music interspersed with advertisements. As a bonus Ceylon also broadcast Australian Test-match commentaries. For the Indians the time difference was ideal. The commentaries would start at about 6 o'clock or 6.30 in the morning and go on till lunch-time. Thus, the 1960–61 Australia–West Indies series was followed by millions of Indians hanging on to every word that Alan McGilvray and Lindsay Hassett uttered. I was then at school, and I would listen to the pre-lunch session, go off to school, hurry home for lunch, catch the close of play score in Australia, and then hurry back with the scores for my class-mates. In at least one Bombay school that winter Australian Test scores were prominently featured on the blackboard, in my case the blackboard of Standard VIII B. If my class-mates were any guide, the Indians were enthusiastic supporters of the Australians in that series. We feared their cricket but we respected them as cricketers.

The Australians, we felt, took India and its cricket seriously.

England always sent what looked like a 'B' team. Before an English tour the Indian press would be full of stories of major players declining the tour. Australia never seemed to have that problem. The great Australian players of the 1950s and 1960s all toured India: Lindwall, Miller, Harvey, Grout, Davidson, Benaud. England also often appointed a tyro captain to lead the side to India, as if it was a training ground, like Nigel Howard, who only ever played for England as captain against India. Whoever was the Australian captain always brought the team to India. So though in the last ten years India had beaten England and never lost a series to them at home while losing twice to Australia it meant more to the Indians to be playing Australia. It was a surer test of ability. Indians felt they were playing a country that did not treat them as an inferior cricket nation.

Simpson's team created even greater interest than the previous visits. It had just retained the Ashes, winning the 1964 rubber 1–0, and could claim to be the world champions. They certainly showed such form in the first Test at Madras where they easily won by 139 runs. But there were several encouraging Indian performances. For the first time in a Test against Australia India took the first-innings lead – of immense psychological importance to Indians as ever. Pataudi himself made a magnificent 128 not out, out of 276, which turned the Indian first innings round after it seemed that McKenzie had shot it to pieces. So despite the defeat India arrived in Bombay for the second Test in remarkably good cheer. The Australians were good, but they were not beyond India.

Bombay had rarely seen a Test match so early – the second week of October. October is quite the worst month in Bombay. May is hotter, but in May the monsoon rains are just a month away. October comes after the monsoon rains and there is no consolation that the rains will soon cool the temperature. It is the month of various festivals which originally marked the gathering of the harvest and have deep religious significance for the Hindus.

The gods certainly seemed to be on the Indian side, for Australia suffered a bizarre misfortune on the morning of the match. Simpson went out to toss thinking he had eleven fit men. He won the toss, decided to bat only to discover that Norman O'Neill had come down with symptoms suspiciously like polio. Fortunately the Australians had had their jabs but it meant that O'Neill could not play in this match and the Australians batted with only ten men in each innings.

For years Indians had grumbled about the slow, dull, dead wickets at the Brabourne. The stadium wicket had now been dug up, relaid with two layers of bricks, then six inches of rubble and the whole bound together. Nobody was sure how it would play but the hope was there would be some life in it for the bowlers as well. Brabourne Stadium had not seen a result for ten years – since December 1955 when New Zealand had been beaten. Since then Australia twice, West Indies, England twice, and Pakistan had all drawn.

That last victory against New Zealand had been engineered by Gupte and for this Test it seemed India had another potential match-winner. Like Gupte he was a leg-spinner but there the similarity between Gupte and Chandrasekhar ended. Gupte was the orthodox, classical leg-spinner, Chandra so unorthodox that he bowled at near medium-pace, his leg-break hardly turned, and his stock ball was the googly. His arrival in Indian cricket was just as extraordinary as his bowling. At seventeen he had gone straight from club cricket in Bangalore into the Mysore side in the Ranji Trophy, and within three months was playing Test cricket. In his first Ranji Trophy season, in a handful of matches, he had taken 31 wickets. He had made his debut in Bombay against Mike Smith's team and took five wickets in the match, but then had taken only five more in the remaining three Tests, largely because Cowdrey joined the tour for the third Test and he was only one of three batsmen – Barrington and Sobers were the others – who faced Chandrasekhar with confidence.

The only Australian who looked like coping well with Chandrasekhar was Burge who in characteristic style hit hard and made 80 before Chandrasekhar caught him off Borde. The other Australians struggled, at one stage they were 146 for 5, before Veivers and Jarman put on 151 for the sixth wicket. Then Chandra caused the decisive collapse and Australia were all out for 320. When India, in reply, were 188 for 6 a big and decisive Australian lead looked likely. But Pataudi now played the first of his two crucial innings of the match. He guided the Indian lower order batting so well that the last four wickets added 153. Apart from Chandrasekhar who could not bat, nos. 8, 9, 10 all made runs with 21, 34, 32. Of course Surti and Nadkarni were capable batsmen but even Indrajitsinhji, the somewhat surprising choice as wicket-keeper for this series, also made runs. They all seemed inspired by Pataudi who made 86 and, for the first time in almost thirty years, the Bombay crowd saw a batsman deliberately lift shots into the vacant outfield. The last man to do it was C. K. Nayudu. The Merchant school had banned the idea: 'Play it along the ground, play it safe.' As the Bombay crowd saw Pataudi use the vast vacant spaces of the Brabourne Stadium to loft the ball they first gasped, then cheered. India gained a small but psychologically important lead of 21 runs.

Australia soon wiped this out and had reached 246 for 3 in their second innings when Pataudi finally found the right bowling combination. He had so far been pairing Chandrasekhar with Durani, or Durani with Nadkarni, now he paired Chandra with Nadkarni. The Australians had shown that Nadkarni's nagging length could get to them. He had taken 5 for 31 and 6 for 91 in Madras. Now Booth was stumped, Cowper caught at the wicket, both off Nadkarni; Chandra then bowled Jarman and had Veivers lbw for 0 and Nadkarni had Martin and McKenzie caught. Australia had gone from 246 for 3 to 274 all out. Chandra finished with 4 for 73, Nadkarni 4 for 33 (off 20.4 overs). The Indians, who had not seen such an opposition collapse since the days of Gupte, were left 254 to get in a few hours of the fourth and all the fifth days.

That generation of Indian cricket followers had never experienced such a situation. They had heard how, in 1948, India had chased a target against the West Indies and nearly won, but few could remember it. In recent years the Tests that had been won at home had generally been because the opposition failed to reach a target. There is something peculiarly exciting and satisfying in winning a cricket match chasing a target.

The 254 total seemed so attainable – this was not one of those distant, 400-plus targets. Yet on a wicket where spinners had taken 23 of the 28 wickets that had fallen it would not be easy. The crowd and the commentators speculated that if the Indians kept all their wickets intact by the end of the day, then next morning they could strike out for victory. But India lost Jaisimha on 4 and this brought in Durani.

Nobody now shouted, 'Sixer, Salim, give us sixer'. Instead they prayed that this mercurial cricketer would exercise caution. As he walked to the wicket Merchant, as ever the expert commentator when Tests were played in Bombay – he never broadcast on Tests outside Bombay – advised caution: 'Steady, Salim, steady.' At the other end was Sardesai, a very dependable batsman, and Merchant hoped Salim would give him the support he needed. India must not lose another wicket tonight. Salim seemed to have heard the advice and the pair took the score to 70 before Durani could not restrain himself and was caught.

Pataudi, keen to protect his main batsmen, Manjrekar and Hanumant, sent in Nadkarni as night-watchman. This can often be a dubious ploy in cricket and he made a duck. Yet another night-watchman was sent in, Surti, but he survived and India finished the day on 74 for 3.

The next day was a holiday, Dassera. This is the climax of the Festival of Durga when the goddess Durga, after slaying the dastardly enemy, half man, half bull, makes her way with her children to her husband Shiva's home. For days before this her image and the act showing the great victory are worshipped, then on Dassera day the images are immersed in the river. Indians have a very personal relationship with their gods and goddesses and this is like wishing someone 'bon voyage'. The goddess is returning home. She will return next year to

236

slay the enemy of man and god again. On this day Indians wear new clothes, sweets are distributed and even strangers greet each other in friendship and hope. Durga, the great goddess of strength, is here again and all is well with the world.

But that morning Indian batsmen seemed powerless in face of McKenzie. Surti had gone early, skying Veivers to Booth in the deep, then McKenzie, in a fine spell, had Sardesai lbw for 56 and bowled Hanumant with a superb yorker. Hanumant had just seen Pataudi play a supreme cover drive and, eager to emulate him, found his stumps go flying. It was barely twelve o'clock, the goddess had not even started on her journey home and India, half an hour before lunch, were 122 for 6.

But because of the night-watchmen the player who should have batted at no. 4, India's most experienced batsman Vijay Manjrekar, was now no. 8. He and Pataudi saw India through to lunch and then, after lunch, slowly saw off McKenzie and then the spinners. The wicket seemed to be slower than on the fourth day, the Australian spinners did not have the pace of Chandra, or, perhaps, the batting was better. By tea the match seemed to be India's. Pataudi and Manjrekar were still there. They had not looked in trouble, and the crowd relaxed. It had been a hot day, they cooled themselves with paper fans, ate sweets, gurgled with the anticipatory thrill of seeing the winning hit.

The only hope Simpson had left was to take the new ball. He did so after tea but when Connolly, bowling from the pavilion end, bowled a bouncer, it sat up like a lap-dog and Manjrekar hooked it imperiously to the square-leg boundary, the ball hitting the fence of the East Stand with tremendous force. Bombay's popular section erupted. India were now 215 for 6, this pair had put on 93 and friendly bets were being taken about who would make the winning hit. But then, suddenly, Connolly had Manjrekar caught.

Still the crowd stayed relaxed. The next batsman was Borde who would also normally have batted higher. He had made 49 in the Madras Test and exuded that calm competence which was his hallmark. Connolly bowled one short outside the off-stump, Pataudi square-cut it viciously. The crowd looked to the boundary. Suddenly the picture seemed to have frozen. Burge materialised at point and had held on to a shot made off the meat of the bat. A great catch to end a great innings. Pataudi had made 53. India were 224 for 8.

Now the tensions of the morning returned. The crowd, laughing and joking a minute ago, fell silent. They put their sweets away. Could Indrajitsinhji stay in with Borde? Little was known about him or why he had been preferred to Engineer, the local Bombay man, or Kunderan for that matter – both better batsmen and better keepers. He was of princely stock, connected with the Ranji family, a tall, awkward-looking man who yet seemed self-assured. But could he withstand the pressure? Simpson, realising that after Indrajitsinhji there was only Chandra, tried everything but Borde shielded him from the strike and played the most sensible cricket: keeping the good ball out and hitting the bad one, he slowly accumulated runs. Half an hour before the close India needed two runs to win when Veivers began to bowl again. Borde calmly on-drove him for four. India had won by two wickets. It was the most exciting Test seen in India since the 1948 one, some said the most exciting Test ever.

The crowds, penned in, could not get on to the playing area but they stood behind the barricades and cheered and cheered and cheered. Eventually Pataudi and the whole Indian team gathered on the CCI balcony to accept the greetings. For the Indians it was like Hutton and The Oval balcony scene of 1953. There English crowds were acknowledging the return of the Ashes, here it was India reclaiming her pride, her ability to do battle and win against the best in the world. Some Indians thought the Test compared with the tied Test in Brisbane. It certainly generated the same feelings and, while the last Test of the series was ruined by rain, after Durani caused an Australian collapse, such had been the euphoria after Bombay that there was a real belief that, under Pataudi, India had begun to turn the corner. On the field his brilliant fielding gave the team a lift, and his batting was always adventurous.

This feeling persisted even for the 1964–65 series against New Zealand that followed a few months later, despite the fact that Pataudi showed several captaincy deficiencies. In the first match he was as negative as any 1950s captain; in the third in Bombay, after India collapsed for 88, her lowest-ever score in India, and followed-on for the first time against New Zealand, he delayed his declaration to enable Sardesai to reach 200. And while this innings saved India, the delay meant that India could not win. For in the end it was the New Zealanders who were hanging on for dear life at 80 for 8. But in the final Test it all came out right as India won by seven wickets. The victory was the achievement of Venkataraghavan, an off-spinner from Madras, who took 8 for 72 in the first innings, 12 for 152 in the match. With Chandra from Bangalore and Venkat from Madras the south was now becoming the land of spin. Pataudi as ever cut it fine and India won with only thirteen minutes to spare but that was just the sort of excitement Indians had come to expect from him.

All this augured well as India prepared for the late 1960s. As at the end of the previous decade India seemed to have arranged a glut of Test matches: between December 1966 and March 1968 fourteen Tests were to be played against four different countries. The first three Tests against the West Indies were the most crucial: the old, almost hysterical, Indian reaction to pace had gone and none of the modern generation of Indian batsmen backed away from fast bowling. Yet India had lost eight of their last ten matches played against the West Indies and the team which Sobers brought to India in 1966–67 looked like true world champions: it had beaten the Australians 2–1 in the West Indies and England 3–1 in England, with the opening bowling in the hands of Hall and Griffith. Since the injury to Contractor Griffith had become a regular member of the West Indian side, even if a controversial one because of certain Australian and English allegations that he chucked.

So would Hall and Griffith once again blow the Indian batsmen away as they had done in the past? Bombay waited just a bit apprehensively for the answer as the first Test began on 13 December. India were soon 14 for 3, two wickets to Hall, but then Borde made a hundred, Pataudi 44 and Durani an almost lyrical 55, hitting Griffith straight back over his head for a six into the first floor balcony of the CCI. It was a typical Durani innings, one minute fulfilling the crowd's fantasy of a six every ball, next minute head in air being bowled by Sobers. India made 296 and then Chandra again seemed to be working his magic. West Indies were 82 for 3, all three wickets to Chandrasekhar, and Hunte, the only one offering resistance, dropped. But now came the crucial miss of the series. Lloyd, on his Test debut, could make nothing of Chandrasekhar. On 8 he edged a straightforward slip catch to Wadekar, who was also making his Test debut. He dropped it. Lloyd went on to make 82, hitting Nadkarni – who had been such a useful foil to Chandra against Australia – out of the attack. Never again did Nadkarni pose a threat in Tests. In the second innings, when West Indies needed 192 to win, Nadkarni did not bowl a single over. Durani was also ineffective. Chandra battled on alone, taking eleven wickets in the match. At one stage in their second innings the West Indies were 90 for 4, all four wickets to Chandrasekhar, but he could not quite win it on his own. Lloyd was more confident and he and Sobers saw the West Indies to a six-wicket victory with Sobers finishing the match off in time to go to the races. He had also announced his engagement to a little known Bombay film star called Anju Mahendra. This turned out to be some bizarre publicity stunt for the girl and, after the Test, nothing more was heard of the engagement.

Nevertheless India went to Calcutta in high hope. One of the miracles of the Indian spirit is that it can always resurrect hope. But this time there was some basis for thinking the West Indians were not that superior. The second Test was a disgrace, however. Not so much for what the players did, though in the end they did not perform very well, as for the actions of the cricket administrators. Cricket was now an extremely popular, extremely profitable sport. But, displaying a greed that was only matched by their own incompetence, the authorities sold too many tickets. Some of the tickets were forgeries, the ticket distribution system deliberately creating artificial shortages, encouraging black market and inflated prices. Eden Gardens then had accommodation for 50,000 people, and decent facilities for less than half that number. Yet 70,000 people crowded in. The first day had already seen problems, the second day, New Year's Day, saw a full-scale riot. The players had taken the field but, with the spectators unable to find places in the stands, crowds spilled on to the field. No Indian Test ground allows spectators on to the grass and the Calcutta police, who have always had a reputation for being tough, decided to charge them with lathis – short wooden batons – to clear the field. Calcutta then was in the middle of its own Maoist movement, the Naxalites, and in any case it is always a volatile city, always threatening to bubble over. The spectators retaliated with bricks, the policemen came back with tear gas. It was a classic Calcutta crowd versus policemen battle, the cricket tensions sparking anger on a whole host of issues. On such occasions the Calcutta crowd can be overwhelming and the police were overwhelmed. The crowd invaded the whole field, dug up the ground, set fire to the stands and made straight for the rich, enclosed sections.

The players fled, the West Indians in confusion in different directions with some players, so hostile with bat or ball, running down Calcutta's famous Red Road in fear for their lives. But the crowd meant them no harm. They were after the officials who had sold the tickets, some of whom cowered under seats in the Indian team coach. 'Please, please,' they pleaded with Pataudi, 'don't let the crowds see us, or we will be killed.' A commission of enquiry eventually established their guilt although it was some years before Calcutta mended its ways. In some ways even more shameful was the behaviour of All-India Radio. Millions all over India tuned in for the day's play. The rioting started just as play was due to begin but instead of referring to it, let alone describing it, All-India Radio had a curt announcement that due to fog – and Calcutta can be foggy in winter – play had been held up. It then went off the air and it was left to next day's newspapers to describe what had happened.

For a time it seemed that the Test would be abandoned, with the West Indies keen to fly home; but with the rest day intervening and after a lot of cajoling, play resumed. Instead of the West Indians being demoralised, however, it was the Indians who were shaken and, on a wicket that had been damaged and was now powdery and dry, Gibbs and Sobers, using various types of spin, took 14 wickets and India lost by an innings and 45 runs.

Yet amazingly, within two weeks, in Madras, India were on the threshold of their first victory against the West Indies. It was an unbelievable transformation started by Engineer who, on the first morning, nearly scored a century before lunch. Engineer had not played in the two previous Tests but, just before this one, the selectors decided to give him a chance. However, instead of dropping Kunderan, which would have been difficult to justify, they put it about that Kunderan was injured when in fact he was not. Engineer opened the batting and was 94 at lunch. India made 404, then, having allowed the West Indies to recover to 406 – Hall and Griffith made 27 and 31 respectively – they set the West Indies to make 322 in four and a half hours. With an hour and a half to go West Indies were 193 for 7, with Griffith, Hall and Gibbs the only remaining support for Sobers.

The wicket was turning and the Indian spinners were making the most of it. But Sobers was dropped twice before he had scored 10 and Griffith supported him by tactics that *Wisden* thought were 'unfortunate'; he used 'his pads more often than his bat and many times even obstructed the ball with his body by going down on his knees'. How he avoided being lbw was a mystery. The West Indies had gained a draw but their performance did not enhance their reputation. It suggested that the great team built by Worrell was beginning to disintegrate.

It was the Indians' turn to feel that they had the makings of a great spin attack. Chandra was still the key bowler but there was an exciting left-arm spinner in Bishan Bedi who had replaced Durani in Calcutta. Prasanna, who had last played in a Test in 1962, also against the West Indies, now made a comeback to international cricket with a vengeance. He seemed to form a natural partnership with Bedi, an off-spinner and a left-armer, both attacking spinners with a similar belief that spinners got wickets by luring batsmen with flight and testing them with frequent variations. It was a more attacking spin option than the one Nadkarni had presented and it had nearly brought India victory at Madras where Bedi and Prasanna took all the seven second-innings West Indian wickets that fell. With Venkat still developing, although he had only taken two wickets in the first two Tests, India had suddenly acquired four high-class spinners.

But these spinners needed dry, hard wickets. Unfortunately the tour to England that followed was in the first and very wet half of 1967. The Indian Board had insisted on that half and the spinners never really had much of a chance. The Indians experienced an horrific May and, when conditions were wet and miserable, heads went down and catches were dropped. Even so, Chandrasekhar with 57 wickets, Prasanna with 45, Bedi with 34 and Venkat with 20 dominated the Indian bowling. The Indians were also badly afflicted by injury. Sardesai, the regular opener, and Guha the opening bowler, were fit for only one Test each; in the final Test even Surti, the makeshift opening bowler, was absent and Pataudi played Kunderan for his batting and opening bowling.

Pataudi cheerfully confessed that he did not know what Kunderan bowled.

India's plight was effectively summed up in the first Test when, with the series barely half a day old, both Surti, who took a fearful blow below the left knee, and Bedi were injured. Neither bowled after that, and they only batted with runners. It was then that Pataudi showed his character. In the first innings after England had made 550, Pataudi alone offered resistance, making 64 out of 164. This so inspired the Indians that, following-on, they made 510. The sun shone and for the first time on the tour, the Indians showed not only that they could bat but that they could bat attractively. Engineer, Wadekar, Pataudi himself, and Hanumant, all made runs, with Pataudi making 148. India were beaten by six wickets but had restored some pride.

That was about as much as India could hope for on this tour and the fightback at Headingley was, in retrospect, the high point of the tour. The second Test at Lord's and the third at Edgbaston were quickly lost although, on the turning wicket there Chandra, Bedi, Prasanna and Venkat – all four played together for the first time – showed their high class. But the batting failed and so India had once again gone to England and come back with nothing: all three Tests lost and only one victory against the counties as opposed to four defeats by the top four county sides.

The Indian cricket followers were disappointed but then they had always had unrealistic hopes. However, the cricketers had come on the tour expecting nothing. Kunderan recalled how it was:

We felt a sense of inferiority even before we got on to the field. We knew when the English came to India they were so well treated, everything was provided for them. The day we arrived in England we had to go to a sports shop to get some equipment. I had to save money from the £1-per-day allowance to buy a bat. Some other boys got money through friends. In those days bat manufacturers did not rush to give you bats and the Indian Board did not provide any equipment. Even the clothes we had were hardly suitable for cricket in England. We had gaberdine flannels that would stick to our knees so we could not bend down. We had a sleeveless sweater and a full sleeve sweater but they were not woollen and did not keep out the cold. In the middle of the tour the boys bought another sweater to wear underneath the Indian sweaters. Our allowance was so meagre that the moment we checked into the hotel, we would have to go looking for a cheap meal. Even in those days you couldn't get much for £1. Some of the boys suffered terribly with food. Venkat and Chandra, being vegetarian, could not eat ham or any of the cold meat salads which were served a lot during cricket matches. For much of the tour they were living on bread and butter. But how much of that can you eat? They were almost starving by the end. The manager, Keki Tarapore, did not help. He did not organise any practice facilities and went round telling the English: we have come to learn, we have come here to learn. He was always crawling to the English.

The Indian Board badly mismanaged the visit. They had chosen the first half of the summer – traditionally the wetter half – because they had packed the Indian cricket calendar that year. On the way back from England the Indians visited East Africa which, in cricketing terms, meant nothing but was a sop to the Indians living there and no sooner were the Indians home than they were preparing for their first visit to Australia in twenty years.

Judging by the statistics, the Australian visit would appear a complete disaster. India did not win a single first-class match and lost all four Tests. But this is a bit misleading. Within hours of the start of the first-class programme Pataudi, while fielding, pulled a hamstring muscle and could only watch as his team lost both their opening first-class match and the first Test. In the second he probably made the mistake of choosing to bat on a green wicket and came in when India were 25 for 5. Yet now, with one good eye and on one good leg, he tamed the Australian attack, combining, said *Wisden*, 'batting genius with courage in a manner which warmed the hearts of all'. *Wisden* went on, 'He was severely restricted in front-foot play by his leg-strain, and refused many singles. Yet he executed aggressive strokes, including several pugnacious hooks.' In India's first innings of 173 he made 75, in the second he made 85 out of 352. It was in this innings that he made McKenzie, who took ten wickets in the match, look quite ordinary as he hit him off the back foot over his head – once nearly for six. As at Headingley it was not enough to save India from defeat but Pataudi's batting in this match and in the series had a 'touch of genius' and he once again gave the battered Indian psyche a lift.

This was such a tonic that the Indians came close to winning the next Test. Chandra, after a leg injury, had gone home. Jaisimha was flown in and went straight into the third Test. To the amazement of the Australians he scored 74 and 101. Was India so rich in cricket talent that they could leave such a player at home? wondered the Australians. But then they did not know how Indians could waste their talent. Prasanna had now developed as a major off-spinner – by the end of this series the Australians were convinced he was the best in the world – he had taken 6 for 141 in Melbourne despite several dropped catches, now he repeated this feat, taking 6 for 104, and Australia were bowled out for 294. The Indians were left 395 to win and, with Jaisimha and

Borde going well, they were 310 for 5. But then Borde was caught off Cowper and India lost by 39 runs, the closest they had come to winning in Australia. India also got into a challenging position in the fourth Test before fading so that, despite losing 4–0, Pataudi felt the Indians were just coming into form as they left Australia.

This seemed to be proved in New Zealand where India won three of the four Tests, the first time India had won a Test match abroad. Perhaps this showed how far New Zealand were behind Australia, but the Indians proved themselves superior in almost every department: batting, fielding and, above all, spin bowling. Prasanna, who had taken 25 wickets in Australia for 27.44, now took 24 for 18.79. Nadkarni, who had managed just 3 wickets for 70 each against Australia, now took 14 wickets at 17.92, heading the averages in his last Test series. New Zealand had no answer to spin. Generously they provided the Indians with spinning wickets and but for some sloppy cricket by the Indians in the second Test – Pataudi sent New Zealand in when he should have batted, then India batted badly – they might have made a clean sweep.

Pataudi returned to India as the first captain to win abroad and with what looked like the makings of a young, attractive team. Surti, who had started the tour scorned in India as the poor man's Sobers, really proved himself as an all-rounder, scoring 967 runs and taking 34 wickets on the tour. Prasanna was now a world-class spinner, Bedi a developing talent, and all the batsmen could bat very attractively. Nobody could now accuse the Indians of being dull, indeed at times they batted too attractively for their own good. In New Zealand some of them had shown they could also play the big innings that was needed – and Indians took particular pleasure from Wadekar's batting. A fine stylish left-handed batsman he seemed unable to score a hundred, making 91 against England at Headingley and 99 against Australia at Melbourne. Now in Wellington he scored 143 and the Indians hoped that this would open the floodgates. As it happened, it turned out to be his only Test century.

16

Tiger's fall
1969-71

The moment of victory is always the most dangerous. Pataudi's fall can be traced to the moment when India won her first Test series abroad in New Zealand. Despite that victory the question marks about Pataudi's captaincy had not entirely vanished. There were specific criticisms like his decision to bat first at Melbourne on a green wicket, then to put Australia in on turning wickets at Brisbane and Sydney. While his fielding was a great influence he never seemed to encourage his bowlers and always appeared a bit removed from the action. Pataudi treated Test cricketers like adults but some of them were not mature enough to appreciate it. Most damaging, Pataudi for all his individual qualities did not quite instil in the Indians the will to win. Bill O'Reilly had commented that the chief weakness of the Indians was 'a shortcoming in the enthusiastic will to win. The Indians do not scrag the opposition severely enough, once they have got them down. Twice they let Australia out of the bag and twice it happened from a lack of concentration at critical periods.'

O'Reilly's criticisms struck a chord in India. Indians believed that man for man they were not inferior to anyone, or any team. What prevented them from scaling the heights was this determination to win that Australians, and Americans, had. This seemed glaringly exposed during the winter of 1969–70 when India stumbled to a draw in a home series against New Zealand when by rights they should have lost, and lost comprehensively to Australia.

In India, at that time, New Zealand evoked the same feelings which India produced in England or Australia. Crowds expected them to be beaten easily. But after India won in Bombay by 60 runs, New Zealand beat India in Nagpur by 167 runs and should have won in Hyderabad where India were bowled out for 89 in their first innings and were 76 for 7 in the second. With two and a quarter hours left there was a violent thunderstorm. However, the ground authorities seemed to do little to dry the ground, forcing Dowling, the New Zealand captain, to come out to help. In the end the match was abandoned.

This Test match seemed to sum up everything that was wrong with Indian cricket. The pitch should have been cut on the rest day but the umpires forgot, and tried to cut it on the third day. Dowling refused to allow this and, on a pitch uncut for three days, India collapsed to New Zealand pace. The third day saw a riot when a youth coming on to congratulate Venkat and Bedi in becoming India's highest scorers when they added 40 for the last wicket, was injured by a soldier: gates were broken down, metal chairs flung on to the ground, fires lit and the crowd attacked by an army unit. No play was possible on the third evening. At the end of the match there was another demonstration and Pataudi left the field to boos.

Pataudi and the players were already in bad odour after the Nagpur match, for the defeat had been accompanied by stories that, on the second evening of the match, the players had spent too much time socialising. Typical of such Indian press reports, there were innuendos and nudge, nudge, wink, wink types of articles which can be the most corrosive of all. After it the Indians played badly, lost, and this reinforced the public tendency to believe that it was demon drink and bad company that had undone them.

The impression that Pataudi was not in control, and did not care, was reinforced during the Australian visit which began shortly afterwards. Australia, led by the canny Bill Lawry, had held on to the Ashes against England in 1968, then beaten the West Indies at home. In India they won the five-Test series 3–1, and everything that could go wrong for India seemed to go wrong. The first Test in Bombay saw India's second-ever defeat in Bombay and the first in the city to be marked by a riot. When Venkat was given out in the second innings the Bombay crowd, which had always been boisterous but never riotous, did riot. In the past Bombay had looked down rather superiorly on riots in Calcutta and Kanpur. Now the decision against Venkat, which was criticised by the commentators, seemed to light the fuse and the East Stand erupted. The hessian surrounding the tennis courts behind the East Stand was set on fire but even as black smoke drifted across the ground Lawry insisted that play continue. For an hour play continued while bottles and chairs were thrown on the ground.

India came back in the third Test at Delhi to win emphatically by seven wickets with a day to spare but in Calcutta there was another riot, and another defeat. Calcutta, then in the grip of Naxalite terror, was inflamed by quite erroneous reports that Walters, who had been called up to do national service, had served in Vietnam. Most Indians opposed the Vietnam war but the left-wing press in Calcutta, always very strong in that city, was particularly vociferous and the issue was whipped up to a frenzy. Despite what had happened in 1967 Calcutta had done little to mend its ways and, on the morning of the fourth day, as 20,000 people who had been queueing all night waited patiently for a ticket, a rumour was spread that there were no more seats. The riot this caused saw six people killed and nearly one hundred injured. How far this affected the Indian players is hard to say, but soon afterwards the Indians collapsed to be all out for 161, of which Wadekar made 62.

The match ended in utter confusion. Lawry, who had almost completely undone all the goodwill that previous Australians had built up, now had an altercation with a photographer. Lawry pushed him and he fell. The photographer claimed he had been struck. As Lawry hit off the winning runs the crowd threw stones. Play was interrupted for fifteen minutes and Pataudi left the field with cries of 'Shame, Pataudi, shame' ringing in his ears. The previous night the crowd, angered by the Indian collapse, had attacked the players' hotel; now they focussed their anger once again on Pataudi.

The final Test at Madras provided Pataudi a chance to redeem all this. Twice India had Australia in its grasp, twice they were allowed to escape. In the first innings at 82 for 4, Walters, on 4, was beaten by Bedi and stranded down the wicket but Engineer missed the stumping. Walters made 102. Then on the third morning Australia, with a lead of 85, were reduced to 24 for 6 by Prasanna. But Redpath was missed twice at the wicket, he made 63, and India were left 249 to win. This looked possible as Wadekar and Viswanath took India to 114 for 2 but then came another collapse and India lost by 77 runs.

There could, argued Pataudi's critics, be no greater proof that under him the Indians did not have the will to win. There was no doubt about the quality of the spin attack. At the end of the series Prasanna and Bedi were being talked of in the same breath as Lock and Laker, Ramadhin and Valentine, and with reason. In Delhi when they shot out Australia for 107 they both took five wickets each and seemed to dovetail so well together. Along with Venkat they dominated the Indian bowling. The three of them bowled 726.3 overs of the 929.1 overs the Indians delivered and took 59 of the 70 wickets. Bedi's 21 wickets had been at 20.57, Prasanna's 26 at 25.84. Prasanna had built on his great achievements in Australia. Bedi had now matured into probably the best left-arm spinner in the world. The Australians never really mastered them. Only thrice had they scored more than 300 in the series and 348 was their highest total.

One reason for the spinners' success was that the close catching, which had often been non-existent, was suddenly electrifying. Pataudi had, over the years, done much to improve the Indian out-cricket. Now Solkar, an exciting youngster, a useful bat and a wonderful close-in catcher, was beginning to bring off the catches that make great bowlers look irresistible. There had been other Indian gains as well. Viswanath, an exciting young batsman from Bangalore, had made his Test debut in Kanpur and scored 137. He was small, no taller than 5ft 4 in., but his lack of height did not seem to affect his timing or his strokeplay. He cut, he drove and he stood up to the fast bowlers quite unafraid of what they might do. Indian hearts sank a little when he scored a century in his first Test – for there was an Indian superstition that batsmen who did that never again scored another hundred – but Viswanath's approach and style suggested he was more than a one-Test wonder.

Wadekar had improved and he and Viswanath were together when India won at Delhi. But despite this the Indians lost the series and Pataudi was blamed. The fact is, Pataudi was to some extent the victim of his own success. His style had made the Indians believe that they could win but now that they did not win as often as they would like, they blamed him. He had raised expectations but failed to fulfil them.

All this may not have mattered had there not been a change in the Selection Committee. The previous year, on 30 September 1968, Vijay Merchant had been appointed Chairman of the Selectors. After his retirement from cricket he had taken little interest in cricket administration. During Bombay Tests he was the great expert and commentator, but he never ventured out of Bombay. Now he had travelled to Calcutta for the Board meeting as the last-minute choice of the Cricket Club of India. There, with the principal factions unable to impose their choice, he had been selected. Merchant brought to his job what he brought to everything else: a businessman's mind. Identify the problem and see what is wrong. As he would later say, he was like the director of a mill which faced the problem of a decline in production. What do you do? Change some of the things you are doing, perhaps change the personnel?

Merchant had followed that policy against New Zealand: bringing in younger players and persisting with it even when New Zealand proved stronger than anticipated. Pataudi had not much liked that and their relationship, never close, was further strained by the Australian visit. Now Merchant thought perhaps he should change the production manager, i.e. the captain, especially as there were tours scheduled to the West Indies in February–April 1971 and to England for the second half of the 1971 season.

Possibly Pataudi did not take this threat too seriously. Throughout the 1960s the stalking horse of the anti-Pataudi faction had been Chandu Borde who, but for the accident to Contractor, might well have succeeded to the captaincy. In a country where seniority matters, he was senior, his Test debut having been in 1958–59. Before the Australian tour Pataudi had even announced his retirement from Test cricket. It seemed Borde's hour had come. Then in a vital Duleep Trophy Match for South Zone against West Zone at the Brabourne Stadium, a match seen as a trial for the tour, Pataudi had scored 200. He had never before batted so determinedly. It made sure that Pataudi would be captain and he had taken the team to Australia with, as ever, Borde as his deputy.

Pataudi had also been in an odd position as captain. He had initially played his cricket in the north, captaining Delhi. He moved south and there he played for Hyderabad and South Zone, neither of which he captained. They were both captained by Jaisimha who was said to have one of the finest cricket brains in the country. Merchant had never liked the Pataudi–Jaisimha axis. When Jaisimha had been flown out as replacement for Chandrasekhar in Australia – which meant that a batsman was replacing a spinner because, although Jaisimha could bowl medium pace and off-breaks, his Test bowling average was 92.11 – Merchant had muttered darkly about this axis. Pataudi's position was a bit like Hutton's when he captained England but not Yorkshire. Apart from India (and Sussex) Pataudi only ever captained one other first-class match, The Rest v. Ranji Trophy Champions. So the first indication of a change in the wind came in December 1970, when the Ranji Trophy Champions, Bombay, met the Rest of India and the Rest was captained by Borde.

Pataudi did his cause little good by not playing for Borde. He claimed he had flu, which looked a weak excuse; but he clearly hoped to repeat what he had done in 1967: score a big hundred in the South Zone versus West Zone match in Bombay. Unfortunately West, led by Borde, were a bit too shrewd for Pataudi. Borde brought on Hattea, a quick bowler, and while Pataudi hooked him for a six and a four, Borde encouraged him to bowl straight and he had Pataudi out lbw for 19. A double-century might have saved his captaincy. Now, it seemed, the anti-forces were gathering momentum.

The selectors met on 8 January 1971. Borde was quickly eliminated however: too old at thirty-six, not fit enough, but he had done his job as a stalking-horse against Pataudi just as Pataudi's father had done in 1936 against Nayudu. The choice narrowed down to Pataudi and, surprisingly, Wadekar, the Bombay captain. To anyone unfamiliar with the intricacies of Indian cricket, Wadekar's rise may seem surprising. But in the often contradictory way Indian cricket politics works it was a most natural choice. With Borde out of the reckoning, Wadekar had emerged as the front-runner almost by elimination – as if he bore a lucky charm.

True, his cricket career had been dotted with lucky episodes. He had made his debut for Bombay in the late 1950s but had to fight to retain his place in a side bristling with talent and where Polly Umrigar – then the supremo of Bombay cricket – did not think highly of him. Once when he scored 151 he was criticised for giving his wicket away. He should have made his Test debut in the mid-1960s. Instead, he had to wait till the 1966–67 West Indies tour of India, where he failed in the first Test. He missed the second match due to illness; but, having avoided the disaster of Calcutta, he made his mark in the third Test at Madras. Here in the second innings, having made 0 in the first, he made a spirited 67, hooking Hall and Griffith.

This launched him on such a successful Test career that he did not miss a single Test over the next three years. He was a fixture in an ever-changing Indian side – a consistent, reliable left-hander at no. 3 (a position India had not filled since the days of Vijay Manjrekar) whose only problem seemed to be that he got out in the nineties but rarely scored a hundred.

His challenge to Pataudi arose not from any particular talent for captaincy – captains of Bombay hardly required talent! – but because his position in the side was not in doubt. Merchant had great faith in him and predicted, when Wadekar was still at college, that he would one day captain India.

However, so precarious is the life of an Indian cricketer that Wadekar himself had not been certain of being selected and asked Pataudi before the meeting, assuming Pataudi would be captain, to put in a good word for him. Now Merchant proposed Wadekar which could be seen as a Bombay man favouring the Bombay captain, but in truth it was because he thought Wadekar was the man for the job. The Selection Committee split 2–2, and Merchant used his casting vote to remove Pataudi. He had been captain for thirty-six Tests, the longest reign in Indian cricket history. It had brought much joy, much good cricket, but not the victories that the Indians wanted. Wadekar was out shopping as the selectors took the decision and returned home to find journalists outside his house.

Pataudi's rejection was greeted with bewilderment and surprise. Pataudi himself took the defeat with poor grace. He had refused to play under Borde. Now he made it appear as if he had never been available to tour by sending a telegram to that effect before the vote. It turned out the telegram was dated 12 January, four days after he was sacked. He compounded his refusal to go on tour by not playing for the South Zone against the East and announced he would stand for Parliament.

Mrs Gandhi was campaigning on the platform of nationalising the banks and removing princely privileges, including privy purse and titles. Pataudi said he would contest a seat in Haryana against the Congress. The Chief Minister there was one Bansi Lal, who was later to earn notoriety, and he summed up the situation pretty well by saying, 'You want to vote for Pataudi? What good will it do to you if he wins this election? To meet him you'll have to get into the stadium first. And you know how difficult it is to get into a cricket stadium in this country. Granting you get in, what will he give you? At most a bat and ball!'

Indians, at least urban Indians, love cricket to distraction. The Australian visit had brought unprecedented crowds to see Test matches with daily attendances of between 35,000 and 50,000. Thousands more wanted to be accommodated. But these crowds did not confuse cricket popularity with politics. Pataudi was a great cricketer, but he had no political standing and was duly trounced.

The Age of the Tiger seemed to have ended. In the typical contradictory way that Indians have, even those who were against him now felt sad. Having done the great deed they felt he had been cheated. And as the dramatic events of the West Indies and England unfolded, this feeling increased. In retrospect the winter of 1970 saw a hiccough in Indian cricket's long love affair with the Tiger. They were miffed but could never be permanently estranged.

17

A genius emerges
1971

A genius, by definition, is not capable of rational explanation. He does things about which other mortals can only fantasise. There is no knowing what he will do or why. The word is often used loosely, particularly in the sporting contest where hyperbole is much favoured. Defeat is usually a disaster, victory a triumph of genius. But in the early months of 1971 a cricket genius did emerge and he, contrary to all expectations, turned out to be a small Indian, so small indeed that even in India there were jokes about his height.

Nothing could have prepared the cricket world for his arrival. That winter England were touring Australia under the canny leadership of Raymond Illingworth and eyes were focussed on the batting of Boycott and the bowling of Snow. In December 1970 Greg Chappell, whose brother Ian was already a leading batsman in the Australian team, had made his debut, scoring a hundred in his first Test – the sixth Australian to do so – and the power and grace of his innings marked him out to be the next great Australian cricketer.

India's tour of the West Indies was supposed to be very much a footnote to all this – indeed it is difficult now to imagine how settled the cricket world looked in 1971. And how centred around England. England under Illingworth were about to regain the Ashes that May had lost to Benaud in 1958–59. The West Indies were the great entertainers of cricket. 'Cricket, lovely cricket' was supposed to have rescued the game from boredom and, in order to accommodate them, England had drastically changed policies. They allowed overseas cricketers into the county sides and made space for more West Indian visits by having twin tours from the supposedly lesser countries of India, Pakistan and New Zealand as well as the West Indies. (But the West Indies were to have full tours as well while since then only Pakistan, in 1987, has enjoyed a full tour.) If there were any challengers to the trinity at the top then it was conceivably the South Africans who produced their best team ever in the late 1960s, but the country's racial policies were catching up with its cricketers and they played no Tests after the 1969–70 series against Australia. They had played their last Tests in England in 1965, on a 'short' tour, and their scheduled series in 1970 was replaced by a Rest of the World team captained by Gary Sobers which included only one Indian, Engineer. Now suddenly, quite out of the blue, up popped Sunil Manohar Gavaskar. Gavaskar had been selected for the West Indies tour of 1970–71 on his reputation as a promising player. He had played twelve first-class matches stretching back to 1966–67, making 811 runs, highest score 176, at an average of 45. What set him apart, though, was that he had shown a capacity for making big scores at school, college and inter-university level. In school matches double-centuries were common and in one university match he had scored 327. Yet not even Wadekar, who had a big part in selecting Gavaskar for the tour, believed he would break any records.

Later much was made of Gavaskar's unusual upbringing. Certainly there was a stroke of luck when, shortly after his birth in July 1949, an observant uncle noticed that he had a punctured earhole and when, at the hospital, Sunil was confused with a fisherman's child, the uncle quickly spotted the mistake. Other aspects of Gavaskar's cricket upbringing only came to seem unusual because of his subsequent fame. His mother used to bowl to him, but it is not unknown for Indian mothers to bowl to their sons. He played all his early cricket on a narrow fifteen-foot balcony outside the flat in central Bombay where he lived, and honed his batting playing 'matches' in the courtyard of his building where, of necessity, he had to hit straight and keep the ball along the ground. The ball just could not be hit above four feet because otherwise it would break window panes and cost money. The physical limitations of his surroundings taught him a control that was to prove useful in later life.

But there were other Indian cricketers who grew up in such buildings, played such cricket. What was unusual was that the block of flats Gavaskar lived in, or building as Indians like to call them, was surrounded by other buildings all of which held young boys, just like Sunil, eager to play. Rarely in cricket history can such concentrated talent have developed so early in such a confined area. The buildings formed a close-knit complex and six of the players with whom Gavaskar played his 'gully' matches went on to play for Bombay. So from an early age there was a sharp competitive edge to Gavaskar.

This was sharpened by the encouragement he received from his parents who, unlike other Indian parents, did not see cricket as a damaging distraction to studies. Gavaskar was able to fuse the Hindu version of the Protestant work-ethic, dedication and hard work, with education at one of Bombay's leading schools, the Jesuit-run St Xavier's where discipline and the Jesuit idea of producing the man from the boy shaped his character. So to his natural gifts he brought a resolve, a determination which most other Indian cricketers did not have. Some of them may have been more gifted, but none was so determined.

Concentration was his great weapon and he could concentrate when other cricketers were easily distracted. Ravi Mandrekar, who played in the 'building matches' with Gavaskar from about the age of seven or eight, described him to me. 'In 1966 we were playing in the Police Shield at the Hindu Gymkhana. I was keeping wicket, Sunil was batting. He was struggling for runs. But he batted for three hours to make 64 not out. Throughout this time he did not say a word to me. He knew me very well. We lived next to each other and had been playing together since kids. But he didn't say a word. Then suddenly somebody from the crowd shouted, "Maro, hit out." Sunil said, "Who the hell is he?" But he did not look up, he just muttered and the next minute he was batting again. That was concentration. His philosophy was, there is no place in cricket for chit-chat, pleasantries. You are just concerned with the bowler and the bat. Sunil got runs because he likes to be at the centre of attraction and when he is batting he is at the centre of attraction.'

This had already impressed his great friend Milind Rege who lived in a nearby block of flats, captained him at school and played with him right through to the Bombay team. But for a heart-attack at an early age Milind might well have played for India. He told me: 'Sunil had tremendous talent but he also had tremendous concentration and patience. He can read a book surrounded by 5,000 people. What was unusual about him was that he could sort out his technical problems.' Rege, who knows him better than anyone else, already saw that his friend was special and was convinced of this when he played for the Combined Universities against New Zealand in Bombay in September 1969. He only made 25 and 10 but, 'he really showed his class. Dayle Hadlee and Collinge were good bowlers but on a green-top wicket he played them beautifully off his toes. That was the moment of truth. That was when he arrived, showed his class.' Gavaskar was twenty but Rege was sure he would achieve greatness.

What also set Gavaskar apart was that cricket was never a game to him. He did not have Kunderan's slap-dash, happy approach. Winning mattered to Gavaskar. Even as a child he hated getting out and would get angry when given out. In these childhood matches he was often given out unfairly because otherwise the other children would never have had a bat, and Gavaskar would be furious. Years later, after he had often been doused with champagne, he said that what he remembered most was the sip from a bottle of 'Rodger's' lemonade he had as a child when playing 'matches' with other building teams in central Bombay. That sip, coming after a hard fought 'match' where as a child he had had to concentrate to win, meant more to him than any amount of champagne.

It is hard to imagine any other Indian cricketer making that point but, before Gavaskar, many cricketers of promise had left India with high hopes and returned with nothing to show but a tale of missed opportunity and bad luck. He was the first Indian cricketer to surprise India as much as the cricket world. For, while Gavaskar was seen as a player of promise, outside Bombay few knew him. The real batting star of the future was supposed to be Gundappa Viswanath, whose century against Australia in his first Test had looked like solving the Indian middle-order problem.

Gavaskar began the West Indies tour in 1970–71 much as other Indian players of promise. He developed an injury, a whitlow on his finger aggravated by chewing his finger-nails. He did not play in the initial matches including the first Test. But in his first first-class match of the tour he made 82 and batted with complete authority. He made his Test debut at Port of Spain and made 65 and 67 not out. Wadekar prayed he would not make a century on his debut because of the famous Indian cricket superstition. Indians also have a saying that, if you are too good at something, or too good-looking, you attract the evil eye. The literal saying is 'they are being given the eye' and this is supposed to bring bad luck. So, very good-looking girls are often given a spot to make them look slightly less beautiful and so avoid the evil eye. Gavaskar, by missing his hundred on debut, did the same and kept Wadekar happy. But he was 67 not out as India won her first Test against the West Indies and then in the series he went on to score 116 and 64 not out, 1 and 117 not out, and 124 and 220. In four Tests he made 774 runs at an average of 154.80.

Not only had no other Indian batsman come anywhere near this, but he was threatening all sorts of world records. Only K. D. Walters then had ever scored a century and a double-century in one Test, and since then only Lawrence Rowe and Greg Chappell. His aggregate of 774 was only 5 runs short of Everton Weekes' aggregate of 779, the highest in a series between the two countries. No batsman in a maiden Test series had ever scored so many runs. Headley in four Tests in 1929–30 had scored 703. Only Bradman against South Africa in 1931–32 and India in 1947–48 had a better average. For a young man, just turned twenty-one, who had never before been out of his country except to Sri Lanka, and playing for a country whose batsmen had a history of catastrophic collapses abroad, this was quite sensational. By the end of the tour even the English newspapers managed to subdue their preoccupation with the Ashes to talk about this new, Indian, Bradman.

Gavaskar's batting was the basis of one of the greatest upsets in cricket history. The Indians had never beaten the West Indies; and they had never won away from home except in New Zealand. Now they won the series 1–0. The West Indies were so surprised by Gavaskar that they never, as Charlie Davis, one of their batting successes of that tour, says, developed a plan for the little man. Davis recalls, 'There were ridiculous ideas about getting him out. He was so short that one expert said bowl a full toss at his chest and when he hits it hard the ball will be caught at square-leg. We just didn't know how to catch him out and we paid the price for it.'

In Trinidad where, appropriately in front of the East Indians, the Indian triumph had come, Lord Relator composed a calypso about Gavaskar. 'He's just like a wall . . . We can't get Gavaskar out at all, at all . . . not at all.'

Gavaskar had chosen the perfect time to make his Test debut. The West Indies were in transition though it was Gavaskar's performances that indicated how much of a building job they had. Gibbs was dropped for this series and new bowlers of both speed and spin were required. Sobers was still a great batsman and when the mood took him a wonderful bowler, but Sobers was fallible as a fielder and early in his big innings Gavaskar was dropped by Sobers more than once; but even then what stood out, as it had when he was playing for St Xavier's High School in Bombay or in his building cricket matches, was the sheer determination to succeed, the ability to put a dropped chance behind him and continue. Indeed later Gavaskar would develop the theory that he played his best innings if he started a bit edgily. It gave him a chance to work out the kinks. If his innings started in perfection he rarely scored many.

This was combined with the ability to withstand pain. In the second innings of the final Test, when Gavaskar made his 220, he batted throughout the innings with severe toothache. As a child playing cricket with his mother he had once hit the ball hard at her and hurt her. But she had brushed this aside and continued playing with him. Gavaskar throughout his career was to show this same ability. The value of his 220 cannot be doubted. He batted for eight hours and fifty minutes, and such was his mastery that the next highest Indian score was 54. His innings enabled India to reach 427 in the second innings which was not only enough to save the match but very nearly won it. The West Indies, requiring 262 to win, were left on the brink at 165 for 8. Had Wadekar been a bit more adventurous with his use of spin and introduced it earlier India might well have won.

The other important point about Gavaskar's achievement was that he was almost the first specialist Indian opening batsman. Very early in his school career he had batted in the middle order but that was when he was very small, about ten; after that, for much of his school, college and university career he was an opener and selected as such for this tour. This was a rarity for Indians where it was quite common to get middle-order batsmen to open, particularly on tours.

Their failures, far from condemning the experiment, often condemned the players. Having asked a silly question the Indians were surprised by the answer. Gavaskar, in some ways, was the first genuine Indian opening batsman, given that Merchant was a middle-order batsman who only took to opening during the 1936 tour at the age of twenty-six.

Letting specialist batsmen play in their accustomed position was to be proven even more emphatically in the case of Sardesai. He was the other batting hero of the tour and in some ways an even more surprising success than Gavaskar. Dilip Sardesai had a wretched tour of England in 1967 and of Australia in 1967–68. Opening the batting he got out early so often that the joke was that Renneberg, the Australian opening bowler, came up to him and introduced himself, 'I open the bowling with Graham McKenzie but you probably don't know me. I come on second.' Sardesai was never an opener. He had been made into one on the previous West Indian trip and since he played straight and India had no openers he became one.

He was in danger of becoming the forgotten man of Indian cricket when he was selected as a last-minute choice, very much on Wadekar's insistence. He was not expected to play in the Tests, but before the first match against Jamaica, Viswanath was injured and this gave a chance to Sardesai. In the first Test Sobers put India in and there was another collapse. India were 75 for 5 when Sardesai started rebuilding the innings, first with Solkar, and then with Prasanna, both century partnerships. When he was eventually out for 212 India had made 387, a position of such strength that the West Indies were made to follow-on. They saved the Test but now India held the initiative and never relaxed her grip. After that, in every crisis in the series Sardesai made runs. He scored a century in the second Test to set up India's winning total; his 150 in the fourth prevented the follow-on and but for Gavaskar's quite exceptional scoring would have been the leading batsman: 642 runs at an average of 80.25.

Successful sides create their own momentum and this Indian side did that. Solkar proved a marvellous late-order batsman and an excellent close catcher. With Venkat and Abid Ali also good close to the wicket, for once the spinners found the chances that they created were being accepted. Chandra was still out of the side but Venkat, Prasanna and Bedi were more than a match for the West Indian batsmen. Sobers scored heavily, so did Charlie Davis, but the spinners dominated the Tests by taking 48 of the 68 wickets.

Since Prasanna's return to Test cricket in 1967 Venkat had become the other spinner in a sort of eternal spin triangle. Now, when Prasanna got injured in the second Test and missed the third and fourth, Venkat took over. Unlike Prasanna, flight was never his forte. Venkat bowled a much flatter trajectory, kept a mean length. His height of over six feet was unusual for Indian spinners who, Chandrasekhar apart, have been short men. And on the West Indian wickets Venkat used this height to get unusual bounce. He was what was known as a 'hitter', hitting the pitch from over eight feet. Venkat also benefited from the fact that, unusually, the West Indians had a high proportion of left-handers: Sobers, Carew, Fredericks, Lloyd, and they found Venkat very difficult. He was so accurate, he kept them so pinned down that they could never get after him. Fredericks, Carew, Lloyd averaged no more than 30 in the Tests. Only Sobers, with his genius, broke free and averaged 74.

Almost everything the Indians tried worked. Pataudi may have fallen from grace but his closest cricket friend, Jaisimha, made the trip. Salim Durani, who had last been seen in a Test in Bombay in 1966, also against the West Indies, nonchalantly combing his hair while fielding at third man and acknowledging the cheers of the adoring Bombay crowd, returned. In cold figures neither did much. But Jaisimha's shrewd cricketing brain was of great help to Wadekar. At a crucial stage in the second Test when Prasanna was injured he reminded Wadekar of the presence of Durani. Durani had not bowled in the first innings but the previous night in Jaisimha's room he had promised to get two wickets for India: Sobers and Lloyd. Durani had had some success against Sobers on the 1962 tour and fancied his chances. Wadekar brought him on. He bowled Sobers for a duck, then had Lloyd caught. He took only one other wicket in the series but he had made the crucial breakthrough. Venkat and Bedi ran through the rest of the side, taking 5 for 95 and 2 for 50 respectively. The Indians, left to make 124 to win, won with a day to spare.

After the match Charlie Davis had arranged a party, Port of Spain being his native town, but the fact that he had invited the Indians got him into trouble. The West Indians, normally so gregarious, were now seeing shadows everywhere. The victory led to scenes with which the Indians were very familiar: recriminations, accusations by the press about low morale, drastic changes in the team, with whispers being heard against the captain. In the past West Indian success had pro-duced such devastation in India. Now the Indians were quietly amused to see the West Indians suffer the same symptoms. Even before this, during the first Test, Garfield Sobers had forgotten that, in a four-day match, the follow-on target was 150. Rain had delayed the start of the first Test, making it a four-day match, and when Wadekar went to the West Indian dressing-room to ask Sobers to follow-on – the first time the Indians were in such a position against the West Indians – Sobers for a moment did not know what he was talking about. He was quite shocked. That sense of shock never left him or his team and by the end of the series, as the Indians returned home in triumph, the West Indies were left to pick up the pieces. Sobers was still the greatest all-rounder the game had ever seen but as a captain he was now considered very fallible. Within two years he had lost the captaincy.

The Indians, meanwhile, were tasting the heady delights of a team returning from an overseas trip in triumph. The most momentous period of Indian cricket history had just begun.

18

Glory and despair
1971-74

Cricket has always claimed to be a game that reflects life. Some see this as a disreputable neo-Marxist analysis but the Indian cricket victories in 1971, first in the West Indies and then in England, turning India almost overnight into a major cricketing power, were uncannily reflected in national life. As India was winning in the West Indies, the Bangladesh crisis was just coming to the boil with the Pakistani army launching its desperate attempt to gun down a people who dared to revolt. By the time the Indians had won at The Oval in August 1971, India and Pakistan were heading for war.

England were due to tour India that very winter but, because of this situation, refused. In December India and Pakistan fought a short, sharp war. India won, and this led to the liberation of Bangladesh. Mrs Gandhi noted that it was the first victory won by Indian arms over a foreign enemy for 2,000 years since the days of Chandragupta who had defeated Alexander's successors and secured ancient India's borders. This was a touch melodramatic but victory in the war did establish India as the major power in South Asia and it seemed to go down well in a country that had long known defeat in battle and defeat in cricket. The victories in cricket were certainly a morale-booster, and that year, in more ways than one, India seemed to belong to the top table of the world.

India would have loved to have played a series that winter and, probably, should have tried to arrange a visit to Australia when the South African tour to Australia was cancelled. A Rest of the World team, including Gavaskar, Engineer and Bedi, went instead and India had to rest content with memories of a most glorious year, which gave a considerable boost to cricket literature in the country, while waiting for England to visit in the winter of 1972-73.

Much to Indian anger, England sent yet another team which missed out several key players: Illingworth, Snow, Boycott, all declined to tour. Tony Lewis, like Nigel Howard, had the dubious distinction of making his debut for England as captain. But Lewis and England proved a surprise. India had started the first Test proudly brandishing its status as 'World Champions': by mid-afternoon of the first Test in

Delhi, India were 80 for 6 with Geoff Arnold doing all the damage. India never really recovered from this, despite some remarkable bowling by Chandrasekhar. In the first innings he took 8 for 79. England had got to 61 for no loss when, in eight balls, he dismissed Wood, Fletcher and Lewis between lunch and tea and Knott after the interval. It seemed the magic of The Oval spell was still on England.

But Chandra could not do it all on his own. England gained a small lead, India made only 233 in the second innings and, left to make 207, England reached the target for the loss of six wickets. The result quite shook India. This was the first time India were playing at home since the victories of 1971, and it had resulted in a defeat. Was this again the familiar pattern? A victory followed by a shattering defeat? It seemed as if in a few days Lewis and his team had undone all that had been achieved, after so long, in the West Indies and England. There was a touch of panic in the Indian ranks. Sardesai, whom Merchant had praised after the West Indies tour as the man who had produced the renaissance of Indian cricket, was now dropped. Merchant had retired and the new selectors had no faith in the renaissance man. Sardesai, looking for one last Test series at home, decided to retire. Salim Durani, who had a phenomenally successful domestic season with bat and ball, was recalled for Calcutta.

There was another crucial change. Prasanna was brought back. Ever since he had missed the third Test in the West Indies due to injury he had found his place as India's first spinner usurped by Venkat. He had kept him out of Tests in England and Prasanna had begun to believe the world and Wadekar did not want him. The defeat had unsettled things and now he was needed. Adhikari, still the team manager, moaned that the perfect machine he had created in England, every player knowing instinctively where to go in the field, had now been shattered.

In a desperately close match both Durani and Prasanna made a difference. Prasanna took three wickets, including that of the dangerous Tony Greig in the first innings. Durani made 53 at a crucial stage in the second innings and India won the match by 28 runs. Chandra, of course, was again the key bowler. He had 5 for 65 in the first innings, 4 for 42 in the second. This was the first series between India and England that received extensive English press coverage. In the past the top English cricket writers, like the English players, had given it a miss – neither Arlott, nor Swanton, nor Cardus had ever covered a tour in India: but on this tour most of the top cricket writers were there. Swanton, himself, witnessed the Calcutta Test and the sight of 70,000 or more people crammed into the Eden Gardens every day: the noise, the tumult, the colour, the Indian close-in fielders led by Solkar hemming in the

English batsmen as Chandra, Bedi and Prasanna bowled, made a deep impression.

But if the victory was a relief for India there was a sub-plot which was disquieting for Wadekar. For much of the match he was not well, Engineer captained in his place and it was noticeable what a difference his bright, engaging approach made. Between the second and third Tests Wadekar had even more cause for worry. Pataudi had given up his unrealistic political hopes along with his title. The domestic season of 1971-72 had seen him bat with remarkable fluency under his new name. He was now Mansur Ali Khan Pataudi or M. A. K. Pataudi, with *Wisden* choosing to put Pataudi in brackets after M.A.K. But to Indians he remained their beloved 'Tiger' and they noted how he mixed dash with discipline. In the winter of the year of victory, as 1971 was becoming known in India, Pataudi scored a century against Prasanna and Chandra and did not lift the ball until he had passed 100 runs. Only then did he play one of those characteristic lofted and cross-bat shots that made him such an astonishing spectacle in Indian cricket. This, said the Indians, was a new Tiger, determined to make a comeback.

Now, on the way to Madras, MCC played South Zone at Bangalore and Pataudi scored a splendid hundred. For the first two Tests he had been a journalist in the press box judging the Indian performance. His century gave a clear indication to the selectors that he was ready and willing to play and in Madras he moved back to the Indian dressing-room as if he had never left it. In the endless intrigue that forms a backdrop to everything in India, be it cricket, politics or life itself, the message to Wadekar seemed clear: the old captain, the rightful heir, was back. Pataudi's failure to make himself available for the West Indies had gone down badly, now he had willingly accepted playing under Wadekar, a player who had made his debut when Pataudi was well established as captain, and this made a deep impression. In India a person senior in age or rank very rarely accepts a position under a man who had superseded him. Pataudi's readiness to do so was seen by Indians as a magnanimous act and whatever bitterness was felt about the West Indies decision was instantly dissolved. Wadekar had only lost one Test as captain but another loss, or a defeat, in the series and who could tell?

Pataudi showed what India had missed as soon as he started batting. For the first time in the series the Indian batsmen built on the platform Chandra had constructed. After England had won the toss on a good wicket Chandra bowled so superbly that England slumped to 110 for 7. That ability of his to cut through a batting line-up was still intact. He had Amiss out before lunch: in 26 balls after lunch he removed Greig, Lewis and Old for eight runs. Then he came back after tea to remove Gifford and Pocock in successive overs and deny Fletcher his century, who remained 97 not out.

India had lost three wickets for 89 when Pataudi emerged. Let *Wisden* record the scene: 'Coming in to a royal and tumultuous welcome from a fine crowd he straightaway attacked the bowling with an array of glittering strokes.' He reached his 50 with a 6 and at one stage was in such an attacking mood that England adopted the most desperate defensive fields to stop him. Eventually he made 73 and India passed 300 for the first time in the series.

The lead of 74 was to prove crucial. Chandra quickly got his hundredth wicket but this time Prasanna was the more influential and England were all out for 159. India needed 86 to win with oceans of time but they were made to struggle, and it was Pataudi who steadied matters and with Durani's help saw India home.

India led 2-1 after three Tests and, despite the closeness of the struggle, had justified to her followers that she was the World Champion. As if satisfied with this Wadekar seemed to go into his defensive shell and both the fourth and fifth Tests were drawn. The wickets at Kanpur and Bombay were good batting surfaces and both teams scored freely. Lewis scored the first hundred of the series in Kanpur; in Bombay there were four hundreds in the match – all five hundreds came in the last two Tests – Engineer and Viswanath for India, and Greig and Fletcher for England.

Only Chandra kept on taking wickets to prove that he was a class above the other bowlers in the series. He got four in England's only innings at Kanpur and six, including 5 for 135, on the very flat wicket of Bombay. In the series he took 35 wickets at the astounding average of 18.91. Bedi with 25 wickets, but 80 more overs, was both a contrast in style and looks and a very useful foil, while Prasanna with 10 wickets eclipsed Venkat, who figured only amongst the 'also bowled' in the averages: 54 overs for 1 wicket. With Solkar, as *Wisden* said, leaping 'about in the leg-trap like a hungry trout', there was never any respite for the English batsmen. What had seemed as a one-off at The Oval in August 1971, was now confirmed as the pattern of play. In the memory of those who watched the series English batsmen always seemed to be pushing forward to Chandra or Bedi only to see the hungry 'trout' Solkar claim a catch. The contrast between the spinners of the two teams told the story of the series. England's leading wicket-takers were the fast men, Arnold and Old, with Underwood taking 15 wickets at 30.46.

So despite the problems, India had emerged victorious, boasting the best spin attack in the world, probably one of the best the world has ever seen. In three series since the West Indies series the four spinners' figures read:

1971   West Indies
Venkat: 289.3-67-744-22
Prasanna: 159.5-40-407-11
Bedi: 310.4-95-656-15
(48 out of the 68 wickets the Indians took)

1971   England
Venkat: 150.3-38-350-13
Chandra: 146.1-32-379-13
Bedi: 151.3-46-325-11
(37 of the 48 wickets India took in the three-Test series)

1972-73   England in India
Chandra: 291.1-83-662-35
Prasanna: 84-16-202-10
Bedi: 372.5-134-632-25
Venkat: 54-4-158-1
(71 of the 77 wickets)

India had won all three series. Never before had Indian cricket known such success. Wadekar was the most successful captain in Indian history. He had not known a series defeat, he had lost only one out of thirteen Tests, winning four. During the Bombay Test his autobiography *My Cricketing Years* was published – a rare event in Indian publishing since not many Indian cricketers write autobiographies. Merchant, in a foreword, saw him playing for India for many more years and the book as an interim progress report. Instead it was to prove his epitaph. If Wadekar could have foreseen the future he would have retired after Bombay.

There seemed little reason to doubt India's capacity to continue the success story. England did not look any stronger in 1974. Since their Indian tour they had come close to losing two matches to New Zealand, and they lost 2-0 to the West Indies in England, also in 1973, which had cost Illingworth the captaincy. A new captain, Mike Denness, had taken them to the West Indies in 1973-74 and England were lucky to come back with a 1-1 draw.

And while England were struggling the Indian spinners were proving as voracious as ever. In the winter of 1973-74 Chandra took 55 Ranji Trophy wickets at 16.83, Prasanna 39 and, backed by the batting of Viswanath and an exciting young batsman, Brijesh Patel, Karnataka did the near impossible. They won the Ranji Trophy, ending Bombay's fifteen-year reign as champions. Those who saw the semi-final with Bombay talked for days about the ball from Prasanna, a floater that beat a well-set Gavaskar's forward defensive stroke and bowled him. Karnataka went on to get the first-innings lead and end one of the longest winning streaks in cricket history. Bombay has won the Championship since then and remains the side to beat, but it has been unable to re-establish its old dominance.

However, England in 1974 was different from the 1971 visit. The Indians were now coming in the first, colder, wetter half of the summer. The Indian Board, as ever, had sold their players short. Often enough in Indian cricket history administrators who knew little about the game had taken decisions which made life difficult for the players. Now they agreed to an experimental law for the series which restricted the on-side fielders to just five. Ever since the West Indies trip the Indian spinners, particularly Prasanna, had concentrated on a leg-stump attack with a ring of fielders on the leg-side. Now the Indian officials had helped remove their most potent weapon. It was to have a dramatic impact.

The Indian selectors added to Wadekar's problems by omitting Salgoankar, then the fastest bowler in India. He spent the summer at Alf Gover's school in Wandsworth and never made it to the Test side. Even before the tour began Wadekar was consumed by self-doubt. Perhaps he wished, like Indian batsmen who score a century and then rest on their laurels, that he could have done the same after the series against Tony Lewis's side. Wadekar's diffidence was partly due to his fears about the batting: Gavaskar, after his scores in the West Indies, had averaged only just over 24 in two series against England; there was no Sardesai; and Viswanath would make a delightful 40 and then get out. Wadekar felt he needed Pataudi's batting. He was even prepared to give Pataudi the captaincy if that was the prize, but Pataudi was not to be persuaded.

During the first match against Derrick Robins' XI there was a row between Wadekar and Bedi. The players had seen little reward for the three series India had won. Vast crowds had been attracted to the matches, great stadiums built, but the men who made it possible had been given very little extra. Bedi, always a fretful character, remonstrated with Wadekar and suggested he should tackle the Board about more money for the players. Wadekar saw this as a move by Bedi to become captain and refused to approach the Board. It opened up a dangerous rift between the two which was to plague the tour. Already the team appeared to be split into two camps. Wadekar seemed to regard Bedi as belonging to the Pataudi faction. Bedi and Prasanna were known to be close to Pataudi and Wadekar could see shadows lurking in every corner.

A further complicating factor was Venkataraghavan. He was vice-captain but, with Prasanna in such form and Chandra and Bedi's places secure, the question was, where would Venkat fit in the team? Could the tour Selection Committee, which included Venkat, drop him? This was a very real problem before the first Test. Wadekar had injured his finger and did not want to play but the idea of Venkat captaining the side provoked a revolt. Wadekar played but Venkat also played, with the thought that he could take over if Wadekar could not continue. This meant that Prasanna, who had been much the best of the spinners till then, did not play. With Engineer also nursing a minor injury India went into the match with only nine fully fit men.

England had been working out a theory to face the spinners. Edrich was brought back to provide a left-handed option and the English batsmen, who had so far played the spinners from the crease, now used their feet. With Fletcher the best English player of spin in that era scoring a hundred, England made 328. In contrast everything about the Indians seemed makeshift, including a partner for Gavaskar. Bose and Naik had not come off, so Solkar opened, failed, and it was only a miraculous hundred by Gavaskar, on a cold, bleak day, a stylish 40 by Viswanath plus an aggressive 71 from Abid Ali that kept India in the game. Gavaskar was nearly hugged to death by an Indian supporter soon after reaching his hundred, his first in a Test outside the West Indies. He could have gone on, so secure was he, to make many more, but he was run out.

It was now that the cracks in the Indian side began to appear. When England batted with a lead of 82 the Indians bowled with an astonishing lack of purpose. Wadekar did not seem to care, and the bowlers let the game drift away. Edrich scored a hundred and England set India 296 to win in six hours – which demonstrated how confident England were. This was still a gettable target, but the weather was atrocious, the cold penetrating, and Wadekar decided to settle for a draw. This was the turning point of the series. If the Indians had made a bolder move to strike out for victory and won – despite the rain on Monday evening the wicket rolled out true on Tuesday – the story of the summer might have been different. But apart from Gavaskar and Viswanath there was no fight in the Indians. Gavaskar made a quite beautiful 58 before he got a ball from Old that rose off a length and was caught. Viswanath made an equally scintillating 50 but, after he was out, the last five wickets went for 43 runs.

The Indian innings had started with Basil Easterbrook in the press box appointing himself in charge of the clock to see how the Indian run rate would go as they chased England. When Gavaskar was dismissed he gave up and England won by 113 runs with fifteen overs to spare. It was a cold, grey day, as it had been a cold, grey week in Manchester, and the Indians seemed to take one look at the sky and give up. The lesson of 1971 seemed to have been forgotten. This was more like the India of 1952 and 1959.

Yet even now the English had not completely conquered their fear of the Indian spinners. Amiss was more confident but he remembered how Bedi had deceived him at Old Trafford, twice beating him outside the off stump as he groped forward to balls that curled away. Then Bedi moved Gavaskar from mid-off to first slip. Amiss got a touch to the third floater that lifted and he was caught. But everything seemed to favour Denness. He won the toss on a beautiful Lord's wicket in glorious sunshine. On the first morning after bowling just 9.3 overs Chandra injured his finger and did not bowl again. England's great scourge had been removed and the English batsmen celebrated in grand style. Amiss made 188, Edrich 96, Denness 118, Greig 106 as England made 629, their highest score since they had made 654 for 5 against South Africa in Durban on the 1938-39 tour. Wadekar and Bedi disagreed about field placing, Wadekar wanted Bedi to curb his inclination to flight the ball but he kept tossing it up outside the off stump and Amiss kept hitting it through the covers. Wadekar just seemed to capitulate and let Bedi and Prasanna bowl much as they wished. Bedi took 6 for 226, Prasanna 2 for 166 and the spell in which the Indian spinners had held England for three years was at last broken.

It was still a good batting wicket and the speculation was Gavaskar would score a double-hundred. But he had never liked Lord's, finding it a colonial, starchy place, nor made runs there, and while there was enterprise in the Indian batting, there was no grit. The innings was a series of vignettes. Gavaskar and Engineer put on 131 for the first wicket, Viswanath made 52, Solkar 43 and India 302. The only consolation was that while India was getting beaten, at least they were putting up a fight. But even this changed on Monday morning. India, following-on, had played two overs in their second innings on Saturday night and did not lose a wicket. On Monday, in heavy overcast conditions, the whole Indian innings lasted 17 overs. Arnold was perhaps lucky to have Engineer lbw, for the batsman believed he had got an edge, but after that the Indians collapsed like they had never done before, not even against Trueman. Only one batsman made double figures, Solkar with 18 not out in a score of 42 all out. Gavaskar probably had the explanation: Arnold and Old bowled five good balls, got the top five Indian batsmen and after that there was no resistance.

Just as Indian triumphs can be overwhelming, so their disasters can be complete. It is not enough for India to be beaten. She has to be humiliated as well. Now there took place a chapter of incidents that were both perplexing and absurd. The day after the Lord's Test the Indians were invited to two receptions: one at the State Bank of India, the other at the Indian High Commissioner's house. The State Bank employed Wadekar and eight players of the team, so it was important for them. The Bank's reception was in the

City; the High Commissioner's residence was in Kensington Gardens and it was always likely that in the evening rush-hour traffic the team would be late. They arrived forty minutes late, found the coach too big to squeeze in through the gates and the players got out to walk. Wadekar was in the lead but as he got to the door, the High Commissioner, furious at being kept waiting, told him to 'get out'. The team, dispirited after the defeat, felt insulted and returned to the coach. It took a lot of cajoling to get them to go back to the High Commissioner's residence and even when they did they did not feel like eating or drinking very much. All this was gleefully distorted in the Indian press as an insult by the team to the High Commissioner: they had arrived late, then refused his hospitality.

In fact the lateness was due to another incident. Naik, the opening batsman from Bombay, was accused of stealing two pairs of socks from Marks & Spencer. Naik, who had been shopping for his team-mates, stoutly defended himself, claiming that it was absurd to steal when he had bought and paid for twenty pairs. But he was persuaded to plead guilty and it was in trying to deal with this matter that Adhikari, the manager, got delayed and so did the team. Poor Naik became so depressed he thought of taking his life.

So the Indians went into the last Test utterly crushed. It was in some ways worse than Lord's. They made 165 and 216, England made 459 for 2, one of the rare occasions a side has lost only two wickets in the entire match. Naik showed great character in making 77, the highest Indian score of the match.

In 1971 the triumphs had been greeted with delirium. Now the defeats created an uproar. The disasters on the field coupled with the grossly inflated off-the-field stories full of innuendo, gave the impression that the entire edifice of Indian cricket was in danger. The victory bat installed in Indore after the triumph of 1971 was defaced. Wadekar's house in Bombay was stoned and the team returned in groups with the manager, Adhikari, going off to East Africa on a coaching assignment before returning home, Wadekar lingering in Europe and the seniormost player, Prasanna, taking the team back.

Wadekar could not survive as India's captain but the vindictiveness with which the Indian cricket administrators pursued him was quite staggering. The Ranji Trophy season had just started, in September 1974, when he was sacked as captain of West Zone and dropped from the team. Wadekar would have liked to have played one last Test series against the West Indies and then retire and avail himself of a benefit. The sacking from the West Zone team was a clear straw in the wind. Wadekar found himself in the extraordinary position of trying to justify his place in the regional side and decided he could not bear the humiliation. He announced he was going to retire. As a compensation the Indian Board agreed to give him a benefit match – a player being accorded a benefit then was entirely at the discretion of the Board – and ahead of other players waiting in the queue.

The field had now been cleared for Pataudi to return. Even then he wanted a unanimous choice by the selectors before he would come back. His rejection in 1971 on the chairman's casting vote still hurt.

19

Tiger's last hurrah
1974-75

A problem with Indians is that they tend to have a poor historical sense. This is one explanation offered by V. S. Naipaul for the country's extraordinary history: one ruined civilisation followed by another. Yet if this is indeed true then it can, sometimes, be useful. Indians are better than other peoples at anaesthetising pain. If they are quick to anger, they are quick to forget, ready to take on the next project, face the next day.

This quality proved immensely valuable in the winter of 1974-75 as the West Indies arrived in India. After the debacle in England the crowds might have turned against cricket: instead they turned up in even greater numbers. The Indians had a new Test centre in Bangalore, the Southern city which was beginning to outrival Madras and Hyderabad. The crowds came despite the fact that India lost the first two Tests and that Pataudi's leadership had made no difference – indeed the confusion was at times even worse than on the England tour.

The Board had appointed an Inquiry Committee but this exonerated all the players. The only one to suffer was Bedi who, having refused to appear before the Committee and explain incidents on the tour and on a television programme in England, was dropped from the first Test. But the Indian selectors compounded their problems further in the first Test with some extraordinary cloak and dagger tactics. Gavaskar was appointed vice-captain but told not to tell anyone! When, in the West Indies' second innings, Pataudi suddenly went off the field after dislocating his finger trying to take a catch, no-one knew who was in charge until the substitute Goel came on to the field to inform the others that Gavaskar was taking over. Even with such a shambles the Indian spinners showed they could put the West Indians under pressure, but vital slip catches were missed. Gordon Greenidge, in his first Test, was missed before he had scored and made 93. Then, having conquered his Test nerves, he went on to score a hundred in the second innings. To add to the Indians' problems, Engineer was injured. India, down to nine men in the second innings, lost heavily.

The second Test brought even more confusion. Pataudi was still injured, so Gavaskar was made captain. But he was injured playing for Bombay and the Indians arrived in Delhi not knowing who would captain them. At a reception before the match the Indian manager, Ramchand, who had himself suffered from the caprice of officials, added to the confusion by saying, 'I know who the Indian captain is going to be but I'm not telling.' The President of the Delhi & District Cricket Association said it was to be Engineer. But when Gopinath, the chairman of the selectors, arrived it turned out he had a different person in mind. Half an hour before the match nobody knew who would lead India. Anybody who had played ten or more Tests for India thought he had a chance and some of them wore their blazers to the ground in anticipation. Eventually Chandrasekhar was dropped and Venkataraghavan brought in and made captain. It looked like 1958 all over again. India lost the Test with a day and a half to spare through some wretched batting, particularly on a rain-affected wicket in the second innings, but the match was notable for Vivian Richards. Batting in only his second Test, he made 192 – an innings which made it clear he was going on to be the next great batting talent. India had now lost five Tests in succession. Between January 1971 and June 1974 India had lost just one Test, now in seven months they had lost five.

Calcutta promised no better. Pataudi returned and Venkat, captain in Delhi, was dropped and did not play again in the series. Chandra was brought back and, with Gavaskar still injured, there was a new batsman, Anshuman Gaekwad, and a first Test for Kharsan Ghavri replacing Abid Ali. It did not seem that these changes would have much effect because Naik was out to the first ball of the match and the Indians found in Andy Roberts yet another devastating West Indian fast bowler. He had proved effective in the earlier Tests; now he was irresistible. He took 5 for 50. Pataudi himself was hit in the face by Roberts and had to retire and, although he came back to take 19 in an over off Holder, it was clear he was not the batsman he had been two years ago. India made only 233.

But suddenly the tide turned, helped by West Indian over-confidence but also because Pataudi had worked out a strategy. This was to deny them any chance of easy ones or twos. The Indians would hustle them on the field with smart fielding and deny them short runs. On a slow pitch where the ball did not come on to the bat, they would be forced to hit the bowlers for fours. The tactics worked and the West Indians were bowled out for 240 (Fredericks 100), just 7 runs ahead.

Even then one question remained to be answered: who could keep Roberts at bay? The answer was provided by Viswanath. Ever since he had made his debut against Australia with a century he had looked a class above every other batsman, barring Gavaskar. He had broken the hoodoo of the Indian who scored a century in his first Test, never to score another, but he did not make runs in the quantity his style and ability suggested he could. Now, for the first time, he really made his class tell: an Indian batsman not only defended his wicket, but was able to take charge of the bowling. Viswanath, coming in at 46 for 2, batted with such command that, when he was the eighth batsman out, he had made 139 and India were 301. Lloyd probably made a mistake in resting Roberts on the fourth morning when he had begun by troubling Viswanath. After only three overs, during which he had conceded nine runs and twice found Viswanath's edge, he was taken off. This so added to Viswanath's confidence that India's last four wickets added 110 runs. The West Indians were left with 309 to win.

The pitch was now thoroughly irregular in bounce, and also taking some spin, but the West Indies seemed to be coping easily and they finished the fourth day halfway to their objective with three wickets down. The next morning Lloyd looked like he wanted to finish the match before lunch and launched a devastating attack on Chandrasekhar. Another captain might have taken him off, but Pataudi's nerve held. He kept him on and, as Chandra could so often do, he produced a gem of a ball to bowl Lloyd off his pads. Kallicharran then lashed out at Chandra and was well caught at slip. From 146 for 3 the West Indies had gone to 178 for 5. Chandra had, in 35 minutes, taken two crucial wickets that were to decide the match. Pataudi expertly shuffled his bowlers, now resting Chandra, now bringing Prasanna on, and Bedi. Suddenly the Indian team, which had looked so beaten and depressed for so long, looked more like the side that had won everything between 1971 and 1973. They took every trick and the spinners were back on top. Bedi had 4 for 52, Chandra 3 for 66 and although Prasanna had gone wicketless he had looked like taking a wicket at any time. India won by 85 runs.

As Bedi bowled Roberts for six, the memory of England in 1974, the summer of 42 as it had become known, was expunged. Bonfires were lit, crackers were let off; in Bombay and elsewhere where fans listening to the radio had been firing crackers at the fall of every West Indian wicket, the victory brought them on to the streets and strangers hugged each other and distributed padeas, little round, very sugary Indian sweets. India was back!

This was amply confirmed in Madras where, on the first day, Viswanath played one of the half-dozen great Test innings of recent Test cricket. While Roberts pulverised the rest of the Indian batting, taking 7 for 64, and no other Indian batsman made 20, Viswanath made 97 not out. He would undoubtedly have got his hundred but had to refuse many singles while adding 21 runs with Chandrasekhar, whose status as the world's worst no. 11 had never been in doubt. A batsman in command always shields his partners and Viswanath's mastery is shown by the fact that the last four Indian wickets added 114 runs, with Viswanath making 80 of them. P. N. Sunderesan, the veteran Indian cricket writer, watching the match, reported: 'On this day Viswanath really took his place amongst the greats of the game.'

But even then 190 was no score. It was only made to look quite a good one by the bowling of Prasanna. He had long had an intuitive understanding with Pataudi, responding to his captaincy more than he did with anyone else: indeed, in his autobiography, *One More Over* (1977) he declared he was 'ready to die' for Pataudi. His great deeds had all come under Pataudi's leadership and now he bowled quite beautifully. In 31 balls he removed Lloyd, Richards, Murray, Julien and Boyce for 5 runs. West Indies were bowled out for 192, two runs ahead.

India batted better in the second innings and this time it was not all Viswanath, but he was still batting in a crisis. At one stage India were 85 for 5 but Gaekwad gave him support. He made 80 before, going for a very risky second run, he was run out. Viswanath made 46 and India recovered to 256. The West Indies needed 255 to win. The only real West Indian resistance came from Kallicharran who made 51 before being run out. But the other batsmen did not know how to play the spinners. They either tried defending clumsily or attacking rashly; neither paid off and 45 minutes after lunch on the final day Bedi had Roberts lbw and India won by 100 runs. For the first time India had drawn level in a series after being 2-0 down.

Only Australia had come back from such a position actually to win a rubber – Bradman's Australia against G. O. Allen's team in 1936-37. Could the Indians manage it? For Bombay they had their full-strength side, with Gavaskar back, but Pataudi lost the toss and on a good batting wicket the West Indians made 604 (Lloyd 242 not out). India replied spiritedly with 406, Gavaskar making 86, Solkar 102, and Viswanath, who had had such a splendid series, 95. But it was never going to be enough. India were finally left 403 to get and lost by 201 runs. Had the West Indians, after two defeats, been forced to bat second again, they might not have enjoyed taking the fourth innings. They had the luck of the toss and made the most of it.

Before the match their manager had taken photographs of the wicket, fearing it would break up. It was a brand new wicket in a brand new stadium. The simmering quarrel between the CCI and the Bombay Cricket Association had exploded into war and the BCA – led by Wankhede, a prominent Maharashtra minister – had gone off to construct its own stadium half a mile away from the Brabourne. When the West Indians arrived in India in October the proposed stadium was rubble. When they returned in January for the fifth Test it was complete. The wicket played beautifully. Lloyd's was a great innings, which India helped by dropping him on 8, 70 and 154; but the sheer power of his stroke play restored the West Indian batting after their collapses in Calcutta and Madras.

But while dejected by this defeat, the Indians were not depressed. Indeed, if India had won, Indians would have been surprised. Pataudi was always associated with glorious losses rather than glorious wins. Nor did this diminish the interest in the series which so excited Indian cricket enthusiasts that a book was published despite the series being lost. This is rare in India where publishers reckon that a lost series means lost profits. But this time they knew the series had been an intensely romantic one. Pataudi back, hauling a team 2-0 down to 2-2, then losing the final Test. This was in the great tradition of the Tiger. As a batsman he was a shadow of his former self, averaging only 13. His good eye was losing a bit of its power and that extra yard of pace that Roberts possessed was proving very difficult. In this last Test he batted at no. 9 in the first innings and no. 7 in the second, making 9 on both occasions, and falling to Gibbs each time. But his leadership had restored India's pride and self-respect.

Contemporary opinion could not bestow enough praise on Pataudi. P. N. Sunderesan wrote after the Madras Test:

That Pataudi achieved his triumph despite himself being in utterly poor shape had only added lustre to it and emphasises his calibre as a cricketer. He was not seen on the field musing, head bowed down over his batting failures or the umpiring decisions that did not help him recover his form but was quite alive to the task of captaincy. If I may sum up, Pataudi seemed a more determined and skilful captain in this match – in this series – perhaps because he wanted to make up for what he could not give through his own batting. He showed that he was worth his place in the team for his captaincy alone, a fact which many may have failed to appreciate while running him down as not worth his place in the team on poor batting form. With Wadekar out of the reckoning there was no-one in India who could have done what Pataudi accomplished in the series. It is an outstanding performance which will be judged in its true perspective long after the din and dust of the series has settled down . . . The measure of his success as captain lies in the incontrovertible fact that the series restored India's prestige in international cricket to a remarkable, if not to the full extent.

Pataudi's supporters saw it as yet another rebuilding job that he did so well. He had rescued India from the doldrums of the 1950s. He had now saved India from the excesses of the 1970s. Pataudi, wrote Prasanna, had given Wadekar a team on which to build his victories. Now the next captain would also be inheriting a fighting team. But would he? Pataudi, obviously, did a superb job in the winter of 1974-75. Another shattering defeat against the West Indies might have set Indian cricket back and depressed morale. But in the long view of history was his role quite as glorious as his friends made out? To an extent the deeper problems of Indian cricket had remained and the next three years would show that Pataudi had masked rather than cured them. But then it would have been too much to expect Pataudi to cure them in one series.

20

Roller-coaster years
1975-77

On 7 April 1976 a Test match began in Port of Spain, Trinidad
– the third Test of the 1975-76 series between India and the West
Indies. The match was not meant to be played there. Originally it
was scheduled for Georgetown's Bourda but weeks of incessant rain
meant that the whole of the Guyana leg of the tour was washed out and
this match was switched to Trinidad. The switch was to prove decisive
for India and the match itself was to have dramatic consequences for
West Indian and world cricket.

It had been some time since India lost to the West Indies in
Bombay in January 1975 but, as with everything in India, it had not
been a straight line of progress. The 'fighting unit' which Prasanna
felt Pataudi had left for his successor had not done much fighting
nor distinguished itself. In 1975 India spent a miserable time in the
inaugural World Cup in England with the Indians pleading that they
were not used to this kind of cricket. This was not quite true, since
the Bombay Police and Talim Shield tournaments were limited-over
matches though of a different kind. Outside Bombay, however, there
were little or no limited-over competitions and this showed in the Indian
performance. India not only failed to qualify for the semi-finals but,
at Lord's against England, performed so lamentably that, faced with
England's 334, Gavaskar batted through the 60 overs of the Indian
innings making 36 not out. Later he could not explain why he had
batted this way and he was censured by the Indian manager and former
captain, Ramchand.

This, almost certainly, told against Gavaskar becoming captain.
Pataudi's departure seemed to leave four possible candidates:
Gavaskar, Venkataraghavan, Bedi and Prasanna. Venkat had captained in the World Cup and not distinguished himself. So with
Gavaskar also ruled out this left Bedi – Prasanna was always the
rank outsider in the captaincy stakes – and in the winter of 1975 he
was apppointed captain for the series against Sri Lanka, part of that
country's effort to obtain Test recognition. He had done a wonderful
job with Delhi and North Zone cricket, leading them to the final of
the Duleep Trophy. If his bowling was full of guile, endlessly testing the

batsman, then his captaincy was always likely to explode into brilliance or just explode.

In this 'series' there was evidence of this in allegations of Bedi's 'high-handedness' after the Nagpur 'Test' and he faced another inquiry. It was widely expected he would lose the captaincy but he survived and was made captain of the team to tour New Zealand and West Indies in the early part of 1976. Gavaskar was his deputy on a tour which was a fresh departure for the Indians. Two series of three and four Tests respectively against two countries which were about as far apart as any two Test-playing countries.

Almost ten years before, Pataudi's Indians had beaten New Zealand 3-1, recording India's first win abroad. That victory was based on spin and this form of attack still posed terrible problems for the New Zealanders as Prasanna demonstrated in the first Test. Gavaskar made a century, Surinder Amarnath in his first Test emulated his father and made a century, and India scored 414, their highest-ever score in New Zealand. After this Prasanna was quite irresistible.

On the plane taking him to New Zealand Prasanna had suddenly felt old. A new generation of Indian cricketers was emerging and he felt like the last forgotten remnant of a bygone age. As he looked round the plane and saw the fresh-faced youngsters, some of whom had been no more than schoolboys when he made his Test debut – he could recall Gavaskar coming up to him with his uncle to ask for his autograph – he felt a certain waste of promise and hope, a feeling common to so many Indian sportsmen. Where, he wondered, had all those years gone? What had happened to the high, promising, future held out to him by Frank Worrell in Kingston in 1962? He made his debut that year and within a few weeks of his first Test toured the Caribbean. He had so impressed Sir Frank Worrell during the Kingston Test, the only one he played in that series, that Worrell had playfully tousled Prasanna's hair and predicted a great future for him. But in the fourteen years since then he had played in only thirty-five Tests.

Partly this was his own doing. Less than three weeks after his return from the Caribbean his father died and Prasanna decided that to qualify as an engineer must take precedence over cricket. He did not play a Test for almost five years, returning against the West Indies at Madras in 1967. On at least one occasion he was called for trials but could not attend because of his engineering examinations. But, as Prasanna tells the story, there is also a strong sense of a man whom the Indian selectors forgot.

His success since his comeback, when he dominated the Indian attack with Bedi from 1967 to 1971, should have eased this pain, made him feel fulfilled. But the Prasanna story was never a simple one, and in this tale of hurt and resentment there were to be other twists and turns. Almost from the moment he came back in 1967 Prasanna established himself as one of the world's leading off-spinners. Between 1967-68, when he toured Australia, and 1969-70, when Australia visited India, he had taken 95 wickets in sixteen Tests, eight times taking five wickets in an innings, once taking ten in a match. The Australians had no doubt he was the world's best off-spinner and Prasanna was in his pomp.

But Prasanna, a sensitive man who reacted quickly to any change of circumstances, found the dismissal of Pataudi in 1971 a severe blow from which he never fully recovered. In the way that Indian cricket, and indeed Indian life, works Prasanna saw himself, and was seen by others, as Pataudi's man. Under Pataudi's leadership Pras, as he came to be known, was the first bowler he turned to. With Pataudi gone, Prasanna felt the fates conspiring against him. On the West Indies trip of 1970-71 he was injured, and after that he was constantly the odd spinner out. Chandra and Bedi were the fixed stars and Prasanna had to fight for the third spinning place with Venkat. Prasanna's bowling remained vital, as in the home series against England in 1972-73 and the West Indies two years later, but it was always a case of Pras making a comeback. The man who in age and experience was the most senior of the four great spinners felt he was always having to prove himself. This feeling was reinforced when two of his possible spin rivals, Venkat and Bedi, were made captains. That meant automatic selection for them and bred the sense of waste and resentment that came over Prasanna as he sat on the plane taking him to New Zealand.

Prasanna was being unduly sensitive. For while there may have been the odd miscarriage of justice the change in fortunes since 1971 was more due to the change in the balance of the Indian spin attack. In his years of glory between 1967 and 1971 he and Bedi were the attacking spinners, Venkat the steady foil. The 1971 English tour rediscovered Chandrasekhar as the most destructive spin bowler of his generation. This changed the equation. Now Chandra and Bedi attacked, and Venkat as the steady foil was often preferred to Prasanna, particularly on overseas tours.

However, in the first Test against New Zealand, with Bedi unable to play because of a pulled calf-muscle, Prasanna re-created, if only momentarily, the glories of the late 1960s. Always happier to play under Gavaskar – a batsman as captain held no threat to him – he revelled in the conditions. The pitch could not have been more helpful and, having sweated under covers for nine days, it was turning from the first morning. By the fourth it was providing both turn and bounce. In the first innings Prasanna supported Chandra, and the two with Venkat completed the spin triangle. Chandra took 6 for 94, Prasanna 3 for 64, Venkat 1 for 59. In the second innings it was all Prasanna as he took 8 for 76 and India won by eight wickets with more than a day to spare.

278

It was Prasanna's best ever Test figures, the best by any bowler in an Auckland Test, and his eleven in the match meant he had become the most successful Indian spinner ever, passing Vinoo Mankad's then record of 162 wickets.

Trevor Bailey had always wondered how a man who looked so innocuous could be so deadly with a ball. Bailey felt that Prasanna looked like a factory worker who, having just taken to the cricket field after completing a shift, had been casually tossed the ball by his captain, almost as an afterthought. Perhaps this deceptive appearance, always slightly over-weight, always just that bit dishevelled, fooled batsmen. They could not believe that somebody who looked so ordinary could be so lethal.

Prasanna's looks formed a vivid contrast with his rival Venkat who, over six feet tall and with a shock of dark hair falling over his eyes – which he always seemed to be brushing away – had the appearance of a professor. He reinforced this impression with a certain sense of brahminical pedantry. The physical differences contributed to the technical ones. Prasanna being shorter had to use sharper spin and subtle variations in flight. Venkat, bringing the ball down from somewhere around eight feet was a 'hitter' who relied on variations of pace. Prasanna was always likely to prove the more expensive bowler and he expected to be hit every now and again, but when he was on song he could provide a joy that Venkat could not match. Both bowlers worked hard at exploiting batsmen's weaknesses, constantly trying to think them out, but while Venkat brought to his bowling a certain dogged studiousness, Prasanna suggested real flair.

As it happened, in the next Test Bedi returned, Venkat was dropped and the Kiwis decided to be less hospitable about their wickets. The next two Tests found wickets prepared for pace and India struggled against New Zealand's fast bowlers. This added to the usual problems faced by visiting teams to New Zealand. The Indians, like almost every visiting team to that country, were unhappy about the New Zealand umpiring and the bias of the New Zealand press. In the third Test at Wellington they found a wicket where the grass had been left unmown. India, with Gavaskar injured, were bowled out for 81 in the second innings with Richard Hadlee taking altogether 11 for 58 and New Zealand won by an innings.

So India arrived in the West Indies not exactly full of hope. The West Indies, too, were shattered. They had won the World Cup but then had been devastated by the pace of Lillee and Thomson in Australia, losing 5-1. India lost the first Test in Barbados, a defeat that was largely their own fault. They coped well with the pace of Roberts and Holding but then seemed to relax against the leg-spin of Holford and paid the price. The Indian spinners showed they could still torment the West Indian batsmen, but the fielding which had been so good in New Zealand now failed. Kirmani had taken over from Engineer – who turned down the tour because of business commitments in England – and impressed with his wicket-keeping in New Zealand; but now he had a bad match, dropping catches and missing stumpings.

India should have won the second Test, however. This match seemed to bear a resemblance to the second Test at Port of Spain in 1971 which India had won. Then Fredericks had been bowled by the first ball of the match, now he was bowled second ball. Despite a Richards century India dismissed West Indies for 241, Bedi taking 5 for 82.

India started badly but Gavaskar was back on his favourite ground. He was on his way to becoming a legend at Port of Spain, and this seemed to help him rediscover his concentration. He had been hit on the cheekbone while fielding in New Zealand during the third Test and, perhaps affected by this injury, he was more inclined to slog and in the match against Trinidad, just before the Test, he scored a quick 50. But this had disappointed his many fans in Trinidad, one of whom came up to him and in that direct West Indian manner said, 'We wanna see you bat all day, maan, not just for an hour.' In the Test he proceeded to do exactly that. All he needed was a partner who would stay with him. He found one in Brijesh Patel. Coming together when India were 124 for 4, they put on 204, a record for India's fifth wicket. To the delight of the Indians of Trinidad Gavaskar made yet another century, his third in successive innings there, and Patel made 115. India declared at 402 for 5.

The wicket was now turning, the ball keeping low and Chandra looked to be in one of those moods of his. In a brilliant spell of thirteen overs he removed Kallicharran and should have had Lloyd caught but, as Solkar was about to take the catch, Patel collided with him. India dropped other catches, a couple of decisions went against them, including an lbw appeal when Roberts played back to Chandra, and in the end the West Indies just managed to get a draw. But the Trinidad factor had started working, India looked the superior side and, when the match at Georgetown was rained off, the Indians were quite happy to return to their favourite West Indian ground.

But for much of the third Test luck seemed to desert the Indians. Chandra had the West Indians struggling at 52 for 3, but Richards, missed by Kirmani on 72, went on to make a quite superb 177 and they ended on 359. After three successive hundreds Gavaskar was due a failure on this ground and he was lbw to Holding for 26. India slowly subsided to 228. The West Indies led by 131 and by lunch on the fourth day they had increased it to 402. Lloyd declared, confident that it was only a question of when he would bowl India out.

The Oval, 1971. Not the occasion when India won their first Test in England, but the moment when that seemed likely. England have just been dismissed for 101 in their second innings, and Chandrasekhar is being applauded on all sides, having taken 6 for 38 *(The Cricketer)*.

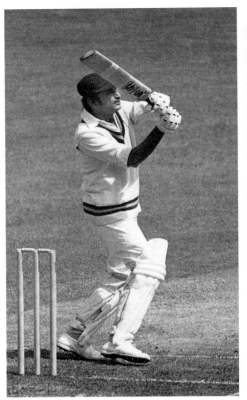

Above left: Ajit Wadekar became a national hero when, in 1971, he led India to unexpected victories in West Indies and England. In 1974, when he lost to England, he discovered how quickly Indian heroes can become villains.

Above right: Eknath Solkar, a fine batsman who is remembered for his close-to-the-wicket catching which made the Indian spinners so much more formidable.

Farokh Engineer, one of the ebullient cricketers who formed part of the Pataudi revival, and one of the few Indians to make an impact on English county cricket
(Patrick Eagar).

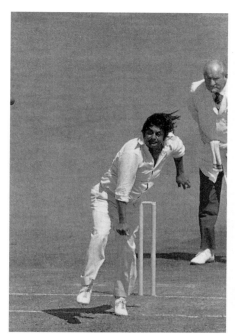

The great quartet of Indian spinners. *Above left:* Prasanna. *Above right:* Chandrasekhar. *Below left:* Venkataraghavan. *Below right:* Bedi. They all played together in only one Test in 1967, but they dominated Indian cricket from the mid-1960s through to the end of the 1970s, producing some famous victories and creating an aura of eternal Indian spin *(Patrick Eagar)*.

Sunil Gavaskar – one of India's great batsman, who was the first to score 10,000 runs in Test cricket and has scored more hundreds in Test matches than any other player. Note the sun hat adapted to accommodate a helmet which he reluctantly agreed to wear towards the end of his career. *Below:* he is batting in the third Test against England in Madras in 1977 *(Patrick Eagar).*

Above left: Mohinder Amarnath playing his favourite hook shot. Later, after several blows to the head, he took to wearing a helmet but remained one of the finest players of fast bowling.

Above right: Dilip Vengsarkar made his debut in 1975–76. He became known as 'the colonel', and recognised as, after Gavaskar, the outstanding Indian batsman of the 1980s. Also the only non-English player to score three separate hundreds in Test matches at Lord's.

Right: Kapil Dev, in his second Test match, against Pakistan at Lahore in 1977–78, the first genuinely quick Indian bowler since Amar Singh and Nissar. Kapil was the mainstay of Indian attack between 1978 and 1994, and for a time was the highest wicket taker in Test history *(Patrick Eagar).*

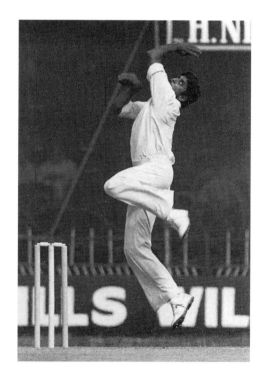

Gundappa Viswanath, one of the best-loved of modern Indian cricketers, here playing his favourite cover-drive during the second Test against Pakistan at Lahore in 1978. Reputed to be more skilful than his brother-in-law Gavaskar, he seldom showed the Bombay man's determination.

Indians from Amritsar crossing the border to Lahore when, in 1978, cricket between India and Pakistan resumed after eighteen years *(Patrick Eagar)*.

Chetan Chauhan, also photographed batting against Pakistan in Lahore, not only helped Gavaskar to put on 213 for their stand against England at The Oval in 1979, but was his most reliable opening partner.

Gavaskar batting during that stand when he made his memorable score of 221 which nearly won India the match when they were set to make 438 runs to win *(Patrick Eagar)*.

A groundsman sweeping the wicket at Eden Gardens, Calcutta, 1977. Old methods neatly combined with modern advertising hoardings which festoon the ground *(All-Sport/Adrian Murrell)*.

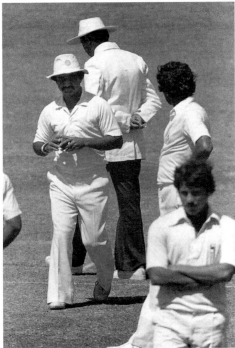

For the Jubilee Test in February 1980, India were captained, for the only time, by Viswanath. Here he is seen recalling Bob Taylor after the batsman protested at being given out caught at the wicket. It was a gesture typical of 'Vishy', but it probably cost India the match *(Patrick Eagar)*.

It was difficult to find even amongst the most partisan East Indians much argument with Lloyd's analysis. He had the pace of Holding who had taken 6 for 65 in the first innings and altogether 12 wickets in four innings against the Indians in the series so far. In addition there was the spin of Padmore, Imtiaz Ali and Jumadeen. On a worn, turning pitch if Holding did not get the Indians, the spinners certainly would. History and precedent were on Lloyd's side.

Few teams in the world chase 400 runs and make them. It had been done only once before and that by the Australians. But that was in 1948 when Bradman was still playing for them. However the Indians were not worried about the target. Gavaskar felt they could save the match and bat out time. He did not think India could win, indeed he did not even entertain the idea, but he felt confident that if the first objective, to bat safely till the end of the day, was achieved, then India could hold out.

After a number of experimentations on the twin tour, Gavaskar had his third opening partner. This time it was Gaekwad, another Indian middle-order batsman who, because he played with a straight bat, had been made into an opener. It had not worked in the first innings but now Gavaskar and Gaekwad put on 69 before Gaekwad was out. This brought in Mohinder Amarnath.

The second son of Lala Amarnath, Mohinder was the classic example of the Indian ability to discover a player and then waste him. He had made his Test debut against Australia in December 1969 more as an opening bowler than a batsman, batting at no. 8. His next Test for India was earlier on this twin tour, in Auckland in January 1976, where his brother Surinder took the limelight. Even by the standards of Indian cricket this was a remarkably long gap. Amarnath was still opening the bowling but by the time the second Trinidad Test came along his batting was being recognised. In the Auckland Test, going in at no. 7 he made 64; now he was no. 3.

Perhaps this long gap had made him determined. His brother Surinder conveyed more of the Amarnath dash but he had done little after his Auckland century and had now been dropped. Mohinder, nicknamed Jimmy by his father who had a penchant for such English names, was more circumspect in his habits and his cricket. Coached by his father he loved to hook the short ball and was not afraid to do so, the only question mark was whether he would lose concentration after scoring 40 or so, as he had done in the past. But in this innings he seemed to show a maturity that much impressed Gavaskar and at the end of the day they were still together with India 134 for 1, Gavaskar 86 not out.

Trinidad was now almost like Gavaskar's home ground and the next day the ground was packed to see him score his hundred.

A good many of the spectators were East Indians, some of whom had gone to the temples in the morning offering prayers for victory and brought back prasads, sweets blessed by the priests. Right from the morning the calypso, which the Trinidadians had composed about Gavaskar being just like a wall whom nobody could get out, was endlessly played. Gavaskar, himself, was not playing as well as he had done the previous day but he got to his hundred, his fourth in five innings in Trinidad, before being caught at the wicket.

India were 177 for 2 with much of the day still to come. Even at this stage there was no thought of victory. Gavaskar was succeeded by Viswanath and if precedent was anything to go by, then Viswanath was due for a failure. The two little men of Indian cricket, Gavaskar and Viswanath, had never made runs in tandem and if one succeeded, the other often failed. But on this occasion Gavaskar seemed to have passed the baton on to Viswanath. For a time runs came slowly but at lunch India were still in the hunt: another 206 in four hours. It was over lunch that the East Indians, gathered in excited groups over their roti, a delicious East Indian bread with fillings, first began to speculate about victory. There were wickets in hand and if India did not lose too many they could still strike out for victory.

This speculation took more concrete shape between lunch and tea as Viswanath and Amarnath slowly piled up the runs. The turning point came when Lloyd took the new ball. Viswanath now set about Julien, who had opened with Holding, and 37 runs came in eight overs. When the spinners came back Viswanath, who probably played spin better than any batsman of his generation, was quickly out of his crease using his feet beautifully to drive them on either side of the wicket. In such a mood Viswanath had no peer and, with Mohinder curbing his strokes and taking singles to give Viswanath the strike, the little man was in his element. His century came out of 147 runs and he and Amarnath had put on 159 and the target of 402 runs was now only 67 runs away when Viswanath was run out, backing up too far. Gavaskar had established the foundations of the innings, Viswanath had built the superstructure, now only the final coat of paint was required.

Five minutes later the mandatory final twenty overs began, with India needing just 65 runs with seven wickets in hand. With the spinners on it was a situation made for Patel and he now played his most confident Test innings. The transformation in the scene was unimaginable. Just twenty-four hours earlier it was the West Indies who looked invincible. Now the Indians oozed confidence and it was as if they were playing at home and the West Indians were the away team. Their bowlers operated to spread-out fields and the East Indians cheered every Indian run. One section of the crowd whose ancestors had come from Uttar Pradesh even began to sing Hindu devotional songs.

The Indians were now sure of victory and, though Amarnath was run out on 85 in the ninth over, Patel cut the last ball of the thirteenth over to the third-man boundary to take India past 402 and to victory by six wickets. Bradman's Australia had made 404 for 3 at Leeds in 1948. India had made 406 for 4. Port of Spain felt like Bombay or Calcutta. The ground seemed to be full of Indians, Indians who had never seen their 'motherland' but who felt intensely proud and fulfilled.

In many ways that was an even more satisfying victory than the one in 1971, largely because it was so unexpected. A sporting upset is always thrilling, and it is wonderfully uplifting if the team you support performs the feat. What was even more remarkable was the dominance of the Indian batting. In the whole day the West Indians had taken only three wickets and two of them were run-outs. Apart from Gavaskar's wicket in the morning, no West Indian bowler had managed to take a wicket. The victory did have one unfortunate political side-effect. In the previous year Mrs Indira Gandhi, the Prime Minister of India, had declared a state of emergency, the closest the Indians had ever come to living under a dictatorship. Some commentators in the State-controlled All-India Radio in a foolish display of excessive zeal ascribed the victory to her 'magnificent emergency' rule.

The interesting cricket question was, though, could the Indians build on it? For a day into the final Test in Jamaica it seemed as if they might. India won the toss and at the end of that day had made 178 for 1. But on the second the West Indians started what the Indians thought was an unfair, 'barbaric', war against their batsmen. Three of the batsmen, Gaekwad, Viswanath and Patel, were sent to hospital, Holding going round the wicket to bowl bouncers and the odd beamer as well. Viswanath had his middle finger broken by a bouncer, Gaekwad was hit on the temple and was in hospital for three days and then Patel was hit on the lips by a short ball from Holder, paying the penalty for taking his eyes off the ball. Holding, who could look like an angel when running in to bowl, now seemed Dracula incarnate.

The Indians complained to the umpires but Gosein claimed that a ridge had suddenly developed, though how such a ridge can develop was never explained. India declared at 305 for 6 to save injury to Bedi and Chandra. *Wisden* accepted that the bounce on this 'virgin' pitch was uneven, but wrote, 'This is not to say there was no short-pitched bowling. There was a surfeit of it – overdone in fact to the extent where the umpires should have intervened. A lot of the short-pitched bowling was delivered by Holding from round the wicket to minimise the batsman's scope of drawing away from his stumps.'

The West Indies had their problems against the Indian spinners but they made 391 and when India batted again they only had six fit men left. When the score reached 97 for 5 the match was over.

At first it seemed the Indians had declared but Bedi made it clear India could not go on because there was nobody else fit enough to bat. West Indies won by ten wickets.

However, world cricket has had a dreadful price to pay for that victory. The lesson the West Indies drew from their defeat in Trinidad and victory in Jamaica was that pace works and spin does not. They had played three spinners in Trinidad and the opposition had made 406 for 4 in the final innings. They had banked on pace, intimidatory, blistering pace in Jamaica, Holding reinforced by Daniel, and they had won. It was after this (and bearing in mind West Indies' own recent defeat in Australia) that Lloyd devised his strategy of pace, pace, pace and pace again. Spinners were ruthlessly discarded. Since that time the West Indies have rarely played a spinner, even on turning Trinidad wickets; in any case never more than one specialist spinner, and nearly always four pace bowlers.

The Indians returned home, said *Wisden*, looking like 'Napoleon's troops on the retreat from Moscow. They were battle-weary and a lot of them were enveloped in plasters and bandages.' But these were seen as campaign ribbons of the tour, evidence of the war they had had to fight. The physical wounds healed but the hurt could not be wiped away as the Indians felt cheated that just when they looked like exercising dominance over the West Indians they had been bounced out of it. However, they drew comfort from the fact that some of their young players had stood up to pace, even the blistering variety in Jamaica. In the second innings of the Test only two Indians made double figures. Amarnath made 59 and Vengsarkar, who had just turned twenty, made 22. In the first innings he had made 39 and in both he impressed by the way he used his six-foot-plus height to deal with the steep bounce.

What was more significant was that he had done it batting in the middle order, his natural position. Vengsarkar had started the tour in New Zealand as part of yet another experiment to make a middle-order batsman into an opener. He hailed from the same Bombay school that had produced Manjrekar, Gupte and Gavaskar. From his bedroom in central Bombay he looked over the patch of the maidan that was the home of Dadar Union, Gavaskar's club; he went to King George's School where Manjrekar had studied, and by the age of eleven he was playing in the highly competitive Harris Shield. With such influence it was hardly surprising that once he had hit his first century in schools cricket, at the age of thirteen, he began to amass big scores, if not like Gavaskar in his schooldays, even so, not far behind.

But he did so batting in the middle order, at nos. 3, 4 or 5. On this tour, however, he was suddenly seen as opener. In his Test debut in Auckland he opened with Gavaskar and continued in that role for the New Zealand series; then, after being dropped for the first Test against the West Indies, he was brought back as an opener in the second, then dropped for the win at Trinidad only to be brought back for Jamaica, but this time in his proper position. It was in his fifth Test that he had his first chance to bat in his normal place and he immediately responded. A middle-order batsman had been rescued and this was to have an important bearing on the future of Indian cricket. If his Test average of 20.33 and tour average of 27 were not remarkable he had hinted at that elusive quality: class. His method of avoiding the bouncer was effective and when a delivery was pitched up he was always quick to drive. India no longer seemed to be just Gavaskar and Viswanath. Another generation of Indian batsmen was emerging and Vengsarkar was to be leader amongst them.

But if all this gave comfort the tour rekindled doubts about Bedi's captaincy. Bedi is a Sikh and the Sikhs are great joke figures in India. Their habit of gathering the hair on top of the head is said to soften the head and there is something called 'Sikh bara baz gaya', Sikh twelve o'clock. The Indian saying is that, at twelve o'clock midday when the sun is high, a Sikh, or Sardarji as they are called, gets very hot and excited by the sun beating on all this hair and is capable of any irrational behaviour. Of course all this is rubbish and superstition, the Sikh is no more irrational, probably a good deal more rational, than most Indians – and certainly more hard-working and straightforward than most Hindus – but they form the basis of Sikh jokes similar to Irish jokes in England or Polak jokes in America.

Despite such jokes Bedi had shown himself to be an astute, imaginative captain who was always willing to take a positive decision. The West Indian tour did raise some question marks about his style of captaincy, however, and as India failed to build on the extraordinary triumph at Trinidad but fell into a morass instead, Bedi appeared increasingly at odds with his cricket. The questions remained muted as long as he was winning; once he started losing the familiar search for scapegoats began.

In the first half of the winter of 1976-77 that followed India beat New Zealand 2-0 in a three-Test series, both Test victories coming by decisive margins: 162 runs and 216 runs. New Zealand had no answer to Bedi who took 22 wickets for 13 runs each while Chandra took 17 at 23 apiece. But even here there was a warning and this concerned the batting. On the face of it the batting looked good. In the first two Tests the totals were: 399, 202 for 4 declared; 524 for 9 declared, 208 for 2. But the batting was over-dependent on Gavaskar and Viswanath and the young hopefuls of the West Indian trip did not really come off. Vengsarkar could not get into the side, Amarnath and Patel, apart from one great knock by Patel, were not consistent and the batting averages were headed by Kirmani who batted at no. 7 and often had to pull India round.

These batting deficiencies were cruelly exposed by England who came to India after the New Zealanders for a five-Test series. For the first time ever a reigning England captain, Tony Greig, led the side. Both India and England were in a similar position. Both had recently been beaten by the West Indies, England having lost the 1976 series at home 3-0. But at the end of the Indian tour, England looked massively superior. For the first time since the Jardine tour, more than forty years before, England won a series in India. The win could not have been more emphatic. England won the first three Tests, something that no other touring team had done. India came back to win the fourth and, since this was just after Mrs Gandhi had announced elections, which eventually led to her downfall and the ending of emergency rule, it was quickly suggested that democracy had revived the Indians. But by then the series was lost and while India had the better of the fifth Test they just could not force a win.

The leading batsman was Surinder Amarnath who was brought in for the fourth Test and made an immediate impression with his belligerence. He was also a rare left-hander in the Indian batting and this helped him cope with England's two principal left-arm bowlers: Underwood and Lever who had so tormented the other Indians. Gavaskar played in patches. In the first Test he made a masterly 71 against Underwood and in the process became the first Indian to score 1,000 runs in a calendar year: 1,024 for 1976. In the fifth he scored the only Indian century of the series in Bombay but between the first and the fifth Tests he passed 50 only once and averaged well below his par, at 39.40. Viswanath averaged 19 with a top score of 79 in Bangalore. It was noticeable that when Gavaskar and Viswanath both came off, as in the second innings of the Bangalore Test, that was when, for the first time, India exerted some pressure on England and won. But as against New Zealand the great hopes of the West Indian trip hardly left a mark. Mohinder Amarnath played in two Tests, one as opener, and made 36 in all, averaging 9. Vengsarkar played in one Test and made 8 and 1, retired hurt.

The Indian spinners never had enough runs to bowl against and, although Bedi with 25 wickets and Chandra with 19 were again the leading wicket-takers and crucial in bowling India to victory at Bangalore, it was Prasanna, making another comeback – he had missed the end of the West Indies trip and the New Zealand tour in India – who looked the best of the spinners. Perhaps the others were exhausted and Prasanna, being fresher, had the edge.

The tour also left a nasty taste in the mouth because in the third Test it was discovered by the umpire that Lever, whose bowling had made a big difference, was carrying on his person a strip of surgigal gauze impregnated with vaseline. Bedi alleged that he had used the vaseline to shine the ball and that this explained why Lever, who hardly swung the ball in England, could do so in India – in the first Test in Delhi his ability suddenly to swing the ball had caused a collapse from which the Indians never recovered. Lever and the MCC denied it, saying that the strips had been used only in the third Test in Madras and only in order to keep the sweat from running into Lever's eyes. By making the allegation in the way he did, when India were about to lose the Test and the series, Bedi gave the impression that he was 'squealing'. But the MCC did not cover itself with glory either and never satisfactorily explained what had happened.

That incident, and others during the tour, showed that even in his own country Bedi could appear as the foreigner while Greig, the white South African-born English captain, astonishingly seemed more at home. Greig, ever the showman, knew Indian crowds from his previous visit and used this knowledge so well that Bedi was always a step behind. In Calcutta he so charmed the crowds that he became known as Greigda, a term of affection. Even in Bangalore, after he had lost, he led his team on a lap of honour while Bedi, the victor of the Test, stood in the press box fuming. India has some of the most demonstrative crowds but also some of the friendliest and any sign of attention – a gesture, a bit of clowning, like that by Randall, who was a great 'hit' with his fielding – captivates them. Greig used all this and more, carefully discriminating between the cheaper stands – where his impressions of a full-breasted woman went down well – and the pricier stands – where he was more decorous – to make Bedi and the Indian cricketers feel as if they were playing away from home. Some of his antics came close to the sort of gamesmanship that should have no place in cricket: if a batsman played and missed Greig, very often fielding at silly mid-on, would snatch his bat and show him how to play the shot. The crowd would roar, but the batsman would lose his concentration.

While Bedi fumbled, Greig never seemed to miss a trick. Lever discovered he could swing the ball in India only when it was changed in the first Indian innings in the first Test in Delhi. The old ball had been used for eleven overs and India had made 43 without loss but then England claimed the ball was out of shape and got it changed. As Mike Selvey, who was on the tour, has since admitted, in a *Guardian* appreciation of Lever, there was nothing wrong with the ball, it was just an English ruse to try to do something, anything, to break up the Indian stand. The 'rogue' ball swung all over, Lever took four wickets in 16 balls, India went from 43 for no loss to 49 for 4 and never recovered. Greig and his Englishmen had used an old English professional trick to undo India. That set a pattern for the series with which Bedi, for all his years in English county cricket, never came to terms.

21

The Gavaskar era
1977-81

In 1976 Gavaskar published his autobiography, *Sunny Days*. Indian cricketers rarely publish their autobiographies – indeed there are only about half a dozen autobiographies and that list does not include such great players as Merchant, Mankad, Lala Amarnath and Gupte. Even the ones who do so usually only publish when their playing days are over.

When *Sunny Days* came out, therefore, it was almost unheard-of for a cricketer to write an autobiography while he was still playing and with the prospect of much of his career still in front of him. Gavaskar discovered a market and started a trend. The book went quickly into paperback and over the years was reprinted several times. This success encouraged publishers to print or reprint memoirs of older cricketers. Autobiographies by Mushtaq Ali and Vijay Hazare now appeared in paperback seeking to exploit the market Gavaskar had opened up.

If this suggests that Gavaskar was the first superstar produced by Indian cricket then that is not far off the mark. To an extent his superstardom was achieved in his very first West Indian tour in 1970-71. But important as Gavaskar became then, he was not the dominant figure in Indian cricket. In a country that respects age inordinately he was still the brilliant young man while Wadekar and Pataudi fought over the captaincy. Now in the winter of 1977, although Bedi was still captain and taking the team to Australia, Gavaskar had become the central figure. For the next ten years everything that happened in Indian cricket revolved around him and in the next five years he was to move from being the dominant Indian batsman to one of the great players in the history of the game.

Inevitably Gavaskar had come down a bit in the world since his arrival in Test cricket with an average of 154. He did not average 50 in a Test series for five years after his first tour, indeed not until he left India again for the twin tours of New Zealand and West Indies in 1975-76. Then he averaged 66 against New Zealand and 55 against the West Indies. But at the age of twenty-seven, after six years of Test cricket, he had already scored 2,776 runs and was closing in on the leading run-getters of Indian Test history: Umrigar and Vijay Manjrekar.

His current average of 47.86 merely reconfirmed his class, a Test average above 42 being a sure sign both of class and staying power. For the next five years, playing cricket in almost every country of the world, he only twice averaged less than 50.

The concentration, dedication and will to succeed that had been his hallmark from childhood remained. But it was his consistency that set him apart from other Indian cricketers who would score a hundred in one innings, be hailed as the great saviour, then hardly score a run in the next dozen innings. India has a surprising number of cricketers who scored a century in their first Test then never scored another Test hundred.*

Gavaskar, in contrast, still had the hunger for runs he had first shown as a schoolboy and that burning desire to succeed. But this was not a Boycott-like hunger, the rather facile comparison often made by English critics. Gavaskar did not make runs in all classes of cricket, all the time. The greater the occasion, the more he lifted his game. Often on tours, in matches outside the Tests, he would score in a breezy, very cavalier fashion. It was as if he saw these games as a release from the arduous task of concentrating during Tests. Even in Tests, however, he could sometimes play with a recklessness that was quite breathtaking. In the first innings of the Bangalore Test against England in January 1977 he opened the batting as if he wanted to score a hundred before lunch. The word was that something or somebody had upset him in the dressing-room and he wanted to get it out of his system.

It is hard to imagine Boycott ever playing like that. Boycott had converted cricket into a nine-to-five job. He scored runs in copious quantities in all classes of cricket, even in charity matches. Every time he went to the crease Boycott gave the impression of wanting to score a hundred. Gavaskar could rarely motivate himself in that fashion. At the end of his Test career Gavaskar had scored 39 per cent of his runs in Test cricket, whereas only 17 per cent of Boycott's runs came from Test cricket. This reflected, of course, apart from temperament, the very different cricket worlds the two men inhabited and a change in international cricket. Indian domestic cricket just did not provide as many opportunities as did the English season, and Gavaskar, coming to cricket a decade after Boycott, was

---

* 53 batsmen have scored a century on their Test debut. The following Indians never scored another:

   Lala Amarnath: 118 v. England, Bombay, 1933-34
   D. H. Shodan: 110 v. Pakistan, Calcutta, 1952-53
   A. G. Kripal Singh 100 v. New Zealand, 1955-56
   A. A. Baig 112 v. England, Manchester, 1959
   Hanumant Singh 105 v. England, Delhi, 1963-64
   S. Amarnath 124 v. New Zealand, Auckland, 1976

a child of the era which saw Test and international cricket dominate the game.

During this period, what may be called the first phase of Gavaskar's cricket, between 1971-76, he scored almost as many runs in domestic competitions as in Tests. Between 1969-70, when he made his first-class debut, and the start of the English visit in 1976, he had scored 2,483 runs in 43 Ranji Trophy innings at an average of 68.97. In the same period he batted 46 times in Test matches scoring 2,123 runs at an average of 51.77. Later the weight of runs in Test cricket increased. Gavaskar was part of the first generation of international cricketers who would play more Test and international cricket than domestic cricket and he adjusted his game accordingly.

This provided the great contrast with Merchant with whom in India he was always being compared. Apart from the fact that it is difficult to compare cricketers of two such different eras, in his first three years Gavaskar had played more Test cricket than Merchant played in his entire career. Gavaskar thrived on international cricket but the daily grind of the game did not always attract him.

This was to become even more evident in the winter of 1977-78 as the Indians prepared for their first visit to Australia in ten years. In nine Test innings Gavaskar scored 450 runs, averaging exactly 50; in five other innings outside the Tests he scored 87 runs, often batting down the order.

But then Gavaskar had even more need to conserve his energies, for the tour was charged with unusual excitement and emotion. Suddenly the Australia-India Test series was a symbol of everything that many people in cricket considered decent, good and worth preserving. Within months of the end of the English tour of India in early 1977, cricket was torn apart by a revolution. Kerry Packer, an Australian magnate, had formed a rival cricket circuit. Having failed to win the right to televise England-Australia Tests, Packer set about organising his own World Series Cricket (WSC) in direct opposition to the traditional game – attracting the leading Australian, West Indian, Pakistani and South African players. England's captain Tony Greig acted as his recruiting sergeant and, of English players, Underwood, Knott and Woolmer were attracted to the 'rebel' cause.

Only India and New Zealand were unaffected. No Indian player was recruited. Indians did not see this as a snub but as a chance to reaffirm the values of traditional cricket organised through the respective Boards and the Indian team to Australia, in the winter of 1977-78, again with Bedi as captain and Gavaskar as vice-captain, was heralded as flying the flag of the traditional game.

Packer's minions rubbished the Test series as a match between an Australian Second XI and an Indian team whose standing in Australia was not very high. But while the Australians had lost some excellent players to Packer even without Packer the team would have needed reconstruction after the 3-0 defeat in England in 1977. And while Packer had taken the established stars there were still some very good players available. They included Jeff Thomson, bowling with rare pace and fire, and young players like Hughes, Dyson, Yallop and Wood who were soon to be a force in Australian cricket. Bob Simpson came out of retirement to lead the Australians and the two teams produced a marvellous Test series. In a head-to-head confrontation with Packer's circus the traditional game proved that nothing could replace real Tests and crowds in fair numbers came to watch.

The Indians responded to the stimulus of the situation very well. They came to the first Test having won all their state matches and they should have won the first Test. But there was a batting failure in the first innings on a good pitch, after Australia had been bowled out for 166, and this left India 341 to win. After Trinidad, chasing such totals did not faze the Indians and, led by Gavaskar who made 113, they lost by only 16 runs. Bedi, who had taken 5 for 55 in bowling Australia out for 166 on the first day, very nearly took India to victory, remaining not out with 26.

The second Test was almost a reverse of the first but just as close. Again Gavaskar scored a century, Mohinder Amarnath nearly scored a century in each innings, 90 and 100, Chauhan made 88 in the first, and in both innings the Indians batted as if they would score a lot more runs. In the first innings India were 229 for 4 but ended on 402, in the second they were 240 for 2 but ended on 330 for 9 declared. Simpson rescued Australia with a dogged 176 and in the final innings Australia were left 339 for victory.

India got an early wicket but this proved a dubious blessing, for the night-watchman, Mann, made a century and, at one stage, the Australians were coasting happily, but magnificent bowling by Bedi so changed the scene that in the end the Australians won by only two wickets.

So the Indians were 2-0 down when they could easily have been 2-0 up, but they were sure they had the beating of the Australians. The third Test at Melbourne was won by 222 runs, the fourth at Sydney was won by an innings and two runs. The Australian victories had been narrow affairs, the Indians had won by thumping margins. The difference was the bowling of Chandrasekhar. In Melbourne he took 12 for 104, the best match figures he had achieved. In Sydney he took 4 for 30 in the first innings as the Australians were bowled out for 131 and never recovered. He took two more wickets in the second innings which meant that in two Tests he had taken 18 wickets. Chandra had a point to prove. He still remembered with bitterness the decision to send him back home on the 1967 tour after he was injured. Then it was said that Chandra could not bowl on Australian wickets. He was determined to prove his critics wrong and, as ever when he was aroused, he bowled with rare determination.

Chandra's bowling was backed by the batting of Gavaskar who scored 118 in the third Test and 49 in the only innings of the fourth. Viswanath, not having reached a 50 so far, now scored 59, 54 and 79 in the third and fourth Tests and the Indians went into the final match with the series marvellously tied at 2-2. Having come back from 2-0 down, the Indians now appeared to have the momentum, so comprehensive had been their victories at Melbourne and Sydney.

But on the first day, and for the first time in the series, the Indian spinners bowled badly, Bedi and Prasanna in particular. Australia got away and eventually reached 505, though Chandra took 5 for 136. India made 269, only Viswanath with 89 and Vengsarkar with 44 providing real resistance. Simpson could have enforced the follow-on. But in a six-day Test he did not fancy facing the Indian spinners on a last-day wicket and decided to bat again. This time the spinners bowled well and Australia were dismissed for 256.

So once again India needed a large total in the final innings to win. They had chased 395 in the first Test and come within 16 runs. Now they chased 492. They would have to do better than their own Trinidad record. If the Trinidad or even the Brisbane example of the first Test was to be followed, Gavaskar would have to make a big hundred. But this time Gavaskar failed. This was the only Test in which he failed to make a decent score in at least one of the innings and the Indian cause looked lost. It was now that the Indians showed remarkable batting depth, that their batting was not solely Gavaskar.

Mohinder Amarnath made 86, Viswanath 73, Vengsarkar 78. At one stage the Indians were 210 for 2. They had reached 348 for 6 when Kirmani, who had batted very well in the first innings and in the series, got together with Ghavri. In the first Test Kirmani and Bedi had nearly brought India victory; now Kirmani and Ghavri took the score to 415, just 65 away. But the second new ball proved too much and though Bedi fought on until the end making 16 and Prasanna was 10 not out, India fell 47 runs short. Only one Indian batsman failed to make double figures, Chandra. It would have been a major sensation if he had made ten. In the third Test at Melbourne, while his bowling arm had been so potent, he had become the first player in Test history to be dismissed for a pair on four occasions.

Defeat yes, but there was consolation in defeat. India's 445 was the second-highest fourth innings total in Test cricket, and the highest score made by any side in the fourth innings to lose a Test. The cricket buff can easily reel off such statistics but what these demonstrated was that the modern generation of Indians was resilient and could fight hard, often against seemingly impossible odds, to try to gain victory. A large fourth-innings target was a spur to the Indians.

Two of the modern Indians who had done well were Mohinder Amarnath who averaged 49.44, just behind Viswanath and Gavaskar, and Dilip Vengsarkar. His average of 35.55 was not earth-shattering, but this tour was a turning point for him. In the previous year, on the twin tours to New Zealand and West Indies, he was still the middle-order batsman the Indians were trying to convert into an opener. In the first match of this series they continued with the experiment, but in the second he was moved down the order to his proper position. And there, for the most part, he stayed although in the 1980s he frequently batted at no. 3.

This was possible because the reserve opener, Chetan Chauhan, had succeeded. This sounds like an important discovery of a new player but Chauhan was no newcomer. He was two years older than Gavaskar, and one of the oldest members of the side. He had made his debut against New Zealand in September 1969, played against Australia later that season, then been discarded for three years. He was recalled against England in 1972-73, then again discarded. Between January 1973, when India had played in Kanpur, and December 1977 when India played in Perth, Chauhan was in the wilderness. He returned for that Test, opening the innings, and suddenly Gavaskar seemed to find the partner he had been looking for for so long. They batted together for the rest of the series and put on 14, 47; 0, 40; 97; 23 and 40; a much more consistent record than many previous opening Indian pairs. For the next few years Chauhan was to provide Gavaskar with his best partner, and the stability this gave the start of the Indian innings was soon evident.

There is no explanation for the treatment of Chauhan, it is just another example of how profligate the Indian selectors can be with their talent. In the Kanpur Test against England, when he helped Gavaskar put on 85, the second best Indian opening partnership in the series, he had suggested he might be the answer to the problem of who should open with Sunil. But the selectors had preferred to experiment and so, for seven seasons, Gavaskar had a new partner every series, sometimes every Test. Sometimes a middle-order batsman like Ashok Mankad, sometimes an all-rounder like Abid Ali, sometimes a wicket-keeper-batsman like Engineer, twice Solkar, once Mohinder Amarnath. But now, almost by chance, the Indians had discovered, or rediscovered, Chauhan. He also had one other virtue – the ability to count prize money and distribute it amongst the players – a gift that was to increase in value over the years. When he was finally sacked he was missed as much for this as his batting.

* * *

So India looked forward to Test cricket in the Packer era with good heart. And while WSC ravaged cricket, producing strife such as the game had never seen, the Indians began to put their international quarrels behind them. In September 1978 the Indians set out for Pakistan. The two countries had not met for eighteen years, they had fought two wars in the meantime and now, in a wave of emotion, they resumed Test cricket. The Pakistanis, who had several players under contract to Packer, had started by refusing to let any of them play in the Tests, but for a series with India, which was almost a substitute for war, they could not afford to field anything less than their best side.

Off the field there was a lot of goodwill as Indians who had been born in Pakistan returned to their former homes and the frontier, so often closed, was now opened. On the field, though, the Pakistanis indulged in a surfeit of bouncers. In the third one-day match at Sahiwal, with India looking set for victory, Sarfraz Nawaz bowled so many bouncers which batsmen could not reach that Bedi protested. When the umpires refused to do anything he conceded the match.

The Pakistani use of the short-pitched delivery was a calculated ploy. As the series progressed the Indian batsmen got tired of ducking and weaving to Sarfraz and Imran; it was common for Imran to bowl three bouncers an over and, by the end of the series, what had started off as a promising batting line-up was looking very sorry. India, having had a comfortable draw in the first Test, lost the second and the third, both by eight wickets. The Pakistani government was so overjoyed that when their team won the second Test they declared the next day a national holiday.

Only one Indian batsman came through the series with an even greater reputation. That, almost inevitably, was Gavaskar. Only once in six Test innings did he really fail, when he made 5 in the first innings of the second Test. His scores were: 89 and 8 not out; 5 and 97; 111 and 137. The two hundreds in the third Test meant that Gavaskar now belonged to another exclusive club. Then, only four other batsmen had performed this feat twice: Herbert Sutcliffe, Headley, Walcott, Greg Chappell. Gavaskar became the fifth.

Those two centuries showed how far ahead he was of the other Indian batsmen. His 111 came in a score of 344 where only one other batsman, Kapil Dev, passed 50; his 137 in the second innings very nearly saved the match for India and came in a score of 300 where again only one other batsman, Mohinder Amarnath, passed 50. He easily headed the Indian Test averages with 447 runs at an average of 89.40. What was remarkable was that outside the Tests, contrary to other tours, Gavaskar also made a lot of runs. He seemed determined to make a big score every time he went to the wicket. He started with 165 not out against Pakistan Bank and went on making runs in nearly every match, finishing with an aggregate of 882 runs at an average of 88.20.

Another success of the tour was Chauhan who finished with an average of 42.40 and three times in five innings helped to put on respectable first-wicket stands: 97, 58 and 192, the last a record opening partnership in Tests between the two countries. He almost overshadowed Viswanath who started the series with his then highest test score of 145, which meant he had scored a hundred against every Test-playing country, but after that he passed 50 only once more, to average 49.80. As the Indians said, 'He would not be Viswanath if he did not fail.'

Gavaskar averaging 88, two other batsmen averaging over 40 suggests a good batting series but, compared to the Pakistani averages – Zaheer Abbas with 194.33, Javed Miandad with 119, Mushtaq Mohammed with 75 – the Indian effort was puny. It exposed an alarming bowling failure. This truly was the last hurrah for the Indian spinners, except that it hardly raised a cheer. Chandra headed the averages but his eight wickets cost 48.12 each. Bedi's six wickets cost 74.83 each and Prasanna's two a horrendous 125.50 each. Venkat did not even get to play in the Tests. Not once did India bowl Pakistan out and *Wisden*'s conclusion, that the spinners were 'over the hill', was unarguable. The great age of Indian spin, perhaps the greatest that cricket has known, was coming to an end.

The only bright spark was provided by a nineteen-year-old from Haryana, Kapil Dev Nikhanj. He made his debut in the first, Faisalabad Test and at the end of the series had had what may be described as a quiet introduction to Test cricket: seven wickets at 60.85, and 159 runs at 31.80. Hidden amongst these unremarkable figures, however, were some very interesting pointers to the future. His highest score of 59 had been made out of 48 balls with two sixes and eight fours. It had come in the first innings of the third Test at a time when the rest of his colleagues, except Gavaskar, had no answer to Imran and Sarfraz. It was in this innings that Gavaskar had made 111 and Kapil's was the next highest score. He had come in to bat at no. 9, with the score 253 for 7, and taken it to 344.

For Indians, what was more significant was that Kapil opened the bowling and this is where he suggested that a new type of cricketer was coming into Indian cricket, or rather a reincarnation of an old, almost extinct type. Since the departure of Nissar and Amar Singh, the Indian opening attacks had mostly meant little more than to get the shine off the ball so that the spinners could come on. If they managed to take a wicket that was considered a wonderful bonus.

There had been fast-medium bowlers like Phadkar and Desai, but they had never been really quick enough or seldom good enough to make much of an impression.

Kapil Dev was different. He looked the part – with a lovely smooth run-up, a beautiful action and genuine pace at the end of it. This was not just a few shuffling steps and military-medium pace. India had not seen a bowler like this since Amar Singh.

Kapil, himself, has never really explained why or how he became a quick bowler. He was brought up in the great era of spin and there was nothing very much in his background to make him a cricketer, let alone a fast bowler. His father, an immigrant from Pakistan who had been born in Rawalpindi, settled in Chandigarh – the Corbusier-designed city. He did not discourage Kapil but he did not play the game himself. It was D. P. Azad, a cricket coach in Chandigarh, who first spotted his potential. Kapil seems to have first begun to think of fast bowling when listening to the radio commentaries on the 1974 tour in England. Indian humiliations at the hands of English pace convinced him then that India needed a fast bowler. But it was a different kind of humiliation, at the hands of an Indian official, that motivated him to try to become one.

This happened in Bombay when Kapil Dev was attending the Indian Board's coaching camp for Under-19 cricketers. Kapil was fifteen and he was a big eater, but at lunch he was served just two dry chappatis and one spoonful of vegetables. He protested that, as a fast bowler, he needed more food and solid food. The Indian Board official, Keki Tarapor, was amused by the very thought of an Indian fast bowler. 'There are no fast bowlers in India,' he mocked. Kapil, hurt and bewildered, vowed to prove him wrong. The story obviously improved in the retelling and would not have made much of an impact unless Kapil had indeed become the fast bowler India hungered for. But in the Kapil Dev canon the missing chappatis and the scornful laugh of Mr Tarapor were to prove decisive. In that sense Tarapor, who was himself a left-arm spinner, had, even though unwittingly, performed a marvellous service for India. Just as the great spinners, perhaps the greatest spin quartet in the history of the game, were declining India had rediscovered pace.

Kapil Dev had timed his arrival with perfection. The Indians returned from Pakistan in November 1978 to face the West Indies at the beginning of December. The long-suffering Indian supporter now felt that, at last, there was a chance of retribution for the long years of being humiliated by West Indian pace, especially as the West Indian side was minus its players committed to World Series Cricket. For all the victories the spinners had won, the Indians had never forgotten their

297

early pace men and hungered for a fast bowler who could answer fire with fire. When Kapil Dev made his debut he was greeted with the sort of disbelief that a childless couple, who have long prayed for a child, experience when they are told that they are going to have a baby.

As Kapil Dev became increasingly prominent in India's cricket story a few initial points need to be made. Not since Amar Singh and Nissar did pace so dominate the Indian attack. But while Kapil Dev was the symbol of this transformation the most successful Indian bowler in the six-Test series against the West Indies was the left-arm medium-pacer Kharsan Devji Ghavri. Ghavri had made his debut against Lloyd's team in 1974-75 and been on the fringes of the Indian team, in and out of Tests, for some time. Ghavri was not all that quick but as a left-armer he provided a different angle and, with Kapil providing the pace at the other end, he blossomed. On the tours of Australia and Pakistan he had shown his potential, now he became the leading wicket-taker with 27 wickets at 23.48. Kapil took 17 wickets but was more expensive, each costing 33. Between them, though, they took 44 wickets, putting the spinners, after three decades of almost total dominance, firmly in the shade. Prasanna had gone, Bedi took 7 wickets at 46.28 each, Chandra 12 at 35.91. Not even the transition from Amar Singh and Nissar to Mankad in the late 1930s had been quite as dramatic. Now it was suddenly nearly all pace.

Only Venkataraghavan, at a very respectable 24.75 runs per wicket, still carried the spin torch. But his contribution showed that, while pace might again become dominant in Indian cricket, if India wanted to win it still needed spin. In the third Test when, after two draws, India had the West Indies on the ropes it was through a combination of the bowling of Ghavri and Venkat who each took four wickets. The West Indies, set 335 to win in 365 minutes, were 197 for 9, with eleven balls left, when the umpires decided that the light was too poor for further play.

Venkat was just as crucial in the next Test at Madras where, on the fastest wicket in India, he took 3 for 60 in the first innings and 4 for 43 in the second. This match illustrated how cricket was changing in India. It came on the third day after India had made 255 in reply to the West Indies' 228.

Let *Wisden* record the moment: 'The match exploded into a bumper war on the third day during which fifteen wickets fell. The Indians for once gave as good as they got. Although there was a provision in the playing conditions for a check on intimidatory bowling, the umpires did not invoke the rules.' Kapil Dev and Ghavri took three wickets apiece, Venkat chipped in with four and the West Indies were bowled out for 151. Sylvester Clarke, at his most furious, retaliated for the West Indians and, at the close, the Indians were 31 for 3.

The Indian crowd had seen nothing like this in living memory. They had seen their batsmen ducking and diving but never their bowlers making the opposition do the same. The West Indies went on trying to bait the Indians with bouncers but while this had some success on the fourth day it played into the hands of Kapil Dev who was happiest when hooking bouncers. Kapil says, 'The bowling was generally around my ears and I stood up and hooked. It was when we were one run short of the target that I told Kiri [Kirmani] we should run as soon as the ball was delivered, for it was unlikely the ball would be anything but a bouncer. I came racing down the track but Kiri took off slowly and to our surprise the keeper missed the stumps with his underarm shy. India won the Test on the bounciest track I had ever seen and the series was decided on that basis.'

In the next Test, India made the West Indies follow-on but rain came to their rescue; seven and a half hours were lost and they easily drew the match. The sixth, like the first and the second, was another high-scoring draw where, for the second successive Test, India made their highest score in Tests. In Delhi it had been 566 for 8, now they reached 644 for 7 declared.

The series was clearly an ideal batting cure for the Indian batsmen after the horror of Pakistan. If Amarnath's average of 142 was slightly artificial – he played in two Tests and made 101 in one of them – Viswanath's 497 at an average of 71 and Vengsarkar's 417 at an average of 59.57 were marks of consistent scoring. For many, however, it was Kapil Dev's batting which caught the eye. He scored 329 with a 126 not out in Delhi which came in only 124 balls and he reached his first Test century in perfect style with a six off Norbert Phillips.

But the basis of the Indian batting domination was Gavaskar. In nine innings he scored 732 runs at an average of 91.50. Almost every time he went to bat he seemed to score a hundred or a double-hundred. In the very first Test in Bombay he scored 205, and a very quick double-century in just over six hours. When he reached his double-century India were 318. In the third Test he scored 107 and 182 not out and became the first batsman in history to score a century in each innings of a Test match three times. The fourth match, when he made 4 and 1, was his only failure but in the fifth he scored another century (120). That century meant that Gavaskar had scored ten centuries against the West Indies, far more than any other batsman. And this was also his eighteenth century in Tests. He now had the same number of centuries as Hutton, in twenty fewer Tests, and was scoring a century better than every fifth time he went to the wicket. Only one other batsman, Donald Bradman, had an even higher scoring rate and his then record total of 29 centuries did not seem that far distant.

Gavaskar's form was all the more remarkable because he was now captain. The defeat in Pakistan had finally brought Bedi's captaincy to an end. Apart from one Test series against New Zealand, he had lost to every other country: West Indies, England, Australia and now Pakistan. The Bedi years had been full of excitement and hope. Under him India had become rather adept at chasing huge totals. India had won Tests they had no right to, but they had also lost Tests they should have won. And they had lost far more Tests than they had won. Bedi, captain since 1975, had led in 23 Tests between 1976 and 1978; India had won 7, lost 11. Both the wins and the losses had been coloured by Bedi's mercurial personality – India conceding matches as in Pakistan, or closing the innings at 97 for 5 as in the West Indies – and the Indians wanted some peace and quiet, some stability. Gavaskar was the natural choice, the logical choice.

The extra burden can sometimes affect form but Gavaskar seemed to thrive on it. Later on there would be accusations that he was too defensive as captain: too much the Bombay school – make sure you are not going to lose, then strike out for victory. But in this series he had been quite willing to attack. In Calcutta, after the West Indies had failed to take a wicket in six hours and they had made 327 in the first innings, Gavaskar had no hesitation in setting them 335 in 365 minutes and came within one wicket of winning the match.

But despite victory in the series there was a question mark over it. The Indians were at full strength; the West Indians, because of Packer, were not. The team was led by the vastly experienced Alvin Kallicharran, Gomes was already established in the side and Bacchus was a fine batsman. There was genuine pace in Sylvester Clarke with good support from Norbert Phillips. This was also a first tour for Malcolm Marshall and, though he hardly played in the Tests, he impressed in the other matches and clearly indicated he would be the pace bowler to watch. But the side was young and inexperienced. Clearly the real test for India would come when they travelled to England for the World Cup, and then a four-Test series against England later in 1979.

For the first time Packer now cast his shadow over Indian cricket. During their tour of Australia there had been approaches to Gavaskar and Bedi. Then in Pakistan, a number of whose leading players were with Packer, there was a visit by Lynton Taylor, a director of WSC. It remains confused who said what and what was on offer. Bedi believed there was an offer for him. But Taylor then withdrew it. Taylor later denied he had ever made Bedi an offer and Bedi, who had an Australian wife then – they were later divorced – wrote an angry letter denouncing Taylor as 'a hollow man'.

Some time afterwards Gavaskar told his biographer, Dom Moraes, that contracts were offered for him and Kirmani, the wicket-keeper who had been a great success in Australia. A lot of money was on offer but there were doubts about whether this would clash with cricket for India, and about travel arrangements. The Indian Board, keen to show that they were untainted by Packer, decided to take severe action. Kirmani was dropped from the team to England and Gavaskar stripped of the captaincy. For the second successive World Cup Venkataraghavan was appointed captain with Viswanath as vice-captain.

Gavaskar's flirtation with Packer – it was little more – remains the most obscure subject in Indian cricket. Gavaskar, despite three cricket books, has never discussed it fully and Kapil Dev formed the fantastic impression that he had actually opted out of the captaincy of the English cricket tour because he did not feel like captaining India. Then when he felt like doing so he told the Board and they reappointed him because, says Kapil, 'he wanted to be back as captain'. Gavaskar certainly had the personality to dictate when and where he would lead the side, but it is possible that Kapil has confused a later episode when he did so opt out and the remarks were made at a time when, as so often in Indian cricket, two strong men were disputing for the captaincy.

It is possible that the Indian Board had taken the action against Gavaskar not so much with Packer in mind as to nip a possible rebellion in the bud. Tony Greig had justified joining Packer on the grounds that he wanted to improve 'the wages of the Glamorgan no. 10'. Gavaskar, who thought deeply about the game, had also begun to question the way the Indian Board treated its players. They made so much money from the players, but what did they give in return? Everyone in India seemed to make money from the players except the players. WSC had made Gavaskar agitate for players' rights, more money and facilities and he began articulating the case against cricket officials, with their obsessions with stadiums. In the years to come he would become the great and best champion the players ever had and this move by the Board was seen as a warning shot across his bows.

But like Nayudu rejecting Mankad before the 1952 tour, this was yet another self-inflicted wound. It is astonishing how often, before an England tour, the Indians seemed intent on committing harikari. Venkat, despite his success against the West Indians, was, at thirty-four, not the bowler he had been. Nor had he ever shown captaincy flair. The Indians began with an appalling World Cup. It was hard for them to do worse than in 1975 when they only beat East Africa, but in 1979 they managed even that. They lost to the

West Indies, lost to New Zealand and, in a sensational match at Old Trafford, also lost to Sri Lanka by 47 runs – the first time an associate member country had beaten a full Test team. India finished the same as Canada, no points after three matches. In contrast Pakistan got to the semi-finals and lost to the eventual champions, the West Indies, by 47 runs.

The Test matches were clearly going to be a struggle and the first, at Edgbaston, suggested that the Indians would be overwhelmed, as they had been in 1974. Here the last rites of the once-famed spin attack were performed. On the morning of the match Bedi woke with a stiff neck and Chandra played. He took none for 113 and never played again for India. Venkat took none for 107 and the only Indian bowler who troubled the batsmen (and took the five wickets that fell) was Kapil Dev whose analysis was 5 for 146. But it was clearly not enough. Boycott made 155, Gower 200, and England declared at 633 for 5.

The rest of the match was a case of whether Gavaskar and Viswanath could stave off an Indian defeat. In both innings they batted well. In the first Gavaskar and Viswanath put on 70, when Gavaskar on 61 was run out. Viswanath went on to make 78 but India followed on 336 behind. Gavaskar and Chauhan put on 124 for the first wicket, Gavaskar made 68 and at one stage, with Viswanath batting well, India were 227 for 4. But then Botham, with the second new ball, claimed 4 wickets for 10 runs in five overs, and India were all out for 253.

The weekend of the Lord's Test felt even more bleak. The Test had begun on an unusual note. Both Brearley and Venkat claimed to have won the toss but, as both wanted India to bat, it did not matter and in the end Venkat was adjudged to have won the toss. He must have wished he had decided to field, for on a day of rain and stoppages, Gavaskar went to the wicket five times during an innings of two and a quarter hours. India were bowled out for 96, only Gavaskar, 42, and Viswanath, 21, offering resistance. England, led by Gower, and with some late hitting by Taylor and Miller, made 419 and India began their second innings facing a deficit of 323.

Again they looked to Gavaskar. Could he at last score the big hundred at cricket's headquarters? But on the fourth afternoon Gavaskar was out for 59, providing Botham's 100th Test wicket. The dismissal was marked by high drama. At the beginning of the Indian second innings, Botham was just one wicket away from this milestone. In the first innings he had taken five wickets coming on second after Lever, bowling from the Pavilion end. Now he opened the England bowling from the Nursery end and as Gavaskar, having leg-stump guard, looked up he saw Botham with the ball. Immediately he had a premonition that he would be Botham's 100th victim. He had felt such a premonition before. In 1974 at Edgbaston he had felt he would be out for a duck and he was. In 1978 in Bangalore he again felt he would be out for a duck and he was out first ball to Sylvester Clarke. But Botham did not get Gavaskar first ball and by the time he began his twelfth over Gavaskar was batting beautifully.

Then suddenly everything changes. Gavaskar drives furiously at the second ball and Randall gets his finger tips to it but cannot hold on to it; the third ball, a bouncer, he fends off and it just fails to carry to Brearley at slip; the fourth ball beats him; off the fifth he is spectacularly caught by Brearley at first slip. The premonition has come true and, as Gavaskar leaves the crease, he offers his hand to Botham in congratulation. It seems as if India is conceding defeat. Gavaskar has lost his famous concentration and India appears doomed.

But Gavaskar's premonition was to contain a sequel that saw Botham dreaming about Gavaskar and in the Test there was unexpected Indian resistance. As Gavaskar departed Viswanath came out to join Vengsarkar and they remained together for the rest of the afternoon. At the end of the day India were 196 for 2.

The next day, interrupted by rain, saw them bat until twenty minutes after tea. In five hours twenty minutes they had put on 210 for the third wicket, just one run short of the 211 which Mankad and Hazare had put on for the third wicket at Lord's twenty-seven years before. Viswanath made 113, Vengsarkar 103. Viswanath was well known, but Vengsarkar's century impressed the English critics who held him up to be the next generation of Indian batsmen. Just as, during the war, the Indian newspapers had spoken of the two Vs, Vijay Hazare and Vijay Merchant, now there was again talk of the two Vs and, with the tour almost half over, the Indians suddenly rediscovered their purpose and form.

The next Test at Headingley was so ruined by rain that only the England innings was completed, but this allowed Botham to play a spectacular innings. For the first time on the tour the new Indian pace attack, led by Kapil Dev, presented a real threat to England. Before the tour Kapil had spent a week in Delhi with Rajinder Pal, a useful seamer. He was keen to learn how to cut the ball and make it come into the batsman. In England Kapil, like Amar Singh before him, was enchanted with the movement that could be obtained and said, 'I loved the experiment I tried out. God gave me my out-swinger but I had to learn the rest.' England helped immensely in the learning process, and while he realised he could not be the genuine pace bowler he had set his heart on being, he now knew he could become a more rounded fast-medium bowler with a great many variations.

He tried some of them at Headingley and in seventeen balls

took three wickets: Boycott, Gooch, Gower. England were 58 for 4 by mid-morning on the first day. Botham came in but a proper contest was prevented by further rain that held up play for the next three days. Botham resumed on Monday and played one of his amazing innings. He had been 9 on Thursday afternoon, he was 108 with four balls to go for lunch on Monday. But evidently he did not realise that a single would have meant a century before lunch and he blocked the four balls. Probably his mind was on another target, the 140 runs he needed to complete the double of 100 wickets and 1,000 runs in Tests. However, by blocking the four balls he did not help his cause, for he eventually fell for 137. Even then it was a magical innings, one that Jim Laker thought was one of the finest he had seen in the last twenty years. England were eventually all out for 270.

When India batted there was some danger of a follow-on at 12 for 3 but Gavaskar made 78, Yashpal Sharma 40 and Vengsarkar, who was not fully fit, 65 not out. The Indians finished on 223 for 6 and proved the resilience of their batting.

Throughout the summer Cornhill, the sponsors of Test cricket, had been distributing posters announcing *It's an Indian Summer*. For the first half of the season it had seemed a wretched pun. Now in the last Test at The Oval there was an Indian summer in the true sense of the words, with a glorious display of Indian batting.

For three and a half days England quite dominated the match. Botham easily got the three runs, which meant he had done the double in twenty-one Tests, two Tests quicker than Mankad. England made 305. India, with Botham again dominant, struggled and only a 62 by Viswanath and 43 not out by Yajuvindra Singh took them to 202. Boycott now made a slow hundred, 125, and England left India 500 minutes in which to make 438. The possibility of an Indian victory was nearly 500-1 against and the only realistic bet was on the time of the England win.

But by the end of the fourth day Gavaskar and Chauhan were still together at 76 for no wicket. The odds on an Indian victory had come down, but only slightly. They were 100-1 outsiders on the morning of the fifth day but somewhat better odds were available on a Gavaskar hundred. Everyone agreed that it would be a good end to the series. He had come so close. An Englishman writing a book about his batting records had been following him around all summer hoping and praying he would score a hundred. When he had made only 13 in the first innings he had wished him luck for the second innings. Maybe, Sunil had said, maybe.

By now Gavaskar had a set routine before he went out to bat. Fifteen minutes before he was due to start an innings, or twenty minutes since this was England and the climate colder, he would start his preparations. A little jog, then a few imaginary strokes, then he would put his pads on, his armguard, a long thin pad for his forearm, then he would check around his neck to see that the two medallions for luck, given to him by an old lady in Bombay and his guru Sai Baba, were there, and then he put on his sunhat, given to him by Zaheer Abbas, and he was ready to go out and bat.

And he did so this fifth morning. As Gavaskar was getting ready Botham had gone ahead of him on to the field. There he looked at the Oval scoreboard and had a premonition about Gavaskar. He seemed to see the numbers turn on the scoreboard again until they registered 200. 'The bugger is going to score a double-century,' thought Botham. Then in the way of professional players such thoughts were put away and battle commenced.

India needed a run a minute to win and the English bowlers were careful. But the runs came: 48 in the first hour, 45 in the second, 44 in the third. Hendrick, the meanest and tightest of bowlers, seemed to keep the batsmen on the leash but no bowler worried Gavaskar. Just once a ball from Edmonds jumped and surprised him a little, but otherwise he was always in command. Chauhan provided his usual support and at lunch the two of them were still together. It was some time after lunch, having batted for five and a quarter hours, that Chauhan finally fell, caught by Botham off Willis for 80; the pair had put on 213 – the best Indian opening partnership for the first wicket against England, bettering the Mushtaq Ali-Merchant 203 set at Old Trafford in 1936.

However, any thought of an England breakthrough was dispelled by Vengsarkar. He was an even better partner for Gavaskar, being an attacking, forceful batsman and, scoring at a run a minute, they had taken India by tea to 304 for 1. Another 133 wanted and now the odds had changed. Suddenly India were favourites.

England seemed to have few options left. Through the series in team meetings, England had discussed Gavaskar and held a theory. They thought that, since he is predominantly an off-side player, he was vulnerable to balls of a good length on or outside the off stump. Hendrick had thought he might be vulnerable to a trap ball: a wide ball delivered after several tight deliveries. Gavaskar might then be tempted to flash at it. In the first three Tests the strategy had worked to an extent but now nothing was working, and Hendrick had disappeared for good with shoulder trouble and the bowling was in the hands of Edmonds and Willey. But now, in an age before a set number of overs had to be bowled, Brearley slowed the game down ruthlessly. In half an hour after tea leading up to five o'clock – when the mandatory final twenty overs started – only six overs were delivered. But still India were in the driving seat. When the last twenty overs began the score was 328 for 1 wicket, 110 runs wanted at just 5 runs an over. A very gettable target given the number of wickets left.

Twelve overs were left, India were 366 for 1 and John Edrich, having to decide on the Man of the Series award and the Man of the Match award could not make up his mind: 'The Man of the Match is easy. It must be Gavaskar. But Man of the Series? So far in this series there has been only one contestant, Botham.' But Gavaskar's batting had begun to push Botham out of the frame and if he were to lead India to victory he would have to plump for him.

It was now that Botham intervened. Having dropped Vengsarkar once, he now caught him off Edmonds for 52. Here Venkataraghavan made a horrendous tactical blunder. He had played long enough for Derbyshire to know all about chasing runs, and this was a typical run chase. A class batsman on a good wicket against an attack under pressure should be able to score at five an over without taking unnecessary risks. Viswanath had class, experience and the technique. But Venkat promoted Kapil Dev up the order. Kapil, far too raw, tried to win it in a few strokes and was quickly out.

Even then Viswanath did not come in but Yashpal Sharma. He and Gavaskar took India to 389 with Gavaskar reaching his double-century. Eight overs were left. 49 were wanted when Brearley, in a bold move, brought back Botham. He had not taken a wicket so far and bowled very ordinarily. But now, having seen his premonition about Gavaskar come true, he decided to retrieve the situation.

Brearley, trying desperately to do something to disturb the little man's concentration, called for drinks. It worked. Gavaskar, after batting for nearly eight hours, played his first false shot and was caught at mid-on off Botham. It was now Viswanath who came in, and India still looked on course.

However, to win such matches you require some luck. Now India was visited by bad luck or rather bad umpiring decisions. Viswanath was given out, caught, Venkat was adjudged to have been run out and Botham swept aside Yashpal and Yajuvindra. Botham's final four overs had brought him three wickets for 17 runs. With two wickets left India needed 15 from the last over. With three balls of the match remaining all four results were possible: an Indian win; an English win; a tie; a draw. In the event, India got another six runs and the match was drawn, with India on 429 for 8, nine runs short.

India had failed to win but cornered the glory. It had been the most exciting Test in England since the 1963 Lord's Test. And nearly all the glory was Gavaskar's. This was the innings in which he stamped himself on the English cricket conscience. England had never seen him bat so well. They had heard of his exploits in the West Indies, in India, in Australia, in Pakistan, but in Tests in England he had played cameo innings: good 50s or 60s that had only once been converted to a hundred. Now he had provided the best, the most satisfying innings England had seen for a long time. In the following Sunday's *Observer* Len Hutton not only acknowledged that Gavaskar was now the most successful opener in history, he had scored three more centuries than Hutton who before him had been the most successful opening bat in history, but that he was something more. Devoting nearly half a page to Gavaskar and his batting score he wrote, 'He has the skill, patience and stamina to become the greatest record-breaking batsman of all time.' *Wisden* chose him as one of its Five Cricketers of the Year, only the fifth Indian to be chosen, and thought that his 'inspiring and technically flawless 221' was of such quality that, had India won, 'there were many Englishmen in the crowd who would not have displayed their customary dejection at the latest defeat'.

Gavaskar had little time to celebrate for, even as the Test match was playing, the Australians had arrived in India. A Test was due to start in Madras in just over a week's time. On the plane back, and with the sort of tactlessness that has always characterised the Indian Board, it was announced that Venkat had been sacked and Gavaskar reinstated as captain. But would the change have been made had Gavaskar's innings actually carried India to victory? Well might we consider.

The next six months was to prove the most hectic Indian cricket had ever known. India were due to play thirteen Tests, six each against Australia and Pakistan and a solitary one, to celebrate the Golden Jubilee of the formation of the Indian Board, against England. By the time that Test finished, in February 1980, India would have played 26 Tests in the space of thirteen months with all the Test-playing countries apart from New Zealand. In between all this had been squeezed the World Cup where India did play New Zealand.

What a contrast this was to the 1950s and 1960s. In the whole of the 1950s India had played 43 Tests. In the whole of the 1960s India played 52 Tests. Partly this reflected the growing acceptance of India as a major Test-playing country, but mostly the expansion was due to Kerry Packer and WSC. The cricket Boards, fearful that if they did not play regular cricket and keep their cricketers employed they would defect to Packer, arranged more and more frequent Test matches. As it happened, while the Indians were in England, the Australian Cricket authorities had been forced to sue for peace with Packer. The series against England in Australia in 1978-79 had lost money – the first time an Ashes series had lost money.

A great reconciliation took place. The Board reasserted itself as the supreme and only body to organise matches in Australia. Packer's promotions company was to help the Board promote the game. It appeared to be a victory for the Australian Board but, as *Wisden* commented, it was a victory of money. And as events were to show, the Australian Board was to prove a small dog wagged by the larger Packer tail. The Packer peace came into effect at the start of the Australian season in 1979-80 and forced radical changes to India's plans. Originally they were due to visit Australia but were asked to postpone it for a year. They were replaced by the West Indies who, along with England, were considered the brand leáders of cricket in Australia. If the Indians were upset, which they had reason to be, they covered it by just playing the Tests at home.

The Australian visit was actually a hangover from the days when the cricket world was still at war. The Australians did not include any of the Packer players. Apart from Kim Hughes, the captain, they had several of the players who were to figure prominently in Australian cricket even after the reunification: Wood, Border, Hogg, Yardley. The Indians had never before started a Test series so early – the second week of September when the departing monsoon rains often deliver a final sting. This badly affected the first two Tests, which were both drawn, but which suggested that, while the Australians might make runs, the Indians would score even more heavily. India had only one complete innings in each Test and made over 400 runs both times.

The third, the first. to be played without interruption, was played on a grassy, unexpectedly fast pitch at Kanpur – it normally is flat and lifeless – which, as the Test went on, produced unexpected bounce. The batting of both teams was just as unpredictable. India made 271, Australia collapsed but recovered to 304, India would have collapsed in the second but for a six-hour 84 by Chauhan, and Australia were left 279 to win in 312 minutes.

But by now the pitch was quite uneven in bounce and they were bowled out for 125, India winning by 153 runs. The line-up of the bowlers who took India to victory showed how the game had changed in India in little over a year. In October 1978 in Pakistan at Faisalabad the bulk of the bowling had been done by Bedi, Prasanna and Chandrasekhar with Kapil Dev in support. Now the three spinners had gone, Bedi having played his last Test at The Oval. His place had been taken in Madras by a thirty-one-year-old spinner, Dilip Doshi, who had been waiting patiently in the wings for Bedi to retire. Yadav, twenty-three and an off-spinner, had come into the second Test at Bangalore. Both had impressed, Doshi in his first Test innings taking six wickets, Yadav in his first Test seven wickets. In the fourth innings at Kanpur Doshi and Ghavri each took one wicket, while Yadav shared the limelight with Kapil, each taking four wickets.

After this the Indians asserted their dominance though they had to wait till the sixth Test before they could make this obvious. In the next Test in Delhi Gavaskar made his first hundred of the series, 115, Viswanath followed with 131, Yashpal Sharma 100 not out, and India made 510 for 7 declared. Kapil Dev took 5 for 83 as the Australians were bowled out for 298. They followed-on but resolute batting and dropped catches helped them save the match. In the fifth match in Calcutta Australia seemed to be prospering as they made 442 and got a lead of 95, but when they set India a target of 247 in 245 minutes the Indians batted so well that by the close they were looking the more likely winners at 200 for 4.

It was in the final Test at Bombay that everything came right for the Indians. Gavaskar scored another hundred: 123. Slowly the target of Bradman's 29 hundreds was being reached. This was century number 22 and meant he was on par with Hammond and Cowdrey. Sobers with 26 was immediately ahead. Gavaskar and Chauhan put on 192 for the first wicket – a record for India-Australia Tests, and with Kirmani restored to the side instead of Reddy for the series against Australia and coming in as night-watchman and making a hundred, India scored 458 for 8 declared. Australia, on a wicket made for spinners and afflicted by injury, collapsed.

Doshi and Yadav wrecked the first innings in four hours, Australia going from 77 for 1 to 160 all out – Doshi 5 for 43, Yadav 4 for 40. They followed-on and now Kapil Dev joined Doshi. He took 4 for 39, Doshi 3 for 60 and Australia were bowled out for 198. India had won by an innings and 100 runs. This gave them the series 2-0, the first time they had won a series against Australia.

If this result was not entirely unexpected the bowling success for the Indians did cause a ripple or two. There are not many bowlers who make their Test debut at thirty-one and go on to take 27 wickets at 23.33. But this was what Doshi had done. The years of waiting for Bedi to depart had meant his left-arm spinning art had matured. Nobody looked less like a cricketer. Doshi resembled a local executive who had unexpectedly strayed on to a cricket field. Not very tall, not very athletic, he gave the impression he was more at ease with a suit and a briefcase than flannels and a ball. He was not a good fielder and, perhaps, just a little better than Chandra with the bat. But as a bowler he was, if not in the Bedi class, not far behind. What is more, he thought about the game, endlessly analysing his opponents, working out new angles, new avenues of attack. A vegetarian who belonged to Jainism, an obscure offshoot of Hinduism, he was quite the most remarkable cricketer ever to play for India, or any country for that matter.

Four days after the Australians had been beaten in Bombay, the Pakistanis began the first match of their tour against Central Zone in Jaipur. This was much the same Pakistani team that had beaten the

309

Indians and effectively ended the spin domination of Bedi, Prasanna and Chandra. They had a new captain in Asif Iqbal but the batting looked awesome and it was hard for the Indians to feel optimistic about the outcome.

The first Test in Bangalore was fairly even. Pakistan made 431 for 9 declared and 108 for 2, India made 416. For much of the second Test India looked in trouble. In reply to Pakistan's 273 they made 126 and were left 390 to win in 550 minutes. Gavaskar left early and Vengsarkar had to control the innings. Defence was not a problem for him but he did not have the little master's knack for picking up runs. On the final day he scored only 17 runs before lunch and in the hour after lunch 31 runs were added. It was only bold hitting by Yashpal that gave India a target of 139 in the 90 minutes after tea. Now Vengsarkar showed the shots he could play and, when the final over began, India at 364 for 6 required another 26 to win. The over was abandoned with Vengsarkar on 146 not out. It meant that he had scored 1,000 runs in a calendar year, but a slightly more positive approach, even an hour earlier, might have combined personal glory with an Indian victory.

Despite this failure the Test proved the turning point of the series. The main problem for the Indians in Pakistan the year before was that they had nobody who could bowl the Pakistanis out. In the Delhi Test Kapil Dev suggested he might be the bowler. He took 5 for 58 in the first innings, 4 for 63 in the second. For the first time since the Test series had been revived the previous year, India managed to bowl Pakistan out – not once but twice, and in the second innings there was quite a collapse: Pakistan went from 210 for 4 to 242 all out in an hour and forty minutes. Kapil Dev had learnt a great deal in England.

Kapil's bowling was not to win India a match till some time later, but the very fact that what had been a formidable batting machine could be halted gave India heart. India indeed took charge of the third Test at Bombay from the moment Gavaskar went for the toss. He won it and batted first on a wicket which was difficult and likely to become worse: the ball turning and coming off at various heights and speeds. India's 334 in the first innings was the crucial score and possible with no. 7, Kirmani, no. 8, Kapil, no. 9, Ghavri, and no. 10, Yadav all making runs and taking India from 154 for 6 to what proved a match-winning total.

Pakistan found both pace and spin a problem, even the medium pace of Roger Binny. Binny, India's first Anglo-Indian cricketer, had made his debut at Bangalore but while he failed to take a wicket before his home crowd, in Bombay the pitch seemed to suit him. Very quickly he had had Majid, Zaheer and Javed out. After that it was spin, Doshi took three wickets, Yadav took three wickets and Pakistan were all out

310

for 173. India collapsed in their second innings for 160, only Gavaskar with 48 and Viswanath with 45 making over 20, but the target of 321 in nine hours and forty minutes on a spiteful pitch was just too much for the Pakistanis. One ball hit Mudassar on the face, the next ball he was lbw. Zaheer was bowled by one that kept low. The wicket was turning so much that Ghavri changed to bowling left-arm slow and took four wickets. Doshi took three, Yadav three, and Pakistan were all out for 190. India had won by 131 runs with a day to spare.

The defeat seemed to unhinge the Pakistanis. They hit out against the Indians in a disgraceful fashion. They accused Indian umpires of cheating, Indian authorities of spoiling the Bombay pitch, and Asif Iqbal talked of calling the tour off.

The fact was that the Pakistanis had, as Indian touring sides had done in the past, created problems for themselves. Even before the tour began they had had their own internal problems. Asif, the captain, felt he could not handle Sarfraz and did not bring him on tour, despite the fact that he was the most successful bowler against India in Pakistan. Pakistani cricket always has a bitter division between Karachi and Lahore and the team seemed split into camps. The rib injury to Imran Khan, which restricted his bowling, did not help but, above all, they could not cope with the pressures of an Indian tour. Imran, writing some years after in *All Round View*, took a more objective stance:

None of the players had any notion of the pressures of an Indian tour. From the moment we arrived it seemed as though the entire country had become a huge spotlight, training solely on us. The relentless publicity, the huge partisan crowds in the jam-packed stadiums, the expectations of our own public – all this was too much for some of our players. Our batting, never famous for its resistance, went to pieces.

Zaheer, who a year ago had averaged 194.33 in Pakistan, now averaged 19.62 and was convinced someone had put a spell on him. Majid and Asif both failed. Asif lost weight and had to take tranquillisers, which explains some of his outbursts, and in the fifth Test at Madras the Pakistani players were so nervous they could not even bear to watch their team bat.

This was the match where Kapil Dev stamped himself as a great all-rounder. On what Imran thought was a perfect batting wicket, Pakistan won the toss and could only make 272, Kapil taking 4 for 90. Then Gavaskar just batted and batted and batted. For seven minutes short of ten hours, 593 minutes, he was at the crease, making 166. Not till Kapil Dev came in to bat at no. 8 did another partner make 50. Then, as Kapil struck a flamboyant 84 in 98 balls, Gavaskar became almost totally stationary. India batted on till the fourth morning, finishing on 430 with a lead of 168.

Pakistan, as Imran recollects, had 'given up'. They were thoroughly despondent – there was an atmosphere of despair in the dressing-room. 'At one stage it seemed as if the match would be over that day.' In little more than an hour and a half after the innings had started Pakistan were 58 for 5, Kapil having taken the first three wickets. Pakistan did finally manage to take the match to the final day but, in the end, India were left to make 75, to win by ten wickets. For the first time since 1952 India had won a series against Pakistan.

Gavaskar could now look down from a personal and collective peak. He had become the first batsman in Test history to score a hundred in each innings three times – still a record. In 1979 for the second time in his career he had scored 1,000 Test runs in one year – 1,555 – and he had beaten the old enemy, Pakistan. So, having done his job, Gavaskar now retired from the captaincy. He had told the selectors he did not want to tour the West Indies, where the Indians were due to visit after the home season, and the last Test was meant to give them a chance to groom another captain. Viswanath, who had now become his brother-in-law, having married his sister, took over. Pakistan had a much better Test than at any time since the first. And with Imran now fully fit there was a fire in their attack. Imran took nine wickets and, at various stages, Pakistan looked like winning, but in the end it was the Indians who came close. Left to make 265 in 280 minutes the Pakistanis eventually had to go on the defensive to force a draw, finishing with 179 for six wickets.

Imran and the Pakistani team dreaded going home. 'No Pakistani team has ever had to face such humiliation, collectively or individually. Our failure was attributed to non-stop partying and a thoroughly irresponsible way of life. Apparently we had all indulged in wining, dining and womanising through the tour. There was little sympathy for my muscle injury, which I had evidently contracted while performing callisthenics with Indian actresses.'

Before the tour, Imran versus Kapil had been seen as a great all-rounder's contest. Kapil had decisively won this round. He headed the bowling with 32 wickets at 17.68 and was fifth in the batting with 278 runs at 30.88. Imran, given his injury, had not done badly. He too headed the Pakistani bowling with 19 wickets at 19.21, but, unlike Kapil, none of his spells had been decisive.

The focus on Kapil tended to obscure the achievements of Doshi who had taken 18 wickets and, having waited so long to make his Test debut, seemed to be in a hurry to catch up. Gavaskar's achievement in scoring 529 runs – more than any other batsman on either side – with an average of 52.90 was also obscured. If he was at times defensive he was always in command and he had provided the essential stability the previous Indian team lacked. In the past India had often fielded almost two whole teams in a series. Now, in a six-Test series, they fielded just twelve players, the same eleven in the first four matches. If the Australian series is taken into account, then in twelve Tests the Indians had fielded a total of sixteen players. Most of them had been playing together for six months and morale and team spirit were high.

But if Gavaskar was not given the credit he deserved then this was because, while he was admired, praised, and even feared, he was not loved. His sheer consistency, in a land where nobody from politicians to cricketers was expected to be consistent, seemed unnerving. Indians pray for their heroes to be infallible but are more comfortable with ones that are not. This had always made Viswanath such a favourite. In terms of class he was not far behind Gavaskar. Gavaskar himself would say, 'Vishi is better. He has four or five shots for every ball, I have just one.' But he would make a beautiful 40 and get out, he just did not play cricket the hard, sometimes relentless, way that Gavaskar did.

This was strikingly illustrated in the Golden Jubilee Test between India and England at Bombay. The Indians, trying to be generous, provided a green wicket, so green that Brearley could scarcely believe it, and Botham gave a startling all-round performance: 13 wickets and 114 runs in an easy ten-wicket England victory. But in a poor match, played by two teams exhausted by non-stop cricket, the great talking point was Viswanath's gesture to Taylor. India had made 242, and England, after being 58 for 5, were recovering through Botham and Taylor at 143 for 5 when Taylor was given out caught at the wicket off Kapil Dev. Taylor appealed to Viswanath and Viswanath, fielding at first slip, withdrew the appeal and got the umpire, Hanumantha Rao, to change his mind. Botham and Taylor went on to add 171 in what proved a match-winning stand. Gavaskar watched from second slip in impassive style and the impression Indians formed generally was that, had he been captain, he would not have intervened. Cricket was a hard game and he played it hard. He gave his best and he asked the players, and the authorities who ran the game, to do so as well.

He seemed to have worked out what he wanted and why. His decisions, like the one not to tour the West Indies, suggested fine calculation. Though he may not have meant it to give the impression that he would pick and choose the Tests he wanted to play in, he was powerful enough to assert his choice. As it happened, his lead was followed by others. The West Indians had problems recruiting their players and the tour was cancelled.

In contrast, Kapil Dev seemed a more natural, spontaneous cricketer, who played for the sheer fun of it. The way the Indians responded to these players showed their feelings. Already, though it was little more than a year since he had made his debut, he was known to millions as Kapil. Gavaskar, after nearly ten years in top-class cricket, was still Gavaskar. Only friends and intimates called him Sunny. Of course by focusing on them in this way the Indians were developing another personality clash, though this was not to become evident for some time. But the seeds of future discord were laid.

22

The rise of the north
1980-83

Kapil Dev's rise also coincided with a general resurgence of cricket in the north of India (see map, page 00) – Punjab, Haryana, Jammu and Kashmir, and Delhi. If Kapil became the symbol of this, the credit really belonged to Bedi. His example had inspired the youth of the Punjab and the north to take to the game, turning away from hockey, and in the late 1970s Bedi fashioned Ranji Trophy teams that took on Bombay and beat them. In 1978-79 Delhi won the Ranji Trophy for the first time, the next year they retained the trophy and it seemed as if nothing could stop Delhi's reign.

But Delhi was often its own worst enemy. The official publication of the Indian Board described what happened in the winter of 1980-81:

Delhi's second successive triumph in the championship of 1979-80 was followed by the formation of the Delhi State Cricket Association by the players, spearheaded by Bishan Singh Bedi and backed by some important Delhi personages. At the function held to form the new body, one was told the purpose was to work in conjunction with the Delhi and District Cricket Association [DDCA], the parent body, that had been running the game for nearly five decades, for the good of the game. However, as it turned out in 1980-81, the season under review, there was bitter confrontation between the two which disrupted the programme in the North Zone. . . . Matters reached a head when Delhi were to play Punjab in the last of their North-Zone league matches. With miscreants digging up the Feroz Shah Kotla pitch, the match could not be played. After the personal intervention of S. K. Wankhede, President of the Indian Cricket Board, an ad hoc committee was formed to choose the Delhi team to play Punjab in a rearranged fixture. However, this time there was utter confusion with two Delhi teams, captained respectively by Surinder Amarnath and Bedi, barging into the home dressing-room and once again the match was not played. Ultimately, Bedi's team – he was dropped from the captaincy for the earlier match for which the team was chosen by DDCA leading to a revolt by senior players – completed the engagement, with a court order restraining the DDCA from interfering with the conduct of the match or even selecting a team. The restraint was removed only after the final between Bombay and Delhi had been completed.

The official summary does not convey some of the high drama and almost farcical scenes that took place. It had begun before the season started when Mohinder Amarnath was appointed captain of Delhi but, when he decided to accept an offer from Australia, his brother Surinder was asked to lead the team instead. This meant that the official vice-captain, Vinay Lamba, had been superseded and Bedi and five senior players – Madal Lal, Rakesh Shukla, Sunil Valson, Arun Lal and Surinder Khanna – insisted Lamba be made captain. Lamba captained in the first Zone match at Srinagar, then resigned. For the second match Surinder Amarnath should have been captain but, upset at not being chosen to tour Australia with the Indian team, he decided not to stand. Bedi had been dropped for this match because of the revolt he had led at Srinagar. On the morning of the second match Shukla and his four fellow rebels walked out. The match started an hour and a half late. The rebel five were suspended, then reinstated for the next match against Punjab but this did not take place as, on the day of the match, a crowd invaded Kotla and shouting 'No Bedi, no match' uprooted the stumps and dug up the pitch. It was when the match was rescheduled that two rival Delhi teams turned up and the Punjab captain was in the unique position of deciding which Delhi team he wanted to play. He chose Bedi, they tossed for the match while Surinder Amarnath, the rival Delhi captain, fumed on the boundary line. The umpires refused to accept this toss and ordered Punjab to toss with Amarnath but Punjab refused and then the umpires disappeared. Eventually the match was played and Delhi, somehow, got to the final.

Given all this, however, it was hardly surprising that Delhi failed in the final. Having beaten Bombay in the semi-final in 1978-79 and the final in 1979-80 they now lost by an innings and 46 runs. And this a Bombay team that was without several Test players on tour in Australia. Mankad and Solkar came out of retirement to lead Bombay to victory.

Bedi announced his retirement at the end of the season but, despite the extraordinary scenes that Delhi cricket had produced, the north had given notice that they were now a cricket power in the land. In a vast country like India regional power balances always keep shifting. In Indian cricket the constant was Bombay, which has always been one of the most important power centres of the game. The question was, which region would challenge Bombay? The north had done so in the 1930s, then faded away to be replaced first by the western states of Maharashtra and Baroda, then the central one of Holkar.

In the 1960s the south had emerged and India's Test resurgence in the 1970s had been largely due to an alliance of southern spin and Bombay batting.

Now a whole range of northern cricketers had begun to emerge who eclipsed the south and began to challenge Bombay's natural assumption that they would always rule Indian cricket. Some of them had been around for some time but it was only in the early 1980s that they came together as a group and a force in international cricket. Kapil was the most outstanding player, then there were Mohinder Amarnath, Yashpal Sharma, Madan Lal, Chetan Chauhan, Kirti Azad. In the 1979-80 Ranji Trophy batting averages eight players from the north had occupied the top twenty batting places, and three of the top bowlers were also from the north.

But this northern dominance of domestic cricket was not reflected in the Indian team that toured Australia and New Zealand in 1980-81 – it contained only five players from the north out of seventeen and Mohinder Amarnath and Madan Lal were left at home. The team for the tour was almost exactly the same that had beaten Pakistan, and once again it was led by Gavaskar with Viswanath as vice-captain.

The tour has come to be known in Indian cricket as 'the great escape'. This refers to a remarkable victory in the third Test in Melbourne which enabled India to leave Australia with the series tied 1-1. *Indian Cricket* wrote, 'Outplayed for 88 days of a three-month tour, the Indians romped home in the final Test to square the series and break a long sequence of failures. Honours were seemingly even at the end but no pragmatic analysis can escape the conclusion that India got away with a trick, Houdini-style.' Given that the Indians came close to forfeiting the match the previous day this was, all in all, a sensational end to a series that Australia dominated.

They won the first Test by an innings and 4 runs. India made 201 in both innings, Australia 406, with Greg Chappell 204 in 296 balls. The match was over in three days. The second Test saw another big Australian score, 528, and this time a double-century by Kim Hughes, 213 from 303 balls. India were in dreadful trouble at 130 for 4 when Sandip Patil played one of those innings which make a man a sporting legend. In the first Test he had been hit on the head by a bouncer when he had made 65, and taken to hospital. He had emerged with a terrible ear-ache and unsure whether he could ever bat again. But although he did bat in the second innings at no. 8 he decided to put on a helmet – they were now becoming common in cricket – and after practising hard with a helmet for a week went into this match. It gave him such confidence that, as *Indian Cricket* said, in an innings of 'raw power, rare charm and enviable elegance' he hit 174 off just 240 balls with 22 fours and a six.

317

That Patil should have succeeded was, perhaps, not surprising. He had emerged from the same great nursery of Bombay cricket as Manjrekar, Gupte, Vengsarkar and even Gavaskar – Shivaji Park; but in many ways he was a very different cricketer. There was a flamboyance about his personality which suggested he had come more from the Bombay film world than its cricket world. His looks, his bearing, his hair, his rather smart clothes, all gave the impression of a man who was aware of his image. And his batting had a violence which that of others lacked. Patil had grown up with Vengsarkar, rivals and friends in their schooldays. But while Vengsarkar was always a correct player, suggesting great reserves of power, Patil radiated a naked strength that soon was to dub him the disco cricketer of India. In some ways he was the first Indian cricket star, even if a brief one, to emerge in the 1980s.

But even his innings might not have saved India for, in the second innings, needing to bat for four and a half hours, they were struggling at 135 for 8 when Ghavri and Yadav saw India to a draw.

Now came the great escape. For the first four days of the Melbourne Test India were thoroughly outplayed. Batting first, India made 237 almost wholly due to Viswanath making 114, his first score above 30 in the series. Australia made another massive score of 419 with Allan Border making a century. India started their second innings with a deficit of 182 and for the first time too Gavaskar made runs. So far in the series he had had a wretched time, making 0, 10, 23, 5, 10. But now he batted with great care, great concentration.

Chauhan, who had enjoyed a rather better series, stayed with him and they had taken the score to 165, almost wiping out the Australian lead when Lillee appealed for lbw against Gavaskar. Gavaskar thought he had edged the ball and, when the umpire gave him out, he lost control and reacted with almost childish petulance. As a child, he had got upset and threatened to hit his fellow players – now in high dudgeon he decided to concede the match. As he walked past Chauhan he ordered him to accompany him back to the pavilion. A bewildered, unhappy Chauhan reluctantly trailed in behind Gavaskar.

Indian cricket was facing its most humiliating situation. Fortunately the Indian manager, Wing-Commander S. K. Durrani, met them at the gate and ordered Chauhan back. The Indian innings continued and when it finished on 324, Australia were left 143 to win. It seemed a formality: all the more so as the Indian principal bowlers had injuries. Kapil Dev had pulled a thigh muscle. Doshi had a fractured instep, and Yadav a fractured toe. That evening Kapil did not even bowl. It was Ghavri and Doshi who did the bowling and they managed to take three Australian wickets. This included the wicket of Greg Chappell who was bowled first ball by Ghavri. Great men can sometimes be undone by simple things.

Chappell in this case played inside the line of a long-hop and was bowled.

The next morning Kapil Dev, dosed with pain-killing injections, appeared at the crease and, while Doshi in considerable pain gave him wonderful support, including bowling Hughes, Kapil bowled unchanged for the next two and a half hours, taking five of the seven wickets to fall. When, with the fifth ball of his seventeenth over, he bowled Higgs for 0, his figures read 16.4-4-28-5. Australia had been bowled out for 83 and India had won by 59 runs. The Melbourne wicket, with its unpredictable bounce, was at fault but for once the Indians had the will to win. Chappell admitted that his side were 'lacking in the areas of anticipation and determination'.

India should have been encouraged by this to take on New Zealand. But here they dissipated all the euphoria of the Melbourne win. Inept batting cost them the first Test at Wellington when, set 253 to win in two days, the batsmen who had failed in Australia, Gavaskar, Viswanath and Vengsarkar, failed again and India were bowled out for 190 and beaten by 62 runs. The second Test was ruined by rain, the third saw the Indians behind for much of the match but fought back in their second innings. New Zealand, needing 157 to win in 242 minutes, struggled a bit and, with four overs of the match remaining, were 95 for 5. Then bad light stopped play.

In Australia Gavaskar had averaged 19.66, Vengsarkar 24.66, Viswanath 35.50. In New Zealand Gavaskar averaged 25.20, Viswanath 12.80. Only Vengsarkar, who headed the averages with 44.50, suggested he might be recovering his form. The brightest spark was provided by Ravi Shastri who had been flown in at the start of the New Zealand leg of the tour to 'cover' the injuries to Doshi and Yadav. An eighteen-year-old Bombay left-arm spinner, he was pulled out of a Ranji Trophy match in Kanpur to find himself flying halfway across the world. After a twenty-hour flight he had a few hours' rest and went straight into a Test match in cold, windy Wellington.

A month before this Shastri had been in university cricket; now he was in a Test match. His first over was a maiden, showing a style that owed more to Nadkarni, who was the assistant manager on this tour, than Bedi. Then came a sharp return catch to dismiss Coney and Test cricket seemed as natural as playing in a college match. In the first innings he took 3 for 54, in the second 3 for 9, helping Kapil to bowl out New Zealand for 100. By the end of the three-Test series he was the leading wicket-taker with 15 wickets at 18.46 and he showed he could bat with composure.

Yet, to an extent, Gavaskar's summoning of Shastri when there was a left-arm spinner like Rajinder Goel available was seen as yet another indication of Bombay lording it over the north. The assistant manager,

Bapu Nadkarni, was from Bombay – Wing-Commander Durrani was not a cricket man – and this was seen as a Bombay plot to keep out such established players as Goel who had already taken over 600 wickets in domestic cricket. Goel might well have played for India had his rise not coincided with Bedi's. Was he not worth a try now? In fact Gavaskar's call for Shastri showed his cricket shrewdness in picking a player who was clearly of Test match class.

But the first whispers about Gavaskar and his 'Bombay attitude' had begun to be heard. Bombay has exercised the same dominance over Indian cricket as Yorkshire has in the past in English cricket, Barbados in the West Indies, and New South Wales in Australia. It is a dominance that is resented and critics were quick to see Gavaskar's approach as exhibiting the Bombay style of leadership: a certain defensive aggressiveness, which seemed to shut out everybody who was not from Bombay.

Gavaskar's personality, or rather his perceived personality, was another factor. Sometime later Pataudi, in an article in *Sunday* entitled 'The Decline of Indian Cricket', was to articulate the case that was building up against Gavaskar.

Gavaskar was the greatest, and while no-one doubted this, it is plain that only some Bombay players paid him sycophantic homage. Perhaps the others were jealous but no matter how hard he tried, many cricketers from elsewhere were unable to give him their full trust. They felt that Gavaskar stood for Gavaskar though he had often clashed with the authorities for the benefit of his team.

What these cricketers forgot was that Gavaskar, now quite a trenchant critic of the Indian Board and its ways, had done more for Indian cricketers than any other player – including Pataudi. Under him, and no doubt influenced by WSC, the Indian cricketer was beginning to earn more money. Gavaskar shrewdly realised that the very people who fussed over a cricketer when he was in the limelight disappeared once he was off the scene, and he set about exploiting it to make money as no other Indian cricketer before him had done. According to Pataudi:

He became the first Indian millionaire through cricket, rich enough to buy a flat in the centre of Bombay. In a capitalist country he would have been considered a financial genius. In India they began to call him a mercenary, and within the team he became the envy of some who felt that their contribution to Indian cricket was not being appreciated. Why should Gavaskar hog all the publicity as well as the money? The answer was simple: he had reached those dizzy heights to which no Indian cricketer in his right mind would ever

320

dream of aspiring. As importantly, he was articulate where others were dumb, he was controversial where others dared not to be, he could even be witty and this made him ideal material for the media and the advertiser.

In the complex, contradictory Indian world, Gavaskar was becoming the besieged hero. Indians who loved flawed heroes such as Viswanath and Kapil Dev found this one with his certainties and his determination increasingly difficult to live with.

Perhaps none of this would have mattered if Gavaskar had continued to lead India to victory. But the lost series to New Zealand, the first to that country, once again started the perennial debate: whither Indian cricket? This headline was used so often in Indian newspapers that some people suggested it should be kept in permanent type. Gavaskar's record as captain was an excellent one. He had beaten the West Indies, Australia, and Pakistan at home, drawn with Australia abroad, and only lost to New Zealand. In 24 Tests under his leadership India had lost two and won six Tests.

Perhaps this helped to mute the critics during the winter of 1981-82 as England toured India. For some time it seemed as if the tour might not take place at all because two of the England players, Geoff Boycott and Geoff Cook, were on the blacklist of players who had played in South Africa. The Gleneagles Agreement enjoined Commonwealth countries to discourage their sportsmen from visiting South Africa, but did this mean that if a *team* contained players who had been to South Africa it should be banned? The black countries argued this case and earlier that year a Test match in Guyana was abandoned because the government of Forbes Burnham objected to the presence of Robin Jackman of Surrey in the English side.

Now the Indians objected to Boycott and Cook. After hectic diplomatic negotiations in London, India and Mexico, where Mrs Gandhi was attending a conference, the issue was finally solved by 'Madam', as Mrs Gandhi was known in India. Just days before the tour was to start, Madam, with that astute political touch of hers, sanctioned it, saying that she had found a reference in Boycott's book that said he abhorred apartheid. In fact the full sentence read that he abhorred apartheid and communism, but such niceties did not matter. Unknown to anybody, however, Boycott had for some time been helping to organise a rebel tour of South Africa and halfway through the Indian tour, unhappy with the country, he left – or rather was encouraged by the English management to leave – and soon after the end of the Indian tour a party of rebel English cricketers, including Boycott, Gooch, Emburey and Underwood – all of whom had been in India – went off to tour South Africa.

Much to Gavaskar's annoyance England started the 1981-82 tour as favourites. England had beaten Australia 3–1 in England in 1981, in quite the most absorbing series seen in recent Test history; now they began their Indian tour with victories in four of their first five matches including the first one-day international. This was the very first time India had played an international limited-overs match at home and the England players easily asserted their greater competence and familiarity with the game.

England held this advantage in the first Test at Bombay until the afternoon of the second day. India, on winning the toss, were bowled out for 179. England were 95 for 1, but then Boycott made a mistake and Doshi swept through the English innings. Almost literally. The English batsmen tried to sweep the left-armer and were either caught or lbw. Fletcher, the captain, Botham and Emburey all fell in that way. Tavaré was also caught off a sweep and Doshi had taken four wickets in five overs for nine runs. England were bowled out for 166.

The English were desperately unhappy about some of the decisions. Fletcher, Botham and Emburey all felt that they had been got at by the Indian umpire. It is now a common enough reaction of a Test team playing away from home to suspect that the foreign umpire is incompetent or crooked. But England chose to make their feelings public and the English press played up these stories.

On tour in India comments by the English press are extensively reported back and the Indians did not take them kindly. All the more so as they appeared in the Indian press on the very day that they were pressing for victory. Nor did it help England. For on that sunny Saturday afternoon in Bombay England seemed to take on the air of a team that believed it had run out of luck. And though India also collapsed, to 90 for 5, they were allowed to recover to 227. England were left 241 to win with a day and a half to get the runs, but now in a thoroughly defeatist frame of mind they were comprehensively beaten. Kapil Dev and Madan Lal, who had last played for India against Australia in Perth five years ago, bowled almost unchanged through the innings. In 25 overs they bowled out England for 102, Kapil taking 5 for 70, Madan 5 for 23. There were further lbw decisions in this innings but England could have no complaints – the ball was keeping low and some batsmen got hit on the ankle. India won by 138 runs with a day and a half to spare.

This match effectively decided the series. The English, shocked, used the next two Tests to try to recover. At Bangalore they won the toss, made a big first-innings score but batted too slowly to dictate terms. With the pitch providing little help to the bowlers there was never any chance of a result. It was a game that suited Gavaskar perfectly. He was on the field for all but four balls of the match as, in reply to England's 400, India made 428 with Gavaskar making 172 in 708 minutes – the longest Test innings played by an Indian. Frustration crept in for England and Fletcher, when caught at the wicket, hit his own wicket as he walked back to the dressing-room; later he apologised.

Now all that was left in the series were moments of personal glory. In Delhi Boycott passed Sobers' record number of runs in Tests: 8,032. His instant response was to remind everyone that, contrary to myths, he did not always think in terms of a record. Gavaskar, walking by, watched the scene sardonically and said he hoped Boycott would enjoy the moment, he knew he was not far behind. Delhi also saw Viswanath, who again had been having a lean time – there was talk of dropping him – recover his form. He had been so wretched that he had gone to one of India's most famous temples and offered the gods gold if they would help him make runs. The prayers worked so well that in Delhi Viswanath made a century. In Madras in the fifth Test he made a double-century, 222, then the biggest score by an Indian in a Test. It had come after England put India in and India lost two early wickets, including Gavaskar's. But Viswanath so dominated the bowling that India went from 51 for 2 to 466 for 3. For a whole day, the second, England did not take a wicket although, due to injury to Vengsarkar, the stand actually involved three players, Viswanath as the common factor, Vengsarkar and Yashpal Sharma. During the hours that these three batsmen were making these runs India's population was estimated to have increased by 75,000. It was in this match that Gavaskar showed a certain defensive tendency. India at 481 for 4 could have gone for a 500-plus score to give a large follow-on target to England. But he declared and England, with Gooch to the fore, made a strong reply.

The sixth and last Test was ravaged by rain with the only interest being the working out of the Botham versus Kapil Dev duel. Botham made a hundred, 142 off 214 balls. Kapil replied with 116, off just 83 balls – the fastest of the series. He batted like a rackets player, hitting down the line off almost any length.

Clearly Botham versus Kapil Dev would be the main attraction of India's tour of England that followed hard on the heels of this one. Once before, in 1952, there had been a similar pattern. Such back-to-back arrangements can often lead to dull games and the early summer of 1982 was only redeemed by Kapil Dev's performance.

From the first morning of the Test series, at Lord's in June, when he took the first three English wickets, reducing England to 37 for 3 and bringing echoes of the Test fifty years ago in 1932, Kapil was always in the centre of the action. At one stage in the match England were 166 for 6 but then Randall with a hundred and Edmonds rescued them. A batting collapse by India – only Gavaskar with 48 and Kapil Dev with 41 making double figures in a score of 128 – virtually lost India the match. India made a fight of it in the second innings, led by a superb 157 by Vengsarkar. He seemed to have a special fondness for Lord's – this was his second Test century there in successive matches.

But again it was Kapil Dev who cornered the glory by saving the innings defeat and taking the match to a fifth day. He made 89 off only 55 balls. His bat, said *Wisden*, made the sound of gunfire as he hit 13 fours and 3 sixes. Then, with England requiring 67 to win, he took all three wickets. England were 18 for 3 (they had been 19 for 3 in the first innings in 1932) before they won.

Botham's reply came in the second Test at Old Trafford when he made 128 out of 169 balls, with his first 50 coming in 46 balls. England made 425 and India were in danger of following-on at 173 for 6 when Kapil Dev came on the scene. Once again he seemed on course for the fastest century as he hit 65 in 55 balls before he was out. Such was his hitting that even Patil, who had come in before him, was happy just to push and nudge. But once Kapil went Patil produced his own brand of hitting. As in Australia he had been hit on the head in the course of his innings but this time, protected by a helmet, he carried on and when Willis took the second new ball his first over went for 24 runs. Willis had not helped by bowling a no-ball but Patil had been quite merciless in his cover-driving and straight-driving of England's captain. Patil moved from 73 to 104 in just nine balls. With the last day washed out the Test did not even see two completed innings.

The duel between Botham and Kapil was building up to quite a finish and Botham seemed to have settled in at The Oval when he made a massive 208. It was his highest Test score and a very quick double-century: 200 out of 220 balls in 268 minutes. In the process he also put Gavaskar out of the match. Gavaskar had come to field very close-in, received a nasty blow on his shin and took no further part in the match. One six off Doshi by Botham made a hole in the pavilion roof. England made 594 and, as throughout the series, the question was, could the Indian batting hold up?

Almost everybody batted well except Vengsarkar who was forced to open with Shastri and did not relish it. Shastri had been pushed into opening in the previous Test but now he showed his versatility by making 66. But the principal innings came, inevitably, from Kapil Dev. He made 97 in 93 balls. He did not have Botham's discipline but it was, perhaps, even more entertaining, including 2 sixes and 14 fours. By the time he was out India had virtually avoided the follow-on and the match was drawn. Kapil did not make a century in the series but each of his Test innings had been memorable, recalling the greatest hitters in the game. This was clean batting, not cross-bat shots, through the line and often very straight.

So England had quickly reversed their defeat in India by defeating India 1-0. Yet despite Kapil Dev's brilliance and the batting of Vengsarkar, Patil and Shastri, the England tour had shown an alarming weakness. India could bat but it just could not bowl sides out cheaply. England's only three completed innings in the series were 433, 425, 594. Doshi was the most successful Indian bowler but even he had taken 13 wickets at 35 runs each. Kapil with ten wickets was even more expensive: 43.90. Twice India had England in trouble: 166 for 6 at Lord's and 161 for 5 at Old Trafford, and twice the bowlers had failed to press the advantage home. In the days of the great spinners this would not have happened.

The alarm signals grew when the Indians played Sri Lanka in Madras in September 1982 for the first time in a Test match. India batted very well in the first innings, making 566 for 6 declared with Gavaskar 155 and Patil 114 not out, but Sri Lanka showed they could bat too; they made 346 and 394. India were left 175 runs to win in 135 minutes, tried hard, got into trouble and Gavaskar, injured, had to come in at no. 9 to make sure that India drew, with the score on 135 for 7.

By now India had not won a Test match since Bombay in November 1981. There was a chorus of complaints against Gavaskar. Doshi, the spinner, felt he had not been treated well, not bowled at the right ends; and the northerners felt discriminated against. In England, the disaffected players from the north, both those selected and those not, had talked about this man Gavaskar and how he promoted the Bombay players. Just before the Indians came on the tour the Ranji Trophy finals had taken place between Delhi and Karnataka. This could have been a match between Merchant's Bombay and Hazare's Baroda or Nayudu's Holkar. Karnataka made 705, with four century-makers. Karnataka batted till the morning of the fourth day. Delhi was expected to surrender but their batsmen played so well that, by the end of the fifth day even the first innings was not completed and it went on till the afternoon of the sixth when Delhi reached 706 for 8. Mohinder Amarnath made 185, yet this was not good enough to gain him a place in the England tour for which Bombay players like Nayak were preferred.

But Amarnath did find a place in the side to tour Pakistan in the winter of 1982-83, and it was just as well he did. For in one of the greatest disasters in Indian cricket Gavaskar and India's bowlers were overwhelmed. India emerged with a creditable draw in the first Test, but then lost the second by an innings and 86 runs, the third by ten wickets, and the fourth by an innings and 119 runs. The fifth and the sixth were drawn, with India making 393 for 8 declared in the sixth but this was small consolation.

The Indian bowling was torn to shreds by the Pakistani batsmen. Their principal scores in the first four Tests were 485, 452, 652, 581 for 3 declared. And every time that India batted there was Imran. In quite the most devastating fast bowling ever seen on the sub-continent he took 40 wickets at the staggering low cost of 13.95 each. It is not often that one man can win an entire series and win it so convincingly. But Imran did in this case. His dominance can be judged from the fact that Sarfraz's 19 wickets cost 33.31 which was not much better than Kapil Dev's 24 wickets at 34.62. Imran towered over the series with the ball and no Indian batsman apart from Gavaskar and Mohinder Amarnath faced him with confidence.

Amarnath had been flitting in and out of the Indian side for more than a decade, but this was mainly a reflection on Indian selection policy. Now Amarnath showed that he had the grit and consistency that others lacked. He had been hit on the head by Imran and, still not afraid to hook, he made 584 runs, averaging 73 and scoring three hundreds. Imran regarded him as the best player of pace he had ever seen.

The other Indian batsmen only showed odd moments of defiance and one great batsman failed altogether. Viswanath had been a star before Gavaskar made his debut. Now he failed dismally. In six innings he scored 134 runs averaging just 16.75. His highest score was a 53 in the third Test; that apart he did nothing and to no-one's surprise he was dropped. Clearly India needed to rebuild, find some bowlers to replace Doshi, whose 8 wickets had cost 61 runs apiece, and rebuild the batting around Amarnath. The next tour was to the West Indies and Amarnath had never lacked courage against pace.

By his own standards Gavaskar did not have a great series. But given the ruins amidst which he batted it was another remarkable performance. He was almost as consistent as Amarnath, scoring 434 runs at an average of 48.22. There was just one century, 127 not out at Faisalabad, but he carried his bat there, the first Indian to do so, and that century was his 26th in Tests. He had equalled Sobers, and was three behind Bradman. The innings showed how much the Indians depended on Gavaskar and Amarnath. Apart from Gavaskar and Amarnath, who made 78, no other Indian batsman made over 16 in a score of 286.

But if as a batsman Gavaskar was indispensable, as captain he was very dispensable. The mutterings that had first begun to be heard after the end of the Australian-New Zealand tour now reached a crescendo of criticism. Gavaskar in his heyday had ruffled too many feathers, made too many enemies. They were eager to bring him down. It was hardly his fault if the batsmen, Amarnath apart, could not face up to Imran, or that the bowlers could not take wickets. Even now his record as captain was one of the better ones in Indian cricket. He had won as many Tests as he had lost, six; and the series score was also even, 3–3. But as the Indians were being hammered in Pakistan talk about a change of captaincy had mounted. There were stories of how Gavaskar had become defeatist. He would lose a toss to Imran, return to the dressing-room and announce that he expected the Pakistanis to make a big score on the wicket and seemingly be resigned to it. Indian cricket, eager to find a scapegoat, settled on Gavaskar.

At the end of the Pakistan tour Kapil Dev and some of the other players wanted to cross back into India at the Wagah border by road and fly home from Amritsar. But Bedi, one of the selectors, who had been in Pakistan, told him to fly back with the team. He was being considered for the captaincy. Bedi, himself, had been sacked when he returned beaten from Pakistan; he believed that Gavaskar had been behind both that and his being dropped from the team. As soon as the Indians returned Gavaskar was sacked and Kapil was appointed captain for the tour to the West Indies.

The northern dominance of Indian cricket was now complete.

23

World Champions
1983-85

On 29 March 1983 the Indians met the West Indies in a one-day international at Berbice in Guyana. This was Indian country, the heart of the sugar territory of Guyana, the land of the Indo-Guyanese. By the time this match was played the Guyanese of Indian descent had lost everything. The political power they had aspired to under the leadership of Cheddi Jagan, who had been the first Premier of British Guiana from 1961–64, had gone. They were the majority in the country but the blacks lorded it over them through the ruthless government of Forbes Burnham.

Even their cricket hopes had died long ago. Kanhai, Solomon, Ivan Madray, the heroes who had promised a sporting redemption to make up for a political failure, had also gone. Kanhai had retired but in any case he had not played in Berbice for ten years, between 1961 and 1970. His batting, as he smashed the bowlers, whether his fellow West Indians or those from other countries, had been a balm to wounded political feelings but now even that was not available. The Indian victories of 1971 and 1976 provided some consolation but they had taken place in Trinidad.

Now in early 1983, there was another Indian touring team – a young, somewhat experimental side which looked as if it might resist the West Indians but could never topple them. They had lost the first Test in Kingston, Jamaica, by four wickets, more through inexperience than anything else, drawn the second, and lost the first one-day international at Port of Spain by 52 runs. Even then the Berbice Indians turned up in their thousands to watch the cricketers from 'home'. What they saw was astonishing. For one brief moment the pain and grief of recent years were forgotten.

The West Indies won the toss and Lloyd asked India to bat. So far Gavaskar had done little on this tour. He was no longer the wall he had been in 1971 or 1976, he no longer seemed able to concentrate. The West Indies had four fast bowlers: Holding, Roberts, Davis and Marshall, and normally, particularly in one-day matches, they exercised such a stranglehold that few batsmen in the world could cope with them. They seemed almost to throttle the life out of batsmen.

328

But probably the Berbice Indians inspired Gavaskar that day. He played an innings that their hero and his, Rohan Kanhai – Gavaskar's son was named Rohan – would have been proud of. While Shastri, who was developing into a good one-day opener, kept things steady at one end, Gavaskar scored at almost five runs an over right from the first ball. The opening pair put on 93, then, at 152 for 2, Kapil Dev came in and Gavaskar and Kapil together added 72. Gavaskar went on to make 90 before being run out. Kapil made 72 in 38 balls with 3 sixes and 7 fours. India, who finished on 282 for 5 in 47 overs, had never made so many runs in a one-day match, nor had any side ever made so many runs against the West Indies in this sort of cricket.

Faced with such a huge score some of the self-confidence of the West Indians seemed to dissipate. Kapil Dev, Sandhu, Madan Lal all bowled well, the spinners kept the game tight and, in the end, to the delight of the mainly Indian crowd of 15,000, the West Indies just could not cope. India won by 27 runs. It was India's first limited-overs victory over the West Indies. And though this was not to become apparent for some three months it was a decisive moment in both Indian cricket and world cricket.

In the context of the tour the victory was a brief Indian moment of joy in what was a forlorn struggle. The Indians did not have the bowlers to repeat the glories of 1971 or even the splendid moments of 1976. India drew the Guyana Test, with Gavaskar scoring his only century of the tour, 147 not out, but this was to be his least happy West Indian tour, with an average of 30. The fourth Test in Barbados was lost and the fifth drawn. So the series was lost 2-0. The consolation was that the Indians had put up a better show than most countries were managing against the West Indies at that time when they were in the middle of assuming total domination of world cricket. Twice in the Test series India made over 450 runs in an innings but this was largely the work of Mohinder Amarnath who had an even better series than his one against Pakistan. In nine innings he made only two scores under 40. They were: 29, 40; 58, 117; 13; 91, 80; 54, 116; a total of 598 runs at an average of 66.44. The West Indies players repeated what Imran had said: Mohinder, or 'Jimmy', was the best player of pace they had seen.

But where were the bowlers? Apart from Kapil Dev, who took 17 wickets at 24.94, the other bowlers seemed just cannon fodder for the West Indian batsmen. The Indians had introduced a new leg-spinner, Sivaramakrishnan, but he was no Gupte. In his only Test he bowled 25 overs, gave away 95 runs, and did not take a wicket.

Yet the Indians were not too depressed. The fight back at Trinidad, when Amarnath and Kapil Dev had scored centuries, and the victory at Berbice had made them feel they could turn the tide if not in Tests at least in one-day cricket. Here at least the West Indians looked fallible.

With the third (Prudential) World Cup due to be held in England in the summer of 1983 there was an early chance for the Indians to apply the lessons learnt from Berbice. India's first match, as it happened, was against the West Indies at Old Trafford. The West Indies were firm favourites. They had never lost a World Cup match and India had only won once: against East Africa in 1975. If anything the bookmakers' odds of 66-1 against the Indians winning the Cup seemed not over-generous.

As at Berbice West Indies put India in and they were soon struggling at 76 for 3 but Yashpal Sharma made 89 and India finished on 262 for 8 in 60 overs – their best score in a World Cup match. Rain had delayed the start, so the match became a two-day affair and, at the end of the first day, the West Indies were 67 for 2. The match looked finely balanced but early the next day Vivian Richards was out and the West Indies collapsed – so dramatically indeed that, at one stage, they were 157 for 9 before a last-wicket partnership of 71 between Roberts and Garner began to cause India some anxiety. It was finally broken through a brilliant Kirmani stumping off Shastri and India won by 34 runs. The Berbice victory, the Indians discovered, was not a flash in the pan. It could be repeated.

This Indian victory did not cause much of a sensation, however. The previous day Zimbabwe had beaten Australia and the Indian victory seemed just a hiccup on the way to another West Indian triumph. India met Zimbabwe in their next match and won by 5 wickets, but then lost heavily to Australia and in the return match with the West Indies. The West Indians bowled with fury and India seemed to be beset with her old problems. Kapil was clearly not getting on with Gavaskar, who was unfit for the match against Australia and was dropped against the West Indies – the only time in his career he was not selected when available.

In the hot-house atmosphere in which Indian cricket had always been played, Kapil had been 'offended' by Gavaskar's attitude. Gavaskar had failed in the first two matches and Kapil had in effect told him, 'Come on, put your head down and get your game together.' Soon after that Gavaskar told the manager, 'If you think I am not trying, you are welcome to drop me.' Kapil was 'hurt' by the remark. Kapil had spoken to Gavaskar in English – their only common language – but Kapil's English is not very good and he felt Gavaskar had misunderstood him. But even if he had, should he react like that? Kapil felt Gavaskar had taken words of encouragement as a slur on his integrity.

Certainly in the next match against Zimbabwe the Indians seemed to be falling apart. India, batting first on a difficult Tunbridge Wells wicket, lost Gavaskar on nought and were soon 9 for 4. Kapil Dev joined Yashpal only to see him get out and reduce India to 17 for 5. India had to win this match to keep in touch with Australia and have any chance of qualifying for the semi-finals. Kapil had decided to bat first because he wanted to get a run-rate better than Australia's. As he watched the wickets fall and saw the possibility of an ignominious exit from the competition he felt he was in a trance. But he saw the innings through to lunch, scoring most of his runs through deflections.

After lunch, with the wicket easing, Kapil, realising what a small ground it was, decided to counter-attack. Curran had been the principal Indian tormentor and he took him on, hitting him for sixes into the hospitality tent and some clean hits out of the ground. He hit six sixes in all and with Binny and Madan Lal providing support 17 for 5 became 140 for 8. Then Kirmani joined him and the pair put on 126 for the ninth wicket. Just as the morning had been one for shocks the afternoon was one for records. The stand with Kirmani was a record for the ninth wicket in the competition, Kapil Dev's 175 not out was the highest score made by any batsman in the competition, and the Indian total of 266 was a match-winning one. Even then Zimbabwe put up a gallant fight and India eventually won by only 31 runs.

India now needed to beat Australia and this they did at Chelmsford when, after India had made 247, Australia were devastated by Binny who took 4 for 29, and Madan Lal, 4 for 20. Australia could only make 129 and lost by 118 runs.

For the first time in three World Cups India were through to the semi-finals. The Indians were pleased that their semi-final against England was at Old Trafford, where they had started the campaign with a win over the West Indies. In the other semi-final West Indies met Pakistan, as they had done in two previous World Cups, and everyone in England seemed to be looking forward to a West Indies-England final. But while the West Indies won easily, England found India a very different proposition. The win over Zimbabwe had given India the feeling that their name was on the cup, and they played a classic one-day game. On a slow wicket England were not allowed to break free. They made only 213 and India, requiring just over three runs an over, won quite easily by six wickets.

England blamed herself for preparing a pitch to suit India and many people in England felt that the final would be a bore. Indeed, outside India, the contest was widely seen as a mismatch. Perhaps it would be a nice day – 'Well, let us hope the Indians put up a good show' – but nobody could see the Indians having more than a walk-on role in another West Indian celebration. Few in England had paid any notice to the Berbice win while India's victory at Old Trafford over the West Indies was felt to have been cancelled out by their subsequent loss at The Oval. Indeed since the defeat in the opening match the West Indies had won all their matches by large margins: 101 runs, eight wickets, 66 runs, seven wickets, ten wickets and eight wickets. That one defeat was an isolated example of a great team caught on a bad day.

Lord's on 25 June 1983 looked a picture, 'groomed like a high-born lady', thought *Wisden* and from early in the morning the West Indian bands seemed to be preparing for the victory to come. Lloyd won the toss, asked India to bat and India lost Gavaskar with the score on 2. It continued his wretched World Cup in which he had made 14, 4, 0, 9, 25, 2. With their best batsmen gone what could the Indians expect: perhaps a few blows from Srikkanth, an explosive opening batsman? He played some unorthodox strokes, did make 38 and that turned out to be the highest score of the innings. The West Indian bowling of Roberts, Garner, Marshall and Holding was just too tight and India were all out for 183 with six overs and two balls remaining.

The West Indians in the stands spreading out from the Tavern started celebrating and the English and Australian pressmen in the box cursed the Indians for putting up such a poor show. In fact it seemed no contest when Richards, coming in with the score on 5 for 1, batted with such contemptuous ease that he was soon 33 and the West Indies 50 for 1. He looked in arrogant command but perhaps he was a touch too arrogant. Madan Lal, having been made to look like a net bowler, produced a ball with a bit more bounce, Richards hooked it, mistimed it and Kapil Dev running back took a splendid catch over his shoulder. This was the turning point of the match. Slowly the West Indian steel bands fell silent. Madan Lal removed Haynes and Gomes, three wickets falling for 16 runs in 19 balls. Lloyd came and went, so did Bacchus. From 50 for 1 the West Indies had slid to 76 for 6.

There was a hint of a revival between Dujon and Marshall but then Amarnath, bowling his medium-paced 'wobblers' very shrewdly, removed them both. Kapil got Roberts lbw and it was 126 for 9. However, at Old Trafford the last wicket pair had added 71. Then it was Roberts and Garner, now it was Garner and Holding. Could they thwart India? They put on 14 before Amarnath had Holding lbw and India had won the World Cup by 43 runs. The team nearly everybody had written off had provided one of the greatest upsets in cricket history.

Perhaps the victory was due to West Indian over-confidence, certainly Richards seemed to display a contempt for the bowling that almost invited a fall, but this was a well-drilled Indian team, a team that worked out its plans. It preferred to bat first, make a score, and then use it to pressurise the chasing team. Also there was remarkable cohesion in the team, the leading players being all from the north. Apart from Binny in the match against Australia, in every successful match the Indian man of the match award went to a northern cricketer: Yashpal Sharma, Madan Lal, Kapil himself and, in the semi-final and final, Amarnath. The final itself saw five players from the north and Sandhu, though playing for Bombay, was a Sikh from the north. Neither Shastri nor Vengsarkar, who in the two previous Test matches at Lord's had made hundreds, got a look in.

Most of all it showed how well the Indians now adapted to playing away from home. England was no longer a foreign, hostile country. The growth of the Indian community, the position it held with restaurants, corner shops and newsagents, gave the players a warmth and comfort that made them feel very much at home. In Berbice they had drawn strength from the Indians of Guyana. Now they drew on the prosperity and hospitality of the Indians in England.

West Indians had often seen victories on the cricket field as an affirmation of their nationalism. Indians did not need cricket to define their nationalism; rather, they saw this victory as a sign that they could compete with the best in the world. Apart from their triumphs in hockey, now fast fading from memory, this was the first major world championship that India had won in sport and the emotional satisfaction it provided was immense. 'It shows we can do it,' said Mrs Gandhi, much as if she was opening a new high-tech factory. But if this represented a technological leap forward it also represented a complete about-turn. It is as if a country which had always believed that its energy resources would come from coal had now turned to nuclear power.

India had played its first international one-day match at home less than two years before the World Cup victory of 1983. Even the previous year, 1982, during the tour of England, Raj Singh, the Indian manager, had decried one-day cricket. Now suddenly one-day cricket became the rage and the subsequent history of Indian cricket is the story of one-day cricket challenging the traditional game and quickly, devastatingly, taking over from the traditional game. In 1981 English cricket writers, visiting India for the first time and mistaking the enthusiasm for cricket as an unshakeable loyalty to the five-day game, had predicted that, whatever happened, Test cricket would never die in India. When they returned to India in 1984-85 they found Test cricket not dead but sickly. 'Where are these vast crowds we have been told come to these matches?' the English players kept asking as, outside Calcutta, Test matches were being played to empty stadiums. The English could not reconcile what they had been told about India with the evidence of their eyes which showed that Indians at all levels were excited and enthusiastic for the one-day game, but increasingly cool about Test cricket.

It demonstrated again how cricket in India was tamasha, an entertainment, and how easy it was for Indians to move from one form of entertainment to another. If the Indian victory at Lord's was a great triumph, it was also a defeat. Just as the victories of 1971 had changed public expectations – after that the Indians were expected to win Test matches – so after 1983 Indians, both the public and the Board, concentrated on one-day cricket to the detriment of the real version of the game.

This change began to manifest itself as early as the winter of 1983-84. In India people often talk of fevers and waves. Before a Test match one can get Test fever, and elections are won on waves. In 1984, when Rajiv Gandhi won the election, he is supposed to have benefited from the sympathy wave generated by his mother's assassination. Now, in September 1983, a sort of one-day cricket wave swept the country. India played two one-day internationals against Pakistan, and a day-night match under floodlights in Delhi, the first such match in India and modelled on WSC matches in Australia. India won both the internationals and the day-night match which was looked on by Indians as a splendid new toy. Crowds in large numbers came to these matches; but few came to the Tests that followed.

Bangalore, a city rich in cricket traditions, saw crowds of 15,000, poor by Indian standards, for the first of three Tests against Pakistan. Jullundur, hosting its first Test, did not attract many more despite the fact that it is a Punjab city and most of the Pakistanis are from the other side of the Punjab. Only Nagpur for the third Test attracted sizeable crowds. This suggested that Test cricket would have to extend beyond traditional areas although the lack of Indian spectators may also have been a comment on the series with Pakistan, which was a poor one and never looked like producing a result. At Nagpur India made an effort to win but Pakistan, cautiously led by Zaheer Abbas, were happy to draw. About the only incident of note was Gavaskar scoring his 28th Test century when he made 103 not out in the first Test match. It showed a welcome return to form even if the century came in almost farcical circumstances for, with the match a certain draw, the Pakistanis were reluctant to continue and had to be forced by the umpires to finish the match and ensure that Gavaskar scored his hundred. He was now just one century short of Bradman's record of 29 Test hundreds.

The West Indies series, which followed immediately afterwards, confirmed this growing popularity of one-day cricket. Even before the Test series with the Pakistanis had ended the West Indians arrived. Judging on results this was an overwhelming victory for the

West Indies. They won the six-Test series 3-0 and they won all the six one-day internationals – a complete revenge for the World Cup. But the margin was not quite as wide as this suggests. The first one-day international was won by the West Indians on a faster scoring rate. Played at Srinagar, in the midst of a hostile Muslim crowd that was vehemently anti-Indian, the Indians felt much as the West Indians feel in Port of Spain or Berbice – that they were the away team. The second was won by four wickets when better Indian fielding might have made the difference. After that the Indians were massacred, as the West Indians seemed determined to prove that the Lord's result had been a fluke.

The Tests were also a closer affair than the margin suggests. India lost the first heavily with Greenidge dominant with 194 in a score of 454, and Marshall taking eight wickets in bowling India out for 207 and 164. Vengsarkar with 65 was the only Indian to score a 50 in the match.

But the second, third, fourth and fifth all saw the Indians build up positions which they eventually frittered away. The fight-back was started by Gavaskar. He had come back from the first Test at Kanpur feeling as if all this was getting a bit too much. After his failure in the World Cup there had been talk of retirement and Marshall seemed to add urgency to such talk. He was out to Marshall in both innings for 0 and 7. In the second innings it had been the throat ball, the bat flew from his hand as he tried to play it and the ball spooned to Davis.

Gavaskar came back to his office in Bombay and told Vasu Pranjpe, the closest he has to a cricketing mentor, 'I just didn't see that ball.' At that moment Gavaskar probably came close to quitting. Pranjpe spoke to him about cricket history and about how, in 1932, faced by bodyline, McCabe had taken the attack to Larwood. 'Why don't you do the same, Sunny? That fast bowling has never been contained, it has to be counter-attacked.'

The next Test was in Delhi. Kapil won the toss, the Indians batted. Gavaskar made a shaky start, then counter-attacked so vigorously that in 37 balls he had reached his 50. In the very first over Marshall bowled a bouncer, Gavaskar hooked it for four and felt it was going to be his day. His second 50 was a bit slower, but only compared to the first. His century in 94 balls is one of the fastest in Test history. And, of course, in making the century he had made history. For this was Test century no. 29 and he had now equalled Sir Donald Bradman's record. Gavaskar's example was followed by Vengsarkar, who made 159, and India totalled 464. They had the West Indians in some bother at 173 for 5 but in what would become the pattern for the series Lloyd, batting at no. 7, pulled the innings together. He made 103 and it was India who had to fight hard in the second innings to get a draw.

Gavaskar again led from the front in the third Test at Ahmedabad, the first time a Test was being played there. After the West Indies had made 281 he opened with such ferocity that he made 40 out of the first 50 in only nine overs. Gavaskar had made 90, only ten short of passing Bradman's record, when Holding got him with an unplayable ball – lifting from just short of a length – but by then he had set another record. When he had made 83 his total Test runs had passed 8,114, and this meant he had surpassed Boycott's record as the highest run-scorer in Tests. Now no-one had scored more centuries than Gavaskar and he had scored more runs than anyone else. Gavaskar's innings had given the Indians a splendid platform and they were 174 for 2 at one stage but Kapil Dev had made the fatal mistake of batting second on a new Test wicket, which had never been played on. It grew worse as the match went on. On the third day India collapsed to 241 all out. Fifteen wickets fell on that day, eight Indian, seven West Indian. West Indies were eventually bowled out for 201 but the Indians, left 242 to win on such a pitch, never had the heart for battle. They were bowled out for 103 and lost by 138 runs.

The fourth Test in Bombay was an opportunity set up for Gavaskar to pass Bradman's record, but he now went into a temporary decline, making 12 and 3. Vengsarkar took over as the senior scorer, making exactly 100, and with Shastri and Binny making runs too India reached 463. Again they had a chance to pressurise the West Indians but Richards was dropped twice, he went on to make 120, and Lloyd and Dujon were allowed to add 119 with the two batsmen being given five chances between them. By the end of the West Indian innings at 393 the Indians had dropped nine catches, but the lead was never enough to force a decision. However, when Kapil Dev set the West Indies 243 to get in 156 minutes, West Indian nervousness about the turning ball saw them slide to 68 for 4 before Lloyd and Gomes arrested the slide and earned their side a draw.

The great difference between the two sides was already clear. The West Indies, with their quartet of fast bowlers led by Malcolm Marshall reaching his peak – he took 33 wickets at 18.81 – always had the depth of bowling to test the Indians. The Indians might make a big score, or get away to a good start but the West Indians would always strike back. India would take five, six or seven wickets but could never prevent Lloyd organising a rescue. Kapil Dev was their only Test-class bowler. He did almost as well as Marshall, taking 29 wickets at 18.51, but he could not bowl the West Indians out on his own. The next Test at Calcutta illustrated this very well.

Calcutta was still enthusiastic for Test cricket and a huge crowd came to see Gavaskar pass Bradman's record. But he was out to the first ball of the match bowled by Marshall. India, thanks to

Kapil, made 241 and had the West Indians at 88 for 5 when Lloyd, playing a dour innings, turned the match around. He and Roberts – who made 68 – put on a record 161 for the eighth wicket. India just could not get Lloyd out. He made 161 not out and India, batting as if shell-shocked, were bowled out for 90 and beaten by an innings. A match that had been close for two-and-a-half days became a rout on the fourth.

Eden Gardens now had the facilities to rival the best grounds in the world but the Calcutta crowd was still a volatile one and it took the defeat badly. In particular it felt betrayed by Gavaskar. In the second innings he had made a quick 20, raised expectations that he would score his 30th Test century, but then got out to a very poor shot. There was something feverish about this innings by Gavaskar, like at Delhi and Ahmedabad, but without the control or judgement. He tried an extravagant square drive and was caught off Holding. As wickets were crashing all round him this shot was seen as very irresponsible. At the end of the day's play the crowd started shouting at him and the police had to usher him away from the ground.

The World Cup success was in ruins and, as always happens in India, the hunt was on for scapegoats. The fantastic Indian rumour mills spread a tale of Gavaskar, the deposed captain, not trying in order to spite Kapil Dev. Kapil, himself, did not help with an interview which somehow suggested that players were more interested in money than the game. On the rest day of the Calcutta Test, after he had got out to Holding, Gavaskar had spent time in a Calcutta bookshop autographing copies of his latest book, and some people saw this as evidence of where Gavaskar's loyalties lay. In fact the signing session had been arranged long ago but a crowd eager to find scapegoats could not be reasoned with.

Gavaskar, in turn, was unhappy about Kapil's statement which seemed to imply that he was not giving one hundred per cent effort. At The Oval six months before, Kapil Dev was hurt by what Gavaskar had said. Now Gavaskar was hurt. Gavaskar rang up Mr Salve, then President of the Board, and told him that if Kapil felt he was not giving his best he would not play in Madras. Salve asked Gavaskar to meet him in Delhi. Kapil also happened to be in Delhi and the three met. The meeting did not really resolve anything except that Gavaskar should bat lower down the order. Kapil pleaded the usual excuse: he had been misquoted in the press and agreed to issue a statement.

Even this did not clear matters. Gavaskar was not happy with Kapil's statement and he was beginning to feel that, if cricket was going to be such a bother, he would rather not play in the Madras Test. Mantri, his uncle, suggested he should feign an injury. This was the traditional Indian way, but Gavaskar had never faked an injury and for days he wrestled with the decision. He came to it almost in cliché fashion. One day while he was shaving, always the great moment of truth for any man, he decided he would not quit. Pranjpe had remonstrated with him about his Calcutta performance. As he did so, Gavaskar had put up his hands, 'Please, enough, wait for Madras.'

In some ways the situation was similar to earlier West Indies Tests in Madras, thirty years before. Then, too, the Indians had been wracked by quarrels and collapsed. It was a sign of the growing maturity of Indian cricket that this was now avoided. The West Indies won the toss and made 313, only Dujon passing 50. Gavaskar may have been 'irresponsible' in Calcutta but without him to open the innings Marshall nearly wrecked it. In his second over Marshall took two wickets in successive balls, Gaekwad and Vengsarkar, and when Gavaskar walked out to bat it was as if he was opening. The score was still 0 for 2. The respite Gavaskar had hoped for did not come.

Gavaskar saved the hat-trick and slowly built up his innings. Had Lloyd posted two gulleys he might have gone, but he survived through to the end of the day which saw some unusual crowd disturbances. Madras normally has the best facilities and the best crowd, but on the third day play was held up by half an hour when Davis was hit by a missile and Lloyd took his players off the field. It needed reassurance from the State Governor before he would come back. The West Indians eventually trooped back looking far from pleased.

The next morning they looked even more displeased. After rain had delayed the start by an hour Marshall bowled the first over. His second ball lifted at Gavaskar's face, hit his forearm protector just above the wrist and flew to third slip. The West Indians were already in their established celebratory routine when they realised that the umpire, Swaroop Kishen, the Oliver Hardy look-alike, had given Gavaskar not out. Surprise turned to anger and throughout his innings their attitude to Gavaskar was a mixture of petulance and anger. Such things had never concerned Gavaskar. His ability to cocoon himself in his own time-frame is legendary and now, with India 92 for 5, he found a partner who could stay with him. So far Gavaskar had been the only one holding the West Indians up. Now Shastri joined him.

Shastri was just the partner Gavaskar wanted – not too flashy as a stroke-maker but with enough solidity and patience to make sure Gavaskar did not have to worry about the other end. The rest of the match was now nearly all Gavaskar. Halfway between lunch and tea on the fourth day Gavaskar pushed Davis for a single to reach his 30th Test century. Bradman's record had been passed. None of the West Indians applauded but Gavaskar hardly noticed in the applause of 40,000 spectators. At tea he gave his bat to Dujon, as he had promised to do, and overcame cramp to continue. In the last over of the day Shastri was out, they had put on 170 for the sixth wicket, an Indian record against the West Indies. Gavaskar was 149 not out.

Other records beckoned. But could he make many more? The next day Binny quickly went and so did Kapil Dev. But Kirmani had often proved obdurate in the past and, this being his birthday, he had a special incentive to succeed. There was, of course, nothing left in the match except individual glory and Gavaskar went past 200, then past his own best of 221, Viswanath's 222 and then Mankad's 231. When he had made 236 and the ninth-wicket pair had put on 143 undefeated runs the innings was declared closed.

Towards the end the West Indians almost gave up. Lloyd left the field, so did Richards, and Greenidge was left in charge. Gavaskar cornered all the glory and a car, a prize for his record century, and his innings lifted the spirit of the Indians. Once again India had a champion who was a world beater.

In the past such euphoria may have obscured the overall team performance. But now individual glory no longer redeemed collective failure, merely highlighted it. This partly reflected the higher expectations of Indians brought about by the success of players like Gavaskar. The World Cup had raised it even further and Indians now expected to beat everyone all the time. They did not appreciate that, since the decline of the great spinners, India did not have the quality bowlers who could bowl out Test-match sides.

The averages of the two sides bore this out. Kapil and Marshall were not far apart: average 29 and 33 wickets respectively, averages 18.51 and 18.81. But Marshall was supported by Holding whose 30 wickets cost 22.10 while Kapil's next best support came from Shastri, whose 12 wickets cost 47.25 each.

In contrast the batting differences were not that great. The first three Indian batsmen, Vengsarkar, Gavaskar and Malhotra, averaged 40 or more, the first three in the West Indian side, Lloyd, Dujon, Greenidge, averaged over 50 and while Gavaskar, with 505 runs, had the best aggregate Lloyd with 496 runs, but at an average of 82.66, had played the more crucial innings. Clearly the Indians missed Amarnath who had one of the most dramatic falls ever seen in cricket. Little more than six months before, against the same bowlers, he had averaged 66.44. Now for six innings his average was 0.16. His highest score was a single and he made: 0, 0, 1, 0, 0, 0. Perhaps the sheer pressure of playing such relentless pace from a battery of fast bowlers had taken its toll. But the Indians, who love their legends and intrigue, spun stories about how Mohinder's father had an argument with Kapil Dev and that this made them less determined.

All this was not helped by a growing and very dangerous trend in Indian cricket journalism. Suddenly what had always been a Victorian pursuit, long and at times boring summaries of play, became a copy of the English tabloid press – and this in a country which has no tabloid press. The ghosted player's column from the English tabloids had caught the fancy of Indian editors. It became fashionable for different newspapers to sign up different players. The Indian Board banned the players from writing, and the newspapers then signed up the visiting West Indians. It became common to see Indian reporters follow the visiting players round with tape-recorders to record their precious words. This meant that Lloyd and his men had ample scope in the Indian newspapers to criticise Kapil Dev who grew increasingly frustrated at not being able to reply.

Personality clashes have always been part of Indian cricket, but this style of reporting in what were the Indian equivalents of quality newspapers highlighted it. Kapil versus Gavaskar was now an even bigger story than Merchant versus Hazare or Hazare versus Amarnath or Pataudi versus Borde. There was money involved now, on a scale unimaginable before. Mohinder and Kapil had refused to share the prize money they had won on the England tour of 1982 and the Pakistan and West Indies ones later. Kapil Dev eventually did so but throughout the 1983-84 season Mohinder refused. Later there would be allegations that Gavaskar took a larger share of a match he had arranged than he should have. This was all complicated by the contrasting personalities of Gavaskar and Kapil Dev.

Both Gavaskar and Kapil Dev were dominant characters and they often disagreed. One such disagreement had come at tea-time on the last day of the Madras Test and showed how personal factors worked. Gavaskar was on 229, three short of breaking Mankad's record, and Kapil suggested he would declare as soon as Gavaskar had passed 231. Gavaskar did not see much point in the declaration as there were only 90 minutes left. Who wanted to field now? But in that time Kirmani could have scored a hundred and Gavaskar himself gone on to make a triple-century. So Kapil explained that there was a competition between himself and Malcolm Marshall. They were level on points and he, Kapil, wanted to get another wicket and win the prize. He did not get another wicket but it showed the personal level at which cricket was still played. This personality factor was now to dominate Indian cricket and almost ruin its Test chances.

340

24

Pressure-cooker cricket
1984-86

At the end of the 1983-84 season Gavaskar, having climbed all the personal peaks he would wish to conquer – the world's highest Test run-getter, more Test centuries than any other batsman – wrote a book *Runs 'n Ruins*, his third cricket book. No other Indian cricketer had published so many books and this was testimony to his drawing-power. In contrast to most such books, which can be so anodyne, this one was revealing, contrasting his season of personal triumphs against the collective Indian failure. At the end of it he bemoaned how his personal triumphs had been marred by the fact that the magnificent edifice of June 1983, when India won the World Cup, lay in ruins. 'But tomorrow is always there, or is it?'

The question mark, perhaps inserted belatedly, was fully justified. For the tomorrow that dawned brought more heartache for Gavaskar and Indian cricket. A wretched captaincy tug-of-war – quite the most wretched in Indian cricket history – dominated the game. And this at a time when India's World Cup triumphs meant that the success of the one-day game was always threatening to overshadow, even overwhelm, the traditional five-day contest.

India's disasters against the West Indies had led the Board to set up yet another panel of experts – over the years such reports made quite a thick volume – which recommended that tours should not disrupt the domestic programme for the Ranji and Duleep Trophy matches. This was a sensible suggestion and the report, coming from such distinguished ex-cricketers as Pataudi and Umrigar, received a certain amount of press attention. But such reports are never meant to change anything and this was demonstrated by the fact that the 1984-85 season began with a visit by Australia to celebrate fifty years of the Ranji Trophy. Yet the visitors played no Tests but just four one-day internationals. It was as if it was decided to hold a mile race to celebrate a famous 5,000-metres event. The visit was a disaster for the Indians. They not only lost 3-0 (one match not completed because of rain), but the tour arrangements suggested gaps in the Indian ability to organise such events, with one match being delayed by three hours as the baggage of the Australians and of the Indian team got lost. India

341

and Pakistan had already been approved as joint hosts for the 1987 World Cup and there were mutterings about the Indian ability to host the event.

The Australian visit, however, had been overshadowed by the Indian selectors' traditional response to disaster: change the captain. Gavaskar was back as captain. And after the Australian visit, which the Indian players did not appear to take too seriously, his first task was a three-Test tour of the country where, eighteen months ago, his captaincy had come to a cruel end. This was the last of the yearly Tests against Pakistan, another of those ideas which sound marvellous on paper but usually work disastrously in practice. The previous year, when Pakistan had visited India, few had turned up to watch; this time the crowds in Pakistan were not much bigger and there were the by now usual controversies that have beset almost every tour to that country.

In the first Test at Lahore India saved the match after following-on but Gavaskar was bitter about the umpiring, declaring, 'Despite the best efforts of the Pakistan umpires to favour the home team we have managed to draw the Test and that is a miracle. Before embarking on the tour of Pakistan we expected close decisions but what happened in the Lahore Test was pre-planned and pre-determined.' At one stage a bat and pad decision against Gaekwad, given by umpire Shakoor Rana, led to words between Gaekwad and the Pakistan players and both umpires had to intervene. Gavaskar's words caused a storm but there was no controversy in the next Test where India scored 500, their highest total in Pakistan, while Pakistan replied with 674 for 6 and the match was drawn.

Two days later, while India were nearing the end of their innings in a one-day international, news came of the assassination of Mrs Gandhi. The match and the whole tour were abandoned. Although extraordinary and tragic circumstances had led to this decision there were few regrets that this marked the end of yearly tours between the two neighbours. What had started as a grand idea to make up for eighteen years of neglect had proved futile and unworkable.

Mrs Gandhi's assassination also cast a shadow over England's tour of India. Mrs Gandhi was gunned down in her garden by her own bodyguards within hours of the arrival of the English team in India. As India mourned, the English team withdrew to Colombo where for nine days they practised before returning to India to play five Tests under a revised itinerary.

But there seemed to be a climate of violence in the air. Less than four weeks after Mrs Gandhi's assassination, and on the eve of the first Test in Bombay, Percy Norris, a British diplomat, who the previous evening had entertained the English cricketers, was murdered. The English cricketers were close to coming home, the English press certainly wanted them to, but after discussions with the Foreign Office the tour continued.

England who had suffered a 'blackwash' at home in 1984 against the West Indies, losing all five Tests, were completely outplayed in this first Test. Sivaramakrishnan, playing his second Test, took his first Test wicket with a full toss but then developed into such an ogre that he finished with 12 for 181, six wickets in each innings and, while there was resistance from England in the second innings with Gatting scoring his first Test century, England just could not come to terms with his leg-spin. England left with bruised egos and a burning sense of resentment about the umpiring, as they had done three years ago on the same ground during Keith Fletcher's tour. Indians were not very impressed that every time England lost they complained about the umpiring, and the Indian mood was summed up at the end of the Test, which India won by eight wickets, by the Indian who held up the banner 'Brownwash'. If this was overstating the Indian victory then it was, perhaps, understandable. This was India's first Test victory since that victory against Fletcher's team, 31 Tests previously. And, as so often, the victory seemed to change everything. Suddenly all seemed rosy in the Indian cricket garden.

But nothing in India remains the same for long. Two weeks later, on the fifth afternoon of the second Test in Delhi, the garden had suddenly become barren. Rarely, even in India's turbulent cricket history, can a change have come about so quickly. That final afternoon India, facing a deficit of 111, had got a small lead and, with wickets in hand, the match looked drawn. Then Patil, frustrated at being pegged down, had a swing and was caught and Kapil Dev, having hit Pocock for a six, tried to hit another and was also caught. India were bowled out for 235 and England easily made the 127 runs required for victory. A match that should have been a draw had been thrown away and the Indian anger was concentrated on Kapil Dev.

That evening the selectors met. Chandu Borde, then chairman of the selectors, recalls what happened: 'We debated the point [Kapil Dev's shot] for nearly nine hours and then came to the conclusion that Kapil had indeed shown irresponsibility by playing a poor shot at a psychologically delicate moment for India. I have always believed that the game is bigger than the player, and that no player should take his place for granted.' Kapil was dropped but, as Borde admits, the selectors did not announce 'right away that Kapil had been disciplined. That caused us a lot of embarrassment.' Nor was Kapil told about his sacking but heard of it from friends. What followed was in the great Indian tradition of making a drama out of almost nothing. India quickly polarised into two camps, one for sacking Kapil, the other for retaining him.

With the third Test being held in Calcutta the whole affair acquired an extra emotional edge and, inevitably, politics crept into it. In the meantime Rajiv Gandhi, who had succeeded his mother Indira as Prime Minister, had called for elections and rumours flew about that Kapil Dev was about to contest the elections in support of Rajiv's Congress Party. The press built up the dispute as a simple Gavaskar versus Kapil affair.

In the days preceding the Test Calcutta was a hot-house of rumour and counter-rumour. Before the Test series began the Indian cricketers had played in a single-wicket contest in Varanasi. Kapil had told a journalist how he had been unhappy that Gavaskar had got paid more for the match than he had. This had led Sandip Patil to write an article, in a Marathi cricket magazine which he edited, declaring his loyalty to Gavaskar in somewhat sycophantic terms. N. K. P. Salve, the Board President and then a Minister in the government, summoned both Gavaskar and Kapil to his home in Nagpur to try and understand what the supposed feud was about. Three days before the Test the selectors met again, at the request of Salve, to reconsider the Kapil sacking. It seems Gavaskar was now in favour of bringing Kapil back following Kapil's 'repentance' but the selectors decided unanimously not to reinstate him. They also decided that a young Muslim batsman from Hyderabad, Mohammed Azharuddin, would play instead of Srikkanth whom Gavaskar had preferred as this would allow him to go down the order.

All this was hardly a conducive atmosphere for playing a Test match and the Calcutta game was a dreadful affair with the Indian first innings lasting till the fourth afternoon. Although there had been interruptions from rain – only about four overs were bowled on the second day – there was also some very slow batting by the Indians. So slow that when, after lunch on the fourth day, Gavaskar seemed inclined to carry on, there was some danger of crowd trouble, with sections of the crowd shouting 'Gavaskar, down, Gavaskar out'. One Indian commentator told the BBC that the police had told Gavaskar that if he did not declare there would be a threat to law and order, but Gavaskar denied any such warning. However, after Edmonds had started reading a newspaper in the outfield he did declare. Eight hours were left when England's first innings started.

Inevitably there was a draw and the only bright spark was provided by Azharuddin scoring a century in his first Test. He had already scored 52 not out and 151 against the England attack and now he showed a technique and a class that stamped him out as a major Indian discovery. Particularly strong on the on-side he not only did not seem to have any discernible weakness but an ability to play the sort of long innings that marks out the best of Test cricketers. He batted for 443 minutes over three days interrupted by rain.

Kapil returned for the fourth Test at Madras and once again some of the hysteria that had marked Delhi returned. Indians, it seemed, could not settle on a policy; either they played as if they were in a timeless Test or as if every Test were a limited-overs match. In Madras India played her first innings as if this was a one-day match, England played it like a proper Test and won. Gavaskar tried hard to square the rubber in Kanpur, India made 553 for 8 declared, but on a slow, dead pitch England after some trouble saved the follow-on and the match. They became the first touring side in India to come from behind to win a rubber.

Only Azharuddin's achievements were some consolation for India. He followed his century at Calcutta with another in Madras and then one at Kanpur, the only batsman in history to score a hundred in his first three Tests. In his first five Test innings he made: 110, 48, 105, 122 and 54 not out, easily heading the averages with 109.75 for 439 runs in all. His first-class average for the season just failed to reach a hundred: 99.10. Before his first Test he had scored a 121 and 105 not out in a Ranji Trophy match for Hyderabad against Andhra. (Though Hyderabad is the capital of the state of Andhra, like Bombay, and in deference to its old cricket status when it was the state of Hyderabad ruled by the Nizam, it is allowed to keep its own team.) In a season that had gone horribly wrong India had discovered a hero and an unusual one at that.

Azharuddin was from the Muslim lower-middle-class area of Hyderabad, a city that is largely Muslim dominated. Its twin city Secunderabad, built by the British, is laid out like a Raj city and more upper-class Hindu in character. It is not an area that has produced a great many world-class batsmen. Abbas Ali Baig, the other major Muslim batsman to emerge from Hyderabad, was from the well-off Muslim upper-class. Azharuddin a shy, retiring twenty-one-year-old was very different. Baig's rise reflected a certain cosmopolitan tradition in Indian cricket. He had been discovered playing for Oxford, Azharuddin came from gulli cricket, playing it in the old MLA quarters of the city, where the Members of the Legislative Assembly usually lived. Brought up strictly as a Sunni Muslim by his maternal grandfather, who died just as Azharuddin was about to reach greatness as a cricketer, he was very much in the mould of what Azharuddin himself later described as a tradition of 'pray and play side by side'. Praying five times a day and maintaining all the fasts required by the Muslim faith were always as much part of his upbringing as playing straight as a batsman.

The traditions of gulli cricket saw his natural talent harnessed to a fierce self-belief. By the time he was in the eight standard – about fourteen years old – he was convinced that he was going to become a cricketer. 'I played cricket,' he would later say, 'seriously, never for the heck of it.' So while the rest of India once again debated the old question, whither Indian cricket? Azharuddin returned to Hyderabad a hero. After the Kanpur Test police in ceremonial attire escorted him home from the airport at the head of a throng which held up posters simply reading: Azhar. That is the name he became known by in India, a mark of respect and affection.

But even here there was controversy. Indian newspapers put it about that when Azharuddin got to his hundred Gavaskar was the only absentee from the players' balcony. 'Is Gavaskar jealous of Azharuddin?' asked the magazine *Sunday* in the sort of mixture of innuendo, gossip and bizarre cricket analysis that was becoming all too common. Gavaskar replied that he was standing behind the other players applauding Azharuddin but because he was short he was not seen. It is the sort of thing that might just make the *Spitting Image* comedy show, trivia dressed up as farce, but in India it became a major story, *Sunday* devoting almost a whole page to discussing this issue. The press and the public, feeding on each other, had made Indian cricket a pressure-cooker and Gavaskar was being singed by the heat. His batting in the series was dismal, he averaged 17.5 – his worst ever average in a Test series and his worst Test series since the dismal one against Australia in 1980-81. Ever a meticulous man he studied his problems deeply. Videos of his batting showed him bringing the bat down from third man, feet in the wrong position, right hand too far across in his grip. He knew what was going wrong, he just could not solve it.

However, he was appointed to lead India for the Benson and Hedges World Championship in Australia. He accepted but decided that this would be the last time he would captain the side. This was one of those artificial one-day tournaments that are now quite frequent. It was meant to mark the 150th anniversary of the founding of the state of Victoria. The Indians arrived with no expectations but in an astonishing turnaround, almost as great as the one between the Bombay and Delhi Tests, they surprised themselves as much as anyone else. While the English and the Australian press speculated about an Australia-England final India stole the honours and in great style. In their first match they beat Pakistan by six wickets, after that they beat England by 86 runs and Australia by eight wickets to qualify for the semi-finals. There they beat New Zealand by seven wickets and then, in the final, beat Pakistan by eight wickets. As India lifted the Benson and Hedges Trophy the Indian players gathered around Gavaskar and drenched him in champagne. It was, says his biographer Dom Moraes, not only an act of affection 'but a sort of awe'.

If so this was a very appropriate gesture because, if the defeat by England was partly his fault, then the transformation was almost entirely due to the way Gavaskar led the side. Away from the pressure-cooker world at home, where the expectations of the crowd and the often hysterical writing in the press gave him no respite, he now seemed relaxed, assured, at peace with himself and this communicated itself to his players. His tactical thinking was shrewd. He himself dropped down the order and opened with Srikkanth the blaster, with Shastri as his partner. The tall, elegant Shastri could be an effective nudger and pusher, though earlier in the Indian season he had hit 36 in an over off the left-arm slow bowler Tilakraj. In that innings he hit 13 sixes, breaking C. K. Nayudu's Indian record and two short of Reid's 15 sixes, scoring exactly 200 runs in 113 minutes off 123 balls. Shastri and Srikkanth almost always gave the innings a good start. But most significant of all was Gavaskar's use of Sivaramakrishnan. Leg-spinners are not supposed to survive in this form of cricket but Gavaskar knew they did well in Australia and on the bigger Australian grounds, some of them 90 or 100 yards, it would not be easy to hit Siva, as he was now known, out of the ground. He could only be hit straight or cross-bat and in a quite revolutionary move Gavaskar used the leg-spinner as a strike bowler in the competition. The gamble paid off handsomely. In every one of the six matches he either bowled nine or very often the full quota of ten overs for about 30 runs, taking some two or three wickets – excellent limited-overs cricket bowling.

But the victory could not persuade Gavaskar to stay on as captain. He was going out on a high note and Kapil, who had long since been forgiven for his indiscretion at Delhi, took the team to the desert of Sharjah where a four-nation Rothman's tournament between England, Australia, Pakistan and India was held. The tournament consisted of each team playing just two matches. In the first semi-final India beat Pakistan and then, in the final, Australia (who had beaten England in the other semi-final).

It was the Indian victory over Pakistan that was most remarkable, not only against the old enemy but as evidence of a new spirit in Indian cricket. India were bowled out for just 125, Azharuddin with 47 being the only batsman to come to terms with a damp pitch which turned sharply when spin was applied. Such a score should have been impossible to defend. Pakistan needed to score just two runs an over but the Indians, led by Kapil Dev, bowled so magnificently that Pakistan were bowled out for 87. Kapil Dev, delighted that his return to the captaincy had meant yet another one-day trophy, saw it as the discovery of that long cherished dream 'killer instinct'. He wrote in his autobiography, 'That we won handsomely by 38 runs after being shot out for 125 speaks of the killer instinct in the Indian cricketers that seemed to be non-existent in the past.' Indians had long searched for this much envied American and Australian quality and now seemed to find it in one-day cricket. Between June 1983 and March 1985 India had won five one-day competitions, two of them in Sharjah, the Benson and Hedges World Championship Cricket in Australia and, of course, the World Cup. Willis, sponsors of the one-day game in India, brought out a slim volume hailing India as 'champions of one-day cricket'.

But could the one-day triumphs be extended to the Test matches? Could the killer instinct in the limited-overs matches become part of proper cricket? The answers came a few months later that year at the start of the 1985-86 season and it showed that the much advertised discovery of an Indian killer instinct was a bit like discovering the yeti or the Loch Ness monster: everybody claimed to have glimpsed it, nobody could prove it existed.

The killer instinct remained as elusive as it had ever been.

The lack of it was most evident when, over Christmas of that year, India played Australia in the second Test at Melbourne. By the time that the Indians began their tour, much of the euphoria of March had disappeared. In August 1985, having played little or no cricket since their one-day triumphs, India went to Sri Lanka for a series of three Tests. It was more of a diplomatic initiative, a thank-you gesture to Sri Lanka who had supported the Indian application to hold the World Cup, rather than a proper cricket tour; but the administrators and the players underestimated the Sri Lankans, treating the tour as a sort of picnic and paid the price. Two weeks before the tour was due to take place it was not certain that it would. The Indians were so casual that they arrived in Colombo just the day before the first match and this lack of preparation was worsened by bad umpiring. The Indians lost the second Test, Sri Lanka's first victory in Tests, and with it the series, despite a gallant effort by India to win the third Test. So India had the dubious distinction of providing Sri Lanka with both her maiden Test triumph and a first series victory. In November there followed another defeat in a one-day competition in Sharjah. The Australian visit came shortly after that.

Australian cricket was then at its lowest ebb and in the drawn first Test India had scored a massive 520 but rain made a result impossible. In the second an Indian victory looked certain when the last day's play began. Australia were 45 ahead with two wickets standing. But one of them was that of Allan Border whose defiance of the Indian attack on the fourth day had carried Australia thus far. Now he continued to frustrate the Indians helped by the fact that Kapil Dev followed the most curious of strategies. Faced with a good batsman shielding tail-enders he fell into the trap of letting Border have a single so as

348

to attack the supposedly weaker tail-ender. This is always a dubious strategy and it backfired. Border and Gilbert added 77 for the last wicket of which Gilbert, the no. 11, made 10. This took up five minutes short of two hours. Yet it still left the Indians 126 to win with almost all of the post-lunch session. However, at tea, with India on 59 for 2, the rains came and the match ended in a draw.

Kapil Dev blamed the weather and the umpiring. The Indians believed Gilbert had been caught off the first ball he received but Kapil's bowling tactics were not very clever and, knowing the weather would break, his batsmen had shown no sense of urgency. R. Mohan, writing in *Indian Cricket* saw it as the old weakness of failing to 'drive home an advantage'. India had snatched a draw from the jaws of victory, as so often before.

This inability to push for victory when the chance was there was demonstrated also in the third Test where India made 600 for 4 wickets declared. But having ended the first day at 334 for 1, Gavaskar and Mohinder Amarnath, who put on a record second-wicket partnership of 224 against Australia (at that stage it was the highest for any wicket against Australia) made just 64 runs before lunch on the second day. Kapil Dev had to promote himself to no. 4 to get the score moving and then Azharuddin, belatedly coming into form, played brilliantly for his 59 not out to make sure India scored 600 for the first time outside India. Rain again interrupted this match and in the end it was inept Australian batting on the last day, when twelve wickets fell, that nearly brought the Indians victory. Australia followed-on and they were 115 for 6 with seven overs remaining but held out for a draw.

So Kapil Dev, after twenty Tests as captain, had yet to win a Test and the contrast with his one-day record was becoming glaring. Kapil Dev could and did point to the umpiring and the luck with the weather. In an unusually wet Australian summer every first-class match on the tour, bar one, was interrupted by rain. The only match to avoid rain was the one against South Australia and this the Indians comprehensively won. Kapil could also point to the fact that the Indians probably had the best batting side in the world. The Test averages testified to that. Gavaskar, enjoying his best ever visit to that country, made 352 runs at an average of 117.33. On a previous visit Bradman had described him as an ornament to the game, now he shone there as never before and scored his 31st Test century in Adelaide, Bradman's home town. It ended Gavaskar's longest Test famine. He had not scored a century since January 1984 in Madras, nearly two years and three Test series before this one. Having relinquished the captaincy he seemed to be at peace with himself and his batting. Before the tour he had been reluctant to open; now he formed a perfect partnership with Srikkanth.

Srikkanth, in some ways, was the great success of the tour. Before this he had been seen as an explosive, temperamental opening batsman – good for one-day matches but not quite secure enough for Test cricket. He had made his debut against England in Bombay in November 1981 but had then been in and out of Test sides, only making his place sure through good performances in one-day internationals on the Sri Lankan tour of 1985. But even as he journeyed to Australia doubts about his temperament for Test cricket persisted. Many recalled the moment in his first Test when he wandered out of his ground in a sort of absent-mindedness and was quickly run out. It was the sort of thing you expected in a public park, not in a Test match. But then he could often bring the abandon and sheer fun of a public park very successfully to Test matches and his 97-ball century in Sydney demonstrated that. On the Australian tour he combined such explosive batting with a much needed consistency and finished the series with an average of 72.75.

Srikkanth's success solved the problem of an opening partner for Gavaskar, never satisfactorily answered since Chauhan had been dropped – interestingly, it was ten years previous to this on another Australian tour that Chauhan had come to the fore. It also gave India probably her best batting line-up ever: Gavaskar and Srikkanth followed by Amarnath, Vengsarkar, Azharuddin, Shastri, with Kapil Dev batting no. 7 and virtually no tail. India could always score runs. The problem was still that India could not stop other teams scoring runs as well. The gap left by the retirement of the four great spinners had never been filled and, as it had been for several seasons, the attack was still Kapil Dev, who took 18 wickets at 19.77, and an assorted collection of spinners. On this tour Yadav, who had been around for almost a decade, had one of his best series: 19 wickets at just over 25 runs apiece, but then Sivaramakrishnan, of whom so much was expected, proved extremely disappointing and became yet another young promise that had not bloomed.

India's lack of support bowling for Kapil Dev was further exposed in a one-day competition in Sharjah. In the final India met Pakistan and seemed to have the match under control but brilliant batting by Javed Miandad and some inept bowling by Chetan Sharma led to a sensational defeat. Pakistan needed a four to win off the last ball. Sharma prevented that but conceded a six. It was Pakistan's first major success in limited-overs competitions and made Miandad an immediate hero.

It was against this background that India came to England in the first half of the summer of 1986. They had toured in the first half of 1982, so should have come in the second half but with two tours scheduled for the winter of 1986-87 the Indian Board wanted their players fresh at the start of the season. It seemed as if the Indian Board had once again condemned its players to the most unfavourable conditions – in the traditionally wetter part of the summer when spinners can usually do little.

But for once the Indian Board got it right. More through luck than judgement, true, but it worked. The turning point of the tour came in the match against Northampton in early June. At this stage the Indians had lost a third of their playing time due to the weather and there was renewed talk of friction between Kapil Dev and Gavaskar about remarks made by Kapil Dev in a new book. On the Saturday of the match, while the rain teemed down, only eight balls were bowled, and the Indian manager, Raj Singh, called the press in for a hurried conference in the Indian team coach. Both Kapil Dev and Gavaskar were present and their feud, which at times had more often been in the fevered imagination of the Indian press, was laid to rest.

The next day the Indians showed why they were rated so highly as a batting side. Amarnath scored a hundred before lunch, Azharuddin also hit a hundred and then Kapil Dev, helped by Sharma and Binny, bowled out Northants, one of Kapil's old counties and one of the best batting sides in the country, for 118. Northants, following-on, saved the match, as Kapil Dev spared himself and gave his other bowlers practice. But the game had proved that, in English conditions, Indian seam bowling could prove potent against modern English batsmen. In the Northants rout of 118 the Indians had not bowled a single over of spin. In the second innings when Northants recovered spin had been used.

It was this lesson that was to prove invaluable a couple of days later when the first Test began at Lord's. England had come back battered and bruised from a tour of the West Indies. Beaten 5-0, many of their batsmen were shell-shocked after facing West Indian pace. Nevertheless England went into this Test oozing with confidence. India had only ever won one Test in England, at The Oval in 1971, and Gower's team had won in India in 1984-85. India would probably bat deep and long but, Kapil apart, who could bowl England out?

For three days of the first Test this seemed to be the case as England made 294 and India replied with 341. The Indian batting promised more than it delivered and the lead of 47 was almost entirely due to a quite marvellous 126 by Vengsarkar. At one stage, with Vengsarkar and Azharuddin going well, India were 232 for 3, but this soon became 264 for 8 and Vengsarkar on 81 looked as if he would be stranded. But More, a combative wicket-keeper batsman from the same cricket school as Vijay Manjrekar, gave him support and so did Maninder Singh at no. 11 and Vengsarkar reached his century – the first overseas batsman to score three hundreds in Tests at Lord's. Boycott,

Compton, Hutton, John Edrich and Hobbs had done so but, of course, for England.

The match turned on the morning of the fourth day. The Monday sports pages had predicted a boring draw. England were 8 for 0, and no other result seemed possible. But that morning Kapil Dev removed Gooch, Robinson and Gower for one run in 19 balls. After that England were always struggling and at 5.40 were all out for 180, leaving India 134 to get and the whole of the last day in which to get it. Seam bowling had done the early damage which was then completed by the left-arm spin of Maninder Singh. A Sikh, like Bedi, though leaner in build and not quite as mercurial in temperament, Maninder had made his debut, at the age of seventeen, four years previously, against Pakistan. After that he had been in and out of Test teams and was not selected for the tour of Australia. It was the decline there of Sivaramakrishnan that provided Maninder with his chance to tour England and he seized the opportunity on that fourth afternoon at Lord's. In 20.4 overs he took 3 for 9, and no English batsman faced him with confidence.

The next day India had a slight attack of nerves as they went for their first victory at Lord's but Kapil Dev came in and took 18 off one over from Edmonds, hitting three fours before pulling him into the Grandstand for a six to win the match. It was his first victory as captain, and India's first at Lord's.

In the past Indian defeats had led to confusion and chaos, but now India's victory led to English muddle. Gower was sacked as England's captain and replaced by Gatting. Many felt that Gatting's sergeant-major style was more suited than Gower's laid-back approach. England were already without Botham, who had admitted that he had smoked cannabis and was suspended from cricket between 29 May and 31 July. The day before the Test Gower was injured so for the first time since 1978 England went into a Test without either Botham or Gower on a ground where they had a poor record of late and with a pitch which even the Leeds groundsman accepted was not very reliable.

India had the confidence that comes from victory and this was not dented when, first, Amarnath and then on the evening before the match Chetan Sharma withdrew due to injury. Chetan, like Kapil also from Haryana, is a bustling, aggressive cricketer – at times a bit too aggressive, and in the previous match at Leicester he had been the subject of a brief police enquiry when he was alleged to have punched an over-eager autograph hunter in the face. He had taken six wickets at Lord's and appeared to have achieved a certain mastery over Gatting, clean bowling him twice. But the Indians were not fazed by his loss. Madan Lal, playing for Ashton in the Lancashire League, was called up and his inclusion was to prove significant. It showed what victory and confidence can do. When in 1952 after the Leeds debacle Mankad was called up, also from League cricket, that was a sign of desperation. Now in very different circumstances and with India dictating terms this seemed a challenging move.

Even then England, outwardly at least, were confident. This was boosted by a press which saw the Lord's defeat as an aberration. They accepted that England were inferior to the West Indies but the thought that they were inferior to India was anathema. After all, in more than fifty years of Test cricket India had never won outside London and the summer of 1985 had been a glorious one for English cricket when Australia had been routed. At the end of the Lord's Test the BBC Cricket Correspondent, Christopher Martin-Jenkins, had been confident that England would win at Leeds and at the end of the first day's play most of the tabloid press was already hailing Gatting as the rejuvenator of English cricket.

As the English press saw it the Indians had made all the mistakes. Kapil had won the toss and batted when the recent Headingley tradition was to field. Then India had made 235 for 8, a steep decline from 203 for 4. Twenty-four hours later the newspapers were announcing that the English revival was a mirage. That Friday's play was one of the most dramatic in Indian cricket history, wiping away some of the awful memories of Indian collapses in England – even to some extent the 0 for 4 at Leeds in 1952.

India made 272. England went into bat and now Kapil Dev's decision to call in Madan Lal was vindicated. He bowled Slack and Chris Smith in quick succession, two obdurate county openers who were not expected to fall in that fashion. By lunch England were 41 for 4. That lunch-time I was a guest of a firm of stockbrokers in one of those entertainment boxes that are now so much part of the Test scene in England. Trueman and Graveney – who had, of course, played in the Leeds Test of 1952 – joined us and the look of disbelief on their faces told the story. This became even more pronounced through the afternoon as Binny, who had removed Lamb before lunch, now got rid of Gatting, Pringle and Emburey – four wickets for 17 runs in 37 balls. England were 63 for 7 and might have been in even worse trouble had Athey been run out. But he survived and helped England save the follow-on. But he could do little about the innings. England were all out for 102, Binny, who had been treated as a bit of a joke bowler by sections of the English press, finishing with 5 for 40, Madan Lal 3 for 18 and India had a lead of 170.

English batting had been humiliated before, but by Australia, by the West Indies. English crowds, at least the ones outside London, were still not used to the idea that India, Pakistan or New Zealand could do this with impunity. The last rout in England at the hands of the Indians, Oval 1971, was at the hand of Chandrasekhar. It could be explained in terms of the mystery of Indian spin. But to be routed by Indian seam and by Roger Binny was almost incomprehensible. As I sat that day amongst the urbane stockbrokers and their clients I could feel the first stirrings of a profound realisation of the state of English cricket and the shifting balance of world cricket. It was probably on that afternoon that the phrase much used now, 'there are no easy Test matches', was born. Later I wandered around the ground and could sense a real sense of anger amongst the Yorkshire crowd. Not long ago they would have dismissed these Indians as not worthy of serious cricket attention. Now the Indians provoked almost the same feelings as the Australians. In the afternoon when India batted the crowd, out of frustration and a desire to make up for English deficiencies, started indulging in the Mexican wave made popular during the World Cup then going on in Mexico. This wave effect was created by the synchronised waving of arms and sections of the crowds alternately rising and sitting. It was so astonishing for the Indians that Azharuddin lost his composure and fell lbw. Raj Singh, the Indian manager, was moved to protest that not even the noisiest of Indian crowds behaved like this.

But no amount of Mexican waving could save England. Indian batting on a pitch very dubious by now had its problems; 29 for 3 became 70 for 5 but Vengsarkar, who had made 61 in the first innings, showed how well he could bat even on a bad wicket. He was known to the Indian team as Chota Nawab, junior Lord, or colonel, and he showed he could command a wicket like no-one else.

He was 33 not out on Friday evening, preventing an English breakthrough. On Saturday morning he quite dominated the bowling. As at Lord's he protected the tail while scoring his hundred: 102 in an Indian innings of 237. Two figures show his mastery. In that Indian innings the next highest score was 31. And in the entire match no other batsman, Indian or English, reached 40. The match was virtually over on Saturday night as England, set 408 to win, were reduced to 90 for 6 by Maninder and Shastri. They had discovered that not only was the bounce unreliable but the pitch was taking spin as well. Only 75 minutes were needed on Monday to bowl England out for 128 and complete an Indian victory by 279 runs.

A 'brownwash', winning all three Tests, was thwarted at Edgbaston though this was partly due to a reappearance of India's old failings. On the first morning England, having been 0 for 2, were 88 for 4 when Gatting was dropped. He edged the ball, it looked like going to Gavaskar at first slip but More the wicket-keeper dived across to take it, obscured his vision and the catch was spilled. Gatting went on to make 183 and England 390. India, showing the depth of their batting also made 390 and then bowled out England for 235. Requiring

236 to win India were well placed at 101 for 1, but good bowling by Edmonds turned the match England's way. Then came a stoppage of 48 minutes for bad light and rain. This meant that India did not have the time to go for the runs and the match was left drawn with India on 174 for 5.

If this last Test was a trifle disappointing for the Indians, the overall gains from the tour seemed immense. The strength and depth of the Indian batting had been amply demonstrated. Certainly in English seaming conditions they had the seamers, Chetan Sharma with 16 wickets was the leading wicket-taker while Maninder seemed to improve with every match. He headed the Test averages with 12 wickets at 15.58. At last, it seemed, a successor to Bedi had been found. Above all there was the captaincy of Kapil Dev. A winning captain can do no wrong and the grumbles about his tactical appreciation of the game disappeared. Wise heads nodded and applauded his ideas.

India's choosing to bat first at Leeds had seemed a mistake, but long before the end of the match it was being hailed as a bold, winning move. India finished the short tour on a high note, beating Yorkshire for the first time ever. If this meant little, given the current quality of cricket in that county, it meant India had gone through an English tour without a first-class defeat. There were only two defeats, both in one-day non-first-class matches. One was against England in a one-day international, but so comprehensive had been India's victory in the first one-day international that they won the Texaco Trophy. India had never had such a successful tour of England. A new dawn seemed to be beckoning Indian cricket.

25

One-day revolution and after
1986-89

In the three years since 1986 much has happened to make what had perhaps looked like a new dawn, leading to a glorious sunny day, turn into very murky, overcast weather where the odd, dazzling ray of victory has been more than clouded by depressing defeats. It is the old Indian cricket story: one step forward, two back.

This began almost as soon as India returned home from her triumphs in England. They were expected to prove too strong for the Australians, but in the first Test they were nearly made to follow-on – they just saved it – even though this was completely overshadowed by what happened on the final day.

India were set 348 to win and as in most of these run-chases since that historic win in Trinidad Gavaskar played a major part. He made a quite superb 90 and when the final twenty overs began India needed 118 with seven wickets in hand. But then Gavaskar was out, the later batsmen panicked but with Shastri providing a cool head India had 30 balls in which to score 18 runs with 4 wickets in hand. Now two wickets fell in one over, soon after another fell and when the last over began India were 344 for 9 with Shastri on strike.

He got a two off the second ball, a single off the third which meant the scores were level. Maninder Singh defended the fourth but was lbw to the fifth. For the second time in 1,052 Test matches, there was a tie. And for the second time Australia had been involved. This was very different to the first tied Test in 1960–61. That had been a fluctuating match, now the West Indies, now Australia dominant. Here Australia had dominated three days, India the last, and if anything the Indians felt they should have won on the last afternoon but had let the match slip away. Maninder also questioned his lbw decision, claiming he had hit the ball, and this kept the pot of controversy, which had been simmering ever since the first one-day international ten days before the Test, bubbling away.

That controversy had involved Sunil Gavaskar. The selectors announced that he would be dropped from the first one-day international as they wanted to give other possible one-day openers a chance to stake their claim for the coming World Cup. The selectors had debated this

356

long and hard and finally decided by a 3–2 majority. It was not an ignoble idea. Gavaskar, who was thirty-seven, could not go on for ever and had never really cared for the one-day game. But it was so badly handled that it raised a storm of protest. Borde, as chairman of selectors, had announced the decision and the public anger was vented on him. He received obscene telephone calls, there were threats to march on his house in Pune, as Poona is now known, and 'gherao' it – a very effective Indian form of demonstration where a vast throng of people surrounds a house or factory and effectively blockades it, sometimes for days or even weeks. The selectors protested that Gavaskar had not been dropped but was only rested. Nobody believed them and in the end they gave way and reinstated him.

The euphoria created by the tied Test obscured this earlier controversy but it could not mask what was now a grave and somewhat ironic problem for India. India bowled best in English conditions. Outside England they could not bowl sides out. In that sense the victory in England, far from being a platform for further success, was an aberration where in helpful conditions the seamers had proved match-winners. In India the seamers did nothing, the bowling was dominated by the spinners, with Yadav, who had not played a Test in England, heading the averages against the Australians but his eight wickets had cost an astronomical 44.87 runs each while Maninder had taken five wickets at 70.40 each. India played two more Tests against Australia and while their batsmen scored runs so did the Australians.

For a time it seemed that India might not be able to bowl out even Sri Lanka. They were the next visitors in this the busiest Test season for India with three countries touring India: Australia, Sri Lanka and Pakistan. In the first Test in Kanpur, Sri Lanka made 420, their highest total against India. India replied with 676 for 7, their highest-ever and the highest in any Test in India. Gavaskar scored his 34th, and what proved to be his last, Test hundred, which was all the more sweet as it came in the town where his wife Pammi, who had been a big influence on him since their marriage, had grown up. Azharuddin, who had not scored a hundred since his three in succession against England in his first three Tests, now scored 199. But with one day abandoned due to fog and rain the Indian first innings was not yet over when the match ended.

In the next two Tests the Indians did rediscover their spinning fingers but that was largely because they were played on very different pitches as the description 'sporting' suggests. The one at Nagpur turned from the first day, Yadav took 5 for 76, his best figures in Tests, and with Maninder providing support Sri Lanka were bowled out for 204 before tea on the first afternoon. Sri Lanka did not have the bowlers for the wicket and India, relishing the conditions, made 451 for 6 declared,

Amarnath 131, Vengsarkar 153, while Gavaskar, who owing to fever had batted at no. 5, scored 74 in only 79 balls. The need was for quick runs and he showed he could score as quickly as anyone. The second Sri Lankan innings again saw Indian spin dominant. This time Maninder took 7 for 51, his career best figures, while Yadav provided support. Sri Lanka, bowled out for 141, were beaten by an innings and 106 runs.

India also won the third Test at Cuttack by an innings. This time India batted first and Vengsarkar, on a wicket that was virtually unprepared, showed, as at Headingley, what a wonderful technique he possesses. While only one other batsman passed 50 in the entire match, Kapil Dev with 60, Vengsarkar made 166, his highest Test score. India totalled 400, Sri Lanka collapsed to Maninder and Kapil Dev who, exploiting the wicket, bowled at slow-medium pace and produced shooters at will. One such shooter bowled Ratnayake, giving Kapil his 300th Test wicket and he joined Botham on the 'double' of 300 wickets and 3,000 runs in Tests. With Shastri also taking 4 for 11 in eight overs, the match finished minutes after lunch on the fourth day. It was India's first series win at home since the defeat of Fletcher's England side in 1981–82.

The Sri Lankan visit, however, gave clear indication that, unless wickets were deliberately prepared for spinners, Indian bowlers would struggle to bowl sides out twice. This was soon to be emphasised as India prepared to receive Pakistan. Any series with Pakistan is emotive. This one had overlays of political considerations with General Zia using the third Test as a cricket lever to put political pressure on the Indian government. Cricket for peace was the slogan.

As it happened, that match saw the need for some urgent cricket diplomacy when, on the third day, Imran, the Pakistan captain, claimed that the sprinkling of sawdust on the field to dry it had changed its nature. Imran refused to carry on with the match and the umpires abandoned the third day's play. There were other incidents in the series and, as *Wisden* noted, some of Imran's colleagues 'were guilty of over-dramatisation on the field. Their orchestrated appealing, and various other practices designed to put the umpires under severe pressure, gave an unhappy aspect to their cricket.' The Pakistani behaviour had an impact on the crowds which did not come out of this very well, particularly those at Ahmedabad and Bangalore where, often reacting to theatrical Pakistani behaviour, they pelted the players with all sorts of missiles and rubbish.

Some of this reflected the overheated atmosphere in which the Tests were being played, and the fact that the first four Tests were all drawn did nothing to reduce the emotional temperature. The feature of those Tests were shirt-front wickets with India scoring 400 in one or other of the innings in all but one of the Tests. Pakistan did not score quite so heavily but India never looked like bowling them out twice. Almost in frustration the fifth Test was played on a deliberately under-prepared wicket. The ball turned sharply on the first day and Maninder, making the most of it, took 7 for 27. Pakistan were bowled out for 116, their lowest-ever score against India. India looked well placed at 119 for 4 with Vengsarkar, who made 50, once again showing how to bat on a wicket which other batsmen found nightmarish. But as soon as he was out the rest of the batsmen panicked and, as the wicket became progressively worse, tried to hit their way out of trouble. India collapsed to 145 all out. Even though the wicket continued to deteriorate, Maninder did not bowl quite as well in the second innings and Pakistan were allowed to make 249, the last-wicket pair adding 51 crucial runs. India needed 221 to win.

Now the wicket was so helpful to the bowlers that even an off-spinner could bowl bouncers. It required technique and patience. The Indians had the technique but not the patience, apart from Gavaskar who was the only one to combine both qualities. In the previous Test in Ahmedabad he had become the first batsman to score 10,000 runs in Tests, a delicate late-cut taking him to this exclusive mark. Retirement beckoned and, in what turned out to be his last Test innings, he showed all the qualities that had made him a batting legend. While nobody in the entire match had passed 50 – Vengsarkar was the only other batsman to reach it – and the highest Pakistani score was 47 – Gavaskar batted as if he would score his 35th Test century. At the end of the fourth day's play he was 51 not out in an Indian score of 99 for 4 with Srikkanth, Amarnath and Vengsarkar out. Next morning he made only three in an hour but by lunch he had reached 82, skilfully rotating the strike as he lost partners. Nothing seemed to shake his concentration and it was the antics of the Pakistani players and, ironically, the Indian crowds that broke it. After an appeal against him had been rejected the Pakistanis put on such a show of petulance that the crowds showered missiles on to the ground and play was held up for ten minutes. Gavaskar who had shut himself off from the world was suddenly reintroduced to it. His concentration was broken. For 5 hours 23 minutes he had defied the Pakistani bowlers; soon after the restart, when he reached 96, he got a ball that kicked off a length and he was caught at slip.

He had almost conjured up a victory, but India fell short by 16 runs. Imran celebrated this first series victory in India and only the third in any series outside Pakistan, while India could only rue some slap-happy batting in both innings for the defeat. If only one batsman had stayed with Gavaskar in that final innings it might have been a different story.

However, the overall difference between India and Pakistan was more than the margin of 16 runs. Pakistan had won the one-day international series 5–1, and even the one Indian victory had been due to a colossal blunder by Abdul Qadir who ran himself out off the last ball going for a second run. Had he been content with a single Pakistan would have won that match as well. His run-out gave India the match because they had lost fewer wickets. Ever since the Miandad six at Sharjah in April 1986, India had lost its traditional dominance over Pakistan in one-day cricket and this seemed ominous for the country's chances of retaining the World Cup.

For the first time the World Cup was to be held outside England. India's victory in 1983 had made this possible, another breakthrough which Indian cricket could claim. India and Pakistan had successfully got together to co-host the event with group matches in both countries, the semi-finals in Lahore and Bombay, and the final in Calcutta. India and Pakistan were in different groups and the script suggested they should meet in the final at Eden Gardens.

But such scripts have a habit of going wrong and there were plenty of sceptics who thought that India and Pakistan could never even stage the play. Some in England, particularly the tabloid press, resented having to go to the sub-continent for the World Cup. Their attitude was not dissimilar to Ian Botham's comment after a tour of Pakistan that he would not send his mother-in-law there, and pre-Cup publicity highlighted all the things that could go wrong. The BBC refused to televise the matches, only relenting for the final, but then England were involved.

Yet in a quite remarkable display of organisational skill the Indians and the Pakistanis proved the sceptics wrong. *Wisden* wrote, 'The fourth World Cup was more widely watched, more closely fought and more colourful than any of its predecessors held in England.' The travelling involved was immense, it was like holding a tournament in Europe, one match in Vienna followed by another in Paris. But it worked. The first four matches set the tone. Sri Lanka nearly beat Pakistan, England made 35 in the last three overs to beat the West Indies, Zimbabwe came within three runs of beating New Zealand, and India lost to Australia by one run.

That Indian defeat showed that the maturity which they had displayed in winning the World Cup in 1983 was no longer there. Requiring 270 to win India needed 15 runs from the last four overs with four wickets in hand but contrived to lose. And while India picked themselves up marvellously after that and won their remaining matches to head their group, there was always the fear that in a run-chase the wheels would come off the chariot. However, as India qualified for the semi-final in Bombay as the head of the group, just what they wanted since this meant avoiding a semi-final with Pakistan in Lahore, this fear appeared to have been exorcised.

As in 1983 their semi-final opponents were England. In the 1983 competition India had never lost batting first, their two defeats had come chasing runs. But in 1987 Kapil was more inclined to chase runs, putting the opposition in when he won the toss. This is what he proceeded to do now, thinking the ball might swing. It did not swing, and India was forced to rely on their spinners. However, in a reversal of what had taken place in two previous Bombay Tests against India, England swept away the spinners, Maninder and Shastri, and prospered to make 254. As India began batting, news that Pakistan was losing at Lahore was coming through but instead of encouraging the Indians this seemed to make them reckless, as if the greatest danger to their hold on the Cup had gone. India lost Gavaskar early, Kapil could not resist trying to slog the ball out of the ground, and the match was lost by 19 runs. India's reign as one-day world champions was over.

What made this result strange and unexpected was that India had the most brilliant batting of the tournament but evidently not the most effective. As the semi-final demonstrated all too often the Indian batsmen were dictated to by the crowds demanding spectacular hitting, and with sponsors awarding large sums of money for fours and sixes there was a brittleness that England mercilessly exposed.

The final in Calcutta was an England-Australia affair. In Australia, a final, say between India and Pakistan, might have produced sparse crowds. But Calcutta was full for this final and the crowd quickly adopted Australia as the home team; and Australia, to their delight, won. The enthusiasm of the crowd and the organisational skill won over even some of the sceptics. India may not have retained the World Cup but, contrary to many English and Australian doubters – or, not to put too fine a point upon it, the mistrust of white cricket officialdom and press – the sub-continent had organised a superb World Cup.

India took some comfort from the praise that now flowed in but this was small consolation for losing the World Cup, the winning of which had made Indians feel that, at last, they were at cricket's top table. The defeat should have been a moment for introspection, for a cool look at the state of the game in the country and a considered appraisal of whether it meant the country was exiled from the top table or merely temporarily excluded. But defeat is nearly always a bad moment for sober judgement. As Tacitus said, 'Success has a thousand fathers, defeat is an orphan' and the Indians took it out on the man who seemed to have made them a cricket orphan. Kapil Dev had both won the World Cup and lost it. Now only the loss was remembered. Even the most comprehensive Indian victory ever in a Test series in England, just eighteen months ago, was forgotten too while the failures were listed in an orgy of masochism: failure to beat Australia, loss to Pakistan, only one series victory at home and that against Sri Lanka. Kapil had looked like making India the Rome of cricket but now her rank was just above Sri Lanka, the Guatemala of international cricket.

Few people seemed to recall that, before Kapil, India had only ever won one World Cup match and that against East Africa and had even lost to Sri Lanka, not then a Test country. Kapil was paying the price for promising too much, arousing too many expectations. He had to go. So for the second time Kapil Dev was sacked as captain. In the past such sackings had often ruined a cricket career, as with Wadekar, but if Indian cricket could do without Kapil as leader it could not do without Kapil as bowler.

Ravi Shastri had looked the likely successor. He was vice-captain, Gavaskar saw him as a future captain as did Kapil Dev himself in his autobiography, written after the English tour when Kapil probably thought he was safe as captain for some time. Shastri, a Brahmin, brought up in Bombay, but originally from the port of Mangalore in Karnataka in south-western India, was also India's answer to Imran, at least in looks and popular sex appeal. Bombay's gossipy film magazines were always 'marrying him off' to various film stars. Perhaps this aspect of his character worried the selectors, because for the West Indian visit that followed Dilip Vengsarkar was appointed captain.

Vengsarkar's rise to the captaincy not only meant the end of Kapil's second coming but also the end of another great era in Indian cricket. Kapil Dev was losing the captaincy just as Gavaskar was bowing out of first-class cricket. In August 1987 Gavaskar had played for the Rest of the World against the MCC in the match to celebrate the bicentennial of the Marylebone Cricket Club. The man who had scored more Test hundreds than any other batsman had never scored a hundred at Lord's and everyone, barring perhaps the MCC bowlers, wished he would now make up for it. It was recognised that, at thirty-eight, this would be perhaps his last chance to play at Lord's. The Indians were not due to visit England again until 1990 when Gavaskar would be forty-one.

He came in to bat at 2.15pm on the Friday after the MCC had declared at 455 for 5. The first ball Marshall bowled to him was a no-ball, the second ball was legitimate, struck him low and hard, most people thought it was lbw. Umpire Harold Bird did not. Perhaps Gavaskar was lucky, we shall never know.

But that is the sort of luck greatness conjures up. For what followed was a classic Gavaskar innings and just what the crowd wanted. In a match that reminded us how cricket used to be played, and still can be when the deadly rivalry of petty nationalism is removed, we saw some fine bowling and some great batting on a perfect batting wicket. In this wealth of batting on display, Gavaskar played the outstanding innings. By the Friday evening, when he was 80 not out in a score of 169 for 3, it was clear Gavaskar had his sights set on his first Lord's hundred. That evening in a committee room near the players' dressing-room at Lord's he declared that he would play no more Test cricket. He would play in the World Cup and then retire. He was asked why he had never scored a century at Lord's but he could give no explanation. But with a twinkle in his eye he reminded the press that there was the next day's play to come and sure enough on this quite glorious Saturday, with Lord's looking a picture, he went to his hundred. He seemed on course for a double-hundred but on 188 was caught and bowled by Shastri. Now, it seemed, all that he wanted to achieve had been done. It would have been fitting had he bid good-bye to cricket at the World Cup final in Calcutta but when India lost in the semi-final in Bombay he announced his retirement then from all first-class cricket.

A few months later Gundappa Viswanath also announced his retirement from first-class cricket. He had played no Test cricket since the disastrous Pakistan tour in 1982–83 but continued playing for Karnataka. It was very appropriate that these two great little men of Indian cricket, once linked through their promise for the future and now through marriage, should have bowed out together. Almost twenty years ago, in 1969, Viswanath had made a spectacular entry into international cricket with a century against Australia in his first Test. Then he seemed destined to become the dominant Indian batsman of his generation. Two years later Gavaskar had emerged and while he had quickly overhauled Viswanath the two players' careers had gone in tandem until Gavaskar had proved his greater staying power and determination. In the end their Test careers had diverged, with Gavaskar becoming the most prolific batsman in Test history: 10,122 runs at an average of 51.12 compared to Viswanath's 6,080 runs at an average of 41.93. But their Ranji Trophy figures were similar. Gavaskar's 5,335 runs, Viswanath's 5,653 runs, except that Viswanath's runs had come from 93 matches and with an average of 45.95 while Gavaskar had played in only 66 matches and averaged 70.19. Figures can be misleading but this statistic does indicate the difference between these two heroes of Indian cricket.

The choice of Vengsarkar as captain was an odd one. His ability as a batsman was not in doubt, but even in Bombay he had only recently been thought of as captain and that not too very highly. The appointment was more in line with change for change's sake. It meant that India had moved from an extrovert, larger than life man who was loved by millions of India's cricket followers, to an intense, introverted figure who was respected but provoked no adulation. In a sense Vengsarkar was another in a long line of Bombay Maharashtrians, like Wadekar, who gave the impression that they had a chip on their shoulder and rarely found it easy to express their feelings or communicate outside a closed, generally Maharashtrian circle. Such insularity is not confined to Maharashtrians, of course, various Indian groups display it; Vengsarkar merely provided the Maharashtrian example. While Kapil motivated those round him by his character and his personality, Vengsarkar could only do so by his batting example and it soon became clear that this was not enough.

On the face of it he did not have a bad first series. India drew the four-Test series with the West Indies 1–1. Given that in the previous three seasons the West Indies had twice beaten England 5–0, both at home and away, and beaten Australia 3–1 in Australia this looked a very good result. But as *Wisden* commented it was not a 'true index of the strength of the teams'. 2–1 would have been more appropriate and the solitary Indian victory came in the last Test on a wicket that made a 'mockery of Test cricket'.

Vengsarkar started his first series as captain inauspiciously. Choosing to bat on a damp wicket in Delhi, the Indians were bowled out in 145 minutes for 75, their lowest-ever score against the West Indies. Kapil and Sharma then bowled the West Indians out for their lowest-ever score against India, 127, and India, led by 102 from Vengsarkar, made 327 in the second innings to leave the West Indies a target of 276. The wicket was now helping spin, India had three spinners (which was the reason why Vengsarkar batted first), but Vivian Richards played so brilliantly that the West Indies won by five wickets.

Rain and some stubborn batting by Vengsarkar saved India in the second Test; and the third, played on a plumb wicket, saw a high-scoring draw, both teams making over 500, India 567, in the first innings. Vengsarkar made another century but then a rising ball from Davis broke a finger on his left hand and he retired from the match and the rest of the series. This at last provided Shastri with the chance to captain India.

Almost immediately Indian fortunes changed. After eight consecutive one-day defeats against the West Indies, India beat them by 56 runs. Then came the last Test in Madras. The Indian answer to pace, pace, and pace from the West Indies was to prepare, or rather under-prepare, a wicket to such an extent that the ball turned from the outset. India won the toss and made 382 largely due to Kapil who, coming in at 156 for 5, made 109 off only 119 balls, including seventeen fours.

The West Indies were already demoralised by the way the wicket helped spinners which had thrown out of gear the traditional West Indian bowling patterns. In the Indian innings there had been forty-two overs of assorted spin from Butts, Richards and Hooper. Now when they came to bat they faced their old nemesis, leg-spin, in the shape of Narendra Hirwani, a twenty-year-old making his Test debut. Just a year previously they had collapsed to Abdul Qadir, being bowled out for 53. Hirwani was no Qadir, or not yet anyway, but six weeks before this Test, at the start of the West Indies' tour, Hirwani had played for the Indian Under-25 XI and in the second innings, with the ball keeping low, had taken all the six West Indian wickets to fall.

Hirwani looked an unlikely cricketer, bespectacled, small, and born in Gorahkpur to a Sindhi family which did not care for cricket. He played for Madhya Pradesh which is an unfashionable cricket centre, except that Hirwani's cricket was nurtured in Indore. The great C. K. Nayudu would have valued the young man's dedication – forsaking a well-off family and living in a rented one-room apartment to further his cricket – while C. S. Nayudu would have recognised in him a kindred spirit. What distinguished Hirwani was that, for a leg-spinner, he was accurate and, right from the beginning, when he took wickets he took them in quantity, developing a knack of taking five or more wickets in an innings, a sure sign of bowling command. In his debut match at the age of sixteen he took 5 for 101 in the only opposition innings and continued to display this hunger for wickets as he moved through the ranks of Indian Under-19 and youth teams. On an Under-19 tour of Australia he took 23 wickets in three 'Tests'.

Shastri brought Hirwani on as the fifth bowler and right from the beginning he showed good control over line and length. The West Indies had lost one wicket by the time Hirwani came on, and his first wicket in Test cricket came from a long-hop when Richardson hit it to backward point. After this he just took charge, taking eight wickets in all: batsmen no. 3 to no. 10, including Richards bowled for 68. This was the crucial moment of the Test. Hirwani bowled Richards on the third morning and in seven overs and three balls he took all five remaining wickets as the West Indies, resuming at 147 for 5, were all out for 184. West Indies just managed to avoid the follow-on and Hirwani finished with 8 for 61, only the fourth bowler in Test history to take eight wickets on his debut.

India took their time to build on their advantage, eventually declaring at 217 for 8 which left the West Indies 415 to make. On a wicket now taking even more spin and Hirwani already something of an ogre, the West Indies stood little chance. The medium-pacers bowled six overs, then Shastri brought on Hirwani and the West Indies effectively conceded the match the moment he did so. They played like men who felt condemned to lose. They attacked recklessly and while there were some spectacular innings there was never any suggestion of a realistic fight. Hirwani started the slide himself by removing both openers and then just carried on exploiting the help given by the wicket but also beating batsmen in flight. There were five stumpings in the innings, four of them off Hirwani, and another eight wickets for him in this innings, 8 for 75, making sixteen in the match for 136 runs. It was the most sensational debut in Test cricket since Bob Massie's at Lord's against England in 1972 when he, too, took sixteen wickets.

The West Indies were all out for 160 and India won by 255 runs, their heaviest margin of victory over the West Indies and the first for ten years. The West Indies complained that the match was a fix but it was not that easy to dismiss Hirwani's bowling. True he had a helpful wicket and his real worth would be proved on a less helpful one, but apart from Hirwani there were seven other spinners in the match; they bowled 154 overs, but took only seven wickets between them. Butts, the West Indian off-spinner, bowled eleven more overs than Hirwani but did not take a wicket. If the wicket helped Hirwani then Hirwani was good enough to exploit it. The other spinners were not.

The victory may have produced a mirage of equality with the champions but this was good for the Indian ego – still bruised after the World Cup defeat – and useful in a country where the one-day tail was increasingly wagging the five-day dog. Indeed the West Indies tour had revealed how dominant the one-day game had become. India's defeat in the World Cup proved to be no check on its growing popularity. Six years after the Indians had first experienced a one-day international it was now the one-day game that was dictating the shape of Tests. The administrators, instead of trying to make sure that the one-day game did not overwhelm the more important four- and five-day game, merely succumbed to its greater drawing power.

The Board even forgot the recommendations of the report, made at the end of the previous West Indies visit in 1984, which had said how important it was that touring teams should not disrupt the domestic programme of four-day cricket. Now the Board, keen to earn more money, began to play ducks and drakes with the Test matches. Originally this had been meant to be a five-Test series. But at the last minute the Test at Nagpur was changed to two one-day internationals, one at Nagpur, one at Calcutta. This cast doubt on the status of the one-day match at Ahmedabad which was originally part of the itinerary. Eventually it was played as a charity one-day international. So instead of a conventional five-Test series plus six one-day internationals, four Tests and eight one-day internationals were played. The reason was that this is what the Indian crowds wanted and, in financial terms, the one-day game was subsidising the five-day one.

Crowds for the Test matches had simply melted away. Not one day of the Tests saw a capacity crowd. Only the final Test in Madras made a small profit and that was because crowds came during the later stages of the match, drawn by the prospect of an Indian victory. But the one-day internationals were well patronised and the administrators, ever ready to realise the potential for money, sought to make the most of them. That this short-sighted policy was jeopardising Indian Test cricket did not seem to bother them.

Indeed the longer game was in such a sad state that, although that year, after thirty-three years, Tamil Nadu won the Ranji Trophy and the final was played in Madras, hardly anybody turned up on the final morning to watch. Chidambaram Stadium was empty except for a handful of spectators, most of them officials of Tamil Nadu. The Board's response to this was characteristic. They proposed yet another one-day tournament. As they saw it, the way to renew the Ranji Trophy would be by having a one-day tournament for the 1988–89 season that would feature New Zealand and England, the two teams due to visit the country.

The 1987–88 season, indeed, ended on a note that was even more worrying. Maninder Singh and Manoj Prabhakar, playing in a tournament in Delhi, came to blows after exchanging words on the field. As if this was not enough Vengsarkar himself persisted in writing a newspaper column, thereby breaking his contract with the Board, and he was banned from cricket for six months. He missed the knock-out stages of the Ranji Trophy which saw Bombay lose in the quarter-final, and also missed the Sharjah Cup in March 1988. To make matters worse, in an inter-company match in Bombay his persistent argument with the umpires led to his team being disqualified from the tournament. A certain bloody-mindedness and greed, dressed up as commercialism, seemed to be operating in Indian cricket and, with no proper leadership, it was difficult to see how it could be restrained.

The 1988–89 season provided little evidence of leadership either on the field or off it. It began promisingly enough with a three-Test series against New Zealand which India won 2–1. Vengsarkar was back as captain and India won the first Test at Bangalore and the third at Hyderabad. The second, in Bombay, was unaccountably lost, with Vengsarkar explaining that the Bombay defeat was due to the fact that the Indians relaxed after their victory in the first Test.

During the series Richard Hadlee attempted to become the first bowler to reach a total of 400 Test wickets. He took 18 wickets at an average of 14.00, and held the record for the greatest number of Test victims; but the series was dominated by the Indian spinners. Hirwani took 20 wickets at 19.50 each. In the first Test he took eight wickets which meant that, in just two Tests, he had taken 24 wickets. By the end of the series his Test career read: played 4 Tests, bagged 36 wickets, an average of 9 wickets per Test – a phenomenal rate of striking. But even his achievement was overshadowed by Arshad Ayub who headed the averages with 21 wickets at 13.66. Just turned twenty he was an off-spinner very much in the Ghulam Ahmed mould: a Muslim from Hyderabad. He had made his debut against the West Indies in the first Test at Delhi and, if his figures at the end of that series, 6 wickets at 66.66 each, were very expensive, he had bowled more overs than any other Indian bowler and had done enough to suggest that India might have found the makings of another good off-spinner, a rare creature since Venkataraghavan had retired.

The New Zealand series showed how well Arshad Ayub had come on. In the first Test he took eight wickets, six in the second and seven in the third. Just as Venkat had used a previous New Zealand visit, that of 1965, to announce himself, so now had Ayub. Hirwani and Ayub's achievements suggested that, a decade after the great spinners had gone, another pair was emerging who might match some of their achievements.

The visit by England that was due to follow should have tested the spinners more fully, but the tour never took place. With India keen to establish her anti-apartheid credentials and England led by unintelligent, ill-advised management, such an outcome always seemed inevitable. Gooch, who had been contracted to play for Western Province in South Africa, was persuaded to change his mind and lead the team to India. Indians remembered how, straight after the 1981–82 tour, he had gone on a rebel tour of South Africa. He had been allowed to play in the World Cup but that was a special dispensation and it had been made clear then that the International Cricket Conference needed to resolve the South African situation. This it failed to do in its meetings in the summer of 1988 and the Indians were faced with a touring party that included several players on the United Nations blacklist.

The choice of Gooch, Emburey and six other players with South African connections was seen by the Indians as a provocative gesture, as if daring the Indians to cancel the tour. The selection committee, headed by Peter May, was obtuse rather than Machiavellian, with May arguing that the wider political considerations did not signify. This was naive and the chairman of the TCCB, Raman Subba Row, was sufficiently incensed about the selection of Gooch and the others to consider calling a meeting to sack the selectors. But this did not happen. The Indians refused to give visas to the offending eight; the TCCB would not withdraw their names; and the tour was cancelled. However, some good did come out of this, for the shock of the cancellation was such that, in January 1989, the International Cricket Conference met again and formulated its strategy for South Africa: players going there now faced a ban.

Indian cricketers, deprived of the English tour, busied themselves in domestic competitions before their tour of the West Indies in early 1989. Any tour to the West Indies requires careful thought and preparation but the Indian selectors seemed to give it little consideration, except to lobby for more one-day internationals. They successfully persuaded the West Indian authorities to have more one-day internationals at the expense of Tests. So instead of five Tests there were only four, and they allowed themselves to be bogged down in petty squabbles. When Mohinder Amarnath, who had in the past decade proved himself to be the best player of fast bowling, criticised the selectors, calling them clowns and jokers, he was dropped, a classic case of cutting off your nose to spite your face. So instead of taking a team of reasonably experienced batsmen India went on their first post-Gavaskar tour with only one major batsman who had played in the West Indies before: Vengsarkar. Shastri and Kapil Dev had toured there but they were in the side as all-rounders; the rest were all newcomers to the Caribbean, including Srikkanth, who was now the vice-captain.

This unbalanced team was made even more lop-sided when, in the fifth one-day international, one of the extra ones the Indian Board had insisted upon, Srikkanth had his left forearm broken by a ball from Ian Bishop. He flew home, another youngster flew out and four days later India began the Test series.

The first in Guyana was drawn with rain washing out the last three days' play. In the next three Tests the Indians were overwhelmed. Vengsarkar, who had started the tour as the leading batsman in the new Deloitte ratings, just could not make runs. He averaged 18.33, having averaged 101.66 against the same team a year earlier in India. Srikkanth's absence was felt in the opening position where India's highest partnership was 35. Navjot Sidhu, the Sikh who had made his debut in 1983–84 against the West Indies, was pushed into the opening position and did not make a bad job of it, with a century in the last Test in Jamaica. He evidently liked the Sabina Park wicket for in the preceding island match he made 286 against the Red Stripe champions of the Caribbean, the highest-ever score by an Indian on tour. What was even more remarkable about Sidhu's performance was that, at one stage, it had looked extremely doubtful if he would tour at all. Just before the tour he had been accused of being involved in the death of a man and faced certain charges. He came on the tour only after being granted bail and after certain Caribbean countries were satisfied that he was not a dangerous criminal.

However, with Vengsarkar failing and no Mohinder Amarnath, there was no solidity to the Indian middle-order. Once Marshall, or Walsh, or Bishop, had made the initial thrust the floodgates just opened and the West Indian pacemen poured through. Only one batsman, Sidhu apart, distinguished himself: Sanjay Manjrekar, the twenty-four-year-old son of Vijay Manjrekar. Ever since his debut in first-class cricket in 1984–85 he had been making runs for Bombay in the Ranji Trophy. In one of his early innings for Bombay in his debut season, in the quarter-final against Haryana, he made 57 out of a score of 195, keeping Bombay in the game. But in a Bombay team where competition for places is always high he did not play in the semi-finals or finals and it was in another year, and in another quarter-final, that he next had the chance to shine, making 44. He really announced himself in the 1986–87 season when in six innings he averaged 76.40 – the average was not bolstered by not-out innings – scoring two hundreds and one fifty.

Unlike in England, youngsters of promise quickly get their chance and the next season, 1987–88, when he was twenty-three, Sanjay came into the national reckoning. He almost doubled the number of innings he had played previously, making 678 runs at an average of 67.80. This included the 5 and 10 which he had made in his first Test against the West Indies, but the 10 in the second innings was an uncompleted innings when he had to retire hurt as a ball from Winston Benjamin flew up off a length and hit him over the left eye. Before that accident he had shown great composure, batting for 78 minutes and helping Vengsarkar pull the innings round.

A blow like that in a first Test might have finished off a lesser batsman, and in England several promising Test careers have been ruined after an initial encounter with the West Indians, but Sanjay Manjrekar has some of the fibre of his father Vijay. 'Chip off the old block' is a cliché which is appropriate in his case. He came back to cricket, made runs for Bombay and managed to force himself on to the West Indies tour. It was said to be very much of a last-minute choice at the insistence of Vengsarkar himself. It was probably the best decision Vengsarkar made. In the second Test at Barbados, while all collapsed round him, Manjrekar, putting the Delhi injury behind him, stood firm. He and Azharuddin put on 71 in 18 overs, and then he and Kapil Dev added 79 in 12 overs. Sanjay showed just the right mixture of defence and aggression to cope with the West Indian pace and went on to score an excellent 108. After that he had little luck, getting a bad decision in Trinidad in the next Test, but he did enough in the fourth Test to suggest that he was going to be the next major Indian batsman.

But if the batting on the tour was a disappointment, against such high, relentless pace it was always going to be difficult. The real disaster was the bowling. Before the tour there were high hopes that the gap left by the departure of Chandra, Prasanna, Bedi and Venkat were now going to be filled by Hirwani and Arshad Ayub. Ayub did take 5 for 104 in the first innings of the Guyana Test but Hirwani took 1 for 106 and that set the pattern for the series. The West Indies were determined to lay the ghost of Madras and by the time the fourth Test of the series came along Hirwani was dropped. He had taken six wickets in three Tests, ten less than he had taken in Madras alone, and each of them had cost 57.33 runs. The man who could do nothing wrong in Madras, could do nothing right in the Caribbean. His bowling style, his failure to decide which side of the stumps to attack, and his field placings drove Subash Gupte, watching from his home in Trinidad, to despair.

The Trinidad Test provided a sharp and dispiriting contrast between the Indian spinners of the late 1980s and the great ones of the 1970s. The Indians won the toss and elected to field on a turning wicket. Old Trinidad hands looked at the wicket and speculated that, with the great spinners operating, the West Indies would have done well to reach 150. Ayub did take 5 for 117, Hirwani had just 2 for 59, but neither could really exploit the wicket and the West Indies made 314. India's best bowler was Kapil Dev who took 2 for 45 in the first and 5 for 58 in the second innings, nearly bringing India back into the match. But the Indian batting, put under pressure by Marshall, collapsed so badly that for the first time since 1962 India lost a Test in Trinidad, only their second loss there. The loss in Jamaica was more predictable and with it the series, 3–0. India had not had such a miserable tour of the Caribbean since 1962.

Even before the Tests the performances in the one-day internationals had made the East Indians of Trinidad, who had so looked forward to the tour, condemn this as a second-rate Indian team. Team of money players, big-shot players, they said derisively: surely a country like India with its vast population could produce something better?

The charge that money ruled the game was revived when, after the West Indian tour, some of the Indian cricketers went on an unofficial tour in the United States. There was no pretence that this was anything other than a money-making venture and it so enraged Indian officials that six of the players – including Vengsarkar, Kapil Dev and Shastri – were banned for a year. After a furore, including the threat of legal action, the ban was lifted and they were free to play in the 1989–90 season.

Yet the disaster in the West Indies and the subsequent fuss over the US trip underlined the fact that, as Indian cricket goes into the 1990s, it faces many problems. The defeat led to the usual inquests, with Pataudi alleging that Vengsarkar had put Indian cricket back ten years. If this was an exaggeration clearly his brief, curious reign as captain had been a sad one – yet another of those interludes which

371

never seem to lead to the main piece. A great batsman, he was no leader of men, he could not communicate, he could not impress his personality. But now, with Shastri no longer the dauphin, the mantle fell on Srikkanth.

In a sense this was similar to the reaction of the English selectors after their Caribbean debacle of 1986. Then Gower had been sacked and Gatting, who had been injured during the tour, was brought in as saviour. Now Srikkanth was offered as the panacea for the nation's cricket ills. A swashbuckling batsman, he had virtually no track record as captain. Tamil Nadu's great success in the 1987–88 final was not under his leadership, indeed he did not even play in the final. And what the selectors forgot was that the ills of Indian cricket cannot be solved by one man, they go deeper than that. In the five years since India won the World Cup in 1983, Indian cricket had changed dramatically and this was taking toll of its Test cricket. The main problem, as the West Indian trip had shown, was that it no longer had world-class bowling. Kapil Dev had been the best bowler with 18 wickets at 21.44 but he was a product of the pre-one-day cricket period and it was the failure to produce either successful spinners or quick bowlers that was making the task of regenerating Indian cricket so difficult. Ironically Kapil's leadership had made India a formidable one-day cricket side, but the price for that had been the loss of bowlers who could take wickets in Tests. India, it seemed, could not square the circle.

26

The boy master
1988-91

On the afternoon of 23 February 1988 a fourteen-year-old went out to bat in a school match in Bombay. The match was at the Sassanian Club ground in Azad Maidan. At the far end of the ground stands Bombay Gymkhana, where, as we have seen, India played her first-ever Test on home soil.

As opposed to the colonial comforts of Bombay Gymkhana, still beautifully maintained by the Indians – who having been denied membership of such clubs during British rule, are now even more eager to maintain old colonial traditions – the young boy emerged from a battered tent that had been specially erected for the match. He walked past the curtained-off portion of the tent where he had changed, and which also acted as the loo, and then past a rickety table in front of the tent where some of his schoolmates sat keeping the score and making sure the portable wooden scoreboard was up-to-date.

As he headed for the pitch he had to be careful not to tread on stones, dirt, cow dung, dog shit and other rubbish that littered the outfield and made fielding such a hazard. The pitch was the only bit of this vast ground that had been properly maintained, although, like all such pitches in India, it was almost wholly brown with hardly a blade of grass to be seen.

There seemed no reason to think that what would happen to the youngster in the match would be worth recording beyond the small world of Bombay schools cricket. The match was hardly special. It was a fixture in the Harris Shield Tournament for senior boys in Bombay schools, Giles being the tournament for junior boys. The young boy was playing for Shardashram Vidyamandir (English), the English in brackets signifying the fact that at his school all the subjects were taught in English.

The bracket was necessary as the same school had another unit with the words Marathi in brackets, indicating that its medium of instruction was Marathi. This was the mother tongue of the fourteen-year-old and the local language of most of the residents of Bombay, but by now, more than forty years after Indians had gained their freedom from British rule, it was being widely recognised that English was the language of the world and worth knowing. But although the boys were taught in English, the school saw itself more in the Indian tradition, rather than the westernised tradition represented by their opponents, St Xavier's High School.

This was a Jesuit school, although like all such schools in India most of the pupils were not Catholics, or even Christians, but drawn from the many other religious communities that make up India. It was seen as one of the westernised schools of Bombay where, four times a day, the boys said the Lord's Prayer, but did so without compromising their own faiths. Xavier's was not a big name in Bombay cricket, although it had produced Sunil Gavaskar two decades earlier. Even when Gavaskar played, however, the school had won little, and since then had virtually disappeared as a force in Bombay schools cricket. However, as a Jesuit school, its pupils were drawn from the more afflu-ent classes of Bombay. Xavier's was proud of its cosmopolitan mix of pupils; a mix that reflected nearly all the communities and faiths that make up India and, in that sense, it was more Anglicised. Shardashram, on the other hand, was more authentically Indian, in particular Maharashtrian, and this introduced a certain needle into this match.

As the young boy walked to the wicket the three-day match seemed to be tilting Xavier's way. They had taken two wickets and the score stood at 84 for 2. At the crease was the young boy's best friend, a sixteen-year-old who had a reputation at school for being a character. Years later the young boy, now a grown man, would have a precise recollection of what followed:

The wicket was wet in the morning and both of us decided that we were going to hang around until lunchtime. We felt forty minutes for lunch would make a lot of difference, help the wicket get dry.

After lunch the wicket did dry and, by the end of the day, the young boy and his partner had batted so well that the score stood at 450 for 2. By lunchtime the next day they were still batting and the score had reached 748 for 2 – both batsmen had made triple centuries and some of the Xavier boys were in tears saying they did not want to bowl any more.

At lunch the fourteen-year-old received an urgent message to ring his school coach, a certain Ramakant Achrekar.

I got a message saying 'you have to call up your coach because he is very angry with you'. When I called he said, 'You shouldn't have played for such a long time. If you cannot get a team out for 500 runs you do not deserve to win. You should not be scoring 700 runs. The moment you go back to the dressing room you should tell the umpires you have declared. Otherwise it is not fair on the opponents.'

The young boy, who was also captain, did so aware that he and his sixteen-year-old friend had put on an unbroken partnership of 664 runs for the third wicket, a world record that still stands.

Such records are often curiosities and in *Wisden* this one is listed under records of Minor Cricket. It is followed by the record 175-yard hit by Rev W. Fellows, while practising at the Christ Church Ground in Oxford in 1856, and the records of throwing the cricket ball by Robert Percival on the Durham Sands Racecourse, Co. Durham in 1882 and Ross Mackenzie at Toronto in 1872.

However, the record that the young man helped create at the Sassanian Club ground that February day has proved more than a mere cricketing curiosity. Over the following decade the boy was to became a cricket wonder and acclaimed as such by no less an authority than Sir Donald Bradman who, shortly before his death, declared that the young man's style was the closest to that of Bradman himself. Today that fourteen-year-old is widely recognised as the best batsman in the world.

That fourteen-year-old boy was, of course, Sachin Tendulkar. His sixteen-year-old partner was Vinod Kambli. Interestingly, Kambli had the more decisive influence in this match. He scored 349 not out hitting three sixes and 49 fours and followed it by taking 6 for 37, bowling off-breaks, as St Xavier's were dismissed for 145, leaving Shardashram Vidyamandir (English) the winners by 603 runs. Tendulkar himself scored 326 not out, hitting one six and 48 fours. Given what Tendulkar has since achieved and the astonishing aura he has cast, both over Indian and world cricket, it is worth recording this first spectacular scorecard of his career, one of many that have since startled world cricket.

Shardashram Vidyamandir (English)

A. Ranade c N.Dias b Sanghani 42
R. Mulye* c Bahutule b Sanghani 18
V. Kambli not out 349
S. Tendulkar (capt) not out..................326
Extras (B 5, LB 3, W 5) 13

1/29, 2/84 ....(2 wkts dec.) 748

A. Muzumdar, P.Bhiwandkar, M. Phadke, S.Sinha, S.Jadhav, R.Bashte, S.Ambapkar did not bat
Bowling: A.Sanghani 22-1-98-2; S.Sansur 14-0-79-0; M.Walalwalkar 22-0-161-0; J. Kothari 7-0-38-0; S. Bahutule 27-0-182-0; S.Saherwala 2-0-31-0; K. Apte 26-0-149-0.

Remarkably, three of the cricketers besides Tendulkar who played in that match went on to achieve distinction in the wider cricket world. Kambli will figure more prominently later in the book, but the most poignant story must be that of Amol Muzumdar. He was due to bat no. 5 and had sat padded up in the tent for two days waiting for Tendulkar and Kambli to get out. In the 1993-94 season, as a nineteen-year-old, he finally got his chance when making his debut for Bombay and seized it so well he immediately broke a world record. Playing in a Ranji Trophy pre-quarter-final match against Harayana at Faridabad he scored 260 from 516 balls, batting for 639 minutes and hitting 31 fours. In the process he easily beat a record that had lasted for more than 70 years, that of the highest score on first-class debut. W.F.E. Marx playing for Transvaal against Griqualand West at Johannesburg had held it since the 1920-21 season. But while Muzumdar has since played capably for Bombay and even captained them, he has not quite made the international grade. His world record is a bit like that of B.B. Nimbalkar's 443. This is the fourth highest first-class score in cricket history, but while the three that precede him are Brian Lara, Hanif Mohamed and Donald Bradman, Nimbalkar's name does not mean much even to modern Indian cricket followers, let alone to the wider world.

And dreadful as Xavier's bowling was made to look by Tendulkar and Kambli it did have one name which made it into Test cricket. While Sairaj Bahutule went for 0 for 182 in that match, he was good enough in the decade that followed to became a colleague of Tendulkar's for Bombay and even played for the Indian team, making his debut in the epic series against Australia in March 2001. He has also headed the averages for Bombay, and in India, where the search for leg-spinners in the mould of Gupte and Chandrasekhar is relentless, Bahutule has been touted as a possibility. But the fact that he made his debut when he was twenty-eight, by which time Tendulkar was not only the master batsman but more often used as a leg-spinner, showed the enormous difference in class between the two.

In a remarkably short time all of Bombay was talking about Tendulkar. Before this feat Tendulkar had scored a century at the age of 12 in the Giles Shield and his 329 not out was sandwiched between 207 and 346 in five innings in the Harris Shield. Soon word of mouth spread the fame of the young boy and crowds were gathering in the various Maidans of south and central Bombay to see the matches involving Shardashram Vidyamandir (English), more numerous than crowds at first-class cricket in Bombay that season.

Initially, both Tendulkar and Kambli were hailed as child prodigies and to have two of them at the same time seemed like a miracle. The gods who had so often mocked Indian cricket were finally, it appeared, smiling on it. But even at this stage there were signs that Tendulkar was something else. Despite the fact that he was two years younger than Kambli, which in teens can be quite a big gap, he seemed to be more mature than his elder team-mate and not only more voracious in his run getting, but also more disciplined and ambitious. Kambli was soon

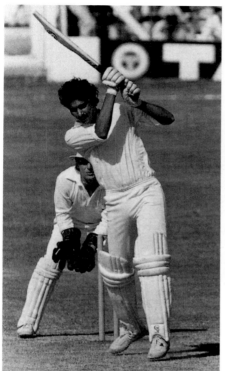

Above left: Ravi Shastri made his debut in February 1981 at the age of eighteen. A talented all-rounder, he was seen, at least according to the film world, as India's answer to Imran Khan.

Above right: Syed Kirmani, India's best wicket-keeper since Engineer, suffered from the vagaries of the selectors. He was an effective lower-order batsman and had the reputation of being as good at 'sledging' as Tony Greig and the Australians.

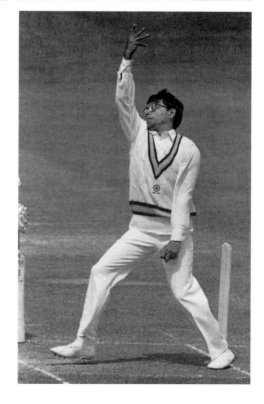

Right: Dilip Doshi, the last of the great era of Indian spinners, had to wait for Bedi's retirement to make his debut at the age of thirty-two, but managed to take 114 wickets in thirty-three Tests (*Patrick Eagar*).

Kapil Dev, *above left,* a wonderful hitter as a batsman, was appointed to lead India after the 3–0 defeat by Pakistan in 1982–83. *Above right:* Krishnanachari Srikkanth, a 'cavalier' of Indian cricket, added an extra 'k' to his name, presumably for luck; but in 1989 he found himself sacked from the captaincy after one tour of Pakistan *(Patrick Eagar). Below:* A panoramic view of the scooter park (and the bicycle park in the background) outside the Karnataka State Cricket Association stadium in Bangalore, an occasional Test match ground since 1974 *(All-Sport).*

The 1983 World Cup, when Indian fantasies came true.

Top right: The odds given by the Patel bookies show the new spirit among Indian supporters in England, both self-mocking and adventurous.

Top left: Mohinder Amarnath's 'mean' medium-pace wobblers were the cornerstone of a famous victory. Here he takes the vital wicket of Jeff Dujon.

Below right: Kapil Dev with the cup, and Amarnath, his vice-captain.
(Patrick Eagar).

Scenes from Indian cricket – two views of the Azad Maidan, Bombay. The tents, improvised pavilions, contain curtained-off portions at the back which serve as changing rooms and loos *(Patrick Eagar)*.

Top left: Sivaramakrishnan, one of a line of Indian spinners in the 1980s who proved to be 'one-Test wonders'; but he bowled effectively in the 1984–85 World Championship.
Top right: He captures Tim Robinson's wicket at Bombay in 1984–85, caught by Kirmani.
Below: The Indian team parading the World Championship of Cricket Trophy on 10 March 1985 in Melbourne; unexpected winners who had shown their ability often to perform better away from home *(Patrick Eagar)*.

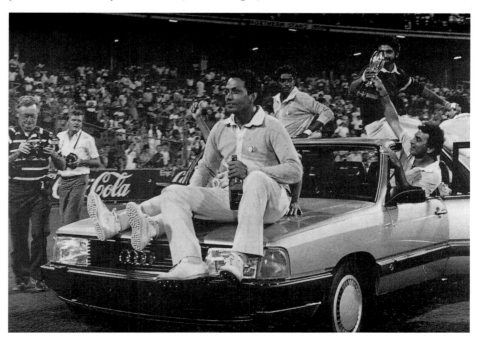

India won their first Test at Lord's in 1986, when Dilip Vengsarkar scored his third Test century there. He also scored 61 and 102 not out in the following Test at Headingley which gained India the Cornhill Trophy, 2–0.

Kapil Dev being presented with the trophy while, in the background, 'Jackie' Baroda, the former Maharajah, happily reflects on changes in fortune since he managed the dismal tour of 1959 *(Patrick Eagar)*.

The Reliance Cup, 1987. *Above:* In the semi-final at Wankhede Stadium, Bombay, India were eliminated by England. *Below:* The final at Eden Gardens, Calcutta, was between England and Australia, with Australia the crowd's favourite.

Kapil Dev lost the captaincy after India's defeat; but the organisation of the tournament by Pakistan and India was a great success *(Patrick Eagar)*.

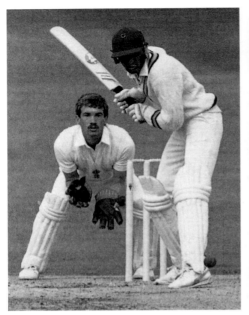

Above left: Mohammed Azharuddin began with three successive centuries in his first three Tests, and while he scored heavily on Indian wickets, he was often found out on pacier, bouncier overseas wickets *(Patrick Eagar)*. *Above right:* Narendra Hirwani lost his place on the tour to the Caribbean in 1988–89, and although he attempted periodic comebacks, he remains a supreme example of the one series spinning wonder *(Graham Morris)*. *Below:* Sanjay Manjrekar, son of Vijay, emerged on the scene in 1989 and suggested he would be the next major Indian batsman. Well as he did, he has been eclipsed by the genius of Tendulkar, and in Indian cricket, his father is still considered the dominant figure *(All-Sport/Ben Radford)*.

showing signs, confirmed over the years, that the world record he set with Tendulkar was a millstone round his neck and not a spur. He was a fine batsman as the record testifies, but he was given little chance to be judged on his own merits. He was always being compared with the promise he had held out that February day on the Sassanian ground, more so as his partner Tendulkar had so amply fulfilled that promise.

The world record had come towards the end of the 1987-88 cricket season. The following season Vengsarkar, captain of Bombay, invited Tendulkar to the team's net practices, a bit like a command to appear at the old Yorkshire nets at Headingley. On 10 December 1988, at just 15 years, 7 months and 17 days old, Tendulkar walked out on to the Wankhede Stadium with the rest of the Bombay team for his first-class debut. His schoolmates, including Kambli, were busy with their studies, but Tendulkar had been given special leave from his standard X class, the equivalent of O-levels, to play first-class cricket for Bombay against Gujarat.

The next day, with the Bombay score at a healthy 206 for 2, he went out to bat – the previous day Gujarat had been bowled out for 140 – and scored exactly 100. It came in 186 minutes off 129 balls and contained 14 fours. Tendulkar remains the youngest player to have scored a century on debut in India's premier first-class tournament and the speed with which he scored the runs was an early indication of how the young man would play in the future. While the match was drawn, there was no doubt Tendulkar had arrived.

On 17 December in Rajkot, near the birthplace of Mahatma Gandhi, Tendulkar came in to bat with Bombay 0 for 2 against Saurashtra and helped add 133 for the third wicket making 58. In the second innings, as Bombay searched for victory, Tendulkar hit 89. On the last day of that year, Tendulkar the bowler emerged. Playing in the Thane suburb of Bombay, he bowled four overs conceding 11 runs without taking a wicket against Baroda. He failed with the bat for the first time, making 17, but by the time Bombay went to Aurangabad to play Maharashtra, Tendulkar's batting form had returned as he made 81, putting on 109 for the third wicket with Chandrakant Pandit.

Thus far it could have been said that he had only played against teams that Bombay normally dominate and against bowlers unlikely to figure in international cricket. The pre-quarter-final against Hyderabad was different. At the Secunderabad Gymkhana Ground from 3–6 February 1989, he found himself pitted against bowlers who were either playing for India or about to. Arshad Ayub was then established as the Indian off-spinner, Venkatapathy Raju was to became the left-arm spinner and Hyderabad were led by Azharuddin. Bombay looked in considerable trouble at 79 for 4 against Hyderabad's 287 with Ayub having taken three quick wickets. At this stage

Tendulkar joined Vengsarkar and put on 118 in a crucial partnership making what *Indian Cricket* called a 'pleasing 59'. It helped Bombay get a small but psychologically important first-innings lead and then the batting of Sanjay Manjrekar and Ravi Shastri led them to victory.

The quarter-final against UP at Wankhede was even more significant. Batting first Tendulkar made 7, failing like many of the Bombay batsmen, but in the second innings, despite the uneven bounce and the wicket taking spin, he made a classy 75 as Bombay amassed 422 and easily beat UP. Less than a year earlier Tendulkar was a schoolboy and yet to go out to bat on the Sassanian ground. With this innings he was to pass 500 runs in 10 innings for Bombay, the only Bombay batsman to reach this landmark that season, and in Ranji terms as rarely achieved as 1,000 runs in an English season.

The next month, in the semi-final against Delhi, Tendulkar's 78 was the highest score in the Bombay innings of 321. This gave him a Ranji aggregate that season of 583, 100 more runs than the next-highest Bombay scorer, the opener Lalchand Rajput, and an average of 64.77. The effort was in vain as Bombay could not match Delhi's 409, with the match like so many others decided on a first-innings lead.

Impressive, even staggering, as these achievements were for a mere fifteen-year-old, Tendulkar was not happy. By the time the semi-final against Delhi came along the Indian team were in the West Indies and three of Bombay's best were in the touring squad: Vengsarkar, captaining the side, Sanjay Manjrekar and Ravi Shastri. Tendulkar wanted to be there facing the West Indies of Malcolm Marshall rather than the Delhi bowling of Madan Lal and Manoj Prabhakar.

It says something about how Indians select their players that there had been urgent debate as to whether Tendulkar should be selected for that India tour. It says even more about Tendulkar that he was sure he could face the best pace attack in the world in their own backyard.

Many years later, when Tendulkar was being hailed as a master, I asked him about it and he seemed surprised by my question.

I was not really worried about facing the West Indian fast bowlers, probably because I didn't know what it meant to play at international level. At that stage I didn't have enough time to watch matches. I was too busy practising very hard and involved in my own cricket. I didn't really bother with anyone else, I was just worried about my own batting and getting runs for my team.

The contrast with other countries like England is marked. The following year the England selectors were to drop Michael Atherton for a tour of the West Indies to protect him. Atherton, by then having graduated from university, had played some years of first-class cricket.

In England the Atherton decision was applauded. In India Tendulkar's omission was criticised and the selectors were accused of not recognising the old adage that if they are good enough they are old enough. Even if Tendulkar's fame had not quite spread all over India by this stage, it was clear that he was exceptional and set apart from his contemporaries. They, often a year or two older than him, would have to follow the conventional route to try and get into the Indian team; Tendulkar on the other hand had just arrived and his batting proclaimed him ready for his country.

In the 1988-89 season, as Tendulkar was making his mark for Bombay, Ajay Jadeja and Nayan Mongia were trying to make the grade by playing for the India Under-19 side. That team toured Pakistan that year and won. The following season other players such as Anil Kumble and Saurav Ganguly were to exhibit their promise in another Under-19 Test series against Pakistan, this time at home and which brought another Indian victory. Through the 1990s Jadeja, Mongia, Kumble and Ganguly would all be prominent in Indian cricket, but Tendulkar did not need to serve such an apprenticeship. He had no need to follow the conventional script. He made his own history.

In the decade that has followed, Tendulkar has made history in such a remarkable way that almost everything in Indian cricket has, at times, appeared to be a reflection of what Tendulkar has done. As the 1990s began, the question was how would Tendulkar fulfill his promise and whether he would be another Gavaskar. Early on in the decade he answered that question fairly emphatically. Unlike Gavaskar he would not be an accumulator but an entertainer. Then through the decade, as India continued to underachieve, the question was when would Tendulkar became captain and by the end of the decade, having had the captaincy not once but twice, the question of Tendulkar regaining the captaincy for a third time resurfaced. All the while one thing was not in doubt. As long as Tendulkar was at the crease India were capable of doing something. And as the decade progressed it was not merely Tendulkar with the bat who could swing a match India's way but also Tendulkar with the ball, particularly in one-day matches.

Indians, probably the world's greatest optimists, are always ready to believe that a leader who will solve everything will emerge from around the next corner, that the next series will, miraculously, conjure up a world-beating cricket team. Some of this is due to the Indian belief in the circular theory of time where a dark age is supposed to be replaced by a glorious one before it is in turn destroyed by another dark age. Some of it is due to the extraordinary faith, and this extends well beyond cricket to all walks of life, in the redemptive power of the leader. The majority of Indians, who are not Christians, may not share the vision of a Christian Messiah, but they do believe in a leader who can set the world right – and often enough in Indian history a leader has arrived, quite unexpectedly, who has taken on the world and emerged triumphant. In many ways it is the Indians' continuing faith in the power of the individual to set right every wrong that prevents them from reading their history and going mad. They need faith if only to believe that the future cannot be as awful as the past.

The brightest moments in Indian cricket history have been associated with such leaders or brilliant individuals. In the 1960s it was Pataudi who revitalised the game and convinced Indians that a dull draw, and denial of defeat, may not be the limit of their ambitions. Then in the 1970s Wadekar conjured up totally unexpected wins in the West Indies and England, helped by a quartet of world-class spinners and the sudden emergence of a master batsman. Nobody could have predicted Gavaskar's feats in the West Indies in 1971, achievements which set new standards for both Indian and world cricket and led to the renaissance of the Indian game. In the 1980s Kapil Dev provided both a potent symbol of all-round excellence to challenge the world and won the World Cup – the ultimate accolade.

The 1990s have been all about Tendulkar. But even here Tendulkar has been an exception. In the past when India has produced a great batsman they had Indian contemporaries against whom they were always being compared. Merchant had Hazare, Gavaskar had Viswanath, but Tendulkar has been on his own. There are many Tendulkar clones, but no-one has come close to matching his mastery of the art of batsmanship.

The other big factor has been that during this Tendulkar decade there have also been vast changes in both Indian politics and society. His arrival on the world stage coincided with the opening of the Indian economy. For four decades after its independence in 1947, India had followed the socialist style of development ushered in by Nehru. Then, in 1991, with the collapse of the Berlin Wall, the fall of communism and under World Bank pressure, India was forced to open up its hitherto sheltered economy and become part of the global economy. This, combined with the arrival of satellite television, meant Tendulkar came to prominence in a totally new India. India was now part of the global sports village, and in Tendulkar it had a star it could market easily to the world.

Since the mid-1990s India has became such an essential component of the global sports village that most Indians can see more sports from around the world than most sports fans in Britain. There is not only live coverage of all Indian international matches but of all international cricket even when India is not playing. A visitor to India any winter can start the day by getting up at six o'clock in the morning to catch the cricket from Australia – an even earlier start is necessary if cricket is being played in New Zealand – then at lunchtime, as the Australian day comes to a close, the action switches to South Africa for cricket from there and, finally, they can stay up late at night to watch cricket from the West Indies. In addition to this there is live coverage of Premiership matches and matches in the Italian and Spanish leagues and sports from all over the world including American baseball, basketball and even ice hockey.

Before Tendulkar, the Indian cricket follower had few opportunities to see their stars, unless they could actually go to a Test Match. And when India played overseas all they had were radio commentaries on All India Radio, which were often of a dubious standard and not always available. The deeds of Gavaskar in the West Indies in 1971 could be followed at best on radio with poor-quality commentaries provided by All India Radio.

Indians did watch Kapil Dev's triumph in the World Cup of 1983, but the historic match against Zimbabwe, when Kapil Dev took India from 17 for 5 to a match-winning 266, making 175, was not considered worthy of BBC cameras and Indians only heard dim and distant reports of it. Tendulkar comes into their living room in live glorious colour and this gives him a status not far removed from a god.

Sometimes this can lead to misleading conclusions about Tendulkar. One such example was provided by Raja Mukherjee, himself a cricketer of no mean repute in Bengal, when writing in *Indian Cricket 2000* he described Tendulkar as 'An Abhimanyu Reborn'.

No Indian child brought up on Hindu myths needs to be told the story of Abhimanyu. He was the son of Draupadi, the woman who was married to all five Pandava brothers. As she carried Abhimanyu she was told the story of how to get into a convoluted tunnel as part of a battlefield manoeuvre. But she fell asleep as the story was being told and did not hear how one could get out. Abhimanyu, a live foetus in Drapuadi's womb, heard part of the tale and when the Pandavas fought their wicked cousins, the Kauravas, for the throne of Indraprashtra, as ancient India was known, he happily got into such a tunnel. Even though he did not know how to get out, it still took seven Kauravas warriors to slay him. His story is the story of the indomitable warrior who may die but will always give his best.

Mukherjee does not explain how Tendulkar's story matches that of Abhimanyu. Although Tendulkar has made enemies, there are no wicked Kauravas waiting to pounce on him, let alone seven of them, nor has he ventured into a tunnel from which he cannot get out. If Mukherjee sees the captaincy as the tunnel then Tendulkar has got in and out of it several times.

If Tendulkar is to be compared to a mythical Hindu warrior then the better comparison is with Arjuna, one of the Pandava men who was married to Draupadi and who was, probably, the father of Abhimanyu. He was the supreme archer of his time, had no peers with bow and arrow but was reluctant to fight his cousins and had to be coaxed by the god Krishna to do so as part of his duty. Even then the comparison is not quite exact since Arjuna always achieved his goal and made sure his side, the Pandavas, won the battle with the Kauravas, but it is nearer the mark.

What this shows is that even for Indians it is very difficult to place Tendulkar and this has been the case from the beginning.

Mukherjee is on surer ground when he writes:

Sachin Tendulkar was no Indian in his method. His batsmanship was of the West Indian mould. Never before did an Indian batsman treat the ball as he did. His method was aggression, his weapon, power. The niceties of grace and classic conventional technique were not for this valiant kid of the 90s generation.

He was born in independent India. An India free from the shackles and insults of colonialism. An India of self-reliance, of candour, he knew not the uncertainties, nor the enforced servility of the pre-independence era. He was born free, free to chart his own course.

So what makes Tendulkar special?

Partly this is something in the man himself. At the age of fifteen, facing the first of many television interviews, he was asked who his best friend was. Everyone expected him to reply Vinod Kambli. Instead Tendulkar knitted his eyebrows as children might do if they are asked if they wanted cough drops and said, 'My bat.'

In 1992, when he became the first non-white to play for Yorkshire – breaking Yorkshire's tradition of never having anyone not born in the county – I asked him about the interview and he replied: 'If you name someone as your friend then the others might not feel so good. If you name the bat nobody can feel left out.' Such sagacity at the age of fifteen is remarkable indeed.

Tendulkar himself has never been able to explain where he gets the qualities which have set him apart from all his contemporaries. In essence, his background, a product of the congested Maharastrian world of north Bombay where the work ethic is high, is not that far removed from Gavaskar's.

He comes from a close-knit family, his father having been a professor, and right from the beginning he has had close support from his family, led by his older brothers Ajit and Nitin.

Like nearly all schoolboys in Bombay, he began by playing tennis-ball cricket with other boys of his age in a rather dingy collection of nine buildings, called a 'colony', in the Bombay suburb of Bandra where he grew up. The trees in the forecourt of the colony shaped the way he plays. He once told me, 'In our colony, the moment the ball touched the trees you were not out, even if somebody took a catch after the ball had hit the tree. That is the reason I developed the habit of hitting the ball in the air. I knew I would not be out if I touched the tree or even a leaf.'

It was his brother Ajit who first detected there was something special about him and suggested he move up from tennis-ball cricket in the colony into serious cricket. Ajit also encouraged him to change schools to take advantage of Achrekar's coaching.

Tendulkar told me: 'Changing schools was a very big decision. From Bandra I had to come all the way to Dadar (another Bombay suburb but nearer to the centre of the city). I was only eleven, so naturally my parents were a little bit scared to let me travel all by myself.'

The way round this was to let young Sachin live during the school week with an uncle and aunt who had no children and who lived near the school. At weekends he went home, but this gave Sachin time to practise cricket: three hours every day after school, seven hours every day during holidays. And every evening Mr. and Mrs. Tendulkar came to Dadar from Bandra to spend time with young Sachin. It was an unusual upbringing meant to produce an exceptional cricketer.

How exceptional he was began to emerge in the winter of 1989 when he was selected to tour Pakistan, having hit 103 not out in the Irani Trophy match between the previous year's Ranji champions, Delhi, and the Rest of India at the Wankhede Stadium.

The selectors, led by the chairman Raj Singh Dungarpur, had a long discussion about including Tendulkar. Some of the selectors were worried that, promising as he was, a tough tour of Pakistan might not be the place to blood him. What if Tendulkar failed? Naren Tamhane, the selector from Tendulkar's home state said, 'Tendulkar never fails,' and Raj Singh recalls: 'When Naren said that we knew Tendulkar had to be selected.'

India went to Pakistan under yet another new captain, Srikkanth, India's seventh change of captaincy in the 1980s. Pakistan is usually a graveyard for Indian cricket teams and captains. Note how uncannily this reflects Indian history. Some of India's great, historic battles have been fought on the fields of Punjab and Sind, now part of Pakistan, and defeats in such battles often subjugated India culminating, in the middle ages, to the rule of triumphant Islamic armies. Cricket defeats have led to the captains being sacked: Bedi after his defeat in Pakistan in 1978; Gavaskar after his defeat in 1982-83.

Srikkanth, managing to draw all four Tests, had little time to feel pleased for he was sacked on his return – his own form during the tour had been woeful. He did lead a side lacking some of the great cricketers of the 1970s and 1980s. Not only had Gavaskar gone but there was no Vengsarkar or Mohinder Amarnath.

Yet Sanjay Manjrekar, building on his performance in the West Indies, held the batting together with as fine and authoritative a display as any that his father Vijay had provided. Indeed, like his father, many of his innings on this tour were played in adversity: India always behind Pakistan and battling hard to save the match, apart from the fourth Test, when India enjoyed her only moment of dominance. Manjrekar hardly ever failed, scoring 569 runs in seven innings – the highest aggregate on either side – at an average of 94.83. His scores of 3, 113 not out, 76, 83, 218 (run out), 72 and 4 told their own story and suggested his only problem was whether he could live up to such achievements in the future. Round him a post-Gavaskar batting solidity seemed to have emerged, with Navjot Sidhu finally coming good and Azharuddin, almost miraculously, reclaiming his place and recovering some of the form that he had shown against David Gower's England team in 1984-85.

There was a bit of luck in this. Azharuddin got a chance to play in the first Test in Karachi because Raman Lamba pulled out at the last minute with a broken toe. At least one senior Indian Board member was convinced Lamba was fit enough to play but that he had chickened out. We shall never know.

There had been increasing doubts about Azharuddin's ability to play pace, and while nobody doubted his supreme wristy style, there was now much muttering in India that he was essentially an eye player whose technique was not quite right. It might do on the low, slow wickets of India but on fast, pacey wickets abroad he would be found out. Had Lamba played there is no knowing what might have happened, his injury was Azharuddin's fortune and he seized it. Lamba never made it in international cricket, while Azharuddin's comeback was to prove very important in the decade that followed, both on and off the field. On such issues as broken toes do cricket fortunes change, more, perhaps in India than anywhere else.

In Karachi, Azharuddin made 35 in both innings, but equalled the world record for five catches by a fielder – some of them quite brilliant takes in the slips. In the second Test in Faisalabad, shedding his diffidence against pace, he made 109, followed by 77 in the third and 52 in the fourth and a total of 312 runs at a very respectable average of 44.57.

In getting to his century in Faisalabad, Azharuddin had run out Tendulkar. For the young man, even though this was only his second Test, this misfortune was the sort of thing he could already take in his stride.

On 16 November 1989, at sixteen years and 201 days, Tendulkar went out to bat in a Test for the first time facing a bowling attack comprising Imran Khan, Wasim Akram, Waqar Younis and Abdul Qadir. The atmosphere could not have been more intimidating. The previous day, the first of the Test, a bearded Pakistani zealot had run on to the pitch to try and hit Srikkanth in the face. He failed, but managed to wrench some buttons off his shirt. Later in the series, when the Indians returned to Karachi for the one-day international, there were so many crowd problems that the match had to be abandoned. With Pakistan struggling on 28 for 3, the crowd began stoning the Indians and then, as police fired on students outside, the match was called off.

None of this seemed to affect Tendulkar. In that first Test he had made only 15, being bowled by Waqar Younis. In the second he made 59 (lbw to Imran) and 8, run out by Azharuddin desperate to move from 99 to 100. In the third Tendulkar made 41, bowled by Qadir, and in the fourth 35 and 57, falling to Wasim, the bowler of the series, and Imran. All his runs came at a time when his side needed him most and his second 50 of the series in the second innings of the fourth Test at Sialkot showed that the sixteen-year-old, not yet able to vote, was already a cricketing man.

He had come into bat on the third day when India, leading by 74 from the first innings, were 38 for 4 and Manjrekar out for 4, his rare failure of the tour. The crowd could not have been more hostile. They had already pelted the Indian fielders with oranges and other harder missiles and were now baying for the blood of the Indian batsmen as Pakistan, frustrated in the series, scented victory.

Led by Wasim, the Pakistani bowlers repeatedly bounced Tendulkar. It got so bad that the English umpire John Holder – the first time that neutral umpires had been used – had to warn them. Waqar Younis hit Tendulkar on the nose and blood started to flow. Imran, concerned about the sixteen-year-old, came up to ask about his welfare. Tendulkar brushed him aside, then, after a quick repair, took up his stance and settled down to face the next ball from Waqar. It was of full pitch, swinging a little and Tendulkar square drove it for four. The one after that was short outside the off stump and Tendulkar, getting up on his toes, hit it past cover for four. Cover did not even have time to react. Tendulkar batted for three-and-a-quarter hours putting on 101 with Sidhu which was enough to save the Test. *Indian Cricket* wrote that Tendulkar, looking positively brilliant from the word go, was 'willing to take the war to the opponent's camp and produced daring strokes on the front foot'.

Perhaps the most revealing moment, however, came a couple of days later in Peshawar on 16 December when India and Pakistan played their first one-day international of the series. Rain washed out the match so they had an exhibition game of 20 overs. Soon Abdul Qadir was bowling, but before he delivered his first ball he sauntered down the wicket to Tendulkar and asked, 'Should you not be busy with books at your age?'

Tendulkar replied he had come to learn from the great master. Tendulkar hit Qadir for three successive sixes and a four, 27 in all in that over and Qadir was left shaking his head in wonder. Tendulkar's unbeaten half-century came in just 18 balls, with five sixes. Although the match meant nothing, it indicated that while Tendulkar might have some of Gavaskar's tenacity, he was essentially an entertainer – if the ball was there to be hit he would hit it.

However, Tendulkar's attitude at the time did worry some Indians. They felt the innings, as Ayaz Memon, one of India's leading cricket writers wrote, had 'a regressive and potentially dangerous influence on the youngster's mind'.

Memon wrote those words in 1991 and for a time it seemed that Tendulkar's carefree attitude was part of wider Indian batting malaise. The solidity the batting had shown in Pakistan did not seem to hold.

Less than a month after the Indians flew home from Pakistan they were in New Plymouth in New Zealand playing a NZCC President's XI. That first match summed up the tour. In the first innings the Indians made 512 in 119 overs, barely more than a day's play, and they were in such a dominant position that the President's XI were in danger of following-on. However, in the second innings they lost four wickets for 6 runs, Tendulkar with 47 shored things up, and although they won by 195 runs there was a recklessness about their batting that would resurface in the Tests and cost them the series. In the first Test, as *Wisden* noted, the Indians played 'too many airy, imaginative strokes' which was the reason for their defeat.

In the second Test recklessness certainly cost Tendulkar his chance to become the youngest-ever century maker in Test history. By the end of the second day he had reached 80 of 258 balls with strong driving and deft placements. He had come to the wicket with his side in a crisis, at 152 for 4, and would put on a record Indian seventh-wicket stand against New Zealand of 128 with Kiran More. The next morning he hit two fours of Danny Morrison to reach 88, then, going for a third boundary, gave a straightforward catch to wide mid-off.

This proved to be Tendulkar's only substantial Test innings of that series. He averaged 29.25 in Tests, the lowest average of his career, and a tour average of 30.14. In the two one-day internationals he made 0 and 36 and was dropped for the two other one-day internationals – for one because he did not wear studs and upset the Indian cricket manager, Bishen Singh Bedi, a new position in Indian cricket and following the trend set in England and other countries.

If some of Tendulkar's performances were just a case of the young man still learning his game, it also reflected the wider truth that the

Indians as a team were just not getting their cricket together around the young man. In the Tests they had batted as if they were one-day internationals, in one-day internationals as if they were Tests. This was so in the notorious one-day match against Australia, played as part of a triangular series. Chasing 187 India were 154 for 6 but still managed to lose by 18 runs. It was after this that Bedi made his famous comment that the 'team should be dumped into the Pacific Ocean'.

As the team for the 1990 England tour was announced, there were those who argued that perhaps Tendulkar should be dumped. India is a land that has an enormous capacity to waste its talented young hopefuls. Many flash across like meteors only to fall and be destroyed, and at this stage there were fears that Tendulkar might be one of them. In the minds of the selectors, however, there was never any doubt about selecting him.

That season England had John Morris making his Test debut for England at the age of twenty-eight, so a sixteen-year old already claiming a regular place in the Indian Test side was sensational and, right from the moment the Indians arrived, Tendulkar was an object of intense curiosity. Bedi added to it by revealing to the press that Tendulkar was receiving hundreds of letters from women of all ages, some wanting to mother him, others wanting something even more intimate. For much of the summer as the sun shone – the conditions were so dry that a ban on the use of hosepipes was introduced – Tendulkar played like an exceptionally gifted child always capable of breathtaking performances but, perhaps, not yet quite capable of changing the course of a match or an innings.

Against Derbyshire he scored 105, going to his century with a six off Ian Bishop, which steered India to victory. The innings saw Kim Barnett, the Derbyshire captain who himself scored a century in the match, drool over Tendulkar saying, 'It was quite simply an astonishing innings. Even the great players in the game would have been proud of that.'

In the two Texaco Trophy one-day internationals, both of which India won in some style, Tendulkar showed glimpses of his class in an overall performance where Manjrekar, Azharuddin, Shastri and Vengsarkar were dominant. Then, at Lord's, he took a breathtakingly athletic catch, which made the crowds gasp in wonder and many a mother claim him. However, he failed with the bat in both innings.

This belief, that Tendulkar was an exceptional boy who might one day become an exceptional cricketer but not quite yet, lasted until the final day of the second Test at Old Trafford. Then, with India facing defeat, Tendulkar showed he was a man and what is more, unlike the rest of his Indian colleagues, he could not only entertain but also shape the course of a match.

At this stage in the summer the Indians had been superb entertainers, but in the major productions of the summer they had had at best cameo roles while the lead roles were played by the English.

This was so in the first Test of the series at Lord's. India's batting in the one-day internationals suggested it could be awesome and going into the Test England seemed to be genuinely worried about it. But Azharuddin, on winning the toss, decided to field, which, as Mike Brearley wrote, was a pusillanimous decision. Azharuddin was never able to explain satisfactorily why he chose to field, although he could argue that had Kiran More, the wicket-keeper, held on to a simple catch by Gooch when he had not scored many, the match might have been different. He did not and Gooch went on to score 333 and England 653 for 4 declared. Gooch followed this by a hundred in the second innings, which gave him a record match aggregate of 456 runs. Against this the Indians, led by Azharuddin's batting, could offer wonderful cameos but no real resistance to the English advance.

Azharuddin himself made a magnificent 121, but such was the English dominance that on the fourth day when the last man Hirwani came to bat India still needed 24 to avoid the follow-on. Kapil Dev rightly decided that he could not trust Narendra Hirwani and in an over off Eddie Hemmings struck the last four balls for successive sixes into the Nursery End which was then full of scaffolding. The very first ball of the next over saw Hirwani get out. India needed persistence and application to avoid defeat and this they did not have. In the second innings they were required to bat out just under four sessions, something a good batting side on a not-too-difficult Lord's wicket should have done, but the batsmen did not show the required professional, disciplined approach. It proved that the Indians of the 1990s had long cast away the dull dog tags of the 1950s, but they lacked grit, which meant their entertainment always seemed to end in defeats.

The second Test at Old Trafford followed this pattern until Tendulkar took charge in the most dramatic fashion. Again England made a huge score, India replied brilliantly, led by another magical Azharuddin innings of 179, but when the final day began India were set 408 to win.

They looked doomed at 183 for 6 when Tendulkar, who had helped Azharuddin add 112 for the fifth wicket in the first innings while making his first Test 50 in England, was joined by Manoj Prabhakar.

What followed showed that while his fellow Indians could entertain but not always finish what they had begun, Tendulkar could do both. He had style and grit. He and Prabhakar put on an unbeaten 160, Tendulkar going on to his first Test hundred, 119 not out, and by the time the match was over India, at 343 for 6, had earned a very creditable draw.

Six months earlier in Napier, Tendulkar had missed the chance of beating Mushtaq Mohammed's record of being the youngest-ever century maker in Tests, but Mushtaq, after watching Tendulkar at Old Trafford, said, 'I would easily trade that record to play an innings like this.'

Now there was a new tone to the English appreciation of Tendulkar. He was not merely an exceptional schoolboy, but a rare batting talent and Bedi declared him to be the most exciting young talent in the world.

The draw Tendulkar had earned his team provided India with a glimmer of hope of winning the last Test and squaring the series. For the first time in the summer they seemed to get things right. They won the toss, batted and made their highest score in England, 606 for 9 declared, with Shastri making 187 and Kapil Dev scoring 101.

India then forced England to follow-on, but a 176-run first-wicket stand between Gooch and Atherton, followed by a superb Gower century, saw England to safety. Their batting exposed India's essential lack of match-winning bowlers. However, it also created yet another Indian might-have-been. What would have happened had Azharuddin not decided to field at Lord's? Such speculation has always consoled Indian cricket and the summer of 1990, when India promised so much, entertained so well, but still went home defeated, was no exception.

But then that was in keeping with India's topsy-turvy summer. Bedi, despite being manager, was reported to have disassociated himself from Azharuddin's decision to field at Lord's, but then said he was misreported. However, his views on Sunil Gavaskar's refusal of an MCC membership was clear. It emerged during the Lord's Test that Gavaskar had turned down the honour because he felt Lord's gatemen were rude and had once stooped him from entering. Bedi put out a press statement saying this was wrong of Gavaskar and he had insulted the Indians of Britain. This public spat between two of India's greatest cricketers underlined that, for all the promise of young Indian talent and the wonderful future Tendulkar held out as India entered the 1990s, the old problems of petty rivalries remained. For India it seemed the future may be bright, but the past was being constantly recreated.

The rest of the that season provided further proof of that. On their return to India they had a hurriedly arranged Test against Sri Lanka – their first at home for two years. During that time India had played fourteen Tests abroad without a win. Now there was a new venue, Sector 16 Stadium in Chandigarh. It was, as *Indian Cricket* said, 'expertly underprepared' – the poor Sir Lankans stood no chance and India duly won.

It was Azharuddin's first win as captain and India's first win for two years. Kapil, who took 5 wickets in the match, equalled Botham's 376-wicket haul, but India's victory was due to Raju, who bowled his left-arm spin so efficiently that he took 6 for 12 in 17.5 overs as Sri Lanka went from 50 for 2 to 82 all out. Although India had made just 288, this was enough to enforce the follow-on and win the match.

Raju's inclusion in the match showed that, Tendulkar apart, the muddle that is Indian cricket had not changed. Raju had made his debut in New Zealand, then gone to England where he got injured and came home. He only played in Chandigarh because Shastri, who was being used as a left-arm bowler, said he was not confident about his bowling, which made Bedi accuse him of chickening out and refused to consider him for the Man of the Match award, despite his making the highest score of the match: 88.

The Sri Lankans also played three one-day matches and this brought Tendulkar's first Man of the Match award in one-day internationals when, in the second game at Pune, he opened the bowling with Kapil and took 2 for 39 in 9 overs, and batting at no. 5, made 53 as India passed Sri Lanka's 227 with six wickets and 4.3 overs to spare. This second successive victory gave them the three-match one-day series.

The rest of the season, with no other international cricket, was dismal and at times alarming and, but for Tendulkar, would have been quite dreadful.

The Duleep Trophy final in Jamshedpur between North and West Zone showed Indian cricket at its worst. On a wicket made for batsmen and where bowlers stood no chance, the behaviour of both teams, many of them very senior players, was shocking. Umpiring decisions were regularly questioned and one captain even went to the umpires' room and berated them. The lowest point came when the West Zone bowler Rashid Patel, having aimed a beamer at Lamba playing for North Zone then took a stump and charged down the wicket at the batsman. With both of them mouthing obscenities at each other, Patel was heard to say that he knew where he would shove the stump and Lamba waved his bat in self-defence. After five days cricket, when only two innings had been completed, North scoring 721 and West 561, the dreadful atmosphere on the pitch led to a riot in the crowd. The result saw anything suitable being set alight and the match came to a premature conclusion. Patel and Lamba were banned for thirteen and ten months respectively, although this was not before the two had played in a double-wicket tournament as a pair.

Tendulkar had also played in the match, having earlier in the tournament made his by-now-customary century on debut in the quarter-final against East Zone, a top score of 159. But what, once again, set him apart from his fellow players was his behaviour in that notorious final. Having made 25, he was caught at short leg by Jadeja off Kirti Azad, and, without any dissent, walked. *Indian Cricket* wrote, 'It is a saving grace that such an atmosphere has not corrupted a player like Sachin Tendulkar. The youngster walked on being caught at short leg. This is the stuff champions are made of.'

The Ranji Trophy final, at Wankhede Stadium on 3–7 May, was to demonstrate that Indians were realising what a champion Tendulkar was. Bombay played Haryana and when the last day began the match seemed lost. Haryana had gained a first-innings lead, which if the match had ended in an overall draw, as most Ranji matches do, is enough to decide the winner. On the final afternoon Kapil Dev, captain of Haryana, set Bombay 355 to win at 5.22 an over.

As Bombay went after the target, Wankhede, normally empty for such domestic matches, began to fill and soon 4,000 people had come into the ground. For a domestic match this was sensational – Indian domestic cricket attracts such few people that admission is now free – and as soon as news spread that Tendulkar was batting the crowd doubled.

Tendulkar came to the crease after Bombay had lost three quick wickets and set the tempo for the chase, making 96. His departure led to another collapse. However Vengsarkar, the Bombay captain, kept them in the hunt adding 47 for the last wicket. When he was run out, Bombay had fallen short by just two runs. The match had seen 1,526 runs scored and while such aggregates are common in Indian cricket, rarely do matches produce outright results, let alone such a close margin. Haryana won their first Ranji championship. Vengsarkar wept, but it was Tendulkar that everyone talked about.

But not even Tendulkar could do anything about a much more sinister aspect that had entered Indian cricket. The reason the final was played in May, six weeks after it was originally planned, was because of a court battle between the Board and one of the teams. The previous season, as we have seen, it was the players versus the Board over certain players going off to the USA and Canada to play exhibition cricket. Now it was Punjab versus the Board in 'The Case of the Missing Umpire'. On New Year's Day in 1991, Delhi had played Punjab in a North Zone league match at Kotla to decide who would accompany Haryana to the knockout phase of the competition.

The two umpires for the match were Venkataraghavan and C. Nagaraj Rao. But Rao did not turn up, so for the pre-lunch session a local umpire, Anil Choudhary, stood at square-leg at both ends. Incidentally Rao was not the only one missing. Navjot Singh Sidhu did not play for Punjab and *Indian Cricket* wrote, 'Navjot did not play. Nor did he give any reason for his absence.'

After lunch Delhi got Pritam Sood to come in. Punjab had objected to him as an umpire before the match and after they lost by 9 wickets they objected even more strongly.

At first the Board upheld Punjab's protest and they allowed them into the knockout phase. Delhi appealed to the Board, which was deadlocked on the issue. It was decided there would be a drawing of lots for a rematch, but Punjab refused and went to the High Court in their home territory of Patiala and got a stay order. The tournament was suspended and it seemed as though it might never finish. But with summer approaching Punjab had a sudden change of heart, withdrew its court action and the knockout phase finally began with the Delhi versus Bombay quarter-final played in mid-April.

One result of this was that match fixing entered Indian cricket. According to the report later prepared by the Indian Central Bureau of Investigations, some of the Delhi players, who had contracts to play league cricket in England starting in April, deliberately lost the quarter-final against Bombay just to get to England on time. Chasing Bombay's first innings of 390, in which Tendulkar had top-scored with 82, Delhi made 389 after having slumped to 215 for 6. Tendulkar went on to make 125 in the second innings, but that was academic as Bombay won as a result of their first-innings lead.

If Tendulkar was the most wonderful thing to happen to Indian cricket and, since the 1990s, has been the figure perpetually bathed in sunshine, then there were also dark forces in the shadows, who, unknown to him, were ready to tear apart the very soul of the Indian game.

27

How India brought the pariah back
1991-92

The white regime of South Africa has had no role in the history of Indian cricket and whatever interaction it has had has brought it no credit – it has consistently sought to assert the superiority of the whites over both the Indians and the blacks. So much so that in 1929 the South African team touring England successfully forced Duleep – the leading amateur batsman that summer – out of the English cricket team because he was Indian.

After 1932, and following India's emergence as a Test nation, South Africa – as an established Test power – could have done much to help the newcomers but it did not. It could not imagine playing with people it derided as 'coolies'.

It is interesting to contrast white South African cricket with Australia. After India's independence, Australia was the first country that India toured and, since then, Australia has always sent its best teams to India. The result has seen Indians regard Australia as the great land of sporting champions – few in India knew of its immigration policy which, until the 1970s, permitted little or no Indian migration to Australia but allowed any white person to emigrate to Australia for just £10.

Curiously, and this speaks volumes for Indian openness, white South African cricket was reported quite extensively and Indians grew up with an awareness of South African cricketers. However, the reverse was the case in white South Africa.

By the beginning of the 1990s it had been more than 130 years since Indians had arrived in South Africa. During that time, however, they had never been made to feel a part of the land. For very nearly the first one hundred years of their existence in South Africa they were not even allowed to buy land in many parts of the country, and even when they were allowed to do so, they could not move from one province to another without a permit from the appropriate government department, even for a holiday. As late as 1960, they were still denied any citizenship in South Africa.

Indeed, in 1948, the white nationalists had come to power on the twin electoral promise of confining the black Africans to their tribal lands and sending the 'coolies' home. And while apartheid had not ravaged Indians as it had the blacks, it had left its mark. The Indians had seen the nationalist government use laws such as the 'Group Areas Act' to virtually expropriate their property and drive them away from the white business areas – the South African Reserve Bank in Pretoria had been built on land seized from the Indians. After 1948, Indians seeking higher education had to be content with so-called 'tribal' colleges, even the much-vaunted liberal universities of South Africa, like Cape Town or Witwatersrand, required Indians to get special permits before they could study there.

In June 1991, white South Africa, forced to shed its pristine whiteness, suddenly discovered Indian cricket. The release of Nelson Mandela in February 1990 started a process that was to dismantle apartheid, starting with sporting apartheid.

In my book *Sporting Colours* I told the story of how and why white South African sport was isolated and then, as apartheid crumbled, brought back into the international arena. In this case, it is the Indian end of the cricket story that is relevant.

In March 1991, Ali Bacher, head of white cricket in South Africa, travelled to Harare with Steve Tshwete, a leading ANC member, to meet the High Commissioners of India and Pakistan. Even a few months previously such a journey would have been impossible, but now, in the New World created by Mandela's release, anything was possible. Bacher, a Jew of Lithuanian extraction, had been at the centre of white cricket in South Africa for nearly two decades. In 1970, he had been captain of the last white team and then, after the country's racist sporting polices had finally caught up with it, he had become an administrator. During that time he had built up a reputation as the 'evil prince' of cricket, the great pirate who had lured the English, Australian, West Indian and even Sri Lankan cricketers with South African gold to play rebel tours in South Africa. He justified it on the grounds that he had to keep white cricket going, and also pointed to his pioneering role in taking cricket to the black townships of Soweto and Alexandria, as if the virtues of this expiated any guilt he felt towards the rebel tours.

With Mandela's release the whole picture had been transformed. The ANC was ready to back South Africa's readmission to international sport. Bacher realised rebel tours were now impossible and that he had to unify his cricket which, due to apartheid, was divided along racial lines. He now began to work with Steve Tshwete, who like Mandela was a former graduate of Robben Island. It had taken years for the world to be persuaded that the old white sporting regime should be isolated; their readmission would take just a few months.

394

Bacher returned from Harare full of hope. Both the Indian and Pakistani High Commissioners had been polite and courteous. He was working to a tight timetable for South Africa's readmission. In June, the two South African cricket bodies, white and non-white, were due to be united – the first time in South African cricket history that it would have one non-racial cricket board. In July, the ICC was to have its annual meeting and Bacher's aim was to ask for the readmission of his unified body.

Back in Johannesburg, Bacher opened an Indian front to speed up the process. He had long known David Richards, then chief executive of the Australian Board – contact had first been established during the rebel tours – and Richards was then negotiating with India over their proposed tour to Australia in the winter of 1991. Richards put Bacher in touch with Jagmohan Dalmiya, the then secretary of the Indian Board.

Sometime in April 1991, Bacher, who can use the phone like an extension of his own self, rang an astonished Dalmiya in Calcutta. Dalmiya's first words were, 'I didn't know you could ring India from South Africa.'

The two struck up an instant rapport. Between that first call in April and the ICC meeting in July, Bacher made about 40 calls to Dalmiya, although it was only in July in London that they first set eyes on each other. By then they both felt they knew each other intimately.

At this stage Bacher, like most white South Africans, was totally ignorant of Indian cricket. In the winter of 1989 I had asked him if he knew who had the second-highest first-class average in cricket. The first, of course, is Don Bradman, a particular hero of Bacher, who worships Australian cricket. Vijay Merchant holds the second-highest average. It was not surprising that Bacher did not know the answer. What was illuminating was that, at that stage, he did not even know who Merchant was.

But Bacher is a fast learner and what set him apart from most of his white sporting contemporaries was that he was ready to acknowledge the evils of apartheid. He knew that the support of the Indians would be crucial if he was to get his new South Africa back into the fold. In March 1991, just before his trip to Harare, Bacher had been in touch with Colin Cowdrey, then chairman of the ICC, and Cowdrey had told him that after the formal ICC meeting the members would be prepared to meet the newly formed United Cricket Board for an informal chat. The agenda for the meeting was already prepared and South Africa's readmission would have to wait for another year. 'No way' replied an angry Bacher. 'We are not coming for a cup of tea at Lord's. We are going for a full application.'

Cowdrey's call was made from Barbados where he was consulting with Clyde Walcott, head of the West Indies Board. The West Indies, along with India and Pakistan, had been a firm opponent of white South Africa and Bacher knew he had to start his own diplomacy to try and get support, and this meant the ANC.

In June, the United Cricket Board held its unity banquet in Johannesburg and one of the guests of honour was Sunil Gavaskar, making his first-ever visit to the country and the first to South Africa by an Indian cricketer. Bacher, a shrewd networker, had rung me up in London to get Gavaskar's telephone number in Bombay. Just before the dinner, Bacher took Sobers and Gavaskar to Soweto. Mandela met, or more correctly granted an audience with, the pair in his Soweto home. Gavaskar astonished Mandela by asking for a memento of the visit, and Mandela gave him a present.

By the time the ICC meeting was held in July, Bacher, with the help of Mandela, had persuaded Cowdrey to place South Africa's readmission on the ICC agenda. The crucial date for South Africa's readmission to cricket was set for 10 July, or, as Tshwete liked to put it, the country's admission, since the previous occupants had been an all-white body that did not represent the whole country.

By now such was Bacher's friendship with Dalmiya that India had agreed to propose the motion, but as Bacher arrived in London for the meeting things suddenly started to go wrong. The next day Dalmiya rang from the apartment he had hired in London – like many Indians he preferred apartments to hotels – to say that many in India were questioning his strategy of proposing South Africa for membership. He told Bacher, 'They are saying what the hell are you doing proposing them?' He was also under pressure from the West Indies, who did not like the idea of the proposal of a resolution after the agenda had already been decided, and Pakistan, who were lukewarm about the prospect. 'Ali,' said Dalmiya, 'you have got to do something. You had better get somebody to talk to Scindia (Madhavrao Scindia, the Board president who had not come to London).'

Bacher decided that the call could only be made by Tshwete. He, however, was still busy with the first-ever ANC Congress in Durban, bringing together the exiles and the internal members in a historic meeting. The moment Tshwete arrived in London, Bacher tried to ring Scindia in India. 'All day I was trying to get hold of him. Eventually I was told he would be at a certain place at four o'clock on Monday afternoon. Steve had gone to sleep. Just before four I went to wake him up and then I got through to Scindia. I did not know Scindia, although Cowdrey had mentioned his name. I introduced myself. I spoke to him for about twenty minutes saying who I was. Then I said I have got somebody from the ANC, and I gave the phone to Steve.'

Tshwete spoke for about fifteen minutes and it was one of the most nerve-wracking fifteen minutes Bacher had ever spent. Then Tshwete put the phone down and, coming over to Bacher, put his arms on his shoulders. 'Don't worry about it. It has been done.' Half an hour later the phone rang. It was Dalmiya. 'Well done. Scindia has instructed me to propose South Africa.'

There was still opposition from Pakistan who, in a meeting with Tshwete, kept saying that his statements were contradicted by others. An exasperated Tshwete finally said, 'We are the best doctors in the South African situation.'

There was a slight hitch at the ICC as they had lost copies of the constitution of the new United Cricket Board, and fresh copies had to be faxed on the morning of the meeting from Johannesburg. In the end it all came right, as India proposed and Australia seconded.

Australia was also very keen for South Africa to take part in the 1992 World Cup in Australia and this was left for a special ICC meeting in Sharjah in October. Cowdrey had agreed to hold the special meeting, but as an economy measure did not take the ICC secretary Lt-Col Stephenson, who was also secretary of the MCC, along with him.

However, by the time Bacher arrived in Sharjah, he found that changes had taken place in India.

Dalmiya returned from London and the merry-go-round of Indian cricket administration resumed. The Dalmiya-Scindia partnership was an uneasy one as they were from opposed camps in Indian cricket. The previous year had seen one of the stormiest annual general meetings of the Indian Board in history, fit to join the ranks of the infamous Mad Hatters Tea Party of 1946, when Duleep was voted off the selection committee, or the one in the Imperial Hotel in Delhi in 1951 when De Mello was ousted. This one, held in Calcutta's Taj Bengal in September 1990, had seen a fight for the control of the Board with Scindia and Dalmiya in opposing camps. The elections saw the use of the most dubious tactics, including 'goondas', hired thugs used to intimidate cricket officials. Dalmiya's faction, which was supporting the reelection of Bengal's B.N. Dutt, lost and Scindia, who was then also a government minister, became president. Dalmiya, himself, however, defeated the Scindia camp's nominee Nagaraj to become secretary by one vote. But, in September 1991, after Dalmiya returned from London, the annual general meeting saw Scindia get his man Nagaraj as secretary and Dalmiya was cast in the wilderness.

So in Sharjah it was Scindia instead of Dalmiya who came to the meeting. And although he had been sweet-talked by Tshwete to propose South Africa's readmission, he was still very cautious about allowing South Africa to take part in the 1992 World Cup. He felt things were going too fast. The West Indies also opposed their admission to the World Cup, but, urged on by Australia, the South

Africans got their way.

Four days after the Sharjah meeting, Bacher and the South African officials travelled to India, partly as a gesture of thanks for India's help in getting South Africa back into the international fold, and partly to get to know the country. None of them had ever been there, but no sooner had they arrived in India they found the Indians facing a crisis of their own. Pakistan, due to come to India for a short tour, had cancelled due to mounting tension between Hindus and Muslims in India. The Indians were left contemplating a situation where, for the first time since 1988 they had not had an official cricket tour, barring a short, hurriedly organised, one-Test visit by Sri Lanka.

In Sharjah the South Africans had been invited as guests of the Indian Cricket Board for the matches against Pakistan, now they were invited to take over from them as the official tourists. Bacher and his group were due to return to South Africa on 2 November and the plan was that the South Africans would be back to play their first match in Calcutta on 10 November. Never has a cricket tour been organised at such short notice and in such fashion between two countries that did not recognise each other. India, whose diplomat had been thrown out of South Africa after 1948, still officially recognised the ANC regime.

The tour made little or no cricket sense. The Indians were about to embark on a gruelling tour of Australia, their first in six years, followed by the World Cup. The South Africans were just about to start their season. But this was too good an opportunity to miss and Bacher knew this would be more than just a cricket tour.

On the evening of South Africa's readmission to international cricket, Bacher had held a small dinner in an Italian restaurant next to Westbury Hotel – the normal headquarters for the South Africans in London. The dinner guests consisted of two Englishmen who had long argued the case for white establishment South Africa: John Woodcock, former cricket correspondent of *The Times* and former editor of *Wisden*; and Jack Bannister, a former Warwickshire bowler and now television commentator. The new friends of the new non-racial South Africa were reflected in the presence of Sunil Gavaskar. I was invited as well and during the dinner Bacher freely speculated on who South Africa's first opponents might be. He was certain he wanted it to be India or some other non-white country.

'Why?' asked Woodcock quite distressed. 'If you think along such racial lines then you are back in the old thinking.'

Bacher was deeply grateful to Woodcock for his help over the years, but now he disagreed. 'No, no, it is very important. We have never played them. And after 102 years of playing international cricket, the new South Africa has to start with them.'

So this unexpected tour of India meant he could kill several birds with one stone, something that really pleased Bacher.

Although Dalmiya was out of power at the Board, he still ran Calcutta and he proposed to host a game in his home city against the South Africans. Scindia matched this with an offer for his native Gwalior and a third match was proposed for Delhi.

The deal was done at Scindia's home in Delhi and it showed how the 'new' South Africa conducted sporting relations. South African and Indian cricket officials met over a typical Indian meal, also present was Anand Sharma, the then-ruling Congress Party's spokesman on South Africa, whose wife is a South African-born Indian and the ANC representative in Delhi, whom the Indians treated as the South African ambassador. Keen as Dalmiya was for the tour, Scindia would not move until he had ANC support. He got it over the tandooris and naans and the deal was struck.

The most curious mix of politics and sports came when Bacher got to Calcutta and was ushered into the Writers' Building, built by Robert Clive and now a rabbit warren housing Bengal's top ministers and civil servants, to see the communist chief minister Jyoti Basu.

Basu, an unreconstructed Stalinist, came in, took one look at Bacher and said 'I want you to play cricket in Calcutta next week' and then swept out. The thought of a communist, who even a few months earlier would have been leading the protests against the old white South Africa, now urging the new South Africa to come back into international sport, overwhelmed Bacher.

Bacher was very keen for the matches to be televised in South Africa, as the symbolic significance of seeing a South African team take on the Indians in India was tremendous. This produced a twist to the story, and one which would have a dramatic impact on Indian cricket throughout the 1990s.

Before the South Africans arrived in India, the Indians had never sold their television rights, either at home or abroad. With Indian television state-owned the broadcasters just televised the matches and paid nothing for the rights. Now the Indian Board was faced with two competing South Africans companies: the South Africa state-owned television one and M-Net, South Africa's cable network.

Amrit Mathur, a close confidant of Scindia and an Indian Board representative, did not even know whether the Indian Board owned the rights. Mathur recalls, 'We had to find out first who owned the rights and then how much they were worth.' Mathur discovered that the rights belonged to the Indian Board. He then consulted Dalmiya about how much the Indians should charge for them. Ask for $10,000, suggested Dalmiya. Mathur doubled this and thought he would ask for $20,000. The South Africans came on the line and offered $200,000. Mathur had barely recovered from this when M-Net offered even more.

But again Bacher intervened. It was very important, he told Mathur, that the television rights should go to the state channel as that was available for everyone. M-Net was only available for subscribers, which mainly meant the rich white South Africans. All South Africans should see this highly symbolic contest. Mathur, delighted with getting more from the television rights than he could ever have imagined, readily agreed and rejected M-Net. The loss of money was marginal. For the Indians, the major revelation was that their cricket rights could be worth so much money. Until the South Africans had opened their eyes, they were not even aware of it. The next decade would see them exploit this knowledge in a masterly fashion.

Bacher's acute commercial radar had already scented the possibility of having even this tour, arranged at only four days' notice, sponsored. Panasonic was quickly recruited to sponsor the team. But what about spreading the net wider? The Boeing 707 taking the team could seat 170 and, even allowing for officials, their wives and the media, this would still leave some space for supporters. And the most likely supporters were the Indians of South Africa. Bacher turned to Liq Nosarka, a cricket official in Transvaal and a prominent Indian businessman. The Indians could not wait to clamber on to the aircraft.

One of the consequences of apartheid was that it kept the different races totally apart. So much so that even newspapers were segregated. A major South African newspaper like *The Sunday Times* would have an edition for the whites, its main edition. But when the same paper was distributed in the Indian area or the black area, this main edition would be wrapped around a special supplement of Indian or black news. The result of this was that while all the races knew about the main news, which featured only white people, the whites had no knowledge of Indian or black news.

Bacher was aware that few whites knew anything of their Indian counterparts. For many of the white officials and players on board, that plane journey was probably the closest they had come to meeting any significant number of Indians, and whilst few of them would have shared a plane with quite so many Indians before, there would have been a number of people on that plane who would not have realised that most of their fellow travellers were also fellow South Africans.

One such person was a high Board official, Ewie Cronje. His son, Hansie, was one of the players chosen for the trip, and father, mother and son were going to India representing Orange Free State. In Afrikaner history, Orange Free State has a certain resonance, but the word 'free' in the title shows how the truth can be distorted. It meant freedom for Afrikaners and whites to do what they wanted while consigning others not fortunate to be whites right out of the state. So until the mid-1980s Indians were not even allowed to live in the state.

At best they could journey through on a 24-hour pass. If by accident they overstayed, they would find themselves locked up in jail and hurriedly transported outside the state borders.

India was something Ewie Cronje had read about in books. He had studied geography at university and knew where the rivers and the mountains in India were. He had seen the video of Gooch's Indian summer chronicling the Indian tour of England in 1990 and knew a bit about the Indian players. As he prepared to board the plane he was aware that he had never really met so many Indians in a social setting, let alone shared a cricket tour with them.

I was a good tennis player. Indeed I was a better tennis player than cricketer (representing his state at both tennis and cricket). I used to go to Natal for tennis or holidays and there I would see Indians serving in hotels. When I played tennis there, there would be ball boys and some of them would come up to me and ask me for autographs.

Ewie Cronje just did not know what to expect. Nor for that matter did many of the Indians who had come along. For them this was a journey into the unknown. No-one felt it more acutely than Hossein Ayob. He was director of coaching of the Cricket Board and for him this journey was a fulfillment of long-cherished dreams.

Hossein, a tall, attractive man with an eye for ladies, was a fast-medium bowler who played his entire cricket in the apartheid system. This meant, as he says, 'atrocious grounds. We never had a blade of grass. It would be littered with stones and glass where we had to prepare and mark the wicket. We would roll the pitch ourselves and lay the mat and our cars provided the only changing rooms.' He might have played for South Africa, but white cricket offered no opportunity for him. The best he could do was play for his own race in South Africa's peculiar brand of inter-race games, where all the other races – coloured, Indians, Malays (descendants of slaves brought to South Africa by the Dutch East India company) and Africans – played against each other. None of them, however, could match their skills against the whites.

Apartheid extended even to watching cricket. So when he went to the Wanderers to watch the white South African team play against a visiting side, he would have to sit behind cages in a particular part of the ground. Until the cages came down he had never seen cricket at the Wanderers from behind the bowler's arm – a great deprivation for a bowler whose trade was to make the ball swing and swerve.

In the 1980s, looking to move to better accommodation, Hossein bought a house in a white suburb. Under apartheid laws, however, he

401

could not do that in his own name. So it was bought through the 'nominee system' whereby a company was formed, 51 per cent of which was owned by François Weidemau, an Afrikaans, while 49 per cent of the shares were owned by Hossein. Of course Hossein paid all the money, but if the police questioned it he could always say he was not breaking the law as the house was technically owned by a white man. A separate legal arrangement between the two protected Hossein from Weidemau taking over the house. Not that Hossein had any fears of that: Weidemau was a cricket coach who worked for Hossein at the Cricket Union and a gentler more soft-spoken man could not be imagined, but the whole thing illustrated the cruel absurdity of apartheid's laws. Now the law had gone and Weidemau had stopped working for him, but the arrangement continued, as it was rather expensive to unwind. Hossein, long used to apartheid's lash, no longer felt the humiliation of it all. Occasionally he recalled the chilling experience of being allowed into a hitherto white restaurant. Already a grown man, the experience of it all was so unnerving that, presented with a finger bowl, he nearly drank the water thinking this was how it was done in the smart restaurants.

Bacher and his fellow cricket officials arrived back in Johannesburg on Saturday, 2 November 1991. On the evening of Thursday, 7 November, the South African team, along with players, officials and wives gathered at Jan Smuts airport in Johannesburg. They knew they were making history. The flight they were about to take was so strange that even the pilot was unfamiliar with the flight plan. He was an experienced enough pilot who had often the flown the South African State president, F.W. De Klerk, on the same aircraft on important missions, but a South African plane had never flown to this destination before.

As the plane swept over the paddy fields and hutments near Calcutta, Hossein felt a dread. This dread increased as the plane landed and, as Hossein looked out of the window, his heart sank. All he could see were hundreds of people milling around and he felt 'Oh, another protest against South Africa. They will demonstrate against us'. But, instead, it was a welcome party, the grandest welcome party any cricket team, probably any sporting team, has ever received. Even more so when you consider that the welcome came from hosts who had neither met them nor even seen them before. Calcutta, the city of hujuks – sudden, extraordinary emotions – was to produce a spectacular hujuk which, even by this city's standards, was quite exceptional. Dalmiya was keen to put on a show for his friend Ali, and he and his people did not fail.

The first part of the welcome was the sort that is traditional in India. Women in saris applied tilak, a red mark on the forehead; every South

African was garlanded and flower petals thrown over them. Then, as the South Africans got into the buses and cars that had been arranged for them, they found themselves part of an immense cavalcade escorted by more than one hundred motor cyclists sporting the red tee-shirts of the Bengal Cricket Association. It was Calcutta's equivalent of a ticker-tape parade. There were cheering crowds lining almost every stretch of the fifteen-mile journey, many of them holding up banners welcoming South Africa. Twice the cavalcade stopped and, at specially erected platforms, Dalmiya, Bacher and other South Africans spoke. Other vehicles stopped and the people inside just cheered.

For white South Africans this was a novel experience. Ever since the days of isolation and growing worldwide protest against apartheid, white South Africans had been made to realise that they were the pariahs of the world.

'We were,' recalls Ewie Cronje, 'overwhelmed by the reception. That will leave a lasting impression, the highlight of my life. We were just treated like kings.' The joke in South African cricket afterwards was that the Cronjes, having been treated like kings by the Indians, would return with nearly all the silk of India as they went on a shopping mission to buy up virtually the whole country.

The welcome did not stop when the South Africans arrived at Calcutta's Grand Hotel. The next day they were taken to see Mother Teresa, whose knowledge of cricket may have been non-existent, but who was a symbol of modern Calcutta. Clive Rice, the South African captain, shook hands with her and the picture, which suggested Mother Teresa was blessing the South African captain, seemed to sum up a divine dispensation for the tour. Wherever they went Indians seemed to want to meet the South Africans, touch them and not just the players, but the officials and even the journalists. Soon after arrival, Shira Bacher, wife of Ali, walked with Ali's then secretary Bridget to Eden Gardens a few hundred yards away from the Grand. Bridget is blonde and looks a bit like Steffi Graf and immediately a crowd started following them chanting, 'Stefffi, Steffi.'

What made the welcome extraordinary is for many South Africans, particularly the whites in the party, this was their first introduction to the third world. Although they often said how in their own country the first world lived next door to the third, for most white people the poverty of the South African third world was carefully hidden. The black township of Alexandria is on the doorstep of Sandton, which under apartheid was a whites-only suburb, but few whites went to Alexandria and it might as well have been in Calcutta.

In Calcutta, on the other hand, the poverty was everywhere. Hossein, not given to sentiment, found himself crying as he looked out on the streets of Calcutta.

However, as the day of the match dawned, Hossein and people like him experienced a different dilemma: whom should they support? For the South African Indians who had come as supporters this was no problem. Their hearts and minds were with India. They wanted India to win so that their white counterparts could understand that Indians could also play cricket. The coolie could beat the 'baas', the term for the whites meaning boss. If they won at cricket, the Indians could also claim to be human beings with the same status as the white man. Hossein, as an official of the Cricket Board, supported South Africa and even took bets against India winning, but he did want the Indians to do well, to put up a show. The day before, he had gone to see the Indians practise in the nets and his heart had sunk. They looked so frail, so young. Compared to the heavy, muscular white bodies of the South Africans, they looked like school kids. He turned to Jimmy Cook, the South African batsman and said, 'This looks like a team from Lenasia (the Indian area outside Johannesburg where under the Group Areas Act Indians were forced to live). You will them beat easily.' Cook smiled and said, 'I hope so.'

Later, after the Indians had won the first two games to take the three-match series, Hossein would feel both humbled and proud. 'I had underestimated the Indians. I really thought the South Africans would beat them. The innings Manjrekar played in Delhi touched me and showed that Indians could play. It made a lot of white South Africans realise that Indians can also play cricket and for the first time they thought that Indians should be treated as human beings, just like the whites.'

Many in the South African party – both black and white – would echo that at the end of this extraordinary, week-long tour. After the series was over and the South Africans had returned home, satiated by the welcome they had received, not only in Calcutta but also in Gwalior and Delhi – in Gwalior they were the guests of Scindia at his palace and received the almost-cliched Indian welcome of snake charmers and fireworks – Richard Snell, one of the players, turned to Hossein and said, 'Eck man, it took me to go to India to realise how warm the Indians were.' He would only have had to drive a few miles out of the white suburbs of northern Johannesburg to Lenasia to meet his fellow Indians. But apartheid meant that he did not and now, as apartheid died, he had journeyed thousands of miles to discover his own countrymen. Nothing could have illustrated more vividly the effects of apartheid on the South Africans and how much this short tour had changed them.

The legacy of apartheid touched other Board officials as well. Some of the officials, particularly those who had come from the non-racial side, had to take stock and ask: which team do I support. Krish

Mackerdhuj had only a year ago been the head of the non-racial Cricket Board and a sworn enemy of both Bacher and what he saw as the racist, arrogant white cricket officials. Now he was vice-president of the United Cricket Board and at the first one-day international in Calcutta he suddenly realised, 'This is my team. I had always supported the opposition. For the first time I was supporting South Africa.'

The dilemma was even more acute for one of his colleagues in the non-racial Board. S.K. Reddy had been a convenor of selectors of the non-racial Board. Now he was a selector with the United Board and had chosen the South African team. As he watched the Indian captain Azharuddin go out for the toss with Rice, he could not help thinking of the time a few years ago when he had met Azharuddin in India. There was talk of Ali Bacher organising a rebel tour from India. Bacher had held secret talks with Mohinder Amarnath and had come close to finalising a team from India. Reddy had warned Azharuddin, 'Don't ever think of stepping foot in South Africa. You will not be welcome.' Azharuddin had assured him that no Indian player would be lured by Bacher's money and plans for a rebel Indian tour had collapsed.

Like Mackerdhuj, Reddy had also wanted South Africa to win, but he could not forget the humiliation apartheid had inflicted on him. Tears still welled in his eyes as he remembered that day in 1962 when his father had lost his home because their area was suddenly declared white. It was in Riverside, a beautiful area in Natal close to the Blue Lagoon. His father, a schoolteacher, worked nights as a wine waiter in a white hotel in Durban to build this beautiful home with a terrific sea view. But, once it had been declared a white area, he had to move and the government offered him a paltry 750 rands for a house worth many times more. Determined not to sell it to the government, he sold it to the first person that inquired, a Rhodesian, for 700 rands. He never owned a house again and died a broken man; the house he had to sell was, by 1991, worth 250,000 rands.

Reddy saw the South African team and experienced feelings similar to Neville Cardus. Cardus loved the Australian Victor Trumper, and when Australia played England he prayed that Trumper would score a century in an Australian all-out total of 105. So Reddy wanted the Indians to show that they too could play cricket and then get beaten. His wife had no such dual loyalties. She desperately wanted India to win. For her all this talk of new South Africa was just talk. The memories of the old South Africa were too recent, too deep – like the occasion in Durban when she had gone to a shop to buy cold drinks. She had just started drinking it when the white shopkeeper said, 'I am sorry dear, but you cannot drink it here.'

'Why not,' asked Mrs Reddy.

'I am sorry that is the law.'

Non-whites could buy drinks from the shop but not drink inside it, just as they could buy clothes from Woolworth's but not use its fitting rooms to try them on. Mrs Reddy slammed the drinks down on the counter and left.

'Have your drink. I don't want it.'

It was a petty humiliation from the days of petty apartheid, but as the Indians took to the field in Calcutta, she hoped her sporting heroes would humiliate the team her husband had helped to select and exact some revenge for the pain she had endured.

It is unlikely that the Indian cricketers who took to the field for the three one-day matches were aware of the burdens they carried or what was riding on their performances. For them it was another one-day series, more meaningless than most. The Indians, vastly more experienced than the South Africans, won both, at Calcutta and Gwalior, more convincingly than the margins suggested. Almost inevitably, Tendulkar won the Man of the Match award in Calcutta with a 62 which was crucial to the Indian victory. Some white South Africans who just believed that they could continue where they had left of when the boycott came in 1970 were rudely awakened. The whole South African team, apart from Kepler Wessels, was making its debut and it showed. However, some of the old attitudes of white supremacy appeared to linger on. The South Africans took defeat so badly in Calcutta that they complained about the Indians gouging the ball, but later withdrew their protest and apologised. As *Wisden* commented, 'it was too soon for them to turn so quickly from cricket's pariah to cricket's preacher.'

The best match was the third, when, with the series decided, India made a seemingly impregnable 287 for 4. South Africa surprised themselves and the Indians by making 288 for 2 and winning by 8 wickets. More than a year after this match, during the winter of 1992, I was in South Africa covering the first-ever Indian tour of the country and the first by a non-white team. One of the questions I was asked by a group of Indian-born South Africans was: how much money did the Indians take to lose the Delhi match?

As it happens Azharuddin, who had led India in the first two one-day matches, did not play in the third. Shastri captained them and there is no suggestion that the match was fixed, but it showed the feelings of the South African Indians who, having seen their champions easily beat their tormentors, could not understand how they could lose a match in which they had scored 287. It was also the first time I had heard about match-fixing in cricket. Little did I realise then that it was perhaps already in the air and ready to poison both Indian and world cricket.

Later on in that 1992-93 tour of South Africa, when India played South Africa in the second one-day international in Port Elizabeth, there was an incident that further raised all the old fears of the South African Indians. The Indians had lost the first one-day international at Cape Town by six wickets. In the second, Kapil Dev did what the Australians in 1947 called a 'Mankad'. As he ran up to bowl, seeing Peter Kirsten out of his ground, he ran him out as he backed up at the non-striker's end. Kapil had not warned the batsman, having done so three times previously on the tour, and Kirsten was furious. His captain Wessels shared his anger. Later in the over Wessels appeared to have collided with Kapil. Kapil complained that Wessels had actually whacked him on the shins with the bat, but Clive Lloyd, the match referee, found the charge unproven.

South African Indians were convinced the Port Elizabeth incident reflected white racist attitudes and I was asked by many if either Kirsten or Wessels had called Kapil names such as coolie. In fact there were no racial overtones to this incident and this was the only incident that marred what was billed as the Friendship Tour, with South Africans still talking of the tremendous hospitality they had received in India. Although the white regime was still in power and negotiations for South Africa's first free elections, allowing all its citizens irrespective of colour the vote, were still not sure of success, sporting apartheid, which had brought institutional racism into sport, had been eliminated.

The white regime in South Africa had been unique in trying to dictate to the sporting world how to play sport along racial lines; no country, not even Hitler's Germany had done that. Hitler and the Nazis were horrified by Jesse Owens, a man the Nazis portrayed as an ape, winning four gold medals in the 1936 Olympics, but could do nothing about it. The white South African regime not only refused to have their own black and brown South Africans playing with them, but also told the world that they would not play them if they included people of colour. After the boycott was instituted, the regime tried to fool the world by pretending it had changed, but this only led to absurdities such as the proposal that South Africa send alternate black and white teams to the Olympics, as under apartheid's laws blacks and whites were not allowed to be in the same changing rooms.

In 1992, however, such restrictions had gone. Nelson Mandela, whose picture was banned from South African papers until his release in February 1990, came to the Saturday of the second Test in Johannesburg. On his previous visit, in 1949, he had to sit in cages reserved for blacks and cheered Neil Harvey, now he was there as a guest of the Cricket Board and, cheered on by the mainly 21,000 white crowd, he supported the new South Africa. The first Test in Durban also saw Omar Henry make history as the first coloured South African to play for his country and players on both sides got on very well, with the South Africans much taken by Raju, the smallest of the Indian cricketers and quite the most delightful. If the Indian cricket team encountered any racist attitudes it was in Harare, where they had gone for Zimbabwe's inaugural Test match. There, despite ten years of black rule, Indians found that the old racist attitudes of the white settlers still lived on.

The Indians had gone to Zimbabwe before going on to South Africa and had hardly distinguished themselves on the field. On a lifeless Harare track, Zimbabwe became the first Test debutants since Australia, back in 1876-77 when Test cricket began, to avoid defeat. Indeed they came close to embarrassing India, totalling 456, and then forcing India to battle hard to avoid the follow-on, which they did with a dogged Manjrekar century. Even then the Indians had conceded a first-innings lead of 149.

The match provided a portent for the South African tour where the Indians lost the one-day series, which came in the middle of the four-Test series, by 5–2, and the four-Test series 1–0. This defeat in the third Test in Port Elizabeth was largely due to the bowling of Allan Donald who had figures of 12 for 139 in the match and a dogged hundred by Cronje.

The defeat showed up all the Indians' old frailties against high-class pace bowling, although the South Africans also benefited from some dubious umpiring decisions.

The Indians could argue that what luck there was always went for the South Africans and, but for a decision by West Indian umpire Steve Bucknor, they would have come to Port Elizabeth already 1–0 ahead in the series. The first Test in Durban had been even with Praveen Amre, another Achrekar product, scoring a century on debut. In the second in Johannesburg, South Africa, batting first, were reduced to 26 for 4 (three for Prabhakar) on the first morning. Jonty Rhodes and Brian McMillan were putting together a rescue stand when, with score on 61 and Rhodes on 28, he was run out by a direct hit. However, Bucknor, being poorly positioned, was unsighted and refused to call the third umpire, in spite of Indian pleading to do so. Rhodes went on to make 91, MacMillan a century and South Africa ended up with 292.

Having one neutral umpire was an innovation for Test cricket and using television replays to settle controversial decisions, such as run outs, stumpings and hit-wickets, was another first. For the first time in Test history a third umpire sitting in the stands could, after watching replays, signal with either a green light or a red light to indicate whether a batsman was out or not. The Indians, and in particular Tendulkar, had been the first-ever victims of it when, in Durban, the camera showed that Rhodes had run out Tendulkar. Without the help of television replays the umpire would have had to give Tendulkar not out. But in Johannesburg Bucknor's refusal to call for television replays meant they could not benefit from it and the advantage of that first morning in Johannesburg was never consolidated.

In the end it required a century from Tendulkar to keep the Indians in the second Test. His 111 out of 227 – the next higher scorer was Kapil Dev with 25 – made him the youngest batsman, at 19 years 217 days, to reach 1,000 Test runs, displacing Kapil Dev who had reached it at 21 years 21 days.

Johannesburg was crucial because after that the teams played a series of one-day matches before resuming the Tests. Until that point the South Africans, playing in their first home series for 22 years, had looked more than a trifle nervous, but the victories in the one-day series gave them a tremendous lift and, much as the Indians felt hard done by at Johannesburg – although they did not help themselves by dropping catches – they could have no quarrels with South Africa's overall supremacy. They were the better all-round side in a drab series.

The might-have-beens of the South African tour were, of course, déjà vu for the Indians. They had had a similar story to tell about their Australian trip the year before, in the winter of 1991-92. Here again there were umpiring decisions that did not go for them and then the weather also conspired against them at crucial times.

This was the first series in Test history which saw the appointment of a match referee, but he do could little, for the umpires were both Australians; the umpiring got so bad that halfway through the second Test at Melbourne the Indian tour manager asked the Australians not to appoint a particular umpire. *Wisden* commented, 'There were other occasions when the Indians expressed dissatisfaction with the umpiring. As often as not, television showed their complaints to be justified. At one stage India's cricket manager, Abbas Ali Baig, drew attention to the disparity in lbw decisions given against the two sides. "Perhaps," he noted dryly, "there are changes in the law with which we have not been made aware."'

Had everything gone for the Indians they could have gone into the fifth Test in Perth all square.

The Indians had made their usual bad start and before the tour was a month old the Indians were 2–0 down in the Test series, the only surprise being that the tour predictions had been proved wrong. Prior to the tour, the pundits had suggested that the Indians would bat well, but bowl abysmally. As things turned out, the Indian bowling often tested the Australians and it was the batting that failed in both of the first two Tests. When it did come good, luck ran out for the tourists.

In the third Test at Sydney, having bowled out Australia for 313, they made their best score of the series, 483, led by Shastri's 206. He put on 196 with Tendulkar, who made 148, becoming the youngest batsman to score a Test century in Australia. One of the bowlers he annihilated was Shane Warne, who, making his Test debut, bowled 45 overs taking 1 for 150. But with rain and bad light robbing 49.1 overs, Australia, at 173 for 8 in their second innings, just about held on for the draw with Warne batting out time with Border.

The fourth Test at Adelaide again had moments when it seemed as though India might take charge. Australia were bowled out for 145 in their first innings and India seemed to be ready to repeat the mighty run chases of the 1970s. Set 371 to win, India came to within 38 runs of victory led by Azharuddin's spectacular 106. However, two crucial lbw decisions went against Vengsarkar and Tendulkar, both of which *Wisden* felt were harsh and then, as so often, the Indians did not help themselves with Manjrekar being run out when going well on 45.

The final Test at Perth, which India lost by 300 runs and with it the series 4–0, perhaps made the gulf between the two sides appear greater than it really was. At Sydney, Tendulkar had provided the Australians with a glimpse of his class. Now he underlined it with an innings that had them in raptures. In the first innings he came in with the score on 69 for 2 facing an Australian first innings of 346. He was ninth out at 240, making 114 from 161 balls. In the process he put on a record Indian ninth-wicket stand against Australia of 81 with Kiran More. As he ran out of partners he stepped up the pace, his second 50 coming in just 55 balls. The Australians won the match, but the critics were unanimous in hailing Tendulkar as a genius.

The Indians, who have a dreadful record in Australia, were not on the whole surprised by the Test results, but hoped that in the World Cup that followed they could come good. In 1985 they had gone to Australia having been beaten by David Gower's Englishmen, but then went on to win the Benson and Hedges Cup which was very much like a World Cup involving the other Test playing nations.

But the 1992 World Cup proved another disappointment and merely added more grist to the ever-productive mills churning out the tearful tales of Indian cricketing might-have-beens. They lost to England in their opening match by 9 runs, then rain caused their match against Sri Lanka to be abandoned and against Australia they had to be content with a new rule which penalised sides batting second in a match shortened by rain. Chasing Australia's 237 from 50 overs, rain reduced the match by three overs but the Indian target was reduced by just one run and they failed by two to get them. So after the first four matches India had just three points and did not make it to the semi-finals, all the more galling as Pakistan, like India, made a shocking start – they were also beaten by India in a match in which Tendulkar starred – but then went on to win the World Cup.

The Indians, great believers in fate, could not blame it all on luck. Their cricket administration had to take responsibility for the shocking way they prepared for major tours. The South African visit to India in November 1991 may have been great theatre and good cricket politics, but it had done little for Indian cricket. Nine days after the day-night match in Delhi, the Indians were in Lismore playing their opening match of the Australian tour against New South Wales. As so often the Indian Board had shot itself in the foot. Despite the fact that the Indians needed to adjust to the very different Australian conditions, the Indian Board insisted that they did not need more than one first-class match before going into the Tests. The cricketers on the field paid a heavy price for such short-sightedness.

By the following year, and the first-ever Indian visit to southern Africa, the Board did not appear to have learned any lessons from the Australian tour. They sent the team to Harare without acclimatization to altitude, and only a one-day match as preparation for the Test. The players were still adjusting to the conditions by the time the Test was over and lost a chance to beat a novice team and gain a much-needed boost before an important Test series.

But much as they cursed their luck and their administrators, the Indians had to accept that the two successive tours of Australia and South Africa merely showed how far Indian cricket had declined since the heady days of 1986 and their 2–0 triumph in England.

The South African tour had been their sixth overseas tour since the triumphant English one in 1986 and during that period the Indians had failed to win a single Test abroad, let alone a series. If at times during the six years Indian cricket had taken one step forward, and the arrival of Tendulkar was a giant leap forward, then it was followed with two or even three or four steps back. India, it seemed, was always caught trying to walk up on the down escalator.

This was clearly the case with the batting. The Indians had come to England in 1990 with a formidable batting line-up and had made their record Test score in England. But, by 1992, many of the batting stars of the tour, who had looked like being major players, had either retired or were in decline. There was no solution to the opening batting problem. Sidhu and Shastri who had looked a decent pair for England had gone. Halfway through the Australian tour, just after Shastri had made his 206 at Sydney, he injured his knee and Srikkanth was unexpectedly recalled. Neither he nor Sidhu made it to South Africa, where India began with Shastri and Jadeja, neither real openers. Then Woorkeri Raman, yet another middle-order batsman, was pushed up to open in the lost Port Elizabeth Test and then Prabhakar, an all-rounder who normally batted in the lower order, opened in the fourth

Test in Cape Town. The failure to find a proper opening pair may not have mattered in India, but abroad this often caught the Indians out. It is perhaps not surprising that 1986 was the last time India had Gavaskar touring abroad, and since then India had failed to find any sort of replacement for him and their batsmen had rarely made a decent start.

This lack of openers meant the Indian middle-order was always trying to rescue innings rather than build on them and this took its toll. Manjrekar, the find of the 1989 West Indies tour, began with a century in Harare but then declined, averaging 23.20, and the middle-order appeared to be a case of new discoveries one season only to be found wanting the next. Praveen Amre seemed a great prospect when making his century in his Durban Test debut, but in the rest of the series he did not pass 50 once and ended with an average of 33.80.

In some ways the bowling was more encouraging. Prabhakar, whose eight wickets in England in 1990 had cost 69.25 each, did very much better in Australia, taking 19 wickets at 35.78 each and bowled with both great heart and character. He was more expensive in South Africa, but did have, as we have seen, one golden spell in Johannesburg and was seen as a great hero for the Indians of South Africa. This, though, did cause some amusing incidents – if only to reveal the absurdities of apartheid.

An article presenting him as a raunchy Indian sex hero was the main feature in the Durban paper on the Sunday of the first Test. In the press box that day the article was much discussed by the journalists. Normally in a South Africa-India series there would not be any English cricket writers present, but as this was South Africa's first home Test series since 1970, when the white team had played Australia, the English press was there to witness history being made and amongst them was Peter Johnson, then cricket correspondent of the *Daily Mail*.

That Sunday morning he was a bit nonplussed by all the talk of Prabhakar as a sex symbol. He had the same paper as the rest of us, but could not find this feature which everyone was talking about. He turned to me and I, giving him my Indian edition, said, 'Peter, as a white man you have the main white edition, this is in the Indian edition and in this instance you have missed out because you are not an Indian.' Peter, a lovely, sweet man, who could not imagine what apartheid could be like, laughed, but the little incident showed how the wretched system still operated.

The South Africa tour saw the further development of the find of the Australian tour, that rare thing: a new Indian fast bowler. He was said to be the fastest since Nissar and Amar Singh. He was Javagal Srinath from Karnataka.

Players from this state usually come from Bangalore and in the past

412

had been mainly spinners. Srinath was from the semi-urban or moffusil areas of the state and was actually spotted by a Bangalore journalist. Then he was more of a dashing batsman than a bowler. However, it was as a bowler he impressed Viswanath in a club match and, since he was also a Karnataka selector, Srinath was soon called up for the state. On his Ranji debut in 1989-90 he took 5 wickets in the first innings including an hat-trick, but he played in just six matches that season, taking 24 wickets, as Karnataka were eliminated early from the competition. At this stage it was by no means certain he would be more than a useful state bowler. He was studying engineering and in India, where the divide between the richer cities and the semi-urban moffusil areas where he came from is wide, the travelling involved in cricket was proving too much.

But the following season when Karnataka played Maharashtra on the batsman-friendly wicket of the Nehru Stadium in Pune, Srinath showed he could rise far above the mediocrity of Indian opening bowlers. Maharashtra, facing Karnataka's 638, had begun well and were 221 for 3, with Srinath having taken two wickets. He came back with such an inspired spell of reverse swing bowling that Maharashtra were all out for 311, and he had finished with 7 for 93.

A few months later he was bowling on the bouncy, quick tracks of Australia, and while his Australian performances did not appear that wonderful, he made a mark with his bowling. At the end of the Australian trip his figures were far from wonderful, his 10 wickets came at an average 55.30, but he had impressed with his pace, overall class, his ability to cut the ball back in to right-handers from wide of the crease and with a bit of luck might have had better figures. Srinath continued to progress through the South African series, taking 12 Test wickets at 26.08 and coming on first change, after Kapil and Prabhakar. India now had an opening attack which was more than merely Kapil Dev.

The South African series also confirmed the Test place of another Karnataka bowler who had also done well in the Maharashtra match of two years ago, except not with the ball but with the bat. Anil Kumble, batting at no. 8, had made 111 – Srinath had made 59 – and this match was part of Kumble's efforts to make the Indian selectors look at him again. He had been on the 1990 England tour, headed the Test averages, but his three wickets at 56.66 each showed how the Indian bowlers had suffered during that hot summer. At 6 feet 2 inches he was unusually tall for an Indian, wore glasses and was more famous that season for Brian Johnson linking his name with Apple Crumble.

Kumble was dropped after the tour and, as he had toured England with Hirwani, there was the depressing thought that he might be another in a long line of one-series leg-spinners – as both Hirwani and, before him, Sivaramakrishnan had proved to be. But unlike them Kumble was both persistent and a good learner. He went back home to work on his bowling.

Like Srinath he studied engineering, but unlike Srinath he had learned his cricket in Bangalore, which by this time was India's fastest growing city and is now the centre of its Silicon Valley. There, on matting wickets spread over baked mud, he had changed, at the age of fifteen, from medium pace to leg-spin, at the suggestion of his brother, and using his height got considerable bounce. He was not a classical leg-spinner, more a quickish wrist-spinner who did not turn the ball much, and many batsmen played him like a medium-pacer.

After his failure in England, Kumble shed his glasses and proved so effective a bowler in domestic cricket – his Ranji Trophy performances included a hat-trick – that, having missed the Australian tour, he forced the selectors to bring him back for South Africa. He easily headed the Indian bowling averages with 18 wickets at 25.94, taking 6 for 53 in the South African second innings in Johannesburg when they were bowled out for 252. On wickets not made for spin, Kumble troubled all the South African batsmen and his performances held out the hope that India might at last have found a spinner who was here to stay.

Throughout all these ups and downs, Tendulkar had continued to blossom as though nothing could stop him from fulfilling his destiny to become the master batsman of his generation. In 1990, in England, Tendulkar had averaged 61.25. A year later in Australia he averaged 46 in Tests and 47.17 in the World Cup. At this stage he was still batting in the middle-order in one-day internationals, but nevertheless still won the only two Man of the Match awards India got in the competition. In South Africa he seemed to take a step back, averaging 33.66, with more than half of his runs coming in the 111 he made at the Wanderers. If this was a decline it was noticeable how the South Africans celebrated when they got him out to a dubious decision in Port Elizabeth, knowing that his fall meant the end of real Indian resistance.

The decline may also have been due to the fact that the virtually non-stop cricket in the past twelve months had finally caught up with the young man: a tour of Australia, followed by a first-ever season in English cricket and then South Africa. That first season in county cricket had seen Tendulkar become a pioneer and reflected how far and how fast he had come since his previous visit to England in 1990. On that first visit he was the wonder kid and the older players would joke with him; sometimes on plane trips as the air hostesses came round offering drinks they would suggest a glass of milk for Tendulkar. When he came to England in the summer of 1992, he was not merely an exceptional young cricketer but one who could help break age-old racial and social barriers.

Yorkshire had decided to have an overseas player for the first time and the initial choice was Craig McDermott, then the Australian fast-bowling spearhead. But when he broke down, Solly Adams, an Indian who had made Bradford his home, persuaded Yorkshire to go for Tendulkar. He would not only be the first foreigner to play for Yorkshire but the first Asian and this, Adams felt, would help break the racial divide in Yorkshire cricket. This was so entrenched that by then, almost half a century after Asians had started coming to Yorkshire in numbers, not a single Asian cricketer had made it to the all-white Yorkshire cricket teams.

Tendulkar was not that keen to come: not because he was worried about being a cricketing pioneer, but because he wanted a rest from cricket. When Adams, who is close to Gavaskar, rang him in Bombay, Tendulkar said, 'Solly I have just come back from Australia. In October I go to South Africa. Come off it, I'm not coming.'

Adams pleaded, 'Listen, these people have never shared a dressing room with a coloured bloke for 128 years. It is my dream to get an Asian to play for Yorkshire. We don't want an Australian or a South African. We have got a chance. I don't want to see it go.'

Eventually, after involved negotiations with Sunil Gavaskar, who acted as his adviser, Tendulkar agreed to come. But first Yorkshire had to agree to a condition. Gavaskar and Tendulkar wanted to know how much Yorkshire had promised McDermott. The Australian was offered £30,000, yet Yorkshire offered Tendulkar only £20,000. Tendulkar insisted he must be on the same terms as the Australian and when Yorkshire agreed the deal was done.

Yorkshire made much of Tendulkar both as their first overseas player and as an Asian. On his arrival in London he held a press conference and when he got to Headingley he was, under the gaze of television cameras, shown round the Yorkshire dressing rooms by Geoffrey Boycott. It was billed as Yorkshire's greatest-ever batsman meeting Yorkshire's best current batsman. Boycott took him to his special corner in the dressing room and advised Tendulkar to grab a corner as soon as possible. Then, with a wink, he mentioned that there were four or five girls in the Yorkshire office who liked a curry and that Tendulkar would be wise to take them out and get to know them.

Tendulkar smiled and did all the right things, but two relatively trivial moments showed the character of this exceptional young man. The first was at the press conference in London where he kept referring to Gavaskar as Mr. Gavaskar, never Sunil or Sunny, and the politeness of the young man, just turned nineteen, impressed the English cricket writers.

Years later when I asked Tendulkar about this he seemed surprised by my question. As a well brought up Indian he would not dream of addressing Gavaskar as anything other than Mr.

But polite as he was, he also had a sharp value of his own worth. This showed not only in making sure Yorkshire paid him as much as they were prepared to pay McDermott, but also in a revealing moment at the Headingley nets. I had gone there with a photographer for a feature on Tendulkar. As the photographer started taking pictures Tendulkar intervened and, pushing aside some of the equipment, said, 'No, I don't want those photographed. I have finished with that sponsorship.'

Tendulkar had arrived in Yorkshire just after celebrating his nineteenth birthday, when pictures of him cutting the cake made the front pages of the Bombay papers, pushing aside weightier political news. The burden he was asked to carry in Yorkshire was far too great, and while he scored 1,000 runs and averaged 46.52, hitting four centuries, he could not be a miracle worker.

How much the Yorkshire experience affected Tendulkar in South Africa is difficult to say, but the series in South Africa was notable for the fact that it was perhaps the last when Tendulkar took second billing to another Indian cricketer, Kapil Dev. Throughout the tour to South Africa, Kapil Dev was the one Indian cricketer every Indian in South Africa wanted to see. The Indian tourists were inundated with invitations from the South African Indians who felt that after 130 years of humiliation and hurt they could at last look their fellow whites in the eye and say, 'We coolies can also play cricket.' Kapil was inevitably the star of these Indian parties and at one of them he was presented with a car.

The Australian series had seen Kapil Dev pass 400 Test victims and his 25 Test wickets was his best-ever series abroad. His South Africa bowling was steady rather than spectacular, but he showed that he could still conjure magic out of nothing. In the second innings of the Port Elizabeth Test he came into bat with India reeling at 27 for 5 in the second innings – still 37 behind and facing a three-day defeat. Kapil then took the attack to the South African bowling in such style, unmatched by anybody else in that drab series, that his 129 in 177 balls was made out of the 188 runs India added to take the match to a fourth day – the next highest score was 17. India set South Africa 155, and while they made it with 9 wickets and a day to spare it made a match of it. It says something of the Indian batting on this tour that Kapil's 129 meant his Test aggregate came to 202 and he easily headed the Indian batting averages with 40.40.

However, this was an old Indian story – a heroic knock in a losing Indian cause – and the Indians returned from South Africa thoroughly depressed. As so often the talk turned to the captaincy. Azharuddin had been captain since 1990 and India had lost four Test series and only scraped a draw against debutants Zimbabwe. As the Indians and South

Africans batted out a dull draw in Cape Town, Indian journalists began writing obituaries of Azharuddin's captaincy and looked forward to the return of Kapil Dev. No sooner had the plane touched down in Bombay, than Kapil Dev was asked to step to one side for an important message from the selectors.

But in Indian cricket nothing is as it seems. Azharuddin's record was dreadful, but then he had only captained India once at home and won that Test against Sri Lanka. Abroad he could show no victories, at home he had a 100 per cent record. His defeats abroad were magnified because the Indian Board had so managed its cricket affairs that between the tour of the West Indies in 1989 and South Africa in 1992-93, India had played only one Test at home.

Indians rarely did well away from home and perhaps this swayed the selectors. Perhaps there were other factors, like a report by the South African tour manager Ajit Wadekar. Kapil was immensely sought after by the South African Indians, but he had not been popular on the tour with the players or the management, behaving in what was seen as a prima-donna fashion. There was talk that Gavaskar, who had been commentating on the tour on television, had a word with his old captain and neighbour Wadekar and swung things Azharuddin's way. Kapil, himself, told the selectors he would only take the job if Azharuddin gave it up. Azharuddin was not inclined to do so although he was clearly very much on trial. India's first home series, for five years, would start with two one-day internationals and then three Tests, the first in Calcutta. The Selectors announced that Azharuddin would be Captain until Calcutta. They did not have to say that if India did not start turning things around that was the last time he would be Captain.

Keith Fletcher, the England tour manager, had been to South Africa during the Johannesburg Test and said he had not seen anything from India to worry him. England had not toured India for almost a decade and came in a jaunty mood under Graham Gooch. They were already playing in India as the Cape Town Test was on and there seemed no reason why the Indians should approach their first home series since 1988 with any great confidence.

Not for the first time, however, Indian cricket was to prove to be full of surprises and, for a change, it was India surprising its opponents rather than the other way round.

28

Indian cricket's Ram Rajya
1993-94

Indian cricket has had many ups and downs, but the fourteen months it had between January 1993 and March 1994 were unparalleled in its history. Everything it touched turned to gold, and for a moment Indians could dream that their cricket team was finally fulfilling its destiny to be world-beaters. Ram Rajya, the kingdom of the god Ram, the mythological Hindu age of perfection, was finally here.

In those fourteen months India played seven Test matches at home against three different opponents and won them all, six of them by an innings. India also won its first Test and series abroad since 1986. If the one-day record was not quite as overwhelming – as part of the growing trend since the World Cup win of 1983, India played four times as many one-day internationals as Tests – it was still impressive: 17 victories in 29 one-day internationals against nearly all the Test playing countries. The home victories meant that, since 1988, India had won eleven of the twelve Tests it had played at home and both the team and individuals had broken records along the way.

Yet such an outcome seemed most unlikely mid-afternoon on 29 January 1993. At that stage in the first Test at Eden Gardens, as Azharuddin came out to bat, India, on winning the toss, were 93 for 3. Azharuddin knew this was his last chance. If he failed he would undoubtedly be sacked as captain. His reappointment was for the two one-day internationals and the first Test. India had lost the first one-day match, won the second and Azharuddin with the bat had made 6 and 36.

Now, on the ground where he made a century on his Test debut against Gower's team, he proceeded to play a quite amazing innings. His 182 so totally dominated the Indian innings of 371 that only Tendulkar, with 50, made any other significant runs. England played into his hands by going in with four seamers on a dry, brown but firm wicket. The Indians read the wicket much better and went into the game with three spinners: Kumble leg-spin; Raju left-arm; and a Test debut for off-spinner Rajesh Chauhan. But, nevertheless, Azharuddin still had to bat well and he made the most of conditions that suited his wristy stroke play.

Azharuddin's innings changed both the match and the series. India's 371 began to look much more formidable when the three spinners got going. Taking three wickets each they forced England to follow-on and, although England saved themselves from an innings defeat, they lost by eight wickets as the spinners picked up up 17 of the 20 wickets to fall in the match.

For Azharuddin the moment was all the sweeter as this was India's first home Test win since the victory over New Zealand in his native Hyderabad on 6 December 1988, when Azharuddin had been India's top scorer with 81. Azharuddin was confirmed as captain for the series and, almost in an instant, the gloom of South Africa vanished. The Indians visibly grew in the remaining two Tests and there followed many moments of special Indian delight.

In Madras, two weeks later, India made 560 for 6 declared, their highest-ever score against England in India. Sidhu scored a first-day century, Tendulkar a second-day century, 165, with 24 fours and a six, which took six hours. He might have been run out when he was on 9 – the use of the third umpire had not become universal – but this could not take anything away from the majesty of his innings, which saw some breathtaking square driving. Tendulkar was in such command that when he fell to Ian Salisbury he was visibly angry at missing out on his double century. This time the follow-on was even more difficult to avoid, the innings defeat was inevitable and the eventual margin of victory, an innings and 22 runs, was the biggest victory by an Indian side over England.

Indians were sent scurrying back to the record books to find the last time they had beaten England by an innings. It was, of course, the first time they had won a Test, also in Madras, with Mankad proving too much for the English batsman. This time it was Kumble who created the problems for the English. He took 2 for 61 in the first innings and 6 for 64 in the second, with the three spinners, as at Calcutta, taking 17 of the 20 wickets.

However, in many ways, the sweetest triumph came in Bombay a week later. Although Tendulkar was by now almost a veteran, this was the first time he was playing in a Test in Bombay. In this he was like his hero Gavaskar, who had to wait two years after his debut before playing his first Test in Bombay and that, too, was against England.

It was also, of course, Kambli's first Bombay Test and the city buzzed with speculation as to how the two Shardashram boys would do in their first Bombay Test together. Kambli, who had long been left behind by Tendulkar, had had to be content, since 1990, with making copious runs in domestic cricket. In his first three seasons for Bombay he had made 2,400 runs from twenty matches, with nine hundreds, at an average of 85.71. Domestic runs are cheap, but the selectors had to take note and on his debut in the first one-day international at Jaipur he had scored 100 not out. But, until Bombay, and thanks to India's dominance, he had only had three innings scoring 16, 18 not out and 59. Now in Bombay, with their former coach Achrekar watching, Kambli seized his moment and, for a time on the second day as he and Tendulkar batted together, it was a bit like Shardashram versus England. If their partnership was not quite a world record, it was a very formidable 194 for the third wicket.

Tendulkar joined Kambli with India already in command at 174 for 2. By the time Tendulkar was out for 78, India had reached 368 and were already 21 runs ahead of England's 347.

Kambli was determined to emerge from the shadow of Tendulkar. So far he had done so by being different. In a society that is very colour conscious, he was very dark, or ebony coloured as the Indians called him, and he consciously seemed to model himself on the West Indians. He was known as 'Des' after Desmond Haynes, a hero of Kambli, and, in a society which liked its young men to be conformists, Kambli stood out as a bit of a rebel and very different to Tendulkar or other young cricketers. So as his school mate grew in cricket stature, Kambli became a character. The day Tendulkar went out to bat for the first time in Headingley on his Yorkshire debut, Kambli stood at the boundary edge machine gunning the crowd in mock horror. Tendulkar would never have indulged in such antics, Kambli thought it was a huge joke.

His cricket also emphasised this difference. As a left-hander he was bound to be very different in an Indian line-up where good left-handers have always been rare. His batting had always had an element of the West Indian about it, and during this innings he so captivated the crowd that *Wisden* described it as an 'innings of rare quality, full of daring stroke play, with a joyfulness that rippled around the ground'.

At the end of the third day with India on 397 for 3, already 50 ahead of England, Kambli, on 164 not out, could set his sights on all sorts of records. No Indian has ever made a triple hundred in Tests. But he fell for 224, which was still the highest score by an Indian against England. By the time India were all out, they had broken their Madras record against England with a score of 591.

Graeme Hick had scored his maiden Test century in the first innings, but in the second there was less resistance and the winning margin of an innings of 15 runs was only seven less than at Madras. Kumble took 7 wickets in the match and finished the series with 21 wickets at 19.80. For a man who less than two years ago had thought of giving up cricket because he was not selected for the Australian tour, this was a remarkable comeback, one matched by the entire Indian team.

Never before had India won every Test in a series and at end of the

Bombay Test, at a highly charged press conference, Gooch took responsibility and spoke of quitting. The Indians, who two months ago could not wait to get rid of Azharuddin, now could not dream of having any other captain. Between 29 January and 23 February his position had changed from being untenable to being unassailable.

The English failure, which was both a cricketing and a cultural one, led to an inquest in England. The cricketing failure was partly due to smugness. In Johannesburg, seeing the Indians in totally different conditions, Fletcher had said that England had nothing to fear. Having watched Kumble he said, 'I didn't see him turn a single ball from leg to off. I don't believe we will have many problems with him.' Geoffrey Boycott, also seeing them in South Africa, described the Indians as the worst side in international cricket for twenty-eight years, and Illingworth pilloried the selectors for choosing Fairbrother and Hick for India. They were, he said, sure to make runs in India since it had such a popgun attack. But would they make them against Australia? In the event Hick made runs, heading the English averages with 52.50, Fairbrother averaged 33.50.

The cultural failure was more devastating. For, as the Indians saw it, the English reaction to defeat was to blame the Indian conditions: too much smog, the wrong kind of prawns and some sharp practice by the Indians.

The prawns story was the most curious. The night before the Madras Test, Gooch and Gatting had eaten in the hotel's Chinese restaurant and had an extra plate of prawns. Just before the toss Gooch fell ill and withdrew from the Test. During the match, Mike Gatting and Robin Smith, who had eaten chicken in his hotel room, left the field feeling ill. The English accusations over Indian food so upset the hotel, one of the best in India, that it pointed out that other members of the team had eaten there without any problems.

This complaint came after the one following the defeat in the Calcutta Test when Dexter, chairman of the England selectors, pointed to smog in the city as the cause and said a study on pollution levels in Indian cities had been commissioned.

To say that smog contributed to the English defeat in Calcutta was strange, as the smog, though bad, was probably a little better than in 1976 when Tony Greig's side easily beat India. The English also complained of Indian batsmen ruining the pitch in Madras by running on it with their spikes. For the Indians it seemed an old English problem in India. They just could not accept defeat from a country they had once lorded over. Teams do not win three successive Tests by such margins because of these factors. If so, how did England consistently manage to lose to Australia through much of the 1930s and 1940s when smog was a factor in London?

As *Wisden* commented, Dexter's remarks were a bit of a smoke screen and nothing further was ever heard of his investigation into pollution. The essential failure was that the English batsmen could not play the turning ball, and by the end of the tour Fletcher bemoaned the lack of such wickets in England.

But such excuses merely exposed the greater cultural failure. Why Englishmen – who have known India for over 300 years and ruled it for all but 200 years, giving it many of the institutions it still cherishes including cricket – should find the place so incomprehensible is one of the great mysteries of the Occident. It would be tempting to say that the fault lies with the present generation of cricketers, the products of council houses and comprehensives. But even in the past, with honourable exceptions, the English have struggled to come to terms with India.

This tour underlined the fact that the Indian subcontinent is like no other place on earth. Although modern air travel had reduced distances, and although some of the best hotels in the world can be found there, India was still not part of the all-night disco, quick food, easy sex, sun and sand environment that is the norm in Australia, South Africa or even the West Indies. And although there was plenty of booze, and Indians can be hard drinkers, it tended to be whisky rather than the modern Western cultural favourites of beer and wine. The India of 1993 was more akin to a 1950s England than a 1990s Australia, and the English cricketers found the cultural gap just too big to bridge.

The tour marked another significant innovation for Indian cricket. The Board, having discovered via the South Africans that television rights for matches had a commercial value, now sold their television rights to TWI, the television arm of Mark McCormark's marketing company, IMG. In England, the matches were shown on Sky, every ball of every one-day international and Test, the first time that such broadcasts had taken place from India to England. This had another curious result.

The technology allowed for viewers to choose the language of the commentary team. The main commentary, which was broadcast on Sky to England, was in English. But at Sky's headquarters in Isleworth there was a subsidiary team which spoke in Hindi and which was clearly aimed at the Indians living in England. I was part of that commentary team, along with Faroukh Engineer, and while the main team of Gower, Bob Willis, Boycott and Gavaskar were in India, we were in a little room in Isleworth commentating on the pictures broadcast from there. It was a bit of a con. It had arisen from a suggestion by the Indian High Commission in London and Sky clearly saw it as a marketing tool. It is not known how many more viewers Sky got as a result, but it showed how sports broadcasts could reach places that other broadcasts could not, and also highlighted the growing international appeal of Indian cricket.

The Indians, revelling in their victory, went on to beat Zimbabwe, winning the solitary Test in Delhi by an innings and 13 runs and the three-match one-day series 3–0. The win in the Delhi Test came despite losing a day to rain – a commentary on woeful Indian covers – with India making its third-successive first-innings score of over 500, 536, with Kambli scoring 227. He was now reaching the dizzy heights attained by Hammond and Bradman: successive Test double hundreds. Zimbabwe, helped by a day's loss of play, seemed to have made the Test safe before a sudden rush of blood by Andy Flower led to a first-innings collapse, follow-on and defeat by an innings and 13 runs.

But these were victories at home. What about when India went abroad? In July, India left for only their second-ever tour of Sri Lanka. In 1985 on the first tour, as we have seen, they had provided Sri Lanka with its first-ever Test triumph. Now on 1 August, at the Sinhalese Sports Club ground in Colombo, India won their first overseas Test for seven years.

The first Test in Kandy had been the shortest-ever Test match, with only 12 overs and forty-nine minutes of play possible due to rain. But it had also shown that the Indian bowling might trouble the Sri Lankan batsman and this proved to be the case at the Sinhalese ground. Again Kambli led the batting. His century meant that since Bombay he had scored 224, 227 and now 127, and his innings totally dominated the Indian total of 366. Sri Lanka's reply of 254, with Kumble taking 5 for 87, gave India a lead of 112.

In the second innings Kambli failed, and reacted so badly when given out for 4 that he was reluctant to leave the crease, and only did so after shedding some tears. The Indians felt this was one of many bad decisions. The age of the independent umpire had not yet dawned, and the Test saw many Indian complaints. The Indians felt that the Sri Lankans' umpiring was so poor that they had to take more than 20 wickets to win a Test and at one stage, in mid-Test, there had to be a meeting between the two sides to cool matters down. Victory restored Indian spirits, although even on the final morning it had looked unlikely.

Sri Lanka, set 472 to win in nine hours, were 180 for 3, but then Prabhakar, with the new ball, took two wickets in five balls, Sri Lanka collapsed and India won by 235 runs, ending an abysmal away record which read ten defeats and sixteen draws since Headingley in June 1986.

India were also in with a chance of winning the final Test in Colombo, on a different ground to the second, with Kambli making another hundred, 120, and, as in Bombay, recreating his old school partnership with Tendulkar, putting on 162 in 204 minutes with Tendulkar who made 71.

On the final morning, Sri Lanka, 95 behind, were perilously placed at 157 for 4 but Roshan Mahanama with 151 and Hashan Tillakaratne with 86 saw them to safety.

In January 1994 Sri Lanka returned to India. As in 1990 they came at short notice, with Pakistan having cried off on security fears, and their reward was the biggest drubbing any visiting team had received since the West Indies toured England for the first time in 1928. For only the second time in Test history, a team won every Test in a series by an innings.

The Indian victories read: Lucknow, an innings and 119 runs, Bangalore an innings and 95 runs, Ahmedabad an innings and 17 runs.

Both in Lucknow – in a stadium named after local boy K.D. Singh Babu, India's legendary hockey hero – and in Ahmedabad, India made over 500. This meant that since February 1993 in Madras, India at home had made: 560 for 6 declared, 591 (against England), 536 for 7 declared (against Zimbabwe), 511 and 541 for 6 declared (against Sri Lanka).

True, the wickets were doctored, but as *Wisden* commented, 'Not even an Asian side, accustomed to such conditions, could resist the Indian juggernaut, running on the wheels of wristy batsmanship and spiteful spin bowling.'

Against England, in January 1993, Sidhu, omitted from the South African tour and playing for the Indian Board President's XI against England, had decided to hit Emburey, who had come on the tour as the main England spinner, out of the attack. He hit him for four sixes in each innings. The result was that Emburey was not chosen for Calcutta and played such a marginal role in the series, only playing in Bombay, that in the tour averages his figures were listed in the 'also bowled' column at the end of the bowling averages: 2 for 144 in 59 overs.

Now at the K.D. Singh Babu Stadium, Sidhu decided to deal with Muralitharan emerging as the bright hope of Sri Lankan cricket. He hit him for six of his eight sixes, only two short of Wally Hammond's Test record of ten sixes against New Zealand in 1932-33. Muralitharan did get Sidhu's wicket after he had made 124, took 5 for 162 and was the pick of the Sri Lankan spinners in the series, but neither he nor the other Sri Lankan spinners were as effective as their Indian counterparts. Muralitharan averaged 35 for each of his 12 wickets, whereas Raju, who headed the Indian bowling, averaged 14.25 for each of his 16, and Kumble 17.61 for each of his 18 wickets, which included his then-best figures of 7 for 59 in the second innings when Sri Lanka managed 174. In contrast, Muralitharan apart, the other Sri Lankan spinners averaged over 70 for their wickets.

The Indians, playing like a team that expected to win, turned every situation to their advantage. In Lucknow, Tendulkar, coming in at 84 for 2, put on 121 with Sidhu and went on to make 142. In Bangalore and

Ahmedabad it was Azharuddin. After his 182 at Calcutta against England he had not done much except hit his first Test 50 in Sri Lanka on two tours. But in Bangalore while the top order got in and then failed to make a hundred – Sidhu 99, Kambli 82, and Tendulkar 96 – Azharuddin held his nerve to make 108. In Ahmedabad he was just masterly.

On a doubtful wicket, where on the first day Sri Lanka on winning the toss were bowled out for 119, with Raju taking 5 for 85, Azharuddin played as if he was batting on a totally different wicket to anyone else. *Widen* described his 152 as 'near miraculous. He batted for a minute over six hours – the next longest innings was Sidhu at three hours – and with virtually no durable support. He looked as if he was on a plumb pitch, despatching the bad balls for fours while keeping out the good ones with polished defence.'

Before the victory at Ahmedabad there was one other very special moment for Indian cricket. The tour of Sri Lanka and their return visit had seen Kapil set new records and get close to a world record. In the second Test at the Sinhalese Sports Club, he had become the second most-capped player in Test history. On the fourth day of the third Test at Colombo's Saravamuttu Stadium he passed Lance Gibbs' record of 27,115 deliveries in Test cricket.

His main goal was to overhaul Richard Hadlee's record Test tally of 431 Test wickets. In Bangalore he took 5 wickets to equal Hadlee's record, prompting Azharuddin to present him with his Man of the Match award. As the Indians took to the field in Ahmedabad on the morning of 8 February, the only question was when would Kapil go past Hadlee.

Just after the first drinks break of the day, Kapil had Tillakaratne caught at short-leg by Manjrekar. The batsman would not walk – like the Indians in Sri Lanka, the visitors felt they had been hard done by the Indian umpiring. In this instance there was no doubt about the decision, and Tillakaratne's reluctance to walk meant Narasimhan, umpiring in his first Test, knew that in raising his finger he would make history for both India and Kapil. The Indians celebrated long and hard and if there were critics who said that Kapil had played 44 more Tests than Hadlee, he could argue that 65 of his 130 Tests were in India while Hadlee's home Tests were on the much more seamer-friendly pitches of New Zealand.

As it was, Kapil had a chance to bowl in Hamilton six weeks later as Indians persuaded New Zealand to add a Test to the four one-day matches. But this was not much of a seamer's wicket, Kapil got just two wickets and the Indian victory roll was stopped. Rain delayed the start and much of the cricket was dismal apart from Tendulkar. His 43 came off only 47 balls and saw him pass 2,000 runs in only thirty-two Tests – he was not yet twenty-one.

The one-day matches also saw a new role for Tendulkar and, as so often, this was due to someone else's injury. New Zealand had won the first one-day match by 28 runs. Tendulkar, still batting in the middle-order, made 15.

But in the second in Auckland, Sidhu had a neck strain and so Tendulkar went out to open the innings. It was not a completely new experience for him. In 1992, he had opened for Yorkshire in the Sunday League, but this was a first at international level. He hit 82 from 49 balls with 15 fours and two sizes. With Jadeja he put on 61 in 9 overs, with Kambli he put on 56 in 6 overs. The result was that India, chasing a moderate 142, won by 7 wickets with only 23.2 overs bowled.

Tendulkar the one-day opener had arrived. In the next match his 63 gave India victory and a 2–1 lead. He made 40 in the fourth and put on 50 in the first 8 overs with Jadeja, but the rest of the batting could not sustain the momentum and New Zealand squared the series.

This opening role for Tendulkar in one-day matches completed his dominance of this form of the game. Tendulkar as a match-winning bowler had already emerged. A wonderful example of this had come in the Hero Cup – the name is that of a commercial company in India – held in November 1993. Pakistan withdrew for fear of violence between Hindus and Muslims, but Sri Lanka, the West Indies, South Africa and Zimbabwe came.

Tendulkar was still batting in the middle-order and India struggled for much of the tournament. In the group matches they tied with Zimbabwe and lost heavily to the West Indies.

The decisive match was the semi-final against South Africa in Calcutta on 24 November. This was the first match played under lights at Eden Gardens and some bombs had to be detonated to deter a swarm of insects, although *Wisden* observed that a local mongoose remained and fielded enthusiastically in this and the two matches that followed. India had earlier beaten South Africa by 43 runs in Mohali. In Calcutta, India made a modest 195 with Azharuddin 90 and Tendulkar just 15.

South Africa needed 45 from the last five overs and when the final over began they needed six runs with three wickets in hand. Kapil, who had bowled 8 overs taking 1 for 31, should have bowled, but it was Tendulkar who took the ball. The idea seems to have been that of the wicket-keeper and Tendulkar was very enthusiastic. He had not bowled before in the match, but now he bowled so well that South Africa lost two more wickets and only scored three runs, giving India victory by two runs. The night sky rang out with triumphant Indian shouts and the crowds lit fires with their newspapers making it look like a Roman amphitheatre fit to salute the man they knew was now becoming the greatest of Indian cricketing heroes.

In the final there was more joy as India easily beat the West Indies by 102 runs, Tendulkar bowling Brian Lara, who opened, for 33, but it was Kumble's match. Coming on as the sixth bowler, he took 6 for 12, his 6 wickets coming in 26 balls for just 4 runs. Such was the devastation, the West Indies went from 57 for 1 to 123 all out.

But the joy was to prove a prelude for much misery. In Hindu mythology Ram Rajya had been followed by darker ages and this was to prove the case here. Even as India notched up record victories, a bank clerk turned illegal bookmaker was, it emerged, corrupting cricketers.

During the 1994 Sri Lankan tour of India, two of the Sri Lankans, it was later alleged, had agreed to 'underperform'. Indian cricketers were already in this former bank clerk's net and one of them had introduced him to an English cricketer during England's tour of India in 1993. According to the testimony later provided by the illegal bookmaker, this cricketer had refused to throw matches, but had taken his money to provide information about match conditions.

It would be some years before all this would emerge, and another six before the illegal bookmaker's name became known. In the midst of heavy defeats the Indians had consoled themselves by saying that the darkest moment always comes before the dawn. Now fourteen months of continually brilliant days were to be followed by the most utter and totally unaccountable darkness.

29

Indian cricket's Kali Yuga
1994-2000

The Hindus believe that there are four ages of man starting with Ram Rajya, the age of perfection when the great Hindu god Rama came down to earth to take a human form. However, such goodness could not last and it was followed by progressively worsening ages until humans reached the fourth and worst age, Kali Yuga (in Sanskrit the word Yuga means age).

This age is symbolised by Kali, the fearsome mother goddess, whose naked form, garlanded by a skull of her beheaded enemies and standing on the body of her drunk husband Shiva, is worshipped by Indians. Indian revolutionaries seeking to free India from British rule would offer prayers to Kali before going off to fight the colonials. The Hindus believe that in Kali Yuga human beings are capable of behaving in the most depraved and evil fashion and as the *Vishnu Puranas*, an ancient Indian text, said:

> Corruption will be the universal means of subsistence. At the end, unable to support their avaricious kings, the people of Kali Age will take refuge in the chasm between mountains, they will wear ragged garments, and they will have too many children. Thus in the Kali Yuga shall strife and decay constantly proceed, until the human race approaches annihilation.

In 1994, just when it seemed Indian cricket had entered Ram Rajya, it found itself in the middle of the Kali Yuga with the evil of match-fixing eating away its soul. The four ages represent the four sides of a dice and neither gambling nor crooked bookmakers were new to Indians, but their introduction to cricket was totally unexpected.

Gambling comes naturally to Indians. Mahabharata, one of the two great myths of Hinduism, turns on a loaded game of dice. It was played between the Pandavas and the Kauravas, two lots of cousins who were both claiming the throne of Indraprastha, the legendary capital of ancient India.

In this epic story of good and bad the Pandavas were the goodies, the Kauravas were the baddies. The leader of the Pandavas, Yuddisthara, who was the embodiment of goodness and honour – he never told a lie in his life – agreed to a game of dice with his wicked cousins to settle the fate of ancient India. The Pandavas duly lost, but unknown to them a wicked Kaurava uncle had loaded the dice. When the Pandavas found out they decided the dice game could not be allowed to stand and went to war to reclaim their just rewards. It was on this historic battlefield that the Hindu god Krishna enunciated his philosophy, which is enshrined in the Bhagavat Gita, the closest the Hindus have to a bible.

This preamble is necessary to understand the extraordinary cricket betting scandal that engulfed Indian cricket in the 1990s and whose repercussions are still being felt today.

In modern India, whose many laws still reflect the legacy of Britain, gambling is only legally permissible on racetracks – as was the case in Britain before the betting shops were legalised in the 1960s. Outside that all other forms of gambling are illegal. Such restrictions have not stopped gambling, merely pushed it underground. When I was growing up in Bombay in the 1950s gambling would take place at street corners and the most popular form of gambling was betting on the closing prices of the New York Cotton Exchange. This produced a set of numbers every day and the bet involved predicting what the numbers would be. As New York is ten hours behind Bombay, by the time the Cotton Exchange closed it would be the next morning in Bombay and one of my early childhood memories is the excited hubbub of conversations as the numbers came through from America.

Inevitably, as gambling was illegal, much of the money involved was what Indians call 'black' money, untaxed money. India has a thriving black economy and almost every major transaction in India involves some element of black money. Such transactions are not uncommon in Britain, let alone other parts of Europe such as Italy, but whereas in Britain it generally means paying cash to the plumber, the electrician, builder or the handyman, in India it touches all the major commercial activities. So a person selling a flat or a house is always asked: how much in black? The government accepts they cannot eliminate it and every now and again announce sweeping measures to try and curb it. Such measures take the form of amnesties for those who voluntarily come forward and declare their black hoard. They are not then subject to penal taxes or other penalties that are laid down in the law.

This, in turn, leads to a constant effort to try and make black money white, and one favoured way is by buying the winning jackpot ticket from the successful punter at a horse race meeting. The winner is approached with an offer higher than he could collect from the tote and the black money holder can then claim that his untaxed money is not as a result of evading taxes, but from his winnings on the racecourse.

The closing prices of the New York Cotton Exchange remained the favourite bet of the Indian punter until the mid-1960s when Matka, the Indian numbers game, took over. Again it was centred around Bombay, and every evening around seven o'clock, a hush would descend at street corners of the city – an unnerving sight given the constant ceaseless noise – and indeed across many street corners in urban India as the Matka numbers were eagerly awaited. Then from the secret Matka centre somewhere in central Bombay the numbers would emerge and the hush would dissolve into a cauldron of noise – either of joy or desolation. The Matka game still goes on, but in the 1980s the Indian gamblers found a new game: cricket.

The earliest story of something odd going on in an Indian match comes from the Test series against Pakistan in 1979-80. The Indians had won the series 2–0 by the time the last and sixth Test began in Calcutta. With Gavaskar, the captain, having decided not to go to the West Indies – as we have seen the tour was eventually called off – Viswanath captained India. He went out to toss with Asif Iqbal, the Pakistan captain. The allegation is that Iqbal had already agreed with Calcutta bookmakers that India would win the toss. As Viswanath tossed the coin in the air, and even before it had properly landed, Asif turned to him and said, 'You have won' and walked off. Viswanath was bemused and narrated this story to others including Raj Singh Dungarpur, a former president of the Indian Board. The story gained such currency that it was mentioned in a Pakistani inquiry into match-fixing, although Asif has always vigorously denied it.

Three years later a lowly bank clerk in Delhi began to take an interest in cricket and match-fixing took on a wholly different meaning. This man was Mukesh Kumar Gupta. His story starts after India's unexpected victory in the 1983 World Cup. One evening Gupta was walking near his home in the grimy by-lanes of old Delhi when he saw some people betting for small amounts on a cricket match. This, as he would later tell the Indian Central Bureau of Investigation, India's equivalent of the FBI, 'caught his imagination.' He found the people who were betting neither well educated nor well informed about cricket and Gupta began to hone his cricket knowledge by listening to the BBC.

Over the next decade Gupta was to travel the world following cricket, meeting many of the game's top cricketers including Mark Waugh, Alec Stewart, Aravinda de Silva, Arjuna Ranatunga, Brian Lara, lunching at Martin Crowe's home with his wife Simone and bribing Mohammed Azharuddin, Hansie Cronje, Manoj Prabhakar, Salim Malik, Ajay Jadeja and many others. Given that Gupta does not speak very good English it says much for his self-belief and confidence that he could parley with international cricketers of such a diverse nature. It also says something about international cricketers and the curious world they inhabit.

Gupta's first cricket contact was with Ajay Sharma. Although Sharma, a Delhi player, made the international headlines only after the betting scandal came to the attention of the western press, he was a well-known Indian cricketer. *Indian Cricket* featured him as one of their cricketers of the year and in 1990 in New Zealand, Tendulkar's first overseas tour outside the Indian subcontinent, Sharma replaced him in a one-day international after Bedi, the Indian cricket manager, dropped Tendulkar. Sharma eventually played in 33 one-day internationals and one Test, but more significantly almost from the start of his career he formed a close friendship with Azharuddin. Sharma may not have set the cricket world alight, but for Gupta he formed a vital conduit to other cricketers.

Gupta first met Sharma at a club tournament in Delhi in 1988 when, impressed by the way he batted, he went up to him and thrust Rupees 2,000 (the equivalent of about £100 at the time) into his pocket. Gupta saw this as an investment for the future and it was to prove a shrewd move. Within two weeks Sharma rang him and soon the two men had formed a bond.

On the 1990 New Zealand tour Sharma provided Gupta with information about the weather, pitch etc and Gupta used this to make money. Through Sharma, Gupta met Prabhakar and on the 1990 England tour Prabhakar, keen to get a new car, offered, says Gupta, to 'underperform' in a Test. It is not clear which Test this was, possibly the Test at The Oval, the only one India dominated. According to Gupta, Prabhakar got his car and it meant more cricket contacts for Gupta.

The 1990-91 season had seen one match in the Ranji Trophy fixed. As we have seen the court action involving Punjab had delayed the final stages of the competition and, as Delhi finally played Bombay in the quarter-final, several of the Delhi players were worried that if they won and progressed they would have to miss out on the lucrative league contracts they had secured in England. The result was they fixed the match and Delhi lost to Bombay by one run.

Bombay made 390, Delhi after a good start suddenly lost wickets including that of Prabhakar, but then a stand between the two Sharmas, Ajay and Sanjeev appeared to rescue them before Ajay got out and they could only get to 389. Bombay's lead by a run on the first innings was enough to take them through to the semi-final.

The picture Gupta gave of his match-fixing activities to the CBI shows how frighteningly casual the whole thing was.

Gupta goes to Prabhakar's Delhi home for dinner. Prabhakar rings Gus Logie, the West Indian middle-order batsman, but he refuses to help. Soon there are some festival matches in Sri Lanka where several international players are involved. Gupta rings Prabhakar who tells him they are all staying at the same hotel in Colombo. Gupta flies out to Colombo and Prabhakar introduces him to Dean Jones, Arjuna Ranatunga and Brian Lara.

Gupta claims to have offered $40,000 to Dean Jones for information. Jones promises to think about it but does nothing. Mark Waugh, says Gupta, takes £14,250 to provide information on a Hong Kong tournament. Gupta also says that on other occasions Waugh refuses to help. So does Salim Malik, then Pakistan captain, but with him, it seems, it is not a point of principle because he has already agreed to fix matches for other bookies. However, he twice fixes one-day matches for Gupta, one against India, the other Australia.

Waugh has since denied taking Gupta's money and been cleared by an Australian cricket investigation.

According to the CBI, the 1993 England tour of India saw Gupta meet an English cricketer. Prabhakar told the CBI that he had introduced Alec Stewart to Gupta and Gupta claimed he paid Stewart £5,000 for information but that Stewart refused to throw matches. The CBI report emerged as England were touring Pakistan in the winter of 2000 and Stewart not only denied receiving any money but said he did not knowingly remember meeting Gupta. After an investigation by the England and Wales Cricket Board he was cleared of any wrongdoing.

Gupta's next foray into international cricket was during the Sri Lankan tour of India in 1994. With Prabhakar acting as his agent, Gupta was introduced to Aravinda de Silva. Gupta's version is that Aravinda and Ranatunga agreed to 'underperform', helping Sri Lanka lose the first Test for which Aravinda was paid £10,000. There was talk of fixing other Tests, but the odds were very low.

Aravinda and Ranatunga denied Gupta's allegations and an investigation by the Sri Lankan cricket authorities cleared their cricketers.

If Gupta is to be believed then Aravinda's involvement did not end there. On the phone he introduced Gupta to Martin Crowe. Gupta got on so well with him that when he visited New Zealand he lunched at Crowe's home. Gupta said he paid Crowe £14,000 for information but that, like Stewart, he refused to fix matches.

Crowe would later claim that he thought he was dealing with a journalist and was duped and was cleared by the New Zealand cricket authorities after an investigation.

These cricketing inquiries in England, New Zealand and Sri Lanka were held only as a result of the CBI investigation, and while the CBI is a government agency the cricketing ones were at the behest of private bodies. The CBI could just pick up Gupta and question him. The cricket authorities were hamstrung by the fact that having spilled the beans to the CBI, Gupta refused to back up his claims by testifying to them or to the Anti-Corruption Unit set up by the ICC to investigate these allegations.

432

Gupta's next alleged hit was during the West Indies tour of India in 1994, when he claimed Brian Lara agreed to 'underperform' in two one-day matches for £27,000. Lara denied the allegations and the West Indies Cricket Board appointed an investigator to look into the claims. At the time of writing, the results of the investigation had not been released.

Even if these allegations had never surfaced the West Indies tour of India would still be a curious cricketing episode, when, for the first time, the march of the Indian cricket juggernaut was halted.

The West Indians nearly did not come to India at all and until the last morning of the tour, during the third Test at Mohali when they suddenly turned the tables on the Indians, they must have wished they had stayed at home. An outbreak of bubonic plague in Gujarat made the tour doubtful; the West Indies arrived a week late; and Brian Lara never adjusted to the conditions, averaging just 33 in the three Tests. For most of the tour, this looked a pale shadow of a team that since March 1980 had not lost a Test series anywhere in the world.

On all previous West Indian tours, apart from 1978-79, when they came without their Packer players, the West Indians had proved the masters of India, inflicting some of the most crushing defeats the Indians had ever suffered at home. Since the 1948-49 series, when the West Indians had had to time waste in order to avoid defeat in the last Test at Bombay, they had lost just four Tests in India on seven visits spread over nearly half a century.

But in 1994, even before the Test series began, they looked a broken side. They lost their record of never having lost a one-day series in India, going down 4–1 in the five-match series, and then lost the opening Test in Bombay. The Test was a new beginning for India in other ways as well. For the first time in nearly two decades there was no Kapil Dev. Srinath played his first home Test, three years after his Test debut in Australia, won the Man of the Match award with his five wickets, and his crucial 60 in the second innings contributed to an Indian victory by 96 runs.

The victory was India's tenth successive home Test triumph and it made Azharuddin, with ten victories, the most successful Indian captain ever. At this stage there seemed no reason why India should not go on and win every home Test. But having achieved the record Azharuddin appeared to rest on his laurels rather than make sure the West Indians lost their fifteen-year unbeaten record.

In the second Test at Nagpur India went back to scoring over 500 in the first innings, 546, but the hunger for success of the recent Tests was missing. Unaccountably India, who dominated the match, batted slowly in the second innings and Azharuddin did not declare until just before lunch on the fifth day. India reduced the West Indies to 132 for 5 but there was never enough time to win. It had provided the West

Indies an escape route and this was expertly piloted by Courtney Walsh and his fast bowling colleagues in the third Test.

For the first time the West Indies could dictate a match. They set India 357 to win and Walsh and Winston Benjamin bowled so decisively that, in a replay of the old Indian horrors against West Indian pace, India were bowled out for 114, in just 35.2 overs. Prabhakar had his nose broken by Walsh before he had scored and did not bat again, Sidhu 11, Manjrekar 17, Tendulkar 10, Azharuddin 5 and Kambli 0 were all out on the final morning in just 21 overs and nobody could argue about the winning margin of 243 runs.

After this match, for the first time, there were murmurs that something not quite right had gone on in that last morning at Mohali, but nobody could prove anything and the Indian failure to inflict their first series defeat on the West Indies since 1980 was put down to that well-known Indian failing: lack of killer instinct.

The really peculiar goings-on came during the course of that winter's numerous one-day matches. After the one-day matches against the West Indies and just before the Tests, India played a three-nation one-day tournament, the Wills World Series, involving New Zealand. At Kanpur, on 30 October 1994, one of the strangest one-day matches in the history of cricket took place. India had already qualified for the final, the question was would they play the West Indies or New Zealand. Set a target of 257, they required 63 from nine overs when Nayan Mongia, the wicket-keeper, joined Prabhakar at the crease. The pair proceeded to stonewall as if this was a Test match they had to save and made only 16 runs. India lost by 46 runs and the match referee Raman Subba Row accused the pair of 'not making an effort to win the match' and docked India two points. The Indians protested about Row's decision and the ICC rescinded it. However, the Indian selectors dropped them from the series. Prabhakar, who had made 102, and Mongia have always protested their innocence.

Many years later Prabhakar speaking about the incident said, 'When we were chasing the West Indies score, Mongia came in to bat and conveyed the management's instructions to try and get as close to the target as we could. The resultant hullabaloo about my going slow should be directed towards the team management and not me as I was doing so under their instructions. Of the 48 balls in that period, I faced only 11. I scored 9 runs off those 11 balls. In fact, it was someone else's fault that I was dropped and humiliated.'

After match-fixing was finally disclosed Prabhakar, armed with a hidden video recorder, went and recorded conversations with several of his former colleagues including Mongia and the then general secretary of the Board, Jayant Lele.

His conversation went:

Mongia: Because of the Kanpur incident, my name is always coming up.

Manager: But what happened?

Prabhakar: That is something even I don't know still.

With Lele, Prabhakar's secret conversation went as follows:

Prabhakar: Sir, I cannot understand that incident. In Kanpur, where I was dropped. What happened? Why?

Lele: Yes, yes, two-match suspension. I was there.

Prabhakar: You were there, sir. That was wrong.

Lele: Yes, everything was happening on the telephone. Instructions were coming from Dalmiya and Mr. Bhindra.

Prabhakar: Like what?

Lele: That suspend them [Mongia and Prabhakar] for two matches.

Prabhakar: Sir, but the mistake was Wadekar's [the Indian cricket manager].

Lele: I am not denying that. I know that.

Prabhakar: Wadekar, Jadeja, Azharuddin, they were all involved. Look how many run outs we had in that match? Three run outs! Azharuddin, Ajay Jadeja, Sidhu . . . All three were run out. Mongia came afterwards.

Lele: Oh, they sent him last.

But these disclosures came six years later. At the time the cricket went on. India met the West Indies in the final and won with some ease.

This was their second victory in a multi-national one-day series that season, having won the Singer Cup in Sri Lanka in September. It featured India, Pakistan, Sri Lanka and Australia and produced one quite extraordinary match, and an amazing match-fixing story about another match that was never played.

On 7 September 1994, at the Sinhalese Sports ground, Australia played Pakistan. Australia made just 179 and Pakistan, captained by Salim Malik, seemed well placed at 80 for 1 but then Saeed Anwar on 43 pulled a hamstring, retired and by the time he returned at 124, Pakistan were five down and lost the match by 28 runs.

Five years later in evidence given to the inquiry conducted by Justice Malik Mohammed Qayyum, a serving High Court judge in Pakistan, it was alleged that Pakistani players had been bribed to throw the match. Anwar was told to come off, and a Pakistani bookmaker told the judge that he had paid two Pakistani players to fix the game. Both players denied it and the judge could not find corroborative evidence to prove the allegation.

One observer watching the match felt that both Australia and Pakistan were trying to lose.

Eight days later came, potentially, the most explosive match-fixing story. This was the match between India and Pakistan, which was due to be played at the Premadasa Stadium in Colombo on 15 September. It rained both that day and on the reserve day on 16 September and the match had to be abandoned. The match was crucial to see whether India or Australia would go through to the final. The one point that India got as a result of the rain washout meant that India went through and beat Sri Lanka by six wickets in the final.

However, sometime before the match, Prabhakar, who was sharing a room with Sidhu, was allegedly visited by a fellow member of his team. Prabhakar alleged his colleague asked him 'to play below my usual standards' to which Prabhakar's response was: 'I told him to get out of my room.'

No match-fixing incident in India has been more closely examined. Every detail has been scrutinised, starting with the exact whereabouts of Sidhu when this player came calling: was he in the bathroom, was he out of the room, was he in the corridor outside the room?

In December 1998, a magazine carried a Calcutta-based journalist's version of the incident. Sakyasen Mitra, who was covering the tournament, was a friend of Prashant Vaidya, one of the Indian players. He roomed next to Prabhakar and Sidhu. The two rooms had a connecting door, which was, on most occasions, open. Mitra said, 'The incident in question happened after some time when it became obvious that Manoj was talking with someone in his room. When he shouted, all of us became conscious of what was happening. I overheard Prabhakar shouting "What do you think you are doing? Can you buy me out in an Indo-Pakistan match? No amount of lakhs is going to buy me out." He also said, "How can a person in your position do this?"' But then, says Mitra, 'Vaidya rose and closed the adjoining door so we never heard who Prabhakar was talking to.'

Although at the time Prabhakar told his captain, manager and some other people, it took the cricket corruption crisis of 2000 for the world to learn the name of the player who allegedly went to Prabhakar's room.

There were other incidents during this Sri Lankan Singer World Series which also remained secret for many years, but there was no doubt they took place.

Sometime during the Sri Lankan trip Mark Waugh and Shane Warne were approached by an Indian bookie who they only knew as John. He asked them to begin giving him apparently innocent information about the weather and the state of the pitch – less, they felt, than they might routinely give free of charge to journalists. John paid Waugh about £2,500 and Warne around £2,000.

Immediately after this series the Australians went to Pakistan to try and win their first Test there since 1959. Waugh, Warne and Tim May were approached by Salim Malik, captain of Pakistan, and were asked to throw a Test match and a one-day match. They refused and told the Australian authorities. The Australians made this public and for the first time match-fixing emerged into the daylight. The picture presented was of upright Australians setting the crooked world of the subcontinent right.

But even as this light was being shone on match-fixing the Australian Cricket Board was involved in a cover up with the help of the International Cricket Council, the only known incident of two cricket bodies colluding to conceal cricketers' involvement with match-fixing.

When the Australian Board discovered the involvement of Waugh and Warne with the bookies they secretly fined them, roughly twice what they had been paid by John, but persuaded the ICC, whose chief executive was another Australian, David Richards, and whose chairman was Clyde Walcott, not to let on. Not only did they not tell the world, they did not even inform the other members of the ICC, in particular Pakistan, who following the Malik approach to Warne, Waugh and May had started their own independent investigation into match-fixing.

The result of all this was that from 1994 cricket was played partly in light, but mostly in darkness. Match-fixing in Pakistan was now under the spotlight and the authorities began the first of four inquiries – the fourth was ongoing at the time of writing. Newspapers there and in India wrote about it.

However, in the rest of the cricket world, thanks to the cover-up by the Australians and the ICC, little attention was paid to match-fixing and even when it was, it was seen as something exotic, a subcontinental speciality. Even Indians took a rather smug and superior view of it all, thinking that while the bookmakers may be Indians, the corrupt cricketers were all Pakistanis.

Away from the light the bookies were, of course, busy. In the winter of 1994-95 Pakistan toured Southern Africa and the 'John' who paid Waugh and Warne and knew Salim Malik approached Hansie Cronje, who had just been appointed captain of South Africa, with an offer to throw a one-day final in the Mandela Cup between South Africa and Pakistan.

In June 2000, Cronje giving evidence before the South African Commission of Judge Edwin King, which inquired into cricket corruption, would describe how John, claiming to be a journalist from India, asked him for an interview. Cronje went to John's hotel room to be interviewed. This is not a usual thing for a captain to do but he would make light of this, saying that he liked to be accessible to Indian journalists as persons from the Free State were not supposed to like

Indians, an interesting way of presenting the fact that Cronje had grown up in the 'Free State' where Indians were not allowed to live during apartheid. In the hotel room John turned out to be a bookie and made Cronje an offer. He discussed it with other South African players, then rejected it.

As it happens Gupta was also known as John. However, all the evidence suggests that Gupta was not the John who paid Waugh and Warne and approached Cronje in 1994-95. We do not know what happened to this John, he vanishes from our story as suddenly as he had emerged.

The John who was Gupta carried on and in 1995 began an intense and close relationship with Azharuddin. Sharma had introduced Azharuddin to Gupta in 1995 at Delhi's Taj Palace, the hotel used by the Indian Board and also visiting cricketing teams. For the next two years, until 1997, the two men would be close. During that period, says Gupta, not only 'Azhar', as Azharuddin is popularly known in India, but his second wife Sangeeta Bijlani got involved and, Gupta claims, he paid Azhar 90 lakh Rupees (£150,000). However Gupta, finding that some of Azhar's 'predictions proved incorrect', asked for his money back and was repaid 30 lakh Rupees, about £40,000.

On and off the field of play this was a crowded period for Indian cricket. While Gupta was being transformed from a lowly bank clerk to cricket's most notorious match-fixer, and enriching himself in the process, cricket was being reinvented largely by the Indians. This meant that by the mid-1990s the Ashes series, which had been the bedrock of the international game for 120 years, was sidelined in favour of one-day internationals.

By 1996 and the heyday of Gupta the match-fixer, there had been an enormous spread of such one-day matches, the greatest expansion in the history of the game, with series in Sharjah, Singapore and Toronto. The Indians call these 'masala matches', masala meaning spice or something made up and not quite real. There were many reasons why such masala matches developed: Sharjah had started as benefit matches for Indian and Pakistani cricketers who have no English-style benefit system; Toronto provided a North American haven for India versus Pakistan matches, often not possible for political reasons in the subcontinent; Singapore and other tournaments represented the commercial opportunities that one-day cricket provided to those seeking to reach the new emerging Indian middle-classes.

It is the economic power of this class of Indians that had fuelled the reinvention of cricket. Companies like Singer and Pepsi, both American but with extensive interests in south Asia, saw the marketing advantages of being associated with Indian cricket and sponsored many of these mini series. Television companies, in particular Rupert

Murdoch's Star Television, were also keen to reach this important economic group. It is estimated that every second person watching cricket in the world is an Indian and with India's growing economic muscle, and an insatiable appetite for the one-day game, this was a market worth cultivating. Ex-cricketers like Tony Greig, Ian Chappell, Geoff Boycott and Barry Richards, have also been well aware of this and now spend much of their time in the subcontinent commentating on the game.

Not surprisingly, this economic power also stimulated the ambitions of the region's cricket administrators, who instead of seeking to combat the likes of Gupta, combated each other instead. The first indication of this growing Asian economic power came in the 1996 World Cup which was held in the Indian subcontinent for the second time in a decade. The decision to give the subcontinent the right to host the World Cup was controversial, but the event itself was to prove a marketing bonanza for the game there.

In 1993 India, Pakistan and Sri Lanka, after the most fractious meeting ever of the International Cricket Council, won the right to stage the 1996 World Cup. The key to victory was the way the three countries got the ICC's Associate Members – hitherto treated much as the Soviet Union used to treat its eastern European satellites – on their side by promising them £100,000 each. England, who believed they had had a gentleman's agreement guaranteeing them the 1996 tournament, had offered them £60,000 each, and throughout the meeting acted as if this was yet another cosy old boys' gathering; after all the MCC secretary was also the secretary of the ICC and the meetings were held at Lord's, the headquarters of English cricket.

The Asians, no longer willing to follow their former colonial masters meekly, looked up the rules and decided to use them to the full. They wheeled in politicians and lawyers and treated the event as if it were an American presidential convention. They outflanked England, and won a rich prize. How rich only became evident when the 1996 World Cup began.

Unlike the Olympic Games, or soccer's World Cup and European Championships, the cricket World Cup was then an event not owned by the international authority that runs the game. The country staging it, in effect, owned the competition. In five previous World Cups this had made little difference: the host country had made money, but not so much as to raise eyebrows. The 1996 World Cup, however, changed everything.

As soon as they had won the rights to stage the competition, the hosts set about selling it. Their biggest success was auctioning the television rights for a staggering $US14 million, using a hitherto unknown agent, Mark Mascarenhas, an Indian born in Bangalore who

439

had successfully established himself in the US media world. The UK rights alone fetched $7.5 million, compared to $1 million in 1992. In addition, the tournament was marketed on a scale never before seen in cricket. There was an official sponsor for every conceivable product, including the official World Cup chewing gum.

Even a few years earlier, Coke, the world's most famous soft drink manufacturer, had not been allowed to sell their products in India, and in 1988 Pepsi was allowed in only after accepting torturous conditions. Now Coca-Cola and Pepsi battled it out to be the official drink supplier. Coke won – but they had to pay $3.8 million, more than Benson and Hedges paid the Australians to be the main sponsor for the 1992 World Cup. The main sponsors Wills, the Indian tobacco offshoot of BAT, paid four times as much: $12 million.

Pepsi, not to be outdone, got some of cricket's leading lights, including Sachin Tendulkar and umpire Dickie Bird, to advertise their product and had huge banners outside the grounds and around the country proclaiming: 'Not the official thing.'

The organisers loved the rivalry. They were aware that they could keep all the profits, once they had met their expenses, which included a fee of £250,000 to each of the competing Test countries. This amount did not even cover the expenses of some of the teams and while they lost money, India and Pakistan pocketed a profit of almost $50 million. Contrast this with the 1996 European Soccer Championship in England, where UEFA, as owners of the championships, made a profit of £69 million whereas England, the hosts, made a loss of £1.7 million.

It could be argued that the cricket administrators of the rest of the world were naïve to agree to such an arrangement. But in five previous World Cups nobody had sought, let alone achieved, such commercial success. Not everyone on the subcontinent foresaw it. The Sri Lankans, co-hosts of the tournament along with India and Pakistan, clearly had doubts; they did not agree to underwrite the costs and so did not participate in any of the profits.

The man who drove this commercial juggernaut was Jagmohan Dalmiya whose official title was Convenor of the Pakistan India Sri Lanka Organising Committee (PILCOM). In 1993, Dalmiya had returned as secretary of the Indian Board. In yet another merry-go-round in Indian cricket he had teamed up with the high-ranking Indian civil servant from Punjab Inderjit, Singh Bhindra, and with Bhindra as president and Dalmiya as secretary the two formed a strong team.

Dalmiya hails from the Marwari community of India whose business skills are both feared and respected. The joke in India is that a Marwari can do business with a Scotsman and a Jew and still make money. The other joke, less flattering, is that if you should see a Marwari and a snake together in the jungle, you should shoot the Marwari first.

Left: Mohammed Azharuddin watches as Kepler Wessels tosses the coin in the first ever Test between South Africa and India played at Durban in November 1992. By then India had been playing Test cricket for 60 years, South Africa for 103 years, but the fact that it had taken so long for these two countries to meet shows how the evil of the 'whites only' sports policy followed by the South Africa regime poisoned cricket (*Allsport/Mike Hewitt*).

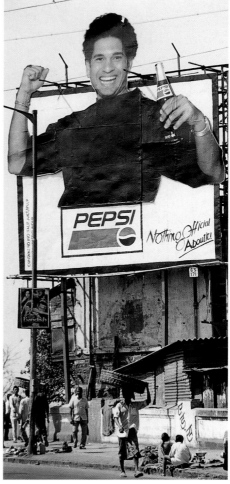

Right: A poster during the 1996 World Cup of Tendulkar. The 1996 World Cup held in India, Pakistan and Sri Lanka demonstrated to the world that India was now the economic powerhouse of cricket. The selling of television rights, marketing and sponsorship proved so successful that India and Pakistan as joint hosts (Sri Lanka did not share in the profits) made a profit of $50m (*Allsport/Shaun Botterill*).

Above: Mohammed Azharuddin batting against Pakistan in Bangalore during the 1996 World Cup quarter-final. India won the match and dreamt of glory in Lahore, only to lose in shameful fashion to Sri Lanka in the semi-final when, with India on the verge of defeat, a crowd riot halted the match and it was awarded to Sri Lanka (*Patrick Eagar*).

Left: Tendulkar salutes the crowd after his 177 against England at Trent Bridge in 1996. He has made more runs against England than against any other country (*Da id Munden*).

Right: By conventional standards, Vinod Kambli has much to be proud of. He played with Tendulkar for India, averaging over 50, but these runs were made mostly in India on slow wickets. His problem was that he could not live with the genius that is Tendulkar. Fame had come early to Tendulkar and he has more than fulfilled his promise. Kambli, not as gifted, has found it impossible to handle the fame and has not made the most of his talents (*Da id Munden*).

Above: Javagal Srinath bowling to Nasser Hussain during the 1996 tour of England. The fastest bowler India has produced since Nissar and Amar Singh retired, his career has illustrated all the problems of being a fast bowler in India. Three years after he made his Test debut in Australia, he played his first home Test, reflecting how redundant such species of bowlers can be in India (*Patrick Eagar*).

Below: Ventkatesh Prasad has formed, with Javagal Srinath, the best opening pair since India's first ever pairing of Mohammed Nissar and Amar Singh (*Allsport/Hamish Blair*).

Above: Sachin Tendulkar flicking Shane Warne to leg during the Sydney Test in January 2000 (*Allsport/Hamish Blair*).

Right: India has had an opening batting problem ever since Gavaskar retired, and a succession of openers have tried to fill the great man's shoes. Navjot Singh Sidhu, while nowhere near the master, proved one of the more durable openers, showing both good defence and a strong capacity for attacking play, particularly against the spinners (*Sportline Photographic/David Munden*).

Above: Saurav Ganguly and Rahul Dravid do the high fives during their epic stand in the second match against Sri Lanka in Taunton. Their batting lit up the 1999 World Cup and provided the only cheer in yet another underachieving performance by Indian cricketers. Ganguly has been proved a controversial captain (*Patrick Eagar*).

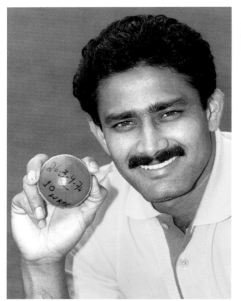

Above left: Anil Kumble holds up the ball after taking all ten Pakistani wickets in the second innings of the Feroze Shah Kotla Test in February 1999, only the second time in cricket history such a feat has been performed (*Sportline Photographic/David Munden*).

Above right: Controversy always seemed to follow Manoj Prabhakar. He was plagued by allegations of throwing on the field and was portrayed as a stud off of it. However, he will be best remembered for his role in match-fixing. He first alleged that Kapil Dev had offered him money to throw a match, but it then emerged that he was himself involved with bookies and was banned from Indian cricket. Kapil, on the other hand, was exonerated of any misdeeds (*Sportline Photographic/David Munden*).

Left: Nayan Mongia, probably the best wicket-keeper India has had since Syed Kirmani. But following the corruption crisis it was alleged he was involved with bookmakers, and while he successfully fought the charges, his career prospects dipped and he has never quite recovered (*Patrick Eagar*).

Below: V.V.S. Laxman cover driving in the Calcutta Test against Australia in March 2001. Purists may say that he is not quite technically correct, but during that innings this tall, erect Karnataka player stood up so well to the Australian bowlers that he turned the Test on its head. His 281 is the highest Test score by an Indian, and it allowed India, having been forced to follow on, to win the match and became only the third team in history to achieve such a feat (*Allsport/Hamish Blair*).

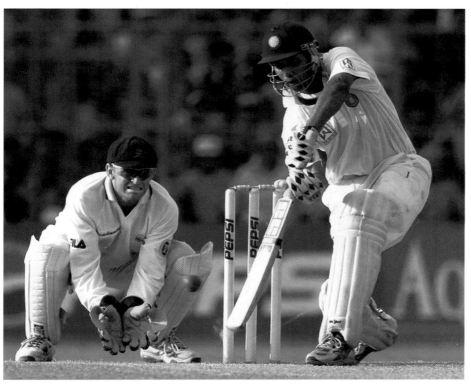

Above: Harbhajan Singh, known as the Turbanator, raises a clenched fist in triumph to mark two remarkable Indian comeback Test wins against Australia in the epic series of 2001. Harbhajan's 32 wickets, in a series where no other Indian bowler took more than three, hustled the Australians to their series defeat (*Allsport/Shaun Botteril*).

Left: Jagmohan Dalmiya, known to his friends as 'Juggu', is the most controversial official in Indian cricket history. A marwari, he is a shrewd businessman who has made a lot of money for Indian and world cricket, but who has also made a lot of enemies. Long the money man of Indian cricket, he decided, in 1996, to go for the highest office and became the first Asian president of the International Cricket Council. His tenure was marked by the ICC making more money than ever before, but this was accompanied by controversy. By the end of his reign he was being investigated by the Indian CBI over a television deal he had negotiated for the ICC. In September 2001, surprisingly, he was elected president of the Indian Board and was immediately the centre of major cricketing controversies (*Patrick Eagar*).

Not everyone, even within the Indian Board, were enamoured of Dalmiya, and the World Cup began badly for him. He was responsible for the opening ceremony in Calcutta, which was widely regarded as a disaster. The designer, an Italian who had designed the 1990 Italian World Cup opener, did not take into account that Calcutta could be windy and the compère Saeed Jaffrey got the names of some teams wrong.

But there was no doubting Dalmiya's financial acumen and he now began to use it to extend his power outside India. At this stage, even in India, Dalmiya had not been the top man, having been Board secretary or treasurer, never president, but just before the World Cup it was suggested to him that he should go for the top job in cricket. The commercial success of the World Cup made this a very real possibility.

Dalmiya's decision to stand was triggered by Australia's refusal on security grounds to go to Colombo to play their World Cup group matches. The West Indies decided to take their cue from Australia and refused to go as well. With the ICC impotent to force the Australians and the West Indians to go to Colombo, the organisers did not know what to do. They even organised a joint India–Pakistan team to play in Colombo and prove security fears were groundless but the Australians would not budge. The opening ceremony in Calcutta was only days away and as they gathered in the foyer of Taj Bengal, the luxurious Calcutta hotel just opposite the city's zoo, there was both anger and resentment. Gathered in the foyer that day were all the leading cricket administrators of the subcontinent.

One of them, Anna Puchi Hewa, president of Sri Lankan cricket, turned to Dalmiya and said, 'We should have an Asian as the next president of the International Cricket Council.' The idea was immediately supported by Joe Bazalio, representative of Gibraltar, and while at the time the other representatives jokingly urged Dalmiya on, the Marwari took it seriously. In strict theory Bhindra, as Indian Board president, should have been the Indian nominee, but the fact that it was Dalmiya showed that the man who until now had been the money man and allowed others to be king now wanted to be king himself.

Dalmiya ran his election as if it was an American presidential race, energetically wooing the associates, but despite twice winning the vote of the ICC members, he found the old powers reluctant to accept him. The bitter power struggle, essentially a brown versus white (and black) battle with England, Australia, New Zealand and the West Indies ranged against the subcontinent, was so vicious that it left scars which have never healed. The Asian countries resented the grudging acceptance of them by England and Australia, while the old powers felt that the new kids on the block were not following the gentlemanly ways and were also doing nothing about cricketing corruption.

The first battle came to a head just after the World Cup during the annual ICC meeting at Lord's in July 1996. With Sir Clyde Walcott coming to the end of his term, Dalmiya stood for the chairmanship, along with Malcolm Gray from Australia and Krish Mackerdhuj of South Africa. On the first round of votes Dalmiya was ahead of Gray and Mackerdhuj, with 13 associates and three Test countries – India, Pakistan and Sri Lanka – supporting him.

In the second round, with Mackerdhuj having dropped out, Dalmiya got a fourth Test playing country, Zimbabwe, although South Africa abstained. Bacher may have found Dalmiya very useful when getting South Africa back into the international cricketing fold in 1991, but now the two men were very distant. Dalmiya also got more associate votes, 18 in all and was ahead well of Gray. However, the ICC rules as they then stood required him to get a majority of Test playing countries' votes and, crucially, he did not have the support of England and Australia, who had the veto. The rules were less than clear and the Indians, having taken the advice of a QC, contended that the election should be decided by a simple majority. Walcott argued that any successful chairman must have the backing of a two-thirds majority of the Test playing countries: six out of nine. Underlying this was the concern about what a Dalmiya chairmanship might do to international cricket. The Indians and the Asians saw it as racism, while the others presented it as a simple concern for cricket.

Soon after this meeting Eshan Mani, the Pakistani representative, David Richards, chief executive, Dalmiya himself and Sir John Anderson, representing New Zealand, flew to Singapore and it was agreed that the way forward was to accept Dalmiya but to restructure the ICC. It would now be an incorporated body and would have various committees including an executive board and the man at the top would be called a president not chairman. It was clearly a move by the old colonial powers to accept the new boy but to make sure that he was properly fenced in.

Mani's suggestion of rotating the presidency had also been accepted and it was agreed Dalmiya would be succeeded by Gray. But what the four wise man could not agree on was how long the term should be. Dalmiya said as Walcott had had three years, he should have three as well, Anderson and Richards wanted to give him only two. The matter was unresolved until another meeting of all Test-playing countries a few months later in Kuala Lumpur when Mani came up with the idea that both Dalmiya and Gray should serve three years, but after that it would be two. If a future president wanted to serve a three-year term, the country he represented would have to wait 27 years between turns. Dalmiya took over in June 1997, but even as he reveled in his success, he had left behind problems in India which have haunted both him and Indian cricket since.

During the protracted voting at Lord's in 1996, England and Australia had approached Bhindra, who was the Indian Board president, and said that if he not Dalmiya was India's representative they would support India and the whole matter would be resolved. This may have been a ruse to split the Asians, but at Lord's it did not work. The Asians told Bhindra that they must remain united behind Dalmiya. However, Bhindra went back and reported this to the Indian Board and the bond between Bhindra and Dalmiya got increasingly frayed until it finally dissolved into public acrimony.

The whole exercise had shown how the Asians were now ready to flex their economic muscles. As one Asian official put it, 'We do not want to come to Lord's for the ICC and just nod our heads like little schoolboys as we used to. Now we come with fully prepared plans and want to be heard as equals.'

An inkling of these revolutionary plans had come during the summer of 1996, when it emerged that the Indians proposed to hold a tournament in May 1997, to mark fifty years of Indian independence. Until the beginning of the 1990s, the summer months from May to August were reserved for English cricket. No one else played then and the rest of the world fitted in its cricket during the other eight months. But Sri Lanka, wracked by civil war and desperate for cricket, began playing Tests and one-day internationals from July and now Indians proposed the seemingly impossible: a one-day tournament in May. Temperatures then can be as high as 110 degrees Fahrenheit in the shade and most Indian children would not be allowed to play by their parents. But the Indians, having used the World Cup profits to install lights, proposed to use them to minimise the heat.

Dalmiya was determined to have the tournament and he proposed a start time for matches at five o'clock in the evening and ending at eleven. He also made arrangements with the Indian government for public transport until two o'clock in the morning. His delight at his success was immense. 'When we suggested it, a lot of people laughed, but these were the first genuine night matches, and our innovation worked.'

The tournament held between 9 May and 27 May 1997 symbolised everything about the new world of one-day cricket in India. Pepsi sponsored it, hence the Pepsi Independence Cup, and India, Pakistan, Sri Lanka and New Zealand played three matches each and there were two finals, one in Mohali and the other in Calcutta. If the economic power of India's growing middle-classes had made this tournament possible it did not translate on to the field, where India won just one match, against New Zealand by eight wickets thanks to Tendulkar scoring his twelfth one-day international century. He was not only established as opener but had found a partner in Saurav Ganguly, who made 62, putting on 169 in 32 overs. In the match against Pakistan, the

443

Indian bowlers had the mortification of seeing Saeed Anwar score 194, the highest score in one-day cricket.

But it was Sri Lanka who confirmed their rise to one-day cricketing supremacy power by winning the tournament. Improvised as their cricket had been, wracked by a civil war which had entered its second decade, Sri Lanka had produced some of the world's most exciting batsmen and proved that if you have batsmen who are willing to strike the ball from the first over of a one-day innings then you can create a momentum that is irresistible. They scored over 300 in both finals and defeated Pakistan twice with ease.

It should have come as no surprise for just over a year earlier they had won the 1996 World Cup in grand style. India, who were drawn in a tough group featuring Australia, appeared to have done all the hard work when they won their quarter-final in Bangalore against Pakistan. India made 287, led by Sidhu's 93, and Pakistan, after a good start, lost their way and were comfortably beaten by 39 runs.

India's semi-final opponents were Sri Lanka, who had defeated England, and with the match in Calcutta the Indians were already looking forward to the final in Lahore. Yet in the group match Sri Lanka had surprised the Indians after the home side had made 271 for 3 in their 50 overs. The Sri Lankans replied so savagely that they made 42 in the first three overs and eventually won by six wickets.

This fear of the Sri Lankan batting seemed to play on the Indian minds. In the semi-final India put Sri Lanka in, and although it appeared to have paid off when Sri Lanka lost two wickets in the first four balls of the match, and were soon 35 for 3, Aravinda with 66 saw Sri Lanka to 251. The Indians began their reply confidently and led by Tendulkar were 98 for 1, but Tendulkar was stumped and there followed an amazing Indian collapse when seven wickets fell for 22 runs. The Calcutta crowd's joy turned to anger, bottles were thrown, seats set on fire and Clive Lloyd, the match referee, had to call the players off and eventually abandon the match giving Sri Lanka the game by default.

The Indians were embarrassed by it all; even as the game was being called off some of the more ashamed spectators held up a banner apologising to the Sri Lankans and later advertisements were taken in the Sri Lankan press full of remorse, but it remains a black day for Indian cricket and did not reflect much credit on the organisers in Dalmiya's home town.

This match marked the end of the Azharuddin reign. Just as the semi-final defeat against England in the 1987 World Cup in Bombay put Kapil Dev's captaincy on the line, so Azhar was now on notice.

If he could have conjured up a win on the 1996 English tour that followed he might still have been safe, but even before the tour began things started going wrong. Kambli, despite averaging 50 in Tests, did not make the tour after reports had emerged that he had been partying wildly late at nights, and Prabhakar, mauled by the Sri Lankans, was also not included. To add to the Indian problems, they lost Sidhu, not through injury but because he felt his pride and honour had been hurt in what proved to be their most bizarre tour of England since 1936.

Sidhu had been dropped for the third one-day international in Old Trafford. However, as a result of the clumsy way in which the tour was managed, neither Azharuddin nor Sandip Patil, the cricket manager, spoke to him. All they did was pin the team sheet up on the dressing room. The result was that Sidhu, unaware that he had been dropped, sat in the Old Trafford pavilion expecting to play. As Azharuddin on winning the toss signalled from the middle that India would bat, Sidhu started padding up.

The rest of the team, aware he was dropped, started laughing and one or two also made jokes about Sikhs (Sidhu being a Sikh), which are common in India. Many of the remarks had come from the younger members of the side and Sidhu, a senior player, felt all the more insulted. In an Indian culture where older people expect to be treated with respect, such behaviour was likely to cause grave offence and it did. Sidhu felt so insulted that despite the efforts of Board president, and fellow Sikh, Inderjit Singh Bhindra, he refused to carry on with the tour.

As he left the tour he made this dramatic declaration, 'I promised my father on his deathbed that I would live my life with integrity and respect. As long as I stay on this tour I cannot do that.'

So India went into the first Test with a makeshift opening pair and, batting first on a sporting wicket at Edgbaston, India were bowled out for 214 after tea on the first day and would not have even made that but for the 52 from Srinath.

Srinath also brought back India into the match taking the wickets of Knight and Thorpe and had Hussain caught of his glove by Mongia when on 14. Umpire Darryl Hair for some reason did not see it that way, however. Hussain went on to make 128 and changed both the course of the match and the series. India again batted badly in the second innings and only a quite brilliant century by Tendulkar restored some Indian pride. As Euro '96 began, Tendulkar, with almost nobody giving him support, made 122 from 176 balls with Manjrekar, 18, being the next highest scorer. The target of 121 was never likely to test England and they romped home by eight wickets with a day to spare.

The Indians had much the better of the second Test at Lord's and the third at Trent Bridge. At Lord's, India discovered two new batsmen who, since then, have been the mainstay of their batting.

Ganguly had been taken to Australia in 1991-92 then discarded. He had shown his potential in the Old Trafford one-day international – a rare Indian success in a dismal one-day series which they lost badly – and should have played at Edgbaston where he might have made the difference. At Lord's he was the key player, holding India together after Tendulkar fell. Batting with an elegance that comes naturally to left-handers, he scored a quite beautiful century on his debut. And this playing in front of a crowd that was more interested in events taking place at the same time in another part of north London in a totally unrelated sport. On that Saturday many spectators in the Warner Stand, and elsewhere at Lord's, turned their back on Ganguly and the cricket and watched soccer on television. At one stage play was stopped due to cheering as England finally beat Spain on penalties in the Euro '96 quarter-final at Wembley. But Ganguly did not allow himself to be fazed by such distractions and went on to make his century.

Ganguly had batted at no. 3, Rahul Dravid, also making his Test debut, batted at no. 7 and made 95. On the final day at Lord's, India had their chances of winning when England, at 168 for 6, were only 83 ahead. But dogged English resistance, helped by more poor umpiring and a lack of support for Srinath and Venkatesh Prasad, saw England earn a draw.

It was a similar story at Trent Bridge. India batted first, Tendulkar scored his second century of the series, Ganguly joined an exclusive club of two West Indian batsmen – Alvin Kallicharran and Lawrence Rowe – who had scored two successive Test centuries in their first two Test innings. India made 521. Had Dravid held on to a catch Atherton offered when he was on 0 off Srinath it might have been a different story. But superbly as Srinath and Prasad bowled, Atherton, riding his luck and often playing and missing, scored a big hundred in a strong England reply. In the end the only interest was whether Ganguly could start a club of which only he could claim membership: a century in each of his first three Test innings. On 48 he was out and for the second successive tour of England India had lost the series as a result of losing the first Test.

The major pluses of the tour had been the discovery of Ganguly and Dravid (who had made 84 in the first innings of the Trent Bridge Test). The two debutants made an interesting contrast. Both are brahmins, but are very different in both upbringing and character. Ganguly hails from a well-off Calcutta family, part of the bhadralok, gentlemanly traditions of the upper castes of the province. His older brother had played for Bengal and like many rich Bengali kids was known as Raja, king. When Saurav came along he was nicknamed Maharaja, greater king and the story, probably apocryphal, was that on his first tour of Australia, when he was asked to be twelfth man, he refused to carry drinks as at home that was the work of servants.

Dravid, a Maharashtrian, born to a food scientist in Indore, but brought up in Bangalore, had made his way through all the various stages of Indian cricket starting with St Joseph's Boys School in Bangalore. He was part of the Indian Board's Under-15 and Under-19 sides and captained the Indian juniors to victory over New Zealand in 1992. Ganguly had shown great character to reclaim his place in the Indian side after his experiences in Australia in 1991-92; Dravid had displayed both persistence and patience in waiting for his call, which had been a long time coming, but which finally came in 1996.

In Prasad, also from Bangalore, India had found an ideal partner for Srinath. *Wisden* had no doubt about their ability: 'Srinath and Prasad were magnificent. They were the best bowlers on either side, and with more fortune, could have inflicted greater damage on England's batting.'

Srinath was simply wonderful, said *Wisden*, 'but dropped catches, poor umpiring and endless playing and missing worked against them.'

But encouraging as these signs were they were not enough to save Azharuddin, who even during the tour gave the impression he did not care much. His batting was abysmal, only 42 runs in three Tests with an average 8.40. And apart from the Sidhu incident there was his dalliance with Sangeeta Bijlani. What a player does in his private life is best left private, but Miss Bijlani, although not married to Azharuddin, is worthy of comment because in many ways she was a team member. She travelled on the team bus, attended official receptions for the Indians and on the team coach sat in the front row of seats reserved for the captain. Azharuddin, a devout Muslim, not only does not drink but does not like the smell of drink and on the tour he would not allow the likes of Tendulkar and others who had the odd drink to sit near him.

Soon after the Indians returned from England Azharuddin was sacked and Tendulkar was made captain. With it came a return to Test victories; Tendulkar started his captaincy with a victory in the one-off Test against Australia at Delhi. On a bone dry, fractured pitch, the first day wicket appeared to be three days old, and Kumble, who had taken just 5 wickets for 334 runs in three Tests in England, now had 5 wickets for 65 in the Australian first innings, and with Mongia making 152 India's winning margin was 7 wickets. Kumble's failure in England, where the previous summer playing for Northamptonshire he was the only bowler in the country to take 100 wickets, was explained away as a result of having been found out by the English batsmen, and the wintry conditions of the 1996 summer did not help. The Australians did not know Kumble, and a dry Delhi was a very different proposition to a cold, wet England.

But did Mukesh Kumar Gupta make the Delhi wicket even drier and dustier? Five years later Gupta confessed to the CBI that with the help of Ajay Sharma and the groundsman he had doctored the pitch at

Delhi's Feroze Shah Kotla ground to help ensure an Indian win in three-and-a-half days.

Azharuddin was no longer captain, but he had not stopped his liaison with Gupta. He was proving unreliable, however, and Gupta was showing such a loss on Azharuddin's 'predictions' that he went with Sharma to see Azhar in Hyderabad. Azhar promised to make it up during the Titan Cup one-day tournament between India, Australia and South Africa, which was held following the Australian Test. India won the final in Bombay, now renamed Mumbai, by 35 runs beating South Africa, and according to Gupta Azharuddin's predictions did not work out.

The South Africans were staying on for their first Test series in India and Gupta says Azharuddin promised to make correct predictions during the series. He predicted the first Test at Ahmedabad would not be a draw, India won and Gupta made money. He then predicted an Indian defeat in the second, India lost and again Gupta made money. By this time Gupta had made up sixty per cent of his previous losses and through Sharma also met Ajay Jadeja.

He was still unhappy about Azhar's reliability as a forecaster and felt he should cultivate the South Africans just to make sure.

The third Test was in Kanpur and Gupta travelled there and asked Azhar to introduce him to Cronje. The devout Muslim and the born-again Christian may seem odd bedfellows, but on that tour Cronje and Azhar were inseparable. Cronje was in constant demand from the Indian cricket fans, having to field endless calls in his hotel room and often went to Azhar's room to escape. They also had a common friend in Hamid 'Banjo' Cassim, a South African of Indian origin. He befriended the South African players by giving them biltong, dried meat, and the Indians by bringing them biryani. In the Cape Town Test that followed a few weeks after the Kanpur Test, the sight of Banjo hauling up biryani via a rope to the Indian dressing room was a spectacle that caught many eyes. What everyone missed, however, was that after this public display of eating there often followed private intrigues on match-fixing.

On the evening of 10 December 1996, after play had ended on the third day of the Kanpur Test, Azharuddin asked Cronje to come up to his room and introduced him to Gupta, describing him as a diamond merchant. Gupta quickly told Cronje he was a match-fixer, and that he wanted to be sure that the South Africans, who were already facing defeat, ironically thanks to a brilliant 163 from Azharuddin, would lose the Test.

Cronje would later tell the King Commission, 'I led him to believe I would. This seemed an easy way to make money But I had no intention of doing anything.' He accepted £20,000 from Gupta, as 'money for jam', hid it in his kit bag and after South Africa had lost the Test and the series 2–1, smuggled it out of India, into and out of South Africa, and finally to a bank account in England, violating the foreign exchange rules of both India and South Africa.

That established the Cronje-Gupta relationship. Cronje says he lied to Gupta about match-fixing but took his money nevertheless. The last match of the Indian tour was a one-day international, meant as a benefit match for Mohinder Amarnath. The South Africans did not want to play the match, they were upset by the loss of the Test series and by then most of their players hated India. Its heat, its poverty, its people and its ways had proved too much for these supposedly new South Africans. They could not wait to get home.

How much India upset the South Africans – still a near all-white team – can be seen from this article Gary Kirsten wrote on his return home in a Cape Town newspaper. Addressed as a letter to his fellow Capetonians it read in part:

I felt like kissing the airport tarmac when we walked down the steps of the plane on Sunday. The drive from the airport was very confusing, not to mention disappointing. Not a single cow, pig or camel in sight, never mind on the road with us. And no Scooters . . . not even a single blast from a car hooter. And no piles of rotting garbage. These things have been an intricate part of life for the last nine weeks; to be suddenly deprived of all of them was quite a shock. Nine weeks. Nine weeks. I'm not sure people realise how long that really is when you are on the road as we were in India. It has only just started sinking in with me since we were arrived back. I also couldn't help noticing how many of my close friends seem to have been eating . . . or maybe I am just comparing them to myself because everyone tells me I've lost a lot of weight and they all look like they've gained weight to me!! Being a great salad eater, one of my most exciting moments came when I went into a small restaurant and I realised that I could order a Greek salad, knowing that it would not only be fresh but also . . . safe. I didn't need to check whether the lettuce had been washed in bottled water! Speaking of clean water, cleaning my teeth with the stuff that comes out of the tap has been another great thrill. You won't believe how many times I ran out of bottled water with my mouth full of toothpaste in India!!'

Kirsten, being white, had clearly never been to the black townships near Cape Town, let alone Alexandria or Soweto, where he would have seen sights far worse than anything in India. The article summed up the mood of this team as it took the flight to Bombay for this unwanted last match. On the plane, Cronje approached some of the players and asked them whether they would like to throw it. In Bombay the entire South African team debated whether to accept £170,000 from Gupta, and Pat Symcox told the King Commission, 'Some guys, including myself, said it was a lot of money and we should look at it. Some guys were for it, some against.' In the end it was rejected, but it remains the only known instance of an entire team discussing match-fixing. Cronje met Gupta at 3 am on the morning of the match to tell him it was not on.

As Cronje flew home with Gupta's money in his kit bag, the Indians followed him to South Africa for a series of back-to-back Tests and one-day internationals. The relationship Cronje had struck up in India with Gupta endured. Cronje says he kept lying to Gupta about throwing matches but took his money. Gupta says that when Cronje, like Azhar, proved an unreliable forecaster and Gupta suffered huge losses, Cronje apologised and promised to make amends. Here we have a touch of comic opera.

According to Gupta, Cronje had promised that South Africa would lose some matches during the one-day series against India. When they did not he told Gupta that India played so badly and missed so many chances he could not do anything about the result. Gupta had bribed both sides, yet could still not get the result he wanted. It is possible other players were in hock to some other bookies seeking a different fix, we shall never know.

The one-day matches, which also involved Zimbabwe, had come after the three Tests where the South Africans had repaid the Indians for their spinning wickets with seaming ones. In India, the South African cricket manager, the former Kent man Bob Woolmer, had complained long and hard about how Indians prepared wickets for their spinners. The Indians, with more stoical grace, just accepted that the first Test in Durban would be on an unplayable seamer's wicket. Even then the bowling of Allan Donald was quite majestic. He took 9 wickets in the match, bowling India out for 100 in the first innings, which lasted barely three hours, and 66 in the second, which lasted 34 overs and one ball. In the entire match India batted for just 73 overs and two balls.

Srinath and Prasad did their best. They took 15 wickets between them, Prasad taking five wickets in both innings, and South Africa were bowled out for 235 and 259. But these scores looked huge compared to the puny Indian batting effort.

The second Test in Cape Town saw another heavy Indian defeat, but at least the Indians had the consolation of producing the best batting seen in the South African season and for many a Test. Replying to South Africa's 529 for 7 declared India were 58 for 5 when Tendulkar was joined by Azharuddin. What followed was beyond the control of any match-fixer. They put on 222 in only 40 overs in what those privileged to watch felt was the most enjoyable of all Test afternoons. In one six-over spell after lunch, Lance Klusener was hit for 30. Azharuddin, always the more exotic, made his 115 from 110 balls, before he ran himself out. Tendulkar stayed to help India avoid the follow-on with two wickets remaining and went on to make 169, his highest Test score against South Africa.

But it was a bit like the charge of the light brigade; the carnage of India could not be avoided and, set 426 to win, India made only 144 and were beaten by 282 runs.

However, having lost the series the Indians seemed to discover themselves. They came close to winning the third Test in Johannesburg and might have done so but for the weather and some dogged resistance by Daryll Cullinan. Dravid, having threatened to make a hundred during the course of the series, finally made it with 148, India made 410, then through the bowling of Srinath, who took 5 for 104, they got a lead of 89. With Dravid making 81 in the second innings, India set South Africa 355 and on the final day South Africa were 77 for 5.

But then came a thunderstorm, resumption was unduly delayed and while two more wickets fell, Klusener then settled in with Cullinan and with the light dimming and India unable to use their faster bowlers South Africa escaped.

So like many Indian captains Tendulkar had started with home victories and overseas defeats.

This trend should have come to an end on 3 April 1997. On that day at Bridgetown, Barbados, once the impregnable heart of West Indian cricket, India were set a mere 120 to win with not a cloud in the sky. But in a Test series where in no completed innings did the Indians fail to pass 300 – in the first innings of this Test they had made 319 – they now made only 81, losing by 38 runs. Well as the West Indians bowled, the defeat was shattering and for hours afterwards Tendulkar could not explain it saying, 'I can't believe it' and wondered when India might get another such chance. Madan Lal, the cricket manager said, 'I don't know what to say about such a team, which can't even make 120.'

It would be tempting to say that this was the old lack of killer instinct and Indians were to agonise long and hard about the might-have-beens. They had some bad luck before the tour began, Srinath crying off before a ball was bowled, and during the Test there were some bad umpiring decisions. In the first innings of this Test with India on 212 for 2 and Tendulkar on 92, seemingly set for a huge score and a big lead, he was given caught off a no ball that the umpire did not see. India went on to make 319, but this was only a slender lead. However, they bowled the West Indians out for 140, which should have been less for they were 107 for 9, and while the wicket helped West Indian pace, 120 was still a very gettable target.

Such defeats are always shattering and what made it worse was that the Indians knew that they had not had such an opportunity since 1971, when they had won in the West Indies for the first and only time. The Indians dominated most of the Tests, and, three hours of madness in Barbados apart, had been superior without having anything to show for it. There is little doubt that if India had made the 120 the recent history of Indian cricket would have been different. The tale of tigers at home and pussy cats abroad would have had to be rewritten and Tendulkar, in only his third series as captain and his second away, would have shown that just as his batting was taking Indian cricket to a new frontier, his captaincy could do the same.

But it was not to be. And the nature of the defeat, combined with some astonishing collapses in the one-day matches – in St Vincent chasing 249, India were 201 for 3, before falling to 231 all out and losing by 18 runs – now began to feed rumours of match-fixing. On the tour a bookie approached an Indian journalist and asked him whether it would be possible to make an offer to Tendulkar. Before the Barbados Test there had been talk of a fix. Following this series *Outlook* magazine started an investigation and in May 1997 published an article which for the first time publicly spoke of match-fixing. Gupta was mentioned, but he was identified only as MK, and Prabhakar went public on the Sri Lankan offer of 1994. He gave the figure he was offered, £40,000, but not the name of the player who made the offer.

The Indian Board appointed a former Chief Justice of the Supreme Court, Justice Chandrachud, to investigate. Prabhakar refused to tell him the name of the player, Chandrachud interviewed other players but drew a blank and concluded there was no match-fixing.

Three years later, Prabhakar, using a secret video camera recorded Irani, the Indian team physio, recalling his testimony in front of Chandrachud.

> Know what Chandrachud asked me? 'Did any of the boys talk in front of you [about match-fixing]?' I said, 'No.' He asked, 'Do you think it happens?' I said, 'Sir, my duty is to report. Even if they are doing, they won't do it in front of me. They respect me. They treat me like a father, brother, mother, everything.' Then Chandrachud gave me his shoulder to rub. He said, 'My shoulder is paining, my leg is paining.'

The net result of all this was truly Indian and bizarre. After four years of innuendo and allegations the only victim was a journalist. The *Hindu* decided to part company with its long-standing and much-respected correspondent Ramswamy Mohan. He had been mentioned in the *Outlook* magazine article as a journalist who used to bet and had contacts with bookies. It was implied that he was a conduit for players, an allegation Mohan denied. He continues to be *Wisden*'s cricket correspondent in India.

It is with this cloud hanging over the game that in August 1997 Tendulkar led the Indians on a tour of Sri Lanka, and while India drew both Tests and Tendulkar himself made runs, the Sri Lankans made even more and shattered the Indian bowling. In the first Test, replying to India's 537, Sri Lanka made 952 for 6 declared. Sanath Jayasuriya made 340, Mahanama made 225, setting up all sorts of records. The second wicket pair batted for two consecutive days, the whole of the third and fourth, having come together on the evening of the second, when India, having taken an early wicket, must have had illusions of winning the Test. By the time they were finally out on the morning of the fifth day, the Indian bowlers must have felt like those of Xavier's at the hands of Tendulkar and Kambli all those years ago.

Their partnership of 576 was the highest for any wicket in Tests and only just short of Hazare and Gul Mahomed's all-time first-class record. India drew the match but could not avoid defeat in the one-day matches and Tendulkar the master batsman looked the novice captain in this his fourth series, three of them having been away from home.

I interviewed him shortly after this series and he still looked very calm, composed and touchingly thoughtful. As I struggled to balance the tea his wife had served me with my tape recorder he said finish your tea then you can ask questions. However, for the first time he was getting a bad press in India and it got worse as the Sri Lankans returned and India, having won all three Tests by an innings in 1994, now drew all three Tests. In both the first and third Test – the second was ruined by rain – India had the advantage but could not force wins. The one-day series was drawn and by the end of 1997, with Tendulkar having been captain for little more than a year, it was clear the Indians felt the experiment had failed. India under Tendulkar had won just three Tests out of 17, all at home and 17 of 54 one-day games.

Tendulkar was replaced with Azharuddin, with Ramakant Desai, now chairman of selectors, saying, 'Azhar was removed in 1996 because he was going through a difficult phase in his personal life. He needed to be rested. This is a good decision for India and we are confident that Azhar will be able to lead the team well. We removed Tendulkar because he could not take the pressure of both batting and captaincy.'

Critics argued that the captaincy had affected Tendulkar's batting, but that was overstating things. Apart from the first home series against South Africa when he averaged 27.66, the lowest of his career in a three-Test series, he had averaged 40.16 in South Africa, 57.80 in the West Indies, 96.66 in Sri Lanka and 49.75 against Sri Lanka at home.

More than anything else, Tendulkar's downfall came through his record in one-day matches, which in India were being increasingly treated on a par with Tests.

The week after his appointment, Azharuddin led India in a one-day tournament in familiar surroundings, a limited-overs tournament against Pakistan and Bangladesh in Dhaka, and India started winning one-day tournaments again, even matches that seemed lost. In Dhaka in January they beat Pakistan in the finals 2–1 and the final match saw India, set 314, make 316 for 7 to win in splendid style.

Azharuddin, already India's most successful captain with 10 Test victories, followed this with a home series against Australia, the first such series in India since 1986 and the tied Test drama. The Australians were on a roll. They had won nine Test series since their Ashes win of 1994-95, their only defeat coming in the one-off Test at Kotla in Tendulkar's first as captain.

The 1998 series was billed as Tendulkar versus Shane Warne, their first encounter since Warne's Test debut in Sydney in the 1991-92 series, with Warne having missed the Kotla encounter. Since then both players had travelled a long way, with Warne in a sense going much further. In Sydney, Tendulkar already looked a genius in the making while Warne had looked hopeless. But then, in 1993, came the ball at Old Trafford with which he bowled Mike Gatting, reckoned to be the ball of the century, and by the time he came to India for his first visit in February 1998 he was clearly the world's best bowler and, probably, the greatest spinner in the history of the game.

Tendulkar prepared himself meticulously for Warne's arrival. Before the tour he practised against local leg spinners getting them to bowl on rough crater-like surfaces. He led Mumbai in the Australian tour opener which was played at the old CCI ground and scored the first double century of his first-class career, 204 not out from 192 balls. Mumbai won by ten wickets, a rare result in a tour match and an even rarer defeat in such a match for a visiting team to India.

But in the first innings of the first Test in Madras, now known as Chennai, it was Australia who were on top, with Warne getting Tendulkar for just four. Tendulkar drove his first ball past the bowler, the fifth dipped and as he jumped out he was caught. But in the second innings it was a different story. Sidhu had served the starter by softening up Warne, Tendulkar provided the main course which was as rich as anything ever seen. *Wisden* wrote, 'Tendulkar's belligerence was awesome and his short placement enthralling.' Warne, having taken 4 for 85 in the first innings, was now reliving the horrors of his Test debut against Tendulkar at Sydney and finished with 1 for 122. Tendulkar's 155 was his third century against Australia and India won by 179 runs.

Tendulkar only made 79 in Calcutta in the second Test, but this was an awesome all-round Indian performance. India made 633 for 5 declared, their highest score against Australia, their highest ever at Eden Gardens, and no Indian batsman made less than 65 with Azharuddin, on his favourite ground, making 163. Srinath took two wickets in his first over and India won by an innings and 219 runs. Tendulkar scored 177 in the third Test at Bangalore, but India had one of its collapses in the second innings and with Australia showing resolution there was a consolation Australian victory.

There was, however, no doubt who had won the Tendulkar-Warne duel. In three Tests Tendulkar had scored 446 runs at a strike rate of 80.65 per hundred balls received and a series average of 111.50. Warne was said to have nightmares of Tendulkar hitting him for sixes. Warne has always said Tendulkar is the best batsman he has bowled to, his ability to judge a length being uncanny.

Tendulkar further emphasised this when, after India lost the one-day series which also featured Zimbabwe, the two teams then travelled to Sharjah for the Coca-Cola Cup which also featured New Zealand. Tendulkar, almost single-handedly, won India the tournament.

It was his batting that pulled India through to the final and against Australia he scored 80, 143 and 134, this last coming in the final when, after Australia had made 272 for 9 in their 50 overs, India passed it with only four wickets down. In five innings he had scored 435 runs at an average of 87.00.

Tendulkar's performances against Australia reassured Indians that the rock on which their batting had been based since 1993 was secure. As long as Tendulkar was there India had a chance of winning any match; if he went then it became doubtful; and if he went cheaply in an overseas Test then there was no chance.

This became very evident later that year on India's tours of Zimbabwe and then New Zealand. The Zimbabwe tour was arranged at short notice to help provide cricket for Zimbabwe after the cancellation of the mini World Cup. The tour involved three one-day internationals and a one-off Test. In the first one-day match Tendulkar made 127 and India won by eight wickets. India also won the second, but in the third Tendulkar made 2 and India could not chase 259.

The Test demonstrated this dependence on Tendulkar even more sharply. Tendulkar made 34 and 7 and India, set a modest 235, failed by 71 runs. Others like Dravid made runs, he made 118 and 44, but unlike Tendulkar they could not win matches on their own.

The tour to New Zealand between December 1998 and January 1999 emphasised this even more. In the very first innings of the first tour match against Central Districts in Napier Tendulkar made 5, India 103 and although Tendulkar made 154 in the second innings, India lost by seven wickets.

After the first Test at Dunedin had been washed out, the second at Wellington provided the deciding Test. In the first innings Tendulkar's 47, was overshadowed by Azharuddin's 103 which gave India some respectability with 208. Facing a deficit of 144, it required a Tendulkar century, 113, to make a match of it. At one stage it seemed as though India might even win its first Test abroad since 1993 when New Zealand, set 215, were struggling on 74 for 5, but New Zealand lost only one more wicket in reaching their target.

India failed to force a win in the third Test, although Dravid joined Gavaskar and Hazare as the only Indians to score a century in each innings, 190 and 103 not out. Dravid's place in the Test side had not been in doubt since Lord's in 1996, but he had not been considered for the one-dayers, the theory being his innings contained too many dot balls. In New Zealand in the four one-dayers which were shared 2–2 he made 123 not out, 38, 68 and 51, and his one-day place was secure.

The Indians returned home to finally play Pakistan at home. Threat of violence had cancelled it in 1991, 1993 and 1994. As in 1991, when the pitch at Wankhede was dug up, this time it was the one at Kotla, but the government was determined to resist fanatics and the tour went ahead amidst unprecedented security.

The first Test at Chennai was once again a case of 'as long as Sachin is there we will do it'. India allowed Pakistan to recover from 91 for 5 to make 238. Tendulkar made 0 and India, batting fitfully, gained a slender lead of 18. With Shahid Afridi making 141, Pakistan set India a target of 273. It looked all over at 82 for 5, but among the unbeaten five was Tendulkar and with Mongia he now began what looked like a match-winning partnership. They had taken India to 218 when Mongia rather rashly got out. Tendulkar, despite a bad back, struggled on but on 136 he tried to hit Saqlain Mushtaq out of the ground and was out. India still had three wickets remaining and required only 17 runs for victory, but they failed by 12.

The second Test at Kotla was a rare one for India, when Tendulkar did nothing but nevertheless India won. Tendulkar made 6 and 29, did not take a catch or bowl a ball but India won thanks to a quite unique performance by Kumble. India's batting was mostly Sadagopan Ramesh, 60 and 96, which gave him an average of 51 in his debut series. Ganguly with 62 also helped in setting Pakistan a target of 420, a significant number as it is the number of the Indian penal code for crimes like robbery and burglary.

Kumble's 4 for 75 had restricted Pakistan to 172 in the first innings. In the second neither he nor any other bowler seemed to make much of an impression as Pakistan got to 101 for no loss at lunch on the fourth day. But after lunch Kumble changed ends, from the Football Stand End to the Pavilion End, and in 19 overs and three balls took all 10 wickets, only the second time since Jim Laker had done so against Australia in 1956 that a bowler had taken all 10 wickets in an innings. Pakistan's defeat by 212 runs, gone from its lunch score to 207 all out after tea, could not have been more comprehensive.

This marked the end of the two Test series. India and Pakistan played a third Test, but it was part of the Asian Test championship. And here it was back to modern Indian cricket's theme song: if Sachin goes, down goes India.

India appeared to have won the match on the first day when Pakistan were 26 for 6, Srinath and Prasad sharing the wickets. But then India, as so often, failed to kill them off, Pakistan made 185, and although it did not look much, it kept them in the game and was the launch pad of their ultimate success.

Even more so when Shoaib Akhtar bowled Tendulkar for 0 and Dravid for 24, as India's 223 did not given them much of an advantage. Pakistan made 316 in their second innings and India were set 278 to win.

Then came the incident which ignited Calcutta and shamed Indian cricket. Tendulkar, on 9, hit a ball to the boundary and going for a third – his second had taken him past 5,000 Test runs – he collided with Akhtar at the bowler's end and was run out. The crowd felt Akhtar had deliberately blocked him and forced the game to come to a stop. Tendulkar and Dalmiya, the ICC president, had to appeal to them before play could resume. But the crowd were on edge. Their hopes rested on Ganguly. But at that stage he was hardly in the right frame of mind. The Indians were due to go to Sri Lanka for the next instalment of the Asian Test Championship and the Selectors wanted him as Vice Captain. However, when the decision was brought to Raj Singh Dungarpur, the Board President for approval, he expressed his disagreement saying Ganguly was not a leader, was too aloof, too arrogant, and not the right man to be Captain-in-waiting. Ganguly was told of Raj Singh's views and it seems to affect his play. On the final morning, with their hero out and India at 251 for 9, facing defeat, they rioted. The police evicted all the spectators and with about 200 people present made up of VIPs, officials and the press, Pakistan won by 26 runs. If the defeat after the stirring deeds of Delhi was shattering, the behaviour of the fans and the incompetence of the authorities were both sad and dishonourable for Indian cricket. It revived memories of the World Cup semi-final against Sri Lanka and, for the second time, a match in Dalmiya's home town had ended in shaming circumstances.

By this time the age of Gupta the match-fixer appears to have ended, probably around May 1998. There is some evidence to suggest that the high tide of cricket match-fixing drawn to a close, although Majid Khan, former chief executive of Pakistan cricket, remains convinced that Pakistan's two World Cup losses to India and Bangladesh in 1999 were fixed and an inquiry is being held in Pakistan now to determine the truth of that.

India did little in the World Cup and could claim their victory against Pakistan, which was genuine, was one of their few high points as was the batting of Dravid and Ganguly, particularly against Sri Lanka. Dravid headed the World Cup run scorers with 461 runs and Ganguly with 379 was third. It was their batting against Sri Lanka at Taunton which had everyone talking. India lost their first wicket, that of Ramesh at 6, but then Ganguly, 183 in 158 balls with 16 fours and seven sixes, and Dravid, run out for 145, took India to 324. They eventually made 373 and Tendulkar was not required; he made 2 coming in at no. 4.

The match was played on the day that Manchester United did the treble, winning their first European Cup since the triumph of 1968 and it is a measure of the Indian batting that it still made some impact.

But while Ganguly and Dravid batted well in other matches as well, India failed to qualify for the semi-finals and again Tendulkar was the key. In the early hours of the morning of the second match against Zimbabwe, Tendulkar learnt his father had died and flew home. India should still have won but they did not and while Tendulkar returned with a century against Kenya, that defeat against Zimbabwe effectively meant that India could not go through to the semi-finals. That match summed up the Indian defects; they bowled so slowly they were deducted three overs when they batted and there seemed neither method nor madness in Azharuddin's captaincy. As often after a World Cup, India looked for a change and for the second time it was Tendulkar's turn. But this time he had Kapil Dev as coach and Indians, always optimistic, hoped for the best.

Tendulkar began his first Test back as captain in dire straits against New Zealand. On a wicket offering seam movement, India were bowled out for 83, with Tendulkar making 18. In the second innings, however, he made an unbeaten century, there was one from Dravid and India nearly forced a win. India won the second Test at Kanpur on the sort of under-prepared wickets suited for its spinners. However, the talking point of the tour came in the third Test when India failed to enforce the follow-on at Ahmedabad.

India batting first made 538 with Tendulkar scoring his first Test double hundred, 217. India, 275 ahead, could have asked New Zealand to follow-on but did not and New Zealand escaped with a draw. Reports suggested Kapil Dev had insisted that the follow-on should not be imposed. Whatever happened, the incident joins one of the many mysteries of Indian cricket.

India's victory against New Zealand was placed in perspective when India toured Australia. Lele forecast that India would lose all three

Tests and they duly did. Worse they lost to Queensland and even a one-day match against the Prime Minister's XI made up of aspirants in one of the worst ever displays by a touring Indian side. Tendulkar made his customary Test century, averaging 46, and in the final Test at Sydney Laxman suddenly came good with 167, but defeats by 285 runs, 180 runs and innings and 141 runs told their own story.

There was a brief moment when India, on the first morning at Adelaide in the first Test, had Australia at 52 for 4. Then when India batted, Tendulkar on 61 was given out caught off Warne when television replays showed he was not out and after that India were rarely in the game.

The only consolation for the Indians was that nobody could beat them at home; not since the defeat by Pakistan in 1986-87 had India lost a series at home. However, the South Africans were coming back for a two-Test series and with India in such disarray after Australia there were fears that this time the dominance at home might end. The fears proved justified as the Indian batting failed in both Tests and perhaps, more significantly, there was disagreement between the team management and the authorities on who was responsible for the preparation of the pitches. The result was there was not enough time to prepare a truly spinning wicket in Mumbai for the first Test; India lost in three days and just after the match Tendulkar came to the terrace of the CCI and said he was quitting as captain. He led India in Bangalore, where Azharuddin, omitted from Australia, played and scored a hundred in a defeat by an innings and it now seemed the cup of Indian misery was complete. India could be thrashed both at home and away. Ganguly was chosen to succeed Tendulkar but there was no real hope of any change. Just then the Kali Yuga exploded and match-fixing finally began to be taken seriously, thanks to Cronje suddenly deciding that he could not do without bookies and a Delhi policeman. As Cronje would tell Judge King, his behaviour was like that of an alcoholic who can abstain for some time but returns to it when he has one drink.

His match-fixing urge returned when, a few weeks after the end of the series against England in South Africa in 2000, Hamid 'Banjo' Cassim introduced him to Sanjay Chawla, another Indian bookie in Durban's Beverly Hills intercontinental. By the time he left Chawla's room, Cronje was clutching a mobile phone box filled with perhaps as much as £55,000, having promised to fix matches on the Indian tour. It was to prove a fatal relationship. Cronje felt so invincible, he did not seem to care who knew about his match-fixing discussions with Chawla and when he got to India happily talked about it on a mobile phone given to him by Chawla. He asked Peter Strydom to play badly in the first Test in Bombay, which Strydom refused to do. In the second there was an offer to other team members, but this was rejected and Cronje tried to present it as a joke.

On 9 March 2000, South Africa played India in a one-day match in Kochi. They made 301 but India, in Ganguly's first match as captain, made 302, winning by three wickets. That evening in a small poky office in Delhi, a Delhi Crime branch detective, Ishwar Singh Redhu was listening to taps that had been placed on certain phones. He was investigating complaints of extorting money with menaces from some Delhi businessman that hot evening of the Kochi match, as he sat listening to telephone taps he had placed on two suspects, suddenly and very unexpectedly the name of Hansie Cronje cropped up and the fixing of the Kochi match.

Ishwar Singh decide to investigate. The South Africans were on their way to Delhi and he watched the Taj hotel where they were staying and saw Chawla go to Cronje's room. He also taped more conversations of match-fixing, this time between Cronje and Chawla.

This showed that on the morning of the final one-day international in Nagpur, Cronje lured Herschelle Gibbs and Henry Williams by offering Gibbs £10,000 if he scored less than 20 runs and Williams a similar sum if his overs cost more than 50 runs. They both agreed, but did not keep to their bargain. Cronje, who had made the offer with a smile, just laughed it off – part of his strategy to convince his players that it could all be a huge practical joke.

Cronje, of course, had no idea the mobile he had got from Chawla was being tapped and went on using it in Sharjah where the South Africans played a one-day tournament after India. The phone taps had convinced Ishwar Singh there might be some match-fixing there as well, but there wasn't.

On 7 April 2000, the Delhi police held a press conference releasing transcripts of conversations between Cronje and Chawla. The immediate reaction to the Delhi police announcement was one of utter disbelief that a born-again white Christian could be involved.

Cronje denied everything, Bacher backed Cronje and the South Africans denounced the tactics of the Delhi police. In London, the *Observer* quoted a South African journalist as saying that he had heard the tapes and that it could not be Cronje's voice as the voice had an Indian accent. It later turned out he had heard Indian actors reading out the transcripts released by the Delhi police. The tapes Ishwar Singh made had been sealed and placed under the jurisdiction of the Delhi High Court and have never been released. Within 48 hours Cronje had made the first of his many confessions and the shadowy world of MK Gupta and his ilk was about to emerge in the public light.

Within two months all the talk of match-fixing that had been rumoured for six years had surfaced in the public. Prabhakar finally

460

revealed that the player who had approached him was Kapil Dev, an allegation he denied and of which he was cleared. In May 2000, the Pakistanis, who had been sitting on a report prepared by Judge Malik Mohammed Qayyum for almost a year, were forced to release it. It recommended life bans for Salim Malik and Ata-ur-Rehman. Qayyum accepted that Waugh, Warne and May had told the truth about Malik seeking to corrupt them, Rehman was found guilty of perjury in relation to evidence about Wasim Akram. Qayyum also imposed fines on Wasim Akram, Mushtaq Ahmed, Waqar Younis, Inzamam-ul-Huq and Saeed Anwar, with the judge suspicious of their actions but unable to find clinching proof.

In June, two weeks after the Qayyum report was published, the South African judicial commission under retired judge Edwin King began to hear devastating evidence from South African players.

The same month saw the ICC, prompted by Lord MacLaurin, hold an emergency session to discuss match-fixing, the first time in six years that the organisation had held such a meeting. In the weeks leading up to the meeting, the various Boards manoeuvred to put themselves in the best possible light. Everyone put pressure on Pakistan to release the Qayyum report while in front of the King commission Ali Bacher made a statement full of hearsay evidence that sought to turn the spotlight away from South Africa on to the world, in particular alleged misdeeds by Pakistani umpires and players.

Then, even before the administrators could gather together, questions were raised in the media about Dalmiya's own conduct during negotiations for television rights concerning the 1998 ICC knock-out tournament held in Dhaka which had brought the ICC £12m, then the biggest deal it had ever done. Just before Dalmiya opened the session, Lord MacLaurin passed round a statement on England and Wales notepaper, which he asked all the ICC delegates to sign, declaring that they were honest men.

Everyone duly complied, but it revealed the curious state of an organisation whose own administrators had to declare they were clean before they could consider the corruption amongst the players. Friends of Dalmiya hinted darkly that this was some English plot. Yet the most persistent questions about the 1998 television deal, where Doordarshan, India's state television, had got the rights were raised in India and by his old comrade Bhindra. Soon there was another CBI inquiry to examine the deal and the links between Dalmiya and Mark Mascarenhas's World-Tel. CBI officers visited Dalmiya's offices in Calcutta and there was also an income tax raid on his home. The CBI report, when it emerges, may reveal the curious ways such television deals are done.

Dalmiya insists he has done nothing wrong. The ICC, he says, did not lose out and if Doordarshan paid over the odds that was their responsibility. As for the raids, he claims the income tax raids had nothing to do with cricket and are common to all business houses in India.

In a sense Dalmiya's remarks sum up the immense cultural divide the cricket corruption issue raises. In Pakistan the Cricket Board is at the mercy of the government, in India it is autonomous, but in both countries the game is played and administered against a background where corruption and police and tax inquiries into prominent persons are part of life. It is interesting to note that AC Muthiah, the then Indian Board president and Uma Bharati, the Indian sports minister, face CBI charges, albeit not related to cricket.

The ICC belatedly took tentative steps setting up an investigation unit under Sir Paul Condon. Yet as Sir Paul himself admitted, he has no legal powers. If he discovers anything it will be reported to the ICC; he can do nothing to administer justice. And in the various countries round the world the investigations reflect the fact that each country does its own thing.

It is noteworthy that on the very afternoon he held a press conference in London to publicise the work of his newly set up unit, the whole thing was overshadowed by the release of the CBI report and Sir Paul had to delay his press conference to deal with it.

The CBI report released in November 2000 proved most far reaching and, concentrating as it did on the illegal bookies, added a new dimension to the match-fixing inquiries. The result was that for the first time a cricketer, Mohammed Azharuddin, confessed that he had thrown three one-day internationals.

Drawing on the information from Gupta and other bookies, the CBI revealed how cricketers from around the world were lured and then corrupted. Azharuddin was banned by the Indian Board, but has since claimed he made no such confession and is fighting his ban.

The CBI is now looking into links between cricketers, bookies and the Indian underworld and could discover more secrets. The high tide of cricket match-fixing may have ended, but the full story of what happened between 1994 and 2000 is yet to be told.

The Hindus believe that the Kali Yuga will end when things will get so bad that the great gods Shiva and Vishnu, who have been asleep, will wake up and send god Rama back to earth to teach mankind how to be good and recreate a new Ram Rajya.

It is too early to say that Indian cricket's Kali Yuga has ended. The gods that guard Indian cricket are yet to awaken from their long sleep and there is, certainly, no sign of the return of Ram Rajya.

30

The new nabobs of Indian cricket
2000-01

Two days before Christmas 2001, a Test match finished in Bangalore between India and England. Both the weather and the conditions were eerily similar to the Test played at The Oval in August 1971 with which this history began.

As was the case during August 1971 a whole day was lost to rain and bad light caused play to stop early on all the other days; the covers kept coming on and off and the overcast weather made the conditions so English that, unusually for Tests in India, the faster bowlers dominated the drawn match. The draw also meant that, as in 1971, a three-Test series ended with India winning 1–0.

But these were superficial, almost trivial, similarities. Everything else about this match and series was different, and emphasised just how far Indian cricket had come since that brilliant August day. Before the Oval Test in 1971, India, on six previous visits to England, had never won a Test, indeed they had only led England once on the first innings. The English press called them the 'dull dogs of cricket' and had suggested that England should play only three-day Tests against them. The Indian cricketers went to England fearful that not only would they make fools of themselves socially, not knowing which knife or fork to use, but that they would also continue to prove inept on the field, unable to play the swinging, seaming ball bowled by these white gods whose fathers had once ruled them.

As we have seen, the totally unexpected victory at The Oval led to dancing in the streets of Bombay and for the first time Indians began to believe in themselves, having won successive series away from home in the West Indies and in England. But despite this, the India of 1971 knew it was very much the supplicant knocking at the door of the centre of world cricket. England's right to see itself as the headquarters of the world game was still unchallenged. India was part of the so-called second tier of cricket nations – Pakistan and New Zealand were the others – who, on a good day, with a favourable wind behind them and with everything else going for them, might give England a game but no more. Until India's victory at The Oval in 1971, none of these three countries had won a Test series in England. Both on and off the field England were the supreme power, having just won back the Ashes and defeated the West Indies, and these were the only two countries it saw as its worthwhile competitors.

In 1971 England were so dominant that, just two days after India's historic triumph at The Oval, they cancelled their tour of India due to take place that winter. Ray Illingworth, the defeated England captain who was never to tour India, told the English selectors he was not prepared to lead the side to the subcontinent, several other leading English cricketers also expressed similar reservations and the English authorities cancelled the tour. It was not unusual for leading English cricketers to duck out of a tour of India; the heat, the food, the people and the culture were always too much for some of them. As we have seen in the past, the English authorities got round this by sending B teams, often led by men who had never before played for England, let alone captained it. But the events at The Oval had demonstrated that India could not be taken so lightly and England had a very plausible excuse for not touring India.

Earlier that year, the brutal suppression of the freedom movement in then East Pakistan by the mainly West Pakistan army had ignited a freedom struggle that led to ten million refugees pouring into neighbouring India. By the end of the year there was a short, sharp war when India defeated Pakistan, liberated East Pakistan from Pakistan army control – where 90,000 of its men surrendered in Dacca – and created what is now called Bangladesh. However, in August 1971, it was not at all certain the two neighbours would go to war. President Richard Nixon wanted to keep Pakistan sweet as a reward for its role as the postman as he reopened American links with China in an effort to outflank the Soviet Union in the Cold War. And Nixon made it clear that as far as America was concerned its Cold War battle with the Soviet Union was more important than the freedom of the oppressed Bengalees of Bangladesh. Nixon was so determined to help Pakistan that he even ordered the American Seventh Fleet to the Bay of Bengal to deter any Indian military action. Indeed, in August 1971, Mrs Indira Gandhi, the Indian prime minister, was going round the world seeking to drum up support to counter this American military might and create a world coalition which could come to the aid of the suppressed Bengalees of Pakistan.

The Indian Board, eager to host an England tour within months of its epic win at The Oval, tried to reassure England that, despite the problems in the east, conditions in India were normal, but English cricket, sure of its status, brushed aside the Indian protests and said they could not come to India and would tour the following year. The Indians had no other option but to accept. The cancellation of the tour was considered so unimportant that *Wisden* dismissed it on page 1087 of its 1972 edition in a mere eleven lines. England knew India needed England and its cricket more than it needed India and it could, and did, call the shots.

2001 could not have been more different. For weeks before the tour the England cricketers, alarmed by the 11 September attacks on New York and Washington, expressed their fears about touring the country. Their fears were magnified by some alarmist reporting in the English tabloid press about the impact of the American action in Afghanistan on India. At that stage the events of 11 September had had little impact on India, for they had been coping with their own terrorism in Kashmir for more than a decade and the country was much calmer than it had been in 1993, when England had previously toured India. Then the dreadful destruction of the Babri Majid mosque by Hindu fanatics had led to tremendous violence between the Hindus and Muslims, and India's own version of 11 September, when bomb blasts in the Bombay Stock Exchange, Air India towers and other places had led to over 700 people being killed. But these events had made little impact in the British media and the English cricketers, oblivious to this, had toured India with their main worries, as we have seen, being the traditional ones of Indian food and the awful pollution in Indian cities.

The biggest difference between 1971 and 2001 was the attitude of the English cricket authorities. Just before the tour was due to begin, Lord MacLaurin, chairman of the ECB, had made noises at an ICC meeting in Kuala Lumpur suggesting that the American action in Afghanistan made an Indian tour difficult. However, unlike in 1971, India did not meekly accept this. They told MacLaurin that as Osama Bin Laden's men had crashed a plane into the Twin Towers and the Pentagon and that as Britain was standing 'shoulder to shoulder' with America, it was Britain that was more at risk from terrorists. Buckingham Palace might be the next target and the Indian cricketers had more to fear from visiting England. If England did not come then India might not tour England in 2002.

The ECB was alarmed. The rights of the summer's Indian Tests had been sold to ESPN Star Sports in India for around £10m. If India were to pull out of the tour, then the ECB stood to lose that money. In theory Sri Lanka, who are due to play three Tests, could have occupied the whole summer. However Sri Lankan television had paid a measly £100,000 for the rights and it could not make up the Indian loss. The ECB knew that Indians could now rightly claim to be the centre of world cricket, the economic powerhouse that generated more than 60 per cent of world cricket's income and the Indian threat made the ECB change its tune instantly.

Within days they changed from seeming to side with the English players who did not want to tour, to becoming so eager for a tour to India to take place that they even roped in the British High Commissioner in India, who was on leave in England, to reassure their cricketers. As added reassurance the ECB sent John Carr, head of its cricket operations, to India accompanied by MacLaurin's son-in-law, the former Derbyshire batsman Tim O'Gorman, who is a lawyer and represented the players on a hectic forty-eight hour trip. Andrew Caddick and Robert Croft could not be reassured, but England found replacements. The English Board knew economics dictated they tour India and they did.

Then, just as England arrived in India, there was even more dramatic evidence of Indian cricket's economic muscle. As in 1993, the Indians were in South Africa as England started their tour of India. But on the third day of the second Port Elizabeth Test a huge storm was generated in India by the decision of the match referee to penalise more than half of the Indian Test team. Five of the players were banned for excessive appealing with one of them, Virender Sehwag, banned from the third Test, while Sachin Tendulkar was given a suspended sentence for cleaning the ball without the permission of the umpires.

The Indians were outraged. The decision made by the match referee Mike Denness, the former England captain, raised all the old colonial hackles. It is possible that had he not penalised Tendulkar, the Indian reaction might not have been so extreme. As we have seen he is the Indian icon and the one cricketer whose deeds have helped Indians keep their faith in the game through the traumatic match-fixing crisis. He occupies a quite unique position in India. In a country that desperately wants to be a sporting superpower but has to live with its sportsmen under-performing, Tendulkar's status as the world's greatest batsman comes as some solace. Now he was touched by scandal and this was just too much to bear.

The Indian reaction was extraordinary, and amidst wild claims of racism, one journalist wrote, 'A majority of former players and administrators are seriously speculating on whether India should continue playing in white majority countries partial to the colour of one's skin.'

The *Asian Age* even ran a front-page story suggesting this was some form of bizarre South African revenge on India for the Delhi police unmasking Hansie Cronje. It accompanied the story with a photograph of Marlon Aronstam, the South African bookie who persuaded Cronje with gifts of a leather jacket and 5,000 Rands to declare during the Pretoria Test against England which led to an England victory. Aronstam was at the Port Elizabeth match and the headline on the piece read: 'Did Hansie bookie take his revenge?'

Such ridiculous suggestions showed how high feelings were. They were further inflamed by the television channels that feed India's sporting appetite, some of them owned by Rupert Murdoch. In the last decade they have built up a group of commentators, mainly ex-players from all over the world, who act like India's version of the tabloid press. They were at their most vociferous on this issue, taking a very hostile view of the decisions and their number included Geoff Boycott. As a player he hated the idea of going to India, as a commentator aware of the riches there, he cannot stay away. He amongst others advised the penalised Indian players to go to the law to challenge the rulings. His and other commentators' comments did much to fuel Indian feelings on this issue.

Not that the Indians needed much encouragement. In the days that followed there were endless television replays in India of sledging by South Africans of Indian batsman with Saurav Ganguly, the Indian captain, being abused by one South African after he had played and missed. He was supposed to have said, 'f*** your mother.'

It added to the growing feeling in India that the cricket world did not give the country its due and highlighted the enormous cultural differences between Asian and white cricketers.

In a sense this was cricket's equivalent of Latins diving in football which so angers English players who tend to have their own tricks.

The Indians were quick to see double standards in everything. One reason for Denness' harsh actions was the fact that two months earlier, Malcolm Speed, the new chief executive of the International Cricket Council, had written to match referees and umpires saying they should be tougher with players who misbehaved.

But what about Michael Slater, cried the Indians. Early in 2001, Speed, then chief executive of Australian cricket, was in Mumbai for the first Test when Australia started their tour of India. During that Test Slater claimed a catch off Rahul Dravid, which television replays showed was not clean. Slater got so incensed he abused Dravid and then Venkat, the Indian umpire, but got away with no more than a slap on the wrist from match referee, the West Indian Cammie Smith. The Indians pointed to this as evidence that match referees discriminated between white and Indian cricketers.

To make matters worse the ICC had left loopholes that fuelled this controversy. Match referees are not only given total discretion to dole out punishment, but the various categories of offences and the punishments that go with them are not properly defined. Also, unlike other sports, the ICC, fearing law suits, did not allow appeals against a referee's decisions or even allow match referees to talk to the media. This led to the ridiculous situation in Port Elizabeth where Denness attended a press conference, but like the proverbial wise monkey was dumb, further inflaming Indian journalists. Ravi Shastri, the lead Indian commentator, stood up at a press conference and asked, 'What is he doing here then, we know what he looks like.'

Such verbal language was matched by a ruthless use of economic muscle. The summer 2001 Indian visit to Zimbabwe had wiped out the accumulated losses of the Zimbabwe Board. The New Zealand Board had announced figures which showed that while they had made money from the Indian tour of 1998-99, they had lost money the following year when Pakistan were the visitors. Now the Indians made noises suggesting they might pull out of the third Test due to start at Centurion Park which alarmed the South Africans. If the third Test was not played, South Africa stood to lose 10 million Rands (£1 million). Also most of the sponsorship income for the 2003 World Cup, which is to be held in South Africa, comes from Indian-based companies. The punishments on Tendulkar and others had also been the subject of debate in the Indian parliament and the South African president, Thabo Mbeki, got into the act saying nothing must be done to damage relations with India, an important trading partner.

So South Africa agreed to ban Mike Denness from the third Test. The ICC declared it an unofficial Test but the Indians carried on as if it was official. Dennis Lindsay, the former South African cricketer who had been selected as the ICC match referee for the India-England series, was chosen by the South Africans to stand in the Centurion Test as well and India omitted Sehwag from the Test, saying this now meant he had met the Denness ban.

The ICC refused to accept this and the question was what would happen in the next Test which was the first of the three Test series against England in Mohali. The Indians chose Sehwag in the squad and the ICC gave the Indians an ultimatum that if they played Sehwag that Test would also be unofficial. England made it clear that in that case they would come home as they had not gone to India to play unofficial Tests.

For days the phone lines between England, India and Australia hummed as a compromise was sought. The ICC extended the deadline given to the Indians and a compromise was worked out. The Indians accepted that Sehwag could not play in the first Test against England in Mohali. In return the ICC agreed to appoint a three-man committee to look into how Denness had reached his decisions and whether he had followed the proper procedures.

But even as the Test series got underway, the Indian cricket administrators made it clear to the English that they were now dealing with a very different India to the one in 1971. The England tour of 2001-02 was divided into Tests followed by a short Christmas break for the England players, then a return to India to play five one-day internationals. The Indians insisted England play a sixth one-day international to make up for the fact that while England were playing only three Tests, India would play four Tests in England in the summer. England had letters showing the Indians had agreed to this arrangement, but this counted for little. England knew that if they did not give into the Indians they stood to lose some of the £10m they had earned from selling the rights of the series to Indian television. While India and England battled it out in the middle, off the field intense negotiations took place between the Indian and English Boards before England gave in.

To further emphasise this new Indian status, the Indian Board secretary told Tim Lamb, chief executive of the ECB, when he visited Mohali that, like England, India would send its own team to England to check on the security. Aside from the Osama Bin Laden threat, there had been race riots in the summer of 2001 between Asians and whites and with India playing in Manchester and Leeds, near the riot areas, the Indians wanted to be reassured that their players and fans would be safe.

The Indians also referred to the fact that in the 2001 summer fans had run onto the ground leading both to injuries to players and England conceding a one-day match. The Indians would also check that since England got five star hotels in India, the Indians had equivalent accommodation. In the past Indian players, many of whom are vegetarians, had complained about the food available at grounds and the Indian Board wanted reassurance on this.

All this Indian tough talking was hugely complicated by the re-emergence of Jagmohan Dalmiya. In September 2001 at the annual election for the Indian Board, Dalmiya, who had appeared to have been frozen out after his term as ICC president ended, decided to challenge Dr A.C. Muthiah for the presidency of the Indian Board. Board officials are elected annually, but normally a president is allowed three terms and is not challenged in his second and third year. By this convention Muthiah should have been given a third term, but Dalmiya decided to ignore this convention and what is more won, proving his remarkable ability to organise winning campaigns.

This added a further, explosive, twist. Dalmiya feels acutely resentful that although as ICC president he made enormous amounts of money for the ICC through lucrative television contracts and funded the match referee programme, the ICC did not defend him when allegations of corruption were made about his role in those television contracts. Friends of Dalmiya see this as racism, although as we have seen the allegations were first made by his colleagues in Indian cricket and it is the Indian Central Bureau of Investigation who is carrying out the investigation.

Dalmiya rode the nationalist bandwagon launched by the Denness decision, and after that his goal was to get the penalties imposed by Denness set aside and make the Centurion Test, which was declared unofficial by the ICC, official.

Here Dalmiya could point to the South African precedent. In 1961, after the South African apartheid regime withdrew from the Commonwealth, it automatically ceased to be a member of the then Imperial Cricket Conference. The ICC met soon after at Lord's and decided that as South Africa was no longer a member of the ICC that winter's Test series between South Africa and New Zealand would be unofficial. The 1962 *Wisden* faithfully recorded this, but subsequent *Wisdens* do not record any further discussion on this subject. However, by some mysterious process the Tests became official, as did all of white South Africa's Tests between 1961 and 1970 when the sporting boycott started.

Dalmiya in all this used India's economic power, aware that if the ICC sought to ban Indian cricket it could severely damage many Test-playing countries.

One ICC insider told me, 'Should India be thrown out of the ICC as a result of this controversy, then England and Australia would survive but the other countries would find it very difficult, if not impossible. The West Indies Board is very dependent on selling its television rights to the Indian market and without such sales it will be in trouble. One of the features of the Indian market is that they not only show the matches involving India, but also Test matches involving two neutral countries, as the Indians buy not only matches involving India but all Test-playing countries.'

It is possible Dalmiya could overplay his hand. When the ICC appointed its commission to look into the Denness decisions, Dalmiya refused to accept the nominees and even some of his friends felt it was one confrontation too many.

Dalmiya was subject to much press criticism in England, but one revealing episode underlined just how far Indian cricket had come since 1971. In August 1971 when India won at The Oval, Ian Wooldridge wrote a warm piece congratulating Wadekar. It was the piece of a generous English journalist acknowledging something unexpected. In December 2001 he came to India for the Mohali Test and went back and wrote a piece damning Dalmiya and sounded alarmed by what the Indian businessman had done. While the piece was critical of the Indian Board, it recognised that India was different.

Yet if all this showed how powerful Indian cricket had become off the field, on the field, as India entered 2002, its cricketers continued to under-perform and create the familiar angst. Once again commentators spoke of a lack of the killer instinct amongst Indians

470

and a former Army general even suggested that the problem lay in the fact that Indians were far too reliant on Gandhi's ethos of non-violence and should adopt more of the violent, military ethos of Subhas Bose.

On the field, 2001 had ended on a familiar note: India were the great mavericks of the game – at times capable of astonishing brilliance and beating the best but never able to sustain such performances and some marvellous victories were followed by humiliating, totally bewildering defeats.

In many ways the record of Indian cricket between 2000 and 2001 was the classic Indian one of one step forward, two steps backs.

The chain of events caused by the Delhi police unmasking Cronje had also undone Kapil Dev. Although he protested his innocence and even shed tears on BBC World when asked about the Prabhakar allegations, he could not carry on as coach and for the ICC Knock Out tournament in Nairobi, the Indians brought back Anshuman Gaekwad in his place.

This seemed to work an Indian miracle. India beat Australia and South Africa to get to the final, but having proved winners as underdogs they were installed as favourites against New Zealand in the final and failed. Gaekwad, who worked well with Ganguly, felt Ganguly erred in his bowling changes in the final, but even then this was the first final of a one-day tournament of all the Test-playing countries India had been in since their triumph in Australia in 1985 and it seemed Indian cricket was on its way back.

The euphoria lasted a few days. The Indians flew from Nairobi to Sharjah and there in the final of the Coca-Cola Cup, they allowed Sri Lanka to smash 299 for 5. India were then bowled out for 54, their lowest score in one-day cricket ever. The loss by 245 runs was the worst defeat suffered by any team in one-day matches at the time.

Indian cricket was in deep gloom. Gaekwad carried on as coach for Bangladesh's inaugural Test, which was also Ganguly's first Test as captain. India won, and while this was technically India's first overseas victory since the one in Sri Lanka in 1993, there was little reason for euphoria. The match was being played in Dacca against novice opponents who made over 400 in their first innings and the manner of the victory was hardly convincing.

By this time the Indians had already decided they needed a foreign coach and looked at several candidates including Geoff Marsh and Greg Chappell of Australia and John Wright of New Zealand. Ganguly was very keen on Wright. In the summer of 2000 he played for Lancashire and the moment he heard Kapil was out he rang Raj Singh Dungarpur from England to tell him that Wright should be selected. Rahul Dravid, who was playing for Kent that season, knew Wright as he was the Kent coach and was also keen on him. The decision was finalised in Nairobi when the senior players, including Tendulkar, Ganguly and Dravid, met Board officials and decided on Wright.

So with Wright as coach India took on Zimbabwe in the home Test series winning the two-match series 1–0, but there was little optimism as the Australians, having won fourteen consecutive Tests, arrived in India in February 2001. Whatever little confidence there was dipped even further when Australia won the first Test at Mumbai in three days by 10 wickets. Tendulkar made runs, but did not dominate as he had done during 1997-98 series, making 76 and 65 in Mumbai. With no Anil Kumble, whose shoulder injury meant he was out of cricket for sometime, it did not look as though India could mount any sort of challenge.

This mood of utter gloom deepened even further during the first three days of the Calcutta Test. Australia made 445 and India were bowled out for 171 in 58.1 overs and followed on 274 runs behind. The only Indian batsman to do anything was V.V.S. Laxman who made 59 batting at No. 6. In the second innings he came in at No. 3 and then something happened which was without parallel in Indian cricket and has only happened twice before in Test history.

Laxman just kept on batting. He lost Tendulkar for 10 and Ganguly for 48, but in Dravid, who having batted at No. 3 now batted at No. 6, he found a soul mate. By the end of the third day India had made match of it at 254 for 4, Laxman 109 not out, Dravid 7 not out. Even then it did not seem as though anything could stop Australia's sixteenth-consecutive Test triumph, merely delay it.

However Laxman and Dravid batted the whole of the fourth day, by the end of which Laxman was 275 not out, having scored more runs in a Test innings than any other Indian and Dravid was 155 not out. India were 589 for 4 and could even think of a declaration.

Ganguly delayed the declaration until India had reached 657 by which time Laxman was out for 281, maintaining the record of no Indian ever having scored 300 runs in a Test innings.

India had left themselves little more than two sessions to bowl Australia out and at this stage the Indians seemed to be looking at no more than a draw. Even that would be an achievement as it would have meant stopping the Australian victory roll. By tea the match seemed destined for a draw with Australia, needing 383, on 161 for 3. However, in the first innings Harbhajan Singh had taken a hat-trick, the first Indian bowler to do so in Tests. He was now installed as the senior spinner in the absence of Kumble and had taken two of the three Australian wickets to fall by tea. But after tea he really got to work and Australia declined so dramatically that in the final session they lost seven wickets in 23 overs, with Harbhajan taking five of them to finish with 7 for 63 and India won by 171 runs.

For the first time India, having followed on, had won, matching the only two previous occasions this had been achieved in Test history, both by England against Australia.

The Indians could hardly believe what they had done and the self confidence this gave them carried them through to victory in Chennai in the third Test with Harbhajan proving virtually unplayable. He had been a bystander when Kumble had taken all ten wickets against Pakistan, his action had been questioned, with Fred Titmus helping him to get it right, and he had proved a troublesome young cricketer for Indian cricket officials to handle. But now, having taken 32 wickets in the series, he was being hailed in the class of Saqlain and like him he had a 'doosra' ball, the one that drifted the other way and caused batsmen immense problems.

The Indians were understandably euphoric about the win. Woorkeri Raman wrote about the change in the attitude of the Indians and 'the biggest gain in the last months has been the self-belief shown by some individuals which has made a tremendous impact on the team as a whole. Gone are the days when fortunes were dependent on Tendulkar alone'.

Yet a year later as this is being written it seems as though Indian cricket is back to where it has been for much of the 1990s – if Tendulkar performs then the team does. Since then India have drawn a series in Zimbabwe, where having won the first Test a few bad batting hours in the second in Harare cost them the match and led to a 1–1 series draw.

This was followed by a 2–1 defeat in Sri Lanka where Muralitharan proved a match winner while Harbhajan, whose duel with Muralitharan was much anticipated, failed. Worse was to come in South Africa where in the first Test Tendulkar yet again rescued India with help from a splendid debut Test century by Sehwag, but despite making 379 in the first innings, after being put in, India bowled so badly that they allowed South Africa to make 563 and lost the first Test by 9 wickets. They did get a draw in Port Elizabeth, but this was overshadowed by controversy and they then played dreadful cricket in the unofficial Centurion Test and lost comfortably.

As we have seen India returned home to beat England, but while the margin of victory in the only Test decided, ten wickets in Mohali, was convincing enough, England had much the better of the other two Tests. Given that this was a very inexperienced England team, by the time 2001 ended all the old doubts and questions about Indian cricket had resurfaced.

After much debate John Wright was retained as coach until the 2003 World Cup, but there was much public debate as to whether Ganguly was the right captain. Raj Singh felt his attitude was all wrong, his batting form was poor and he was the wrong man for the job. But

Gaekwad defended him saying he had a wonderful rapport with the young players.

Ganguly could argue that his record, as Indian captains go, was not a bad one. In his short span he has already won as many Tests as any other Indian captain abroad – three, although two of them were against Bangladesh and Zimbabawe. Moreover in the first year of his captaincy he had been without Kumble for much of the year. The England series, where Kumble became the first Indian spinner to reach 300 wickets, showed he was coming back to form. Also in Sri Lanka he had been without Tendulkar, for the first time since Tendulkar made his debut in 1989, and his batting might have made all the difference. And while India did lose, they showed some fight in winning the second Test in Sri Lanka when Ganguly himself batted reasonably well.

In a sense the debate about Ganguly is a familiar one. How can this country of talented cricketers be moulded into a team. However what makes this old debate very different now is that there is a growing gap between India's economic power and its performances on the field. Indian cricket is rich and Indians are becoming more demanding of their players.

Also the power of the Indian Board has never been stronger. As we have seen, Indian cricket has had many patrons over the years, starting with the princes then moving on to corporations and businesses keen to employ cricketers and have their own cricket teams.

However, fewer and fewer Indian businesses can now afford to maintain cricket teams and employ people whose only job is to play cricket. Until recently a cricketer could get a job on his playing ability alone, never do a proper day's work but merely play cricket every now and again for his office team. Now such jobs are disappearing. In contrast, the Indian Board, fed by huge amounts of television money, is now the richest Board in the world and Indian cricketers are looking to it for the sort of contracts that are common in Australia, England and South Africa. Cricketers are also seeking such contracts at state level.

We have seen how Indian cricket made the transition from the era of princely patronage to that of big business. How Indian cricket adjusts to the power of a rich Board is very difficult to say. It could prove the most difficult transition for Indian cricket to make, and if the Board does not get it right and Indian cricketers continue to under-perform, then is it possible that the Indian public may turn away from the game?

This may seem a stupid question to ask. However, it is not quite as daft as it seems. Things can change very quickly in India. Before 1983 it seemed India would always be the land for Test cricket, with no time for the one-day game. After the 1983 World Cup triumph Indians moved away from Test to one-day cricket almost overnight. So much so that even for the England tour of India in 2001 there were empty stands for all days of the three Tests. Indians are now exposed to vast amounts of international sport through television and, while they love their cricket, their love is more for individuals like Tendulkar, or Kumble in Bangalore. There is less of a team identification. What is more, Indians do not care for their domestic game, admission for domestic matches is free, and the earlier, deep-rooted nature of their love for the game appears to have disappeared.

The modern enthusiasm for cricket is more like a film buff's identification with his cine heroes and unless the Indian Board, whose officials are the new nabobs of the game, show leadership and skill, the new phase of Indian cricket may be fraught with much danger. Indians live in hope, but Indian cricket for all its riches does not provide much hope now and without the right leadership it may never fulfil the often unrealistic hopes of the Indian public.

Cricket remains the one game India is any good at and Indians are desperately keen to become a superpower in sport. However, India does not run cricket. The game is still run by the English and the Australians. What is more it is the Australian team that is dominant on the field of play. Indians are not even a close second and this produces tensions and breeds resentments in India which could lead to more problems as time goes on. Unless Indian cricket achievements on the field of play can match their economic muscle off it, there may well be deep disillusionment with both cricket and cricketers and Indians may be lured to taking up some other sport.

Forty years ago, when India ruled the hockey world – it did not lose a match in the Olympics between 1928 and 1960 – hockey was almost on a par with cricket in prestige and power. But then India lost its great winning run, it was poorly served by wretched administrators who allowed Europeans to impose artificial pitches which robbed the Indians of the power their magical dribbling and stickwork had given them, while benefiting the more muscular power play of the Europeans. Periodically since then, Indians have threatened to produce a world-class team but the international game is dominated by the Europeans and the Australians and hockey is now very much a second-class sport in India.

I hope such a fate does not befall Indian cricket but it would be foolish to ignore the danger signals. When, after independence, Indian cricket developed and became the dominant sport in the country, outclassing all others, the rapid industrialization of the country – helped by the prejudices of the country's elite – helped cricket's rise. It is interesting to note that cricket's rise in the 1960s and 70s came just as Indian hockey was suffering its great fall. Indians desperately wanted a world sport to excel in and cricket was ideal.

However cricket, and even more hockey, are fairly limited in their international appeal and in the last decade, through television, India is being exposed to the sport than can truly claim to be the most popular in the world: football. As we have seen there has always been a tremendous grass roots enthusiasm for football and, today, domestic football matches attract crowds more numerous than domestic cricket matches.

The problem has been the failure of Indian football administrators, a byword for incompetence, to harness this enthusiasm and translate it into a national team Indians could be proud of. The appetite for world-class football is immense. Millions of Indians, through television, can watch, almost nightly, the deeds of David Beckham, Michael Owen and many other international stars. Indeed one of the most prominent ads during the last England Test series in India was one about football. Promoting the brand name of Nike it showed Beckham being sent off, borrowing a coke from a fan who turns out to be a Juventus fan. Indian cricket administrators confess that their children are keener on Beckham and Owen than they are on Steve Waugh or Shane Warne. If Indian football could get its act together – and it is a big if – then it could become a major force.

What all this suggests is Indian cricket has entered its most critical phase. When it was growing up in the years after independence it could plead poverty. Now it has money to finance its dreams, but unless its administrators can provide the far-sighted leadership the game desperately needs, the danger is there may be a growing gap between boardroom riches and on-field poverty leading to a growing public disillusionment from which Indian cricket may find it difficult to recover.

It survived the match-fixing scandal but already there are signs the Indian media is getting impatient with its cricketers. After the Indians, through cautious batting, drew the second Ahmedabad Test against England, many Indian newspapers chose to lead on a hockey success abroad rather than the Test, as if to say we will not put up with cricketing under-performance. As this history has shown, Indians are not the slow, patient people they are made out to be, who will put up with anything, nor is it a country that never changes. Indians are a people given to hujuks, sudden enthusiasms, they are volatile, they want success and want it now and things can change very quickly in the country.

If Indian cricket does not heed the dangers it may find that, like hockey, it no longer shapes events but is shaped by events beyond its control.

Appendixes

Appendix A

THE RANJI TROPHY 1934 TO 2000–01

Founded as 'The Cricket Championship of India' at a meeting of the Board of Control for Cricket in India in July 1934. The first Ranji Trophy fixtures took place in the 1934–35 season. The Trophy was donated by H.H. Sir Bhupendra Singh Mahinder Bahadur, Maharajah of Patiala in memory of His late Highness Sir Ranjitsinhji Vibhaji of Nawanagar. See map, page xviii.

In the main the Ranji Trophy is composed of teams representing the states that make up India. As the political states have multiplied, so have cricket teams, but not every state has a team. However, as if to compensate, some states have more than one cricket team, e.g. Maharashtra and Gujerat. There are also 'odd' teams like Railways, and Services representing the armed forces.

The various teams are grouped into *zones* – North, West, East, Central and South – and the initial matches are played on a league basis within the zones. The format has changed frequently in thelast decade. From 2002–03 season, the Ranji Trophy will adopt the two division format of the English county championship. The historic zonal basis will be abandoned and the whole country divided into two divisions with promotion and relegation between the divisions. The changes reflect the need to make this competition more relevant to the needs of Indian cricket and the ease of travel which enables teams from the various parts of the country to travel long distances to play cricket matches.

Andhra	Formed 1953, originally northern part of Madras Presidency. *South Zone.*
Army	See Services. *North Zone.*
Assam	See Bengal. *East Zone.*
Baroda	Part of Gujerat until 1937. Joined 1937–38, *West Zone.*
Bengal	Formed as Cricket Association of Bengal and Assam in 1928. Assam seceded 1938. East Bengal partitioned off as East Pakistan, 1947. Bangladesh independence declared, 1971. West Bengal played as Bengal after Partition in *East Zone.*

479

Bihar	Formed 1935. Played since 1936–37, *East Zone*.
Central India	Formed 1932. Played in *East Zone* until 1939–40. In 1941 jurisdiction taken over by Holkar.
Central Provinces and Berar	Formed Nagpur 1934. Played intermittently until 1949–50 when taken over by Madhya Pradesh.
Delhi	Founded 1932 as Delhi & District Cricket Association. Joined 1934–35, *North Zone*.
Goa	Liberated from Portuguese rule in 1960 it only emerged as a Ranji team in the 1990s, playing in the *West Zone*, and its ground has staged many one day internationals.
Gujerat	Formed 1934 (see Bombay). Joined 1934–35, *West Zone*.
Gwalior	Now part of Madhya Pradesh.
Haryana	Formed from part of South Punjab, 1970–71, *North Zone*.
Himachal Pradesh	A new state whose capital is Shimla, the summer capital of the Raj and which plays in the *North Zone*.
Holkar	See Central India. Played 1941–42 to 1951–52 in *East Zone*. Transferred to Central Zone 1952–53. Changed title 1955–56 to Madhya Bharat. Now part of Vidarbha, *Central Zone*.
Hyderabad	Formed *c*. 1930. Joined 1934–35, *South Zone*. Like Bombay, the team represents the city; but the city is the political capital of the state of Andhra Pradesh which has its own team. See Andhra.
Jammu & Kashmir	Joined 1959–60, *North Zone*.
Karnataka	Formerly Mysore. Changed name 1973–74. *South Zone*.
Kerala	Formerly Travancore-Cochin, until 1957–58. Joined 1951–52, *South Zone*.
Madras	Madras Cricket Association formed 1933. Played in *South Zone* until 1969–70. Name changed 1970 to Tamil Nadu. See Tamil Nadu and Andhra.
Madhya Bharat	Played as Holkar until 1954–55, and as Madhya Bharat in 1955–56 and 1956–57. Now part of Vidarbha, *Central Zone*.
Madhya Pradesh	Originally part of Central India Cricket Association. Formed separate association and joined *South Zone* 1950. Since 1952–53, *Central Zone*.
Maharashtra	Formed out of Bombay Presidency, 1934. Joined 1934–35, *West Zone*.

Mumbai	Bombay until 1996. Bombay Presidency Cricket Association formed 1930. Joined Ranji Trophy, 1934–35. Gujerat and Maharashtra seceded that year. Is now Mumbai Cricket Association, comprising only the city of Mumbai. *West Zone.*
Mysore	Formed 1930. Changed name to Karnataka, 1973–74.
Northern India	Joined 1934–35. Now in Pakistan.
Nawanagar	Played in *West Zone* from 1936–37 to 1947–48. Now part of Saurashtra.
North-West Frontier Province	Played in *North Zone* between 1937–38 and 1946–47. Now part of Pakistan.
Orissa	Originally southern part of Bihar. Formed Cricket Association and joined 1949, *East Zone.*
Patiala	Went through various transformations, once appearing under its name before changing to Southern Punjab in 1959–60. See Punjab.
Punjab	Historically the Punjab was divided by Partition, the East remaining in India. Punjab Cricket Association formed 1968–69 from Northern and Southern Punjab; part of the South seceded in 1970–71 to become Haryana following the formation of the political state. *North Zone.*
Railways	Based in Delhi. Joined the competition and *North Zone* 1958–59 but transferred in 1975–76 to *Central Zone.*
Rajasthan	Formerly Rajputana, formed 1931. Has played as Rajasthan since 1956–57 and since 1952–53 in *Central Zone.*
Saurashtra	Originally part of Western India States, and played previously as Kathiawar. Formed 1950 and joined 1951–52, *West Zone.*
Services	Formed as Army Sports Control Board 1919. Appeared in first Ranji Trophy season, and reappeared in 1949–50 as the Services Sports Control Board (India). Based in Delhi. *North Zone.*
Sind	Played in *West Zone* 1934–35 until 1947–48. Now part of Pakistan.
Tamil Nadu	Formerly Madras. Joined 1970–71, *South Zone.*
Travancore-Cochin	See Kerala.
Tripura	A new state on the eastern borders of India, it plays in the *East Zone.*
United Provinces	Formed 1934. Moved to *East Zone* 1938–39. Changed

481

name to Uttar Pradesh 1950–51. Since 1952–53 *Central Zone.*

Uttar Pradesh	Formerly United Provinces, changed to Uttar Pradesh 1950–51. Since 1952–53 *Central Zone.*
Vidarbha	Originally Holkar, 1941–42 until 1951–52, then Madhya Bharat until 1956–57. *Central Zone.*
Western India States	Founded 1934, consisting of four Prant clubs: Halar, Sorath, Jhalawat and Gohelwad. Played in *West Zone* until 1945–46 when its jurisdiction was taken over by Kathiawar. See Saurashtra.

RANJI TROPHY WINNERS

1934–35	Bombay	1974–75	Bombay
1935–36	Bombay	1975–76	Bombay
1936–37	Nawanagar	1976–77	Bombay
1937–38	Hyderabad	1977–78	Karnataka
1938–39	Bengal	1978–79	Delhi
1939–40	Maharashtra	1979–80	Delhi
1940–41	Maharashtra	1980–81	Bombay
1941–42	Bombay	1981–82	Delhi
1942–43	Baroda	1982–83	Karnataka
1943–44	Western India	1983–84	Bombay
1944–45	Bombay	1984–85	Bombay
1945–46	Holkar	1985–86	Delhi
1946–47	Baroda	1986–87	Hyderabad
1947–48	Holkar	1987–88	Tamil Nadu
1948–49	Bombay	1988–89	Delhi
1949–50	Baroda	1989–90	Bengal (on run quotient)
1950–51	Holkar	1990–91	Haryana
1951–52	Bombay	1991–92	Delhi
1952–53	Holkar	1992–93	Punjab
1953–54	Bombay	1993–94	Bombay
1954–55	Madras	1994–95	Bombay
1955–56	Bombay	1995–96	Karnataka
1956–57	Bombay	1996–97	Mumbai
1957–58	Baroda	1997–98	Karnataka
1958–59	Bombay	1998–99	Karnataka
to	(15 years)	1999–00	Mumbai
1972–73		2000–01	Baroda
1973–74	Karnataka		

THE DULEEP TROPHY, 1961 TO 1989–90

The Duleep Trophy competition was started by the Board of Control for Cricket in India in 1961–62 with the aim of providing a greater competitive edge in domestic cricket – because, apart from the knock-out stages of the Ranji Trophy, that competition proved predictable, with Bombay winning for fifteen consecutive years. The Duleep was also meant to help the selectors in assessing form.

Five teams, drawn from the five zones, play each other on a knock-out basis. Since 1961–62 the winners have been:

Season	Winners	Season	Winners
1961–62	West Zone	1982–83	North Zone
1962–63	West Zone	1983–84	North Zone
1963–64	West Zone/	1984–85	South Zone
	South Zone (joint)	1985–86	West Zone
1964–65	West Zone	1986–87	South Zone
1965–66	South Zone	1987–88	North Zone
1966–67	South Zone	1988–89	North Zone/
1967–68	South Zone		West Zone (joint)
1968–69	West Zone	1989–90	South Zone
1969–70	West Zone	1990–91	North Zone
1970–71	South Zone	1991–92	North Zone
1971–72	Central Zone	1992–93	North Zone
1972–73	West Zone	1993–94	North Zone
1973–74	North Zone	1994–95	North Zone
1974–75	South Zone	1995–96	South Zone
1975–76	South Zone	1996–97	Central Zone
1976–77	West Zone	1997–98	Central Zone/
1977–78	West Zone		West Zone (joint)
1978–79	North Zone	1998–99	Central Zone
1979–80	North Zone	1999–00	North Zone
1980–81	West Zone	2000–01	North Zone
1981–82	West Zone		

Appendix B

INDIA'S TEST MATCH RESULTS AGAINST OTHER COUNTRIES

INDIA v ENGLAND

CAPTAINS

SEASON	INDIA	ENGLAND	T	I	E	D
1932	CK Nayudu	DR Jardine	1	0	1	0
*1933–34	CK Nayudu	DR Jardine	3	0	2	1
1936	Maharaj of Vizianagram	GO Allen	3	0	2	1
1946	Nawab of Pataudi, sr	WR Hammond	3	0	1	2
*1951–52	VS Hazare	ND Howard (1)	5	1	1	3
1952	VS Hazare	L Hutton	4	0	3	1
1959	DK Gaekwad (2)	PBH May (3)	5	0	5	0
*1961–62	NJ Contractor	ER Dexter	5	2	0	3
*1963–64	Nawab of Pataudi, jr	MJK Smith	5	0	0	5
1967	Nawab of Pataudi, jr	DB Close	3	0	3	0
1971	AL Wadekar	R Illingworth	3	1	0	2
*1972–73	AL Wadekar	AR Lewis	5	2	1	2
1974	AL Wadekar	MH Denness	3	0	3	0
1976–77	BS Bedi	AW Greig	5	1	3	1
1979	S Venkatarghavan	JM Brearley	4	0	1	3
*1979–80	GR Viswanath	JM Brearley	1	0	1	0
*1981–82	SM Gavaskar	KWR Fletcher	6	1	0	5
1982	SM Gavaskar	RGD Willis	3	0	1	2
*1984–85	SM Gavaskar	DI Gower	5	1	2	2
1986	Kapil Dev	MW Gatting (4)	3	2	0	1
1990	M Azharuddin	GA Gooch	3	0	1	2
*1992–93	M Azharuddin	GA Gooch (5)	3	3	0	0
1996	M Azharuddin	MA Atherton	3	0	1	2
*2001–02	SC Ganguly	N Hussein	3	1	0	2
	In India		46	12	10	24
	In England		41	3	22	16
	TOTALS		87	15	32	40

* Played in India
Notes: The following deputised in one or more Test Match:
(1) DB Carr (Fifth). (2) Pankaj Roy (Second). (3) MC Cowdrey (Fourth and Fifth).
(4) DI Gower (First). (5) AJ Stewart (Second).

INDIA v SOUTH AFRICA

CAPTAINS

SEASON	INDIA	SOUTH AFRICA	T	I	SA	D
1992–93	M Azharuddin	KC Wessels	4	0	1	3
*1996–97	SR Tendulkar	WJ Cronje	3	2	1	0
1996–97	SR Tendulkar	WJ Cronje	3	0	2	1
*1999–00	SR Tendulkar	WJ Cronje	2	0	2	0
2001–02	SC Ganguly	SM Pollock	2	0	1	1
	In India		5	2	3	0
	In South Africa		9	0	4	5
	TOTALS		14	2	7	5

* Played in India

INDIA v AUSTRALIA

CAPTAINS

SEASON	INDIA	AUSTRALIA	T	I	A	D	TIE
1947–48	L Amarnath	DG Bradman	5	0	4	1	0
*1956–57	PR Umrigar	IW Johnson (1)	3	0	2	1	0
*1959–60	GS Ramchand	R Benaud	5	1	2	2	0
*1964–65	Nawab of Pataudi, jr	RB Simpson	3	1	1	1	0
1967–68	Nawab of Pataudi, jr (2)	RB Simpson (3)	4	0	4	0	0
*1969–70	Nawab of Pataudi, jr	WM Lawry	5	1	3	1	0
1977–78	BS Bedi	RB Simpson	5	2	3	0	0
*1979–80	SM Gavaskar	KJ Hughes	6	2	0	4	0
1980–81	SM Gavaskar	GS Chappell	3	1	1	1	0
1985–86	Kapil Dev	AR Border	3	0	0	3	0
*1986–87	Kapil Dev	AR Border	3	0	0	2	1
1991–92	M Azharuddin	AR Border	5	0	4	1	0
*1996–97	SR Tendulkar	MA Taylor	1	1	0	0	0
*1997–98	M Azharuddin	MA Taylor	3	2	1	0	0
1999–00	SR Tendulkar	SR Waugh	3	0	3	0	0
*2000–01	SC Ganguly	SR Waugh	3	2	1	0	0
	In India		32	10	10	11	1
	In Australia		28	3	19	6	0
	Totals		60	13	29	17	1

* Played in India
Notes: The following deputied in one or more Test Match:
(1) RR Lindwall (Second). (2) CG Borde (First). (3) WM Lawry (Third and Fourth).

INDIA v WEST INDIES

CAPTAINS

SEASON	INDIA	WEST INDIES	T	I	WI	D
*1948–49	L Amarnath	JDC Goddard	5	0	1	4
1952–53	VS Hazare	JB Stollmeyer	5	0	1	4
*1958–59	Ghulam Ahmed (1)	FCM Alexander	5	0	3	2
1961–62	NJ Contractor (2)	FMM Worrell	5	0	5	0
*1966–67	Nawab of Pataudi, jr	GStA Sobers	3	0	2	1
1970–71	AL Wadekar	GStA Sobers	5	1	0	4
*1974–75	Nawab of Pataudi, jr (3)	CH Lloyd	5	2	3	0
1975–76	BS Bedi	CH Lloyd	4	1	2	1
*1978–79	SM Gavaskar	AI Kallicharran	6	1	0	5
1982–83	Kapil Dev	CH Lloyd	5	0	2	3
*1983–84	Kapil Dev	CH Lloyd	6	0	3	3
*1987–88	DB Vengsarkar (4)	IVA Richards	4	1	1	2
1988–89	DB Vengsarkar	IVA Richards	4	0	3	1
*1994–95	M Azharuddin	CA Walsh	3	1	1	1
1996–97	SR Tendulkar	CA Walsh (5)	5	0	1	4
	In India		37	5	14	18
	In West Indies		33	2	14	17
	TOTALS		70	7	28	35

* Played in India
Notes: The following deputies in one or more Test Match:
(1) PR Umrigar (First), V Mankad (Fourth), HR Adhikari (Fifth). (2) Nawab of Pataudi, jr
(Third, Fourth and Fifth). (3) S Venkataraghavan (Second). (4) RJ Shastri (Fourth).
(5) BC Lara (Third).

NEW ZEALAND v INDIA

CAPTAINS

SEASON	INDIA	NEW ZEALAND	T	I	NZ	D
*1955–56	PR Umrigar (1)	HB Cave	5	2	0	3
*1964–65	Nawab of Pataudi, jr	JR Reid	4	1	0	3
1967–68	Nawab of Pataudi, jr	GT Dowling (2)	4	3	1	0
*1969–70	Nawab of Pataudi, jr	GT Dowling	3	1	1	1
1975–76	BS Bedi (3)	GM Turner	3	1	1	1
*1976–77	BS Bedi	GM Turner	3	2	0	1
1980–81	SM Gavaskar	GP Howarth	3	0	1	2
*1988–89	DB Vengsarkar	JG Wright	3	2	1	0
1989–90	M Azharuddin	JG Wright	3	0	1	2
1993–94	M Azharuddin	KR Rutherford	1	0	0	1
*1995–96	M Azharuddin	LK Germon	3	1	0	2
1998–99	M Azharuddin	SP Fleming	2	0	1	1
*1999–00	SR Tendulkar	SP Fleming	3	1	0	2
	In India		24	10	2	12
	In New Zealand		16	4	5	7
	Totals		40	14	7	19

* Played in India
Notes: The following deputed in one Test Match:
(1) Ghulam Ahmed (First). (2) BW Sinclair (First). (3) SM Gavaskar (First).

INDIA v PAKISTAN

CAPTAINS

SEASON	INDIA	PAKISTAN	T	I	P	D
*1952–53	L. Amarnath	A.H. Kardar	5	2	1	2
1954–55	V. Mankad	A.H. Kardar	5	0	0	5
*1960–61	N.J. Contractor	Fazal Mahmood	5	0	0	5
1978–79	B.S. Bedi	Mushtaq Mohammad	3	0	2	1
*1979–80	S.M. Gavaskar(1)	Asif Iqbal	6	2	0	4
1982–83	S.M. Gavaskar	Imran Khan	6	0	3	3
*1983–84	Kapil Dev	Zaheer Abbas	3	0	0	3
1984–85	S.M. Gavaskar	Zaheer Abbas	2	0	0	2
*1986–87	Kapil Dev	Imran Khan	5	0	1	4
1989–90	K. Srikkanth	Imran Khan	4	0	0	4
*1998–99	M Azharuddin	Wasim Akram	2	1	1	0
*1998–99#	M Azharuddin	Wasim Akram	1	0	1	0

In India	.27	5	4	18	
In Pakistan	.20	0	5	15	
Totals	.47	5	9	33	

* Played in India.
\# Part of Asian Test Championship
Note: The following captained in one Test Match:
(1) G.R. Viswanath (Sixth).

INDIA v SRI LANKA

CAPTAINS

SEASON	INDIA	SRI LANKA	T	I	SL	D
*1982–83	SM Gavaskar	B Warnapura	1	0	0	1
1985–86	Kapil Dev	LRD Mendis	3	0	1	2
*1986–87	Kapil Dev	LRD Mendis	3	2	0	1
*1990–91	M Azharuddin	A Ranatunga	1	1	0	0
1993–94	M Azharuddin	A Ranatunga	3	1	0	2
*1993–94	M Azharuddin	A Ranatunga	3	3	0	0
1997–98	SR Tendulkar	A Ranatunga	2	0	0	2
*1997–98	SR Tendulkar	A Ranatunga	3	0	0	3
1998–99#	M Azharuddin	A Ranatunga	1	0	0	1
2001	SC Ganguly	ST Jayasuriya	3	1	2	0

In India	.11	6	0	5	
In Sri Lanka	.12	2	3	7	
Totals	.23	8	3	12	

* Played in India
\# Part of Asian Test Championship

INDIA v ZIMBABWE

CAPTAINS

SEASON	INDIA	ZIMBABWE	T	I	Z	D
1992–93	M Azharuddin	DL Houghton	1	0	0	1
*1992–93	M Azhaaruddin	DL Houghton	1	1	0	0
1998–99	M Azharuddin	ADR Campbell	1	0	1	0
*2000–01	SC Ganguly	HH Streak	2	1	0	1
2001	SC Ganguly	HH Streak	2	1	1	0

In India	3	2	0	1	
In Zimbabwe	4	1	2	1	
Totals	7	3	2	2	

* Played in India

INDIA v BANGLADESH

CAPTAINS

SEASON	INDIA	BANGLADESH	T	I	B	D
2000–01	SC Ganguly	Naimur Rahman	1	1	0	0

In India	0				
In Banglasdesh	4	1	2	1	
Totals	7	3	2	2	

\# Part of Asian Test Championship

TOTALS Out of 349 Test matches played since June 1932 and until 31 December 2001 India has won 68 matches, her opponents 117, there has been 1 tie and 163 drawn games.

INDIA'S COMPOSITE INTERNATIONAL RESULTS BY OPPONENT

TEST MATCHES 1932–2001

OPPONENT	IN INDIA					OVERSEAS					TOTALS				
	M	W	L	D	T	M	W	L	D	T	M	W	L	D	T
England	46	12	10	24	–	41	3	22	16	–	87	15	32	40	–
Australia	32	10	10	11	1	28	3	19	6	–	60	13	29	17	1
West Indies	37	5	14	18	–	33	2	14	17	–	70	7	28	35	–
Pakistan	27	5	4	18	–	20	–	5	15	–	47	5	9	33	–
New Zealand	24	10	2	12	–	16	4	5	7	–	40	14	7	19	–
Sri Lanka	11	6	–	5	–	12	2	3	7	–	23	8	3	12	–
Zimbabwe	3	2	–	1	–	4	1	2	1	–	7	3	2	2	–
South Africa	5	2	3	–	–	9	–	4	5	–	14	2	7	5	–
Bangladesh				–		1	1	–	–	–	1	1	–	–	–
TOTALS	185	52	43	89	1	164	16	74	74	–	349	68	117	163	1

LIMITED-OVER INTERNATIONAL MATCHES 1974–2001

OPPONENT	IN INDIA					OVERSEAS					TOTALS				
	M	W	L	T	AB	M	W	L	T	AB	M	W	L	T	AB
England	16	7	9	–	–	20	9	10	–	1	36	16	19	–	1
East Africa	–					1	1	–	–	–	1	1	–	–	–
New Zealand	19	15	4	–	–	42	16	23	–	3	61	31	27	–	3
Pakistan	14	4	10	–	–	71	25	42	–	4	85	29	52	–	4
West Indies	26	9	17	–	–	40	14	24	1	1	66	23	41	1	1
Sri Lanka	26	17	8	–	1	44	19	21	–	4	70	36	29	–	5
Australia	25	11	11	–	3	42	14	28	–	–	67	25	39	–	3
Zimbabwe	14	12	1	1	–	22	16	5	1	–	36	28	6	2	–
Bangladesh	3	3	–	–	–	5	5	–	–	–	8	8	–	–	–
South Africa	15	9	6	–	–	27	5	21	–	1	42	14	27	–	1
UAE	–					1	1	–	–	–	1	1	–	–	–
Kenya	4	3	1	–	–	6	5	1	–	–	10	8	2	–	–
TOTALS	162	90	67	1	4	321	130	175	2	14	483	220	242	3	18

487

Appendix C

SELECTED TEST MATCH SCORECARDS 1952–2001

The hardback edition featured all the scorecards between 1932 and 1989. However, the growth of cricket in the last decade has made it impossible to carry all Test Match scorecards and the author has made a selection of the 12 most significant ones, plus one Limited-Over International.

1. Fifth Test, India v England, Chepauk, Madras, February 1952

2. Fifth Test, India v New Zealand, Corporation, Madras, January 1956

3. Fourth Test, New Zealand v India, Eden Park, Auckland, March 1968

4. Third Test. England v India, Kennington Oval, August 1971

5. Third Test, West Indies v India, Port-of-Spain, Trinidad, April 1976

6. Fourth Test, England v India, Kennington Oval, Aug–Sept 1979

7. Second Test, England v India, Headingley, June 1986

8. First Test, India v Australia, Chepauk, Madras, September 1986

9. Third Test, India v England, Wankhede, Mumbai, February 1993

10. First Test, India v Australia, Chepauk, Madras, March 1998

11. Second Test, India v Pakistan, Feroz Shah Kotla, Delhi, February 1999

12. Second Test, India v Australia, Eden Gardens, Calcutta, March 2001

13. Prudential World Cup Final, India v West Indies, Lords, 25 June 1983

FIFTH TEST: INDIA v ENGLAND
6, 8, 9 and 10 February 1952 at Chepauk, Madras

ENGLAND

	First innings		Second innings	
FA Lowson	b Phadkar	1	c Mankad b Phadkar	7
RT Spooner+	c Phadkar b Hazare	66	lbw b Divecha	6
TW Graveney	st Sen b Mankad	39	c Divecha b Ghulam Ahmed	25
JDB Robertson	c & b Mankad	77	lbw b Ghulam Ahmed	56
AJ Watkins	c Gopinath b Mankad	9	c & b Mankad	48
CJ Poole	b Mankad	15	c Divecha b Ghulam Ahmed	3
DB Carr*	st Sen b Mankad	40	c Mankad b Ghulam Ahmed	5
MJ Hilton	st Sen b Mankad	0	st Sen b Mankad	15
JB Statham	st Sen b Mankad	6	c Gopinath b Mankad	9
F Ridgway	lbw b Mankad	2	b Mankad	0
R Tattersall	not out	2	not out	0
	b4, lb4, nb3	11	b7, lb2	9
		266		**183**

	First innings				Second innings			
	O	M	R	W	O	M	R	W
Phadkar	16	2	49	1	9	2	17	1
Divecha	12	2	27	0	7	1	21	1
Amarnath	27	6	56	0	3	0	6	0
Ghulam Ahmed	18	5	53	0	26	6	77	4
Mankad	38.5	15	55	8	30.5	9	53	4
Hazare	10	5	15	1				

Fall of Wickets
1-3, 2-71, 3-131, 4-174, 5-197, 6-244, 7-252, 8-261, 9-261, 10-266
1-12, 2-15, 3-68, 4-117, 5-135, 6-159, 7-159, 8-178, 9-178, 10-183

INDIA

	First innings	
Mushtaq Ali	st Spooner b Carr	22
Pankaj Roy	c Watkins b Tattersall	111
VS Hazare*	b Hilton	20
MH Mankad	c Watkins b Carr	22
L Amarnath	c Spooner b Statham	31
DG Phadkar	b Hilton	61
PR Umrigar	not out	130
CD Gopinath	b Tattersall	35
RV Divecha	c Spooner b Ridgway	12
P Sen+	b Watkins	2
Ghulam Ahmed	not out	1
	b8, lb2	10
	(9 wickets dec.)	**457**

	O	M	R	W
Statham	19	3	54	1
Ridgway	17	2	47	1
Tattersall	39	13	94	2
Hilton	40	9	100	2
Carr	19	2	84	2
Watkins	14	2	50	1
Robertson	5	1	18	0

Fall of Wickets
1-53, 2-97, 3-157, 4-191, 5-216, 6-320, 7-413, 8-430, 9-448

Umpires: BJ Mohoni & MG Vijayasarathi
Test Debuts: nil

Toss: England

India won by an innings and 8 runs

FIFTH TEST: INDIA v NEW ZEALAND
6, 7, 8, 10 and 11 January 1956 at Corporation Stadium, Madras

INDIA

	First innings	
MH Mankad	c Cave b Moir	231
Pankaj Roy*	b Poore	173
PR Umrigar	not out	79
GS Ramchand	lbw b MacGibbon	21
VL Manjrekar	not out	0
AG Kripal Singh		
NJ Contractor		
DG Phadkar		
NS Tamhane+		
JM Patel		
SP Gupte		
	b18, lb11, nb4	33
	(3 wickets dec.)	**537**

	First innings			
	O	M	R	W
Hayes	31	2	94	0
MacGibbon	38	9	97	1
Cave	44	16	94	0
Reid	7	3	10	0
Moir	26	1	114	1
Poore	31	5	95	1

Fall of Wickets
1-413, 2-449, 3-537

NEW ZEALAND

	First innings		Second innings	
JG Leggat	lbw b Phadkar	31	c Tamhane b Mankad	61
B Sutcliffe	c Umrigar b Patel	47	c & b Gupte	40
JR Reid	b Patel	44	c Umrigar b Gupte	63
JW Guy	c Umrigar b Gupte	3	st Tamhane b Gupte	9
SN McGregor	c Phadkar b Gupte	10	c Gupte b Mankad	12
AR MacGibbon	c Phadkar b Gupte	10	lbw b Patel	0
MB Poore	lbw b Gupte	15	b Mankad	1
AM Moir	c Umrigar b Patel	30	c Ramchand b Mankad	22
HB Cave*	c Roy b Gupte	9	not out	0
TG McMahon+	not out	4	b Gupte	
JA Hayes	absent ill		absent ill	
	b4, lb10, nb2	16	b1, lb8, nb1	10
		209		**219**

	First innings				Second innings			
	O	M	R	W	O	M	R	W
Phadkar	15	4	25	1	28	13	33	0
Ramchand	4	3	1	0	8	5	10	0
Gupte	49	26	72	5	36.3	14	73	4
Patel	45	23	63	3	18	7	28	1
Mankad	19	10	32	0	40	14	65	4

Fall of Wickets
1-75, 2-109, 3-121, 4-141, 5-144, 6-145, 7-190, 8-201, 9-209
1-89, 2-114, 3-116, 4-117, 5-147, 6-148, 7-151, 8-219, 9-219

Umpires: AR Joshi & MG Vijayasarathi   Toss: India
Test Debuts: nil

India won by an innings and 109 runs

FOURTH TEST: NEW ZEALAND v INDIA

7, 8, 9, 11 and 12 March 1968 at Eden Park, Auckland

INDIA

Batsman	First innings		Second innings	
FM Engineer+	c Bartlett b Motz	44	c & b Alabaster	48
S Abid Ali	c Dowling b Motz	1	c Murray b Taylor	22
AL Wadekar	c Ward b Bartlett	5	b Taylor	1
RF Surti	c Pollard b Bartlett	28	c Burgess b Bartlett	99
Nawab of Pataudi, jr*	c Pollard b Motz	51	lbw b Pollard	6
CG Borde	c Alabaster b Pollard	41	not out	65
ML Jaisimha	c Pollard b Alabaster	19	not out	1
V Subramanya	run out	3		
RG Nadkarni	c Burgess b Bartlett	21		
EAS Prasanna	not out	0		
BS Bedi	c Murray b Motz	36		
Extras	b9, lb3, w2, nb22		b6, lb4, nb9	19
Total		252	(5 wickets dec.)	261

	First innings				Second innings			
	O	M	R	W	O	M	R	W
Motz	26.4	12	51	4	16	4	44	0
Bartlett	26	11	66	3	15	1	40	1
Taylor	17	4	49	0	22	4	60	2
Pollard	8	4	9	1	21	8	42	1
Alabaster	13	0	41	1	22	4	56	1

Fall of Wickets

1-6, 2-13, 3-69, 4-132, 5-175, 6-215, 7-226, 8-244, 9-251, 10-252

1-43, 2-48, 3-112, 4-127, 5-253

NEW ZEALAND

Batsman	First innings		Second innings	
GT Dowling*	c Engineer b Surti	8	b Bedi	37
BAG Murray	c Engineer b Surti	17	c Jaisimha b Surti	3
BE Congdon	c Abid Ali b Nadkarni	27	c Surti b Nadkarni	3
MG Burgess	c Subramanya b Prasanna	11	c Bedi b Surti	18
BW Sinclair	b Bedi	20	b Prasanna	12
V Pollard	run out	3	b Bedi	0
GA Bartlett	c Wadekar b Prasanna	0	(8) b Prasanna	11
BR Taylor	c Abid Ali b Bedi	7	(9) b Prasanna	0
RC Motz	c & b Prasanna	18	(10) c Engineer b Bedi	6
JT Ward+	not out	10	(7) b Prasanna	5
JC Alabaster	c Bedi b Prasanna	13	not out	6
Extras	b4, nb9		b3, lb2, nb1	
Total		140		101

	First innings				Second innings			
	O	M	R	W	O	M	R	W
Surti	10	2	32	2	11	2	30	2
Jaisimha	7	3	14	0	3	1	5	0
Nadkarni	14	6	16	1	2	1	5	1
Prasanna	28.1	11	44	4	27	15	40	4
Bedi	17	8	21	2	17.4	11	14	3
Subramanya	1	1	0	0	1	0	5	0

Fall of Wickets

1-30, 2-33, 3-67, 4-74, 5-77, 6-88, 7-103, 8-106, 9-124, 10-140

1-10, 2-15, 3-55, 4-74, 5-78, 6-78, 7-94, 8-95, 9-101, 10-101

Umpires: DEA Copps & WT Martin
Test Debuts: nil

Toss: New Zealand

India won by 272 runs

THIRD TEST: ENGLAND v INDIA
19, 20 (no play), 21, 23 and 24 August 1971 at Kennington Oval

ENGLAND

	First innings		Second innings	
BW Luckhurst	c Gavaskar b Solkar	1	c Venkataraghavan b Chandrasekhar	33
JA Jameson	run out	82	run out	16
JH Edrich	c Engineer b Bedi	41	b Chandrasekhar	0
KWR Fletcher	c Gavaskar b Bedi	2	c Solkar b Chandrasekhar	0
BL D'Oliveira	c Mankad b Chandrasekhar	90	c sub (K Jayantilal) b Venkataraghavan	17
APE Knott+	c & b Solkar	11	c Solkar b Venkataraghavan	1
R Illingworth*	b Chandrasekhar	11	c & b Chandrasekhar	4
RA Hutton	b Venkataraghavan	81	not out	13
JA Snow	c Engineer b Solkar	3	c & b Chandrasekhar	0
DL Underwood	c Wadekar b Venkataraghavan	22	c Mankad b Bedi	11
JSE Price	not out	1	lbw b Chandrasekhar	3
	b4, lb15, w1	20	lb3	3
		355		**101**

	First innings				Second innings			
	O	M	R	W	O	M	R	W
Abid Ali	15	2	47	0	3	1	5	0
Solkar	15	4	28	3	3	1	10	0
Gavaskar	1	0	1	0				
Bedi	36	5	120	2	1	0	1	1
Chandrasekhar	24	6	76	2	18.1	3	38	6
Venkataraghavan	20.4	3	63	2	20	4	44	2

Fall of Wickets:
1-5, 2-111, 3-135, 4-139, 5-143, 6-175, 7-278, 8-284, 9-352, 10-355
1-23, 2-24, 3-24, 4-49, 5-54, 6-65, 7-72, 8-72, 9-96, 10-101

INDIA

	First innings		Second innings	
SM Gavaskar	b Snow	6	lbw b Snow	0
AV Mankad	b Price	10	c Hutton b Underwood	11
AL Wadekar*	c Hutton b Illingworth	48	run out	45
DN Sardesai	b Illingworth	54	c Knott b Underwood	40
GR Viswanath	b Illingworth	0	c Knott b Luckhurst	33
ED Solkar	c Fletcher b D'Oliveira	44	c & b Underwood	1
FM Engineer+	c Illingworth b Snow	59	not out	28
S Abid Ali	b Illingworth	26	not out	4
S Venkataraghavan	lbw b Underwood	24		
BS Bedi	c D'Oliveira b Illingworth	0		
BS Chandrasekhar	not out	0		
	b6, lb4, nb1	11	b6, lb5, nb1	12
		284	(6 wickets)	**174**

	First innings				Second innings			
	O	M	R	W	O	M	R	W
Snow	24	5	68	2	11	7	14	1
Price	15	2	51	1	5	0	10	0
Hutton	12	2	30	0				
D'Oliveira	7	5	5	1	9	3	17	0
Illingworth	34.3	12	70	5	36	15	40	0
Underwood	25	6	49	1	38	14	72	3
Luckhurst					2	0	9	1

Fall of Wickets:
1-17, 2-21, 3-114, 4-118, 5-125, 6-222, 7-230, 8-278, 9-284, 10-284
1-2, 2-37, 3-76, 4-124, 5-134, 6-170

Umpires: CS Elliott & AEG Rhodes
Test Debuts: nil

Toss: England

India won by four wickets

THIRD TEST: WEST INDIES v INDIA

7, 8, 10, 11 and 12 April 1976 at Queen's Park Oval, Port-of-Spain

WEST INDIES

Batsman	First innings	R	Second innings	R
RC Fredericks	c Amarnath b Chandrasekhar	27	c Solkar b Chandrasekhar	25
LG Rowe	c Viswanath b Chandrasekhar	18	c Kirmani b Venkataraghavan	27
IVA Richards	c Chandrasekhar b Bedi	177	c Solkar b Venkataraghavan	23
AI Kallicharran	b Chandrasekhar	0	not out	103
CH Lloyd*	c Gaekwad b Chandrasekhar	68	c Viswanath b Chandrasekhar	36
DL Murray+	b Chandrasekhar	11	c Solkar b Bedi	25
BD Julien	c Viswanath b Bedi	47	c Kirmani b Venkataraghavan	6
MA Holding	lbw b Bedi	1	not out	17
Imtiaz Ali	not out	0		
AL Padmore	c Gavaskar b Bedi	0		
RR Jumadeen	lbw b Chandrasekhar	0		
Extras	lb7, nb2	9	b1, lb7, nb1	9
Total		**359**	(6 wickets dec.)	**271**

First innings	O	M	R	W
Madan Lal	6	1	22	0
Amarnath	5	0	26	0
Solkar	9	2	40	0
Bedi	30	11	73	4
Chandrasekhar	32.2	8	120	6
Venkataraghavan	27	7	69	0

Second innings	O	M	R	W
Madan Lal	11	2	14	0
Amarnath	11	3	19	0
Bedi	25	3	76	1
Chandrasekhar	27	5	88	2
Venkataraghavan	30.3	5	65	3

Fall of Wickets
1-45, 2-50, 3-52, 4-176, 5-227, 6-334, 7-357, 8-358, 9-358, 10-359
1-41 2-78, 3-81, 4-162, 5-214, 6-230

INDIA

Batsman	First innings	R	Second innings	R
SM Gavaskar	lbw b Holding	26	c Murray b Jumadeen	102
AD Gaekwad	c Murray b Julien	6	c Kallicharran b Jumadeen	28
M Amarnath	st Murray b Padmore	25	run out	85
GR Viswanath	b Ali	41	run out	112
ED Solkar	b Holding	13		
BP Patel	c Fredericks b Holding	29	(5) not out	49
Madan Lal	c Richards b Holding	42	(6) not out	1
S Venkataraghavan	b Ali	13		
SMH Kirmani+	lbw b Holding	13		
BS Bedi*	b Holding	0		
BS Chandrasekhar	not out	0		
Extras	b11, lb6, w4	21	b8, lb12, w1, nb8	29
Total		**228**	(4 wickets)	**406**

First innings	O	M	R	W
Julien	13	4	35	1
Holding	26.4	3	65	6
Lloyd	1	0	1	0
Padmore	29	11	36	1
Ali	17	7	37	2
Fredericks	16	7	33	0

Second innings	O	M	R	W
Julien	13	3	52	0
Holding	21	1	82	0
Lloyd	6	1	22	0
Padmore	47	10	98	0
Ali	17	3	52	2
Jumadeen	41	13	70	2
Fredericks	2	1	7	0

Fall of Wickets
1-22, 2-50, 3-86, 4-112, 5-147, 6-182, 7-203, 8-225, 9-227, 10-228
1-69, 2-177, 3-336, 4-392

Umpires: R Gosein & CF Vyfhuis
Test Debuts: Imtiaz Ali & AL Padmore

Toss: West Indies

India won by six wickets

FOURTH TEST: ENGLAND v INDIA
30, 31 August, 1, 3 and 4 September 1979 at Kennington Oval

ENGLAND

Batsman	First innings		Second innings	
G Boycott	lbw b Kapil Dev	35	b Ghavri	125
AR Butcher	c Singh b Venkataraghavan	14	c Venkataraghavan b Ghavri	20
GA Gooch	c Viswanath b Ghavri	79	lbw b Kapil Dev	31
DI Gower	lbw b Kapil Dev	0	c Reddy b Bedi	7
P Willey	c Singh b Bedi	52	c Reddy b Ghavri	31
IT Botham	st Reddy b Venkataraghavan	38	run out	0
JM Brearley*	b Ghavri	34	b Venkataraghavan	11
DL Bairstow+	c Reddy b Kapil Dev	9	c Gavaskar b Kapil Dev	59
PH Edmonds	c Kapil Dev b Venkataraghavan	16	not out	27
RGD Willis	not out	10		
M Hendrick	c Gavaskar b Bedi	0		
Extras	lb9, w4, nb5	18	lb14, w2, nb7	23
Total		**305**	(8 wickets dec)	**334**

Bowling	First innings				Second innings			
	O	M	R	W	O	M	R	W
Kapil Dev	32	12	83	3	28.5	4	89	2
Ghavri	26	8	61	2	34	11	76	3
Bedi	29.5	4	69	2	26	4	67	1
Yajurvindra Singh	8	2	15	0	2	0	4	0
Venkataraghavan	29	9	59	3	26	4	75	1

Fall of Wickets
1-45, 2-51, 3-51, 4-148, 5-203, 6-245, 7-272, 8-275, 9-304, 10-305
1-43, 2-107, 3-125, 4-192, 5-194, 6-215, 7-291, 8-334

INDIA

Batsman	First innings		Second innings	
SM Gavaskar	c Bairstow b Botham	13	c Gower b Botham	221
CPS Chauhan	c Botham b Willis	6	c Botham b Willis	80
DB Vengsarkar	c Botham b Willis	0	c Botham b Edmonds	52
GR Viswanath	c Brearley b Botham	62	(6) c Brearley b Willey	15
Yashpal Sharma	lbw b Willis	27	lbw b Botham	19
Yajurvindra Singh	not out	43	(7) lbw b Botham	1
Kapil Dev	b Hendrick	16	(4) c Gooch b Willey	0
KD Ghavri	c Bairstow b Botham	7	(9) not out	3
B Reddy+	c Bairstow b Botham	12	not out	5
S Venkataraghavan*	c & b Hendrick	2	(10)	6
BS Bedi	c Brearley b Hendrick	1	(8) run out	
Extras	b2, lb3, w5, nb3	13	b11, lb15, w1	27
Total		**202**	(8 wickets)	**429**

Bowling	First innings				Second innings			
	O	M	R	W	O	M	R	W
Willis	18	2	53	3	28	4	89	1
Botham	28	7	65	4	29	5	97	3
Hendrick	22.3	7	38	3	8	2	15	0
Willey	4	1	16	0	43.5	15	96	2
Gooch	2	0	6	0			9	0
Edmonds	5	1	17	0	38	11	87	0
Butcher					2	0	9	0

Fall of Wickets
1-9, 2-9, 3-47, 4-91, 5-130, 6-161, 7-172, 8-192, 9-200, 10-202
1-213, 2-366, 3-367, 4-389, 5-410, 6-411, 7-419, 8-423

Umpires: DJ Constant & KE Palmer
Test Debuts: DL Bairstow & AR Butcher

Toss: England

Match drawn

SECOND TEST: ENGLAND v INDIA

19, 20, 21 and 23 June 1986 at Headingley

INDIA

	First innings		Second innings	
SM Gavaskar	c French b Pringle	35	c French b Lever	1
K Srikkanth	c Emburey b Pringle	31	b Dilley	8
RJ Shastri	c Pringle b Dilley	32	lbw b Lever	3
DB Vengsarkar	c French b Lever	61	lbw b Lever	102
M Azharuddin	lbw b Gooch	15	b Lever	2
CS Pandit	c Emburey b Pringle	23	b Pringle	17
Kapil Dev*	lbw b Lever	0	(8) c Gatting b Lever	31
RMH Binny	c Slack b Emburey	6	(10) lbw b Pringle	26
Madan Lal	c Gooch b Dilley	20	run out	22
KS More+	not out	36	(7) c Slack b Pringle	16
Maninder Singh	c Gooch b Dilley	3	c Gatting b Pringle	8
	lb5, nb5	10	b4, lb4	8
		272		237

	First innings				Second innings			
	O	M	R	W	O	M	R	W
Dilley	24.2	7	54	3	17	2	71	1
Lever	30	4	102	2	23	5	64	4
Pringle	27	6	47	3	22.3	6	73	4
Emburey	17	4	45	1	7	3	9	0
Gooch	6	0	19		7	2	12	0

Fall of Wickets:
1-64, 2-75, 3-128, 4-163, 5-203, 6-203, 7-211, 8-213, 9-267, 10-272
1-9, 2-9, 3-29, 4-35, 5-70, 6-102, 7-137, 8-173, 9-233, 10-237

ENGLAND

	First innings		Second innings	
GA Gooch	c Binny b Kapil Dev	8	c Srikkanth b Kapil Dev	5
WN Slack	b Madan Lal	0	c Gavaskar b Binny	19
CL Smith	b Madan Lal	6	c More b Shastri	28
AJ Lamb	c Pandit b Binny	10	c More b Binny	10
MW Gatting*	c More b Binny	13	not out	31
CWJ Athey	c More b Madan Lal	32	(8) c More b Maninder Singh	8
DR Pringle	c Srikkanth b Binny	8	(9) c Azharuddin b Kapil Dev	8
JE Emburey	c Kapil Dev b Binny	0	(10) c Vengsarkar b Maninder Singh	5
BN French+	b Binny	8	(11) run out	2
GR Dilley	b Shastri	10	(7) c More b Maninder Singh	0
JK Lever	not out	0		0
	b1, lb2, nb4	7	lb9, nb2	11
		102		128

	First innings				Second innings			
	O	M	R	W	O	M	R	W
Kapil Dev	18		36	1	19.2		24	2
Madan Lal	11.1	3	18	3	9.4	2	30	0
Binny	13		40	5	8	1	18	2
Shastri	3	1	5	1	10	3	21	1
Maninder Singh					16.3	6	26	4

Fall of Wickets:
1-4, 2-14, 3-14, 4-38, 5-41, 6-63, 7-63, 8-71, 9-100, 10-102
1-12, 2-46, 3-63, 4-77, 5-90, 6-90, 7-101, 8-104, 9-109, 10-128

Umpires: J Birkenshaw & DJ Constant
Test Debuts: BN French & CS Pandit

Toss: India

India won by 279 runs

FIRST TEST: INDIA v AUSTRALIA

18, 19, 20, 21 and 22 September 1986 at Chepauk, Madras

AUSTRALIA

	First innings		Second innings	
DC Boon	c Kapil Dev b Sharma	122	(2) lbw b Maninder Singh	49
GR Marsh	c Kapil Dev b Yadav	22	(1) b Shastri	11
DM Jones	b Yadav	210	c Azharuddin b Maninder Singh	24
RJ Bright	c Shastri b Yadav	30		
AR Border*	c Gavaskar b Shastri	106	(4) b Maninder Singh	27
GM Ritchie	run out	13	(5) c Pandit b Shastri	28
GRJ Matthews	c Pandit b Yadav	44	(6) not out	27
SR Waugh	not out	12	(7) not out	2
TJ Zoehrer+				
CJ McDermott				
BA Reid				
	b1, lb7, w1, nb6	15	lb1, nb1	2
	(7 wickets dec.)	**574**	(5 wickets dec)	**170**

	First innings				Second innings			
	O	M	R	W	O	M	R	W
Kapil Dev	18	5	52	0	1	0	5	0
Sharma	16	8	70	1	6	0	19	0
Maninder Singh	39	8	135	0	19	2	60	3
Yadav	49.5	9	142	4	9	2	35	0
Shastri	47	8	161	1	14	2	50	2
Srikkanth	1	0	6	0				

Fall of Wickets
1-48, 2-206, 3-282, 4-460, 5-481, 6-544, 7-574
1-31, 2-81, 3-94, 4-125, 5-165

INDIA

	First innings		Second innings	
SM Gavaskar	c & b Matthews	8	c Jones b Bright	90
K Srikkanth	c Ritchie b Matthews	53	c Waugh b Matthews	39
M Amarnath	run out	1	c Boon b Matthews	51
M Azharuddin	c & b Bright	50	c Ritchie b Bright	42
RJ Shastri	c Zoehrer b Matthews	62	(7) not out	48
CS Pandit	c Waugh b Matthews	35	(5) b Matthews	39
Kapil Dev*	c Border b Matthews	119	(6) c Bright b Matthews	1
KS More+	c Zoehrer b Waugh	4	lbw b Bright	0
C Sharma	c Zoehrer b Reid	30	(8) c McDermott b Bright	23
NS Yadav	c Border b Bright	19	b Bright	8
Maninder Singh	not out	0	lbw b Matthews	0
	b1, lb9, nb6	16	b1, lb3, nb2	6
		397		**347**

	First innings				Second innings			
	O	M	R	W	O	M	R	W
McDermott	14	2	59	0	5	0	27	0
Reid	18	4	93	1	10	2	48	0
Matthews	28.2	3	103	5	39.5	7	146	5
Bright	23	3	88	2	25	3	94	5
Waugh	11	2	44	1	4	1	16	0
Border					4	3	12	0

Fall of Wickets
1-62, 2-65, 3-65, 4-142, 5-206, 6-220, 7-245, 8-330, 9-387, 10-397
1-55, 2-158, 3-204, 4-251, 5-253, 6-291, 7-331, 8-334, 9-344, 10-347

Umpires: DN Dotiwalla & V Vikramraju
Test Debuts: nil

Toss: Australia

Match tied

THIRD TEST: INDIA v ENGLAND
19, 20, 21, 22 and 23 February 1993 at Wankhede Stadium, Mumbai

ENGLAND

	First innings		Second innings	
GA Gooch*	c More b Kapil Dev	4	b Prabhakar	8
AJ Stewart	run out	13	lbw b Prabhakar	10
MA Atherton	c Prabhakar b Kumble	37	c More b Prabhakar	11
RA Smith	c More b Raju	2	b Kumble	62
MW Gatting	c Kapil Dev b Raju	23	st More b Chauhan	61
GA Hick	c Kapil Dev b Prabhakar	178	c Amre b Kumble	47
RJ Blakey+	lbw b Kumble	1	b Kumble	0
CC Lewis	lbw b Kumble	49	c More b Raju	3
JE Emburey	c More b Kapil Dev	12	c Tendulkar b Kumble	1
PAJ DeFreitas	lbw b Kapil Dev	11	st More b Raju	12
PCR Tufnell	not out	2	not out	2
	b4, lb5, w2, nb4	15	b4, lb6, w1, nb1	12
		347		229

First innings	O	M	R	W
Kapil Dev	15	3	35	3
Prabhakar	13	2	52	1
Raju	44	8	102	2
Kumble	40	4	95	3
Chauhan	23	7	54	0

Second innings	O	M	R	W
	7	1	21	0
	11	4	28	3
	26.5	7	68	2
	26	9	70	4
	12	5	32	1

Fall of Wickets
1-11, 2-25, 3-30, 4-58, 5-116, 6-118, 7-211, 8-262, 9-279, 10-347
1-17, 2-26, 3-34, 4-155, 5-181, 6-181, 7-206, 8-214, 9-215, 10-229

INDIA

	First innings	
NS Sidhu	c Smith b Tufnell	79
M Prabhakar	c Blakey b Hick	44
VG Kambli	c Gatting b Lewis	224
SR Tendulkar	lbw b Tufnell	78
M Azharuddin*	lbw b Lewis	26
PK Amre	c DeFreitas b Hick	57
Kapil Dev	c DeFreitas b Emburey	22
KS More+	c Lewis b Emburey	0
A Kumble	c Atherton b Tufnell	16
RK Chauhan	c Atherton b Tufnell	15
SLV Raju	not out	0
	b5, lb14, w5, nb6	30
		591

First innings	O	M	R	W
DeFreitas	20	4	75	0
Lewis	42	9	114	2
Emburey	59	14	144	2
Tufnell	39.3	6	142	4
Hick	29	3	97	2

Fall of Wickets
1-109, 2-174, 3-368, 4-418, 5-519, 6-560, 7-560, 8-563, 9-591, 10-591

Umpires: PD Reporter & S Venkataraghavan
Test Debuts: nil

Toss: England

India won by an innings and 15 runs

FIRST TEST: INDIA v AUSTRALIA

6, 7, 8, 9 and 10 March 1998 at Chepauk, Madras

INDIA

	First innings		Second innings	
NR Mongia+	c Healy b Kasprowicz	58	lbw b Blewett	18
NS Sidhu	run out	62	c Ponting b Robertson	64
R Dravid	c Robertson b Warne	52	c Healy b Robertson	56
SR Tendulkar	c Taylor b Warne	4	not out	155
M Azharuddin*	c Reiffel b Warne	26	c SR Waugh b ME Waugh	64
SC Ganguly	lbw b Robertson	3	not out	30
A Kumble	c SR Waugh b Robertson	30		
J Srinath	c Taylor b Warne	1		
R K Chauhan	c Healy b Robertson	3		
Harvinder Singh	not out	0		
SLV Raju	b Robertson	0		
	b8, lb6, nb4	18	b18, lb6, nb7	31
		257	(4 wickets dec.)	**418**

	First innings				Second innings			
	O	M	R	W	O	M	R	W
Kasprowicz	21	8	44	1	14	6	42	0
Reiffel	15	4	27	0	9	1	32	0
Warne	35	11	85	4	30	7	122	1
Robertson	28.2	4	72	4	27	4	92	1
ME Waugh	1	0	4	0	9	0	44	1
SR Waugh	4	1	11	0	8	0	27	0
Blewett					10	2	35	1

Fall of Wickets
1-122, 2-126, 3-130, 4-186, 5-195, 6-247, 7-248, 8-253, 9-257, 10-257
1-43, 2-115, 3-228, 4-355

AUSTRALIA

	First innings		Second innings	
MA Taylor*	c Mongia b Harvinder Singh	12	(2) c Srinath b Kumble	13
MJ Slater	c Dravid b Kumble	11	(1) b Srinath	13
ME Waugh	b Kumble	66	(5) c Dravid b Kumble	18
SR Waugh	c Mongia b Raju	12	(6) c Dravid b Raju	27
RT Ponting	lbw b Chauhan	18	(7) lbw b Raju	2
GS Blewett	c Dravid b Kumble	9	(3) c Dravid b Kumble	5
IA Healy+	c Ganguly b Raju	90	(8) not out	32
PR Reiffel	c Tendulkar b Kumble	15	(4) c Azharuddin b Raju	8
SK Warne	c Dravid b Kumble	17	c Kumble b Chauhan	35
GR Robertson	c Mongia b Srinath	57	b Chauhan	0
MS Kasprowicz	not out	11	c Srinath b Kumble	4
	b1, lb6, nb3	10	b4, lb3, nb4	11
		328		**168**

	First innings				Second innings			
	O	M	R	W	O	M	R	W
Srinath	17.3	3	46	1	6	4	9	1
Harvinder Singh	11	4	28	1	2	0	9	0
Kumble	45	10	103	4	22.5	7	46	4
Chauhan	25	3	90	1	22	7	66	2
Raju	32	8	54	3	15	3	31	3

Fall of Wickets
1-16, 2-44, 3-57, 4-95, 5-119, 6-137, 7-173, 8-201, 9-297, 10-328
1-18, 2-30, 3-31, 4-54, 5-79, 6-91, 7-96, 8-153, 9-153, 10-168

Umpires: S Venkataraghavan & G Sharp
Test Debuts: Harvinder Singh & GR Robertson

Toss: India

India won by 179 runs

SECOND TEST: INDIA v PAKISTAN
4, 5, 6 and 7 February 1999 at Feroz Shah Kotla, Delhi

INDIA

	First innings		Second innings	
S Ramesh	b Saqlain Mushtaq	60	c & b Mushtaq Ahmed	96
VVS Laxman	b Wasim Akram	35	b Wasim Akram	8
R Dravid	lbw b Saqlain Mushtaq	33	c Ijaz Ahmed b Saqlain Mushtaq	29
SR Tendulkar	lbw b Saqlain Mushtaq	6	c Wasim Akram b Mushtaq Ahmed	29
M Azharuddin*	c Ijaz Ahmed b Mushtaq Ahmed	67	b Wasim Akram	14
SC Ganguly	lbw b Mushtaq Ahmed	13	not out	62
NR Mongia+	run out	10	lbw b Wasim Akram	0
A Kumble	c Yousuf Youhana b Saqlain Mushtaq	0	c Ijaz Ahmed b Saqlain Mushtaq	15
J Srinath	lbw b Saqlain Mushtaq	0	c Ijaz Ahmed b Saqlain Mushtaq	49
BKV Prasad	run out	1	b Saqlain Mushtaq	6
Harbhajan Singh	not out	1	b Saqlain Mushtaq	0
	b11, lb9, nb6	26	b13, lb9, nb9	31
		252		**339**

First innings	O	M	R	W
Wasim Akram	13		23	1
Waqar Younis	13	5	37	0
Mushtaq Ahmed	26	5	64	2
Saqlain Mushtaq	33.5	9	94	5
Shahid Afridi	4	1	14	0

Second innings	O	M	R	W
	21	3	43	3
	12	2	42	0
	26	4	86	2
	46.4	12	122	5
	8	1	24	0

Fall of Wickets:
1-88, 2-113, 3-122, 4-191, 5-231, 6-240, 7-243, 8-247, 9-248, 10-252
1-15, 2-100, 3-168, 4-183, 5-199, 6-199, 7-231, 8-331, 9-339, 10-339

PAKISTAN

	First innings		Second innings	
Saeed Anwar	c Mongia b Prasad	1	c Laxman b Kumble	69
Shahid Afridi	b Harbhajan Singh	32	c Mongia b Kumble	41
Ijaz Ahmed	c Dravid b Kumble	17	lbw b Kumble	0
Inzamam-ul-Haq	b Kumble	26	lbw b Kumble	6
Yousuf Youhana	c & b Kumble	0	b Kumble	15
Salim Malik	c Azharuddin b Prasad	31	(7) b Kumble	0
Moin Khan+	lbw b Srinath	14	(6) c Ganguly b Kumble	37
Wasim Akram*	c Laxman b Harbhajan Singh	15	c Laxman b Kumble	1
Mushtaq Ahmed	c Laxman b Harbhajan Singh	12	c Dravid b Kumble	0
Saqlain Mushtaq	lbw b Kumble	2	lbw b Kumble	6
Waqar Younis	not out	1	not out	0
	b1, lb8, nb9	18	b15, lb2, w2, nb10	29
		172		**207**

First innings	O	M	R	W
Srinath	12	1	38	1
Prasad	11	2	20	2
Harbhajan Singh	17	5	30	3
Kumble	24.3	4	75	4

Second innings	O	M	R	W
	12	2	50	0
	4	1	15	0
	18	5	51	0
	26.3	9	74	10

Fall of Wickets:
1-1, 2-54, 3-54, 4-60, 5-114, 6-130, 7-139, 8-167, 9-168, 10-172
1-101, 2-101, 3-115, 4-115, 5-127, 6-128, 7-186, 8-198, 9-198, 10-207

Umpires: AV Jayaprakash & SA Bucknor
Test Debuts: nil

Toss: India

India won by 212 runs

SECOND TEST: INDIA v AUSTRALIA

11, 12, 13, 14 and 15 March 2001 at Eden Gardens, Calcutta

AUSTRALIA

	First innings			Second innings	
MJ Slater	c Mongia b Khan	42	(2)	c Ganguly b Harbhajan Singh	43
ML Hayden	c sub (HK Badani) b Harbhajan Singh	97	(1)	lbw b Tendulkar	67
JL Langer	c Mongia b Khan	58		c Ramesh b Harbhajan Singh	28
ME Waugh	c Mongia b Harbhajan Singh	22		lbw b Raju	0
SR Waugh*	lbw b Harbhajan Singh	110		c sub (HK Badani) b Harbhajan Singh	24
RT Ponting	lbw b Harbhajan Singh	6		c Das b Harbhajan Singh	0
AC Gilchrist+	lbw b Harbhajan Singh	0		lbw b Tendulkar	0
SK Warne	c Ramesh b Harbhajan Singh	0		lbw b Tendulkar	0
MS Kasprowicz	lbw b Ganguly	7	(9)	not out	13
JN Gillespie	c Ramesh b Harbhajan Singh	46	(10)	c Das b Harbhajan Singh	6
GD McGrath	not out	21	(8)	lbw b Harbhajan Singh	12
Bonus runs					5
Extras	b19, lb10, nb7	36		b6, nb8	14
		445			**212**

	First innings				Second innings			
	O	M	R	W	O	M	R	W
Khan	28.4	6	89	2	8	4	30	0
Prasad	30	5	95	1	3	1	7	0
Ganguly	13.2	3	44	0	1	0	2	0
Raju	20	2	58	1	15	3	58	1
Harbhajan Singh	37.5	7	123	7	30.3	8	73	6
Tendulkar	2	0	7	0	11	3	31	3

Fall of Wickets
1-103, 2-193, 3-214, 4-236, 5-252, 6-252, 7-252, 8-269, 9-402, 10-445
1-74, 2-106, 3-116, 4-166, 5-166, 6-167, 7-173, 8-174, 9-191, 10-212

INDIA

	First innings			Second innings	
SS Das	c Gilchrist b McGrath	20		hit wicket b Gillespie	39
S Ramesh	c Ponting b Gillespie	0		c ME Waugh b Warne	30
R Dravid	b Warne	25		run out	180
SR Tendulkar	lbw b McGrath	10	(6)	c Gilchrist b Gillespie	10
VVS Laxman	c SR Waugh b Kasprowicz	59		c Gilchrist b McGrath	281
NR Mongia+	c Hayden b Warne	4		c Ponting b McGrath	48
Harbhajan Singh	c Gilchrist b Kasprowicz	4	(3)	b McGrath	8
Z Khan	c Ponting b Gillespie	3	(9)	not out	8
SLV Raju	b McGrath	4	(8)	not out	23
BKV Prasad	not out	7			
Extras	lb2, nb12	14		b4, lb14, w2, nb14	34
		171		(7 wickets dec.)	**657**

	First innings				Second innings			
	O	M	R	W	O	M	R	W
McGrath	14	8	18	4	39	12	103	3
Gillespie	11	0	47	2	31	6	115	2
Kasprowicz	13	0	39	2	35	6	139	1
Warne	20.1	3	65	2	34	3	152	0
ME Waugh					18	1	58	0
Ponting					12	1	41	0
Hayden					6	0	24	0
Slater					2	0	4	0
Langer					1	0	3	0

Fall of Wickets
1-1, 2-34, 3-48, 4-88, 5-88, 6-92, 7-97, 8-113, 9-129, 10-171
1-52, 2-97, 3-115, 4-232, 5-608, 6-624, 7-629

Umpires: SK Bansal & P Willey
Test Debuts: nil

Toss: Australia

India won by 171 runs

PRUDENTIAL WORLD CUP FINAL: INDIA v WEST INDIES

25 June 1983 at Lord's

INDIA

		R
SM Gavaskar	c Dujon b Roberts	2
K Srikkanth	lbw b Marshall	38
M Amarnath	b Holding	26
Yashpal Sharma	c sub (AL Logie) b Gomes	11
SM Patil	c Gomes b Garner	27
Kapil Dev*	c Holding b Gomes	15
K Azad	c Garner b Roberts	0
RMH Binny	c Garner b Roberts	2
Madan Lal	b Marshall	17
SMH Kirmani+	b Holding	14
BS Sandhu	not out	11
Extras	b5, lb5, w9, nb1	20
	(54.4 overs)	**183**

	O	M	R	W
Roberts	10	3	32	3
Garner	12	4	24	1
Marshall	11	1	24	2
Holding	9.4	2	26	2
Gomes	11	1	49	2
Richards	1	0	8	0

Fall of Wickets
1-2, 2-59, 3-90, 4-92, 5-110, 6-111, 7-130, 8-153, 9-161, 10-183

WEST INDIES

		R
CG Greenidge	b Sandhu	1
DL Haynes	c Binny b Madan Lal	13
IVA Richards	c Kapil Dev b Madan Lal	33
CH Lloyd*	c Kapil Dev b Binny	8
HA Gomes	c Gavaskar b Madan Lal	5
SFAF Bacchus	c Kirmani b Sandhu	8
PJL Dujon+	b Amarnath	25
MD Marshall	c Gavaskar b Amarnath	18
AME Roberts	lbw b Kapil Dev	4
J Garner	not out	5
MA Holding	lbw b Amarnath	6
Extras	lb4, w10	14
	(52 overs)	**140**

	O	M	R	W
Kapil Dev	11	4	21	1
Sandhu	9	1	32	2
Madan Lal	12	2	31	3
Binny	10	1	23	1
Amarnath	7	0	12	3
Azad	3	0	7	0

Fall of Wickets
1-5, 2-50, 3-57, 4-66, 5-66, 6-76, 7-119, 8-124, 9-126, 10-140

Umpires: HD Bird & BJ Meyer
Debuts: Nil

Toss: West Indies
Man of the Match: M Amarnath

India won by 43 runs

Appendix D

LIMITED-OVER INTERNATIONAL RESULTS 1974–2001

Date	Comp	Venue	Opponent	WON	LOST	OTHER
1974						
13.7.74		Headingley	Eng		4w	
16/17.7.74		Oval	Eng		6w	
1975						
7.6.75	WC	Lord's	Eng		202r	
11.6.75	WC	Headingley	EAf	10w		
14.6.75	WC	Old Trafford	NZ		4w	
1975–76						
21.2.76		Christchurch	NZ		9w	
22.2.76		Auckland	NZ		80 r	
1.10.78		Quetta	Pak	4r		
1978–79						
13.10.78		Sialkot	Pak		8w	
3.11.78		Sahiwal	Pak			(Ind concede)
1979						
9.6.79	WC	Edgbaston	WI		9w	
13.6.79	WC	Headingley	NZ		8w	
16/18.6.79	WC	Old Trafford	SL		47r	
1980–81						
6.12.80 *		MCG	Aus	66r		
9.12.80 *		Perth	NZ	5r		
18.12.80 *		SCG	Aus		9w	
21.12.80 *		Brisbane	NZ		3w	
23.12.80 *		Adelaide	NZ	6r		
8.1.81 *		SCG	Aus		9w	
10.1.81 *		MCG	NZ		10w	
11.1.81 *		MCG	Aus		7w	
15.1.81 *		SCG	Aus		27r	
18.1.81 *		Brisbane	NZ		22r	
14.2.81		Auckland	NZ		78r	
15.2.81		Hamilton	NZ		57r	

Date	Comp	Venue	Opponent	WON	LOST	OTHER
1981–82						
25.11.81		**Ahmedabad**	Eng		5w	
20.12.81		**Jullundur**	Eng	6w		
27.1.82		**Cuttack**	Eng	5w		
1982						
2.6.82		Headingley	Eng		9w	
4.6.82		Oval	Eng		114r	
1982–83						
12.9.82		**Amritsar**	SL	78r		
15.9.82		**Delhi**	SL	6w		
26.9.82		**Bangalore**	SL	6w		
3.12.82		Gujranwala	Pak		14r	
17.12.82		Multan	Pak		37r	
31.12.82		Lahore	Pak	FSR		
21.1.83		Karachi	Pak		8w	
9.3.83		Port-of-Spain	WI		52r	
29.3.83		Berbice	WI	27r		
7.4.83		Grenada	WI		7w	
1983						
9/10.6.83	WC	Old Trafford	WI	34r		
11.6.83	WC	Leicester	Zim	5w		
13.6.83	WC	Trent Bridge	Aus		162r	
15.6.83	WC	Oval	WI		66r	
18.6.83	WC	Tunbridge Wells	Zim	31r		
20.6.83	WC	Chelmsford	Aus	118r		
22.6.83 SF	WC	Old Trafford	Eng	6w		
25.6.83 F	WC	Lord's	WI	43r		
11.9.83		**Hyderabad**	Pak	4w		
1983–84						
2.10.83		**Jaipur**	Pak	4w		
13.10.83		**Srinagar**	WI		FSR	
9.11.83		**Baroda**	WI		4w	
1.12.83		**Indore**	WI		8w	
8.12.83		**Jamshedpur**	WI		104r	
17.12.83		**Gauhati**	WI		6w	
8.4.84		Sharjah	SL	10w		
13.4.84		Sharjah	Pak	54r		
1984–85						
28.9.84 *		**Delhi**	Aus		48r	
1.10.84		**Trivandrum**	Aus			Abandoned
3.10.84		**Jamshedpur**	Aus			Abandoned
5.10.84		**Ahmedabad**	Aus		7w	
6.10.84		**Indore**	Aus		6w	
12.10.84		Quetta	Pak		46r	
31.10.84		Sialkot	Pak			Abandoned
5.12.84		**Pune**	Eng		4w	
27.12.84		**Cuttack**	Eng		FSR	
20.1.85		**Bangalore**	Eng		3w	
23.1.85		**Nagpur**	Eng	3w		

503

Date	Comp	Venue	Opponent	WON	LOST	OTHER
27.1.85		**Chandigarh**	Eng		7r	
20.2.85 *		MCG	Pak	6w		
26.2.85 *		SCG	Eng	86r		
3.3.85		MCG	Aus	8w		
5.3.85 * SF		SCG	NZ	7w		
10.3.85 * F		MCG	Pak	8w		
22.3.85 *		Sharjah	Pak	38r		
29.3.85 *		Sharjah	Aus	3w		

1985–86

Date	Comp	Venue	Opponent	WON	LOST	OTHER
25.8.85		Colombo, SSC	SL	2w		
21.9.85		Colombo, Sav	SL		14r	
22.9.85		Colombo, Sav	SL			Abandoned
17.11.85		Sharjah	Pak		48r	
22.11.85		Sharjah	WI		8w	
11.1.86		Brisbane	NZ	5w		
12.1.86		Brisbane	Aus		4w	
16.1.86 *		MCG	Aus	8w		
18.1.86		Perth	NZ		3w	
21.1.86 *		SCG	Aus		100r	
23.1.86 *		MCG	NZ		5w	
25.1.86		Adelaide	NZ	5w		
26.1.86		Adelaide	Aus		36r	
31.1.86		MCG	Aus	6w		
2.2.86		Launceston	NZ	21r		
5.2.86 F1 *		SCG	Aus		11r	
9.2.86 F2 *		MCG	Aus		7w	
10.4.86		Sharjah	NZ	3w		
13.4.86		Sharjah	SL	3w		
18.4.86 F		Sharjah	Pak		1w	

1986

Date	Comp	Venue	Opponent	WON	LOST	OTHER
24.5.86		Oval	Eng	9w		
26.5.86		Old Trafford	Eng		5w	

1986–87

Date	Comp	Venue	Opponent	WON	LOST	OTHER
7.9.86		**Jaipur**	Aus	7w		
9.9.86		**Srinagar**	Aus		3w	
24.9.86		**Hyderabad**	Aus			Abandoned
2.10.86		**Delhi**	Aus	3w		
5.10.86		**Ahmedabad**	Aus	52r		
7.10.86		**Rajkot**	Aus		7w	
27.11.86 *		Sharjah	SL	7w		
30.11.86 *		Sharjah	WI		33r	
5.12.86 *		Sharjah	Pak		3w	
24.12.86		**Kanpur**	SL		117r	
11.1.87		**Gauhati**	SL	8w		
13.1.87		**Delhi**	SL	6w		
15.1.87		**Baroda**	SL	94r		
17.1.87		**Bombay**	SL	10r		
27.1.87		**Indore**	Pak		3w	
18.2.87		**Calcutta**	Pak		2w	
20.3.87		**Hyderabad**	Pak	Lost fewer wkts		

504

Date	Comp	Venue	Opponent	WON	LOST	OTHER
22.3.87		**Pune**	Pak		6w	
24.3.87		**Nagpur**	Pak		41r	
26.3.87		**Jamshedpur**	Pak		5w	
2.4.87		Sharjah	Eng	3w		
5.4.87		Sharjah	Aus	7w		
10.4.87		Sharjah	Pak		8w	
1987–88						
9.10.87	WC	**Madras**	Aus		1r	
14.10.87	WC	**Bangalore**	NZ	16r		
17.10.87	WC	**Bombay**	Zim	8w		
22.10.87	WC	**Delhi**	Aus	56r		
26.10.87	WC	**Ahmedabad**	Zim	7w		
31.10.87	WC	**Nagpur**	NZ	9w		
5.11.87 SF	WC	**Bombay**	Eng		35r	
8.12.87		**Nagpur**	WI		10r	
23.12.87		**Gauhati**	WI		52r	
2.1.88		**Calcutta**	WI	56r		
5.1.88		**Rajkot**	WI		6w	
7.1.88		**Ahmedabad**	WI		2r	
19.1.88		**Faridabad**	WI		4w	
22.1.88		**Gwalior**	WI		73r	
25.1.88		**Trivandrum**	WI		9w	
25.3.88		Sharjah	SL	18r		
27.3.88		Sharjah	NZ	73r		
1.4.88 F		Sharjah	NZ	52r		
1988–89						
16.10.88		Sharjah	WI	23r		
19.10.88		Sharjah	Pak		34r	
21.10.88		Sharjah	WI		8w	
27.10.88		Chittagong	Bang	9w		
29.10.88		Dhaka	SL		17r	
31.10.88		Dhaka	Pak	4w		
4.11.88 F		Dhaka	SL	6w		
10.12.88		**Visakhapatnam**	NZ	4w		
12.12.88		**Cuttack**	NZ	5w		
15.12.88		**Indore**	NZ	53r		
17.12.88		**Baroda**	NZ	2w		
7.3.89		Bridgetown	WI		50 r	
9.3.89		Port-of-Spain	WI		6w	
11.3.89		Port-of-Spain	WI		6w	
18.3.89		St John's	WI		8w	
21.3.89		Georgetown	WI		101r	
1989–90						
13.10.89		Sharjah	WI		5w	
15.10.89		Sharjah	Pak		6w	
16.10.89		Sharjah	WI	37r		
20.10.89		Sharjah	Pak		38r	
22.10.89		**Ahmedabad**	SL	6r		
23.10.89		**Delhi**	WI		20r	
25.10.89		**Kanpur**	Eng	6w		

Date	Comp	Venue	Opponent	WON	LOST	OTHER
27.10.89		**Bangalore**	Aus	3w		
28.10.89		**Calcutta**	Pak		77r	
30.10.89	SF	**Bombay**	WI		8w	
18.12.89		Gujranwala	Pak		7r	
20.12.89		Karachi	Pak			Aban (riots)
22.12.89		Lahore	Pak		38r	
1.3.90		Dunedin	NZ		108r	
3.3.90		Christchurch	Aus		18r	
6.3.90		Wellington	NZ	1r		
8.3.90		Hamilton	Aus		7w	
25.4.90		Sharjah	SL		3w	
27.4.90		Sharjah	Pak		26r	

1990

Date	Comp	Venue	Opponent	WON	LOST	OTHER
18.7.90		Headingley	Eng	6w		
20.7.90		Trent Bridge	Eng	5w		

1990–91

Date	Comp	Venue	Opponent	WON	LOST	OTHER
1.12.90		**Nagpur**	SL	19r		
5.12.90		**Pune**	SL	6w		
8.12.90		**Margao**	SL		7w	
25.12.90		**Chandigarh**	Bang	9w		
28.12.90		**Cuttack**	SL		36r	
4.1.91 F		**Calcutta**	SL	7w		

1991–92

Date	Comp	Venue	Opponent	WON	LOST	OTHER
18.10.91		Sharjah	Pak	60r		
19.10.91		Sharjah	WI	19r		
22.10.91		Sharjah	WI	7w		
23.10.91		Sharjah	Pak		4r	
24.10.91 F		Sharjah	Pak		72r	
10.11.91		**Calcutta**	SA	3w		
12.11.91		**Gwalior**	SA	38r		
14.11.91		**Delhi**	SA		8w	
6.12.91		Perth	WI			TIED
8.12.91		Perth	Aus	107r		
10.12.91		Hobart	Aus		8w	
14.12.91		Adelaide	WI	10r		
15.12.91		Adelaide	Aus		6w	
11.1.92		Brisbane	WI		6w	
14.1.92 *		SCG	Aus		9w	
16.1.92 *		MCG	WI	5w		
18.1.92 * F1		MCG	Aus		88r	
20.1.92 * F2		SCG	Aus		6r	
22.2.92 *	WC	Perth	Eng		9r	
28.2.92	WC	Mackay	SL			Abandoned
1.3.92	WC	Brisbane	Aus		1r	
4.3.92 *	WC	SCG	Pak	43r		
7.3.92	WC	Hamilton	Zim	55r		
10.3.92	WC	Wellington	WI		5w	
12.3.92	WC	Dunedin	NZ		4w	
15.3.92	WC	Adelaide	SA		6w	

Date	Comp	Venue	Opponent	WON	LOST	OTHER
1992–93						
25.10.92		Harare	Zim	30r		
7.12.92 *		Cape Town	SA		6w	
9.12.92 *		Port Elizabeth	SA		6w	
11.12.92 *		Pretoria	SA	4w		
13.12.92 *		Johannesburg	SA		6w	
15.12.92 *		Bloemfontein	SA		8w	
17.12.92 *		Durban	SA		39r	
19.12.92 *		East London	SA	5w		
18.1.93		**Jaipur**	Eng		4w	
21.1.93		**Chandigarh**	Eng	5w		
26.2.93		**Bangalore**	Eng		48r	
1.3.93		**Jamshedpur**	Eng		6w	
4.3.93		**Gwalior**	Eng	3w		
5.3.93		**Gwalior**	Eng	4w		
19.3.93		**Faridabad**	Zim	67r		
22.3.93		**Gauhati**	Zim	7w		
25.3.93		**Pune**	Zim	8w		
1993–94						
25.7.93		Colombo, Khett	SL	1r		
11.8.93		Colombo, Khett	SL		8r	
14.8.93		Moratuwa	SL		4w	
7.11.93		**Kanpur**	SL	7w		
16.11.93		**Ahmedabad**	WI		69r	
18.11.93		**Indore**	Zim			TIED
22.11.93		**Chandigarh**	SA	43r		
23.11.93	SF	**Calcutta**	SA	2r		
27.11.93	F	**Calcutta**	WI	102r		
15.2.94		**Rajkot**	SL	8r		
18.2.94		**Hyderabad**	SL	7w		
20.2.94		**Jullundur**	SL		4w	
25.3.94		Napier	NZ		28r	
27.3.94		Auckland	NZ	7w		
30.3.94		Wellington	NZ	12r		
2.4.94		Christchurch	NZ		6w	
13.4.94		Sharjah	UAE	71r		
15.4.94		Sharjah	Pak		6w	
19.4.94	SF	Sharjah	Aus	7w		
22.4.94	F	Sharjah	Pak		39r	
1994–95						
4.9.94		Colombo, Khett	SL			Abandoned
5.9.94		Colombo, Khett	SL		7w	
9.9.94		Colombo, Khett	Aus	31r		
17.9.94	F	Colombo, SSC	SL	6w		
17.10.94		**Faridabad**	WI		96r	
20.10.94		**Bombay**	WI	FSR		
23.10.94		**Madras**	WI	4w		
28.10.94		**Baroda**	NZ	7w		
30.10.94		**Kanpur**	WI		46r	
3.11.94		**Delhi**	NZ	107r		

Date	Comp	Venue	Opponent	WON	LOST	OTHER
5.11.94 F		**Calcutta**	WI	72r		
7.11.94		**Visakhapatnam**	WI	4r		
9.11.94		**Cuttack**	WI	8w		
11.11.94		**Jaipur**	WI	5r		
16.2.95		Napier	NZ		4w	
18.2.95		Hamilton	SA		14r	
22.2.95		Dunedin	Aus	5w		
5.4.95		Sharjah	Bang	9w		
7.4.95		Sharjah	Pak		97r	
9.4.95		Sharjah	SL	8w		
14.4.95 F		Sharjah	SL	8w		

1995–96

Date	Comp	Venue	Opponent	WON	LOST	OTHER
15.11.95		**Jamshedpur**	NZ		8w	
18.11.95		**Amritsar**	NZ	6w		
24.11.95		**Pune**	NZ	5w		
26.11.95		**Nagpur**	NZ		99r	
29.11.95		**Bombay**	NZ	6w		
18.2.96	WC	**Cuttack**	Ken	7w		
21.2.96	WC	**Gwalior**	WI	5w		
27.2.96	WC	**Bombay**	Aus		16r	
2.3.96	WC	**Delhi**	SL		6w	
6.3.96	WC	**Kanpur**	Zim	40r		
9.3.96 QF	WC	**Bangalore**	Pak	39r		
13.3.96 SF	WC	**Calcutta**	SL			Default (riots)
3.4.96		Singapore	SL	12r		
5.4.96		Singapore	Pak		8w	
12.4.96		Sharjah	Pak		38r	
14.4.96		Sharjah	SA		80r	
15.4.96		Sharjah	Pak	28r		
17.4.96		Sharjah	SA		5w	
19.4.96 F		Sharjah	SA		38r	

1996

Date	Comp	Venue	Opponent	WON	LOST	OTHER
23/24.5.96		Oval	Eng			Abandoned
25.5.96		Headingley	Eng		6w	
26/27.5.96		Old Trafford	Eng		4w	

1996–97

Date	Comp	Venue	Opponent	WON	LOST	OTHER
28.8.96		Colombo, Prem	SL		9w	
1.9.96		Colombo, SSC	Zim	7w		
6.9.96		Colombo, SSC	Aus		3w	
16.9.96		Toronto	Pak	8w		
17.9.96		Toronto	Pak		2w	
18.9.96		Toronto	Pak	55r		
21.9.96		Toronto	Pak		97r	
23.9.96		Toronto	Pak		52r	
17.10.96		**Hyderabad**	SA		47r	
21.10.96		**Bangalore**	Aus	2w		
23.10.96		**Jaipur**	SA		27r	
29.10.96		**Rajkot**	SA		5w	
3.11.96		**Chandigarh**	Aus	5r		
6.11.96 F		**Bombay**	SA	35r		

Date	Comp	Venue	Opponent	WON	LOST	OTHER
14.12.96		**Bombay**	SA	74R		
23.1.97 *		Bloemfontein	SA		39r	
27.1.97 *		Paarl	Zim			TIED
2.2.97		Port Elizabeth	SA		6w	
4.2.97 *		East London	SA		6w	
7.2.97 *		Pretoria	Zim		3w	
9.2.97		Benoni	Zim	6w		
12.2.97		Durban	SA			Abandoned
13.2.97 F		Durban	SA		17r	
15.2.97		Bulawayo	Zim		8w	
26.4.97		Port-of-Spain	WI		8w	
27.4.97		Port-of-Spain	WI	10w		
30.4.97		St Vincent	WI		18r	
3.5.97		Bridgetown	WI		10w	
14.5.97		**Bangalore**	NZ	8w		
17.5.97		**Bombay**	SL		5w	
21.5.97		**Madras**	Pak		35r	
1997–98						
18.7.97		Colombo, Prem	SL		6w	
20.7.97		Colombo, SSC	Pak			Abandoned
24.7.97		Colombo, SSC	Bang	9w		
26.7.97 F		Colombo, Prem	SL		8w	
17.8.97 *		Colombo, Prem	SL		2r	
20.8.97 *		Colombo, Prem	SL		7w	
23.8.97		Colombo, SSC	SL			Abandoned
24.8.97		Colombo, SSC	SL		9r	
13.9.97		Toronto	Pak	20r		
14.9.97		Toronto	Pak	7w		
17.9.97		Toronto	Pak			Abandoned
18.9.97		Toronto	Pak	34r		
20.9.97		Toronto	Pak	7w		
21.9.97		Toronto	Pak		5w	
28.9.97		Hyderabad	Pak		5w	
30.9.97		Karachi	Pak	4w		
2.10.97 *		Lahore	Pak		9w	
11.12.97 *		Sharjah	Eng		7r	
14.12.97 *		Sharjah	Pak		4w	
16.12.97 *		Sharjah	WI		41r	
22.12.97		**Gauhati**	SL	7w		
25.12.97		**Indore**	SL			Aban (pitch)
28.12.97		**Goa**	SL		5w	
10.1.98		Dhaka	Bang	4w		
11.1.98		Dhaka	Pak	18r		
14.1.98 F1 *		Dhaka	Pak	8w		
16.1.98 F2 *		Dhaka	Pak		6w	
18.1.98 F3 *		Dhaka	Pak	3w		
1.4.98		**Cochin**	Aus	41r		
5.4.98		**Baroda**	Zim	12r		
7.4.98		**Kanpur**	Aus	6w		
9.4.98		**Cuttack**	Zim	32r		
14.4.98 F		**Delhi**	Aus		4w	

509

Date	Comp	Venue	Opponent	WON	LOST	OTHER
17.4.98 *		Sharjah	NZ	15r		
19.4.98 *		Sharjah	Aus		58r	
20.4.98 *		Sharjah	NZ		4w	
22.4.98 *		Sharjah	Aus		26r	
24.4.98 F *		Sharjah	Aus	6w		
14.5.98 *		**Chandigarh**	Bang	5w		
20.5.98 *		**Bangalore**	Ken	4w		
25.5.98 *		**Bombay**	Bang	5w		
28.5.98 *		**Gwalior**	Ken		69r	
31.5.98 F *		**Calcutta**	Ken	9w		

1998–99

Date	Comp	Venue	Opponent	WON	LOST	OTHER
19.6.98		Colombo, Prem	SL	8w		
23.6.98		Colombo, Prem	NZ			Abandoned
1.7.98		Colombo, SSC	SL		8r	
3.7.98		Colombo, SSC	NZ			Abandoned
7.7.98 F		Colombo, Prem	SL	6r		
12.9.98		Toronto	Pak	6w		
13.9.98		Toronto	Pak		51r	
16.9.98		Toronto	Pak		77r	
19.9.98		Toronto	Pak		134r	
20.9.98		Toronto	Pak		5w	
26.9.98		Bulawayo	Zim	8w		
27.9.98		Bulawayo	Zim	8w		
30.9.98		Harare	Zim		37r	
28.10.98 *		Dhaka	Aus	44r		
31.10.98 SF *		Dhaka	WI		6w	
6.11.98 *		Sharjah	SL	3w		
8.11.98 *		Sharjah	Zim	7w		
9.11.98 *		Sharjah	SL	81r		
11.11.98 *		Sharjah	Zim		13r	
13.11.98 F *		Sharjah	Zim	10w		
9.1.99 *		Taupo	NZ		5w	
12.1.99 *		Napier	NZ	2w		
14.1.99 *		Wellington	NZ			Abandoned
16.1.99		Auckland	NZ	5w		
19.1.99 *		Christchurch	NZ		70r	
22.3.99		**Nagpur**	SL	80r		
24.3.99		**Jaipur**	Pak		143r	
30.3.99		**Pune**	SL	51r		
1.4.99 *		**Mohali**	Pak		7w	
4.4.99 F *		**Bangalore**	Pak		123r	
8.4.99 *		Sharjah	Pak		116r	
9.4.99 *		Sharjah	Eng	20r		
11.4.99 *		Sharjah	Eng	9r		
13.4.99 *		Sharjah	Pak	6w		
16.4.99 F *		Sharjah	Pak		8w	

1999

Date	Comp	Venue	Opponent	WON	LOST	OTHER
15.5.99	WC	Hove	SA		4w	
19.5.99	WC	Leicester	Zim		3r	
23.5.99	WC	Bristol	Ken	94r		

510

Date	Comp	Venue	Opponent	WON	LOST	OTHER
26.5.99	WC	Taunton	SL	157r		
29/30.5.99	WC	Edgbaston	Eng	63r		
4.6.99	WC	Oval	Aus		77r	
9.6.99	WC	Old Trafford	Pak	47r		
12.6.99	WC	Trent Bridge	NZ		5w	

1999–2000

23.8.99		Galle	Aus		8w	
25.8.99 *		Colombo, Prem	SL		7w	
28.8.99		Colombo, SSC	Aus		41r	
29.8.99		Colombo, SSC	SL	23r		
4.9.99		Singapore	Zim	115r		
5.9.99		Singapore	WI		42r	
7.9.99 F1		Singapore	WI			Abandoned
8.9.99 F2		Singapore	WI		4w	
11.9.99		Toronto	WI	8w		
12.9.99		Toronto	WI		70r	
14.9.99		Toronto	WI	88r		
26.9.99		Nairobi	SA	8w		
29.9.99		Nairobi	Ken	58r		
1.10.99		Nairobi	ZIm	107r		
3.10.99 F		Nairobi	SA		26r	
5.11.99		**Rajkot**	NZ		43r	
8.11.99		**Hyderabad**	NZ	174r		
11.11.99		**Gwalior**	NZ	14r		
14.11.99		**Gauhati**	NZ		48r	
17.11.99		**Delhi**	NZ	7w		
10.1.00 *		Brisbane	Pak		2w	
12.1.00 *		MCG	Aus		28r	
14.1.00 *		SCG	Aus		5w	
21.1.00		Hobart	Pak		32r	
25.1.00 *		Adelaide	Pak	48r		
26.1.00 *		Adelaide	Aus		152r	
28.1.00 *		Perth	Pak		104r	
30.1.00		Perth	Aus		4w	
9.3.00		**Cochin**	SA	3w		
12.3.00		**Jamshedpur**	SA	6w		
15.3.00		**Faridabad**	SA		2w	
17.3.00		**Baroda**	SA	4w		
19.3.00		**Nagpur**	SA		10r	
22.3.00 *		Sharjah	SA		10w	
23.3.00 *		Sharjah	Pak	5w		
26.3.00 *		Sharjah	Pak		98r	
27.3.00 *		Sharjah	SA		6w	
30/31.5.00 *		Dhaka	Bang	8w		
1.6.00 *		Dhaka	SL		71r	
3.6.00 *		Dhaka	Pak		44r	

2000–01

3.10.00		Nairobi	Ken	8w		
7.10.00		Nairobi	Aus	20r		
13.10.00 SF		Nairobi	SA	95r		

511

Date	Comp	Venue	Opponent	WON	LOST	OTHER
15.10.00 F		Nairobi	NZ		4w	
20.10.00 *		Sharjah	SL		5w	
22.10.00 *		Sharjah	Zim	13r		
26.10.00 *		Sharjah	Zim	3w		
27.10.00 *		Sharjah	SL		68r	
29.10.00 F *		Sharjah	SL		245r	
2.12.00		**Cuttack**	Zim	3w		
5.12.00		**Ahmedabad**	Zim	61r		
8.12.00		**Jodhpur**	Zim		1w	
11.12.00		**Kanpur**	Zim	9w		
14.12.00		**Rajkot**	Zim	39r		
25.3.01 *		**Bangalore**	Aus	60r		
28.3.01		**Pune**	Aus		8w	
31.3.01		**Indore**	Aus	118r		
3.4.01		**Visakhapatnam**	Aus		93r	
6.4.01		**Margao**	Aus		4w	
24.6.01		Harare	Zim	9w		
27.6.01		Bulawayo	Zim	4w		
30.6.01		Bulawayo	WI	6w		
4.7.01		Harare	WI	6w		
7.7.01 F		Harare	WI		16r	
20.7.01 *		Colombo, Prem	NZ		84r	
22.7.01 *		Colombo, Prem	SL		6r	
26.7.01		Colombo, Prem	NZ		67r	
28.7.01		Colombo, Prem	SL	7w		
1.8.01		Colombo, SSC	SL	46r		
2.8.01		Colombo, SSC	NZ	7w		
5.8.01 F *		Colombo, Khett	SL		121r	
5.10.01 *		Johannesburg	SA		6w	
10.10.01 *		Centurion	SA	41r		
12.10.01 *		Bloemfontein	Ken	10w		
17.10.01 *		Port Elizabeth	Ken		70r	
19.10.01 *		East London	SA		46r	
24.10.01 *		Paarl	Ken	186r		
26.10.01 F *		SA			6w	

Notes:
WC =   Cricket World Cup
* =   Played under floodlights
QF/SF/F = Quarter-final/Semi-final/Final
Venues in bold are games played in India
Matches described as abandoned all started play

Matches where no play was possible:

Date	Venue	Opponent	Date	Venue	Opponent
19.12.88	**Jammu**	NZ	12.2.97	Durban	SA
16.12.89	Peshawar	Pak	16/17.2.97	Harare	Zim
15/16.9.94	Colombo, Prem	Pak	25.6.98	Galle	SL
20.11.95	**Margao**	NZ	29.6.98	Galle	NZ
27.10.96	**Cuttack**	Aus	15.1.99	Wellington	NZ

Appendix E

INDIAN TEST PLAYERS
AND THEIR TEST AVERAGES

Note: The first lines give the name by which the players are usually known and recorded. The second line gives his full name, if different, and, where appropriate, his nickname. The details are made up to 31 December 2001. (Acknowledgements to *Register of Indian Test Cricketers* and Anant Gaundalkar.)

	Tests	I	NO	HS	Runs	Avge	100	Ct	St	Balls	Runs	Wkts	Avge	BB
ABID ALI S. Syed Abid Ali Sardar Ali b Hyderabad 9 Sept 1941	29	53	3	81	1018	20.36	–	32	–	4164	1980	47	42.12	6-55
ADHIKARI, H.R. Hemachandra Ramachandra 'Hemu' Adhikari, b Baroda 31 July 1919	21	36	8	114*	872	31.14	1	8	–	170	82	3	27.33	3-68
AGARKAR, A.B. Ajit Bhalchandra Agarkar b Bombay 4 December 1977	10	16	1	41*	124	8.26	–	3	–	1968	932	24	38.83	3-43
AMARNATH, L. Lala Amarnath Nanik Bhardwaj b Lahore 11 Sept 1911, d 5 Aug 2000	24	40	4	118	878	24.38	1	13	–	4241	1481	45	32.91	5-96
AMARNATH, M. Mohinder Amarnath Bhardwaj b Patiala 24 Sept 1950	69	113	10	138	4378	42.50	11	47	–	3676	1782	32	55.68	4-63
AMARNATH, S. Surinder Amarnath Bhardwaj b Kanpur 30 Dec 1948	10	18	0	124	550	30.55	1	4	–	11	5	1	5.00	1-5
AMAR SINGH, L. Amar Singh Ladha Nakum b Rajkot 4 Dec 1910, d 20 May 1940	7	14	1	51	292	22.46	–	3	–	2182	858	28	30.64	7-86
AMIR ELAHI b Lahore 1 Sept 1908, d 28 Dec 1980	1	2	0	13	17	8.50	–	–	–	–	–	–	–	–

	Tests	I	NO	HS	Runs	Avge	100	Ct	St	Balls	Runs	Wkts	Avge	BB
AMRE, P.K. Pravin Kulyan Amre b Bombay 14 August 1968	11	13	3	103	425	42.50	1	9	–	–	–	–	–	–
ANKOLA, S.A. Salil Ashok Ankola b Sholapur 1 Mar 1968	1	1	0	6	6	6.00	–	–	–	180	128	2	64.00	1-35
APTE, A.L. Arvindrao Laxmanrao Apte b Bombay 24 Oct 1934	1	2	0	8	15	7.50	–	–	–	–	–	–	–	–
APTE, M.L. Madhavrao Laxmanrao Apte b Bombay 5 Oct 1932	7	13	2	163*	542	49.27	1	2	–	6	3	0	–	–
ARSHAD AYUB b Hyderabad 2 Aug 1958	13	19	4	57	257	17.13	–	2	–	3663	1438	41	35.07	5-50
ARUN, B. Bharathi Arun b Vijaywada 14 Dec 1962	2	2	1	2*	4	4.00	–	2	–	252	116	4	29.00	3-76
ARUN LAL, J. Jagdish Arun Lal b Moradabad 1 Aug 1955	16	29	1	93	729	26.03	–	13	–	16	7	0	–	–
AZAD, K.B.J. Kirtivardhan Bhagwat Jha Azad b Purnea 2 Jan 1959	7	12	0	24	135	11.25	–	3	–	750	373	4	124.33	2-84
AZHARUDDIN, M.A. Mohammed Azizuddin Azharuddin b Hyderabad 8 Feb 1963	99	147	9	199	6215	45.03	22	105	–	13	16	0	–	–
BADANI, H.K. Hemang Kamal Badani b Madras 14 November 1976	4	7	1	38	94	15.66	–	6	–	48	17	0	–	–
BAHUTULE, S.V. Sairaj Vasant Bahutule b Bombay 6 January 1973	2	4	1	21*	39	13.00	–	1	–	366	203	3	67.66	1-32
BAIG, A.A. Abbas Ali Baig b Hyderabad 19 March 1939	10	18	0	112	428	23.77	1	6	–	18	15	0	–	

	Tests	I	NO	HS	Runs	Avge	100	Ct	St	Balls	Runs	Wkts	Avge	BB
BANERJEE, S.N. Sarobindu Nath 'Shute' Banerjee b Calcutta 3 Oct 1911, d 14 Oct 1980	1	2	0	8	13	6.50	–	–	–	306	181	5	36.20	4-120
BANERJEE, S.S. Sudwangsu Sekhar 'Mantu' Banerjee b Calcutta 1 Nov 1919, d 14 Sept 1992	1	1	0	0	0	0.00	–	3	–	273	127	5	25.40	4-54
BANERJEE, S.T. Subroto Tara b Patna 13 February 1969	1	1	0	3	3	3.00	–	–	–	108	47	3	15.66	3-47
BAQA JILANI, M. Mohammed Baqa Jilani Khan b Jullundur 20 July 1911, d 2 July 1941	1	2	1	12	16	16.00	–	–	–	90	55	0	–	–
BEDI, B.S. Bishan Singh Giansingh Bedi b Amritsar 25 Sept 1946	67	101	28	50*	656	8.98	–	26	–	21,364	7637	266	28.71	7-98
BHANDARI, P. Prakash Bhandari b Delhi 27 Nov 1935	3	4	0	39	77	19.25	–	1	–	78	39	0	–	–
BHARADWAJ, V.R. Raghvendrarao Vijay 'R Vijay' Bharadwaj b Bangalore 15 August 1975	3	3	0	22	28	9.33	–	3	–	247	101	1	101.00	1-26
BHAT, R.A. Raghuram Adwai Bhat b Puttar 16 April 1958	2	3	1	6	6	3.00	–	–	–	438	151	4	37.75	2-65
BINNY, R.M.H. Roger Michael Humphrey Binny b Bangalore 19 July 1955	27	41	5	83*	830	23.05	–	11	–	2870	1534	47	32.63	6-56
BORDE, C.G. Chandrakant Gulabrao 'Chandu' Borde b Poona 21 July 1934	55	97	11	177*	3061	35.59	5	37	–	5695	2417	52	46.48	5-88
CHANDRASEKHAR, B.S. Bhagwat Subramaniam Chandrasekhar b Bangalore 17 May 1945	58	80	39	22	167	4.07	–	25	–	15,963	7199	242	29.74	8-79
CHAUHAN, C.P.S. Chetan Pratap Singh Chauhan b Bareilly 21 July 1947	40	68	2	97	2084	31.57	–	38	–	174	106	2	53.00	1-4

	Tests	I	NO	HS	Runs	Avge	100	Ct	St	Balls	Runs	Wkts	Avge	BB
CHAUHAN, R.K. Rajesh Kumar Chauhan b Ranchi 19 December 1966	21	17	3	23	98	7.00	–	12	–	4749	1857	47	39.51	4-48
CHOPRA, N. Nikhil Chopra b 26 December 1973	1	2	0	4	7	3.50	–	–	–	144	78	0	–	–
CHOWDHURY, N.R. Nirode Ranjan Chowdhury b Calcutta 23 May 1923, d 14 Dec 1979	2	2	1	3*	3	3.00	–	–	–	516	205	1	205.00	1-130
COLAH, S.H.M. Sorabjee Hormasjee Munchersha Colah b Bombay 22 Sept 1902, d 11 Sept 1950	2	4	0	31	69	17.25	–	2	–	–	–	–	–	–
CONTRACTOR, N.J. Nariman 'Nari' Jamshedji Contractor b Godhra 7 March 1934	31	52	1	108	1611	31.58	1	18	–	186	80	1	80.00	1-9
DAHIYA, V. Vijay Dahiya b Delhi 10 May 1973	2	1	1	2*	2	–	–	6	–	–	–	–	–	–
DANI, H.T. Hemachandra Tukaram 'Bal' Dani b Dudhani 23 May 1932, d 19 Dec 1999	1	–	–	–	–	–	–	1	–	60	19	1	19.00	1-9
DAS, S.S. Shiv Sunder Das b Bhubaneshwar 5 November 1977	16	29	2	110	1053	39.00	1	23	–	18	7	0	–	–
DASGUPTE, D. Deep Dasgupte b Calcutta 7 June 1977	5	9	1	100	291	38.37	1	10	–	–	–	–	–	–
DESAI, R.B. Ramakant Bhikaji Desai b Bombay 20 June 1939, d 27 April 1998	28	44	13	85	418	13.48	–	9	–	5597	2761	74	37.31	6-56
DIGHE, S.S. Sameer Sudhakar Dighe b Bombay 8 October 1968	6	10	1	47	141	15.66	0	12	2	–	–	–	–	–
DILAWAR HUSSAIN b Lahore 19 March 1907, d 26 Aug 1967	3	6	0	59	254	42.33	–	6	1	–	–	–	–	–

	Tests	I	NO	HS	Runs	Avge	100	Ct	St	Balls	Runs	Wkts	Avge	BB
DIVECHA, R.V. Ramesh Vithaldas Divecha b Bombay 18 Oct 1927	5	5	0	26	60	12.00	–	5	–	1044	361	11	32.81	3-102
DOSHI, D.R. Dilip Rasiklal Doshi b Rajkot 22 Dec 1947	33	38	10	20	129	4.60	–	10	–	9322	3502	114	30.71	6-102
DRAVID, R. Rahul Dravid b Indore 11 January 1973	53	92	10	200*	4257	51.91	9	61	–	66	21	0	–	–
DURANI, S.A. Salim Aziz Durani b Kabul 11 December 1934	29	50	2	104	1202	25.04	1	14	–	6446	2657	75	35.42	6-73
ENGINEER, F.M. Farokh Manekshaw Engineer b Bombay 25 Feb 1938	46	87	3	121	2611	31.08	2	66	16	–	–	–	–	–
GADKARI, C.V. Chandrasekhar Waman Gadkari b Poona 3 Feb 1928, d 11 Jan 1998	6	10	4	50*	129	21.50	–	6	–	102	45	0	–	–
GAEKWAD, A.D. Anshuman Dattajirao Gaekwad b Bombay 23 Sept 1952	40	70	4	201	1985	30.07	2	15	–	334	187	2	93.50	1-4
GAEKWAD, D.K. Dattajirao Krishnarao Gaekwad b Baroda 27 Oct 1928	11	20	1	52	350	18.42	–	5	–	12	12	0	–	–
GAEKWAD, H.G. Hiralal Ghasulal Gaikwad b Nagpur 28 Aug 1923	1	2	0	14	22	11.00	–	–	–	222	47	0	–	–
GANDHI, D.J. Devang Jayant Gandhi b Bhavnagar 6 September 1971	4	7	1	88	204	34.00	–	3	–	–	–	–	–	–
GANDOTRA, A. Ashok Gandotra b Rio de Janeiro 24 Nov 1948	2	4	0	18	54	13.50	–	1	–	6	5	0	–	–
GANESH, D. Doddanarasiah 'Dodda' Ganesh b Bangalore 30 June 1973	4	7	3	8	25	6.25	–	–	–	461	287	5	57.40	2-28

	Tests	I	NO	HS	Runs	Avge	100	Ct	St	Balls	Runs	Wkts	Avge	BB
GANGULY, S.C. Sourav Chandidas Ganguly b Calcutta 8 July 1973	51	87	9	173	3155	40.44	7	36	–	1802	1012	23	44.00	3-28
GAVASKAR, S.M. Sunil 'Sunny' Manohar Gavaskar b Bombay 10 July 1949	125	214	16	236*	10,122	51.12	34	108	–	380	206	1	206.00	1-34
GHAVRI, K.D. Kharsan Devji Ghavri b Rajkot 28 Feb 1951	39	57	14	86	913	21.23	–	16	–	7036	3656	109	33.54	5-33
GHORPADE, J.M. Jayasingh Mansingh Ghorpade b Panchgani 2 Oct 1930, d 29 Apr 1978	8	15	0	41	229	15.26	–	4	–	150	131	0	–	–
GHULAM AHMED b Hyderabad 4 July 1922, d 28 Oct 1998	22	31	9	50	192	8.72	–	11	–	5650	2052	68	30.17	7-49
GOPALAN, M.J. Morappakam Joysam Gopalan b Maduranthakam 6 June 1909	1	2	1	11*	18	18.00	–	3	–	114	39	1	39.00	1-39
GOPINATH, C.D. Coimbatarao Doraikunnu Gopinath b Madras 1 Mar 1930	8	12	1	50*	242	22.00	–	2	–	48	11	1	11.00	1-11
GUARD, G.M. Ghulam Mustafa Guard b Surat 12 Dec 1925, d 13 Mar 1978	2	2	0	7	11	5.50	–	2	–	396	182	3	60.66	2-69
GUHA, S. Subroto Guha b Calcutta 13 Jan 1946	4	7	2	6	17	3.40	–	2	–	674	311	3	103.66	2-55
GUL MOHAMMED Gulzar Mohammed b Lahore 15 Oct 1921, d 8 May 1992	8	15	0	34	166	11.06	–	3	–	77	24	2	12.00	2-21
GUPTE, B.P. Balakrishna Pandharinath 'Baloo' Gupte b Bombay 30 Aug 1934	3	3	2	17*	28	28.00	–	–	–	678	349	3	116.33	1-54
GUPTE, S.P. Subash Pandharinath 'Fergie' Gupte b Bombay 11 Dec 1929	36	42	13	21	183	6.31	–	14	–	11,284	4403	149	29.55	9-102

	Tests	I	NO	HS	Runs	Avge	100	Ct	St	Balls	Runs	Wkts	Avge	BB
GURSHARAN SINGH Gursharan Singh b Amritsar 8 Mar 1963	1	1	0	18	18	18.00	–	2	–	–	–	–	–	–
HANUMANT SINGH Hanumant Singh Banswara b Banswara 29 Mar 1939	14	24	2	105	686	31.18	1	11	–	66	51	0	–	–
HARBHAJAN SINGH Harbhajan Singh b Jullundur 3 July 1980	20	29	9	55	255	12.75	–	3	–	5138	2367	81	29.22	8-84
HARDIKAR, M.S. Monahar Shankar Hardikar b Baroda 8 Feb 1936, d 4 Feb 1995	2	4	1	32*	56	18.66	–	3	–	108	55	1	55.00	1-9
HARVINDER SINGH Harvinder Singh b Amritsar 23 December 1977	3	4	1	6	6	2.00	–	–	–	273	185	4	46.25	2-62
HAZARE, V.S. Vijay Samuel Hazare b Sangli 11 Mar 1915	30	52	6	164*	2192	47.65	7	11	–	2840	1220	20	61.00	4-29
HINDLEKAR, D.D. Dattaram Dharmaji Hindlekar b Bombay 1 Jan 1909, d 30 Mar 1949	4	7	2	26	71	14.20	–	3	–	–	–	–	–	–
HIRWANI, N.D. Narendra Deepchand Hirwani b Gorakhpur 18 Oct 1968	17	22	12	17	54	5.40	–	5	–	4298	1987	66	30.10	8-61
IBRAHIM, K.C. Khan Mohammad Cazzambhoy Ibrahim b Bombay 26 Jan 1919	4	8	0	85	169	21.12	–	–	–	–	–	–	–	–
INDRAJITSINHJI, K.S. Kumar Sri Indrajitsinhji Jadya b Jamnagar 15 June 1937	4	7	1	23	51	8.50	–	6	3	–	–	–	–	–
IRANI, J.K. Jamshed 'Jenni' Khudadaad Irani b Karachi 18 Aug 1923, d 25 Feb 1982	2	3	2	2*	3	3.00	–	2	1	–	–	–	–	–
JADEJA, A. Ajaysingh 'Ajay' Jadeja b Jamnagar 1 Feb 1971	15	24	2	96	576	26.18	–	5	–	–	–	–	–	–

	Tests	I	NO	HS	Runs	Avge	100	Ct	St	Balls	Runs	Wkts	Avge	BB
JAFFER, W. Wasim Jaffer b Bombay 16 Feb 1978	2	4	0	23	46	11.50	–	3	–	–	–	–	–	–
JAHANGIR KHAN, M. Mohammed Jahangir Khan b Jullundur 1 Feb 1910, d 27 July 1988	4	7	0	13	39	5.57	–	4	–	606	255	4	63.75	4-60
JAI, L.P. Laxmidas Purushottamdas Jai b Bombay 1 Apr 1902, d 29 Jan 1968	1	2	0	19	19	9.50	–	–	–	–	–	–	–	–
JAISIMHA, M.L. Motganhalli Lakshminarsu Jaisimha b Secunderabad 3 Mar 1939, d 6 July 1999	39	71	4	129	2056	30.68	3	17	–	2097	829	9	92.11	2-54
JAMSHEDJI, R.J.D. Rustomji Jamshedji Dorabji Jamshedji b Bombay 18 Nov 1892, d 5 Apr 1976	1	2	2	4*	5	–	–	2	–	210	137	3	45.66	3-137
JAYANTILAL, H.K. Hirjee Kenia Jayantilal b Hyderabad 13 Jan 1948	1	1	0	5	5	5.00	–	–	–	–	–	–	–	–
JOHNSON, D.J. David Jude Johnson b Arasikere 16 Oct 1971	2	3	1	5	8	4	–	–	–	240	143	3	47.66	2-52
JOSHI, P.G. Padmanabh 'Nana' Govind Joshi b Baroda 27 Oct 1926, d 8 Jan 1987	12	20	1	52*	207	10.89	–	18	9	–	–	–	–	–
JOSHI, S.B. Sunil Bandacharya Joshi b Gadag 6 June 1969	15	19	2	92	352	20.70	–	7	–	3451	1470	41	35.85	5-142
KAIF, M. Mohammad Kaif b Allahabad 1 Feb 1980	4	8	1	37	141	20.14	–	1	–	18	4	0	–	–
KAMBLI, V.G. Vinod Ganpat Kambli b Bombay 18 January 1972	17	21	1	227	1084	54.20	4	7	–	–	–	–	–	–
KANITKAR, H.H. Hrishikesh Hemant Kanitkar b Poona 14 November 1974	2	4	0	45	74	18.50	–	–	–	6	2	0	–	–

	Tests	I	NO	HS	Runs	Avge	100	Ct	St	Balls	Runs	Wkts	Avge	BB
KANITKAR, H.S. Hemant Shamsunder Kanitkar b Amravati 8 Dec 1942	2	4	0	65	111	27.75	–	–	–	–	–	–	–	–
KAPIL DEV, N. Kapildev Ramlal Nikhanj b Chandigarh 6 Jan 1959	131	184	15	163	5248	31.05	8	64	–	27,740	12,867	434	29.64	9-83
KAPOOR, A.R. Aashish Rakesh Kapoor b Madras 25 March 1971	4	6	1	42	97	19.40	–	1	–	642	255	6	42.50	2-19
KARDAR, A.H. Played for India as Abdul Hafeez b Lahore 17 Jan 1925, d 21 Apr 1996	3	5	0	43	80	16.00	–	1	–	–	–	–	–	–
KARIM, S.S. Syed Saba Karim b Patna 14 November 1967	1	1	0	15	15	15.00	–	1	–	–	–	–	–	–
KARTIK, M. Murali Kartik b Madras 11 September 1976	4	5	0	43	61	12.20	–	1	–	885	309	9	34.33	3-123
KENNY, R.B. Ramnath Baburao Kenny b Bombay 29 Sept 1930, d 21 Nov 1985	5	10	1	62	245	27.22	–	1	–	–	–	–	–	–
KHAN, Z. Zaheer Khan b Shrirampur 7 October 1978	9	13	3	45	85	10.50	–	3	–	1681	956	22	43.45	4-76
KIRMANI, S.M.H. Syed Mujtaba Hussein Kirmani b Madras 29 Dec 1949	88	124	22	102	2759	27.04	2	160	38	19	13	1	13.00	1-9
KISHENCHAND, G. Gogumal Kishenchand Harisinghani b Karachi 14 Apr 1925, d 16 April 1997	5	10	0	44	89	8.90	–	1	–	–	–	–	–	–
KRIPAL SINGH, A.G. Amritsar Govind Singh Kripal Singh b Madras 6 Aug 1933, d 27 July 1987	14	20	5	100*	422	28.13	1	4	–	1518	584	10	58.40	3-43
KRISHNAMURTHY, P. Pochiah Krishnamurthy b Hyderabad 12 July 1947, d 28 January 1999	5	6	0	20	33	5.50	–	7	1	–	–	–	–	–

	Tests	I	NO	HS	Runs	Avge	100	Ct	St	Balls	Runs	Wkts	Avge	BB
KULKARNI, N.M. Nilesh Moreshwar Kulkarni b Dombivili 3 April 1973	3	2	1	4	5	5.00	–	1	–	738	332	2	166.00	1-70
KULKARNI, R.R. Rajiv 'Raju' Ramesh Kulkarni b Bombay 25 Sept 1962	3	2	0	2	2	1.00	–	1	–	366	227	5	45.40	3-85
KULKARNI, U.N. Umesh Narayan Kulkarni b Alibagh 7 Mar 1942	4	8	5	7	13	4.33	–	–	–	448	238	5	47.60	2-37
KUMAR, V.V. Vaman Viswanath Kumar b Madras 22 June 1935	2	2	0	6	6	3.00	–	2	–	605	202	7	28.85	5-64
KUMBLE, A. Anil Kumble b Bangalore 17 Oct 1970	66	87	15	88	1286	17.86	–	32	–	20,664	8412	300	28.04	10-74
KUNDERAN, B.K. Budhisagar 'Budhi' Krishnappa Kunderan b Mangalore 2 Oct 1939	18	34	4	192	981	32.70	2	23	7	24	13	0	–	–
KURUVILLA, A. Abey Kuruvilla b Mannar 8 August 1968	10	11	1	35*	66	6.60	–	–	–	1765	892	25	35.68	5-68
LALL SINGH Lall Singh Narayan Singh b Kuala Lumpur 12 Dec 1909, d 19 Nov 1985	1	2	0	29	44	22.00	–	1	–	–	–	–	–	–
LAMBA, R. Raman Lamba b Meerut 2 Jan 1960; 23 Feb 1998	4	5	0	53	102	20.40	–	5	–	–	–	–	–	–
LAXMAN, V.V.S. Vangipurappu Venkata Sai 'VVS' Laxman b Hyderabad 1 November 1974	29	49	3	281	1703	37.02	2	40	–	150	68	0	–	–
MADAN LAL, S. Madanlal Udhouram Sharma b Amritsar 20 Mar 1951	39	62	16	74	1042	22.65	–	15	–	5997	2846	71	40.08	5-23
MAKA, E.S. Ebrahim Suleman Maka b Daman 5 Mar 1922	2	1	1	2*	2	–	–	2	1	–	–	–	–	–

	Tests	I	NO	HS	Runs	Avge	100	Ct	St	Balls	Runs	Wkts	Avge	BB
MALHOTRA, A.O. Ashok Omprakash Malhotra b Amritsar 26 Jan 1957	7	10	1	72*	226	25.11	–	2	–	18	3	0	–	–
MANINDER SINGH Maninder Singh Harbansingh Billa b Poona 13 June 1965	35	38	12	15	99	3.80	–	9	–	8218	3288	88	37.36	7-27
MANJREKAR, S.V. Sanjay Vijay Manjrekar b Mangalore 12 July 1965	37	61	6	218	2043	37.14	4	25	1	17	15	0	–	–
MANJREKAR, V.L. Vijay Laxman Manjrekar b Bombay 26 Sept 1931, d 18 Oct 1983	55	92	10	189*	3208	39.12	7	19	2	204	44	1	44.00	1-16
MANKAD, A.M. Ashok Mulvantrai Mankad b Bombay 12 Oct 1946	22	42	3	97	991	25.41	–	12	–	41	43	0	–	–
MANKAD, M.H. Mulvantrai 'Vinoo' Himatlal Mankad b Jamnagar 12 Apr 1917, d 21 Aug 1978	44	72	5	231	2109	31.47	5	33	–	14,686	5236	162	32.32	8-52
MANTRI, M.K. Madhav Krishanji Mantri b Nasik 1 Sept 1921	4	8	1	39	67	9.57	–	8	1	–	–	–	–	–
MEHERHOMJI, K.R. Khorshedji Rustomji Meherhomji b Bombay 9 Aug 1911, d 10 Feb 1982	1	1	1	0*	0	–	–	1	–	–	–	–	–	–
MEHRA, V.L. Vijay Laxman Mehra b Amritsar 12 Apr 1938	8	14	1	62	329	25.30	–	1	–	36	6	0	–	–
MERCHANT, V.M. Vijay Madhavji Merchant Thackersey b Bombay 12 Oct 1911, d 27 Oct 1987	10	18	0	154	859	47.72	3	7	–	54	40	0	–	–
MHAMBREY, P.L. Paras Laxmikant Mhambrey b Bombay 20 June 1972	2	3	1	28	58	29.00	–	1	–	258	148	2	74.00	1-43
MILKA SINGH, A.G. Amritsar Govindsingh Milka Singh b Madras 31 Dec 1941	4	6	0	35	92	15.33	–	2	–	6	2	0	–	–

	Tests	I	NO	HS	Runs	Avge	100	Ct	St	Balls	Runs	Wkts	Avge	BB
MODI, R.S. Rusi Sheriyar Modi b Surat 11 Nov 1924, d 17 May 1996	10	17	1	112	736	46.00	1	3	–	30	14	0	–	–
MOHANTY, D.S. Debasis Sarbeswar Mohanty b Bhubaneshwar 20 July 1976	2	1	1	0*	0	–	–	–	–	430	239	4	59.75	4-78
MONGIA, N.R. Nayan Ramlal Mongia b Baroda 19 December 1969	44	68	8	152	1442	24.03	1	99	8	–	–	–	–	–
MORE, K.S. Kiran Shankar More b Baroda 4 Sept 1962	49	64	14	73	1285	25.70	–	110	20	12	12	0	–	–
MUDDIAH, V.M. Venkatappa Musandra Muddiah b Bangalore 8 June 1929	2	3	1	11	11	5.50	–	–	–	318	134	3	44.66	2-40
MUSHTAQ ALI, S. Syed Mushtaq Ali Yakub Khan b Indore 17 Dec 1914	11	20	1	112	612	32.21	2	7	–	378	202	3	67.33	1-45
NADKARNI, R.G. Rameshchandra Gangaram 'Bapu' Nadkarni b Nasik 4 Apr 1932	41	67	12	122*	1414	25.70	1	22	–	9165	2559	88	29.07	6-43
NAIK, S.S. Sudhir Sakaram Naik b Bombay 21 Feb 1945	3	6	0	77	141	23.50	–	–	–	–	–	–	–	–
NAOOMAL, J. Jeoomal Naoomal Makhija b Karachi 17 Apr 1904, d 18 June 1980	3	5	1	43	108	27.00	–	–	–	108	68	2	34.00	1-4
NARASIMHA RAO, M.V. Modireddy Venkateshwar Narasimha Rao b Secunderabad 11 Aug 1954	4	6	1	20*	46	9.20	–	8	–	463	227	3	75.66	2-46
NAVLE, J.G. Janardan Gnyanoba Navle b Poona 7 Dec 1902, d 7 Sept 1979	2	4	0	13	42	10.50	–	1	0	–	–	–	–	–
NAYAK, S.V. Surendra 'Suru' Vithal Nayak b Bombay 20 Oct 1954	2	3	1	11	19	9.50	–	1	–	231	132	1	132.00	1-16

	Tests	I	NO	HS	Runs	Avge	100	Ct	St	Balls	Runs	Wkts	Avge	BB
NAYUDU, C.K. Cottari Kanakaiya Nayudu b Nagpur 31 Oct 1895, d 14 Nov 1967	7	14	0	81	350	25.00	–	4	–	858	386	9	42.88	3-40
NAYUDU, C.S. Cottari Subbanna Nayudu b Nagpur 18 Apr 1914	11	19	3	36	147	9.18	–	3	–	522	359	2	179.50	1-19
NAZIR ALI, S. Syed Nazir Ali b Jullundur 8 June 1906, d 18 Feb 1975	2	4	0	13	30	7.50	–	–	–	138	83	4	20.75	4-83
NEHRA, A. Ashish Nehra b Delhi 29 April 1979	4	5	3	17*	26	13.00	–	–	–	772	441	14	31.50	4-72
NISSAR, MOHAMMED b Hoshiapur 1 Aug 1910, d 11 Mar 1963	6	11	3	14	55	6.87	–	2	–	1211	707	25	28.28	5-90
NYALCHAND, S. Shah Nyalchand b Dhragandhra 14 Sept 1919, d 3 Jan 1997	1	2	1	6*	7	7.00	–	–	–	384	97	3	32.33	3-97
PAI, A.M. Ajit Manohar Pai b Bombay 28 Apr 1945	1	2	0	9	10	5.00	–	–	–	114	31	2	15.50	2-29
PALIA, P.E. Phiroz Edulji Palia b Bombay 5 Sept 1910, d 9 Sept 1981	2	4	1	16	29	9.66	–	–	–	42	13	0	–	–
PANDIT, C.S. Chandrakant Sitaram Pandit b Bombay 30 Sept 1961	5	8	1	39	171	24.42	–	14	2	–	–	–	–	–
PARKAR, G.A.H.M. Ghulam Ahmed Hasan Mohammed Parkar b Kalusta 24 Oct 1955	1	2	0	6	7	3.50	–	1	–	–	–	–	–	–
PARKAR, R.D. Ramnath Dhondu Parkar b Bombay 31 Oct 1946, d 11 August 1999	2	4	0	35	80	20.00	–	–	–	–	–	–	–	–
PARSANA, D.D. Dhiraj Devshi Parsana b Rajkot 2 Dec 1947	2	2	0	1	1	0.50	–	–	–	120	50	1	50.00	1-32
PATANKAR, C.T. Chandrakant Trimbak Patankar b Penn 24 Nov 1930	1	2	1	13	14	14.00	–	3	1	–	–	–	–	–

	Tests	I	NO	HS	Runs	Avge	100	Ct	St	Balls	Runs	Wkts	Avge	BB
PATAUDI, I.F.K. Iftikar Ali Khan Pataudi (Nawab of Pataudi, Sr) b Pataudi 16 Apr 1910, d 5 Jan 1952	3	5	0	22	55	11.00	–	–	–	–	–	–	–	–
PATAUDI, M.A.K. Mansur Ali Khan Pataudi (Nawab of Pataudi, Jr) b Bhopal 5 Jan 1941	46	83	3	203*	2793	34.91	6	27	–	132	88	1	88.00	1-10
PATEL, B.P. Brijesh Parasuram Patel b Baroda 24 Nov 1952	21	38	5	115*	972	29.45	1	17	–	–	–	–	–	–
PATEL, J.M. Jasubhai Motibhai Patel b Ahmedabad 26 Nov 1924, d 12 Dec 1992	7	10	1	12	25	2.77	–	2	–	1725	637	29	21.96	9-69
PATEL, R.G.M. Rashid Ghulam Mohammed Patel b Sabarkanta 1 June 1964	1	2	0	0	0	0.00	–	1	–	84	51	0	–	–
PATIALA, YUVRAJ OF Yuvraj Yajuvendra Singh Patiala b Patiala 17 Jan 1913, d 17 June 1974	1	2	0	60	84	42.00	–	2	–	–	–	–	–	–
PATIL, S.M. Sandeep Madhusudan Patil b Bombay 18 August 1956	29	47	4	174	1588	36.93	4	12	–	645	240	9	26.66	2-28
PATIL, S.R. Sadashiv Raoji Patil Kolhapur 10 October 1933	1	1	1	14*	14	–	–	1	–	138	51	2	25.50	1-15
PHADKAR, D.G. Dattatreya 'Dattu' Gajanan Phadkar b Kolhapur 12 Dec 1925, d 17 Mar 1985	31	45	7	123	1229	32.34	2	21	–	5994	2285	62	36.85	7-159
PRABHAKAR, M. Manoj Prabhakar b Ghaziabad 15 Apr 1963	39	58	9	120	1600	32.65	1	20	–	7475	3581	96	37.30	6-132
PRASAD, B.K.V. Bapu Krishnarao Venkatesh Prasad b Bangalore 5 August 1969	33	47	20	30*	203	7.51	–	6	–	7041	3360	96	35.00	6-33
PRASAD, M.S.K. Mannava Sri Kanth Prasad b Guntur 24 April 1975	6	10	1	19	106	11.77	–	15	–	–	–	–	–	–

	Tests	I	NO	HS	Runs	Avge	100	Ct	St	Balls	Runs	Wkts	Avge	BB
PRASANNA, E.A.S. Erapalli Anantarao Srinivasrao Prasanna b Bangalore 22 May 1940	49	84	20	37	735	11.48	–	18	–	14,353	5742	189	30.38	8-76
PUNJABI, P.H. Pamanlal Hotchand Punjabi b Karachi 20 Sept 1921	5	10	0	33	164	16.40	–	5	–	–	–	–	–	–
RAI SINGH, K. Kanwar Rai Singh b Darkati 24 Feb 1922	1	2	0	24	26	13.00	–	–	–			–	–	–
RAJINDERNATH, V. b Amritsar 7 Jan 1928; d 22 Nov 1989	1	–	–	–	–	–	–	–	4	–		–	–	–
RAJINDER PAL b Delhi 18 Nov 1937	1	2	1	3*	6	6.00	–	–	–	78	22	0	–	–
RAJPUT, L.S. Lalchand Sitaram Rajput b Bombay 18 Dec 1961	2	4	0	61	105	26.25	–	1	–	–	–	–	–	–
RAJU, S.L.V. Lalchand Sitaram Rajput b Hyderabad 9 July 1969	28	34	10	31	240	10.0	–	6	–	7602	2857	93	30.72	6-12
RAMAN, W.V. Woorkeri Venkat Raman b Madras 25 May 1965	11	19	1	96	448	24.88	–	6	–	348	129	2	64.50	1-7
RAMASWAMI, C. Cota Ramaswami b Madras 16 June 1896, presumed dead	2	4	1	60	170	56.66	–	–	–	–	–	–	–	–
RAMCHAND, G.S. Gulabrai Sipahimalani Ramchand b Karachi 26 July 1927	33	53	5	109	1180	24.58	2	20	–	4976	1899	41	46.31	6-49
RAMESH, S. Sadagoppan Ramesh b Madras 16 October 1975	19	37	1	143	1367	37.97	2	18	–	54	43	0	–	–
RAMJI, L. Ranji Ladha Nakum b Pidhar 10 Feb 1900, d 20 Dec 1948	1	2	0	1	1	0.50	–	1	–	138	64	0	–	–
RANGACHARI, C.R. Commandur Rajagopalachari Rangachari b 14 Apr 1916, d 9 Oct 1993	4	6	3	8*	8	2.66	–	–	–	846	493	9	54.77	5-107

	Tests	I	NO	HS	Runs	Avge	100	Ct	St	Balls	Runs	Wkts	Avge	BB
RANGNEKAR, K.M. Khanderao Moreshwar Rangnekar b Bombay 27 June 1917, d 11 Oct 1984	3	6	0	18	33	5.50	–	1	–	–	–	–	–	–
RANJANE, V.B. Vasant Baburao Ranjane b Poona 22 Jan 1937	7	9	3	16	40	6.66	–	1	–	1265	649	19	34.15	4-72
RATHOUR, V. Vikram Rathour b Jullundur 26 March 1969	6	10	0	44	131	13.10	–	12	–	–	–	–	–	–
RAZDAN, V. Vivek Razdan b Hyderabad 25 Aug 1969	2	2	1	6	6*	6.00	–	–	–	240	141	5	28.20	5-79
REDDY, B. Bharat Reddy b Madras 12 Nov 1954	4	5	1	21	38	9.50	–	9	2	–	–	–	–	–
REGE, M.R. Madhusudan Ramachandra Rege b Poona 18 Apr 1924	1	2	0	15	15	7.50	–	1	–	–	–	–	–	–
ROY, A.K. Ambar Khirid Roy b Calcutta 5 June 1945, d 19 Sept 1997	4	7	0	48	91	13.00	–	–	–	–	–	–	–	–
ROY, PANKAJ Pankaj Khirod Roy b Calcutta 31 May 1928	43	79	4	173	2442	32.56	5	16	–	104	66	1	66.00	1-6
ROY, PRANAB Pranab Pankaj Roy b Calcutta 10 Feb 1957	2	3	1	60*	71	35.50	–	1	–	–	–	–	–	–
SANDHU, B.S. Balwindersingh Harbansingh Sandhu b Bombay 3 Aug 1956	8	11	4	71	214	30.57	–	1	–	1020	557	10	55.70	3-87
SANGHVI, R.L. Rahul Laxman Sanghvi b Surat 3 September 1974	1	2	0	2	2	1.00	–	–	–	74	78	2	39.00	2-67
SARDESAI, D.N. Dilip Narayan Sardesai b Margoa 8 Aug 1940	30	55	4	212	2001	39.23	5	4	–	59	45	0	–	–

	Tests	I	NO	HS	Runs	Avge	100	Ct	St	Balls	Runs	Wkts	Avge	BB
SARWATE, C.T. Chandrasekhar Trimbak Sarwate b Saugor 22 June 1920	9	17	1	37	208	13.00	–	–	–	658	374	3	124.66	1-16
SAXENA, R.C. Ramesh Chandra Saxena b Delhi 20 Sept 1944	1	2	0	16	25	12.50	–	–	–	12	11	0	–	–
SEHWAG, V.C. Virender Sehwag b Delhi 20 October 1978	4	5	0	105	235	47.00	1	5	–	60	32	0	–	–
SEKHAR, T.A.P. Tirimalai Ananthanpillai Sekhar b Madras 28 Mar 1956	2	1	1	0*	0	–	–	–	–	204	129	0	–	–
SEN, P.K. Probir Khokar Sen b Comela 31 May 1926, d 27 Jan 1970	14	18	4	25	165	11.78	–	20	11	–	–	–	–	–
SENGUPTA, A.K. Apoorva Kumar Sengupta b Lucknow 3 Aug 1939	1	2	0	8	9	4.50	–	–	–	–	–	–	–	–
SHARMA, A.K. Ajay Kumar Sharma b Alwar 3 Apr 1964	1	2	0	30	53	26.50	–	1	–	24	9	0	–	–
SHARMA, C. Chetan Jagatram Sharma b Ludhiana 3 January 1966	23	27	9	54	396	22.00	–	7	–	3470	2163	61	35.45	6-58
SHARMA, G Gopal Sharma b Kanpur 3 Aug 1960	5	4	1	10*	11	3.66	–	2	–	1307	418	10	41.80	4-88
SHARMA, P.H. Parthasarathy Harishchandra Sharma b Delhi 5 Jan 1948	5	10	0	54	187	18.70	–	1	–	24	8	0	–	–
SHARMA, S.K. Sanjeev Kumar Sharma b Delhi 25 Aug 1965	2	3	1	38	56	28.00	–	1	–	414	247	6	41.16	3-37
SHARMA, Y.B. Yashpal Barburam Sharma b Ludhiana 11 Aug 1954	37	59	11	140	1606	33.45	2	16	–	30	17	1	17.00	1-6

	Tests	I	NO	HS	Runs	Avge	100	Ct	St	Balls	Runs	Wkts	Avge	BB
SHASTRI, R.J. Ravishankar Jayadritha Shastri b Bombay 27 May 1962	80	121	14	206	3830	35.79	11	36	–	15,751	6185	151	40.96	5-75
SHINDE, S.G. Sadashiv Ganpatrao Shinde b Bombay 18 Aug 1923, d 22 June 1955	7	11	5	14	85	14.16	–	–	–	1515	717	12	59.75	6-91
SHODHAN, D.H. Deepak Harshadlal Shodan b Ahmedabad 18 Oct 1928	3	4	1	110	181	60.33	1	1	–	60	26	0	–	–
SHUKLA, R.C. Rakesh Chandra Shukla b Kanpur 4 Feb 1948	1	–	–	–	–		–	–	–	294	152	2	76.00	2-82
SIDHU, N.S. Navjot Singh Bhagwantsingh Sidhu b Patiala 20 Oct 1963	51	78	2	201	3202	42.13	9	9	–	6	9	0	–	–
SINGH, R. Robin Singh b Delhi 1 January 1970	1	1	0	0	0	0.00	0	1	–	240	176	3	58.66	2-74
SINGH, R.R. Rabindra Ramanarayan 'Robin' Singh b Prince's Town, Trinidad 14 September 1963	1	2	0	15	27	13.50	0	5	–	60	32	0	–	–
SINGH, S. Sarandeep Singh b Amritsar 21 October 1979	2	1	0	4	4	4.00	–	–	–	552	260	9	28.88	4-136
SIVARAMAKRISHNAN, L. Laxman Sivaramakrishnan b Madras 31 Dec 1965	9	9	1	25	130	16.25	–	9	–	2367	1145	26	44.03	6-64
SOHONI, S.W. Shriranga Wasudev Sohoni b Nimbora 5 Mar 1918, d 19 May 1993	4	7	2	29*	83	16.60	–	2	–	532	202	2	101.00	1-16
SOLKAR, E.D. Eknath Dhondu Solkar b Bombay 18 Mar 1948	27	48	6	102	1068	25.42	1	53	–	2265	1070	18	59.44	3-28
SOOD, M.M. Man Mohan Sood b Lahore 6 July 1939	1	2	0	3	3	1.50	–	–	–	–	–	–	–	–

	Tests	I	NO	HS	Runs	Avge	100	Ct	St	Balls	Runs	Wkts	Avge	BB
SRIKKANTH, K. Krishnamachari Srikkanth b Madras 21 Dec 1959	43	72	3	123	2062	29.88	2	40	–	216	114	0	–	–
SRINATH, J. Javagal Srinath b Mysore 31 August 1969	57	80	21	76	831	14.08	–	22	–	13,214	6377	216	29.52	8-86
SRINIVASAN, T.E. Tirumalai Echambadi Srinivasan b Madras 26 Oct 1950	1	2	0	29	48	24.00	–	–	–	–	–	–	–	–
SUBRAMANYAM, V. Venkatraman Subramanyam b Bangalore 16 July 1936	9	15	1	75	263	18.78	–	9	–	444	201	3	67.00	2-32
SUNDERAM, G.R. Gundibail Rama Sunderam b Udipi 29 Mar 1930	2	1	1	3*	3	–	–	–	–	396	166	3	55.33	2-46
SURENDRANATH, R. b Meerut 4 Jan 1937	11	20	7	27	136	10.46	–	4	–	2602	1053	26	40.50	5-75
SURTI, R.F. Rusi Framroz Surti b Surat 25 May 1936	26	48	4	99	1263	28.70	–	26	–	3870	1962	42	46.71	5-74
SWAMY, V.N. Venkatraman Narayan Swamy b Calicut 18 Mar 1924, d 1 May 1983	1	–	–	–	–	–	–	–	–	108	45	0	–	–
TAMHANE, N.S. Narendra Shankar 'Naren' Tamhane b Bombay 4 Aug 1931	21	27	5	54*	225	10.22	–	35	16	–	–	–	–	–
TARAPORE, K.K. Keki Khorshedji Tarapore b Bombay 17 Dec 1910, d 15 June 1986	1	1	0	2	2	2.00	–	–	–	114	72	0	–	–
TENDULKAR, S.R. Sachin Ramesh Tendulkar b Bombay 24 Apr 1973	89	143	15	217	7419	57.96	27	60	–	1896	996	25	39.84	3-10
UMRIGAR, P.R. Pahelam Ratanji 'Polly' Umrigar b Solapur 28 Mar 1926	59	94	8	223	3631	42.22	12	33	–	4725	1473	35	42.08	6-74
VENGSARKAR, D.B. Dilip Balwant Vengsarkar b Rajapur 6 Apr 1956	116	185	22	166	6868	42.13	17	78	–	47	36	0	–	–

	Tests	I	NO	HS	Runs	Avge	100	Ct	St	Balls	Runs	Wkts	Avge	BB
VENKATARAGHAVAN, S. Srinivasaraghavan Venkataraghavan b Madras 21 Apr 1946	57	76	12	64	748	11.68	–	44	–	14,877	5634	156	36.11	8-72
VENKATARAMANA, M. Margasaghayam Venkataramana b Secunderabad 24 Apr 1966	1	2	2	0*	0	–	–	1	–	70	58	1	58.00	1-10
VISWANATH, G.R. Gundappa Raghunath Viswanath b Bhadravati 12 February 1949	91	155	10	222	6080	41.93	14	63	–	70	46	1	46.00	1-11
VISWANATH, S. Sardanand Viswanath b Bangalore 29 Nov 1962	3	5	0	20	31	6.20	–	11	–	–	–	–	–	–
VIZIANAGRAM, Maharajkumar of b Vizianagar 28 Dec 1905, d 2 Dec 1965	3	6	2	19*	33	8.25	–	1	–	–	–	–	–	–
WADEKAR, A.L. Ajit Laxman Wadekar b Bombay 1 Apr 1941	37	71	3	143	2113	31.07	1	46	–	61	55	0	–	–
WASSAN, A.S. Syed Wazir Ali b Delhi 23 March 1968	4	5	1	53	94	23.50	–	1	–	712	504	10	50.40	4-108
WAZIR ALI, S. Syed Wazir Ali b Jullundur 15 Sept 1903, d 17 June 1950	7	14	0	42	237	16.92	–	1	–	30	25	0	–	–
YADAV, N.S. Shivlal Nandalal Yadav b Hyderabad 26 Jan 1957	35	40	12	43	403	14.39	–	10	–	8360	3580	102	35.09	5-76
YADAV, V. Vijay Yadav b Gonda 14 March 1967	1	1	0	30	30	30.00	–	1	2	–	–	–	–	–
YAJUVINDRA SINGH Yajuvindra Singh Jaswant Singh b Rajkot 1 Aug 1952	4	7	1	43*	109	18.16	–	11	–	120	50	0	–	–
YOGRAJ SINGH, B. Yograjsingh Bhagsingh Bhundel b Chandigarh 25 Mar 1958	1	2	0	6	10	5.00	–	–	–	90	63	1	63.00	1-63

The following players have appeared in limited-over internationals but not in Test matches:

BEDADE, A.C.
Atul Chandrakant Bedade
b Bombay 24 September 1966

BHANDARI, A.
Amit Bhandari
b Delhi 1 October 1978

BHUPINDER SINGH
b Hoshiarpur 1 April 1965

BHANDARI, A.
Amit Bhandari
b Delhi 1 October 1978

BOSE, G.K.
Gopalkrishna Bose
b Calcutta 20 May 1947

CHANDRASEKHAR, V.B.
Vakkadai Biksheswaran Chandrasekhar
b Madras 21 Aug 1961

CHATTERJEE, U.
Utpal Chatterjee
b Calcutta 13 July 1964

DAVID, N.A.
Noel Arthur David
b Hyderabad 26 February 1971

DHARMANI, P.
Pankaj Dharmani
b Delhi 27 September 1974

GHAI, R.S.
Rajinder Singh Ghai
b Jullundur 12 June 1960

KHANNA, S.C.
Surinder Chamanlal Khanna
b Delhi 3 June 1956

KHODA, G.K.
Gagan Kishanlal Khoda
b Barmer 24 October 1974

KHURASIYA, A.R.
Amay Ramsevak Khurasiya
b Jabalpur 18 May 1972

KUMARAN, T.
Thirunavukkarasu Kumaran
Born: 30 December 1975, Madras

MARTIN, J.J.
Jacob Joseph Martin
b Baroda 11 May 1972

MONGIA, D.
Dinesh Mongia
b Chandigarh 17 April 1977

MUKHERJEE, S.P.
Saradindu Purnendu Mukherjee
b Calcutta 5 October 1964

PANDEY, G.K.
Gyanendrakumar Kedarnath Pandey
b Lucknow 12 August 1972

PARANJPE, J.V.
Jatin Vasudeo Paranjpe
b Bombay 17 April 1972

PATEL, A.K.
Ashok Kurjibhai Patel
b Bhavnagar 6 March 1957

RANDHIR SINGH
b Delhi 16 August 1957

RAUL, S.S.
Sanjay Susanta Raul
b Cuttack 6 October 1976

SHUKLA, L.R.
Laxmi Ratan Shukla
b Howrah 6 May 1981

SINGH, R.P.
Rudra Pratap Singh
b Lucknow 6 Jan 1963

SODHI, R.S.
Reetinder Singh Sodhi
b Patiala 18 October 1980

SOMASUNDER, S.B.
Sujith Bijjahali Somasunder
b Bangalore 2 December 1972

SRIRAM, S.
Sridharan Sriram
b Madras 21 February 1976

SUDHAKAR RAO, R.
Ramachandra Sudhakar Rao
b Bangalore 8 Aug 1952

VAIDYA, P.S.
Prashant Sridhar Vaidya
b Nagpur 23 September 1967

YUVRAJ SINGH
b Chandigarh 12 December 1981

See Appendix F for 'A Note on Indian Names'.

534

INDIAN LIMITED-OVER INTERNATIONAL PLAYERS
AND THEIR LOI AVERAGES

	M	I	NO	HS	Runs	Ave	100	50	Ct	St	Balls	Runs	Wkt	Ave	BB	4wi
Abid Ali, S	5	3	0	70	93	31.00	–	1	–	–	336	187	7	26.71	2-22	–
Agarkar, A.B.	81	47	15	67	515	16.09	–	1	30	–	4298	3663	124	29.54	4-25	5
Amarnath, M.	85	75	12	102*	1924	30.53	2	13	23	–	2730	1971	46	42.84	3-12	–
Amarnath, S.	3	3	0	62	100	33.33	–	1	1	–						
Amre, P.K.	37	30	5	84	513	20.52	–	2	12	–	2	4	0	–	–	–
Ankola, S.A.	20	13	4	9	34	3.77	–	–	2	–	807	615	13	47.30	3-33	–
Arshad Ayub	32	17	7	31	116	11.60	–	–	5	–	1769	1216	31	39.22	5-21	1
Arun, B	4	3	1	8	21	10.50	–	–	–	–	102	103	1	103.00	1-43	–
Arun Lal, J.	13	13	0	51	122	9.38	–	1	4	–						
Azad, K.B.J	25	21	2	39	269	14.15	–	–	7	–	390	273	7	39.00	2-48	–
Azharuddin, M.	334	308	54	153*	9378	36.92	7	58	156	–	552	479	12	39.91	3-19	–
Badani, H.K.	23	22	5	100	566	33.29	1	3	9	–	60	53	2	26.50	1-7	–
Bahutule, S.V.	7	3	1	11	12	6.00	–	–	3	–	276	259	2	129.50	1-31	–
Banerjee, S.T.	6	5	3	25	49	24.50	–	–	3	–	240	202	5	40.40	3-30	–
Bedade, A.C.	13	10	3	51	158	22.57	–	1	4	–						
Bedi, B.S.	10	7	2	13	31	6.20	–	–	4	–	590	340	7	48.57	2-44	–
Bhandari, A.	1	1		0	0	–	–	–	–	–	60	75	2	37.50	2-75	–
Bharadwaj, R.V.	9	8	4	41	136	34.00	–	–	3	–	348	275	15	18.33	3-34	–
Bhupinder Singh	2	1	0	6	6	6.00	–	–	–	–	102	78	3	26.00	3-34	–
Binny, R.M.H.	72	49	10	57	629	16.12	–	1	12	–	2957	2260	77	29.35	4-29	3
Bose, G.K.	1	1	0	13	13	13.00	–	–	–	–	66	39	1	39.00	1-39	–
Chandrasekhar, B.S.	7	1	1	11	11	–	–	–	–	–	56	36	3	12.00	3-36	–
Chandrasekhar, V.B.	7	7	0	53	88	12.57	–	1	1	–						
Chatterjee, U.	3	2	1	3	6	6.00	–	–	3	–	161	117	3	39.00	2-35	–
Chauhan, C.P.S.	7	7	0	46	153	21.85	–	–	10	–						
Chauhan, R.K.	35	18	5	32	132	10.15	–	–	16	–	1634	1216	29	41.93	3-29	–
Chopra, N.	39	26	6	61	310	15.50	–	1	19	–	1835	1286	46	27.95	5-21	2
Dahiya, V.	19	15	2	51	216	16.61	–	1	19	5						
Das, S.S.	3	3	1	5	9	4.50	–	–	–	–						
Dasgupta, D.	5	4	1	24	51	17.00	–	–	2	1						
David, N.A.	4	2	2	8	9	–	–	–	–	–	192	133	4	33.25	3-21	–
Dharmani, P.	1	1	0	8	8	8.00	–	–	–	–						
Dighe, S.S.	23	17	6	94	256	23.27	–	1	19	5						
Doshi, D.R.	15	5	2	5	9	3.00	–	–	3	–	792	524	22	23.81	4-30	2
Dravid, R.	163	151	14	153	5190	37.88	7	35	81	3	186	170	4	42.50	2-43	–
Engineer, F.M.	5	4	1	54	114	38.00	–	1	3	1						
Gaekwad, A.D.	15	14	1	78	269	20.69	–	1	6	–	48	39	1	39.00	1-39	–

	M	I	NO	HS	Runs	Ave	100	50	Ct	St	Balls	Runs	Wkt	Ave	BB	4wi
Gandhi, D.J.	3	1	0	30	49	16.33	–	–	–	–	30	20	1	20.00	1-20	–
Ganesh, D.	1	1	0	4	4	4.00	–	–	–	–	–	–	–	–	–	–
Ganguly, S.C.	181	175	14	183	7097	44.08	18	41	64	–	2680	2262	67	33.76	5-15	3
Gavaskar, S.M.	108	102	14	103*	3092	35.13	1	27	22	–	20	25	1	25.00	1-10	–
Ghai, R.S.	6	1	0	1	1	1.00	–	–	–	–	275	260	3	86.66	1-38	–
Ghavri, K.D.	19	16	6	20	114	11.40	–	–	2	–	1033	708	15	47.20	3-40	–
Gursharan Singh	1	1	0	4	4	4.00	–	–	1	–	–	–	–	–	–	–
Harbhajan Singh	35	19	4	46	165	11.00	–	–	8	–	1920	1282	44	29.13	3-27	–
Harvinder Singh	16	5	1	3	6	1.50	–	–	6	–	686	609	24	25.37	3-44	–
Hirwani, N.D.	18	5	3	4	8	2.00	–	–	2	–	960	719	23	31.26	4-43	3
Jadeja, A.	196	179	36	119	5359	37.47	6	30	59	–	1248	1094	20	54.70	3-3	–
Joshi, S.B.	69	45	11	61	584	17.17	–	1	19	–	3386	2509	69	36.36	5-6	2
Kambli, V.G.	104	97	21	106	2477	32.59	2	14	15	–	4	7	1	7.00	1-7	–
Kanitkar, H.H.	34	27	8	57	339	17.84	–	1	14	–	1006	803	17	47.23	2-22	–
Kapil Dev	225	198	39	175*	3783	23.79	1	14	71	–	11202	6945	253	27.45	5-43	4
Kapoor, A.R.	17	6	0	19	43	7.16	–	–	–	–	900	612	8	76.50	2-33	–
Karim, S.S.	34	27	4	55	362	15.73	–	1	27	3	–	–	–	–	–	–
Khan, Z.	29	16	9	32	141	20.14	–	–	7	–	1499	1199	42	28.54	4-42	2
Khanna, S.C.	10	10	2	56	176	22.00	–	2	4	4	–	–	–	–	–	–
Khoda, G.K.	2	2	0	89	115	57.50	–	1	–	–	–	–	–	–	–	–
Khurasiya, A.R.	12	11	0	57	149	13.54	–	1	3	–	–	–	–	–	–	–
Kirmani, S.M.H.	49	31	13	48*	373	20.72	–	–	27	9	–	–	–	–	–	–
Krishnamurthy, P.	1	1	0	6	6	6.00	–	–	1	1	–	–	–	–	–	–
Kulkarni, N.M.	10	5	3	5	11	5.50	–	–	2	–	402	357	11	32.45	3-27	–
Kulkarni, R.R.	10	5	3	15	33	16.50	–	–	–	–	444	345	10	34.50	3-42	–
Kumaran, T.	8	3	0	8	19	6.33	–	–	3	–	378	348	9	38.66	3-24	–
Kumble, A.	215	106	36	26	724	10.34	–	–	73	–	11575	8073	281	28.72	6-12	9
Kuruvilla, A.	25	11	4	7	26	3.71	–	–	4	–	1131	890	25	35.60	4-43	1
Lamba, R.	32	31	2	102	783	27.00	1	6	10	–	19	20	1	20.00	1-9	–
Laxman, V.V.S.	29	27	2	101	627	25.08	1	4	14	–	36	32	0	–	–	–
Madan Lal, S.	67	35	14	53	401	19.09	–	1	4	–	3164	2137	73	29.27	4-20	2
Malhotra, A.	20	19	4	65	457	30.46	–	1	18	–	6	–	0	–	–	–
Maninder Singh	59	18	14	8	49	12.25	–	–	4	–	3133	2066	66	31.30	4-22	1
Manjrekar, S.V.	74	70	10	105	1994	33.23	1	15	23	–	8	10	1	10.00	1-2	–
Mankad, A.V.	1	1	0	44	44	44.00	–	–	–	–	35	47	1	47.00	1-47	–
Martin, J.J.	10	8	1	39	158	22.57	–	–	6	–	–	–	–	–	–	–
Mhambrey, P.L.	3	1	1	7	7	–	–	–	–	–	126	120	3	40.00	2-69	–
Mohanty, D.S.	45	11	6	18	28	5.60	–	–	10	–	1996	1662	57	29.15	4-56	1
Mongia, D.	4	4	0	37	51	12.75	–	–	–	–	–	–	–	–	–	–
Mongia, N.R.	140	96	33	69	1272	20.19	–	2	110	44	–	–	–	–	–	–
More, K.S.	94	65	22	42	563	13.09	–	–	63	27	–	–	–	–	–	–
Mukherjee, S.P.	3	1	1	2	2	–	–	–	1	–	174	98	2	49.00	1-30	–
Naik, S.S.	2	2	0	20	38	19.00	–	–	1	–	–	–	–	–	–	–
Nayak, S.V.	4	1	0	3	3	3.00	–	–	–	–	222	161	1	161.00	1-51	–

Name	M	I	NO	HS	Runs	Ave	100	50	Ct	St	Balls	Runs	Wkt	Ave	BB	4wi
Nehra, A.	10	3	2	2	4	6.00	—	—	1	—	526	389	13	29.92	3-30	—
Pandey, G.K.	2	2	1	4	4	4.00	—	—	—	15	78	60	0	—	—	—
Pandit, C.S.	36	23	9	33	290	20.71	—	—	15	15	—	—	—	—	—	—
Paranjipe, J.V.	4	4	1	27	54	18.00	—	—	2	—	—	—	—	—	—	—
Parkar, G.A.H.M.	10	10	0	42	165	18.33	—	—	4	—	—	—	—	—	—	—
Patel, A.K.	8	2	2	6	6	3.00	—	1	1	—	360	263	7	37.57	3-43	—
Patel, B.P.	10	9	1	82	243	30.37	—	1	1	—	—	—	—	—	—	—
Patel, R.G.M.	1	—	—	—	—	—	—	—	—	—	60	58	0	—	—	—
Patil, S.M.	45	42	1	84	1005	24.51	—	9	11	—	864	589	15	39.26	2-28	—
Prabhakar, M.	130	98	21	106	1858	24.12	2	11	27	—	6360	4534	157	28.87	5-33	6
Prasad, B.K.V.	161	63	31	19	221	6.90	—	—	37	—	8129	6332	196	32.30	5-27	4
Prasad, M.S.K.	17	11	2	63	131	14.55	—	1	14	—	—	—	—	—	—	—
Rajput, L.S.	4	4	1	8	9	3.00	—	—	2	—	7	42	0	—	—	—
Raju, S.L.V.	53	16	8	8	32	4.00	—	—	8	—	2770	2014	63	31.96	4-46	2
Raman, W.V.	27	27	1	114	617	23.73	1	3	2	—	162	170	2	85.00	1-23	—
Ramesh, S.	24	24	1	82	646	28.08	—	6	3	—	36	38	1	38.00	1-23	—
Randhir Singh	2	—	—	—	—	—	—	—	—	—	72	48	1	48.00	1-30	—
Rathour, V.	7	7	0	54	193	27.57	—	2	4	—	—	—	—	—	—	—
Raul, S.S.	2	2	0	8	8	4.00	—	—	—	—	36	27	1	27.00	1-13	—
Razdan, V.	3	3	1	18	23	11.50	—	—	4	—	84	77	1	77.00	1-37	—
Reddy, B.	3	2	2	8	11	—	—	—	2	—	—	—	—	—	—	—
Sandhu, B.S.	22	7	3	16	51	12.75	—	—	5	—	1110	763	16	47.68	3-27	—
Sanghvi, R.L.	10	2	0	8	8	4.00	—	—	4	—	498	399	10	39.90	3-29	—
Sehwag, V.	22	30	3	100	459	27.00	1	3	6	—	640	567	13	43.61	3-59	—
Sekhar, T.P.	4	—	—	—	—	—	—	—	—	—	156	128	5	25.60	3-23	—
Sharma, A.K.	31	27	6	59	424	20.19	—	3	6	—	1140	875	15	58.33	3-41	—
Sharma, C.	65	35	16	101*	456	24.00	1	—	7	—	2835	2336	67	34.86	3-22	—
Sharma, G.	11	2	0	7	11	5.50	—	—	2	—	486	361	10	36.10	3-29	—
Sharma, P.H.	2	2	0	14	20	10.00	—	—	—	—	—	—	—	—	—	—
Sharma, S.K.	23	12	4	28	80	10.00	—	—	7	—	979	813	22	36.95	5-26	1
Shastri, R.J.	150	128	21	109	3108	29.04	4	18	40	—	6613	4650	129	36.04	5-15	3
Shukla, L.R.	3	2	0	13	18	9.00	—	—	1	—	114	94	1	94.00	1-25	—
Sidhu, N.S.	136	127	8	134*	4413	37.08	6	33	20	—	4	3	0	—	—	—
Singh, R.P.	2	—	—	—	—	—	—	—	—	—	82	77	1	77.00	1-58	—
Singh, R.R.	136	113	23	100	2336	25.95	1	9	33	—	3734	2985	69	43.26	5-22	2
Sivaramakrishnan, L.	16	4	2	2	5	2.50	—	—	7	—	756	538	15	35.86	3-35	—
Sodhi, R.S.	17	13	3	67	279	27.90	—	2	9	—	462	365	5	73.00	2-31	—
Solkar, E.D.	7	6	0	13	27	4.50	—	—	2	—	252	169	4	42.25	2-31	—
Somasunder, S.	2	2	0	9	16	8.00	—	—	—	—	—	—	—	—	—	—
Srikkanth, K.	146	145	4	123	4091	29.01	4	27	42	—	712	641	25	25.64	5-27	2
Srinath, J.	198	105	31	53	837	11.31	—	1	31	—	10336	7697	268	28.72	5-23	7
Srinivasan, T.E.	2	2	0	6	10	5.00	—	—	—	—	—	—	—	—	—	—

	M	I	NO	HS	Runs	Ave	100	50	Ct	St	Balls	Runs	Wkt	Ave	BB	4wi
Sriram, S.	6	5	1	12	21	5.25	–	–	1		210	194	5	38.80	3-47	–
Sudhaker Rao, R.	1	1	0	4	4	4.00	–	–	1	–						
Tendulkar, S.R.	280	272	25	186*	10803	43.73	31	53	89		5814	4792	103	46.52	5-32	4
Vaidya, P.S.	4	2	0	12	15	7.50	–	–	2		184	174	4	43.50	2-41	–
Vengsarkar, D.B.	129	120	19	105	3508	34.73	1	23	37		6	4	0	–	–	–
Venkataraghavan, S.	15	9	4	26	54	10.80	–	–	4		868	542	5	108.40	2-34	–
Venkatarama, M.	1	1	1	0	0	–	–	–	–		60	36	2	18.00	2-36	–
Viswanath, G.R.	25	23	1	75	439	19.95	–	2	3		–	–				
Viswanath, S.	22	12	4	23	72	9.00	–	–	17		7					
Wadekar, A.L.	2	2	0	67	73	36.50	–	1	1		–					
Wassan, A.S.	9	6	2	16	33	8.25	–	–	2		426	283	11	25.72	3-28	–
Yadav, N.S.	7	12	2	1	1	–	–	–	1		330	228	8	28.50	2-18	–
Yadav, V.	19	12	2	34	118	11.80	–	–	12		7					
Yashpal Sharma	42	40	9	89	883	28.48	–	4	10		201	199	1	199.00	1-27	–
Yograj Singh, B.	6	4	2	1	1	0.50	–	–	2		244	186	4	46.50	2-44	–
Yuvraj Singh	28	24	2	98	498	22.63	–	2	14		642	453	12	37.75	2-24	–

Appendix F

A NOTE ON INDIAN NAMES

Indians have always had a biblical attitude to names. Just as the *Genesis* gives no surnames – Adam begot Seth and Seth begot Enosh, etc. – so Indians have traditionally found surnames superfluous. It was the arrival of the British, with their ideas of property rights tied to families, that encouraged Indians to acquire family names. But even today south India, particularly Tamil Nadu, has a very different attitude to surnames compared to the rest of the country.

There a man is known by his own name, followed by his father's first name; then follow several other names indicating the village, caste, community he comes from but there is no *family* name as such that goes on from father to son through succeeding generations. Thus the Indian tennis player Ramanathan Krishnan did not have Krishnan as a family name, that was the name of his father. His son Ramesh, also a good tennis player, should have been called, by tradition, Ramesh Ramanathan, but he decided to make his grandfather's first name the family name and is known as Ramesh Krishnana – a good example of a family acquiring a surname in the accepted Anglo-Saxon fashion.

Even families that have long established family names can spell them in very different ways. This, of course, is the result of transliteration, trying to convert words from one language into another. In the case of my own family this has led to two, seemingly distinct surnames. Our original Bengali surname is Bosu, some of my uncles call themselves Basu, my father preferred Bose.

There is another complication. Indians, taking their cue from the style of Victorians, rarely spell out a person's first name in public. Thus the present Prime Minister is nearly always referred to as V. P. Singh, not by his full name of Viswanath Pratap Singh. It is only the BBC's almost legendary correspondent in Delhi, Mark Tully, who refers to him in that way. Indians have a similar reticence with cricketers and other public figures. C. K. Nayudu, to the best of my knowledge, has never been referred to by his full names of Cottari

Kanakaiya, indeed I doubt whether many Indians know of them – even the latest study of him does not mention his full name on the title page or the cover but refers to it coyly in the blurb. He is just C. K. Nayudu. Similarly with Prasanna. His full name Erapalli Anantarao Srinivastoo Prasanna was too much even for Indians and he was always E. A. S. Prasanna, even in his auto-biography, while Jaisimha's first names of Motganhalli Lakshminarsu were a mystery to most Indian cricket followers. These first names have only begun to emerge under pressure from English newspaper enquiries and at times it is almost comical to see Indians try to discover the first names of individuals they have known for years. In the cases of Prasanna and Jaisimha it became common to use abbreviations as given by English journalists as a sort of first name. Thus Prasanna became 'Pras', and Jaisimha became 'Jai' which, of course, is a first name in India. A similar abbreviation, if more Indian-inspired, was 'Polly' for Pahelam, Umrigar's proper first name.

In contrast there are certain cricketers who have such romantic first names that they are known only by these. An illustration is Salim Durani, who was universally known as Salim, the name of a great Mughal emperor. It has also been fashionable to acquire nicknames through English associations. Thus Vijay Manjrekar was known as 'Tatt', because he played for Tattershall in the Lancashire League while Lala Amarnath gave his children nicknames such as 'Jimmy' for Mohinder. Lala, in fact, was a pet name given to him and this, again, is a common custom in India. A child will have a proper name which is often, at least amongst Hindus, given after consultation with astrologers and is the one shown on his or her horoscope. But then the doting mother or father bestows a pet name which can be Chand, which means 'moon', or Lal, which means 'beloved', or Raja, which means 'king', and the child can grow up rarely using his proper name. (The nearest Western equivalent perhaps is to call a man named John, Jack, or Robert, Bob, or Margaret, Maggie.)

The way in which names are used is possibly best illustrated by two of India's greatest cricketers, Kapil Dev and Sunil Gavaskar. Sunil Gavaskar is more often known by his initials S.M.G. or 'Sunny', his popular nickname. However Dev is not even Kapil's surname. His real surname is Nikhanj, but this is rarely used and one of the names he was given at birth has become his surname. Even in his own autobiography he has chosen to omit his family name, but in an extraordinary twist his first name, Kapil, has to all practical purposes become his first name and his surname. In *Wisden*'s 'Birth and Deaths of Cricketers' Kapil Dev is listed under 'K' along with Kanhai. In that sense Kapil has returned to the biblical tradition where a man had one name and a family name did not seem to matter.

Appendix G

INDIA'S TEST MATCH GROUNDS

Ahmedabad	Gujerat Stadium
Bangalore	Karnataka State Cricket Association Stadium
Bombay (now Mumbai)	Gymkhana (1933–34) Brabourne Stadium (1948–49 to 1972–73) Wankhede Stadium (since 1975)
Calcutta (now Kolkatta)	Eden Gardens
Chandigarh	Sector 16 (1990–91) Punjab Cricket Association Stadium, Mohali (since 1994)
Cuttack	Barabati Stadium
Delhi	Feroz Shah Kotla
Hyderabad	Lal Bahadur Stadium
Jaipur	Sawai Mansingh Stadium
Jullundur	Burlton Park
Kanpur	Green Park (Modi Stadium)
Lucknow	University Ground (1952) K.D. 'Babu' Singh Stadium (1994)
Madras (now Chennai)	Chepauk (Chidambaram) Stadium (since 1981–82) Corporation (Nehru) Stadium (1955–56 to 1964–65)
Nagpur	Vidarbha Cricket Association Ground

Appendix H

SELECT BIBLIOGRAPHY

Indian cricket literature is not as extensive as English but writing on Indian cricket is still considerable. The following are the books and periodicals that I found most useful when researching and writing the book.

ALLEN, David Rayvern (Ed): *The Essential John Arlott* (Collins Willow, 1989)

ALLEN, David Rayvern (Ed): *A Word from Arlott* (Pelham, 1983)

ALI Mushtaq: *Cricket Delightful* (Rupa, 1981)

ANSARI, Khalid (Ed): *Champions of One-day Cricket* (Orient Longman, 1985)

BHARATAN, Raju: *Indian Cricket – The Vital Phase* (Vikas, 1977)

BAILEY, Philip: *V.M. Merchant* (Association of Cricket Statisticians, 1988)

BERRY, Scyld: *Cricket Wallah* (Hodder & Stoughton, 1982)

BERRY, Scyld: *Cricket Odyssey* (Pavilion, 1988)

BHIMANI, Kishore: *West Indies '76: India's Caribbean Adventure* (Nachiketa Publications, 1976)

BIRBALSING, Frank, and SHIWCHARAN, Clem: *Indo-West Indian Cricket* (Hansib, 1988)

BOSE, Mihir: *Keith Miller, a Cricketing Biography* (Allen & Unwin, 1979)

BOSE, Mihir: *All in a Day, Great Moments in Cup Cricket* (Robin Clarke, 1983)

BOSE, Mihir: *A Maidan View, the Magic of Indian Cricket* (Allen & Unwin, 1986)

BOYCOTT, Geoffrey: *The Autobiography* (Macmillan, 1987)

BRADMAN, Sir Donald: *Farewell to Cricket* (Hodder & Stoughton, 1950)

CASHMAN, Richard: *Players, Patrons and the Crowd* (Orient Longman, 1980)

CHAUDHURI, Nirad: *The Continent of Circe* (Jaico, 1966)

CHAUDHURI, Nirad: *Thy Hand, Great Anarch!* (Chatto & Windus, 1987)

CLARK, C.D.: *The Record-Breaking Sunil Gavaskar* (David & Charles, 1980)

DABYDEEN, David (Ed): *India in the Caribbean* (Hansib, 1987)

DE MELLO, Anthony: *Portrait of Indian Sport* (Macmillan, 1959)

DEODHAR, D.B.: *March of Indian Cricket* (S.K. Roy, 1949)

DOCKER, Edward: *History of Indian Cricket* (Macmillan, India, 1976)

DOUGLAS, Christopher: *Douglas Jardine, Spartan Cricketer* (Allen & Unwin, 1984)

'ESKARI': *C.K. Nayudu: A Cricketer of Charm* (Illustrated News, Calcutta, 1945)

FOWLER, Graeme: *Fox on the Run* (Viking, 1988)

HEADLAM, Cecil: *Ten Thousand Miles through India and Burma* (Dent, 1903)

GOWER, David and LEE, Alan: *David Gower, with Time to Spare* (Ward Lock, 1980)

GAVASKAR, Sunil: *Sunny Days* (Rupa, 1976)

GAVASKAR, Sunil: *Idols* (Rupa, 1983)

GAVASKAR, Sunil: *Runs 'n Ruins* (Rupa, 1984)

GAVASKAR, Sunil: *One-Day Wonders* (Rupa, 1986)

GREEN, Benny (Ed): *Wisden Anthologies: 1864–1900; 1900–1940; 1940-1963;1963–1982* (Macdonald Queen Anne Press, 1979, 1980, 1982, 1983)

GREENIDGE, Gordon: *The Man in the Middle* (David & Charles, 1980)

GOODWIN, Clayton: *Caribbean Cricketers* (Harrap, 1980)

HAZARE, Vijay: *A Long Innings* (Rupa, 1981)

HOWAT, Gerald: *Cricket's Second Golden Age* (Hodder & Stoughton, 1989)

ILLINGWORTH, Ray: *Yorkshire and Back* (Macdonald Futura, 1981)

JAMES, C. L. R.: *Cricket* (Allison & Busby, 1986)

KAPIL Dev: *Cricket My Style* (Allied, 1987)

KHAN, Imran: *All Round View* (Chatto & Windus, 1988)

LEMMON, David: *Cricket Mercenaries* (Pavilion, 1987)

LEWIS, Tony: *Playing Days* (Stanley Paul, 1985)

LLOYD, Clive: *Living for Cricket* (Stanley Paul, 1980)

LORD, John: *The Maharajahs* (Random House, 1971)

MARTIN-JENKINS, Christopher: *The Complete Who's Who of Test Cricketers* (Orbis, 1980)

MCDONALD, Trevor: *Clive Lloyd, The Authorised Biography* (Granada, 1985)

MCDONALD, Trevor: *Viv Richards, The Authorised Biography* (Pelham Books, 1984)

MANLEY, Michael: *A History of West Indian Cricket* (André Deutsch, 1988)

MAY, Peter: *A Game Enjoyed* (Stanley Paul, 1985)

MORAES, Dom: *Sunil Gavaskar – An Illustrated Biography* (Macmillan, India, 1987)

MUKERJEE, Sujit: *Playing for India* (Orient Longman, 1972)

MUKERJEE, Sujit: *Between Indian Wickets* (Orient Longman 1976)

MURPHY, Patrick: *Botham, A Biography* (Dent, 1988)

NAIK, Vasant: *Vijay Merchant* (Bandodkar Publishing House, n.d.)

NAIPAUL, V.S.: *Middle Passage* (André Deutsch, 1962)

NANDY, Ashis: *The Tao of Cricket – on Games of Destiny and the Destiny of Games* (Penguin, 1989)

PATIL, Sandeep: *Sandy Storm* (Rupa, 1984)

PARKER, Eric: *The History of Cricket* (Seeley Service, 1950)

PAVRI, M.E.: *Parsee Cricket* (J.B. Marzban, 1901)

PRASANNA, E.A.S.: *One More Over* (Rupa, 1982)

PURI, Narottam: *Portrait of Indian Captains* (Rupa, 1978)

RAIJI, Vasant: *The Romance of the Ranji Trophy* (Tyeby Press, 1984)

RAIJI, Vasant and DOSSA, Anandji: *CCI & the Brabourne Stadium, 1937–1987* (Cricket Club of India, 1987)

RAIJI, Vasant: *India's Hambledon Men* (Tyeby Press, 1986)

RAIJI, Vasant: *C.K. Nayudu – The Shahenshah of Indian Cricket* (The Marine Sports, 1989)

RAJAN, Sunder: *India v. West Indies, 1974–1975* (Jaico, 1975)

RAMASWAMI, C: *Ramblings of a Games Addict* (Ramaswami, n.d.)

RAMASWAMI, N.S.: *Indian Cricket* (Abhinav, 1976)

RAMCHAND, Partab: *Great Moments in Indian Cricket* (Vikas, 1977)

RAMCHAND, Partab: *Great Indian Cricketers* (Vikas, 1979)

RAMCHAND, Partab: *Great Feats of Indian Cricket* (Rupa, 1984)

ROSENWATER, Irving: *Sir Donald Bradman: A Biography* (Batsford, 1978)

ROSS, Alan: *Ranji*, (Pavilion, 1988)

ROYLE, Trevor: *The Last Days of the Raj* (Michael Joseph, 1989)

SANYAL, Saradindu: *40 Years of Test Cricket including the 41st Year* (Thomson, India, 1974)

SARBADHIKARY, Berry: *Indian Cricket Uncovered* (S.K. Roy, 1945)

SORABJEE, Shapoorjee: *A Chronicle of Cricket Amongst Parsees* (Bombay, c. 1898)

SUNDARESAN, P.N.: *Ranji Trophy, Golden Years 1934–35 to 1983–84* (Board of Control, 1984)

SOBERS, Sir Garfield (With Brian Scovell): *Sobers, Twenty Years at the Top* (Macmillan, 1988)

STOLLMEYER, Jeff: *Everything under the Sun* (Stanley Paul, 1983)

SWANTON, E.W.: *Gubby Allen, Man of Cricket* (Hutchinson, 1985)

VAIDA, Sudhir: *Figures of Cricket* (Bombay Cricket Association, 1976)

WHITTINGTON, R.S.: *The Quiet Australian – The Lindsay Hassett Story* (Heinemann, 1969)

SELECT BIBLIOGRAPHY

WADEKAR, Ajit: *My Cricketing Years* (Vikas, 1973)
WILD, Roland: *The Biography of Colonel His Highness Shri Sir Ranjitsinhji Vibhaji* (Rich & Cowan, 1934)
WILDE, Simon: *Ranji* (Heinemann, 1990)

REFERENCE BOOKS:
Guide to First-Class Cricket Matches played in India, compiled by the Association of Cricket Statisticians (1986)
Barclays World of Cricket (Collins Willow, 1986)
FRINDALL, Bill (Compiler and Editor): *The Wisden Book of Test Cricket, 1877–1999* (Headline, 1999)
FRINDALL, Bill (Compiler and Editor): *The Wisden Book of Cricket Records* (Macdonald Queen Anne Press, 1986)

ANNUALS
Wisden Cricketers' Almanack
Indian Cricket
Pelham Cricket Year: 1979–81
Benson & Hedges Cricket Year: 1982–83
World of Cricket, 1979, 1980
Playfair Cricket Annual

MAGAZINES
The Cricketer
Playfair Cricket Monthly
Wisden Cricket Monthly
Sportsweek
Sportstar
Sportsworld
Sunday
India Today
Illustrated Weekly of India
Outlook

NEWSPAPERS
The Times
Guardian
Daily Telegraph
Times of India
Hindu
Statesman
Independent
Sunday Times
Sunday Observer (Bombay)
Midday
Indian Express
Pioneer

SOUVENIRS
Golden Jubilee Commemoration Volume 1929–1979, Board of Control for Cricket in India, n.d.
Golden Jubilee Commemoration Volume 1930–1980, Bombay Cricket Association
New Zealand and India Tour of Australia 1985–86, ABC, 1985
England Tour of India 1981–82, Hindu

Index